AMMIANUS MARCELLINUS

I

THE ACERENZA BUST

Supposed by some to be a portrait of Julian

This bust, slightly more than life size and made of the local limestone, stood for many years on the gable of the cathedral of Acerenza (Aceruntia), near Horace's birthplace; it is now preserved in the sacristy of the church. It was formerly regarded by the natives as an image of St. Peter. That it might represent Julian was first suggested by Lenormant in 1883; his opinion was accepted by some, but is now generally rejected by the best authorities; for although the bust is probably a work of the fourth century, it does not at all correspond with Ammianus' description of Julian (xxv. 4, 22), or with the coins and a sardonyx gem, which seem to give the only authentic portraits of the emperor.[1]

[1] I am indebted for a full account of the literature on the subject to Dr. George M. A. Hanfmann, Research Fellow of Harvard University, and Professor David M. Robinson, of Johns Hopkins University.

AMMIANUS MARCELLINUS

WITH AN ENGLISH TRANSLATION BY

JOHN C. ROLFE

PH.D., LITT.D.
UNIVERSITY OF PENNSYLVANIA

IN THREE VOLUMES

I

CAMBRIDGE, MASSACHUSETTS
HARVARD UNIVERSITY PRESS
LONDON
WILLIAM HEINEMANN LTD
MCMLXIII

First Printed 1935
Revised and Reprinted 1950, 1956, 1963

Printed in Great Britain at The University Press, Aberdeen

CONTENTS

v

CONTENTS

PREFACE

SOME of the reviews of my previous contributions to the *L.C.L.* make it advisable to say that this is a translation and not a critical edition. Every serious student of the text must use the standard edition of C. U. Clark (Berlin, vol. i, 1910 ; vol. ii, part I, 1915). The translator has, however, attempted to examine all the available critical material, and has deviated in a number of instances from Clark's text, always with hesitation, except in the way of filling out lacunae. To shorten and simplify the critical notes (which are perhaps still too numerous) all instances have been omitted in which the earlier editions have made corrections of Codex V which are generally accepted.

Clark's punctuation according to the metrical *clausulae* (see Introd., p. xxii) is regarded by Novák (*Wiener Studien* 33, p. 293) as no less important in establishing the text than the discovery of a new and valuable manuscript. Although this punctuation differs from the usual system, especially in the case of some relative clauses and in a more abundant use of commas, it has seemed best to follow it except in a few instances, where it might be misleading. It frequently throws light on the writer's meaning.

My obligations to Professor Clark are not confined to the use of his edition. He generously placed at

PREFACE

my disposal the first draft of his translation of Books
xiv-xvii, 11, 4, which has been of great service.
My translation, however, must not be supposed
to reflect his final version. He also lent me his
copy of the somewhat rare translation of Holland.

Anyone who is at all familiar with the constant
problems presented by the text of Ammianus, and by
his Latinity, will view with indulgence an attempt
to render him into English and to retain so far as
possible something of the flavour of the original.

JOHN C. ROLFE.

PHILADELPHIA, *June*, 1935.

INTRODUCTION

THE LIFE OF AMMIANUS

OUR knowledge of Ammianus is derived almost
wholly from his own writings. He was born about
A.D. 330 in Syrian Antioch, of a good Greek family,[1]
and probably received his early education in his
native city. Antioch at that time was one of the
principal cities of the Roman Empire, *orientis apex
pulcher*,[2] and Ammianus took just pride in its material
prosperity.[3] He was not, however, equally proud
of his fellow citizens, a mixed population of Greeks,
Jews, Syrians, and other peoples,[4] united only in
their devotion to luxury and the pursuit of pleasure.
The historian makes no reply to the criticisms
passed upon them by Julian,[5] except to characterize
them as exaggerated. But Greek still maintained
its intellectual leadership, and the opportunities
for education were good.[6] The city produced other
men of distinction, notably Libanius and Joannes
Chrysostom.

Ammianus spent his active life during the reigns
of Constantius II, Julian, Jovian, Valentinian,
and Valens, in the second half of the fourth century,
when, in spite of some memorable victories, the

---

[1] Cf. *ingenuus*, xix. **8**, 6, and xxxi. **16**, 9.   [2] xxii. **9**, 14.
[3] xiv. **8**, 8 ; xiv. **1**, 9.
[4] Mommsen, *Röm. Gesch.* v. 456.
[5] xxii. **14**, 2-3 ; xxiii. **2**, 3-4.   [6] Mommsen, *l.c.*

prestige of the empire was on the wane. The turning-point in its history was the disastrous defeat of Valens by the Goths at Adrianople in 378, in which the emperor himself met his death, and at that date our direct knowledge of Ammianus comes to an end.

At an early age the future historian was made one of the *protectores domestici*,[1] a select corps of the imperial bodyguard, which is further testimony to his good birth. In 353 he was attached by the emperor's order to the staff of Ursicinus, commander-in-chief of the army in the East, and joined him at Nisibis in Mesopotamia.[2] He accompanied his general to Antioch, where Ursicinus was entrusted by Gallus Caesar with the conduct of trials for high treason. Ammianus' early life is closely connected with the career of Ursicinus, to whom he was strongly attached, and with whom he shared prosperity and adversity. Incidentally, he immortalized his chief, of whom little or nothing is known from other sources.

In 354 Ursicinus, who had become an object of suspicion to the emperor, was summoned to the court at Mediolanum,[3] accompanied by Ammianus. There palace intrigues caused Ursicinus to be still more distrusted by Constantius, who accordingly assigned to him the difficult task of suppressing the revolt of Silvanus, who had assumed the purple at Cologne [4]; but although the mission was successful, Ursicinus not only received no commendation

---

[1] See pp. xlii f., below. Their full title, *protector lateris divini Augusti nostri*, appears in an inscription in *Ephem. Epigr.*, v. 121 (no. 4).

[2] xiv. 9, 1. [3] xiv. 11, 4 f. [4] xv. 5, 21 ff.

INTRODUCTION

from the emperor, but was even accused of embezzling some of the Gallic treasure.[1] Ammianus remained with his chief in Gaul until the summer of 357, and hence was in close touch with the exploits of Julian, the newly appointed Caesar. Ursicinus was next summoned by the suspicious emperor to Sirmium in Pannonia, and from there, because of the danger which threatened from the Persians, was once more sent to the East,[2] still accompanied by Ammianus. But when the Persians began hostilities in 359, Ursicinus was again recalled to court, but on reaching the river Hebrus received orders to return to Mesopotamia, which had already been invaded by the enemy.[3]

Since Sabinianus, who in the meantime had been appointed commander-in-chief of the army in the East, took no action, Ursicinus with his staff went to Nisibis, to prevent that city from being surprised and taken by the Persians.[4] From there he set out for Amida, to keep the roads from being occupied, but immediately after leaving Nisibis sent Ammianus back to the city on an errand.[5] In order to escape the hardships of the siege with which Nisibis was threatened, Ammianus after hastily carrying out his orders tried to rejoin his general. He was all but captured on the way, but finally came up with Ursicinus and his following at Amudis, warned them of the approach of the Persians, and accompanied them in their retreat.[6] By a clever stratagem they misled their pursuers into taking the wrong direction, and finally reached

[1] xv. 5, 36. [2] xvi. 10, 21. [3] xviii. 6, 5.
[4] xviii. 6, 8. [5] xviii. 6, 10 ff. [6] xviii. 6, 12 f.

INTRODUCTION

Amida.[1] There by a cipher message from Procopius, who had gone to the Persians as an envoy and was detained by them, they were informed that the enemy's main body had crossed the Tigris, and Ursicinus sent Ammianus, accompanied by a faithful centurion, to the satrap of Corduene, who was secretly a friend of the Romans, in quest of more definite information.[2] From a rocky height Ammianus saw the advance of Sapor's army, witnessed their crossing of the river Anzaba, and reported what he had learned to Ursicinus. He, on hearing of the enemy's advance, resolved to go to Samosata and destroy the bridges by which the Persians were planning to cross the Euphrates [3]; but through the negligence of the Roman cavalry outposts his forces were attacked and scattered.[4] Ammianus after several narrow escapes was forced to return to Amida,[5] where he took part in the stubborn resistance of the city to the Persian attack.[6] When Amida finally fell, he succeeded in making his escape under cover of night and after many adventures met Ursicinus at Melitene in Armenia Minor and with him returned safely to Antioch.[7]

After the deposition of Ursicinus in 360 we hear little definite about the historian's career. He took some part in Julian's Persian campaign of 363, but in what capacity is uncertain; he apparently joined Julian with the arrival of the Euphrates fleet, since it is after that point in his narrative that we find him using the first person.[8] After the return

[1] xviii. 6, 14 ff.　　　[2] xviii. 6, 20 f.　　　[3] xviii. 8, 1.
[4] xviii. 8, 2 ff.　　　[5] xviii. 8, 11.　　　[6] xix. 1-7.
[7] xix. 8, 5-12.　　　[8] xxiii. 5, 7, *profecti . . . venimus.*

of the Roman army to Antioch on the death of
Julian and the accession of Jovian he seems to have
remained in his native city for a considerable time,
since his account of the trials conducted there for
high treason in 371 is clearly that of an eye-witness.[1]
He probably made his home in Antioch until the
defeat and death of Valens, but his residence in the
city was interrupted by journeys to Egypt [2] and to
Greece after the great earthquake of July 6, 366.[3] It
was doubtless in Antioch that he did some of his extensive reading in preparation for the writing of his
History. His military career occupied a compara-
tively brief period of his life,[4] the greater part of which
was devoted to study and writing.

After the events of 378 Ammianus went to Rome
by way of Thrace, where he seems to have inspected
the battlefields,[5] choosing the land route rather than
the more convenient trip by sea in order to get
material for his History. At any rate, he seems to
have taken up his residence in the Eternal City
before 383, and his bitter language about the expulsion of foreigners at that time because of
threatened famine [6] has led some to infer that he
was one of those who were forced to leave. The
words of Symmachus,[7] *defectum timemus annonae,
pulsis omnibus quos exserto et pleno ubere Roma
susceperat*, imply that the expulsion was general,

[1] xxix. **1**, 24 ff.   [2] xvii. **4**, 6 ; xxii. **15**, 1.
[3] xxvi. **10**, 19.
[4] Apparently not more than fifteen years; cf. Klein,
pp. 9 f. (For this and similar references see *Bibliographical
Note*, p. xlix).
[5] xxxi. **7**, 16.   [6] xiv. **6**, 19.   [7] *Epist.* ii. 7.

and Ammianus' unfavourable opinion of the Anicii, who at that time were a powerful family at Rome, may have some bearing on the question.[1] Others believe that his rank as a former *protector domesticus*, which carried with it the title of *perfectissimus*,[2] would have spared him such an indignity. If he was driven out, it seems probable that the hope of Symmachus,[3] *quam primum revocet urbs nostra quos invita dimisit*, was fulfilled, for Ammianus wrote his History in Rome, and acquired a certain position in the city, numbering among his friends Symmachus and Praetextatus,[4] although apparently some circles of distinguished Romans did not admit an *honestus advena* to intimacy.[5]

That Ammianus was not a Christian is evident from many of his utterances, for he speaks of Christian rites, ceremonies, and officials in a way which shows a lack of familiarity with them.[6] At the same time he was liberal in his attitude towards the Church; he twice censures the closing of the schools of rhetoric to Christian teachers,[7] praises the simple life of the provincial bishops,[8] and in general favours absolute religious toleration.[9] He often refers to a supreme power (*numen*), with such adjectives as *magnum*, *superum*, *caeleste*, *divinum*, *sempiternum*, and others of the same kind, and he sometimes speaks of this power as *deus*,[10] but in

---

[1] xvi. **8**, 13.   [2] See pp. xxviii and xliii, below.
[3] *l.c.*   [4] xxi. **12**, 24 ; xxvii. **3**, 3 ; **9**, 8.
[5] xiv. **6**, 12.
[6] xiv. **9**, 7 ; xv. **5**, 31 ; xxvi. **3**, 3 ; xxvii. **10**, 2 ; etc.
[7] xxii. **10**, 7 ; xxv. **4**, 20.   [8] xxvii. **3**, 15.
[9] xxx. **9**, 5.   [10] xvii. **13**, 33 ; xxiv. **1**, 1 ; etc.

much the same sense as the word is used by Horace [1] and other pagan writers. He indicates a belief in astrology, divination, dreams, and other superstitions of his time, and he speaks of *Fortuna* and *fatum* as controlling powers, but shows that they may be overcome or influenced by man's courage and resourcefulness.[2] The view of Dill [3] that " his real creed was probably a vague monotheism with a more decided tendency to fatalism " is rightly questioned by Ensslin,[4] who says that Ammianus was a determinist, but not a passive fatalist, one who in inactive quiet awaited what might come.

When Ammianus died is quite uncertain. The latest allusion in his History is to the consulship of Neotherius in 391.[5] In the same year the Serapeum at Alexandria was burned, but the historian refers to the building as if it were still standing ; [6] other indications are his references to Probus and Theodosius.[7] He was certainly living in 391, and probably in 393, but how much longer his life was prolonged cannot be determined.

His History.

Ammianus set himself the vast project of succeeding Tacitus as an historian, and might have entitled his work *Res Gestae a fine Corneli Taciti* ; but the title which has come down to us is simply *Res Gestae.*[8]

[1] *Odes*, i. 3, 21 ; i. 34, 13.
[2] xviii. **1,** 1 ff. ; xxiv. **3,** 6 ; **4,** 1 ff. ; xxxi. 5, 14 ; cf. xxiii. **5,** 5.
[3] p. 101.
[4] p. 81.   [5] xxvi. 5, 14.   [6] xxii. **16,** 12.
[7] xxvii. **11,** 1   xxix. **6,** 15.
[8] Priscian, *Gr. Lat.* ii. 487, 1, Keil.

INTRODUCTION

It covered the period between the accession of Nerva in A.D. 96 to the death of Valens in 378, and was divided into thirty-one books, of which the first thirteen are lost. Since the surviving eighteen books deal with a period of twenty-five years, from 353, the seventeenth year of the reign of Constantius II, to the battle of Adrianople, the lost books must have given a brief account of the two hundred and fifty-seven years to which they were devoted. In 391 Libanius implies [1] that Ammianus published, and probably recited parts of his work at Rome with great success. Seeck thinks that the part which was published in 390 or 391 ended with the twenty-fifth book; that this was his original plan, and that he was encouraged to go farther by the favourable reception given to a public recitation; that he intended to continue beyond the death of Valens is indicated by his promise to tell of the fate that overtook Maximinus and Simplicius,[2] but his failure to do so may possibly have been an oversight. That the work was published in instalments seems to be indicated by the prefatory remarks at the beginning of Books xv. and xxvi.

There can be no doubt that Ammianus took his task seriously and made careful preparation for it, reading extensively in Latin literature and making copious notes of what he read. He naturally gave special attention to Tacitus, in particular

---

[1] *Epist.* 983, ἀκούω δὲ τὴν Ῥώμην αὐτὴν στεφανοῦν σοι τὸν πόνον καὶ κεῖσθαι ψῆφον αὐτῇ, τῶν μέν σε κεκρατηκέναι, τῶν δὲ οὐχ ἡττῆσθαι. "I hear that Rome herself has crowned your work, and that her verdict is, that you have surpassed some and equalled others."

[2] xxviii. **1,** 57.

to the Histories, and imitated him so far as he could. He also read Livy and sometimes attempts to use his periodic structure, occasionally with success.[1] He also was acquainted with Sallust, although the traces of the Amiternian's diction may be due to the latter's influence on Tacitus. It is of no significance that he nowhere mentions either Tacitus or Livy in his work. To perfect his Latinity he read Cicero, whom he quotes more than thirty times; partly for the same reason and partly for information about Gaul, he read Caesar. In addition to these conspicuous examples he shows acquaintance, not only with such prose writers as Gellius, Valerius Maximus, the elder Pliny, Florus, and others, but also with the poets; for example, Plautus and Terence, Virgil, Horace, Ovid, and Lucan. Of later writers he used the *Annales* of Virius Nicomachus Flavianus, and the work of an anonymous Greek writer who followed the Thucydidean chronology by summers and winters; Ammianus shows in this respect a mixture of the annalistic and the Thucydidean method. He depended also for historical information on the *Diary* of Magnus of Carrhae;[2] and in his excursuses he made use of Seneca, *Naturales Quaestiones*, Solinus, Ptolemy, and others, as well as of the official lists of the provinces (*Notitiae*).

In addition to his literary sources Ammianus relied for a considerable part of his work on his own

---

[1] At the beginning of Books xiv. and xxiv.; see Mackail, *Class. Studies*, p. 163.

[2] On this complicated question see especially Klein, who also reconstructs the fragments of Magnus of Carrhae.

INTRODUCTION

observation and personal experiences, and it is these that give his work its greatest charm. It is evident that he wished to write a history, rather than follow the biographical treatment which had been popular since the time of Suetonius ; he speaks with scorn of those who, *detestantes ut venena doctrinas*, read only Juvenal and Marius Maximus.[1] Yet he could not wholly escape the influence of the followers of Suetonius ; he has a biographical sketch of each of the emperors and Caesars included in his History, besides an encomium of the eunuch Eutherius,[2] but he did not follow any fixed form of biographical composition.[3] He also disapproved of the epitomes which were fashionable in his day, yet he did not hesitate to draw on Eutropius, Rufius Festus, and Aurelius Victor.

Ammianus aimed at strict truthfulness [4] without suppressing anything that was well authenticated or indulging in deliberate invention,[5] faults which he censures in his criticism of the official reports of the emperor Constantius ; [6] and he avoided exaggeration.[7] Although he recognised the danger of speaking freely and frankly of recent or contemporary

---

[1] xxviii. **4, 14.** Mentioned as authors of gossipy works, contrasted with those of solid learning. Marius Maximus (circa A.D. 165-230) wrote *Lives of the Caesars*, in continuation of Suetonius, from Nerva to Elegabalus. His work is lost, but was used by the *Scriptores Historiae Augustae*.
[2] xvi. **7,** 4 ff. ; his account of Julian also has characteristics of the *encomium ;* see M. J. Kennedy, *The Literary Work of Ammianus*, Univ. of Chicago diss., 1912.
[3] See Leo, *Die griechisch-römische Biographie*, pp. 236 ff.
[4] See e.g. xv. i. 1 ; xvi. **1,** 3 ; xxxi. **5,** 10.
[5] xxix. **1,** 15.   [6] xvi. **12,** 69.   [7] xviii. **6,** 23.

personages and events,[1] he does not profess to write
sine ira et studio,[2] but gives free expression to praise
or blame ; he did not hesitate to censure where
censure was due, and he more than once finds faults
even in his hero Julian.[3] In the historical part of
his work he may fairly be said to have attained his
ideal of truthfulness ; that he was less successful
in his numerous excursuses was due in part to lack
of knowledge, and to some extent to an apparent
desire to conceal the extent of his dependence
upon literary sources. If he had heeded Livy's
warning about digressions,[4] his work would have
been more uniformly successful. They could be
omitted without interfering with the course of the
narrative.

Ammianus wrote for Roman readers, and in
particular for the leading literary circle of the
Eternal City, of which Symmachus was a prominent
member. It was for that reason, and not merely
because he was continuing the narrative of Tacitus,
that he wrote in Latin and not in his native language.
His readers and hearers were of course *utriusque
linguae periti*, but they knew their Roman literature
and could appreciate and applaud his echoes of
Livy, Cicero, and other greater writers of the
past.

In modern times Gibbon found him sincere, modest,
loyal to his superior officers, copious and authentic,
an accurate and faithful guide.[5] Mackail calls him
an officer and a gentleman, worthy of a place among

---

[1] xxvi. **1**, 1 ; xxvii. **9**, 4.　　[2] Tac., *Ann.* i. **1**.
[3] xxii. **9**, 12 ; **10**, 7 ; etc.　　[4] ix. 17, 1.
[5] *Passim ;* see Mackail, *Class. Stud.*, p. 164.

the great Roman historians.[1] Seeck [2] praises his
ability in depicting character, all but unexampled
in ancient literature, and ranking him with the first
historians of all time. In ancient times his work
was little known; it is cited only once, by Priscian,[3]
who seems to have had no more of the History
before him than we have to-day. Cassiodorus is
said to have written out the entire work and to have
imitated its author's style.[4]

His Style

That Ammianus gave great attention to the style
of his work is evident. Klein's idea of the manner
in which he composed the History seems plausible,[5]
namely, that he wrote his first draft in his natural
Latin, using also from memory expressions which
he had met in his wide reading. When he wished
to publish, or recite, a part of it, he worked it over
with particular attention to stylistic effect, drawing
heavily on the results of his reading from the notes
which he had collected. Being a soldier, he knew Latin
as the official language of the army; he could speak,
read, and write it, but he did not acquire a thorough
mastery of it, the *Sprachgefühl* of a native Roman.
As Pliny aptly says,[6] *invenire praeclare, enuntiare
magnifice interdum etiam barbari solent; disponere*

[1] *l.c.* [2] Paully-Wissowa, *Real-Enc.* i., p. 1852.
[3] *Gr. Lat.* 2, 487, 1 f., Keil, *ut " indulsi indulsum " vel
" indultum," unde Marcellinus rerum gestarum xiiii* . . .
[4] Teuffel, *Römische Literatur*, 6th ed., p. 299.
[5] *l.c.*, p. 9.   [6] *Epist.* iii. 13, 3.

apte, figurare varie nisi eruditis negatum est. It was
in particular Ammianus' attempt to decorate his
style with ornaments of all kinds, drawn from
every source, combined with his imitation of Tacitus,
that produced his very extraordinary Latin ; in the
words of Kroll,[1] " sein taciteisches Latein ist schwer
zu verstehen, unleidlich geziert und überladen, eine
Qual seiner Leser," a verdict in which the present
translator would take exception only to the last
clause. Some of his peculiarities are an unnatural
word-order, attempted picturesque and poetic forms
of expression, and a general striving for effect, due
in part to the general taste of the time in which
he lived, and in part to the custom of public recitations. There are colloquial features : the use of
the comparative for the positive, of *quod* with the
indicative for the accusative and the infinitive, of
the present for the future, the imperfect for the
pluperfect, and the pluperfect for a preterit ; also
improper uses of the subjunctive, and a disregard of
the sequence of tenses. Naturally, characteristics of
his native language appear ; some of the peculiarities
already noted may be traced to that source, as well
as his extensive use of participial constructions.[2]

In spite of all this, when we consider the high
value which the Romans, even of late times, set
upon form and rhetoric, it does not seem possible
that the success of his public recitations was due
solely to the content of his History, or that his style

---

[1] Teuffel, *Römische Literatur*, 6th ed., p. 297, repeated
from earlier editions.

[2] Norden, *Die Antike Kunstprosa*, pp. 648 ff., who sees
also influence of the Asianic oratorical style.

could have been as offensive to his hearers as it is to the modern reader of his work.

Ammianus' attention to form is further shown by the rhythmical structure of his prose ; for it has long since been observed that he regularly ended his clauses with metrical *clausulae*. These have recently been made the object of special study by Clark [1] and Harmon,[2] with the result that they have been found to be based upon accent and not upon quantity. The system which he uses was a simple one : between the last two accents of a phrase two or four unaccented syllables are placed, never one or three. Quantity makes no difference and final vowels are never elided ; Greek words as a rule retain the Greek accent ; *i* and *u* may be read either as vowels or as consonants. Of course it is possible that in some instances the arrangement of syllables may be accidental, but the number of *clausulae* is too great to be other than designed. In spite of the simplicity of his system Ammianus has considerable variety in his endings, as is illustrated by Clark [3] in the following scheme :

Cursus planus : expeditiónis evéntus, xiv. **1, 1.**

              illúc transitúrus, xiv. **6, 16.**

              Aégyptum pétens, xxii. **5, 5.**[4]

              régna Persídis, xxiii. **5, 16.**[4]

Cursus tardus : pártium ánimis, xiv. **1, 1.**

              instruménta non lévia, xiv. **6, 18.**

---

[1] Ed. of Ammianus, vol. i., Berlin, 1910, pp. vi. ff.

[2] *Trans. Conn. Acad. of Arts and Science*, 16 (1910), pp. 117 ff.

[3] *l.c.*, p. vii. For the value of the *clausulae* for the interpretation of the text, see Preface.

[4] Greek accent retained.

INTRODUCTION

Cursus velox :   frégerat et labórum, xiv. **1, 1.**
relatúri quae audíret, xiv. 1, 6.[1]
obiécti sunt praeter mórem, xiv. **2, 1.**
Aégypto trucidátur, xiv. 11, 32.[4]
gramínea prope rívum, xxiv. 8, 7.
nómine allocútus est, xv. **6, 3.**
incénsas et habitácula, xviii. **2, 19**

ROMAN OFFICIALS IN THE TIME OF AMMIANUS.

The transformation of the Roman Empire into
an oriental monarchy began in A.D. 284, when
Diocletian became sole ruler. He abandoned all re-
publican traditions and undertook the reorganisation
of the civil and military administration. The process was continued by Constantine and his successors,
until the government became a bureaucracy in the
hands of a limited number of high officials. The
powers and rank of these ministers varied during this
period, and involve a number of difficult problems.
For the sake of reasonable brevity the offices are
described so far as possible as they were in the time
of Ammianus.

Diocletian, realising that the rule of the vast
empire was too great a task for one man, took
Maximianus as his colleague, sharing with him also
the title *Augustus.* The authority of the two *Augusti*
was equal and all laws and edicts were issued in their
common name, but practically the empire was
divided into two parts, Diocletian ruling the East,
with his headquarters at Nicomedia, Maximian

---

[1] *Quae* read as dissyllabic.

INTRODUCTION

the West, at Mediolanum. The *Augusti* were not
accountable to any legislative body or magistrate.
They wore the imperial diadem and a robe trimmed
with jewels, and an elaborate ceremonial was required of all who approached them. Everything
connected with the emperor was called *sacer, sanc-
tissimus,* or *divinus.*

Nine years after Diocletian became emperor he
and Maximian chose two Caesars, who stood next
to themselves in rank and dignity ; they were,
however, dependents of the *Augusti,* having no
authority except what was conferred upon them by
their superiors, and receiving a fixed salary. The
administration of the empire was then divided into
four parts ; Diocletian took Thrace, Egypt, Syria,
and Asia Minor, and assigned to Galerius, the
Caesar whom he had nominated, the Danubian
provinces, Illyricum, Greece, and Crete ; Maximian
governed Italy and Africa ; Constantius, his Caesar,
ruled Gaul, Spain, and after 296 Britain. This
division was only for administrative purposes ;
the empire in reality consisted of two parts, of which
the two *Augusti* were the supreme rulers.

The main purpose of the institution of the Caesars
was to provide for the succession, and it was a part
of the plan that when one of the *Augusti* died or
resigned, his place should be filled by one of the
Caesars, who at the time of their appointment were
adopted by the *Augusti.* When Diocletian and
Maximian retired in 306, a series of wars followed
among the Caesars and the *Augusti.* In that year
Constantine I, later surnamed the Great, assumed
the title of Caesar, which was acknowledged by

INTRODUCTION

Galerius; in 308 he was declared Augustus along with Galerius, and Severus and Maximinus were chosen as Caesars. Maxentius, son of Maximian, was proclaimed Augustus by the troops at Rome, but was not acknowledged by the other *Augusti* and Caesars; he defeated and slew Severus in Italy, whereupon Licinius was made an Augustus by Galerius. In 308 there were four *Augusti*: Constantine, Galerius, Licinius, and Maximinus, in addition to the usurper Maxentius. A series of wars followed. Maximinus was defeated by Licinius and died shortly afterward; Galerius had died in 311. Constantine defeated Maxentius at Saxa Rubra in 312 and reigned for a time with Licinius. After two wars, with a brief interval of peace, Constantine defeated Licinius at Adrianople and Chalcedon in 324. In that year he became sole Augustus, with his sons Crispus, Constantine and Constantius as Caesars; in 335 Delmatius and Hannibalianus were added to the list of Caesars, making five in all.

Constantine ruled alone until his death in 337, when his sons Constantinus II, Constantius II, and Constans were declared *Augusti;* Crispus had in the meantime fallen victim to the jealousy of Fausta, his stepmother, and Delmatius and Hannibalianus were now put to death. In 340 war broke out between Constantinus II and Constans; the former was defeated and slain, and Constans became sole emperor in the West. In 350 Constans died, and three usurpers appeared: Magnentius in Gaul, Nepontianus at Rome, and Vetranio at Mursa in Pannonia. The last two were quickly

disposed of; Nepontianus was killed in less than
a month after his elevation to the supreme rank,
and Vetranio was defeated and deposed by
Constantius after ten months. The contest with
Magnentius, who had appointed his brother Decentius
to the position of Caesar, lasted for three years;
Constantius defeated the usurper at Mursa and
drove him into Gaul, where Magnentius was again
defeated and took his own life. Constantius ruled as
sole Augustus until 361; in 351, while the war with
Magnentius was still going on, he had conferred the
rank of Caesar on his cousin Gallus and sent him to
the East, to carry on war against the Persians.
With Gallus' arrogance and cruelty at Antioch the
extant part of Ammianus' narrative begins.

After Constantius became sole emperor his authority was supreme, but the four-fold administrative
division of the empire into the East, Illyricum,
Italy, and Gaul was continued;[1] the divisions
were called prefectures, and were governed by
praetorian prefects, resident at Constantinople,
which Constantine had made the capital of the empire in 330; at Sirmium; at Mediolanum (Milan);
and at Treveri (Trèves) or at Eboracum (York).
The prefectures were divided into dioceses, and the
dioceses into provinces; the provinces were under
the charge of a governor called *consularis*, *corrector*,
or *praeses*.[2] There were thirteen dioceses and 101

[1] The development of the administrative system was
a gradual one from the time of Constantine until the fifth
century, and the exact date of the various changes is in
many instances uncertain.

[2] See note 1, p. 143. Ammianus often uses the word
iudex of governors of provinces and other high officials

provinces (compared with 45 in Hadrian's time), a number which was later increased to about 120.

The purpose of these divisions and of the consequent increase in the number of these and of other officials[1] was to prevent any officer from becoming powerful enough to start a revolution and interfere with the regular succession to imperial power. The same end was sought by a sharp division between civil and military authority,[2] and by the fact that the competence of the various official groups was not always clearly defined, which led to jealousy and rivalry among the officers. Also the subordinates of the higher officials were appointed by the emperor, and the conduct of their superiors was besides watched and reported to the Augustus by a corps of secret service men, the *agentes in rebus*.[3] The effect of all this, and the elaborate ceremonial required in order to approach the emperor, removed him from contact with his subjects and enhanced his dignity and majesty; at the same time he was unable to hear the complaints of the people, since the officials, who often enriched themselves at the expense of the provincials, concealed one another's

(xviii. 6, 12; xx. 5, 7; xx. 8, 14; xx. 9, 1), and transfers it to similar officers among foreign peoples (Quadi, xvii. 12, 21; Goths, xxvii. 5, 6); sometimes he uses *iudex* in its usual sense of " a judge " (xiv. 9, 3). The two meanings are combined in xvi. 8, 6.

[1] See below under the various officials.

[2] These were never held at the same time by the same official; the place of the senatorial and equestrian *cursus honorum* was taken by careers that were mainly civil or mainly military.

[3] See note 2, p. 98, and Index II.

misdemeanors. In fact, the emperor, although in theory all-powerful, was actually a tool in the hands of a hierarchy of powerful ministers; the real control was exercised by the highest civil and military officers, and those in charge of the affairs of the imperial household.

The entire body of officials was divided into a number of grades, each with its own title. All officers who held positions of sufficient importance became members of the senatorial order, with the title *clarissimi*, which was also held by the two higher grades. A smaller group of higher officials had the title *spectabiles*, and a third body, including only the heads of the various administrative departments, made up the *illustres*. The title *nobilissimus* was reserved for the members of the imperial family. Two classes ranking below the *clarissimi* were the *perfectissimi* and the *egregii*; these included only a small number of officials, and the titles gradually went out of use.

Two other orders of a somewhat different character were created by Constantine. A purely honorary title, *patricius*, was open only to those who had held the positions of praetorian prefect, city prefect, commander-in-chief of the army, or *consul ordinarius*. It was held for life and its possessor took precedence of all officials except consuls in office.

To the *comites*, originally merely the companions of an emperor or high official on his travels,[1] Constantine gave importance by making *comes* (count) a title of honour conferred upon the holders of some public offices, or conferred as a reward for service

---

[1] Horace, *Epist.* i. 3.

INTRODUCTION

The counts were attached to the emperor and the ruling house,[1] but it was a natural and easy step to assign them various duties as the emperor's deputies,[2] both in a civil and in a military capacity. There were three grades (*comites primi, secundi, et tertii ordinis*),[3] and counts appear among the *illustres*, the *spectabiles*, and the *clarissimi*. Like other officials, they were variously designated as in actual service (*in actu positi*) ; as *vacantes*, men of inferior position who on retiring from office were given the rank and insignia of counts as a reward for good service ; and as *honorarii*, who received the title by imperial favour or by purchase, but did not have the right to wear the insignia.[4]

The emperors gathered about them a body of advisers, which entirely superseded the senate in importance.[5] It was first called the *auditorium* or *consilium principis*, but Constantine gave it the title of *consistorium principis* or *sacrum consistorium* ; [6] *consistorium* does not appear in inscriptions until 353, and Ammianus seems to be the first writer to use the word. There is difference of opinion as to its membership. It was composed mainly of the

---

[1] *Comes domini nostri Constantini Aug.*, Dessau, 1213 ; *C.I.L.* vi. 1707 ; *comiti dominorum nostrorum Augustorum et Caesarum*, Dessau, 1223 ; *C.I.L.* x. 4752.

[2] *Comes et quaestor, Cod. Theod.* i. 8, 1, 2 ; *comes et magister equitum*, ibid. vii. 1, 9.

[3] A similar division by Tiberius (Suet., *Tib.* 46) seems to have been made for a special occasion only.

[4] See also Index II.

[5] The senate and the senatorial order retained their dignity, but the power of the senate was purely local.

[6] On the use of *sacer*, see p. xxiv, above.

heads of the various departments of administration, certainly of those most intimately connected with the imperial household (*dignitates palatinae*) : the Minister of Finance (*comes sacrarum lagitionum*),[1] the Minister of the Privy Purse (*comes rerum privatarum*), the Quaestor (*quaestor sacri palatii*), who was the emperor's legal adviser, and the Master of the Offices. The prefect, whose seat of government was at the capital (*praefectus praetorio praesens*), was probably a member, as well as the Grand Chamberlain (*praepositus sacri cubiculi*), and some officials of the grade *spectabilis*. The members of the council were called *comites consistoriani* or simply *consistoriani*.[2] It was presided over by the emperor, or in his absence by the Quaestor, who was obliged to give his decisions in writing ; the proceedings were taken down by secretaries and stenographers (*notarii*).[3]

Since the consulship was often held by the emperor, that office was one of high honour and the consul in office ranked next to the emperor himself, above the *patricii* and the prefects. The consuls, however, had little actual power. On the day of their accession to office they held a procession, which the

---

[1] For an account of these high officials see below.

[2] xv. 5, 12.

[3] *Notarii* were of varying ranks ; those who attended the meetings of the consistory were *tribuni et notarii principis*, where *tribuni* is merely a designation of rank, given to the secretaries in the service of the emperor and the praetorian prefect. Besides their clerical duties they were sometimes sent abroad on confidential missions, to keep an eye on suspected persons (xvii. 9, 7 ; xxi. 7, 2) ; and they were often promoted to high positions (xx. 9, 5 ; xxviii. 1, 12 ; xxviii, 2, 5). See also Index II.

emperor himself attended, exhibited games, and freed slaves. The title *consularis*, which was the highest title held by the governors of the provinces,[1] did not necessarily imply that its holder was an ex-consul.

The Praetorian Prefect (*praefectus praetorio*) in the time of Augustus was a military officer, the commander of the praetorian cohorts in Rome, which formed the emperor's body-guard. It was the highest grade in the equestrian *cursus honorum*, and its holder gradually acquired great power. Sejanus was practically the ruler of Rome during the absence of Tiberius, and Titus, although of senatorial rank, assumed the office in order to increase his authority and to have a freer hand.[2] There were ordinarily two prefects, although occasionally there was only one, and in the latter part of the reign of Commodus there were three.

This official, as time went on, became more prominent as a judge and in a civil capacity, and under Septimius Severus and Gallienus he was practically a civil minister, although he retained some vestiges of military authority even under Diocletian. When Constantine abolished the praetorian guard and replaced it by the *scholae Palatinae*,[3] the dignity and rank of the prefect survived and he became the highest civil servant of the emperor, without any participation in military affairs. He was appointed for an indefinite period, but because of his great

---

[1] E.g. Pannonia, xvi. **8**, 3 ; Picenum, xv. **7**, 5 ; Syria, xiv. **7**, 5 ; etc. On *consularis, corrector* and *praeses*, see p. 143, note 1.

[2] Suetonius, *Titus*, **6**. [3] See below, p. xliii.

power he was seldom kept in office for more than a year. Constantine also appointed a *praefectus per Gallias* and a *praefectus per Orientem*, and to these a *praefectus per Illyricum* was later added, so that each of the four grand divisions of the empire was governed by a prefect. The prefect had a number of *vicarii*, each of whom governed one of the dioceses into which his prefecture was divided.[1]

In spite of various restrictions[2] the power of a prefect was very extensive. His office, like that of the other *illustres*, was large and well organized, with assistants, recorders, clerks, shorthand writers and mounted messengers. From the time of Alexander Severus he was a member of the senate. He had complete control of the general tax ordered by the emperor (*indictio*), and through his subordinates took part in levying it ; he held court as the emperor's representative ; he issued edicts, which had the same force as those of the emperor, unless they were annulled by the Augustus ; he supervised the governors and judges of the provinces, proposed their names, and paid their salaries ; and he had a general supervision of the grain supplies, manufactures, coinage, roads and courier-service (*cursus publicus*).[3] His insignia were a lofty chariot, a golden pen-case, a silver inkstand, and a silver tripod and bowl for receiving petitions. He wore a cloak like that of the emperor, except that it

---

[1] E.g. *vicarius Asiae*, xxvii. **9**, 6.

[2] Especially the transfer of some of the prefect's powers to other officials.

[3] This last, with the right of granting free conveyance, he shared with the emperor and the *magister officiorum*.

reached to the knees instead of to the feet; as a mark of his former military rank he carried a sword.[1] Of the four praetorian prefects one who was resident at the court of an emperor or a Caesar seems to have been called *praesens* or *praesentalis*, if the number of *Augusti* and Caesars was less than four.[2]

The Prefect of the City (*praefectus urbis*) in early times had charge of the city of Rome during the absence of the king or the consuls. His duties and powers were gradually taken over by the city praetor (*praetor urbanus*), until Augustus revived the office, in order to provide for the government of Rome during his absence. Under Tiberius, because of his long stay at Capri, the office became a permanent one, and it increased in power and importance until the City Prefect ranked next to the Praetorian. He had command of the city troops (*cohortes urbanae*) and general charge of the policing of the city. In addition to this he had a number of officers under his supervision, through whom he managed the census, the markets, and the granaries, and had power over all the corporations and guilds which carried on business in the city. Within the hundredth milestone he had supreme judicial, military, and administrative power. He convoked and presided over the senate, and made known its wishes to the

[1] Cassiodorus, *Variae*, Books vi. and vii., gives the formulae for conferring the various offices, with a summary of their duties; for the Praetorian Prefect, see vi. 3; there is a condensed translation by T. Hodgkin, London, 1886.

[2] See xiv. 1, 10, note; xxiii. 5, 6; cf. xx. 4, 8. If the *Augusti* and Caesars were four in number, each had his own prefect, and no such designation was necessary.

emperor. His insignia were twelve fasces, he wore
the toga, and shared with the praetorian prefect
alone the privilege of using a chariot within the city.
There was also a city prefect at Constantinople
(xxvi. 7, 2) with corresponding powers.

In very early times the Master of the Horse
(*magister equitum*) was an assistant of the dictator,
and was appointed by him ; he played a particularly
important part between 49 and 44 B.C., because of
the frequent absence of the dictator Caesar from Italy.
Augustus transferred the powers of this official to
the *praefectus praetorio*, who exercised them for a
long time. Constantine in the early part of his
reign, for the purpose of limiting the powers of the
praetorian prefect, revived the office by appointing
two commanders-in-chief of the military forces of
the empire, one of the cavalry (*magister equitum*),
the other of the infantry (*magister peditum*). From
the middle of the fourth century these two officers
began to be called *magistri equitum et peditum*, or
magistri utriusque militiae, and finally, *magistri
militum*. Ammianus uses both titles, as well as
magister armorum,[1] *magister rei castrensis*[2] and
pedestris militiae rector.[3] Constantius added three
more *magistri militum*, for the Orient, Gaul, and
Illyricum, and in the *Notitia Dignitatum* we find
five in the Eastern, and three in the Western Empire.

With the appointment of these officers the organi-

---

[1] xv. 5, 36 ; xvi. 7, 3 ; xx. 1, 2.   [2] xxvii. 10, 6.
[3] xv. 5, 2. In spite of his experience as a soldier,
Ammianus is somewhat loose and inexact in his use of
military titles, although some at least of his terms were
probably due to a desire for variety.

INTRODUCTION

sation of the army was changed. The *limitanei*,
who guarded the boundaries of the empire, were
diminished in number, while the *comitatenses*, or
field-troops under command of the several *magistri
militum*, and the *palatini*,[1] attached to the court
and commanded by the Master of the Offices, were
increased. The *magistri militum* were the judges
of the army under their control, and had the power
of jurisdiction even in some civil cases involving
their soldiers; but their civil powers were very
strictly limited, and in civil matters the decision
ordinarily rested with the provincial judges; an
appeal from their decision went to the *praefectus
praetorio*, and not to the *magister militum*. The
magistri militum were judges over their subordinates,
the *comites rei castrensis* and the *duces*, but not
over the subordinates of the *comites* and *duces*.
They could not move troops from one part of the
empire to another, without the emperor's order,
except in case of a very great emergency.

Next in rank to these three officials was the Grand
Chamberlain (*praepositus sacri cubiculi*). Chamberlains are first mentioned in connection with Julius
Caesar's capture by the pirates[2]; four years later
Cicero alludes to them in such a way as to imply
that they were regular members of the families of
the wealthier citizens[3]; they had considerable
importance as personal attendants of the governors

[1] The *Scholae Palatinae* consisting of five corps of 500
men each at Rome and at Constantinople, to which two
others were later added at Constantinople; see note 3,
p. 56. Besides these there were the *protectores* and
domestici.

[2] Suetonius, *Jul.* 4, 1.   [3] *Verres*, ii. 3, 4, 8.

of provinces, but were not members of their official staff.[1] When Augustus reorganized the palace service, the chamberlains formed a corps under the headship of an officer called *a cubiculo*,[2] who was in close touch with the emperor, later sometimes his companion [3] and confidant, and hence gradually acquired wide influence. Another official of the corps is perhaps the *decurio cubiculariorum*, mentioned by Suetonius in connection with the murder of Domitian.[4] The *praepositi* of the time of Ammianus were eunuchs, and as constant companions of the emperor they had great power; in one instance a *praepositus* who confessed that he had taken part in a conspiracy escaped punishment through the intervention of his fellow eunuchs,[5] and Ammianus ironically says [6] that the emperor Constantius had considerable influence, if the truth be told, with Eusebius, his Grand Chamberlain.

The Grand Chamberlain had a considerable body of subordinates, all of whom were employed in the personal service of the emperor; the *primicerius sacri cubiculi* was the head of those who served as the chamberlains of the emperor's apartment, and the *comes castrensis sacri palatii* of all who were not chamberlains, such as pages, and the throng of palace servants; other subordinates, with appro-

---

[1] Cicero, *Ad Att.* vi. 2, 5 ; *Digest*, l. 16, 203.

[2] Dunlap, pp. 169 ff. ; see note 4, p. xiii.

[3] Philo, *Legatio ad Gaium*, 27.

[4] Suet., *Dom.* 17, 2.   [5] xv. 2, 10.

[6] xviii. 4, 3 ; so Dunlap, p. 181, but as Ammianus is not often, if ever, humorous, the conjecture of *posuit* for *potuit* is a reasonable one, with the meaning that Constantius depended greatly on Eusebius.

priate titles, had charge of the royal wardrobe, of necessary repairs in the palace, and the keeping of any noise from reaching the imperial apartments (the *silentiarii*).

Another important official in close contact with the imperial household was the Master of the Offices (*magister officiorum*). In 321 and 323 we hear of a *tribunus et magister officiorum*,[1] so that the office goes back at least as far as Constantine, although the earliest *magister* who appears in inscriptions held office in 346.[2] Since *tribunus* implies military service, the office is supposed to have originated when Diocletian organized the *officiales* of the palace on a military basis and chose the senior tribune of the praetorian guard to take charge of the various corps of palace attendants, and also to command the soldiers attached to the court.[3] As one of the *dignitates palatinae* the functions of the Master of the Offices came in conflict with those of the Praetorian Prefect, whose power he still further curtailed, and to some extent with those of the Grand Chamberlain. Besides being in command of the five *scholae* of the palace guards,[4] he had supervision over the chiefs of the four imperial *scrinia*, or correspondence bureaus, and over the *schola* of the *agentes in rebus*,[5]

---

[1] Cod. Theod. xvi. 10, 1 ; xi. 9, 1.
[2] Dessau, 1244 ; *C.I.L.* vi. 1721.
[3] Dunlap, pp. 26 f.   [4] Note 3, p. 56.
[5] See p. xxvii, above, and note 3. This was a large corps, numbering 1174 in the Orient in 430, and increased to 1248 by the emperor Leo (457-474). They were divided into five grades, and from the two higher classes chiefs of bureau for the *vicarii* were recruited, as well as *comites*, *duces* and even governors of provinces.

and he also had charge of the *cursus publicus*, or state courier-service. The management of this was at first in the hands of the Praetorian Prefect, but was transferred under Constantine to the Master of the Offices. This control of the means of conveying state dispatches and persons travelling on state business throughout the empire was a very important one, since it included the right to issue passes giving the privilege of using the *cursus*. It brought the Master into frequent collision with the Praetorian Prefect, but the Master had the superior supervision.

The Master of the Offices also had control of the great arsenals and manufactories of arms of Italy, and in particular it was through him that imperial audiences were obtained, and that the ambassadors of foreign powers were received and introduced. Actual entrance into the audience-chamber was under the direction of a *magister admissionum*, and a corps of *admissionales*; in the cases of distinguished applicants for audience the *magister admissionum* functioned [1] and in very exceptional cases the *magister officiorum* himself, regularly in the case of women of distinction. He had a very large corps of assistants and subordinates; his duties were very complex and important, and he was one of the most powerful officials.

The *Quaestor Sacri Palatii* was also numbered among the *dignitates palatinae* and was in close touch with the emperor. In the days of Augustus the quaestorship was the lowest office that gave

---

[1] See note, p. 144.

admission to the senate. It was given additional prestige by the arrangement by which some of its occupants were selected by the emperor himself (called *quaestores candidati* or *quaestores Augusti*, or *principis*), and because one of them was regularly attached to the person of the ruler, to read his letters and other communications to the senate.[1] As the emperor's letters came more and more to have the force of laws and edicts, the Quaestor was considered a legal officer connected with civil jurisprudence, and ranked as one of the highest officials of the court. He had the rank of Count and at the end of the fourth century became an *illustris*. His duties required him to be the mouthpiece of the emperor, and to suggest to the ruler anything that would be for the welfare of the state. He had the right to suggest laws and to answer petitions addressed to the emperor. It was therefore necessary that he should be a trained jurist, in order to be an exact and just interpreter of the law. He also had the supervision of every one who entered the capital; he made inquiries into the character of all who came from the provinces, and found out from what provinces they came and for what reasons, the purpose being to prevent worthless men from taking up their residence in the city.

Theodoric wrote to the senate with regard to the office of Quaestor:[2] " It is only men whom we consider to be of the highest learning that we raise

[1] Suet., *Aug.* 65, 2 ; *Nero*, 15, 2 ; *Titus*, 6, 1.

[2] Cassiodorus, *Varia*, v. 4 (Hodgkin) ; vi. 5 ; viii. 19 ; the *Varia* contain valuable information about all these high officials.

INTRODUCTION

to the dignity of the quaestorship, such men as are fitted to be the interpreters of the laws and sharers of our counsels," and Claudian said of that official [1] " thou comest to give edicts to the world, to make reply to suppliants. A monarch's utterance has won dignity from thine eloquence."

The Count of the Sacred Largesses (*comes sacrarum largitionum*) was the Minister of Finance, who controlled the revenues of the state, except those which passed into the hands of the prefects, the Count of the Privy Purse (*comes rerum privatarum*),[2] the Quaestor, and the Master of the Offices. He had supreme charge of the *sacrum aerarium*, or state treasury, including the former *aerarium* and *fiscus*,[3] exerting it in the provinces through his subordinates, the *comites largitionum*, of whom there was one for each diocese. The latter had subordinates called *rationales summarum*, each of whom collected the money and taxes either of his whole diocese or of a great part of it.

The *Comes Sacrarum Largitionum* also had under his supervision numerous direct and indirect taxes, and the revenues from the provinces were sent to him by the first of March. Through subordinates he had control of the sea-coasts and of merchants, who could not go beyond certain cities prescribed by law ; and the trading in salt, which was a government monopoly, was under his direct supervision,

[1] *Panegyr. dictus Manlio Theodoro*, 34 ff. (*L.C.L.* ii., p. 341.)
[2] See below.
[3] That is, the *aerarium Saturni*, or public treasure, and the emperor's privy purse.

including the granting of licences for the working of the public salt mines, the revenues from which were under his control. Through other subordinates he had charge of the banks in the various provinces, in which the money that was collected was kept until it was sent to him. He controlled the other mines and those who worked in them, the coinage, and the mints. He was general superintendent of the imperial factories, the employees in which could not engage in private work and were hereditarily confined to their special trades ; they were under the direct charge of *procuratores*.

He also had judicial control over his subordinates and the power of confirming the appointments of some judges in the provinces. As his title implies, he administered the bounties of the emperor (the *largitiones*). The disposition of the money under his charge was entirely dependent on the good will of the emperor, either in meeting the demands of the various necessities of state, or in giving presents, or in conferring rewards.

Like the other high officials he had in his office a great number of bureaus of correspondence (*scrinia*) consisting of officials who received the payments made each year by the provinces ; kept accounts of the *sacrae largitiones* through *tabularii* ; made out the fiscal accounts and supervized the *largitiones* ; had charge of all the expenditures for clothing needed in the palace and for the soldiers, whether they belonged to the palace troops or not, of the silverware of the palace, and the like.

The Count of the Privy Purse (*comes rerum privatarum*) had charge of the *aerarium privatum*, con-

INTRODUCTION

sisting both of the *res privatae*, the inalienable crown property, and the *patrimonium sacrum*, the private and personal property of the emperor, which could be inherited by his family. His subordinates were at first the *magistri* (later the *rationales*) *rei privatae*, one for each diocese or province, who took care of all finances within their province, including lands belonging to the temples, and kept a record of the income. He had the superintendence through his *rationales* of the government estates, both at home and in the provinces, as well as of the revenues from estates which were especially assigned to the imperial house. The *res privatae* at this time included also the confiscated property of men who had been condemned or proscribed, which before Tiberius had gone to the state treasury (*aerarium*), as well as all deposited money which because of long lapse of time had no claimant, and property for which there were no heirs.

The Count of the Privy Purse also superintended the collectors of the rents of the imperial property in the provinces, and of the gifts of silver or gold demanded in time of need from those to whom the emperors had made presents of real estate, which was free from taxation.

To the *dignitates palatinae*, or offices whose duties did not call their holders away from the capital, might be added the Counts of the Body Guard (*comes domesticorum equitum* and *comes domesticorum peditum*), who are placed in the *Notitia Dignitatum* immediately after the *Comes rerum privatarum*, although they were not always *illustres*, but sometimes held that rank. With the *domestici* the *protectores* are sometimes coupled,[1] and when Constantine in 312 disbanded the praetorian troops, he gave their rank and duties to the *protectores et domestici*. Thus we have two kinds of palace troops : the *scholae palatinae*[2] under the command of the Master of the Offices, and two corps of *protectores et domestici*, who ranked higher than the members of the *scholae palatinae* and were commanded by the *comites domesticorum*. Ammianus is the first to refer to the *protectores* and *domestici* as also divided into scholae.[3] These consisted of ten divisions of fifty men each, commanded by *decemprimi*, of the rank *clarissimus*, and these were under the supervision of a *primicerius*,[4] of the grade *spectabilis ;* the *protectores* themselves ranked as *perfectissimi*.

In addition to accompanying the emperor when he went abroad, the *protectores* and *domestici* were sent to the provinces to perform various public services, although a part had to be always *in praesenti*, or at court. Sometimes, as in the case of Ammianus, they were sent to a *magister militum* and placed under his orders. Whenever they were sent abroad, their pay, which was already large, was increased.

Tribunus is a title of various military officers in connection with the *domestici*, the *armaturae*, the *scutarii*, and the *protectores ;* also of officers in charge of manufactories of arms[5] and of the imperial stables.[6] As has already been noted, the title was

---

[1] xiv. **10**, 2, *protector domesticus ;* cf. xviii. **8**, 11.
[2] See above, p. xxxi.   [3] xiv. **7**, 9, note ; xxvi. **5**, 3.
[4] xviii. 3, 5.   [5] xiv. **7**, 18 ; xv. **5**, 9, at Cremona.
[6] xiv. **10**, 8 ; xxx. **5**, 19.

given also to civil officials, such as the higher in rank of the *notarii*.[1] *Tribuni vacantes* had the title and rank of *tribuni* without a special assignment.[2]

For further information see Index II, which sometimes supplements also the notes on the Text.

MANUSCRIPTS AND EDITIONS.

There are twelve manuscripts that contain all the surviving books of Ammianus. Two break off at the end of Book xxvi. (PR). and one ends abruptly at xxv. **3**, 13 (D). There are besides six detached sheets which once formed part of a codex belonging to the abbey of Hersfeld; these are now in Kassel, and the manuscript to which they belonged is designated as M. Of the other fifteen manuscripts seven are in Rome (VDYEURP), one each in Florence (F), Modena (Q), Cesena (K), and Venice (W), and the remaining four in Paris (CHTN). V and M are of the ninth century, the rest of the fifteenth. A full description of all these and their relations to one another is given by Clark,[3] who has convincingly shown that of the existing manuscripts only V has independent value. To this are added the readings of M, so far as that manuscript has been preserved,[4] and so far as the readings of its lost part can be restored from the edition of Gelenius, who professed

---

[1] Note 3, p. 339.　　　　　　[2] xvi. **12**, 63 ; xviii. **2**, 2.
[3] *The Text Tradition of Ammianus Marcellinus*, New Haven, 1904.
[4] Fragments of Books xxiii., xxviii. and xxx. ; see H. Nissen, *Frag. Marb.*, Berlin, 1876.

to follow M, but made extensive emendations of his own.

Clark reconstructs the history of the text as follows. A capital manuscript, presumably of the sixth century, was copied, probably in Germany by a writer using the *scriptura Scottica*. In the early Caroline period a copy was made from this insular manuscript, which is the parent of V (*Fuldensis*), and of the one of which the Hersfeld fragments formed a part (M). No copy of the *Hersfeldensis* exists, but many of its readings are found in the edition of Gelenius. Every other manuscript is copied from the *Fuldensis* (V), four directly (FDN and E), and the other nine through F, including Gardthausen's *codices mutili* (P and R), which are copies of V at two removes at least.

Since the text of V is in bad shape, with numerous *lacunae*, some of the readings of the early editions are of value. The first printed edition (S) was that of Sabinus, Rome, 1474, containing Books xiv.-xxvi. ; it is a reprint of R, the poorest manuscript in existence, and hence of little or no value. The next (B), that of Petrus Castellus, Bologna, 1517, was a reprint of S, in which the text was further debased by irresponsible emendations, which vitiated all the subsequent history of the text of Books xiv.-xxvi. A pirated reprint of B by Erasmus (*b*) was published at Basle in 1518.

The first improvement dates from the edition of Accursius (A), Augsburg, May, 1533, who used a manuscript copied from V and corrected from a copy of E, which is itself a transcript of V emended by a humanist. A still greater improvement was made by the edition of Gelenius, Basle, July, 1533, who also was partly dependent on the copy of E, but had access besides to the purer tradition of M.

Subsequent editions were those of Gruter, 1611, who corrected his text from V; of Lindenbrog, Hamburg, 1609, who made use of F and first provided the text with explanatory notes; of Henricus Valesius, Paris, 1636, whose annotations formed the basis of all later commentaries, while his brilliant scholarship and critical acumen led him to make numerous correct emendations, with the help of N (his *codex Regius*). He also recognised the existence of metrical *clausulae*, and says three or four times [1] that certain emendations do not correspond with these. His punctuation also seems to take account of the *clausulae*, and hence is often the same as that of Clark.[2] Also important are the editions of Wagner and Erfurdt, Leipzig, 1808, with a collection of the best material in previous commentaries, and of Ernesti, Leipzig, 1773, with a useful *index verborum*, which, however, is not complete, and gives only the numbers of the chapters, without those of the sections, a practice especially exasperating in the long chapters.

The critical study of the text begins with the edition of Henricus Valesius. His younger brother Hadrianus in his edition (Paris, 1681) had the use of two additional manuscripts, C and the codex Valentinus, which is now lost. Later editors were content with the readings of these editions until

---

[1] E.g. at the end of the annotations on Book **xiv**.
[2] See Preface.

INTRODUCTION

1871, when Eyssenhardt published his text at Berlin, which was followed in 1874-75 by that of Gardthausen (Leipzig). The latter was the first to use the *Petrinus* (P), which he thought was written before V came into Italy, from an archetype on a plane with V, and that a copy of V, corrected from M, was the archetype of E and of Accursius' codex. His readings of P are often erroneous, and it is now recognized, as already said, that P does not represent a tradition independent of V. The standard critical edition is that of C. U. Clark, of which volume one, containing Books xiv.-xxv., and volume two, part one, containing xxiv.-xxxi., were published at Berlin in 1910 and 1915 respectively. The second part of volume two, the indices, has not yet appeared.[1]

[1] A complete *Sprachlicher u. Historischer Kommentar zu Ammianus Marcellinus* is planned by P. De Jonge, who published the notes on xiv, 1-7, as his doctoral dissertation, Groningen, 1935. Part 2 (on xiv, 7-11) appeared in 1939.

BIBLIOGRAPHICAL NOTE

THERE is no commentary in English on Ammianus, and
no full and satisfactory one in any language.[1] He has
been translated into English by Philemon Holland, London,
1609, and by C. D. Yonge, London, 1862 ; into German
by C. Büchele, Stuttgart, 1827 (reprinted 1853-54 ; a
second edition by L. Tross, Ulm, 1898, seems never to
have gone beyond Vol. I, containing Books xiv.-xv.) ; into
French by T. Salvète, with the Latin text, Collection
Nisard, Paris, 1849. All these are based upon texts which
differ from the present standard editions.

Papers and monographs dealing with various phases
of Ammianus and his work are very numerous. On the
text may be mentioned in addition to those cited by
Clark in his Compendia : R. Novák, *Kritische Nachlese
zu Ammianus Marcellinus*, Wiener Studien, 33 (1912),
pp. 293 ff. ; P. H. Damsté, *Adversaria critica*, Mnemosyne,
lv. (1927), pp. 241-259 ; lviii. (1930), pp. 1 ff. ; G. B. A.
Fletcher, *Notes on Ammianus Marcellinus*, Classical
Quarterly, xxiv. (1930), pp. 193 ff., and *A.J.P.* lviii.
(1937), pp. 392 ff. ; J. P. Pighius (G. P. Pighi), *Studia
Ammianea*, Milano, 1935 ; *I Discorsi nelle Storie
d'Ammiano Marcellino* and *Nuovi Studi Ammianei*,
Milano, 1936 ; R. P. Robinson, *The Hersfeldensis and
Fuldensis of Ammianus Marcellinus*, in the Univ. of
Missouri Studies, Columbia, Missouri, 1936. On the
officials : M. Cosenza, *Official Positions after the Time of
Constantine* (Columbia Univ. dissertation), Lancaster, Pa.,
1905 ; A. E. R. Boak, *Roman Magistri in the Civil and
Military Service of the Empire*, Harvard Studies in Class.
Phil., xxvi. (1915), pp. 73 ff., and *The Master of the Offices*,
Univ. of Michigan Studies, xiv., pp. 1-160, New York,
1924 ; J. E. Dunlap, *The Grand Chamberlain*, ibid.,
pp. 161-324. General : Klein, W., *Studien zu Ammianus
Marcellinus*, Klio, Beiheft 13, 1914 ; Ensslin, W., *Zur
Geschichtsschreibung und Weltanschauung des Ammianus*

---

[1] See note, p. xlvii.

xlviii

BIBLIOGRAPHICAL NOTE

Marcellinus, Klio, Beiheft 16, 1923 ; T. R. Glover, *Life and Letters in the Fourth Century*, Camb. Univ. Press, 1901 ; R. B. Steele, *Ammianus Marcellinus*, *Class. Weekly*, xvi., pp. 18 ff. and 27 ff. ; W. Hyde, *Roman Alpine Routes*, American Philosophical Society, 1935 ; A. Hoepffner, in *Rev. des Études Lat.*, xiv. (1936), pp. 119 ff. (on the death of Theodosius) ; E. A. Thompson, *The Historical Work of Ammianus*, Cambridge, 1947. To these may be added : G. B. A. Fletcher, *Ammianus and Solinus*, *Phil.* xci. (1936), pp. 478 ff. ; *Stylistic Borrowings and Parallels in Ammianus Marcellinus*, *Rev. de Phil.* xi. (1937), pp. 378 ff. ; and *Ammianea*, *Amer. Jour. of Phil.* lviii. (1937), pp. 378 ff. ; S. Blomgren, *De Sermone Ammiani Marcellini Quaestiones Variae*, Uppsala Universitets Årsskrift, 1937 ; R. A. Pack, *Studies in Libanius and Antiochene Society under Theodosius*, Univ. of Mich. diss., 1935 ; J. Miller, *Jahresbericht*, 247 (1935), pp. 52 ff., with selected literature on Ammianus, 1925-32 ; H. Hagendahl, *Studia Ammianea*, Uppsala, 1921 ; and *De Abundantia Sermonis Ammianei*, in *Eranos*, xxii, 1924, pp. 161 ff.

SIGLA

A	= the edition of Accursius.[1]
B	= the edition of Castellus.
b	= the edition of Erasmus.
Boxh.	= the edition of Boxhorn, Leyden, 1632.
c.c.	= *cursus causa*, emendations made to correct rhythmical endings.
D	= Codex Vaticanus, 1874 (ends at xxv. **3**, 13).
E	= Codex Vaticanus Lat. 2969.
Eyssen.	= the edition of Eyssenhardt.
G	= the edition of Gelenius.
g	= the edition of Gelenius by R. Stephanus, Paris, 1544.
Gardt.	= the edition of Gardthausen.
H	= Codex Parisinus, Bibl. Nat. Lat. 5819.
Her.	= W. Heraeus, who collaborated with Clark in his edition.
lac.	= *lacuna*.
Lind.	= the edition of Lindenbrog.
M	= Codex Hersfeldensis.
N	= Codex Neapolitanus, Paris, Bibl. Nat. Lat. 6120.
P	= Codex Petrinus, Rome, Basil. S. Petri, E 27 (ends with Book xxvi.).
Pet.	= M. Petschenig.
T	= Codex Tolosanus, Paris, Bibl. Nat. Lat. 5820.
vulgo	= readings unknown to the Valesii, but found in the ed. of Gronov.
V	= Codex Fuldensis, Rome, Vat. Lat. 1873.
Val.	= the edition of Henricus Valesius.
Hadr. Val.	= the edition of Hadrian Valesius.
W	= Codex Venetus, Bibl. S. Marc. 388, Bess.

[1] For a brief description of the principal manuscripts and editions see Introd., pp. xliv ff., and for a full description, Clark's *Text Tradition*; see p. xliv, note 3.

1

AMMIANI MARCELLINI
RERUM GESTARUM
LIBRI QUI SUPERSUNT

AMMIANI MARCELLINI
RERUM GESTARUM
LIBRI QUI SUPERSUNT

LIBER XIV

1. *Galli Caesaris saevitia.*[1]

1. Post emensos insuperabilis expeditionis eventus,
languentibus partium animis, quas periculorum
varietas fregerat et laborum, nondum tubarum
cessante clangore, vel milite locato per stationes
hibernas, fortunae saevientis procellae tempestates
alias rebus infudere [2] communibus, per multa illa et
dira facinora Caesaris Galli, qui ex squalore imo
miseriarum, in aetatis adultae primitiis, ad principale
culmen insperato saltu [3] provectus, ultra terminos

---

[1] These summaries, which are not the work of Ammianus
but of some early editor, are put for convenience at the
beginning of each chapter. Usually the summaries of
each book are put all together at the beginning of that
book, or (e.g. by Eyssenhardt) the summaries of all the
books are collected at the end of the entire text.

[2] *infudere*, HA; *infundere*, V.   [3] *saltu*, Kellerbauer,
Kiessling; *cultu*, V.

---

[1] Flavius Claudius (Julius) Constantius Gallus, nephew
of Constantine the Great and half-brother of Julian.
He was made Caesar by Constantius II. in 351.

2

THE SURVIVING BOOKS OF
THE HISTORY
OF AMMIANUS MARCELLINUS

BOOK XIV

CONSTANTIUS AND GALLUS

1. *The cruelty of Gallus Caesar.*[1]

1. After the survival of the events of an unendurable campaign,[2] when the spirits of both parties, broken by the variety of their dangers and hardships, were still drooping, before the blare of the trumpets had ceased or the soldiers been assigned to their winter quarters, the gusts of raging Fortune brought new storms upon the commonwealth through the misdeeds, many and notorious, of Gallus Caesar.[3] He had been raised, at the very beginning of mature

---

[2] Against Magnentius, who in 350 had assumed the rank of an Augustus in the west, with Veteranio ; but was defeated, in 351, by Constantius at Mursa, on the river Drave, a tributary of the Danube and in the passes of the Cottian Alps in 353. His followers then abandoned him and he committed suicide. See Index.

[3] The title of Augustus was lawfully held only by the reigning emperor, or emperors. Caesar was the title next in rank and was conferred by the emperor on one or more of the imperial family ; see Introd. p. xxiv.

3

potestatis delatae procurrens, asperitate nimia
cuncta foedabat.   Propinquitate enim regiae stirpis,
gentilitateque etiam tum Constantii [1] nominis,
efferebatur in fastus, si plus valuisset, ausurus
hostilia in auctorem suae felicitatis (ut videbatur).
2. Cuius acerbitati uxor grave accesserat incentivum,
germanitate Augusti turgida supra modum, quam
Hanniballiano regi fratris filio antehac Constantinus
iunxerat pater, Megaera quaedam mortalis, inflam-
matrix saevientis assidua, humani cruoris avida
nihil mitius quam maritus.   Qui paulatim eruditiores
facti processu temporis ad nocendum, per clandes-
tinos versutosque rumigerulos, compertis leviter
addere quaedam male suetos, falsa et placentia sibi
discentes, affectati regni vel artium nefandarum
calumnias insontibus affigebant.   3. Eminuit autem
inter humilia, supergressa iam impotentia [2] fines
mediocrium delictorum, nefanda Clematii cuiusdam
Alexandrini nobilis mors repentina ; cuius socrus
cum misceri sibi generum, flagrans eius amore, [3] non

---

[1] *Constantii*, Lind ; *Constantiani*, Val ; *Constantini*, V.
[2] *iam impotentia*, Wagn. ; *impotentia*, Momm. ; *iam potentia*,
V.   [3] *flagrans, eius amorem*, sugg. by Clark.

---

[1] He was married to Constantia, daughter of Constantine
the Great and Fausta, wrongly called Constantina, XIV.
7, 4, etc.
[2] Constantine had given him the rule of Pontus, Armenia
Minor, and Cappadocia, but Constantius II., soon after
his accession, had caused his assassination.

manhood, by an unexpected promotion from the utmost depths of wretchedness to princely heights, and overstepping the bounds of the authority conferred upon him, by excess of violence was causing trouble everywhere. For by his relationship to the imperial stock, and the affinity which he even then had with the name of Constantius,[1] he was raised to such a height of presumption that, if he had been more powerful, he would have ventured (it seemed) upon a course hostile to the author of his good fortune. 2. To his cruelty his wife was besides a serious incentive, a woman beyond measure presumptuous because of her kinship to the emperor, and previously joined in marriage by her father Constantine with his brother's son, King Hanniballianus.[2] She, a Megaera[3] in mortal guise, constantly aroused the savagery of Gallus, being as insatiable as he in her thirst for human blood. The pair in process of time gradually became more expert in doing harm, and through underhand and crafty eavesdroppers, who had the evil habit of lightly adding to their information and wanting to learn only what was false and agreeable to them, they fastened upon innocent victims false charges of aspiring to royal power or of practising magic. 3. There stood out among their lesser atrocities, when their unbridled power had already surpassed the limits of unimportant delinquencies, the sudden and awful death of one Clematius, a nobleman of Alexandria. This man's mother-in-law, it was said, had a violent passion for her son-in-law, but

---

[3] One of the Furies.

impetraret, ut ferebatur, per palatii pseudothyrum
introducta, oblato pretioso reginae monili, id assecuta
est, ut ad Honoratum, tum comitem Orientis,
formula missa letali, homo [1] scelere nullo contactus,
idem Clematius, nec hiscere nec loqui permissus,
occideretur.

4. Post hoc impie perpetratum, quod in aliis quoque iam timebatur, tamquam licentia crudelitati
indulta, per suspicionum nebulas aestimati quidam
noxii damnabantur. Quorum pars necati alii puniti
bonorum multatione, actique laribus suis extorres,
nullo sibi relicto praeter querellas et lacrimas, stipe
collaticia victitabant; et civili iustoque imperio ad
voluntatem converso cruentam, claudebantur opu-
lentae domus et clarae. 5. Nec vox accusatoris ulla
(licet subditicii) [2] in his malorum quaerebatur acervis,
ut saltem specie tenus crimina praescriptis legum
committerentur, quod aliquotiens fecere principes
saevi; sed quidquid Caesaris implacabilitati sedisset,
id velut fas iusque perpensum, confestim urgebatur
impleri. 6. Excogitatum est super his, ut homines
quidam ignoti, vilitate ipsa parum cavendi, ad
colligendos rumores per Antiochiae latera cuncta

---

[1] *homo*, Lind.; *omnino*, EW [2]; *omo* (from *odio*), V.
[2] *subditicii*, Lind.; *subditi et*, V.

---

[1] *Comites* originally were companions of an official
on his travels, as Catullus accompanied Memmius to
Bithynia; cf. Horace, *Epist.* i. 8, 2, etc. They gradually
became his advisers, and later they were appointed to

6

was unable to seduce him; whereupon, gaining
entrance to the palace by a back door, she presented
the queen with a valuable necklace, and thus
secured the dispatch of his death-warrant to
Honoratus, at that time Count of the East;[1] and
so Clematius, a man contaminated by no guilt,
was put to death without being allowed to protest
or even to open his lips.

4. After the perpetration of this impious deed,
which now began to arouse the fears of others also,
as if cruelty were given free rein, some persons were
adjudged guilty on the mere shadow of suspicion
and condemned. Of these some were put to death,
others punished by the confiscation of their property
and driven from their homes into exile, where,
having nothing left save tears and complaints, they
lived on the doles of charity; and since constitutional and just rule had given place to cruel caprice,
wealthy and famous houses were being closed.
5. And no words of an accuser, even though bribed,
were required amid these accumulations of evils, in
order that these crimes might be committed, at
least ostensibly, under the forms of law, as has sometimes been done by cruel emperors; but whatever the implacable Caesar had resolved upon was
rushed to fulfilment, as if it had been carefully
weighed and determined to be right and lawful.
6. It was further devised that sundry low-born men,
whose very insignificance made them little to be
feared, should be appointed to gather gossip in all

various duties as his deputies. They differed in rank;
the *Comes Orientis* was of the second grade (*spectabilis*),
see Introd., p. xviii.

7

destinarentur, relaturi quae audirent. Hi pera-
granter et dissimulanter honoratorum circulis assis-
tendo, pervadendoque divites domus egentium
habitu, quicquid noscere poterant vel audire, latenter intromissi per posticas in regiam, nuntiabant,
id observantes conspiratione concordi, ut fingerent
quaedam, et cognita duplicarent in peius, laudes
vero supprimerent Caesaris, quas invitis compluribus
formido malorum impendentium exprimebat. 7. Et
interdum acciderat, ut siquid in penetrali secreto,
nullo citerioris [1] vitae ministro praesente, pater-
familias uxori susurrasset in aurem, velut Amphiarao
referente aut Marcio, quondam vatibus inclitis,
postridie disceret imperator. Ideoque etiam parietes
arcanorum soli conscii timebantur. 8. Adulescebat
autem obstinatum propositum erga haec et similia
multa scrutandi,[2] stimulos admovente regina, quae
abrupte mariti fortunas trudebat in exitium praeceps,
cum eum potius lenitate feminea ad veritatis humani-
tatisque viam reducere utilia suadendo deberet, ut in
Gordianorum actibus factitasse Maximini truculenti
illius imperatoris retulimus coniugem.

---

[1] *citerioris*, vulgo ; *citeriora eis*, V.   [2] *scrutandi*, V ;
scrutanda, Bent. ; *scrutantis*, sugg. by Clark, cf. xxx. 5,
5 ; xv. 3, 2.

---

[1] Amphiaraüs was a famous seer of the heroic age, who
took part in the hunt of the Calydonian boar, the expedition of the Argonauts, and unwillingly, because he saw the
outcome, in the war of the Seven against Thebes, in which
he lost his life. The prophecies of Marcius, or as some say,
of two brothers of that name, were discovered in 213 B.C.

quarters of Antioch and report what they had heard. These, as if travellers, and in disguise, attended the gatherings of distinguished citizens, and gained entrance to the houses of the wealthy in the guise of needy clients ; then, being secretly admitted to the palace by a back door, they reported whatever they had been able to hear or learn, with one accord making it a rule to add inventions of their own and make doubly worse what they had learned, but suppressing the praise of Caesar which the fear of impending evils extorted from some against their will. 7. And sometimes it happened that if the head of a household, in the seclusion of his private apartments, with no confidential servant present, had whispered something in the ear of his wife, the emperor learned it on the following day, as if it were reported by Amphiaraus or Marcius, those famous seers of old.[1] And so even the walls, the only sharers of secrets, were feared. 8. Moreover, his fixed purpose of ferreting out these and many similar things increased, spurred on by the queen, who pushed her husband's fortunes headlong to sheer ruin, when she ought rather, with womanly gentleness, to have recalled him by helpful counsel to the path of truth and mercy, after the manner of the wife [2] of that savage emperor Maximinus, as we have related in our account of the acts of the Gordians.

According to Livy, xxv. 12, 5, they foretold the defeat at Cannae. Cf. also Pausanias, I. 34. 4 ff. and II. 13. 7. At a later time these prophetic writings were preserved on the Capitol at Rome with the Sibylline books.

[2] Her name is unknown ; she was perhaps the *diva Paulina* whose name appears on a silver coin of the period.

9. Novo denique perniciosoque exemplo, idem
Gallus ausus est inire flagitium grave, quod Romae
cum ultimo dedecore temptasse aliquando dicitur
Gallienus, et adhibitis paucis clam ferro succinctis,
vesperi per tabernas palabatur et compita, quaeritando Graeco sermone, cuius erat impendio gnarus,
quid de Caesare quisque sentiret. Et haec confidenter agebat in urbe, ubi pernoctantium luminum
claritudo dierum solet imitari fulgorem. Postremo
agnitus saepe, iamque (si prodisset) conspicuum se
fore contemplans, non nisi luce palam egrediens ad
agenda quae putabat seria cernebatur. Et haec
quidem medullitus multis gementibus agebantur.

10. Thalassius vero ea tempestate praefectus praetorio praesens, ipse quoque arrogantis ingenii, considerans incitationem eius ad multorum augeri discrimina, non maturitate vel consiliis mitigabat, ut[1]
aliquotiens celsae potestates iras principum mollive-
runt, sed adversando iurgandoque cum parum congrueret, eum ad rabiem potius evibrabat, Augustum
actus eius exaggerando creberrime docens, idque
(incertum qua mente) ne lateret affectans. Quibus[2]
mox Caesar acrius efferatus, velut contumaciae

[1] *ut*, added in G; V omits.   [2] *quibus* *ut* *mox*
(lac. 6 letters), V.

---

[1] That is, Antioch. The brilliant lighting of the city is
mentioned also by Libanius and Hieronymus.

10

9. Finally, following an unprecedented and destructive course, Gallus also ventured to commit the atrocious crime which, to his utter disgrace, Gallienus is said to have once hazarded at Rome. Taking with him a few attendants with concealed weapons, he used to roam at evening about the inns and street-corners, inquiring of every one in Greek, of which he had remarkable command, what he thought of the Caesar. And this he did boldly in a city [1] where the brightness of the lights at night commonly equals the resplendence of day. At last, being often recognized, and reflecting that if he continued that course he would be conspicuous, he appeared only in broad daylight, to attend to matters which he considered important. And all this conduct of his caused very deep sorrow to many.

10. Now at that time Thalassius was the Praetorian Prefect at court,[2] a man who was himself of an imperious character. He, perceiving that Gallus' temper was rising, to the peril of many, did not try to soothe it by ripe counsel, as sometimes high officials have moderated the ire of princes ; but rather roused the Caesar to fury by opposing and reproving him at unseasonable times ; very frequently he informed the emperor of Gallus' doings, exaggerating them and taking pains—whatever his motive may have been—to do it openly. Through this conduct the Caesar was soon still more violently enraged,

[2] This office was originally a military one, but the *praefectus praetorio* under Constantine became the highest civil servant of the emperor. On *praesens*, see Introd. p. xxxiii. In this case the court of Gallus is referred to, and there would also be a *praefectus praetorio praesens* at the court of Constantius.

quoddam vexillum altius erigens, sine respectu
salutis alienae vel suae, ad vertenda opposita,[1] instar
rapidi fluminis, irrevocabili impetu ferebatur.

2. *Isaurorum incursiones.*

1. Nec sane haec sola pernicies orientem diversis
cladibus affligebat. Namque et Isauri, quibus est
usitatum saepe pacari, saepeque inopinis excursibus
cuncta miscere, ex latrociniis occultis et raris, alente
impunitate adulescentem in peius audaciam, ad bella
gravia proruperunt, diu quidem perduelles spiritus
irrequietis motibus erigentes, hac tamen indignitate
perciti vehementer, ut iactitabant, quod eorum capti
quidam consortes, apud Iconium Pisidiae oppidum in
amphitheatrali spectaculo feris praedatricibus obiecti
sunt praeter morem. 2. Atque (ut Tullius ait) ut
etiam bestiae[2] fame monitae plerumque ad eum
locum ubi aliquando pastae sunt revertuntur, ita
omnes instar turbinis degressi montibus impeditis et
arduis, loca petivere mari confinia, per quae aviis[3]
latebrosis sese convallibusque occultantes, cum
appeterent noctes—luna etiam tum cornuta, ideoque
nondum solido splendore fulgente—nauticos obser-
vabant. Quos cum in somnum sentirent effusos,
per ancoralia quadrupedo gradu repentes, seseque

---

[1] *opposita*, Bent.; *sibi o.*, Langen; *supposita*, V
[2] *bestiae*, added by Val., cf. Cic. l.c., note 2; *ferae*, W[2]G.
[3] *auiis*, Kiessling; *uiis*, V.

---

[1] A people dwelling in the mountains of Pisidia in
southern Asia Minor.

and as if raising higher, as it were, the standard of his obstinacy, with no regard for his own life or that of others, he rushed on with uncontrollable impetuosity, like a swift torrent, to overthrow whatever opposed him.

2. *Inroads of the Isaurians.*

1. And indeed this was not the only calamity to afflict the Orient with various disasters. For the Isaurians [1] too, whose way it is now to keep the peace and now put everything in turmoil by sudden raids, abandoned their occasional secret plundering expeditions and, as impunity stimulated for the worse their growing boldness, broke out in a serious war. For a long time they had been inflaming their warlike spirits by restless outbreaks, but they were now especially exasperated, as they declared, by the indignity of some of their associates, who had been taken prisoner, having been thrown to beasts of prey in the shows of the amphitheatre at Iconium, a town of Pisidia—an outrage without precedent. 2. And, in the words of Cicero,[2] as even wild animals, when warned by hunger, generally return to the place where they were once fed, so they all, swooping like a whirlwind down from their steep and rugged mountains, made for the districts near the sea ; and hiding themselves there in pathless lurking-places and defiles as the dark nights were coming on—the moon being still crescent and so not shining with full brilliance—they watched the sailors. And when they saw that they were buried in sleep, creeping on all fours along the anchor-ropes and making their

---

[2] *Pro Cluentio*, 25, 67.

suspensis passibus iniectantes in scaphas, eisdem [1] nihil opinantibus assistebant, et incendente aviditate saevitiam, ne cedentium quidem ulli parcendo, obtruncatis omnibus merces opimas vel utiles nullis repugnantibus avertebant. 3. Haecque non diu sunt perpetrata. Cognitis enim pilatorum caesorumque funeribus, nemo deinde ad has stationes appulit navem, sed ut Scironis praerupta letalia declinantes, litoribus Cypriis contigui navigabant, quae Isauriae scopulis sunt controversa. 4. Procedente igitur mox tempore cum adventicium nihil inveniretur, relicta ora maritima, in Lycaoniam annexam Isauriae se contulerunt, ibique densis intersaepientes [2] itinera praetenturis, provincialium et viatorum opibus pascebantur. 5. Excitavit hic ardor milites per municipia plurima, quae eisdem conterminant, dispositos et castella, et quisque serpentes latius pro viribus repellere moliens, nunc globis confertos, aliquotiens et dispersos, multitudine superabatur vigenti,[3] quae nata et educata inter editos recurvosque ambitus montium, eos ut loca plana persultat et mollia, missilibus obvios eminus lacessens et ululatu truci perterrens. 6. Coactique aliquotiens nostri pedites ad eos persequendos scandere clivos sublimes,

---

[1] *eisdem enim,* V ; *enim* del ' W,' Lit. Centralblatt, 1871, Col. 1084 ; *e. sensim,* Eyssen. ; *e navi,* Traube. [2] *intersaepientis,* Lind. ; *intercipientes,* Traube ; *interasipientes,* V. [3] *uigenti,* Pet., Clark ; *ingenti* (originally *ingentis*), V.

---

[1] A notorious robber slain by Theseus; he haunted the cliffs between Attica and Megara. He not only robbed travellers who came that way, but forced them to wash his feet, and while they were obeying kicked them off into the sea.

14

way on tiptoe into the boats, they came upon the crew all unawares, and since their natural ferocity was fired by greed, they spared no one, even of those who surrendered, but massacred them all and without resistance carried off the cargoes, led either by their value or by their usefulness. 3. This however did not continue long; for when the fate of those whom they had butchered and plundered became known, no one afterwards put in at those ports, but avoiding them as they would the deadly cliffs of Sciron,[1] they coasted along the shores of Cyprus, which lie opposite to the crags of Isauria. 4. Then presently, as time went on and nothing came their way from abroad, they left the sea-coast and withdrew to that part of Lycaonia that borders on Isauria; and there, blocking the roads with close barricades, they lived on the property of the provincials and of travellers. 5. Anger at this aroused the soldiers quartered in the numerous towns and fortresses which lie near those regions, and each division strove to the best of its power to check the marauders as they ranged more widely, now in solid bodies, sometimes even in isolated bands. But the soldiers were defeated by their strength and numbers; for since the Isaurians were born and brought up amid the steep and winding defiles of the mountains, they bounded over them as if they were a smooth and level plain, attacking the enemy with missiles from a distance and terrifying them with savage howls. 6. And sometimes our infantry in pursuing them were forced to scale lofty slopes, and when they lost their footing, even if they reached the very summits by catching hold of underbrush or briars,

CONSTANTIUS ET GALLUS

etiam si lapsantibus plantis fruticeta prensando vel dumos, ad vertices venerint summos, inter arta tamen et invia, nullas acies explicare permissi, nec firmare nisu valido gressus ; hoste discursatore rupium abscisa volvente superne, periculose per prona discedunt, aut ex necessitate ultima fortiter dimicantes, ruinis ponderum immanium consternuntur. 7. Quam ob rem circumspecta cautela observatum est deinceps, et cum edita montium petere coeperint grassatores, loci iniquitati [1] milites cedunt. Ubi autem in planitie potuerint reperiri, quod contingit assidue, nec exsertare lacertos nec crispare permissi tela quae vehunt bina vel terna, pecudum ritu inertium trucidantur.

8. Metuentes igitur idem latrones Lycaoniam magna parte campestrem, cum se impares nostris fore congressione stataria documentis frequentibus scirent, tramitibus deviis petivere Pamphyliam, diu quidem intactam, sed timore populationum et caedum, milite per omnia diffuso propinqua, magnis undique praesidiis communitam. 9. Raptim igitur properantes, ut motus sui rumores celeritate nimia praevenirent, vigore corporum ac levitate confisi, per flexuosas semitas ad summitates collium tardius evadebant. Et cum, superatis difficultatibus arduis, ad supercilia venissent fluvii Melanis, alti et verticosi,

---

[1] *iniquitati*, Horkel ; *iniquitate*, V.

16

the narrow and pathless tracts allowed them neither to take order of battle nor with mighty effort to keep a firm footing ; and while the enemy, running here and there, tore off and hurled down masses of rock from above, they made their perilous way down over steep slopes ; or if, compelled by dire necessity, they made a brave fight, they were overwhelmed by falling boulders of enormous weight. 7. Therefore extreme caution was shown after that, and when the marauders began to make for the mountain heights, the soldiers yielded to the unfavourable position. When, however, the Isaurians could be found on level ground, as constantly happened, they were allowed neither to stretch out their right arms nor poise their weapons, of which each carried two or three, but they were slaughtered like defenceless sheep.

8. Accordingly these same marauders, distrusting Lycaonia, which is for the most part level, and having learned by repeated experience that they would be no match for our soldiers in a stand-up fight, made their way by retired by-paths into Pamphylia, long unmolested, it is true, but through fear of raids and massacres protected everywhere by strong garrisons, while troops were spread all over the neighbouring country. 9. Therefore they made great haste, in order by extreme swiftness to anticipate the reports of their movements, trusting in their bodily strength and activity ; but they made their way somewhat slowly to the summits of the hills over winding trails. And when, after overcoming extreme difficulties, they came to the steep banks of the Melas, a deep and eddying stream, which surrounds the inhabitants like a wall and

qui pro muro tuetur accolas circumfusus, augente
nocte adulta terrorem, quievere paulisper, lucem
opperientes. Arbitrabantur enim nullo impediente
transgressi, inopino accursu apposita quaeque
vastare, sed in cassum labores pertulere gravissimos.
10. Nam sole orto magnitudine angusti gurgitis sed
profundi a transitu arcebantur, et dum piscatorios
quaerunt lenunculos, vel innare temere contextis
cratibus [1] parant, effusae legiones quae hiemabant
tunc apud Siden, eisdem impetu occurrere veloci.
Et signis prope ripam locatis, ad manus comminus
conserendas, denseta scutorum compage, semet
scientissime praestruebant, ausos quoque aliquos
fiducia nandi, vel cavatis arborum truncis, amnem
permeare latenter, facillime trucidarunt. 11. Unde
temptatis ad discrimen ultimum artibus militum,[2]
cum nihil impetraretur, pavore vique repellente
extrusi, et quo tenderent ambigentes, venere prope
oppidum Laranda. 12. Ibi victu recreati et quiete,
postquam abierat timor, vicos opulentos adorti,
equestrium adiumento cohortium, quae casu propin-
quabant, nec resistere planitie porrecta conati,
digressi sunt, retroque cedentes,[3] omne iuventutis
robur relictum in sedibus acciverunt. 13. Et
quoniam inedia gravi afflictabantur, locum petivere
Paleas nomine, vergentem in mare, valido muro

---

[1] *contextis cratibus*, Kiessling ; *contexti sunt ratibus*, V ;
contextis ratibus, BG. [2] *militum*, Clark ; *multum*, V ;
multis, Val. [3] *cedentes*, Novak ; *concedentes*, V.

protects them, the lateness of the night increased their alarm, and they halted for a time, waiting for daylight. They thought, indeed, to cross without opposition and by their unexpected raid to lay waste all before them; but they endured the greatest hardships to no purpose. 10. For when the sun rose, they were prevented from crossing by the size of the stream, which was narrow but deep. And while they were hunting for fishermen's boats or preparing to cross on hastily woven hurdles, the legions that were then wintering at Side poured out and fell upon them in swift attack. And having set up their standards near the river-bank, the legions drew themselves up most skilfully for fighting hand to hand with a close formation of shields; and with perfect ease they slew some, who had even dared to cross the river secretly, trusting to swimming, or in hollowed out tree trunks. 11. From there, after trying the skill of our soldiers even to a final test without gaining anything, dislodged by fear and the strength of the legions, and not knowing what direction to take, they came to the neighbourhood of the town of Laranda. 12. There they were refreshed with food and rest, and after their fear had left them, they attacked some rich villages; but since these were aided by some cohorts of cavalry, which chanced to come up, the enemy withdrew without attempting any resistance on the level plain; but as they retreated, they summoned all the flower of their youth that had been left at home. 13. And since they were distressed by severe hunger, they made for a place called Palaea, near the sea, which was protected by a strong wall. There supplies are

firmatum, ubi conduntur nunc usque commeatus, distribui militibus omne latus Isauriae defendentibus assueti. Circumstetere igitur hoc munimentum per triduum et trinoctium, et cum neque acclivitas ipsa sine discrimine posset adiri[1] letali, nec cuniculis quicquam geri, nec procedebat ullum obsidionale commentum, maesti excedunt, postrema vi subigente maiora viribus aggressuri. 14. Proinde concepta rabie saeviore, quam desperatio incendebat et fames, amplificatis viribus, ardore incohibili in excidium urbium matris Seleuciae efferebantur, quam comes tuebatur Castricius, tresque legiones bellicis sudoribus induratae. 15. Horum adventum praedocti speculationibus fidis, rectores militum tessera data sollemni, armatos omnes celeri eduxere procursu, et agiliter praeterito Calycadni fluminis ponte, cuius undarum magnitudo murorum alluit turres, in speciem locavere pugnandi. Neque tamen exsiluit quisquam, nec permissus est congredi. Formidabatur enim flagrans vesania manus, et superior numero, et ruitura sine respectu salutis in ferrum. 16. Viso itaque exercitu procul, auditoque liticinum cantu, represso gradu parumper stetere praedones, exsertantesque minaces gladios postea lentius incedebant. 17. Quibus occurrere bene pertinax miles explicatis ordinibus parans, hastisque feriens scuta, qui habitus iram pugnantium concitat

---

[1] *possit adiri*, EbG ; *possit adire*, V ; *posset*, A, put before *adiri* by Clark.

regularly stored even to-day, for distribution to the troops that defend the whole frontier of Isauria. Therefore they invested that fortress for three days and three nights; but since the steep slope itself could not be approached without deadly peril, and nothing could be effected by mines, and no method of siege was successful, they withdrew in dejection, ready, under the pressure of extreme necessity, to undertake even tasks beyond their powers. 14. Accordingly, filled with still greater fury, to which despair and famine added fuel, with increased numbers and irresistible energy they rushed on to destroy Seleucia, the metropolis of the province, which Count Castricius was holding with three legions steeled by hard service. 15. Warned of their approach by trusty scouts, the officers of the garrison gave the watchword, according to regulations, and in a swift sally led out the entire force; and having quickly crossed the bridge over the river Calycadnus, whose mighty stream washes the towers of the city walls, they drew up their men in order of battle. And yet no one charged or was allowed to fight; for they feared that band on fire with madness, superior in numbers, and ready to rush upon the sword, regardless of their lives. 16. Consequently, when the army came into view afar off, and the notes of the trumpeters were heard, the marauders stopped and halted for a while; then, drawing their formidable swords, they came on at a slower pace. 17. And when the unperturbed soldiers made ready to meet them, deploying their ranks and striking their shields with their spears, an action which rouses the wrath and resentment of the combatants, they

et dolorem, proximos iam gestu terrebat. Sed eum in certamen alacriter consurgentem, revocavere ductores, rati intempestivum anceps subire certamen, cum haut longe muri distarent, quorum tutela securitas poterat in solido locari cunctorum. 18. Hac ita persuasione reducti intra moenia bellatores, obseratis undique portarum aditibus, propugnaculis insistebant et pinnis, congesta undique saxa telaque habentes in promptu, ut si quis se proripuisset citerius,[1] multitudine missilium sterneretur et lapidum. 19. Illud tamen clausos vehementer angebat, quod captis navigiis, quae frumenta vehebant per flumen, Isauri quidem alimentorum copiis affluebant, ipsi vero solitarum rerum cibo iam consumendo, inediae propinquantis aerumnas exitialis horrebant. 20. Haec ubi latius fama vulgasset, missaeque relationes assiduae Gallum Caesarem permovissent, quoniam magister equitum longius ea tempestate disintebatur, iussus comes Orientis Nebridius, contractis undique militaribus copiis, ad eximendam periculo civitatem amplam et opportunam, studio properabat ingenti. Quo cognito abscessere latrones, nulla re amplius memorabili gesta, dispersique (ut solent,) avia montium petiere celsorum.

[1] *proripuisset*, EBG ; *p. citerius*, Gronov, Fletcher ; *p. interius*, Val. ; *proripuisse* (lac. 3 letters) *terius*, V.

---

[1] See Introd., pp. xxxiv f.   [2] See Introd., pp. xxviii f.

intimidated the nearest of the enemy by their very gestures. But as they were eagerly rushing to the fray, their leaders called them back, thinking it inadvisable to risk a doubtful combat when fortifications were not far distant, under the protection of which the safety of all could be put on a solid foundation. 18. In this conviction, then, the warriors were led back within the walls, the entrances to the gates on all sides were barred, and they took their place on the battlements and pinnacles with rocks gathered from every hand and weapons in readiness, so that, if anyone should force his way near to the walls, he might be overwhelmed by a shower of spears and stones. 19. Still, the besieged were greatly troubled by the fact that the Isaurians, having captured some boats which were carrying grain on the river, were abundantly supplied with provisions, while they themselves had already exhausted the regular stores and were dreading the deadly pangs of approaching famine. 20. When the news of this situation spread abroad, and repeated messages dispatched to Gallus Caesar had roused him to action, since the Master of the Horse [1] was at the time too far removed from the spot, orders were given to Nebridius, Count of the East.[2] He quickly got together troops from every side and with the greatest energy was hastening to rescue this great and strategically important city from danger. On learning this, the freebooters departed without accomplishing anything more of consequence, and scattering (after their usual fashion) made for the trackless wastes of the high mountains.

CONSTANTIUS ET GALLUS

3. *Persarum commentum irritum.*

1. Eo adducta re per Isauriam, rege Persarum bellis finitimis illigato, repellenteque a collimitiis suis ferocissimas gentes, quae mente quadam versabili hostiliter eum saepe incessunt, et in nos arma moventem aliquotiens iuvant, Nohodares quidam nomine e numero optimatum, incursare Mesopotamiam quotiens copia dederit ordinatus, explorabat nostra sollicite, si repperisset usquam locum, vi subita perrupturus. 2. Et quia Mesopotamiae tractus omnes crebro inquietari sueti, praetenturis et stationibus servabantur agrariis, laevorsum flexo itinere, Osdroenae subsiderat extimas partes, novum parumque aliquando temptatum commentum aggressus ; quod si impetrasset, fulminis modo cuncta vastarat. Erat autem quod cogitabat huius modi.

3. Batnae municipium in Anthemusia conditum Macedonum manu priscorum, ab Euphrate flumine brevi spatio disparatur, refertum mercatoribus opulentis, ubi annua sollemnitate prope Septembris initium mensis, ad nundinas magna promiscuae fortunae convenit multitudo, ad commercanda quae Indi mittunt et Seres, aliaque[1] plurima vehi terra marique consueta. 4. Hanc regionem praestitutis celebritati diebus, invadere parans dux ante dictus, per solitudines Aboraeque amnis herbidas ripas,

---

[1] *aliaque*, A, Kiessling ; *alia*, V.

---

[1] Sapor, see Index.

3. *An unsuccessful plot of the Persians.*

1. When affairs had reached this stage in Isauria, the king of Persia,[1] involved in war with his neighbours, was driving back from his frontiers a number of very wild tribes which, with inconsistent policy, often make hostile raids upon his territories and sometimes aid him when he makes war upon us. One of his grandees, Nohodares by name, having received orders to invade Mesopotamia whenever occasion offered, was carefully reconnoitring our territory, intending a sudden incursion in case he found any opening. 2. And as all the districts of Mesopotamia, being exposed to frequent raids, were protected by frontier-guards and country garrisons, Nohodares, having turned his course to the left, had beset the remotest parts of Osdroene, attempting a novel and all but unprecedented manœuvre; and if he had succeeded, he would have devastated the whole region like a thunderbolt. Now what he planned was the following.

3. The town of Batne, founded in Anthemusia in early times by a band of Macedonians, is separated by a short space from the river Euphrates; it is filled with wealthy traders when, at the yearly festival, near the beginning of the month of September, a great crowd of every condition gathers for the fair, to traffic in the wares sent from India and China, and in other articles that are regularly brought there in great abundance by land and sea. 4. This district the above-mentioned leader made ready to invade, on the days set for this celebration, through the wilderness and the grass-covered banks of the river Abora; but he was betrayed by information

suorum indicio proditus, qui admissi flagitii metu
exagitati, ad praesidia descivere Romana, absque
ullo egressus effectu, deinde tabescebat immobilis.

4. *Saracenorum irruptiones et mores.*

1. Saraceni tamen nec amici nobis umquam nec
hostes optandi, ultro citroque discursantes, quicquid
inveniri poterat momento temporis parvi vastabant,
milvorum rapacium similes, qui si praedam di-
spexerint celsius, volatu rapiunt celeri, ac si[1]impetra-
verint, non immorantur.   2. Super quorum moribus
licet in actibus principis Marci, et postea aliquotiens
memini rettulisse,[2] tamen nunc quoque pauca de
eisdem expediam carptim.   3. Apud has gentes,
quarum exordiens initium ab Assyriis, ad Nili
cataractas porrigitur, et confinia Blemmyarum,
omnes pari sorte sunt bellatores, seminudi coloratis
sagulis pube tenus amicti, equorum adiumento
pernicium graciliumque camelorum per diversa
reptantes, in tranquillis vel turbidis rebus ; nec
eorum quisquam aliquando stivam apprehendit, vel
arborem colit, aut arva subigendo quaeritat victum,
sed errant semper per spatia longe lateque distenta,
sine lare sine sedibus fixis aut legibus ; nec idem
perferunt diutius caelum, aut tractus unius sol
illis umquam placet.   4. Vita est illis semper in
fuga, uxoresque mercennariae conductae ad tempus
ex pacto, atque (ut sit species matrimonii,) dotis
nomine futura coniunx hastam et tabernaculum

---

[1] *ac si*, Mommsen ; *aut si*, V.   [2] *memini rettulisse*,
Kiessling ; *meminerit tulisse*, V.

---

[1] In one of the lost books.

given by some of his own soldiers, who, fearing punishment for a crime which they had committed, deserted to the Roman garrison. Therefore, withdrawing without accomplishing anything, he languished thereafter in inaction.

4. *Inroads of the Saracens ; their customs.*

1. The Saracens, however, whom we never found desirable either as friends or as enemies, ranging up and down the country, in a brief space of time laid waste whatever they could find, like rapacious kites which, whenever they have caught sight of any prey from on high, seize it with swift swoop, and directly they have seized it make off.   2. Although I recall having told of their customs in my history of the emperor Marcus,[1] and several times after that, yet I will now briefly relate a few more particulars about them.   3. Among those tribes whose original abode extends from the Assyrians to the cataracts of the Nile and the frontiers of the Blemmyae all alike are warriors of equal rank, half-nude, clad in dyed cloaks as far as the loins, ranging widely with the help of swift horses and slender camels in times of peace or of disorder.   No man ever grasps a plough-handle or cultivates a tree, none seeks a living by tilling the soil, but they rove continually over wide and extensive tracts without a home, without fixed abodes or laws ; they cannot long endure the same sky, nor does the sun of a single district ever content them. 4. Their life is always on the move, and they have mercenary wives, hired under a temporary contract. But in order that there may be some semblance of matrimony, the future wife, by way of dower, offers

27

offert marito, post statum diem (si id elegerit,) dis-
cessura, et incredibile est quo ardore apud eos in
venerem[1] uterque solvitur sexus. 5. Ita autem quoad
vixerint late palantur, ut alibi mulier nubat, in loco
pariat alio, liberosque procul educat,[2] nulla copia
quiescendi permissa. 6. Victus universis caro ferina
est, lactisque abundans copia qua sustentantur, et
herbae multiplices, et siquae alites capi per aucupium
possint, et plerosque nos vidimus frumenti usum et
vini penitus ignorantes.

7. Hactenus de natione perniciosa. Nunc ad
textum propositum revertamur.

5. *Magnentianorum supplicia.*

1. Dum haec in Oriente aguntur, Arelate hiemem
agens Constantius, post theatralis ludos atque circen-
ses ambitioso editos apparatu, diem sextum idus
Octobres, qui imperii eius annum tricensimum
terminabat, insolentiae pondera gravius librans,
siquid dubium deferebatur aut falsum, pro liquido
accipiens et comperto, inter alia excarnificatum
Gerontium, Magnentianae comitem partis, exsulari
maerore multavit. 2. Utque aegrum corpus quas-
sari etiam levibus solet offensis, ita animus eius
angustus et tener, quicquid increpuisset, ad salutis

---

[1] *in venerem,* W[2] BG ; *in venere,* Traube ; *invenire,* V.
[2] *educat,* Lind. ; *inde educat,* Novák ; *deducat,* V.

---

[1] This dates his reign from A.D. 323, when he and his
brothers Constantine and Crispus were appointed Caesars
by Constantine the Great. He became an Augustus with
Constantine II. and Constans in 337, and reigned alone,
after the death of Magnentius, from 353 to 361. The

her husband a spear and a tent, with the right to
leave him after a stipulated time, if she so elect :
and it is unbelievable with what ardour both sexes
give themselves up to passion. 5. Moreover, they
wander so widely as long as they live, that a woman
marries in one place, gives birth in another, and
rears her children far away, without being allowed
any opportunity for rest. 6. They all feed upon
game and an abundance of milk, which is their main
sustenance, on a variety of plants, as well as on such
birds as they are able to take by fowling ; and I have
seen many of them who were wholly unacquainted
with grain and wine. 7. So much for this dangerous
tribe. Let us now return to our original theme.

5. *The torture of the followers of Magnentius.*

1. While this was happening in the East, Constantius was passing the winter at Arelate, where he
gave entertainments in the theatre and the circus
with ostentatious magnificence. Then, on the 10th
of October, which completed the thirtieth year of
his reign,[1] giving greater weight to his arrogance and
accepting every false or doubtful charge as evident
and proven, among other atrocities he tortured
Gerontius, a count of the party of Magnentius,[2] and
visited him with the sorrow of exile. 2. And, as an
ailing body is apt to be affected even by slight
annoyances, so his narrow and sensitive mind,
thinking that every sound indicated something done
or planned at the expense of his safety, made his

actual date seems to have been November 8th, 323 ;
see Dessau, Inser. Lat. 708, note 2, and cf. De Jonge,
p. 124, citing Seeck.   [2] See note, p. 1 and Index.

suae dispendium existimans factum aut cogitatum, insontium caedibus fecit victoriam luctuosam. 3. Siquis enim militarium vel honoratorum aut nobilis inter suos, rumore tenus esset insimulatus fovisse partes hostiles, iniecto onere catenarum, in modum beluae trahebatur, et inimico urgente vel nullo, quasi sufficiente hoc solo, quod nominatus esset aut delatus aut postulatus, capite vel multatione bonorum, aut insulari solitudine damnabatur.

4. Accedebant enim eius asperitati, ubi imminuta esse [1] amplitudo imperii dicebatur, et iracundiae suspicionumque vanitati,[2] proximorum cruentae blanditiae, exaggerantium incidentia, et dolere impendio simulantium, si principis petitur [3] vita, a cuius salute velut filo pendere statum orbis terrarum fictis vocibus exclamabant. 5. Ideoque fertur neminem aliquando ob haec vel similia poenae addictum, oblato de more elogio, revocari iussisse, quod inexorabiles quoque principes factitarunt. Et exitiale hoc vitium, quod in aliis non numquam intepescit, in illo aetatis progressu effervescebat, obstinatum eius propositum accendente adulatorum cohorte.

[1] *inminuta esse*, Traube ; *imminuta uel laesa*, Val. ; *inminutae* (lac. 5 letters), V. [2] *suspicionumque vanitati*, Heraeus ; *suspicionum quantitati*, V. [3] *petitur*, Novák ; *periclitetur*, Gardt. ; *per[di]tur*, V.

---

[1] Over Magnentius. See note, p. 3.
[2] The *honorati* were former civil officials ; cf. xxix. 1, 9, *abunde honoratum ; Asiam quippe rexerat pro praefectis.*

victory[1] lamentable through the murder of innocent men. 3. For if anyone of the military commanders or ex-officials,[2] or one of high rank in his own community, was accused even by rumour of having favoured the party of the emperor's opponent, he was loaded with chains and dragged about like a wild beast. And whether a personal enemy pressed the charge or no one at all, as though it was enough that he had been named, informed against, or accused, he was condemned to death, or his property confiscated, or he was banished to some desert island.

4. Moreover his harsh cruelty, whenever the majesty of the empire was said to be insulted, and his angry passions and unfounded suspicions were increased by the bloodthirsty flattery of his courtiers, who exaggerated everything that happened and pretended to be greatly troubled by the thought of an attempt on the life of a prince on whose safety, as on a thread, they hypocritically declared that the condition of the whole world depended. 5. And he is even said to have given orders that no one who had ever been punished for these or similar offences should be given a new trial after a writ of condemnation[3] had once been presented to him in the usual manner, which even the most inexorable emperors commonly allowed. And this fatal fault of cruelty, which in others sometimes grew less with advancing age, in his case became more violent, since a group of flatterers intensified his stubborn resolution.

[3] That is, a tablet on which the charge and the punishment were recorded. This was sometimes handed to the emperor by a judge, cf. Suet., *Calig.* 27, 1, sometimes issued by the emperor himself; see Amm. xiv. 7, 2; xix. 12, 9.

6. Inter quos Paulus eminebat notarius, ortus in Hispania coluber[1] quidam sub vultu latens, odorandi vias periculorum occultas perquam sagax. Is in Britanniam missus, ut militares quosdam perduceret, ausos conspirasse Magnentio, cum reniti non possent, iussa licentius supergressus, fluminis modo fortunis complurium sese repentinus infudit, et ferebatur per strages multiplices ac ruinas, vinculis membra ingenuorum affligens, et quosdam obterens manicis, crimina scilicet multa consarcinando, a veritate longe discreta. Unde admissum est facinus impium, quod Constanti tempus nota inusserat sempiterna. 7. Martinus agens illas provincias pro praefectis, aerumnas innocentium graviter gemens, saepeque obsecrans, ut ab omni culpa immunibus parceretur, cum non impetraret, minabatur se discessurum; ut saltem id metuens, perquisitor malivolus tandem desineret quieti coalitos homines in aperta pericula proiectare. 8. Per hoc minui studium suum existimans Paulus, ut erat in complicandis negotiis artifex dirus, unde ei Catenae indutum[2] est cognomentum, vicarium ipsum eos quibus praeerat adhuc defensantem, ad sortem periculorum communium traxit. Et instabat ut eum quoque cum tribunis et aliis pluribus, ad comitatum imperatoris vinctum perduceret; quo percitus ille, exitio urgente abrupto,

---

[1] *coluber*, Bentley, Novák; *glaber*, V.   [2] *indutum*, Clark, e.c. (cf. xv. 3, 4); *inditum*, EBG; *indinuum*, V.

---

6. Prominent among these was the state secretary [1] Paulus, a native of Spain, a kind of viper, whose countenance concealed his character, but who was extremely clever in scenting out hidden means of danger for others. When he had been sent to Britain to fetch some officers who had dared to conspire with Magnentius, since they could make no resistance he autocratically exceeded his instructions and, like a flood, suddenly overwhelmed the fortunes of many, making his way amid manifold slaughter and destruction, imprisoning freeborn men and even degrading some with handcuffs ; as a matter of fact, he patched together many accusations with utter disregard of the truth, and to him was due an impious crime, which fixed an eternal stain upon the time of Constantius. **7.** Martinus, who was governing those provinces as substitute for the prefects, deeply deplored the woes suffered by innocent men ; and after often begging that those who were free from any reproach should be spared, when he failed in his appeal he threatened to retire, in the hope that, at least through fear of this, that malevolent man-hunter might finally cease to expose to open danger men naturally given to peace. **8.** Paulus thought that this would interfere with his profession, and being a formidable artist in devising complications, for which reason he was nicknamed " The Chain," since the substitute continued to defend those whom he was appointed to govern, Paulus involved even him in the common peril, threatening to bring him also in chains to the emperor's court, along with the tribunes and many others. Thereupon Martinus, alarmed at this threat, and thinking

33

ferro eundem adoritur Paulum. Et quia languente dextera letaliter ferire non potuit, iam destrictum mucronem in proprium latus impegit. Hocque deformi genere mortis, excessit e vita iustissimus rector,[1] ausus miserabiles casus levare multorum. 9. Quibus ita sceleste patratis, Paulus cruore perfusus, reversusque ad principis castra, multos coopertos paene catenis adduxit, in squalorem deiectos atque maestitiam, quorum adventu intendebantur eculei, uncosque parabat carnifex et tormenta. Et ex his [2] proscripti sunt plures, actique in exsilium alii, non nullos gladii consumpsere poenales. Nec enim quisquam facile meminit sub Constantio, ubi susurro tenus haec movebantur, quemquam absolutum.

6. *Senatus populique Romani vitia.*

1. Inter haec Orfitus praefecti potestate regebat urbem aeternam,[3] ultra modum delatae dignitatis sese efferens insolenter, vir quidem prudens, et forensium negotiorum oppido gnarus, sed splendore liberalium doctrinarum minus quam nobilem decuerat institutus. Quo administrante seditiones sunt concitatae graves ob inopiam vini, cuius [4] avidis usibus vulgus intentum, ad motus asperos excitatur et crebros.

---

[1] *rector*, H. Ernst, Bentley ; *remora*, V.   [2] *et ex his*, Eyssen. ; *tormentae texis*, V.   [3] *urbem aeternam*, E[2]A ; *ur* (lac. of 8 letters) *nam*, V[1], *urbem etate nam*, V[2]. [4]*cuius*, C. F. W. Müller ; *huius*, V.

swift death imminent, drew his sword and attacked that same Paulus. But since the weakness of his hand prevented him from dealing a fatal blow, he plunged the sword which he had already drawn into his own side. And by that ignominious death there passed from life a most just ruler, who had dared to lighten the unhappy lot of many. 9. After perpetrating these atrocious crimes, Paulus, stained with blood, returned to the emperor's camp, bringing with him many men almost covered with chains and in a state of pitiful filth and wretchedness. On their arrival, the racks were made ready and the executioner prepared his hooks and other instruments of torture. Many of the prisoners were proscribed, others driven into exile ; to some the sword dealt the penalty of death. For no one easily recalls the acquittal of anyone in the time of Constantius when an accusation against him had even been whispered.

6. *The faults of the Roman Senate and People.*

1. Meanwhile Orfitus was governing the eternal city with the rank of Prefect, and with an arrogance beyond the limits of the power that had been conferred upon him. He was a man of wisdom, it is true, and highly skilled in legal practice, but less equipped with the adornment of the liberal arts than became a man of noble rank. During his term of office serious riots broke out because of the scarcity of wine ; for the people, eager for an unrestrained use of this commodity, are roused to frequent and violent disturbances.

2. Et quoniam mirari posse quosdam peregrinos existimo, haec lecturos forsitan (si contigerit), quam ob rem cum oratio ad ea monstranda deflexerit quae Romae geruntur, nihil praeter seditiones narratur et tabernas et vilitates harum similis alias, summatim causas perstringam, nusquam a veritate sponte propria digressurus.

3. Tempore quo primis auspiciis in mundanum fulgorem surgeret victura dum erunt homines Roma, ut augeretur sublimibus incrementis, foedere pacis aeternae Virtus convenit atque Fortuna, plerumque dissidentes, quarum si altera defuisset, ad perfectam non venerat summitatem. 4. Eius populus ab incunabulis primis ad usque pueritiae tempus extremum, quod annis circumcluditur fere trecentis, circummurana pertulit bella ; deinde aetatem ingressus adultam, post multiplices bellorum aerumnas, Alpes transcendit et fretum ; in iuvenem erectus et virum, ex omni plaga quam orbis ambit immensus, reportavit laureas et [1] triumphos ; iamque vergens in senium, et nomine solo aliquotiens vincens, ad tranquilliora vitae discessit. 5. Ideo urbs venerabilis, post superbas efferatarum gentium cervices oppressas, latasque leges, fundamenta libertatis et retinacula sempiterna, velut frugi parens et prudens et dives, Caesaribus tamquam liberis suis regenda patrimonii iura permisit. 6. Et olim licet otiosae

---

[1] *laureas et*, Kiessling ; *laureace*, V.

---

[1] Here Ammianus, writing his History at Rome, classes himself as a Roman ; see note on **6, 12,** below, and Introd., p. xiv.

2. Now I think that some foreigners [1] who will perhaps read this work (if I shall be so fortunate) may wonder why it is that when the narrative turns to the description of what goes on at Rome, I tell of nothing save dissensions, taverns, and other similar vulgarities. Accordingly, I shall briefly touch upon the reasons, intending nowhere to depart intentionally from the truth.

3. At the time when Rome first began to rise into a position of world-wide splendour, destined to live so long as men shall exist, in order that she might grow to a towering stature, Virtue and Fortune, ordinarily at variance, formed a pact of eternal peace; for if either one of them had failed her, Rome had not come to complete supremacy. 4. Her people, from the very cradle to the end of their childhood,[2] a period of about three hundred years, carried on wars about her walls. Then, entering upon adult life, after many toilsome wars, they crossed the Alps and the sea. Grown to youth and manhood, from every region which the vast globe includes, they brought back laurels and triumphs. And now, declining into old age, and often owing victory to its name alone, it has come to a quieter period of life. 5. Thus the venerable city, after humbling the proud necks of savage nations, and making laws, the everlasting foundations and moorings of liberty, like a thrifty parent, wise and wealthy, has entrusted the management of her inheritance to the Caesars, as to her children. 6. And

[2] The same figure is used by Florus, *Introd.* 4 ff. (*L.C.L.*, pp. 6 ff.).

sint tribus, pacataeque centuriae, et nulla suffragiorum certamina, sed Pompiliani redierit securitas temporis, per omnes tamen quot orae sunt partesque [1] terrarum, ut domina suscipitur et regina, et ubique patrum reverenda cum auctoritate canities, populique Romani nomen circumspectum et verecundum.

7. Sed laeditur hic coetuum magnificus splendor, levitate paucorum incondita, ubi nati sunt non reputantium, sed tamquam indulta licentia vitiis, ad errores lapsorum atque [2] lasciviam. Ut enim Simonides lyricus docet, beate perfecta ratione victuro, ante alia patriam esse convenit gloriosam. 8. Ex his quidam aeternitati se commendari posse per statuas aestimantes, eas ardenter affectant, quasi plus praemii de figmentis aereis sensu carentibus adepturi, quam ex conscientia honeste recteque factorum, easque auro curant imbratteari, quod Acilio Glabrioni delatum est primo, cum consiliis armisque regem superasset Antiochum. Quam autem sit pulchrum, exigua haec spernentem et minima, ad ascensus verae gloriae tendere longos et arduos, ut memorat vates Ascraeus, Censorius Cato monstravit. Qui interrogatus quam ob rem inter multos ipse [3]

---

[1] *quot orae sunt partesque*, Seguine, Clark ; *quotque sunt partes quae*, V.   [2] *atque*, Harmon, c.c., Clark ; *ac*, Eyssen. ; *ad*, V.   [3] *ipse*, Novák, Pet. ; *solus*, Traube in lac. 3 lett.

---

[1] The thirty-five tribes into which the Roman citizens were divided.

[2] The *comitia centuriata*.

[3] The passage does not occur in the surviving fragments. Plutarch, *Demosthenes*, 1, attributes the same saying to Euripides, " or whoever it was."

[4] See Livy, xl. 34, 5.

although for some time the tribes [1] have been inactive
and the centuries [2] at peace, and there are no contests for votes but the tranquillity of Numa's time
has returned, yet throughout all regions and parts
of the earth she is accepted as mistress and queen;
everywhere the white hair of the senators and their
authority are revered and the name of the Roman
people is respected and honoured.

7. But this magnificence and splendour of the
assemblies is marred by the rude worthlessness of a
few, who do not consider where they were born, but,
as if licence were granted to vice, descend to sin and
wantonness. For as the lyric poet Simonides tells
us,[3] one who is going to live happy and in accord
with perfect reason ought above all else to have a
glorious fatherland. 8. Some of these men eagerly
strive for statues, thinking that by them they can
be made immortal, as if they would gain a greater
reward from senseless brazen images than from the
consciousness of honourable and virtuous conduct.
And they take pains to have them overlaid with gold,
a fashion first introduced by Acilius Glabrio,[4] after
his skill and his arms had overcome King Antiochus.[5]
But how noble it is, scorning these slight and trivial
honours, to aim to tread the long and steep ascent
to true glory, as the bard of Ascra expresses it,[6] is
made clear by Cato the Censor. For when he was
asked why he alone among many did not have a

[5] At Thermopylae in 191 B.C.
[6] Hesiod, *Works and Days*, 289 ff. τῆς δ' ἀρετῆς ἱδρῶτα
θεοὶ προπάροιθεν ἔθηκαν | 'Αθάνατοι· μακρὸς δὲ καὶ ὄρθιος οἶμος
ἐπ' αὐτήν, | καὶ τρηχὺς τὸ πρῶτον· ἐπὴν δ' εἰς ἄκρον ἵκηται, |
'Ρηιδίη δὴ ἔπειτα πέλει, χαλεπή περ' ἐοῦσα.

statuam non haberet, "Malo" inquit "ambigere
bonos, quam ob rem id non meruerim, quam (quod
est gravius) cur impetraverim mussitare."

9. Alii summum decus in carruchis solito altioribus,
et ambitioso vestium cultu ponentes, sudant sub
ponderibus lacernarum, quas in collis insertas iugulis [1] ipsis annectunt, nimia subtegminum tenuitate
perflabilis, exceptantes eas manu utraque et vexantes [2] crebris agitationibus, maximeque sinistra,
ut longiores fimbriae tunicaeque perspicue luceant,
varietate liciorum effigiatae in species animalium
multiformes. 10. Alii nullo quaerente, vultus severi-
tate assimulata, patrimonia sua in immensum extol-
lunt, cultorum (ut putant) feracium multiplicantes
annuos fructus, quae a primo ad ultimum solem se
abunde iactitant possidere, ignorantes profecto
maiores suos per quos ita magnitudo Romana
porrigitur, non divitiis eluxisse, sed per bella saevissima, nec opibus nec victu nec indumentorum vilitate gregariis militibus discrepantes, opposita cuncta
superasse virtute. 11. Hac [3] ex causa collaticia stipe
Valerius humatur ille Publicola, et subsidiis amicorum
mariti, inops cum liberis uxor alitur Reguli, et

---

[1] *insertas iugulis,* W[2], Gronov; *inserta singulis,* V.
[2] *exceptantes eas* (*expendentes eas,* Val.) *manu utraque et
vexantes,* Novák; *explicantes eas,* Bentley, Traube;
per pia uilis expectantes, V[2] in lac. 24 letters. [3] *hac,*
Eyssen.; *hic,* V.

40

statue, he replied : " I would rather that good men should wonder why I did not deserve one than (which is much worse) should mutter ' Why was he given one ? ' "

9. Other men, taking great pride in coaches higher than common and in ostentatious finery of apparel, sweat under heavy cloaks, which they fasten about their necks and bind around their very throats, while the air blows through them because of the excessive lightness of the material ; and they lift them up with both hands and wave them with many gestures, especially with their left hands,[1] in order that the over-long fringes and the tunics embroidered with party-coloured threads in multiform figures of animals may be conspicuous.   10. Others, though no one questions them, assume a grave expression and greatly exaggerate their wealth, doubling the annual yield of their fields, well cultivated (as they think), of which they assert that they possess a great number from the rising to the setting sun ; they are clearly unaware that their forefathers, through whom the greatness of Rome was so far flung, gained renown, not by riches, but by fierce wars, and not differing from the common soldiers in wealth, mode of life, or simplicity of attire, overcame all obstacles by valour. 11. For that reason the eminent Valerius Publicola was buried by a contribution of money,[2] and through the aid of her husband's friends [3] the needy wife of

---

[1] Probably to display their rings; cf. Pliny, *N.H.* xxxiii. 9, *manus et prorsus sinistrae maximam auctoritatem conciliavere auro.*   [2] In 503 B.C. ; see Livy, ii. 16, 7.

[3] Valerius Maximus, iv. 4, 6, says that it was the senate that came to their aid.

dotatur ex aerario filia Scipionis, cum nobilitas
florem adultae virginis diuturnum absentia pauperis
erubesceret patris.

12. At nunc si ad aliquem bene nummatum tumen-
temque ideo, honestus advena salutatum introieris
primitus, tamquam exoptatus suscipieris, et interrogatus multa coactusque mentiri, miraberis numquam
antea visus, summatem virum tenuem te sic enixius
observantem, ut paeniteat ob [1] haec bona tamquam
praecipua non vidisse ante decennium Romam. 13.
Hacque affabilitate confisus, cum eadem postridie
feceris, ut incognitus haerebis et repentinus, hor-
tatore illo hesterno suos enumerando,[2] qui sis vel
unde venias diutius ambigente. Agnitus vero tandem et asscitus in amicitiam, si te salutandi assid-
uitati dederis triennio indiscretus, et per totidem
dierum [3] defueris tempus, reverteris ad paria perfe-
renda, nec ubi esses interrogatus, et ni inde miser [4]
discesseris, aetatem omnem frustra in stipite conteres

---

[1] *ob*, Val. ; *ut*, V.   [2] *suos*, scripsi ; *varia* or *foenera
enumerando*, Wagner ; *clientes n.*, suggested by Clark ;
te non n., Pet. ; *inter miracula n.*, Novák ; *numerando*,
preceded by lac. of 5 letters, V.   [3] *dierum*, added
by Val. ; V omits.   [4] *ni inde miser*, Novák ; *et non
temisero*, in lac. of 10 letters, V[2].

---

[1] Cn. Cornelius Scipio, who wrote from Spain in the
second Punic war, asking to be recalled, that he might
provide a dowry for his daughter ; see Valerius Maximus,
iv. 4, 10.

Regulus and her children were supported. And the daughter of Scipio[1] received her dowry from the public treasury, since the nobles blushed to look upon the beauty of this marriageable maiden long unsought because of the absence of a father of modest means.

12. But now-a-days, if as a stranger[2] of good position you enter for the first time to pay your respects to some man who is well-to-do[3] and therefore puffed up, at first you will be greeted as if you were an eagerly expected friend, and after being asked many questions and forced to lie, you will wonder, since the man never saw you before, that a great personage should pay such marked attention to your humble self as to make you regret, because of such special kindness, that you did not see Rome ten years earlier. 13. When, encouraged by this affability, you make the same call on the following day, you will hang about unknown and unexpected, while the man who the day before urged you to call again counts up his clients, wondering who you are or whence you came. But when you are at last recognized and admitted to his friendship, if you devote yourself to calling upon him for three years without interruption, then are away for the same number of days, and return to go through with a similar course, you will not be asked where you were, and unless you abandon the quest in sorrow, you will waste your whole life to no purpose in paying court to the blockhead.

---

[2] Ensslin, p. 7 (see Bibliography), refers this to Ammianus; cf. note on 6, 2, above.

[3] For *bene nummatum*, cf. Horace, *Epist.* i. 6, 38.

summittendo. 14. Cum autem commodis [1] inter-
vallata temporibus, convivia longa et noxia coeperint
apparari, vel distributio sollemnium sportularum,
anxia deliberatione tractatur, an exceptis his quibus
vicissitudo debetur, peregrinum invitari conveniet,
et si digesto plene consilio, id placuerit fieri, is
adhibetur qui pro domibus excubat aurigarum, aut
artem tesserariam profitetur, aut secretiora quaedam
se nosse confingit. 15. Homines enim eruditos et
sobrios, ut infaustos et inutiles vitant, eo quoque
accedente, quod et nomenclatores, assueti haec et
talia venditare, mercede accepta, lucris quosdam et
prandiis inserunt subditicios ignobiles et obscuros.

16. Mensarum enim voragines et varias volup-
tatum illecebras, ne longius progrediar, praeter-
mitto, illuc transiturus, quod quidam per ampla
spatia urbis, subversasque silices, sine periculi metu
properantes equos velut publicos, ignitis [2] quod
dicitur calcibus [3] agitant, familiarium agmina tamquam praedatorios globos post terga trahentes, ne
Sannione quidem (ut ait comicus) domi relicto.
Quos imitatae matronae complures, opertis capitibus
et basternis, per latera civitatis cuncta discurrunt.
17. Utque proeliorum periti rectores primo catervas
densas opponunt et fortes, deinde leves armaturas,

[1] *commodis*, Val. ; *cum autem commotus*, in lac. of 15
letters, V[2].   [2] *ignitis*, Pet. ; *signatis*, V.   [3] *calcibus*,
Bentley, Traube ; *calcis*, V.

[1] Referring to a plebeian (cf. xxviii. 4, 29), a partisan of
one of the colours.   Cf. also Suet., *Calig.* 55, 3.

14. And when, after a sufficient interval of time, the preparation of those tedious and unwholesome banquets begins, or the distribution of the customary doles, it is debated with anxious deliberation whether it will be suitable to invite a stranger, with the exception of those to whom a return of hospitality is due; and if, after full and mature deliberation, the decision is in the affirmative, the man who is invited is one who watches all night before the house of the charioteers,[1] or who is a professional dicer, or who pretends to the knowledge of certain secrets. 15. For they avoid learned and serious people as unlucky and useless, in addition to which the announcers of names, who are wont to traffic in these and similar favours, on receiving a bribe, admit to the doles and the dinners obscure and low-born intruders.

16. But I pass over the gluttonous banquets and the various allurements of pleasures, lest I should go too far, and I shall pass to the fact that certain persons hasten without fear of danger through the broad streets of the city and over the upturned stones of the pavements as if they were driving post-horses with hoofs of fire (as the saying is), dragging after them armies of slaves like bands of brigands and not leaving even Sannio at home, as the comic writer says.[2] And many matrons, imitating them, rush about through all quarters of the city with covered heads and in closed litters. 17. And as skilful directors of battles place in the van dense throngs of brave soldiers, then light-armed troops, after them the javelin-throwers, and

[2] Terence, *Eun.*, 780, *solus Sannio servat domi.*

post iaculatores ultimasque subsidiales acies (si fors adegerit) iuvaturas, ita praepositis urbanae familiae suspense digerentibus atque[1] sollicite, quos insignes faciunt virgae dexteris aptatae, velut tessera data castrensi, iuxta vehiculi frontem omne textrinum incedit : huic atratum coquinae iungitur ministerium, dein totum promisce servitium, cum otiosis plebeis de vicinitate coniunctis ; postrema multitudo spadonum a senibus in pueros desinens, obluridi distortaque lineamentorum compage deformes, ut quaqua incesserit quisquam, cernens mutilorum hominum agmina, detestetur memoriam Samiramidis reginae illius veteris, quae teneros mares castravit omnium prima, velut vim iniectans naturae, eandemque ab instituto cursu retorquens, quae inter ipsa oriundi crepundia, per primigenios seminis fontes, tacita quodam modo lege vias propagandae posteritatis ostendit.

18. Quod cum ita sit, paucae domus studiorum seriis cultibus antea celebratae, nunc ludibriis ignaviae torpentis[2] exundant, vocabili sonu, perflabili tinnitu fidium resultantes. Denique pro philosopho cantor, et in locum oratoris doctor artium ludicrarum accitur, et bibliothecis sepulcrorum ritu in perpetuum clausis, organa fabricantur hydraulica, et lyrae ad speciem[3] carpentorum ingentes, tibiaeque et histrionici gestus instrumenta non levia.

---

[1] *atque,* added by Novák, cf. Livy, xxii. 59, 16 ; xxvii. 50, 6 ; V omits.　　[2] *torpentis,* vulgo ; *torrentes,* V. [3] *ad,* BG in E[2] ; *de specie,* Eyssen. ; *de speciem,* V.

last of all the reserve forces, to enter the action in case chance makes it needful, just so those who have charge of a city household, made conspicuous by wands grasped in their right hands, carefully and diligently draw up the array; then, as if the signal had been given in camp, close to the front of the carriage all the weavers march; next to these the blackened service of the kitchen, then all the rest of the slaves without distinction, accompanied by the idle plebeians of the neighbourhood; finally, the throng of eunuchs, beginning with the old men and ending with the boys, sallow and disfigured by the distorted form of their members; so that, wherever anyone goes, beholding the troops of mutilated men, he would curse the memory of that Queen Samiramis of old, who was the first of all to castrate young males, thus doing violence, as it were, to Nature and wresting her from her intended course, since she at the very beginning of life, through the primitive founts of the seed, by a kind of secret law, shows the ways to propagate posterity.

18. In consequence of this state of things, the few houses that were formerly famed for devotion to serious pursuits now teem with the sports of sluggish indolence, re-echoing to the sound of singing and the tinkling of flutes and lyres. In short, in place of the philosopher the singer is called in, and in place of the orator the teacher of stagecraft, and while the libraries are shut up forever like tombs, water-organs are manufactured and lyres as large as carriages, and flutes and instruments heavy for gesticulating actors.

47

19. Postremo ad id indignitatis est ventum, ut cum peregrini ob formidatam haud ita dudum alimentorum inopiam pellerentur ab urbe praecipites, sectatoribus disciplinarum liberalium, impendio paucis, sine respiratione ulla extrusis, tenerentur mimarum asseculae[1] veri, quique id simularunt ad tempus, et tria milia saltatricum, ne interpellata quidem, cum choris totidemque remanerent magistris. **20.** Et licet, quocumque oculos flexeris, feminas affatim multas spectare cirratas, quibus (si nupsissent) per aetatem ter iam nixus poterat suppetere liberorum, ad usque taedium pedibus pavimenta tergentis, iactari volucriter[2] gyris, dum exprimunt innumera simulacra, quae finxere fabulae theatrales.

21. Illud autem non dubitatur, quod cum esset aliquando virtutum omnium domicilium Roma, ingenuos advenas plerique nobilium, ut Homerici bacarum suavitate Lotophagi, humanitatis multiformibus officiis retentabant. **22.** Nunc vero inanes flatus quorundam, vile esse quicquid extra urbis pomerium nascitur aestimant praeter orbos et caelibes, nec credi potest qua obsequiorum diversitate coluntur homines sine liberis Romae.

---

[1] *adsaeculae*, V.   [2] *uolucriter*, Gronov ; *uoluetur*, V.

---

[1] This happened in 383 ; see Introd., p. xiii.
[2] I.e. dancing on the mosaic pavements of great houses.
[3] *Odyssey*, ix. 84 ff.
[4] Originally, the line within the city wall, marking the

19. At last we have reached such a state of baseness, that whereas not so very long ago, when there was fear of a scarcity of food, foreigners were driven neck and crop from the city,[1] and those who practised the liberal arts (very few in number) were thrust out without a breathing space, yet the genuine attendants upon actresses of the mimes, and those who for the time pretended to be such, were kept with us, while three thousand dancing girls, without even being questioned, remained here with their choruses, and an equal number of dancing masters. 20. And, wherever you turn your eyes, you may see a throng of women with curled hair, who might, if they had married, by this time, so far as age goes, have already produced three children, sweeping the pavements[2] with their feet to the point of weariness and whirling in rapid gyrations, while they represent the innumerable figures that the stage-plays have devised.

21. Furthermore, there is no doubt that when once upon a time Rome was the abode of all the virtues, many of the nobles detained here foreigners of free birth by various kindly attentions, as the Lotus-eaters of Homer[3] did by the sweetness of their fruits. 22. But now the vain arrogance of some men regards everything born outside the pomerium[4] of our city as worthless, except the childless and unwedded; and it is beyond belief with what various kinds of obsequiousness men without children are courted at

limit within which the auspices could be taken; the term *pomerium* was soon transferred to the strip of land between this line and the actual city wall. Here it means merely the wall of the city.

23. Et quoniam apud eos, ut in capite mundi, morborum acerbitates celsius dominantur, ad quos vel sedandos omnis professio medendi torpescit, excogitatum est adminiculum sospitale, nequi amicum perferentem similia videat, additumque est cautioribus [1] paucis remedium aliud satis validum, ut [2] famulos percontatum missos quem ad modum valeant noti hac [3] aegritudine colligati, non ante recipiant domum, quam lavacro purgaverint corpus. Ita etiam alienis oculis visa metuitur labes. 24. Sed tamen haec cum ita tutius observentur, quidam vigore artuum imminuto, rogati ad nuptias, ubi aurum dextris manibus cavatis offertur, impigre vel usque Spoletium pergunt. Haec nobilium sunt [4] instituta.

25. Ex turba vero imae sortis et paupertinae, in tabernis aliqui pernoctant vinariis, non nulli sub velabris [5] umbraculorum theatralium latent, quae, Campanam imitatus lasciviam, Catulus in aedilitate sua suspendit omnium primus ; aut pugnaciter aleis certant, turpi sono fragosis naribus introrsum reducto spiritu concrepantes ; aut quod est studiorum omnium maximum ab ortu lucis ad vesperam sole fatiscunt vel pluviis, per minutias [6] aurigarum

[1] *cautioribus*, Bentley, *cautionibus*, V. [2] *ut*, added by Lind. ; V omits. [3] *noti hac*, G ; *non hac*, EB ; *non haec*, V. [4] *sunt*, Kiessling ; *est*, V. [5] *nonnulli sub velabris* (*nonnulli*, G ; *uelariis*, Gardt.), Her. ; [*ul*]*ariis non nullis velabris*, V. [6] *per minutias*, Lind. ; *perminuas*, V.

[1] This " legacy hunting," by paying court to childless men and women, is satirized by Horace (*Sat.* ii. 5). The " art " was in vogue as early as Plautus' time (see *Miles*, 705 ff.), but became a " profession " at the end of the

Rome.[1] 23. And since among them, as is natural in the capital of the world, cruel disorders gain such heights that all the healing art is powerless even to mitigate them, it has been provided, as a means of safety, that no one shall visit a friend suffering from such a disease, and by a few who are more cautious another sufficiently effective remedy has been added, namely, that servants sent to inquire after the condition of a man's acquaintances who have been attacked by that disorder should not be readmitted to their masters' house until they have purified their persons by a bath. So fearful are they of a contagion seen only by the eyes of others. 24. But yet, although these precautions are so strictly observed, some men, when invited to a wedding, where gold is put into their cupped right hands, although the strength of their limbs is impaired, will run even all the way to Spoletium.[2] Such are the habits of the nobles.

25. But of the multitude of lowest condition and greatest poverty some spend the entire night in wineshops, some lurk in the shade of the awnings of the theatres, which Catulus [3] in his aedileship, imitating Campanian wantonness, was the first to spread, or they quarrel with one another in their games at dice, making a disgusting sound by drawing back the breath into their resounding nostrils ; or, which is the favourite among all amusements, from sunrise until evening, in sunshine and in rain, they stand open-mouthed, examining minutely the good

Republic (cf. Cic., *Paradoxa*, v. 39) and under the Empire, followed even by some of the emperors (see Suet., *Calig.* 38, 2 ; *Nero*, 32, 2).

[2] In Umbria. On *aurum* see Pliny, *Epist.* x. 116.

[3] See Index, and Val. Max. ii. 4. 6. *Q. Catulus primus spectantium consessum velorum umbraculis texit.*

equorumque praecipua vel delicta scrutantes. 26.
Et est admodum mirum videre plebem innumeram,
mentibus ardore quodam infuso, e dimicationum
curulium eventu pendentem. Haec similiaque
memorabile nihil vel serium agi Romae permittunt.
Ergo redeundum ad textum.

7. *Galli Caesaris immanitas et saevitia.*

1. Latius iam disseminata licentia, onerosus
bonis omnibus Caesar, nullum post haec adhibens
modum, orientis latera cuncta vexabat, nec honoratis
parcens nec urbium primatibus nec plebeis. 2.
Denique Antiochensis [1] ordinis vertices sub uno
elogio iussit occidi, ideo efferatus, quod ei celerari [2]
vilitatem intempestivam urgenti, cum impenderet
inopia, gravius rationabili responderunt ; et peris-
sent ad unum, ni comes orientis tunc Honoratus fixa
constantia restitisset. 3. Erat autem diritatis eius
hoc quoque indicium nec obscurum nec latens, quod
ludicris cruentis delectabatur, et in circo sex vel
septem aliquotiens deditus [3] certaminibus, pugilum
vicissim se concidentium, perfusorumque sanguine
specie, ut lucratus ingentia, laetabatur. 4. Accen-
derat super his incitatum propositum ad nocendum
aliqua mulier vilis, quae ad palatium (ut poposcerat)

---

[1] *Antiochensis*, Lind. ; *antichisis*, V.   [2] *celerari*, Wagner ; *celebrari*, V.   [3] *deditus*, Pet. ; *vetitus*, V.

---

[1] The great Syrian city ; see Index.
[2] See Introd., pp. xviii f.

points or the defects of charioteers and their horses. 26. And it is most remarkable to see an innumerable crowd of plebeians, their minds filled with a kind of eagerness, hanging on the outcome of the chariot races. These and similar things prevent anything memorable or serious from being done in Rome. Accordingly, I must return to my subject.

7. *Atrocities and savagery of Gallus Caesar.*

1. His lawlessness now more widely extended, Caesar became offensive to all good men, and henceforth showing no restraint, he harassed all parts of the East, sparing neither ex-magistrates nor the chief men of the cities, nor even the plebeians. 2. Finally, he ordered the death of the leaders of the senate of Antioch [1] in a single writ, enraged because when he urged a prompt introduction of cheap prices at an unseasonable time, since scarcity threatened, they had made a more vigorous reply then was fitting. And they would have perished to a man, had not Honoratus, then count-governor [2] of the East, opposed him with firm resolution. 3. This also was a sign of his savage nature which was neither obscure nor hidden, that he delighted in cruel sports ; and sometimes in the Circus, absorbed in six or seven contests, he exulted in the sight of boxers pounding each other to death and drenched with blood, as if he had made some great gain. 4. Besides this, his propensity for doing harm was inflamed and incited by a worthless woman, who, on being admitted to the palace (as she had demanded) had betrayed a plot that was secretly

53

intromissa, insidias ei latenter obtendi prodiderat a militibus obscurissimis. Quam Constantina exultans, ut in tuto iam locata mariti salute, muneratam vehiculoque impositam per regiae ianuas emisit in publicum, ut his illecebris alios quoque ad indicanda proliceret paria vel maiora. 5. Post haec Gallus Hierapolim profecturus, ut expeditioni specie tenus adesset, Antiochensi plebi suppliciter obsecranti, ut inediae dispelleret metum, quae per multas difficilisque causas affore iam sperabatur, non ut mos est principibus, quorum diffusa potestas localibus subinde medetur aerumnis, disponi quicquam statuit, vel ex provinciis alimenta transferri conterminis, sed consularem Syriae Theophilum prope adstantem, ultima metuenti multitudini dedit, id [1] assidue replicando, quod invito rectore, nullus egere poterit victu. 6. Auxerunt haec vulgi sordidioris audaciam; et cum ingravesceret penuria commeatuum, famis et furoris impulsu, Eubuli cuiusdam inter suos clari domum ambitiosam ignibus subditis inflammavit, rectoremque ut sibi iudicio imperiali addictum, calcibus incessens et pugnis, conculcans seminecem laniatu miserando discerpsit. Post cuius lacrimosum interitum, in unius exitio quisque

---

[1] *dedit id,* Eyssen. ; *dediti,* V.

being made against him by some soldiers of the lowest condition. Whereupon Constantina, exulting as if the safety of her husband were now assured, gave her a reward, and seating her in a carriage, sent her out through the palace gates into the public streets, in order that by such inducements she might tempt others to reveal similar or greater conspiracies.

5. After this, when Gallus was on the point of leaving for Hierapolis, ostensibly to take part in the campaign, and the commons of Antioch suppliantly besought him to save them from the fear of a famine, which, through many difficulties of circumstance, was then believed to be imminent, he did not, after the manner of princes whose widely extended power sometimes cures local troubles, make any arrangements or command the bringing of supplies from neighbouring provinces ; but to the multitude, which was in fear of the direst necessity, he delivered up Theophilus, consular governor of Syria, who was standing near by, constantly repeating the statement, that no one could lack food if the governor did not wish it. 6. These words increased the audacity of the lowest classes, and when the lack of provisions became more acute, driven by hunger and rage, they set fire to the pretentious house of a certain Eubulus, a man of distinction among his own people ; then, as if the governor had been delivered into their hands by an imperial edict, they assailed him with kicks and blows, and trampling him under foot when he was half-dead, with awful mutilation tore him to pieces. After his wretched death each man saw in the end of one person an image of his own

imaginem periculi sui considerans, documento re-
centi similia formidabat. 7. Eodem tempore Serenianus ex duce, cuius ignavia populatam in Phoenice
Celsein ante rettulimus, pulsatae maiestatis imperii
reus iure postulatus ac lege, incertum qua potuit
suffragatione absolui, aperte convictus, familiarem
suum cum pileo quo caput operiebat, incantato
vetitis artibus, ad templum misisse fatidicum,
quaeritatum praesagia,[1] an ei firmum portenderetur
imperium (ut cupiebat) et tutum.[2] 8. Duplexque
eisdem diebus acciderat malum, quod et Theophilum
insontem atrox interceperat casus, et Serenianus
dignus execratione cunctorum, innoxius, modo non
reclamante publico vigore, discessit.

9. Haec subinde Constantius audiens, et quaedam
referente Thalassio doctus, quem obisse[3] iam compererat lege communi, scribens ad Caesarem blandius,
adiumenta paulatim illi subtraxit, sollicitari se
simulans ne, uti est militare otium fere tumultu-
osum, in eius perniciem conspiraret, solisque scholis
iussit esse contentum palatinis et protectorum, cum
Scutariis et Gentilibus, et mandabat Domitiano, ex
comite largitionum praefecto provecto, ut cum in
Syriam venerit, Gallum quem crebro acciverat,[5]

[1] *praesagia*, W[2]N[2]; *praesa anei*, V.   [2] *tutum*, C. F. W.
Müller; *cũtum*, V.   [3] *quem obisse*, Lind. ; *quẽ movisse*,
V.   [4] *uti est*, Val. ; *uitiae*, V.   [5] *acciuerat*, Val-
esius ; *acciperat*, V.

---

[1] In a lost book.   [2] See ch. i. 10, above.
[3] The *Scholae Palatinae* were the divisions of the household or court troops, a corps of 3500 men : *protectores,
domestici, gentiles, scutarii* and *armaturae.* The *protectores,*
guards, were a body of troops with the rank of officers, also
called *domestici.* The *scutarii* (targeteers) took their name

peril and dreaded a fate like that which he had just witnessed. 7. At that same time Serenianus, a former general, through whose inefficiency Celse in Phoenicia had been pillaged, as we have described,[1] was justly and legally tried for high treason, and it was doubtful by what favour he could be acquitted; for it was clearly proved that he had enchanted by forbidden arts a cap which he used to wear, and sent a friend of his with it to a prophetic shrine, to seek for omens as to whether the imperial power was destined to be firmly and safely his, as he desired. 8. At that time a twofold evil befell, in that an awful fate took off Theophilus, who was innocent, and Serenianus, who was deserving of universal execration, got off scotfree, almost without any strong public protest.

9. Constantius, hearing of these events from time to time, and being informed of some things by Thalassius,[2] who, as he had now learned, had died a natural death, wrote in flattering terms to the Caesar, but gradually withdrew from him his means of defence. He pretended to be anxious, since soldiers are apt to be disorderly in times of inaction, lest they might conspire for Gallus' destruction, and bade him be satisfied with the palace troops only [3] and those of the guards, besides the Targeteers and the Household troops. He further ordered Domitianus, a former state treasurer,[4] and now prefect, that when he came into Syria, he should politely and respectfully urge Gallus, whom he had frequently

from their equipment. The *gentiles* were a cavalry troop enlisted from foreigners: Scythians, Goths, Franks, Germans, etc.

[4] See Introd., p. **xl**.

ad Italiam properare blande hortaretur et [1] verecunde. 10. Qui cum venisset ob haec festinatis itineribus Antiochiam, praestrictis palatii ianuis, contempto Caesare quem videri decuerat, ad praetorium cum pompa sollemni perrexit, morbosque diu causatus, nec regiam introiit, nec processit in publicum, sed abditus multa in eius moliebatur exitium, addens quaedam relationibus supervacua, quas subinde mittebat [2] ad principem. 11. Rogatus ad ultimum, admissusque in consistorium, ambage nulla praegressa, inconsiderate et leviter, " Proficiscere " inquit (ut praeceptum est) " Caesar, sciens quod (si cessaveris) et tuas et palatii tui auferri iubebo prope diem annonas." Hocque solo contumaciter dicto, subiratus abscessit, nec in conspectum eius postea venit, saepius arcessitus. 12. Hinc ille commotus, ut iniusta perferens et indigna, praefecti custodiam protectoribus mandaverat fidis. Quo conperto Montius tunc quaestor, acer [3] quidem sed ad lenitatem propensior, consulens in commune, advocatos palatinarum primos scholarum allocutus est mollius, docens nec decere haec fieri nec prodesse, addensque vocis obiurgatorio sonu, quod si id

[1] *et*, added by BG, omitted by V. [2] *mittebat*, Petschenig; *dimittebat*, V. [3] *acer*, Gronov; *afen*, V; *Afer*, Bentley, Kiessling.

---

[1] I.e. the local *consistorium* of Gallus.

summoned, to hasten to return to Italy. 10. But when Domitianus had quickened his pace because of these instructions and had come to Antioch, passing by the gates of the palace in contempt of the Caesar, on whom he ought to have called, he went to the general's quarters with the usual pomp, and having for a long time pleaded illness, he neither entered the palace nor appeared in public, but remaining in hiding he made many plots for Gallus' ruin, adding some superfluous details to the reports which from time to time he sent to the emperor. 11. At last, being invited to the palace and admitted to the council,[1] without any preliminary remarks he said inconsiderately and coolly : " Depart, Caesar and know that, if you delay, I shall at once order your supplies and those of your palace to be cut off." Having said only this in an insolent tone, he went off in a passion, and although often sent for, he never afterwards came into Gallus' presence. 12. Caesar, angered at this and feeling that such treatment was unjust and undeserved, ordered his faithful guards [2] to arrest the prefect. When this became known, Montius, who was then quaestor,[3] a spirited man but somewhat inclined to moderate measures, having in view the public welfare, sent for the foremost members of the palace troops and addressed them in mild terms, pointing out that such conduct was neither seemly nor expedient and adding in a tone of reproof that if they approved of this course, it would be fitting

[2] See note, p. 56.
[3] Corresponding in the court of Gallus to the *quaestor sacri palatii* of the emperor.

placuerit, post statuas Constantii [1] deiectas, super
adimenda vita praefecto conveniet securius cogi-
tari.   13. His cognitis Gallus ut serpens appetitus
telo vel saxo, iamque spes extremas opperiens, et
succurrens saluti suae quavis ratione, colligi omnes
iussit armatos, et cum starent attoniti, districta
dentium acie stridens, " Adeste " inquit " viri fortes
mihi periclitanti vobiscum.   14. Montius nos tumore
inusitato quodam et novo, ut rebelles et maiestati
recalcitrantes Augustae, per haec quae strepit incu-
sat, iratus nimirum, quod contumacem praefectum,
quid rerum ordo postulat ignorare dissimulantem,
formidine tenus iusserim custodiri."   15. Nihil
morati post haec militares avidi saepe turbarum,
adorti sunt Montium primum, qui devertebat in
proximo, levi corpore senem atque morbosum, et
hirsutis resticulis cruribus eius innexis, divaricatum
sine spiramento ullo ad usque praetorium traxere
praefecti.   16. Et eodem impetu Domitianum praecipitem per scalas itidem funibus constrinxerunt, eosque
coniunctos per ampla spatia civitatis acri raptavere
discursu. Iamque artuum et membrorum divulsa
compage, superscandentes corpora mortuorum, ad
ultimam truncata deformitatem, velut exsaturati
mox abiecerunt in flumen.   17. Incenderat autem
audaces usque ad insaniam homines ad haec
quae nefariis egere conatibus, Luscus quidam
curator urbis subito visus, eosque ut heiulans baiolo-
rum praecentor, ad expediendum quod orsi sunt,

[1] *Constantii,* Valesius ; *Constantini,* **V.**

first to overthrow the statues of Constantius and then plan with less anxiety for taking the life of the prefect. 13. On learning this, Gallus, like a serpent attacked by darts or stones, waiting now for a last expedient and trying to save his life by any possible means, ordered all his troops to be assembled under arms, and while they stood in amazement, he said, baring and gnashing his teeth, " Stand by me, my brave men, who are like myself in danger. 14. Montius with a kind of strange and unprecedented arrogance in this loud harangue of his accuses us of being rebels and as resisting the majesty of Augustus, no doubt in anger because I ordered an insolent prefect, who presumes to ignore what proper conduct requires, to be imprisoned, merely to frighten him." 15. With no further delay the soldiers, as often eager for disturbance, first attacked Montius, who lodged close by, an old man frail of body and ill besides. bound coarse ropes to his legs, and dragged him spread-eagle fashion without any breathing-space all the way to Caesar's headquarters. 16. And in the same access of rage they threw Domitianus down the steps, then bound him also with ropes, and tying the two together, dragged them at full speed through the broad streets of the city. And when finally their joints and limbs were torn asunder, leaping upon their dead bodies, they mutilated them in a horrible manner, and at last, as if glutted, threw them into the river. 17. Now these men, reckless to the point of madness, were roused to such atrocious deeds as they committed by a certain Luscus, curator of the city. He suddenly appeared and with repeated cries, like a bawling leader of porters, urged them to

incitans vocibus crebris. Qui haud longe postea ideo vivus exustus est.

18. Et quia Montius inter dilancinantium manus spiritum efflaturus, Epigonum et Eusebium, nec professionem nec dignitatem ostendens, aliquotiens increpabat, aequisoni[1] his magna quaerebantur industria, et nequid intepesceret, Epigonus e Cilicia[2] philosophus ducitur, et Eusebius ab Emissa Pittacas cognomento, concitatus orator, cum quaestor non hos sed tribunos fabricarum insimulasset, promittentes armorum, si novae res agitari coepissent.[3] 19. Eisdem diebus Apollinaris Domitiani gener paulo ante agens palatii Caesaris curam, ad Mesopotamiam missus a socero, per militares numeros immodice scrutabatur, an quaedam altiora meditantis iam Galli secreta susceperint scripta ; qui compertis Antiochiae gestis, per minorem Armeniam lapsus, Constantinopolim petit, exindeque per[4] protectores retractus, artissime tenebatur.

20. Quae dum ita struuntur, indicatum est apud Tyrum indumentum regale textum occulte, incertum quo locante vel cuius usibus apparatum. Ideoque rector provinciae tunc pater Apollinaris eiusdem nominis ut conscius ductus est, aliique congregati

---

[1] *aequisoni*, Traube ; *qui sint*, V[2]. Her. ; *e Lycia*, EG ; *haec licia*, V. EG ; *conperissent*, PB ; *conpissent*, V. by E[2] BG (B omits *que*) ; V omits. [2] *Cilicia*, Clark, [3] *coepissent*, [4] *per*, added

finish what they had begun. And for that not long afterwards he was burned alive.

18. And because Montius, when about to breathe his last in the hands of those who were rending him, cried out upon Epigonus and Eusebius, but without indicating their profession or rank, men of the same name were sought for with great diligence. And in order that the excitement might not cool, a philosopher Epigonus from Cilicia was arrested, and a Eusebius, surnamed Pittacas, a vehement orator, from Edessa, although it was not these that the quaestor had implicated, but some tribunes of forges,[1] who had promised arms in case a revolution should be set on foot. 19. In those same days Apollinaris, son-in-law of Domitianus, who a short time before had been in charge of Caesar's palace, being sent to Mesopotamia by his father-in-law, inquired with excessive interest among the companies of soldiers whether they had received any secret messages from Gallus which indicated that he was aiming higher; but when he heard what had happened at Antioch, he slipped off through Lesser Armenia and made for Constantinople, but from there he was brought back by the guards and kept in close confinement.

20. Now, while these things were happening, attention was drawn at Tyre to a royal robe that had been made secretly, but it was uncertain who had ordered it or for whose use it was made. Consequently the governor of the province at that time, who was the father of Apollinaris and of the same name, was brought to trial as his accomplice; and many others

---

[1] I.e. in charge of workshops for making arms. *Fabrica* is applied to Vulcan's forge in Cic., *De Nat. Deo.* iii. 22, 55.

sunt ex diversis civitatibus multi, qui atrocium criminum ponderibus urgebantur.

21. Iamque lituis cladium concrepantibus internarum, non celate [1] (ut antea) turbidum saeviebat ingenium, a veri consideratione detortum, et nullo impositorum vel compositorum fidem sollemniter inquirente, nec discernente a societate noxiorum insontes, velut exturbatum e iudiciis fas omne discessit et causarum legitima silente defensione, carnifex rapinarum sequester, et obductio capitum, et bonorum ubique multatio versabatur per orientales provincias ; quas recensere puto nunc opportunum, absque Mesopotamia, iam [2] digesta cum bella Parthica narrarentur,[3] et Aegypto, quam necessario aliud reiciemus [4] ad tempus.

8. *Orientis provinciarum descriptio.*

1. Superatis Tauri montis verticibus, qui ad solis ortum sublimius attolluntur, Cilicia spatiis porrigitur late distentis, dives bonis omnibus terra, eiusque lateri dextro annexa Isauria, pari sorte uberi, palmite viret et frugibus multis, quam mediam navigabile flumen Calycadnus interscindit. 2. Et hanc quidem praeter oppida multa duae civitates exornant, Seleucia opus Seleuci regis, et Claudiopolis, quam deduxit coloniam Claudius Caesar.

---

[1] *concitate*, Her. ; *concelatae*, V.   [2] *iam*, added by Val.; *Mesopotamiam*, V.   [3] *narrarentur*, Her.; *dicerentur*, G ; (lac. of 5 letters) *rentur*, V.   [4] *reiciemus*, Traube; *reici* (lac. of 4 letters), V.

were gathered together from various cities and were
bowed down by the weight of charges of heinous
crimes.

21. And now, when the clarions of internal disaster were sounding, the disordered mind of Caesar,
turned from consideration of the truth, and not
secretly as before, vented its rage ; and since no one
conducted the usual examination of the charges
either made or invented, or distinguished the innocent
from association with the guilty, all justice vanished
from the courts as though driven out.   And while the
legitimate defence of cases was put to silence, the
executioner (trustee of plunderings), hoodwinking
for execution, and confiscation of property ranged
everywhere throughout the eastern provinces.
These I think it now a suitable time to review,
excepting Mesopotamia, which has already been
described in connection with the account of the
Parthian wars,[1] and Egypt, which we will necessarily
postpone to another time.[2]

8. *Description of the Eastern Provinces.*

1. After one passes the summits of Mount Taurus,
which on the east rise to a lofty height, Cilicia spreads
out in widely extended plains, a land abounding in
products of every kind ; and adjoining its right side
is Isauria, equally blest with fruitful vines and
abundant grain, being divided in the middle by the
navigable river Calycadnus.   2. This province too,
in addition to many towns, is adorned by two cities ;
Seleucia, the work of king Seleucus, and Claudiopolis,

---

[1] In a lost book.   [2] See xxii. 15-16.

Isaura [1] enim antehac nimium potens, olim subversa ut rebellatrix interneciva, aegre vestigia claritudinis pristinae monstrat admodum pauca. 3. Ciliciam vero, quae Cydno amni exultat, Tarsus nobilitat, urbs perspicabilis—hanc condidisse Perseus memoratur, Iovis filius et Danaes, vel certe ex Aethiopia profectus Sandan quidam nomine vir opulentus et nobilis — et Anazarbus auctoris vocabulum referens, et Mobsuestia, vatis illius domicilium Mobsi, quem a commilitio Argonautarum, cum aureo vellere direpto redirent, errore abstractum, delatumque ad Africae litus, mors repentina consumpsit, et ex eo caespite punico tecti, manes eius heroici, dolorum varietati medentur plerumque sospitales. 4. Hac duae provinciae, bello quondam piratico catervis mixtae praedonum, a Servilio pro consule missae sub iugum, factae sunt vectigales. Et hae quidem regiones velut in prominenti terrarum lingua positae, ab orbe eoo monte Amano disparantur. 5. Orientis vero limes in longum protentus et rectum, ab Euphratis fluminis ripis ad usque supercilia porrigitur Nili, laeva Saracenis conterminans gentibus, dextra pelagi fragoribus patens, quam plagam Nicator Seleucus occupatam auxit magnum in modum, cum post Alexandri Macedonis obitum successorio iure teneret regna Persidis, efficaciae impetrabilis rex (ut

[1] *Isaura*, Val. ; *Isauria*, W[2]BG ; *Caesaris aurenimante*, V.

---

[1] The Emperor Claudius, A.D. 41-54.

which Claudius Caesar [1] founded as a colony. For
Isaura, which was formerly too powerful, was long
ago overthrown as a dangerous rebel, and barely
shows a few traces of its former glory. 3. Cilicia, however, which boasts of the river Cydnus, is ennobled
by Tarsus, a fair city; this is said to have been
founded by Perseus, son of Jupiter, and Danaë, or
else by a wealthy and high-born man, Sandan by
name, who came from Ethiopia. There is also Anazarbus, bearing the name of its founder, and Mobsuestia, the abode of that famous diviner Mobsus. He,
wandering from his fellow-warriors the Argonauts when
they were returning after carrying off the golden
fleece, and being borne to the coast of Africa, met a
sudden death. Thereafter his heroic remains, covered
with Punic sod, have been for the most part effective
in healing a variety of diseases. 4. These two provinces, crowded with bands of brigands, were long
ago, during the war with the pirates, sent under
the yoke by the proconsul Servilius [2] and made
to pay tribute. And these regions indeed, lying, as
it were, upon a promontory, are separated from the
eastern continent by Mount Amanus. 5. But the
frontier of the East, extending a long distance in a
straight line, reaches from the banks of the Euphrates
to the borders of the Nile, being bounded on the left
by the Saracenic races and on the right exposed to
the waves of the sea. Of this district Nicator
Seleucus took possession and greatly increased it in
power, when by right of succession he was holding
the rule of Persia after the death of Alexander of
Macedon; and he was a successful and efficient

---

[2] P. Servilius Isauricus, in 74 B.C.

indicat cognomentum). 6. Abusus enim multitudine hominum, quam tranquillis in rebus diutius rexit, ex agrestibus habitaculis urbes construxit, multis opibus firmas et viribus, quarum ad praesens pleraeque, licet Graecis nominibus appellentur, quae eisdem ad arbitrium imposita sunt conditoris, primigenia tamen nomina non amittunt, quae eis Assyria lingua institutores veteres indiderunt.

7. Et prima post Osdroenam quam (ut dictum est) ab hac descriptione discrevimus, Commagena (nunc Euphratensis) clementer assurgit, Hierapoli (vetere Nino) et Samosata civitatibus amplis [1] illustris.

8. Dein Syria per speciosam interpatet diffusa planitiem. Hanc nobilitat Antiochia, mundo cognita civitas, cui non certaverit alia advecticiis ita affluere copiis et internis, et Laodicia et Apamia, itidemque Seleucia iam [2] inde a primis auspiciis florentissimae.

9. Post hanc acclinis Libano monti Phoenice, regio plena gratiarum et venustatis, urbibus decorata magnis et pulchris ; in quibus amoenitate celebritateque nominum Tyros excellit, Sidon et Berytus eisdemque pares Emissa et [3] Damascus saeculis condita priscis. 10. Has autem provincias, quas Orontes ambiens amnis, imosque pedes Cassii montis illius celsi praetermeans, funditur in [4] Parthenium

---

[1] *amplis*, EG ; *amplis et*, V.   [2] *Seleucia iam*, Val. ; *Seleuciam*, V.   [3] *et*, A ; V omits.   [4] *in*, added by E, Lind. ; omitted by the other MSS., and by G.

king, as his surname Nicator indicates. **6.** For by
taking advantage of the great number of men whom
he ruled for a long time in peace, in place of their
rustic dwellings he built cities of great strength and
abundant wealth ; and many of these, although
they are now called by the Greek names which were
imposed upon them by the will of their founder,
nevertheless have not lost the old appellations in the
Assyrian tongue which the original settlers gave
them.

7. And first after Osdroene, which ,as has been said,
I have omitted from this account, Commagene, now
called **Euphratensis**, gradually lifts itself into
eminence ; [1] it is famous for the great cities of Hierapolis, the ancient Ninus, and Samosata.

8. Next Syria spreads for a distance over a beautiful plain. This is famed for Antioch, a city known
to all the world, and without a rival, so rich is it in
imported and domestic commodities ; likewise for
Laodicia, Apamia, and also Seleucia, most flourishing
cities from their very origin.

9. After this comes Phoenicia, lying at the foot of
Mount Libanus,[2] a region full of charm and beauty,
adorned with many great cities ; among these in
attractiveness and the renown of their names Tyre,
Sidon and Berytus are conspicuous, and equal to
these are Emissa and Damascus, founded in days
long past. **10.** Now these provinces, encircled by
the river Orontes, which, after flowing past the foot
of that lofty mountain Cassius, empties into the
Parthenian Sea,[3] were taken from the realms of the

---

[1] Above the surrounding country. [2] Lebanon.
[3] Near the Gulf of Issos, in south-eastern Cilicia.

mare, Gnaeus Pompieus superato Tigrane, regnis Armeniorum abstractas, dicioni Romanae coniunxit.

11. Ultima Syriarum est Palaestina, per intervalla magna protenta, cultis abundans terris et nitidis, et civitates habens quasdam egregias, nullam nulli cedentem, sed sibi vicissim velut ad perpendiculum aemulas : Caesaream, quam ad honorem Octaviani principis exaedificavit Herodes, et Eleutheropolim et Neapolim, itidemque Ascalonem Gazam, aevo superiore exstructas. 12. In his tractibus navigerum nusquam visitur flumen, et in locis plurimis aquae suapte natura calentes emergunt, ad usus aptae multiplicium medellarum. Verum has quoque regiones pari sorte Pompeius Iudeis domitis et Hierosolymis captis, in provinciae [1] speciem delata iuris dictione formavit.

13. Huic Arabia est conserta, ex alio latere Nabataeis contigua, opima varietate commerciorum, castrisque oppleta validis et castellis, quae ad repellendos gentium vicinarum excursus, sollicitudo pervigil veterum per opportunos saltus erexit et cautos. Haec quoque civitates habet inter oppida quaedam ingentes, Bostram et Gerasam atque Philadelphiam, murorum firmitate cautissimas. Hanc provinciae imposito nomine, rectoreque adtributo, obtemperare legibus nostris Traianus compulit imperator, incolarum tumore saepe contunso, cum glorioso Marte Mediam urgeret et Parthos.

[1] *provinciae,* Val. ; *provincias,* V.

---

[1] In 64 B.C.   [2] I.e. exactly.   [3] Herod the Great.

Armenians by Gnaeus Pompeius, after his defeat of Tigranes,[1] and brought under Roman sway.

11. The last region of the Syrias is Palestine, extending over a great extent of territory and abounding in cultivated and well-kept lands ; it also has some splendid cities, none of which yields to any of the others, but they rival one another, as it were, by plumb-line.[2] These are Caesarea, which Herodes [3] built in honour of the emperor Octavianus,[4] Eleutheropolis, and Neapolis, along with Ascalon and Gaza, built in a former age. 12. In these districts no navigable river is anywhere to be seen, but in numerous places natural warm springs gush forth, adapted to many medicinal uses. But these regions also met with a like fate, being formed into a province by Pompey, after he had defeated the Jews and taken Jerusalem,[5] but left to the jurisdiction of a governor.

13. Adjacent to this region is Arabia, which on one side adjoins the country of the Nabataei, a land producing a rich variety of wares and studded with strong castles and fortresses, which the watchful care of the early inhabitants reared in suitable and readily defended defiles, to check the inroads of neighbouring tribes. This region also has, in addition to some towns, great cities, Bostra, Gerasa and Philadelphia, all strongly defended by mighty walls. It was given the name of a province, assigned a governor, and compelled to obey our laws by the emperor Trajan,[6] who, by frequent victories crushed the arrogance of its inhabitants when he was waging glorious war with Media and the Parthians.

[4] Augustus.   [5] In 63 B.C.   [6] In A.D. 105.

14. Cyprum itidem insulam procul a continenti [1] discretam et portuosam, inter municipia crebra urbes duae faciunt claram, Salamis et Paphus, altera Iovis delubris, altera Veneris templo insignis. Tanta autem tamque multiplici fertilitate abundat rerum omnium eadem Cyprus, ut nullius externi indigens adminiculi, indigenis viribus, a fundamento ipso carinae ad supremos usque carbasos, aedificet onerariam navem, omnibusque armamentis instructam, mari committat. 15. Nec piget dicere avide magis hanc insulam populum Romanum invassisse quam iuste. Ptolomaeo enim rege foederato nobis et socio, ob aerarii nostri angustias iusso sine ulla culpa proscribi, ideoque hausto veneno, voluntaria morte deleto, et tributaria facta est, et velut hostiles eius exuviae classi impositae, in urbem advectae sunt per Catonem. Nunc repetetur ordo gestorum.

9. *De Constantio Gallo Caesare.*

1. Inter has ruinarum varietates, a Nisibi quam tuebatur accitus Ursicinus,[2] cui nos obsecuturos iunxerat imperiale praeceptum, dispicere litis exitialis crimina [3] cogebatur, abnuens et reclamans, adulatorum oblatrantibus turmis, bellicosus sane milesque semper et militum ductor, sed forensibus iurgiis longe

---

[1] *continenti*, EBG ; *continendisque tam*, V.   [2] *Ursicinus*, E², Val. ; V omits.   [3] *crimina*, W²DE, Clark (c. *iam*, W²DE) ; *lese* (lac. of 2 letters) *mina*, V.

---

[1] Brother of Ptolemy Auletes, King of Egypt from 80 B.C.   [2] Cato Uticensis in 58 B.C.

72

14. Cyprus, too, an island far removed from the mainland, and abounding in harbours, besides having numerous towns, is made famous by two cities, Salamis and Paphos, the one celebrated for its shrines of Jupiter, the other for its temple of Venus. This Cyprus is so fertile and so abounds in products of every kind, that without the need of any help from without, by its native resources alone it builds cargo ships from the very keel to the topmast sails, and equipping them completely entrusts them to the deep. 15. Nor am I loth to say that the Roman people in invading that island showed more greed than justice; for King Ptolemy,[1] our ally joined to us by a treaty, without any fault of his, merely because of the low state of our treasury was ordered to be proscribed, and in consequence committed suicide by drinking poison; whereupon the island was made tributary and its spoils, as though those of an enemy, were taken aboard our fleet and brought to Rome by Cato.[2] I shall now resume the thread of my narrative.

9. *Of Constantius Gallus Caesar.*

1. Amid this variety of disasters Ursicinus, to whose attendance the imperial command had attached me, was summoned from Nisibis, of which he was in charge, and was compelled, in spite of his reluctance and his opposition to the clamorous troops of flatterers, to investigate the accusations in the deadly strife. He was in fact a warrior, having always been a soldier and a leader of soldiers, but far removed from the wranglings of the forum;

73

discretus, qui metu sui discriminis anxius, cum
accusatores quaesitoresque subditivos sibi conso-
ciatos, ex eisdem foveis cerneret emergentes, quae
clam palamve agitabantur occultis Constantium
litteris edocebat, implorans subsidia, quorum metu
tumor notissimus Caesaris exhalaret. 2. Sed cautela
nimia in peiores haeserat plagas, ut narrabimus
postea, aemulis consarcinantibus insidias graves
apud Constantium, cetera medium principem, sed
siquid auribus eius huius modi quivis infudisset
ignotus, acerbum et implacabilem, et in hoc causarum
titulo dissimilem sui.

3. Proinde die funestis interrogationibus praestituto, imaginarius iudex equitum resedit magister,
adhibitis aliis, iam quae essent agenda praedoctis, et
assistebant hinc inde notarii, quid quaesitum esset
quidve responsum, cursim ad Caesarem perferentes ;
cuius imperio truci, stimulis reginae exsertantis ora [1]
subinde per aulaeum, nec diluere obiecta permissi
nec defensi periere complures. 4. Primi igitur omnium statuuntur Epigonus et Eusebius, ob nominum
gentilitatem oppressi. Praediximus enim Montium
sub ipso vivendi termino his vocabulis appellatos,
fabricarum culpasse tribunos, ut adminicula futurae molitioni [2] pollicitos. 5. Et Epigonus quidem
amictu tenus philosophus, ut apparuit, prece frustra
temptata, sulcatis lateribus, mortisque metu admoto,

---

[1] *ora*, Novák, Her. (cf. *Aen.* iii. 425) ; *aura*, V.
[2] *molitioni*, Lind. ; *militioni*, V (*melitioni*, V[3]).

---

[1] See **7, 18**, with note.

accordingly, worried by fear of the danger which
threatened him, seeing the corrupt accusers and
judges with whom he was associated all coming
forth from the same holes, he informed Constantius
by secret letters of what was going on furtively or
openly, and begged for aid, that through fear of
it the well-known arrogance of the Caesar might
subside. 2. But by too great caution he had fallen
into worse snares, as we shall show later, since his
rivals patched up dangerous plots with Constantius,
who was in other respects a moderate emperor, but
cruel and implacable if anyone, however obscure,
had whispered in his ear anything of that kind, and
in cases of that nature unlike himself.

3. Accordingly, on the day set for the fatal
examinations the master of the horse took his seat,
ostensibly as a judge, attended by others who had
been told in advance what was to be done ; and
here and there shorthand writers were stationed who
reported every question and every answer post-
haste to Caesar ; and by his cruel orders, instigated
by the queen, who from time to time poked her face
through a curtain, many were done to death without being allowed to clear themselves of the charges
or to make any defence. 4. First of all, then,
Epigonus and Eusebius were brought before them
and ruined by the affinity of their names ; for
Montius, as I have said,[1] at the very end of his
life had accused certain tribunes of forges called
by those names of having promised support to
some imminent enterprise. 5. And Epigonus,
for his part, was a philosopher only in his attire,
as became evident ; for when he had tried entreaties to no purpose, when his sides had been

turpi confessione cogitatorum socium (quae nulla erant) fuisse firmavit, cum nec vidisset quicquam nec audisset, penitus expers forensium rerum ; Eusebius vero obiecta fidentius negans, suspensus in eodem gradu constantiae stetit,[1] latrocinium illud esse, non iudicium clamans. 6. Cumque pertinacius (ut legum gnarus) accusatorem flagitaret atque sollemnia, doctus id Caesar, libertatemque superbiam ratus, tamquam obtrectatorem audacem excarnificari praecepit, qui ita evisceratus ut cruciatibus membra deessent, implorans caelo iustitiam, torvum renidens, fundato pectore mansit immobilis, nec se incusare nec quemquam alium passus, et tandem nec confessus nec confutatus, cum abiecto consorte poenali est morte multatus. Et ducebatur intrepidus, temporum iniquitati insultans, imitatus Zenonem illum veterem Stoicum, qui ut mentiretur quaedam laceratus diutius, avulsam sedibus linguam suam cum cruento sputamine, in oculos interrogantis Cyprii regis impegit.

7. Post haec indumentum regale quaerebatur, et ministris fucandae purpurae tortis, confessisque pectoralem tuniculam sine manicis textam, Maras nomine quidam inductus est (ut appellant Christiani)

---

[1] *constantiae stetit*, Lind. ; *cunctantia est et id*, V.

furrowed and he was threatened with death, by
a shameful confession he declared that he was
implicated in plans which never existed, whereas
he had neither seen nor heard anything; he was
wholly unacquainted with legal matters. Eusebius
on the contrary, courageously denied the charges,
and although he was put upon the rack, he remained
firm in the same degree of constancy, crying out that
it was the act of brigands and not of a court of
justice. 6. And when, being acquainted with the
law, he persistently called for his accuser and the
usual formalities, Caesar, being informed of his
demand and regarding his freedom of speech as
arrogance, ordered that he be tortured as a reckless
traducer. And when he had been so disembowelled
that he had no parts left to torture, calling on Heaven
for justice and smiling sardonically, he remained unshaken, with stout heart, neither deigning to accuse
himself nor anyone else; and at last, without having
admitted his guilt or been convicted, he was condemned to death along with his abject associate.
And he was led off to execution unafraid, railing
at the wickedness of the times and imitating the
ancient stoic Zeno, who, after being tortured for a
long time, to induce him to give false witness, tore
his tongue from its roots and hurled it with its blood
and spittle into the eyes of the king of Cyprus, who
was putting him to the question.

7. After this, the matter of the royal robe was
investigated, and when those who were employed
in dyeing purple were tortured and had confessed
to making a short sleeveless tunic to cover the chest,
a man named Maras was brought in, a deacon, as

diaconus ; cuius prolatae litterae scriptae **Graeco**
sermone, ad Tyrii textrini praepositum, celerari
speciem perurgebant, quam autem non indicabant ;
denique etiam idem ad usque discrimen vitae
vexatus, nihil fateri compulsus est. 8. Quaestione
igitur per multiplices dilatata fortunas, cum am-
bigerentur quaedam, non nulla levius actitata
constaret, post multorum clades Apollinares ambo
pater et filius, in exilium acti, cum ad locum Crateras
nomine pervenissent, villam scilicet suam, quae ab
Antiochia vicensimo et quarto disiungitur lapide, ut
mandatum est, fractis cruribus occiduntur. 9. Post
quorum necem nihilo lenius ferociens Gallus, ut leo
cadaveribus pastus, multa huius modi scrutabatur.
Quae singula narrare non refert, ne professionis
modum (quod sane vitandum [1] est) excedamus.

10. *Pax Alamannis petentibus datur a Constantio A.*

1. Haec dum oriens diu [2] perferret, caeli reserato
tepore, Constantius consulatu suo septies et Caesaris
iterum, egressus Arelate Valentiam petit, in Gun-
domadum et Vadomarium fratres Alamannorum reges
arma moturus, quorum crebris excursibus vasta-
bantur confines limitibus terrae Gallorum. 2. Dumque ibi diu moratur, commeatus opperiens, quorum

---

[1] *sane uitandum*, Cornelissen, Traube ; *saevitatum*, V.
[2] *diu*, V ; *dira*, Damsté.

---

[1] It was Gallus' third Consulship ; Valesius proposed to
read *tertium* or *ter*.

the Christians call them. A letter of his was presented, written in Greek to the foreman of a weaving plant in Tyre, strongly urging him to speed up a piece of work; but what it was the letter did not say. But although finally Maras also was tortured within an inch of his life, he could not be forced to make any confession. 8. So when many men of various conditions had been put to the question, some things were found to be doubtful and others were obviously unimportant. And after many had been put to death, the two Apollinares, father and son, were exiled; but when they had come to a place called Craterae, namely, a villa of theirs distant twenty-four miles from Antioch, their legs were broken, according to orders, and they were killed. 9. After their death Gallus, no whit less ferocious than before, like a lion that had tasted blood, tried many cases of the kind; but of all of these it is not worth while to give an account, for fear that I may exceed the limits which I have set myself, a thing which I certainly ought to avoid.

10. *The Alamanni sue for peace, which is granted by Constantius Augustus.*

1. While the East was enduring this long tyranny, as soon as the warm season began, Constantius, being in his seventh consulship with Gallus in his second,[1] set out from Arelate for Valentia, to make war upon the brothers Gundomadus and Valomarius, kings of the Alamanni, whose frequent raids were devastating that part of Gaul which adjoined their frontiers. 2. And while he delayed there for a long time,

translationem ex Aquitania verni imbres solito
crebriores prohibebant auctique torrentes, Herculanus advenit protector domesticus, Hermogenis ex
magistro equitum filius, apud Constantinopolim (ut
supra retulimus) popularium [1] quondam turbela
discerpti. Quo verissime referente quae Gallus
egerat coniuxque,[2] super praeteritis maerens, et
futurorum timore suspensus, angorem animi quam
diu potuit amendabat.[3] 3. Miles tamen interea
omnis apud Cabyllona collectus, morarum impatiens
saeviebat, hoc irritatior, quod nec subsidia vivendi
suppeterent, alimentis nondum ex usu translatis.
4. Unde Rufinus ea tempestate praefectus praetorio,
ad discrimen trusus est ultimum. Ire enim ipse
compellebatur ad militem, quem exagitabat inopia
simul et feritas, et alioqui coalito more in
ordinarias dignitates asperum semper et saevum,
ut satisfaceret, atque monstraret, quam ob causam
annonae convectio sit impedita. 5. Quod opera
consulta cogitabatur astute, ut hoc insidiarum
genere Galli periret avunculus, ne eum ut praepotens acueret in fiduciam, exitiosa coeptantem.
Verum navata est opera diligens, hocque dilato,
Eusebius praepositus cubiculi missus est Cabyllona,

---

[1] *popularium*, Pet.; *populari ui*, Mommsen; *populari
ut*, V.   [2] *coniuxque*, Heraeus; *damnis*, BG; *domus
quae*, V (*quae* del. V[3]).   [3] *amendabat*, Bentley, Clark;
emendabat, V.

---

[1] In a lost book.
[2] Châlon sur Saône.
[3] That is, praetorian prefect in Gaul.
[4] *Praefectus praetorio* at this time was a civil, not a
military, official.

waiting for supplies, the transport of which from Aquitania was hindered by spring rains of unusual frequency and by rivers in flood, Herculanus came there, one of his body-guard, the son of Hermogenes, formerly commander of the cavalry and, as we have before related,[1] torn to pieces in a riot of the people at Constantinople. When this man gave a true account of what Gallus and his wife had done, the emperor, grieving over the past disasters and made anxious by fear of those to come, concealed the distress that he felt as long as he could. 3. The soldiers, however, who in the meantime had been assembled at Châlon,[2] began to rage with impatience at the delay, being the more incensed because they lacked even the necessities of life, since the usual supplies had not yet been brought. 4. Therefore Rufinus, who was at that time praetorian prefect,[3] was exposed to extreme danger; for he was forced to go in person before the troops, who were aroused both by the scarcity and by their natural savage temper, and besides were naturally inclined to be harsh and bitter towards men in civil positions,[4] in order to pacify them and explain why the convoy of provisions was interrupted. 5. This was a shrewd plan, cunningly devised with set purpose, in order that by a plot of that kind the uncle of Gallus[5] might perish, for fear that so very powerful a man might whet the boldness of his nephew and encourage his dangerous designs. But great precautions were taken, and when the design was postponed, Eusebius, the grand chamberlain,[6]

---

[5] Rufinus was his mother's brother.

[6] In charge of the imperial household. At this time a very important official; see Introd. pp. xxxv f.

aurum secum perferens, quo per turbulentos sedi-
tionum concitores occultius distributo, et tumor
consenuit militum, et salus est in tuto locata praefecti. Deinde cibo abunde perlato, castra die
praedicto sunt mota. 6. Emensis itaque difficultatibus multis, et nive obrutis callibus plurimis, ubi
prope Rauracum ventum est ad supercilia fluminis
Rheni, resistente multitudine Alamanna, pontem
suspendere navium compage Romani vi nimia veta-
bantur, ritu grandinis undique convolantibus telis ;
et cum id impossibile videretur, imperator cogita-
tionibus magnis attonitus, quid capesseret ambigebat.
7. Ecce autem ex improviso index quidam regionum
gnarus advenit, et mercede accepta, vadosum locum
nocte monstravit, unde superari potuit flumen. Et
potuisset aliorsum intentis hostibus exercitus inde
transgressus, nullo id opinante, cuncta vastare, ni
pauci ex eadem gente, quibus erat honoratioris
militis cura commissa, populares suos haec per
nuntios docuissent occultos, ut quidam existimabant.
8. Infamabat autem haec suspicio Latinum domesticorum comitem et Agilonem tribunum stabuli
atque Scudilonem scutariorum rectorem, qui tunc,
ut dextris suis gestantes rem publicam, colebantur.
9. At barbari suscepto pro [1] instantium rerum ratione
consilio, dirimentibus forte auspicibus, vel congredi
prohibente auctoritate sacrorum, mollito rigore, quo

[1] *pro*, added by G ; V omits.

---

[1] Augusta Rauricorum, modern Augst.
[2] See Introd. p. xlii, and note 3, p. 56.
[3] See Introd., pp. xliii f.   [4] See note 3, p. 56.
[5] Cf. Val. Max. ii. 8, 5, *humeris suis salutem patriae
gestantes* (of Scipio and Marcellus).

was sent to Châlon taking gold with him ; when this had been secretly distributed among the turbulent inciters of rebellion, the rage of the soldiers abated and the safety of the prefect was assured. Then an abundant supply of food arrived and the camp was moved on the appointed day. 6. And so, after surmounting many difficulties, over paths many of which were heaped high with snow, they came near to Rauracum [1] on the banks of the river Rhine. There a great force of the Alamanni opposed them, and hurling weapons from all sides like hail, by their superior numbers prevented the Romans from making a bridge by joining boats together. And when that was obviously impossible, the emperor was consumed with anxious thought and in doubt what course to take. 7. But lo ! a guide acquainted with the region unexpectedly appeared, and, in return for money, pointed out by night a place abounding in shallows, where the river could be crossed. And there the army might have been led over, while the enemy's attention was turned elsewhere, and devastated the whole country without opposition, had not a few men of that same race, who held military positions of high rank, informed their countrymen of the design by secret messengers, as some thought. 8. Now the shame of that suspicion fell upon Latinus, count in command of the bodyguard,[2] Agilo, tribune [3] in charge of the stable, and Scudilo, commander of the targeteers,[4] who were then highly regarded as having in their hands the defence of the state.[5] 9. But the savages, taking such counsel as the immediate circumstances demanded, since the obstinacy which inspired a bold resistance was

fidentius resistebant, optimates misere, delictorum veniam petituros et pacem. 10. Tentis igitur regis utriusque legatis, et negotio tectius diu pensato, cum pacem oportere tribui quae iustis condicionibus petebatur, eamque ex re [1] fore sententiarum via concinens approbasset, advocato in contionem exercitu, imperator pro tempore pauca dicturus, tribunali adsistens, circumdatus potestatum coetu celsarum, ad hunc disseruit modum :

11. "Nemo (quaeso) miretur, si post exsudatos labores itinerum longos, congestosque adfatim commeatus, fiducia vestri ductante, barbaricos pagos adventans, velut mutato repente consilio, ad placidiora deverti. 12. Pro suo enim loco et animo, quisque vestrum reputans id inveniet verum, quod miles ubique, licet membris vigentibus firmius,[2] se solum vitamque propriam circumspicit et defendit, imperator vero officiorum, dum aequis omnibus consulit, plenus,[3] alienae custos salutis, nihil non ad sui spectare tutelam rationes populorum cognoscit,[4] et remedia cuncta quae status negotiorum admittit, arripere debet alacriter, secunda numinis voluntate delata. 13. Ut [5] in breve igitur conferam et ostendam qua ex causa omnes vos simul adesse

---

[1] *re*, E[2]bG ; *re tum*, A ; *rerum*, V.   [2] *firmius*, V, Pet. ; *firmior*, Clark.   [3] *consulit*, *plenus*, added by Novák.   [4] *rationes populorum cognoscit*, BG ; *ratio* (lac. of 33 letters), V.   [5] *ut*, Lind. ; *id*, V.

diminished perhaps because the auspices were unfavourable or because the authority of the sacrifices
forbade an engagement, sent their chiefs to sue for
peace and pardon for their offences. 10. Therefore
the envoys of both kings were detained and the
matter was discussed for a long time in secret ; and
since there was general agreement in the opinion that
peace which was asked for on reasonable conditions
ought to be granted, and that it would be expedient
to do so under the present circumstances, the emperor
summoned an assembly of the army, intending to
say a few words appropriate to the occasion ; and
taking his place upon a tribunal, surrounded by a
staff of high officials, he spoke after this fashion :

11. " Let no one, I pray, be surprised, if after going
through the toil of long marches and getting together
great quantities of supplies, I now, when approaching
the abode of the savages, with my confidence in you
leading the way, as if by a sudden change of plan
have turned to milder designs. 12. For each one
of you, according to his rank and judgment, upon
consideration will find it to be true, that the soldier
in all instances, however strong and vigorous of body,
regards and defends only himself and his own life.
The commander, on the other hand, has manifold
duties, since he aims at fairness to all ; and being
the guardian of others' safety, he realises that the interests of the people look to him wholly for protection and that therefore he ought eagerly to seize
upon all remedies which the condition of affairs
allows, as though offered to him by the favour of
Heaven. 13. To put the matter, then, in a few words,
and to explain why I have wished you all to be present

volui, commilitones mei fidissimi, accipite aequis
auribus quae succinctius explicabo. Veritatis enim
absolutio [1] semper est [2] simplex. 14. Arduos vestrae
gloriae gradus, quos fama per plagarum quoque
accolas extimarum diffundit, excellenter accrescens,
Alamannorum reges et populi formidantes, per
oratores quos videtis, summissis cervicibus, concessionem praeteritorum poscunt et pacem. Quam ut
cunctator et cautus, utiliumque monitor, (si vestra
voluntas adest) tribui debere censeo multa contemplans. Primo ut Martis ambigua declinentur,
dein ut auxiliatores pro adversariis adsciscamus, quod
pollicentur, tum autem ut incruenti mitigemus
ferociae flatus, perniciosos saepe provinciis, postremo
id reputantes, quod non ille hostis vincitur solus,
qui cadit in acie, pondere armorum oppressus et
virium, sed multo tutius etiam tuba tacente, sub
iugum mittitur voluntarius, qui sentit expertus, nec
fortitudinem in rebelles nec lenitatem in supplices
animos abesse [3] Romanis. [4] 15. In summa tamquam
arbitros vos quid suadetis opperior, ut princeps
tranquillus, temperanter adhibere modum adlapsa
felicitate decernens. Non enim inertiae sed modes-
tiae humanitatique (mihi credite) hoc quod recte
consultum est adsignabitur."

16. Mox dicta finierat, multitudo omnis ad quae

---

[1] *absolutio*, E, Madvig, Novák; *absolimo*, V.   [2] *est*,
Novák, deleting *at per* as dittography; *at per est*, V.
[3] *abesse*, Eyssen.; *adesse*, V.   [4] *Romanis*, Günther in
lac. of 8 letters.

here together, my loyal fellow-soldiers, receive with favourable ears what I shall briefly set forth; for perfect [1] truth is always simple. 14. The kings and peoples of the Alamanni, in dread of the rising progress of your glory, which fame, growing greatly, has spread abroad even among the dwellers in far off lands, through the envoys whom you see with bowed heads ask for peace and indulgence for past offences. This I, being cautious, prudent, and an advisor of what is expedient, think ought to be granted them (if I have your consent), for many reasons. First, to avoid the doubtful issue of war; then, that we may gain friends in place of enemies, as they promise; again, that without bloodshed we may tame their haughty fierceness, which is often destructive to the provinces; finally, bearing in mind this thought, that not only is the enemy vanquished who falls in battle, borne down by weight of arms and strength, but much more safely he who, while the trumpet is silent, of his own accord passes under the yoke and learns by experience that Romans lack neither courage against rebels nor mildness towards suppliants. 15. In short, I await your decision as arbiters, as it were, being myself convinced as a peace-loving prince, that it is best temperately to show moderation while prosperity is with us. For, believe me, such righteous conduct will be attributed, not to lack of spirit, but to discretion and humanity."

16. No sooner had he finished speaking than the

---

[1] Cf. Cic., *De Fin.* v. 14, 38, *ex qua virtus est, quae rationis absolutio definitur*, " virtue which is defined as the perfection of reason " (*L.C.L.* p. 437).

imperator voluit promptior, laudato consilio, consensit in pacem, ea ratione maxime percita, quod norat expeditionibus crebris[1] fortunam eius in malis tantum civilibus vigilasse ; cum autem bella moverentur externa, accidisse plerumque luctuosa. Icto post haec foedere gentium ritu, perfectaque sollemnitate, imperator Mediolanum ad hiberna discessit.

11. *Constantius Gallus Caesar evocatur a Constantio*
A. et capite truncatur.

1. Ubi curarum abiectis ponderibus aliis, tamquam nodum et obicem[2] difficillimum, Caesarem convellere nisu valido cogitabat ; eique deliberanti cum proximis, clandestinis colloquiis et nocturnis, qua vi quibusve commentis id fieret, antequam effundendis rebus pertinacius incumberet confidentia, acciri mollioribus scriptis, per simulationem tractatus publici nimis urgentis,[3] eundem placuerat Gallum, ut auxilio destitutus, sine ullo interiret obstaculo. 2. Huic sententiae versabilium adulatorum refragantibus globis, inter quos erat Arbitio, ad insidiandum acer et flagrans, et Eusebius tunc praepositus cubiculi effusior ad nocendum, id occurrebat, Caesare discedente, Ursicinum in oriente perniciose

---

[1] *et crebris,* V ; *e crebris,* E, Momm. ; *e* om. A.   [2] *obicem,*
R. Unger ; *odiem,* V.   [3] *urgentis,* N, Val. ; *argentis,* V.

---

[1] See Ch. **10, 5,** and note 6.

whole throng, fully in agreement with the emperor's wish, praised his purpose and unanimously voted for peace. They were influenced especially by the conviction, which they had formed from frequent campaigns, that his fortune watched over him only in civil troubles, but that when foreign wars were undertaken, they had often ended disastrously. After this a treaty was struck in accordance with the rites of the Alamanni, and when the ceremony had been concluded, the emperor withdrew to Mediolanum for his winter quarters.

11. *Constantius Gallus Caesar is summoned by Constantius Augustus and executed.*

1. There having laid aside the burden of other cares, Constantius began to consider, as his most difficult knot and stumbling-block, how to uproot the Caesar by a mighty effort. And as he deliberated with his closest friends, in secret conferences and by night, by what force or by what devices that might be done before the Caesar's assurance should be more obstinately set upon throwing everything into disorder, it seemed best that Gallus should be summoned by courteous letters, under pretence of very urgent public business, to the end that, being deprived of support, he might be put to death without hindrance. 2. But this view was opposed by the groups of fickle flatterers, among whom was Arbitio, a man keen and eager in plotting treachery, and Eusebius, at that time grand chamberlain,[1] who was sufficiently inclined to mischief, and it occurred to them to say that, if Caesar left the East, it would be dangerous to leave Ursicinus there, since he would

89

relinquendum, si nullus esset qui prohiberet [1] altiora
meditaturum.   3. Eisdemque residui regii accessere
spadones, quorum ea tempestate plus habendi
cupiditas ultra mortalem modum adolescebat, inter
ministeria vitae secretioris per arcanos susurros
nutrimenta fictis criminibus subserentes ; qui ponderibus invidiae gravioris virum fortissimum op-
primebant, subolescere imperio adultos eius filios
mussitantes, decore corporum favorabiles et aetate,
per multiplicem armaturae scientiam, agilitatemque
membrorum, inter cotidiana proludia exercitus,
consulto consilio cognitos : Gallum suopte ingenio
trucem, per suppositos quosdam ad saeva facinora ideo animatum, ut eo digna omnium ordinum
detestatione exoso, ad magistri equitum liberos
principatus insignia transferantur.

4. Cum haec taliaque sollicitas eius aures everbe-
rarent, expositas semper eius modi rumoribus et
patentes, vario animi [2] motu miscente [3] consilia,
tandem id ut optimum factu elegit : et Ursicinum
primum ad se venire summo cum honore mandavit,
ea specie ut pro rerum tunc urgentium captu, disponeretur concordi consilio, quibus virium incrementis, Parthicarum gentium arma minantium
impetus frangerentur.   5. Et nequid suspicaretur
adversi venturus, vicarius eius (dum redit) Prosper
missus est comes ; acceptisque litteris, et copia rei

---

[1] *prohiberet*, EAg ; *prohibeat*, G ; *prohibet*, V ; *pro-
hibebit*, Clark.   [2] *animi*, Her. ; *animo*, V.   [3] *motu
miscente*, Her. (cf. *Aen.* xii. 217) ; *tumiscente*, V.

be likely to think of a loftier station, if there were on one to restrain him. 3. And this faction was supported by the other royal eunuchs, whose love of gain at that time was growing beyond mortal limits. These, while performing duties of an intimate nature, by secret whispers supplied fuel for false accusations. They overwhelmed that most gallant man with the weight of a grave suspicion, muttering that his sons, who were now grown up, were beginning to have imperial hopes, being popular because of their youth and their handsome persons and through their knowledge of many kinds of weapons, and bodily activity gained amidst daily army exercises, besides being known to be of sound judgment ; that Gallus, while naturally savage, had been incited to deeds of cruelty by persons attached to his person, to the end that, when he had incurred the merited detestation of all classes, the emblems of empire might be transferred to the children of the master of the horse.

4. When these and similar charges were dinned into the emperor's anxious ears, which were always attentive and open to such gossip, the turmoil of his mind suggesting many plans, he at last chose the following as the best. First, in the most complimentary terms he directed Ursicinus to come to him, under pretence that, because of the urgent condition of affairs at the time, they might consult together and decide what increase of forces was necessary in order to crush the attacks of the Parthian tribes, which were threatening war. 5. And that Ursicinus might not suspect any unfriendly action, in case he should come, Count Prosper was sent to be his substitute until his return. So, when the letter was

vehiculariae data, Mediolanum itineribus proper-
avimus magnis.

6. Restabat ut Caesar post haec properaret accitus,
et abstergendae causa suspicionis, sororem suam
(eius uxorem) Constantius ad se tandem desideratam
venire, multis fictisque blanditiis hortabatur.   Quae
licet ambigeret, metuens saepe cruentum, spe tamen
quod eum lenire poterit [1] ut germanum, profecta,
cum Bithyniam introisset, in statione quae Caenos
Gallicanos appellatur, absumpta est vi febrium
repentina.   Cuius post obitum maritus contemplans
cecidisse fiduciam qua se fultum existimabat, anxia
cogitatione quid moliretur haerebat.   7. Inter res
enim impeditas et turbidas, ad hoc unum mentem
sollicitam dirigebat, quod Constantius cuncta ad
suam   sententiam   conferens,   nec   satisfactionem
suscipiet aliquam, nec erratis ignoscet, sed ut erat
in propinquitatis perniciem inclinatior, laqueos ei
latenter obtendens, si cepisset incautum, morte
multaret.   8. Eo necessitatis adductus, ultimaque
ni vigilasset opperiens, principem locum, si copia
patuisset, clam [2] affectabat, sed perfidiam proximorum ratione bifaria verebatur, qui eum ut trucu-
lentum horrebant et levem, quique altiorem Constantii fortunam in discordiis civilibus formidabant.
9. Inter has curarum moles immensas, imperatoris

---

[1] *poterit*, Kellerbauer ;   *poterat*, **V.**   [2] *clam*, Her. ;
quam, V.

---

[1] Ammianus was attached to the suite of Ursicinus ;
see ch. **9. 1.**
[2] Cf. ch. **10, 16**, above.

received and abundant transportation facilities were furnished, we [1] hastened at full speed to Mediolanum.

6. After this the next thing was to summon Caesar and induce him to make equal haste, and in order to remove suspicion, Constantius with many feigned endearments urged his sister, the Caesar's wife, at last to satisfy his longing and visit him. And although she hesitated, through fear of her brother's habitual cruelty, yet she set forth, hoping that, since he was her own brother, she might be able to pacify him. But after she had entered Bithynia, at the station called Caeni Gallicani, she was carried off by a sudden attack of fever. After her death the Caesar, considering that the support on which he thought he could rely had failed him, hesitated in anxious deliberation what to do. 7. For in the midst of his embarrassments and troubles his anxious mind dwelt on this one thought, that Constantius, who measured everything by the standard of his own opinion, was not one to accept any excuse or pardon mistakes ; but, being especially inclined to the ruin of his kin, would secretly set a snare for him and punish him with death, if he caught him off his guard. 8. But in such a critical situation and anticipating the worst if he were not on the watch, he secretly aimed at the highest rank, if any chance should offer ; but for a twofold reason he feared treachery on the part of those nearest to his person, both because they stood in dread of him as cruel and untrustworthy, and because they feared the fortune of Constantius which in civil discords usually had the upper hand.[2] 9. Amid this huge mass of anxieties he received constant letters from

scripta suscipiebat assidua, monentis orantisque
ut ad se veniret, et mente monstrantis obliqua, rem
publicam nec posse dividi nec debere, sed pro viribus
quemque ei ferre suppetias fluctuanti, nimirum
Galliarum indicans vastitatem. 10. Quibus sub-
serebat non adeo vetus exemplum, quod Diocletiano
et eius collegae, ut apparitores Caesares non resides
sed ultro citroque discurrentes, obtemperabant, et in
Syria Augusti vehiculum irascentis, per spatium
mille passuum fere pedes antegressus est Galerius
purpuratus.

11. Advenit post multos Scudilo scutariorum
tribunus, velamento subagrestis ingenii, persuasionis
opifex callidus. Qui eum adulabili sermone periuriis [1]
admixto, solus omnium proficisci pellexit, vultu
assimulato saepius replicando, quod flagrantibus
votis eum videre frater cuperet patruelis, siquid [2]
per imprudentiam gestum est, remissurus, ut mitis
et clemens, participemque eum suae maiestatis
assciscet,[3] futurum laborum quoque socium, quos
Arctoae provinciae diu fessae poscebant. 12. Utque
solent manum iniectantibus fatis, hebetari sensus
hominum et obtundi, his illecebris ad meliorum
expectationem erectus, egressusque Antiochia numine
laevo ductante, prorsus ire tendebat de fumo, ut proverbium loquitur vetus, ad flammam ; et ingressus

---

[1] *periuriis*, Clark ; *periis*, V (*seriis*, V[3] EBG).　　[2] *siquid*,
Kiessling ; *quid*, V.　　　　　[3] *adsciscet*, C. F. W. Müller ;
adscisco et, V ; *adscitum ut*, G ; *adscitum et*, B.

the emperor, admonishing and begging him to come
to him and covertly hinting that the commonwealth
could not be divided and ought not to be, but that
each ought to the extent of his powers to lend it aid
when it was tottering, doubtless referring to the
devastation of Gaul. 10. To this he added an
example of not so very great antiquity, that Diocletian and his colleague [1] were obeyed by their
Caesars as by attendants, who did not remain in
one place but hastened about hither and thither,
and that in Syria Galerius, clad in purple, walked
for nearly a mile before the chariot of his Augustus [2]
when the latter was angry with him.

11. After many other messengers came Scudilo,
tribune of the targeteers, a skilled artist in persuasion, under the cloak of a somewhat rough nature.
He alone of all, by means of flattering words mingled
with false oaths, succeeded in persuading Gallus to
set out, constantly repeating with hypocritical expression that his cousin would ardently wish to see him,
that being a mild and merciful prince he would over-
look anything that was done through inadvertence;
that he would make him a sharer in his rank, to be
a partner also in the labours which the northern
provinces, for a long time wearied, demanded.
12. And since, when the fates lay hands upon men,
their senses are apt to be dulled and blunted, Gallus
was roused by these blandishments to the hope of a
better destiny, and leaving Antioch under the lead
of an unpropitious power, he proceeded to go straight
from the smoke into the fire, as the old proverb has

---

[1] Maximianus.   [2] Diocletian.

CONSTANTIUS ET GALLUS

Constantinopolim, tamquam in rebus prosperis et securis, editis equestribus ludis, capiti Thoracis [1] aurigae coronam imposuit, ut victoris.

13. Quo cognito Constantius ultra mortalem modum exarsit; ac nequo casu idem Gallus de futuris incertus, agitare quaedam conducentia saluti suae per itinera conaretur, remoti sunt omnes de industria milites agentes in civitatibus perviis. 14. Eoque tempore Taurus quaestor ad Armeniam missus, confidenter nec appellato eo nec viso transivit. Venere tamen aliqui iussu imperatoris, administrationum specie diversarum, eundem ne commovere se posset, neve temptaret aliquid occulte custodituri; inter quos Leontius erat, postea urbi praefectus, ut quaestor, et [2] Lucillianus quasi domesticorum comes et scutariorum tribunus nomine Bainobaudes. 15. Emensis itaque longis intervallis et planis, cum Hadrianopolim introisset, urbem Haemimontanam, Uscudamam antehac appellatam, fessasque labore diebus duodecim recreans vires, comperit Thebaeas legiones in vicinis oppidis hiemantes, consortes suos misisse quosdam, eum ut remaneret promissis fidis hortaturos et firmis, cum animarentur roboris [3] sui fiducia, abunde per stationes locatae [4] confines, sed observante cura pervigili proximorum, nullam videndi vel audiendi quae ferebant, furari potuit facultatem. 16. Inde aliis super alias urgentibus litteris exire et

---

[1] *capiti Thoracis,* T[2]; *capita ethoracia,* V.   [2] *et,* EG; *ut,* V; *ac,* Traube.   [3] *cum a. roboris,* added by Novák.
[4] *locatae,* Novák; *locat,* V.

it ; and entering Constantinople as if in the height
of prosperity and security, he exhibited horse-races
and crowned Thorax the charioteer as victor.

13. On learning this Constantius was enraged
beyond all human bounds, and lest by any chance
Gallus should become uncertain as to the future and
should try in the course of his journey to take
measures for his own safety, all the soldiers in the
towns through which he would pass were purposely
removed. 14. And at that time Taurus, who had
been sent to Armenia as quaestor, boldly passed that
way without addressing him or going to see him.
Others, however, visited him by the emperor's orders,
under pretext of various matters of business, but
really to take care that he should not be able to
make any move or indulge in any secret enterprise ;
among these was Leontius, then quaestor and later
prefect of the city, Lucillianus, as count commander
of the household troops, and a tribune of the targeteers called Bainobaudes. 15. Thus, after covering
long distances over level country, he had entered
Hadrianopolis, a city in the region of Mt. Haemus,
formerly called Uscudama, and for twelve days was
recovering his strength, exhausted by his exertions.
There he learned that certian Theban legions that
were passing the winter in near-by towns had sent
some of their comrades to encourage him by faithful
and sure promises to remain there, since they were
full of confidence in their strength and were posted
in large numbers in neighbouring encampments ; but
owing to the watchful care of those about him, he
could not steal an opportunity of seeing them or
hearing the message that they brought. 16. Then, as

97

decem vehiculis publicis, ut praeceptum est, usus, relicto palatio omni, praeter paucos tori ministros et mensae, quos avexerat secum, squalore concretus, celerare gradum compellebatur, adigentibus multis, temeritati suae subinde flebiliter imprecatus, quae eum iam despectum et vilem arbitrio subdiderat infimorum. 17. Inter haec tamen per indutias naturae conquiescentis, sauciabantur eius sensus circumstridentium terrore larvarum, interfectorum- que catervae, Domitiano et Montio praeviis, correp- tum eum (ut existimabat in somnis), uncis furialibus obiectabant. 18. Solutus enim corporeis nexibus, animus semper vigens motibus indefessis, ex cogita- tionibus subiectis et curis, quae mortalium sollicitant mentes, colligit visa nocturna, quas φαντασίας nos appellamus.

19. Pandente itaque viam fatorum sorte tristis- sima, qua praestitutum erat eum vita et imperio spoliari, itineribus rectis [1] permutatione iumentorum emensis, venit Petobionem oppidum Noricorum, ubi reseratae sunt insidiarum latebrae omnes, et Barbatio repente apparuit Comes, qui sub eo domesticis praefuit, cum Apodemio agente in rebus, milites ducens, quos beneficiis suis oppigneratos elegerat

---

[1] *rectis*, Lind. ; *eiectis*, V. ; *directis*, Novák.

---

[1] I.e. we Greeks.

[2] The *agentes in rebus* constituted the imperial secret service under the direction of the *magister officiorum*. These were the original *frumentarii*, who at first had charge of the grain supply of the troops, but towards the beginning of the second century A.D. became secret police

letter followed letter, urging him to leave, making use of ten public vehicles, as was directed, and leaving behind all his attendants with the exception of a few whom he had brought with him to serve in his bedroom and at his table, he was driven to make haste, being without proper care of his person and urged on by many, railing from time to time at the rashness which had reduced him, now mean and abject, to submit to the will of the lowest of mankind. 17. Yet all this time, whenever nature allowed him sleep, his senses were wounded by frightful spectres that shrieked about him, and throngs of those whom he had slain, led by Domitianus and Montius, would seize him and fling him to the claws of the Furies, as he imagined in his dreams. 18. For the mind, when freed from the bonds of the body, being always filled with tireless movement, from the underlying thoughts and worries which torment the minds of mortals, conjures up the nocturnal visions to which we[1] give the name of phantasies.

19. And thus with the way opened by the sad decree of fate, by which it was ordained that he should be stripped of life and rank, he hurried by the most direct way and with relays of horses and came to Petobio, a town of Noricum. There all the secret plots were revealed and Count Barbatio suddenly made his appearance—he had commanded the household troops under Gallus—accompanied by Apodemius, of the secret service,[2] and at the head of soldiers whom Constantius had chosen because they were under obligation to him for favours and could

agents. It was Diocletian who changed the name *frumentarii* to *agentes in rebus*.

99

imperator, certus nec praemiis nec miseratione ulla posse deflecti.

20. Iamque non umbratis fallaciis res agebatur, sed qua palatium est extra muros, armatis Barbatio[1] omne circumdedit. Ingressusque obscuro iam die, ablatis regiis indumentis, Caesarem tunica texit et paludamento communi, eum post haec nihil passurum, velut mandato principis iurandi crebritate confirmans, et " Statim " inquit " exsurge," et inopinum carpento privato impositum, ad Histriam duxit, prope oppidum Polam, ubi quondam peremptum Constantini filium accipimus Crispum. 21. Et cum ibi servaretur artissime, terrore propinquantis exitii iam praesepultus, accurrit Eusebius, cubiculi tunc praepositus, Pentadiusque notarius, et Mallobaudes armaturarum tribunus, iussu imperatoris compulsuri eum singillatim docere, quam ob causam quemque apud Antiochiam necatorum iusserat trucidari. 22. Ad quae Adrasteo pallore perfusus, hactenus valuit[2] loqui, quod plerosque incitante coniuge iugulaverit Constantina, ignorans profecto Alexandrum Magnum urgenti matri ut occideret quendam insontem, et dictitanti spe impetrandi postea quae vellet, eum se per novem menses utero portasse praegnantem, ita respondisse prudenter : " Aliam, parens optima, posce mercedem ; hominis enim salus beneficio nullo pensatur." 23. Quo comperto

---

[1] *Barbatio,* added by Damsté.   [2] *valuit,* vulgo ; *voluit,* V.

[1] See note 3, p. 56.

[2] Proverbial ; cf. Virgil, *Aen.* vi. 480, *Adrasti pallentis imago.* Adrastus turned pale at the death of his sons-in-law Tydeus and Polynices (when the seven champions attacked Thebes), and never recovered his colour.

[3] See note 1, p. 4.

not, he felt sure, be influenced by bribes or any feeling of pity.

20. And now the affair was being carried on with no disguised intrigue, but where the palace stood without the walls Barbatio surrounded it with armed men. And entering when the light was now dim and removing the Caesar's royal robes, he put upon him a tunic and an ordinary soldier's cloak, assuring him with frequent oaths, as if by the emperor's command, that he would suffer no further harm. Then he said to him : " Get up at once," and having unexpectedly placed him in a private carriage, he took him to Histria, near the town of Pola, where in former times, as we are informed, Constantine's son Crispus was killed. 21. And while he was kept there in closest confinement, already as good as buried by fear of his approaching end, there hastened to him Eusebius, at that time grand chamberlain, Pentadius, the secretary, and Mallobaudes, tribune of the guard,[1] to compel him by order of the emperor to inform them, case by case, why he had ordered the execution of all those whom he had put to death at Antioch. 22. At this, o'erspread with the pallor of Adrastus,[2] he was able to say only that he had slain most of them at the instigation of his wife Constantina,[3] assuredly not knowing that when the mother of Alexander the Great urged her son to put an innocent man to death and said again and again, in the hope of later gaining what she desired, that she had carried him for nine months in her womb, the king made this wise answer : " Ask some other reward, dear mother, for a man's life is not to be weighed against any favour." 23. On hearing this the emperor, smitten with

irrevocabili ira princeps percitus et dolore, fiduciam
omnem fundandae securitatis in eodem posuit
abolendo. Et misso Sereniano, quem in crimen
maiestatis vocatum praestrigiis quibusdam absolutum esse supra monstravimus, Pentadio quin etiam
notario, et Apodemio agente in rebus, eum capitali
supplicio destinavit, et ita colligatis manibus in
modum noxii cuiusdam latronis, cervice abscisa,
ereptaque vultus et capitis dignitate, cadaver est
relictum informe, paulo ante urbibus et provinciis
formidatum. 24. Sed vigilavit utrubique superni
numinis aequitas. Nam et Gallum actus oppressere [1]
crudeles, et non diu postea ambo cruciabili morte
absumpti sunt, qui eum licet nocentem, blandius
palpantes periuriis, ad usque plagas perduxere letales.
Quorum Scudilo destillatione iecoris pulmones vomi-
tans interiit ; Barbatio, qui in eum iam diu falsa
composuerat crimina, cum ex magisterio peditum
altius niti quorundam susurris incusaretur, damnatus
extincti per fallacias Caesaris manibus [2] illacrimoso
obitu parentavit.

25. Haec et huius modi quaedam innumerabilia
ultrix facinorum impiorum, bonorumque praemia-
trix, aliquotiens operatur Adrastia, (atque utinam
semper !) : quam vocabulo duplici etiam Nemesim
appellamus : ius quoddam sublime numinis efficacis,

---

[1] *oppressere*, NT. Val. ; *oppresse*, V.   [2] *manibus anima,*
V ; *anima*, del. Val.

implacable anger and resentment, rested all his hopes of securing his safety on destroying Gallus; and sending Serenianus, who, as I have before shown, had been charged with high treason and acquitted by some jugglery or other, and with him Pentadius the secretary and Apodemius of the secret service, he condemned him to capital punishment. Accordingly his hands were bound, after the fashion of some guilty robber, and he was beheaded. Then his face and head were mutilated, and the man who a little while before had been a terror to cities and provinces was left a disfigured corpse. 24. But the justice of the heavenly power was everywhere watchful; for not only did his cruel deeds prove the ruin of Gallus, but not long afterwards a painful death overtook both of those whose false blandishments and perjuries led him, guilty though he was, into the snares of destruction. Of these Scudilo, because of an abscess of the liver,[1] vomited up his lungs and so died; Barbatio, who for a long time had invented false accusations against Gallus, charged by the whispers of certain men of aiming higher than the mastership of the infantry, was found guilty and by an unwept end made atonement to the shades of the Caesar, whom he had treacherously done to death.

25. These and innumerable other instances of the kind are sometimes (and would that it were always so!) the work of Adrastia,[2] the chastiser of evil deeds and the rewarder of good actions, whom we also call by the second name of Nemesis. She is, as it were, the sublime jurisdiction of an efficient divine power,

---

[1] Augustus was cured of this disease by Antonius Musa (Suet., *Aug.* 81, 1).　　　[2] See Index.

humanarum mentium opinione lunari circulo super-
positum, vel ut definiunt alii, substantialis tutela
generali potentia partilibus praesidens fatis, quam
theologi veteres fingentes Iustitiae filiam, ex abdita
quadam aeternitate tradunt omnia despectare
terrena. 26. Haec ut regina causarum, et arbitra
rerum ac disceptatrix, urnam sortium temperat,
accidentium vices alternans, voluntatumque nostrarum exorsa interdum alio quam quo contende-
bant exitu terminans, multiplices actus permutando
convolvit. Eademque necessitatis insolubili retin-
aculo mortalitatis vinciens fastus, tumentes in
cassum, et incrementorum detrimentorumque momenta versabilis librans [1] (ut novit), nunc erectas
eminentium [2] cervices opprimit et enervat, nunc
bonos ab imo suscitans ad bene vivendum extollit.
Pinnas autem ideo illi fabulosa vetustas aptavit, ut
adesse velocitate volucri crunctis existimetur, et
praetendere gubernaculum dedit, eique subdidit
rotam, ut universitatem regere per elementa dis-
currens omnia non ignoretur.

27. Hoc immaturo interitu, ipse quoque sui pertae-
sus, excessit e vita, aetatis nono anno atque vicensimo, cum quadriennio imperasset. Natus apud
Tuscos in Massa Veternensi patre Constantio,
Constantini fratre imperatoris, matreque Galla,
sorore Rufini et Cerealis, quos trabeae consulares

---

[1] *versabilis librans*, E. Meurig Davies ; *uersabis*, V[1] ;
uersabilis, V[2].
[2] *eminentium*, Fletcher, C.Q. 1930, p. 193 ; *tumentium*,
Günther ; *mentium*, V.

---

[1] Cf. Cic., *Acad.* ii. 28, 91, *veri et falsi quasi disceptatricem
et iudicem.*

dwelling, as men think, above the orbit of the moon; or as others define her, an actual guardian presiding with universal sway over the destinies of individual men.   The ancient theologians, regarding her as the daughter of Justice, say that from an unknown eternity she looks down upon all the creatures of earth. 26. She, as queen of causes and arbiter and judge [1] of events, controls the urn with its lots and causes the changes of fortune,[2] and sometimes she gives our plans a different result than that at which we aimed, changing and confounding many actions.   She too, binding the vainly swelling pride of mortals with the indissoluble bond of fate, and tilting changeably, as she knows how to do, the balance of gain and loss, now bends and weakens the uplifted necks of the proud, and now, raising the good from the lowest estate, lifts them to a happy life.   Moreover, the storied past has given her wings in order that she might be thought to come to all with swift speed ; and it has given her a helm to hold and has put a wheel beneath her feet, in order that none may fail to know that she runs through all the elements and rules the universe.[3]

27. By this untimely death, although himself weary of his existence, the Caesar passed from life in the twenty-ninth year of his age, after a rule of four years.   He was born in Etruria at Massa in the district of Veternum, being the son of Constantius, the brother of the emperor Constantine, and Galla, the sister of Rufinus and Cerealis, who were distinguished by the

[2] Cf. Ovid, *Metam.* xv. 409, *alternare vices.*
[3] With this description cf. that of Fortune in Pacuvius, inc. xiv., Ribbeck (p. 144), and Horace, *Odes,* i. 34.

nobilitarunt, et praefecturae. 28. Fuit [1] autem
forma conspicuus bona, decente filo corporis mem-
brorumque recta compage, flavo capillo et molli,
barba licet recens emergente lanugine tenera, ita
tamen ut maturius auctoritas emineret; tantum a
temperatis moribus Iuliani differens fratris, quantum
inter Vespasiani filios fuit Domitianum et Titum.
29. Assumptus autem in amplissimum fortunae
fastigium, versabilis eius motus expertus est, qui
ludunt mortalitatem, nunc evehentes quosdam in
sidera, nunc ad Cocyti profunda mergentes. Cuius
rei cum innumera sint exempla, pauca tactu summo
transcurram. 30. Haec fortuna mutabilis et in-
constans fecit Agathoclem Siculum ex figulo regem,
et Dionysium, gentium quondam terrorem, Corinthi
litterario ludo praefecit. 31. Haec Adramytenum
Andriscum, in fullonio natum, ad Pseudophilippi
nomen evexit, et Persei legitimum filium artem
ferrariam ob quaerendum docuit victum. 32.
Eadem Mancinum post imperium dedidit [2] Numan-
tinis, Samnitum atrocitati Veturium, et Claudium
Corsis, substravitque feritati Carthaginis Regulum;
istius iniquitate Pompeius, post quaesitum Magni ex

---

[1] *fuit*, in lac. of 5 letters, EDW²NA (defendo, cf. Suet.,
Aug. 79, 1, *Tib.* 68, 1, *Calig.* 50, 1); *erat*, Brakman (cf.
xxv. 4, 22).　　　[2] *dedidit*, Val.; *dedit*, V.

---

[1] The *trabea* was a toga, or robe, in white, ornamented
with horizontal stripes of purple. It was worn by the
knights on public occasions and by the early kings and
consuls. In the classical period it was, in that form,
the distinctive garb of the *equites* (see Tac., *Ann.* iii. 2;

vesture [1] of consul and prefect. 28. He was conspicuous for his handsome person, being well proportioned, with well-knit limbs. He had soft golden hair, and although his beard was just appearing in the form of tender down, yet he was conspicuous for the dignity of greater maturity. But he differed as much from the disciplined character of his brother Julian as did Domitian, son of Vespasian, from his brother Titus. 29. Raised to the highest rank in Fortune's gift, he experienced her fickle changes, which make sport of mortals, now lifting some to the stars, now plunging them in the depths of Cocytus. But although instances of this are innumerable, I shall make cursory mention of only a few. 30. It was this mutable and fickle Fortune that changed the Sicilian Agathocles from a potter to a king, and Dionysius, once the terror of nations, to the head of an elementary school, at Corinth. 31. She it was that raised Andriscus [2] of Adramyttium, who was born in a fullery, to the title of the Pseudo-Philip, and taught the legitimate son of Perseus the blacksmith's trade as a means of livelihood.[3] 32. She, too, delivered Mancinus, after his supreme command, to the Numantians, Veturius to the cruelty of the Samnites, and Claudius to the Corsicans, and she subjected Regulus to the savagery of the Carthaginians. Through her injustice Pompey, after he had gained the surname Great by his

Val. Max., ii. 2, 9), but it varied in its colour and its use at different periods. One form, wholly of purple, was worn by the kings and later emperors ; another, of purple and saffron, by the augurs.

[2] For Andriscus and other names in 31-33, see Index.

[3] Cf. Plutarch, *Aem.* 37.

rerum gestarum amplitudine cognomentum, ad spadonum libidinem in Aegypto trucidatur. 33. Et
Eunus quidam ergastularius servus ductavit in
Sicilia fugitivos. Quam multi splendido loco nati
Romani,[1] eadem rerum domina conivente, Viriathi
genua sunt amplexi vel Spartaci ? Quot capita
quae horruere gentes funesti carnifices absciderunt ?
Alter in vincula ducitur, alter insperatae praeficitur
potestati, alius a summo culmine dignitatis excutitur.
34. Quae omnia si scire quisquam velit quam varia
sint et assidua, harenarum numerum idem iam
desipiens et montium pondera scrutari putabit.[2]

LIBER XV

1. *Mors Galli Caesaris imperatori nuntiatur.*

1. Utcumque potui veritatem [3] scrutari, ea quae
videre licuit per aetatem, vel perplexe interrogando
versatos in medio scire, narravimus ordine casuum
exposito diversorum ; residua quae secuturus aperiet
textus, pro virium captu limatius absolvemus, nihil
obtrectatores longi (ut putant) operis formidantes.
Tunc enim laudanda est brevitas, cum moras rum-
pens intempestivas, nihil subtrahit cognitioni gestorum.[4]

---

[1] *nati Romani*, Novák ; *nati*, E²BG ; *natura*, V.   [2] *putabit*, E, Val. (in text) ; *posse putabit*, Val. ; *putavit*, V.
[3] *utcumque potui ueritatem*, Traube ; *ut cumippo tum.eri-
tate*, V.   [4] *gestorum*, E, Val. ; *iustorum*, V.

glorious deeds, was butchered in Egypt to give the eunuchs' pleasure. 33. Eunus, too, a workhouse slave, commanded an army of runaways in Sicily. How many Romans of illustrious birth at the nod of that same arbiter of events embraced the knees of a Viriathus [1] or a Spartacus ! [2] How many heads dreaded by all nations has the fatal excutioner lopped off! One is led to prison, another is elevated to unlooked-for power, a third is cast down from the highest pinnacle of rank. 34. But if anyone should desire to know all these instances, varied and constantly occurring as they are, he will be mad enough to think of searching out the number of the sands and the weight of the mountains.

BOOK XV

1. *The death of Gallus Caesar is reported to the Emperor.*

1. So far as I could investigate the truth, I have, after putting the various events in clear order, related what I myself was allowed to witness in the course of my life, or to learn by meticulous questioning of those directly concerned. The rest, which the text to follow will disclose, we shall set forth to the best of our ability with still greater accuracy, feeling no fear of critics of the prolixity of our work, as they consider it ; for conciseness is to be praised only when it breaks off ill-timed discursiveness, without detracting at all from an understanding of the course of events.

[1] Flor., i. 33, 15 ff.   [2] Flor., ii. 8, 3 ff.

CONSTANTIUS ET GALLUS

2. Nondum apud Noricum exuto penitus Gallo, Apodemius quoad vixerat igneus turbarum incentor, raptos eius calceos vehens, equorum permutatione veloci, ut nimietate cogendi quosdam exstingueret, praecursorius index Mediolanum advenit ingressusque regiam, ante pedes proiecit Constantii, velut spolia regis occisi Parthorum ; et perlato nuntio repentino, docente rem insperatam et arduam ad sententiam tota facilitate completam, hi qui summam aulam tenebant, omni placendi studio in adulationem ex more collato, virtutem felicitatemque imperatoris extollebant in caelum, cuius nutu in modum gregariorum militum (licet diversis temporibus) duo exauctorati sunt principes, Veteranio nimirum et Gallus. 3. Quo ille studio blanditiarum exquisito sublatus, immunemque se deinde fore ab omni mortalitatis incommodo fidenter existimans, confestim a iustitia declinavit ita intemperanter, ut " Aeternitatem meam " aliquotiens subsereret ipse dictando, scribendoque propria manu orbis totius se dominum appellaret ; quod dicentibus aliis, indignanter admodum ferre deberet is qui ad aemulationem civilium principum formare vitam moresque suos, ut praedicabat, diligentia laborabat enixa. 4. Namque etiam si mundorum infinitates Democriti regeret, quos Anaxarcho incitante Magnus somniabat Alexander, id reputasset legens vel audiens, quod (ut docent mathematici concinentes),

---

[1] He joined in the attempt of Magnentius ; see note 2, p. 3. The name seems really to be Vetranio.

110

2. Hardly had Gallus been wholly stripped in Noricum, when Apodemius, a fiery inciter of disorder so long as he lived, seized and carried off Caesar's shoes, and with such swift relays of horses that he killed some of them by over-driving, was the first to arrive in Milan as an advance informer. Entering the palace, he cast the shoes at Constantius' feet, as if they were the spoils of the slain Parthian king. And on the arrival of the sudden tidings, which showed that an apparently hopeless and difficult enterprise had been carried out to their satisfaction with perfect ease, the highest court officials, as usual turning all their desire to please into flattery, extolled to the skies the emperor's valour and good fortune, since at his beck two princes, though at different times, Veteranio [1] to wit and Gallus, had been cashiered like common soldiers. 3. So Constantius, elated by this extravagant passion for flattery, and confidently believing that from now on he would be free from every mortal ill, swerved swiftly aside from just conduct so immoderately that sometimes in dictation he signed himself "My Eternity," and in writing with his own hand called himself lord of the whole world—an expression which, if used by others, ought to have been received with just indignation by one who, as he often asserted, laboured with extreme care to model his life and character in rivalry with those of the constitutional emperors. 4. For even if he ruled the infinity of worlds postulated by Democritus, of which Alexander the Great dreamed under the stimulus of Anaxarchus, yet from reading or hearsay he should have considered that (as the astronomers unanimously teach)

111

ambitus terrae totius, quae nobis videtur immensa,
ad [1] magnitudinem universitatis instar brevis optinet
puncti.

2. *Ursicinus, magister equitum per orientem, Julianus,*
Galli Caesaris frater, et Gorgonius, praepositus
Caesariani cubiculi, accusantur maiestatis.

1. Iamque post miserandam [2] deleti Caesaris
cladem, sonante periculorum iudicialium tuba, in
crimen laesae maiestatis arcessebatur Ursicinus,
adulescente magis magisque contra eius salutem
livore, omnibus bonis infesto. 2. Hac enim superabatur difficultate, quod ad suscipiendas defensiones
aequas et probabiles, imperatoris aures occlusae,
patebant [3] susurris insidiantium clandestinis, qui
Constantii nomine per orientis tractus omnes abolito,
ante dictum ducem domi forisque desiderari, ut
formidolosum Persicae genti, fingebant. 3. Sed contra
accidentia vir magnanimus stabat immobilis, ne se
proiceret abiectius cavens, parum tuto loco inno-
centiam stare medullitus gemens, hocque uno tristior
quod amici ante haec frequentes ad potiores des-
civerant, ut ad successores officiorum, more poscente, solent transire lictores. 4. Impugnabat autem
eum per fictae benignitatis illecebras, collegam et
virum fortem propalam saepe appellans Arbitio, ad
innectendas letales insidias vitae simplici perquam

---

[1] *ad*, added by G ; V omits. [2] *miserandam*, E ;
petiserandam, V ; *detestandam*, Traube. [3] *occlusae*,
W[2]AG ; *patebant*, BG ; *occluserat ebant*, V.

the circuit of the whole earth, which to us seems
endless, compared with the greatness of the universe
has the likeness of a mere tiny point.

2. *Ursicinus, commander of the cavalry in the Orient,
Julian, brother of Gallus Caesar, and Gorgonius,
his grand chamberlain, are accused of treason.*

1. And now, after the pitiful downfall of the murdered Caesar, the trumpet of court trials sounded
and Ursicinus was arraigned for high treason, since
jealousy, the foe of all good men, grew more and
more dangerous to his life. 2. For he fell victim
to this difficulty, that the emperor's ears were
closed for receiving any just and easily proved
defence, but were open to the secret whispers of
plotters, who alleged that Constantius' name was
got rid of throughout all the eastern provinces and
that the above-mentioned general was longed for
both at home and abroad as being formidable to the
Persian nation. 3. Yet in the face of events this
high-souled hero stood immovable, taking care not
to abase himself too abjectly, but lamenting from
his heart that uprightness was so insecure, and the
more depressed for the single reason that his friends,
who had before been numerous, had deserted him for
more powerful men, just as lictors are in the habit of
passing, as custom requires, from magistrates to their
successors. 4. Furthermore, he was attacked with
the blandishments of counterfeit courtesy by Arbitio,
who kept openly calling him his colleague and a brave
man, but who was exceedingly shrewd in devising

callens, et ea tempestate nimium potens. Ut enim subterraneus serpens, foramen subsidens occultum, adsultu subito singulos transitores observans incessit, ita ille odio alienae sortis [1] etiam post adeptum summum [2] militiae munus, nec laesus aliquando nec lacessitus, inexplebili quodam laedendi proposito, conscientiam polluebat. 5. Igitur paucis arcanorum praesentibus [3] consciis, latenter cum imperatore sententia diu digesta,[4] id sederat, ut nocte ventura, procul a conspectu militarium raptus, Ursicinus indemnatus occideretur, ut quondam Domitius Corbulo dicitur caesus, in colluvione illa Neroniani saeculi provinciarum fidus defensor et cautus. 6. Quibus ita compositis, cum ad hoc destinati praedictum tempus operirentur, consilio in lenitudinem flexo, facinus impium ad deliberationem secundam differri praeceptum est.

7. Indeque ad Iulianum, recens perductum, calumniarum vertitur machina, memorabilem postea principem, gemino crimine, ut iniquitas aestimabat, implicitum : quod a Macelli fundo, in Cappadocia posito, ad Asiam demigrarat, liberalium desiderio doctrinarum, et [5] per Constantinopolim transeuntem

---

[1] *odio alienae sortis*, Pet. ; *addiemaesortes*, V.   [2] *adeptum summum*, added in lac. of 15 letters, Clark.   [3] *praesentibus*, Heraeus ;   *praefectibus*, V.   [4] *diu digesta*, added in lac. of 9 letters, Novák (cf. xv. 4, 1 ; xiv. 6, 14). [5] *et*, added by G ; V omits.

---

[1] A villa or castle near Caesarea, where Gallus and Julian were brought up.

[2] Julian was devoted to the study of Greek literature and philosophy. He wrote a great many books, some of

deadly snares for a straightforward character and was at that time altogether too powerful. For just as an underground serpent, lurking below the hidden entrance to its hole, watches each passer-by and attacks him with a sudden spring, so he, through envy of others' fortune even after reaching the highest military position, without ever being injured or provoked kept staining his conscience from an insatiable determination to do harm. 5. So, in the presence of a few accomplices in the secret, after long deliberation it was privately arranged with the emperor that on the following night Ursicinus should be carried off far from the sight of the soldiers and slain without a trial, just as in days gone by it is said that Domitius Corbulo was murdered, a man who had been a loyal and prudent defender of the provinces amid the notorious corruption of Nero's time. 6. When this had been so arranged and the persons appointed for it were awaiting the allotted time, the emperor changed his mind in the direction of mercy, and orders were given to postpone the wicked deed until after a second consultation.

7. But then the artillery of slander was turned against Julian, the future famous emperor, lately brought to account, and he was involved, as was unjustly held, in a two-fold accusation : first, that he had moved from the estate of Macellum,[1] situated in Cappadocia, into the province of Asia, in his desire for a liberal education ;[2] and, second, that he had visited his brother Gallus as he passed through

which have been preserved : orations, letters, satires, and a few epigrams.

viderat fratrem. 8. Qui cum obiecta dilueret,
ostenderetque neutrum sine iussu fecisse, nefando
assentatorum coetu perisset urgente, ni adspiratione
superni numinis Eusebia suffragante regina, ductus
ad Comum oppidum Mediolano vicinum, ibique
paulisper moratus, procudendi ingenii causa (ut
cupidine flagravit) ad Graeciam ire permissus est.
9. Nec defuere deinceps ex his emergentia casibus,
quae diceres [1] secundis avibus contigisse, dum puni-
rentur ex iure, vel tamquam irrita diffluebant et
vana. Sed accidebat non numquam, ut opulenti
pulsantes praesidia potiorum, eisdemque tamquam
ederae celsis arboribus adhaerentes, absolutionem
pretiis mercarentur immensis; tenues vero, quibus
exiguae vires [2] erant ad redimendam salutem aut
nullae, damnabantur abrupte. Ideoque et veritas
mendaciis velabatur, et valuere pro veris aliquotiens
falsa.

10. Perductus est eisdem diebus et Gorgonius, cui
erat thalami Caesariani cura commissa, cumque
eum ausorum fuisse participem, concitoremque
interdum, ex confesso pateret, conspiratione spadonum iustitia concinnatis mendaciis obumbrata,
periculo evolutus abscessit.

---

[1] *diceres*, Her. ; *dispice*, V.   [2] *vires*, EA ; *res*, W²G ;
vere serant, V.

Constantinople. 8. And although he cleared himself of these implications and showed that he had done neither of these things without warrant, yet he would have perished at the instigation of the accursed crew of flatterers, had not, through the favour of divine power, Queen Eusebia befriended him ; so he was brought to the town of Comum, near Milan, and after abiding there for a short time, he was allowed to go to Greece for the sake of perfecting his education, as he earnestly desired. 9. Nor were there wanting later actions arising from these occurrences which one might say had a happy issue, since the accusers were justly punished, or their charges came to naught as if void and vain. But it sometimes happened that rich men, knocking at the strongholds of the mighty, and clinging to them as ivy does to lofty trees, bought their acquittal at monstrous prices ; but poor men, who had little or no means for purchasing safety, were condemned out of hand. And so both truth was masked by lies and sometimes false passed for true.

10. At that same time Gorgonius also, who had been appointed the Caesar's head chamberlain, was brought to trial ; and although it was clear from his own confession that he had been a party in his bold deeds, and sometimes their instigator, yet through a plot of the eunuchs justice was overshadowed with a clever tissue of lies, and he slipped out of danger and went his way.

CONSTANTIUS ET GALLUS

3. *In Galli Caesaris amicos et ministros animadvertitur.*

1. Haec dum Mediolani aguntur, militarium catervae ab oriente perductae sunt Aquileiam, cum aulicis pluribus, membris inter catenas fluentibus, spiritum trahentes exiguum vivendique moras per aerumnas detestati multiplices. Arcessebantur enim ministri fuisse Galli ferocientis, perque eos Domitianus discerptus credebatur et Montius, et alii post eos acti in exitium praeceps. 2. Ad quos audiendos Arbetio [1] missus est et Eusebius, cubiculi tunc praepositus, ambo inconsideratae iactantiae, iniusti pariter et cruenti. Qui nullo perspicaciter inquisito,[2] sine innocentium sontiumque differentia, alios verberibus vel tormentis afflictos exsulari poena damnarunt, quosdam ad infimam trusere militiam, residuos capitalibus addixere suppliciis. Impletisque funerum bustis, reversi velut ovantes, gesta rettulerunt ad principem, erga haec et similia palam obstinatum et gravem. 3. Vehementius hinc et deinde Constantius, quasi praescriptum fatorum ordinem convulsurus, recluso pectore patebat insidiantibus multis. Unde rumorum aucupes subito exstitere complures, honorum vertices ipsos ferinis morsibus appetentes, posteaque pauperes et divites indiscrete ; non ut Cibyratae illi Verrini, tribunal

---

[1] *Arbetio*, Kellerbauer ; *Arbitio*, Seeck ; *arborum*, V.
[2] *inquisito*, added by Hadr. Val.

---

[1] Two brothers from Cibyra, in Phrygia, Tlepolemus and Hiero, tools of Verres ; cf. Cic., *Verr.*, iv. 21, 47 ; iv. 13, 30.

3. *Punishment is inflicted on the friends and tools of Gallus Caesar.*

1. While these events were taking place at Milan, troops of soldiers were brought from the East to Aquileia together with several courtiers, their limbs wasting in chains as they drew feeble breaths and prayed to be delivered from longer life amid manifold miseries. For they were charged with having been tools of the savagery of Gallus, and it was through them, it was believed, that Domitianus and Montius were torn to pieces and others after them were driven to swift destruction. 2. To hear their defence were sent Arbetio and Eusebius, then grand chamberlain, both given to inconsiderate boasting, equally unjust and cruel. They, without examining anyone carefully or distinguishing between the innocent and the guilty, scourged and tortured some and condemned them to banishment, others they thrust down to the lowest military rank, the rest they sentenced to suffer death. And after filling the tombs with corpses, they returned as if in triumph and reported their exploits to the emperor, who in regard to these and similar cases was openly inflexible and severe. 3. Thereupon and henceforth Constantius, as if to upset the predestined order of the fates, more eagerly opened his heart and laid it bare to the plotters, many in number. Accordingly, numerous gossip-hunters suddenly arose, snapping with the jaws of wild beasts at even the highest officials, and afterwards at poor and rich indifferently, not like those Cibyrate hounds of Verres [1] fawning upon the tribunal of only one

119

unius legati lambentes, sed rei publicae membra totius per incidentia mala vexantes. 4. Inter quos facile Paulus et Mercurius eminebant : hic origine Persa, ille [1] natus in Dacia : notarius ille, hic a ministro triclinii rationalis. Et Paulo quidem, ut relatum est supra, Catenae inditum est cognomentum, eo quod in complicandis calumniarum nexibus erat indissolubilis, mira [2] inventorum sese varietate dispendens, ut in colluctationibus callere nimis quidam solent artifices palaestritae. 5. Mercurius vero [3] somniorum appellatus est [4] comes, quod ut clam mordax canis interna saevitia [5] summissius agitans caudam, epulis coetibusque se crebris inserens, si per quietem quisquam, ubi fusius natura vagatur, vidisse aliquid amico narrasset, id venenatis artibus coloratum in peius, patulis imperatoris auribus infundebat, et ob hoc homo tamquam inexpiabili obnoxius culpae, gravi mole criminis pulsabatur. 6. Haec augente vulgatius fama, tantum aberat, ut proderet quisquam visa nocturna, ut contra [6] aegre homines dormisse sese praesentibus faterentur externis, maerebantque docti quidam, quod apud Atlanteos nati non essent, ubi memorantur somnia non videri ; quod unde eveniat, rerum scientissimis relinquamus.

7. Inter has quaestionum suppliciorumque species diras, in Illyrico exoritur alia clades, ad multorum

---

[1] *ille,* added by G ; V omits.   [2] *mira,* Gronov, Haupt; *intra,* V.   [3] *vero,* added by Her.   [4] *est,* added by Clark, c.c.   [5] *saevitia,* Hermann ; *vitia,* V.   [6] *ut contra,* Traube ; *ut,* AG, C. F. W. Müller ; *cum,* V.

---

[1] xiv. **5,** 8.   [2] Cf. Herodotus, iv. 184.

governor, but afflicting the members of the whole commonwealth with a visitation of evils. 4. Among these Paulus and Mercurius were easily the leaders, the one a Persian by origin, the other born in Dacia ; Paulus was a notary, Mercurius, a former imperial steward, was now a treasurer. And in fact this Paulus, as was told before,[1] was nicknamed " the Chain," because he was invincible in weaving coils of calumny, exerting himself in a wonderful variety of schemes, just as some expert wrestlers are in the habit of showing excessive skill in their contests. 5. But Mercurius was dubbed " Count of Dreams," because, like a slinking, biting cur, savage within but peacefully wagging its tail, he would often worm his way into banquets and meetings, and if anyone had told a friend that he had seen anything in his sleep, when nature roams more freely, Mercurius would give it a worse colour by his venomous skill and pour it into the open ears of the emperor ; and on such grounds a man, as though really chargeable with inexpiable guilt, would be beaten down by a heavy burden of accusation. 6. Since rumour exaggerated these reports and gave them wide currency, people were so far from revealing their nightly visions, that on the contrary they would hardly admit in the presence of strangers that they had slept at all, and certain scholars lamented that they had not been born near Mount Atlas, where it is said that dreams are not seen [2] ; but how that happens we may leave to those who are most versed in natural science.

7. Amid these dire aspects of trials and tortures there arose in Illyricum another disaster, which

pericula ex verborum inanitate progressa. In
convivio Africani, Pannoniae secundae rectoris,
apud Sirmium poculis amplioribus madefacti quidam,
arbitrum adesse nullum existimantes, licenter imperium praesens ut molestissimum incusabant;
quibus alii optatam permutationem temporum
adventare, veluti e praesagiis affirmabant, non nulli
maiorum augurio [1] sibi portendi, incogitabili de-
mentia promittebant. 8. E quorum numero Gaudentius agens [2] in rebus, mente praecipiti stolidus, rem
ut seriam detulerat ad Rufinum, apparitionis praefecturae praetorianae tunc principem, ultimorum
semper avidum hominem, et coalita pravitate
famosum. 9. Qui confestim quasi pinnis elatus, ad
comitatum principis advolavit, eumque ad suspiciones
huius modi mollem et penetrabilem, ita acriter
inflammavit, ut sine deliberatione ulla Africanus, et
omnes letalis mensae participes, iuberentur rapi
sublimes. Quo facto delator funestus, vetita ex
more humano validius cupiens, biennio id quod
agebat (ut postularat) continuare praeceptus est.
10. Missus igitur ad eos corripiendos Teutomeres
protector domesticus cum collega onustos omnes
catenis (ut mandatum est) perducebat. Sed ubi
ventum est Aquileiam, Marinus tribunus [3] ex campi-
doctore eo tempore vacans, auctor perniciosi sermonis, et alioqui naturae ferventis, in taberna

---

[1] *augurio*, EW[2] N, Mommsen ; *auguria*, G ; *auirio*, V.
[2] *agens*, E, Val. ; *magis*, V ; *magnis*, W[2] BG.   [3] *tribunus*, Val. added in lac. of 8 letters.

---

[1] The principal city of Pannonia ; see Index.
[2] See note 2, p. 98.

began with idle words and resulted in peril to many. At a dinner-party given by Africanus, governor of Pannonia Secunda, at Sirmium,[1] certain men who were deep in their cups and supposed that no spy was present freely criticized the existing rule as most oppressive ; whereupon some assured them, as if from portents, that the desired change of the times was at hand ; others with inconceivable folly asserted that through auguries of their forefathers it was meant for them. 8. One of their number, Gaudentius, of the secret service,[2] a dull man but of a hasty disposition, had reported the occurrence as serious to Rufinus, who was then chief steward of the praetorian prefecture, a man always eager for extreme measures and notorious for his natural depravity. 9. Rufinus at once, as though upborne on wings, flew to the emperor's court and inflamed him, since he was easily influenced by such suspicions, to such excitement that without any deliberation Africanus and all those present at the fatal table were ordered to be quickly hoisted up and carried out. That done, the dire informer, more strongly desirous of things forbidden, as is the way of mankind, was directed to continue for two years in his present service, as he had requested. 10. So Teutomeres, of the emperor's bodyguard,[3] was sent with a colleague to seize them, and loading them with chains, as he had been ordered, he brought them all in. But when they came to Aquileia, Marinus, an ex-drillmaster [4] and now a tribune,[5] who was on furlough at the

[3] See note 3, p. 56.
[4] His office was to drill and exercise the soldiers.
[5] See Introd., pp. xliii f.

relictus, dum parantur itineri necessaria, lateri cultrum longiorem [1] casu repertum impegit, statimque extractis vitalibus, interiit. 11. Residui ducti Mediolanum, excruciatique tormentis, et confessi inter epulas petulanter se quaedam locutos, iussi sunt attineri poenalibus claustris, sub absolutionis aliqua spe (licet incerta). Protectores vero pronuntiati vertere solum exilio, ut Marino eisdem consciis mori permisso, veniam Arbetione meruere precante.

4. *Lentienses Alamanni a Constantio Aug. pars caesi, pars fugati.*

1. Re hoc modo finita, . . .[2] et Lentiensibus, Alamannicis pagis, indictum est bellum, collimitia saepe Romana latius irrumpentibus. Ad quem procinctum imperator egressus, in Raetias camposque venit Caninos, et digestis diu consiliis, id visum est honestum et utile, ut eo cum militis parte ibidem opperiente,[3] Arbetio magister equitum cum validiore exercitus manu, relegens margines lacus

---

[1] *longiorem*, Novák added in lac. of 9 letters, cf. xvi. 12, 39; xvii. 12, 2.   [2] The lac. (12 letters) contained the name of another tribe of the Alamanni, which cannot be supplied.   [3] *ibidem opperiente*, Her. added in lac. indicated by Schneider; *pater* for *parte* without lac., V.

---

[1] Cf. Cod. Just., x. 19, 2, *carcer poenalium*.
[2] See critical note.

time, the originator of that mischievous talk and besides a man of hot temper, being left in a tavern while things necessary for their journey were preparing, and chancing upon a long knife, stabbed himself in the side, at once plucked forth his vitals, and so died. 11. The rest were brought to Milan and cruelly tortured; and since they admitted that while feasting they had uttered some saucy expressions, it was ordered that they be kept in close confinement [1] with some hope (though doubtful) of acquittal. But the members of the emperor's guard, after being sentenced to leave the country for exile, since Marinus with their connivance had been allowed to die, at the suit of Arbetio obtained pardon.

4. *Of the Lentienses, a tribe of the Alamanni, a part were slain and a part put to flight by Constantius Augustus.*

1. The affair thus ended, war was declared on the . . . [2] and Lentienses,[3] tribes of the Alamanni, who often made extensive inroads through the Roman frontier defences. On that expedition the emperor himself set out and came to Raetia and the Campi Canini; [4] and after long and careful deliberation it seemed both honorable and expedient that, while he waited there with a part of the soldiers, Arbetio, commander of the cavalry, with the stronger part of the army should march on,

[3] Dwelling in the neighbourhood of Lentia, modern Lenze.

[4] Plains in Raetia, round about Bellinzona.

Brigantiae pergeret, protinus barbaris congressurus. Cuius loci figuram breviter quantum ratio patitur, designabo.

2. Inter montium celsorum amfractus, immani pulsu Rhenus exoriens, per[1] scopulos extenditur altos,[2] nullos advenas amnes[3] adoptans, ut per[4] cataractas inclinatione praecipiti funditur Nilus. Et navigari ab ortu poterat primigenio copiis exuberans propriis, ni ruenti curreret similis potius[5] quam fluenti lenius amni.[6] 3. Iamque ad plana volutus,[7] altaque divortia riparum adradens, lacum invadit rotundum et vastum, quem Brigantiam accola Raetus appellat, perque quadringenta et sexaginta stadia longum, parique paene spatio late diffusum, horrore silvarum squalentium inaccessum, nisi qua vetus illa Romana virtus et sobria iter composuit latum, barbaris et natura locorum et caeli inclementia refragante. 4. Hanc ergo paludem spumosis strependo[8] verticibus amnis irrumpens, et undarum quietem permeans pigram, mediam velut finali intersecat libramento, et tamquam elementum perenni discordia separatum, nec aucto nec imminuto agmine quod intulit, vocabulo et viribus absolvitur integris, nec contagia deinde ulla perpetiens, oceani gurgitibus intimatur. 5. Quodque

---

[1] *exoriens per*, scripsi; *exoriens per praeruptos*, Val. in lac. of 11 letters; *pulsurhen . . . pulos*, V.   [2] *altos*, scripsi. ;   [3] *nullos advenas am*, Gronov added in lac. of 10 letters   *extenditur . . . nes*, V.   [4] *per*, Val. added in lac. of 3 letters.   [5] *similis potius*, Val. ; *sim* (lac. of 8 letters), *quam*, V.   [6] *lenius amni*, scripsi in lac. of 6 letters.   [7] *ad plana volutus*, Petschenig ; *ad* (lac. 7 letters) *solutus*, V.   [8] *strependo*, G ; *stridendo*, Traube ; *stertendo* from *tertendo*.

skirting the shores of Lake Brigantia,[1] in order to
engage at once with the savages. Here I will describe the appearance of this place as briefly as my
project allows.

2. Between the defiles of lofty mountains the
Rhine rises and pours with mighty current over
high rocks, without receiving tributary streams,
just as the Nile with headlong descent pours over
the cataracts. And it could be navigated from its
very source, since it overflows with waters of its
own, did it not run along like a torrent rather than
a quietly flowing river. 3. And now rolling to
level ground and cutting its way between high and
widely separated banks, it enters a vast round lake,
which its Raetian neighbour calls Brigantia ;[1] this
is four hundred and sixty stades long and in breadth
spreads over an almost equal space ; it is inaccessible through the bristling woods of the gloomy
forest except where that old-time practical Roman
ability, in spite of the opposition of the savages, the
nature of the region, and the rigour of the climate,
constructed a broad highroad. 4. Into this pool,
then, the river bursts roaring with frothing eddies,
and cleaving the sluggish quiet of the waters, cuts
through its midst as if with a boundary line. And
as if the element were divided by an everlasting
discord, without increasing or diminishing the
volume which it carried in, it emerges with name and
force unchanged, and without thereafter suffering
any contact it mingles with Ocean's flood. 5. And

---

[1] The Lake of Constance.

est impendio mirum, nec stagnum aquarum rapido
transcursu movetur, nec limosa subluvie tardatur
properans flumen, et confusum misceri non potest
corpus ; quod, ni ita agi ipse doceret aspectus,
nulla vi credebatur posse discerni. 6. Sic Alpheus
oriens in Arcadia, cupidine fontis Arethusae captus,
scindens Ionium mare, ut fabulae ferunt, ad usque
amatae confinia proruit nymphae.[1] 7. Arbetio qui
adventus barbarorum nuntiarent non exspectans
dum[1] adessent, licet sciret aspera orta bellorum,
in occultas delatus insidias, stetit[2] immobilis, malo
repentino perculsus. 8. Namque improvisi[3] e
latebris hostes exsiliunt, et sine parsimonia quicquid offendi poterat telorum genere multiplici con-
figebant ; nec enim resistere nostrorum quisquam
potuit, nec aliud vitae subsidium, nisi discessu
sperare veloci. Quocirca vulneribus declinandis
intenti, incomposito agmine milites huc et illuc
dispalantes, terga ferienda dederunt. Plerique
tamen per angustas semitas sparsi, periculoque
praesidio tenebrosae noctis extracti, revoluta iam
luce, redintegratis viribus agmini quisque proprio
sese consociavit. In quo casu ita tristi et inopino,
abundans numerus armatorum, et tribuni desiderati
sunt decem. 9. Ob quae Alamanni sublatis animis
ferocius incedentes secuto die[4] prope munimenta
Romana, adimente matutina nebula lucem, strictis

---

[1] *proruit (progreditur,* G) *nymphae, Arbetio . . . expectans,*
BG ; *progrontusque barbaros* (lac. of 2¼ lines) *barbaros
dum,* V.   [2] *insidias stetit,* E, Val. ; *insi* (lac. of 6 letters),
V.   [3] *namque inprovisi,* Langen added in lac. of 7
letters ; . . . *visi,* V.   [4] *secuto die,* Clark ; *se cotidie,* V.

---

[1] The spring of Ortygia, at Syracuse in Sicily.

what is exceeding strange, neither is the lake stirred by the swift passage of the waters nor is the hurrying river stayed by the foul mud of the lake, and though mingled they cannot be blended into one body; but if one's very sight did not prove it to be so, one would not believe it possible for them to be kept apart by any power. 6. In the same way the river Alpheus, rising in Arcadia and falling in love with the fountain Arethusa, cleaves the Ionian Sea, as the myth tells us, and hastens to the retreat [1] of the beloved nymph. 7. Arbetio did not wait for the coming of messengers to announce the arrival of the savages, although he knew that a dangerous war was on foot, and when he was decoyed into a hidden ambuscade, he stood immovable, overwhelmed by the sudden mischance. 8. For the enemy sprang unexpectedly out of their lurking-places and without sparing pierced with many kinds of weapons everything within reach; and in fact not one of our men could resist, nor could they hope for any other means of saving their lives than swift flight. Therefore the soldiers, bent on avoiding wounds, straggled here and there in disorderly march, exposing their backs to blows. Very many however, scattering by narrow by-paths and saved from danger by the protecting darkness of the night, when daylight returned recovered their strength and rejoined each his own company. In this mischance, so heavy and so unexpected, an excessive number of soldiers and ten tribunes were lost. 9. As a result the Alamanni, elated in spirit, came on more boldly the following day against the Roman works; and while the morning mist obscured

mucronibus discurrebant, frendendo minas tumidas intentantes. Egressique repente scutarii, cum obiectu turmarum hostilium repercussi stetissent, omnes suos conspiratis mentibus ciebant ad pugnam. 10. Verum cum plerosque recentis aerumnae documenta terrerent, et[1] intuta fore residua credens haereret Arbetio, tres simul exsiluere tribuni, Arintheus agens vicem armaturarum rectoris, et Seniauchus qui equestrem turmam comitum tuebatur, et Bappo ducens promotos. 11. Qui cum commissis sibi militibus, pro causa communi se velut propria Deciorum veterum exemplo voventes, more[2] fluminis hostibus superfusi, non iusto proelio sed discursionibus rapidis,[3] universos in fugam coegere foedissimam. Qui dispersi laxatis ordinibus, dumque elabi properant impediti, corpora nudantes intecta, gladiorum hastarumque densis ictibus truncabantur. 12. Multique cum equis interfecti iacentes, etiam tum eorum dorsis videbantur innexi; quo viso omnes e castris effusi, qui prodire in proelium cum sociis ambigebant, cavendi immemores, proterebant

---

[1] *et intuta*, Val. ; *intota*, V. [2] *Qui cum commissis . . . uouentes, more*, Her. (cf. xvi. 10, 3 ; xxiii. 5, 19); *promoto* (lac. 30 letters) *missis sibi* (lac. of 11 letters) *causa communis velut propri* (lac. of 18 letters) *ueterum exemplo usuentere*, V. [3] *rapidis*, Her. in lac. of 9 letters.

---

[1] See note 3, p. 56.
[2] A picked body of troops, perhaps the same as the *comitatenses ;* they were divided into several bodies, distinguished by various names.

the light they rushed about with drawn swords, gnashing their teeth and giving vent to boastful threats. But the targeteers [1] suddenly sallied forth, and when they were driven back by the opposition of the enemy's battalions, and were at a standstill, with one mind they called out all their comrades to the fight. 10. But when the majority were terrified by the evidence of the recent disaster, and Arbetio hesitated, believing that the sequel would be dangerous, three tribunes sallied forth together : Arintheus, lieutenant-commander of the heavy-armed bodyguard, Seniauchus, leader of a squadron of the household cavalry,[2] and Bappo, an officer of the veterans.[3] 11. They with the soldiers under their command, devoting themselves on behalf of the common cause, like the Decii of old,[4] poured like a torrent upon the enemy, and not in a pitched battle, but in a series of swift skirmishes, put them all to most shameful flight. And as they scattered with broken ranks and encumbered by their haste to escape, they exposed themselves unprotected, and by many a thrust of swords and spears were cut to pieces. 12. And many, as they lay there, slain horse and man together, seemed even then to be sitting fast upon the back of their mounts. On seeing this, all who had been in doubt about going into battle with their comrades poured forth from the camp, and careless of all precaution trod under foot the horde of savages, except those whom flight

[3] Soldiers who were given a higher rank on account of good service or favour; cf. Vegetius, ii. 3, *legionum robur infractum est, cum per gratiam promoverentur milites, qui promoveri consueverant per labores.*

[4] See Index.

barbaram plebem, nisi quos fuga exemerat morte,
calcantes cadaverum strues, et perfusi sanie peremptorum. 13. Hocque exitu proelio terminato, imperator Mediolanum ad hiberna ovans revertit et
laetus.

5. *Silvanus Francus, magister peditum per Gallias,
Coloniae Augustus adpellatur, et xxviii. imperi
die per insidias opprimitur.*

1. Exoritur iam hinc rebus afflictis, haut dispari
provinciarum malo calamitatum turbo novarum,
exstincturus omnia simul, ni Fortuna moderatrix
humanorum casuum motum eventu celeri consummavit, impendio formidatum. 2. Cum diuturna
incuria Galliae caedes acerbas rapinasque et incendia,
barbaris licenter grassantibus, nullo iuvante perferrent, Silvanus pedestris militiae rector, ut efficax
ad haec corrigenda, principis iussu perrexit,[1] Arbetione id maturari modis quibus poterat adigente, ut
absenti aemulo quem superesse adhuc gravabatur
periculosae molis onus impingeret.[2]

3. Dynamius quidam [3] actuarius sarcinalium principis iumentorum, commendaticias ab eo petierat
litteras ad amicos, ut quasi familiaris eiusdem esset

---

[1] *principis iussu perrexit,* Val. ; *primum ipsius super-
rexit,* V. [2] *gravabatur . . . impingeret,* BG in lac. of
about 3 lines in V. [3] *Dynamius quidam,* Val. added ; G
has lac. of 3 letters.

---

[1] He had charge during campaigns and journeys of
the transportation of the emperor's baggage ; other
actuarii are mentioned in **xx. 5, 9** (see note), and *actuarii*

132

had saved from death, trampling on heaps of dead bodies and drenched with the blood of the slain. 13. The battle thus done and ended, the emperor returned in triumph and joy to Milan, to pass the winter.

5. *Silvanus the Frank, commander of the infantry in Gaul, is hailed as Augustus at Cologne, but is treacherously slain on the twenty-eighth day of his reign.*

1. Now there arises in this afflicted state of affairs a storm of new calamities, with no less mischief to the provinces ; and it would have destroyed everything at once, had not Fortune, arbitress of human chances, brought to an end with speedy issue a most formidable uprising. 2. Since through long neglect Gaul was enduring bitter massacres, pillage, and the ravages of fire, as the savages plundered at will and no one helped, Silvanus, an infantry commander thought capable of redressing these outrages, came there at the emperor's order ; and Arbetio urged by whatever means he could that this should be hastened, in order that the burden of a perilous undertaking might be imposed upon an absent rival, whose survival even to this time he looked upon as an affliction.

3. A certain Dynamius, superintendent of the emperor's pack-animals,[1] had asked Silvanus for letters of recommendation to his friends, in order to make himself very conspicuous, as if he were one

---

a rationibus scrutandis in xxv. **10,** 7. *Actuarius* is an adjective, sc. *scriba.*

133

notissimus. Hoc impetrato, cum ille nihil suspicans
simpliciter praestitisset, servabat epistulas, ut perni-
ciosum aliquid in tempore moliretur. 4. Memorato
itaque duce Gallias ex re publica discursante, bar-
barosque propellente, iam sibi diffidentes et trepidantes, idem Dynamius inquietius agens, ut versutus
et in fallendo exercitatus, fraudem comminiscitur
impiam, subornatore et conscio, ut iactavere rumores
incerti, Lampadio praefecto praetorio, et Eusebio
ex comite rei privatae, cui cognomentum erat inditum Mattyocopi, atque Aedesio ex magistro
memoriae, quos ad consulatum ut amicos iunctissi-
mos idem curarat rogari praefectus ; et peniculo
serie litterarum abstersa, solaque [1] incolumi relicta
subscriptione, alter multum a vero illo dissonans
superscribitur textus : velut Silvano rogante verbis
obliquis, hortanteque amicos agentes intra palatium,
vel privatos, inter quos et Tuscus erat Albinus,
aliique plures, ut se altiora coeptantem, et prope
diem loci principalis aditum petiturum iuvarent.[2]
5. Hunc fascem ad arbitrium figmenti compositum,[3]
vitam pulsaturum insontis, a Dynamio susceptum

[1] *solaque*, Traube ; *sola*, V. [2] *aditum petiturum
iuuarent*, Petschenig ; *aditurum*, without lac., V. [3] *compositum*, Val. ; *co* (lac. of 7 letters) *sit*, V.

[1] See Dessau, Inscr. 4154, note 3.
[2] See Introd., pp. xli. f.
[3] "Glutton," from -κοπέω, "cut," and ματτύα, "deli-
cacies," "delicate food."

of his intimates. On obtaining this request, for
Silvanus, suspecting nothing, had innocently granted
it, he kept the letters, intending to work some mischief at the proper time. 4. So when the above-
mentioned commander was traversing Gaul in the
service of the government and driving forth the
savages, who had now lost their confidence and
courage, this same Dynamius, being restless in
action, like the crafty man he was and practised
in deceit, devised a wicked plot. He had as abettors
and fellow conspirators, as uncertain rumours declared, Lampadius,[1] the praetorian prefect, and
Eusebius, former keeper of the privy purse,[2] who
had been nicknamed Mattyocopus,[3] and Aedesius,
late master of the rolls,[4] all of whom the said prefect
had arranged to have called to the consulship as his
nearest friends. With a sponge he effaced the lines
of writing, leaving only the signature intact, and
wrote above it another text far different from
the original, indicating that Silvanus in obscure
terms was asking and urging his assistants within
the palace or without official position, including
both Tuscus Albinus and many more, to help him,
aiming as he was at a loftier position and soon
to mount to the imperial throne. 5. This packet
of letters, thus forged at his pleasure to assail
the life of an innocent man, the prefect received
from Dynamius, and coming into the emperor's

---

[4] The *magister memoriae* was a subordinate of the
magister officiorum, and head of the *scrinium memoriae*
(first established by Caracalla) consisting of 62 clerks
and 12 *adiutores*. They sent out the *acta* prepared by the
scrinia epistularum et libellorum, and kept on record
answers to petitions.

praefectus imperatori, avide scrutari haec et similia
consueto, secrete obtulit [1] soli, ingressus intimum
conclave in tempore,[2] deinde sperans accepturum se
a principe praemium,[3] ut pervigilem salutis eius cus-
todem et cautum,[4] lectaque consistorio astu callido
consarcinata materia, tribuni iussi sunt custodiri,
et de provinciis duci privati, quorum epistulae
nomina designabant.   6. Confestimque iniquitate
rei percitus Malarichus, gentilium rector, collegis
adhibitis strepebat immaniter, circumveniri homines
dicatos imperio per factiones et dolos minime debere
proclamans, petebatque ut ipse relictis obsidum loco
necessitudinibus suis, Mallobaude armaturarum tribuno spondente quod remeabit, velocius iuberetur
ire ducturus Silvanum, aggredi nihil tale conatum,
quale insidiatores acerrimi concitarunt ; vel contra
se paria promittente, Mallobaudem orabat properare
permitti, haec quae ipse pollicitus est impleturum.
7. Testabatur enim id se procul dubio scire, quod siqui
mitteretur externus, suopte ingenio Silvanus etiam
nulla re perterrente timidior, composita forte turbabit.

8. Et quamquam utilia moneret et necessaria,
ventis tamen loquebatur incassum. Namque Arbetione auctore, Apodemius ad eum vocandum cum

---

[1] *consueto, secrete obtulit*, Haupt; *censue terreret* (second
r added by V[2]) *e* (lac. 8 letters) *id* V.   [2] *conclave in tempore*, Novák ; *caperem tempore*, V.   [3] *accepturum* . . .
praemium, added by Novák.   [4] *et cautum*, added by
Novak in lac. of about 9 letters.

---

[1] The emperor's council, or secret cabinet ; see Introd.,
pp. xxix. f.
[2] The foreign contingent of the household troops ; see
note 3, p. 56.

private room at an opportune time and finding him alone, secretly handed it to him, accustomed as he was eagerly to investigate these and similar charges. Thereby the prefect hoped that he would be rewarded by the emperor, as a most watchful and careful guardian of his safety. And when these letters, patched together with cunning craft, were read to the consistory,[1] orders were given that those tribunes whose names were mentioned in the letters should be imprisoned, and that the private individuals should be brought to the capital from the provinces. 6. But Malarichus, commander of the gentiles,[2] was at once struck with the unfairness of the procedure, and summoning his colleagues, vigorously protested, exclaiming that men devoted to the empire ought not to be made victims of cliques and wiles. And he asked that he himself—leaving as hostages his relatives and having Mallobaudes, tribune of the heavy-armed guard, as surety for his return—might be commissioned to go quickly and fetch Silvanus, who was not entering upon any such attempt as those most bitter plotters had trumped up. Or as an alternative, he asked that he might make a like promise and that Mallobaudes be allowed to hurry there and perform what he himself had promised to do. 7. For he declared that he knew beyond question that, if any outsider should be sent, Silvanus, being by nature apprehensive, even when there was nothing alarming, would be likely to upset the peace.

8. But although his advice was expedient and necessary, yet he was talking vainly to the winds. For by Arbetio's advice Apodemius, an inveterate

137

litteris mittitur, inimicus bonorum omnium diuturnus et gravis. Qui incidentia parvi ducens [1] cum venisset in Gallias, dissidens a mandatis, quae proficiscenti sunt data, nec viso Silvano nec oblatis scriptis ut veniret admonito,[2] remansit adscitoque rationali, quasi proscripti iamque necandi magistri peditum clientes et servos hostili tumore vexabat. 9. Inter haec tamen dum praesentia Silvani speratur, et Apodemius quieta perturbat, Dynamius ut argumento validiore impie structorum adsereret fidem, compositas litteras his concinentes quas obtulerat principi per praefectum, ad tribunum miserat fabricae Cremonensis, nomine Silvani et Malarichi, a quibus ut arcanorum conscius monebatur parare propere cuncta. 10 Qui cum haec legisset, haerens et ambigens diu quidnam id esset—nec enim meminerat secum aliquando super negotio ullo interiore hos quorum litteras acceperat collocutos—epistulas ipsas per baiulum qui portarat, iuncto milite ad Malarichum remisit,[3] obsecrans ut doceret aperte quae vellet, non ita perplexe ; nec enim intellexisse firmabat, ut subagrestem et simplicem, quid significatum esset obscurius. 11. Haec Malarichus subito nanctus, etiam tunc squalens et maestus, suamque

---

[1] *incidentia parvi ducens*, Val. ; *incidentis*, lac. of 27 letters, V ; lac. of 6 letters, G.   [2] *admonito*, AG ; *admonuit*, EB ; *admonit*, V. Clark indicates lac.   [3] *remisit*, Her. ; *misit*, V.

and bitter enemy of every patriot, was sent with a letter to recall Silvanus. He, caring little for what might happen, on arriving in Gaul, departed from the instructions given him on his setting out and remained there without either interviewing Silvanus or citing him to come to court by delivering the letter ; and associating with himself the fiscal agent of the province, as if the said infantry commander were proscribed and now to be executed, he abused his dependents and slaves with the arrogance of an enemy. 9. In the meantime, however, while Silvanus' presence was awaited and Apodemius was disturbing the peace, Dynamius, in order to maintain the credibility of his wicked inventions with a stronger argument, had made up a letter tallying with the one which he had presented to the emperor through the prefect, and sent it to the tribune of the Cremona armory, in the name of Silvanus and Malarichus ; in this letter the tribune, as one privy to their secret designs, was admonished to prepare everything with speed. 10. When the tribune had read this, hesitating for a long time and puzzling as to what in the world it meant (for he did not remember that the men whose letter he had received had ever talked with him about any confidential business), he sent the identical letter back to Malarichus by the carrier who had brought it, and with him a soldier, begging Malarichus to explain openly what he wanted, and not so enigmatically. For he declared that, being a somewhat rude and plain man, he had not understood what had been obscurely intimated. 11. Malarichus, on unexpectedly receiving this, being even then troubled and

et popularis Silvani vicem graviter ingemiscens,
adhibitis Francis, quorum ea tempestate in palatio
multitudo florebat, erectius iam loquebatur ; tumultuando patefactis [1] insidiis reserataque [2] iam fallacia,
per quam ex confesso salus eorum appetebatur.
12. Hisque cognitis statuit imperator, dispicientibus
consistorianis et militaribus universis, in negotium
perspicaciter inquiri.[3] Cumque iudices resedissent,[4]
Florentius Nigriniani filius agens tunc pro magistro
officiorum, contemplans diligentius scripta, apicum-
que pristinorum quasi quandam umbram [5] rep-
periens animadvertit (ut factum est) priore textu
interpolato longe alia quam dictarat Silvanus, ex
libidine consarcinatae falsitatis adscripta. 13.
Proinde fallaciarum nube discussa, imperator doctus
gesta relatione fideli, abrogata potestate praefectum
statui sub quaestione praecepit, sed absolutus est
enixa conspiratione multorum. Suspensus autem
Eusebius ex comite privatarum, se conscio haec

---

[1] *tumultuando patefactis*, Val. ; *tumultua* (lac. of 10
letters) *factis*, V.   [2] *reserataque*, Kiessling ; *refe* (lac.
of 3 letters) *que*, V.   [3] *perspicaciter inquiri*, Her. ;
praeter morem inquiri, Traube, Novák ; *praeterinquiri*, V.
[4] *resedissent*, Novák ; *festidissent*, V.   [5] *umbram*, added
by Her. ; V omits.

---

[1] The *magister officiorum* was a very important official,
to whom many of the former functions of the praetorian
prefect had been transferred (or shared with the prefect).
Along with his many duties was complete charge of the
discipline of the palace. See Introd., pp. xxxvii. f.

sad, and grievously lamenting his own lot and that
of his fellow-countryman Silvanus, called together
the Franks, who at that time were numerous and in-
fluential in the palace, and now spoke more boldly,
raising an outcry over the disclosure of the plot and
the unveiling of the deceit by which their lives were
avowedly aimed at. 12. And on learning this, the
emperor decided that the matter should be investigated searchingly through the medium of his council
and all his officers. And when the judges had
taken their seats, Florentius, son of Nigrinianus, at
the time deputy master of the offices,[1] on scrutinizing
the script with greater care, and finding a kind of
shadow, as it were, of the former letters,[2] perceived
what had been done, namely, that the earlier text
had been tampered with and other matter added
quite different from what Silvanus had dictated, in
accordance with the intention of this patched-up
forgery. 13. Accordingly, when this cloud of deceit
had broken away, the emperor, learning of the
events from a faithful report, deprived the prefect
of his powers, and gave orders that he should be
put under examination; but he was acquitted
through an energetic conspiracy of many persons.
Eusebius, however, former count of the privy
purse,[3] on being put upon the rack, admitted that
this had been set on foot with his cognizance.

---

[2] For the meaning of *apices*, see *Amer. Jour. of Philol.*,
xlviii. (1927), pp. 1 ff. The word is wrongly translated
by Holland, " prickes or *accents* over the letters," and
by Yonge, " some vestiges of the *tops* of former words " ;
rightly by Tross, " einige Spuren der früheren Buchstaben."

[3] See Introd., pp. xli. f.

dixerat concitata. 14. Aedesius omnino nescisse [1]
quid actum sit pertinaci infitiatione contendens,
abiit innoxius, et ita finito negotio, omnes sunt
absoluti quos exhiberi delatio compulit criminosa.
Dynamius vero ut praeclaris artibus illustratus,
cum correctoris dignitate regere iussus est Tuscos
et Umbros.[2]

15. Agens inter haec apud Agrippinam Silvanus,
assiduisque suorum comperiens [3] nuntiis, quae Apodemius in labem suarum ageret fortunarum, et sciens
animum tenerum versabilis principis, timensque ne
trucidaretur [4] absens et inauditus,[5] in difficultate
positus maxima, barbaricae se fidei committere cogitabat. 16. Sed Laniogaiso vetante (tunc tribuno)
quem dum militaret candidatus solum adfuisse
morituro Constanti supra rettulimus, docenteque
Francos, unde oriebatur, interfecturos eum aut
accepto praemio prodituros, nihil tutum ex praesentibus ratus, in consilia agitabatur [6] extrema et
sensim cum principiorum verticibus erectius [7] col-
locutus, eisdemque magnitudine promissae mercedis
accensis, cultu purpureo a draconum et vexillorum

---

[1] *omnino nescisse*, Traube ; *enim minus scisse*, V.
[2] *et Umbros*, Seeck added in lac. of 15 letters.   [3] *con-
periens*, Clark ; *conperiis*, V.   [4] *timensque ne trucidaretur* (*trucidaretur* for *perageretur reus*, Gronov ; *-que* added
by Clark), BG ; (lac. of 15 letters) *aretur*, V.   [5] *inauditus*,
Val. ; *indamnatus*, V.   [6] *agitabatur*, E, Eyssen. ;
cogitabatur, V.   [7] *erectius*, Traube ; *erectus*, V.

14. Aedesius, who maintained with stout denial that he had known nothing of what was done, got off scot-free. And so at the close of the business all those were acquitted whom the incriminating report had forced to be produced for trial; in fact Dynamius, as if given distinction by his illustrious conduct, was bidden to govern Etruria and Umbria with the rank of corrector.[1]

15. Meanwhile Silvanus, stationed at Cologne and learning from his friends' constant messages what Apodemius was undertaking to the ruin of his fortunes, knowing the pliant mind of the fickle emperor, and fearing lest he should be condemned to death absent and unheard, was put in a most difficult position and thought of entrusting himself to the good faith of the savages. 16. But he was prevented by Laniogaisus, at that time a tribune, whom I have earlier stated to have been the sole witness of Constans' death, while he was serving as a subaltern.[2] He assured Silvanus that the Franks, whose fellow-countryman he was, would kill him or on receipt of a bribe betray him. So Silvanus, seeing no safety under present conditions, was driven to extreme measures, and having gradually spoken more boldly with the chief officers, he aroused them by the greatness of the reward he promised; then as a temporary expedient he tore the purple decorations from the standards of

---

[1] *Correctores* in the fourth century were governors of smaller provinces, ranking between the highest (*consulares*) and the lowest (*praesides*). Originally a *corrector* governed the whole of Italy. The title gradually died out, being replaced by *consulares* or *praesides*. See Index II.
[2] See Index II, s.v. *candidatus*.

143

insignibus ad tempus abstracto, ad culmen imperiale surrexit.

17. Dumque haec aguntur in Galliis, ad occasum inclinato iam die, perfertur Mediolanum insperabilis nuntius, aperte Silvanum demonstrans, dum ex magisterio peditum altius nititur, sollicitato exercitu ad augustum culmen evectum. 18. Hac mole casus inopini Constantio icto, quasi fulmine Fati, primates, consilio secunda vigilia convocato, properarunt omnes in regiam. Cumque nulli ad eligendum quid agi deberet, mens suppetere posset aut lingua, submissis verbis perstringebatur Ursicini [1] mentio, ut consiliis rei bellicae praestantissimi, frustraque gravi iniuria lacessiti, et per admissionum magistrum—qui mos est honoratior—accito eodem, ingresso consistorium offertur purpura multo quam antea placidius. Diocletianus enim Augustus [2] omnium primus, externo et regio more [3] instituit adorari, cum semper antea ad similitudinem iudicum salutatos principes legerimus. 19. Et qui paulo antea cum insectatione malivola, orientis vorago, invadendaeque [4] summae rei per filios affectator compellabatur, tunc dux prudentissimus, et Constantini [5]

---

[1] *Ursicini*, Val.; *sic inimentio*, V.   [2] *Diocletianus Augustus* added by Val. (*enim* by Gardt.) in lac. of 16 letters. [3] *extero* (*externo*, Traube, Novák, Her., cf. Livy, xxix. 19, 4) *ritu et regio more*, G; *extortio ei regio re*, V.   [4] *vorago inuadendaeque*, G; *uoragi* (lac. of 8 letters) *uadendaeque*, V.   [5] *Constantii*, suggested by Clark, Her.; *Constantini*, V.

---

[1] The *magister admissionum* was a subordinate of the *magister officiorum;* imperial audiences were obtained

the cohorts and the companies, and so mounted to the imperial dignity.

17. And while this was going on in Gaul, as the day was already drawing to its close, an unexpected messenger reached Milan, openly declaring that Silvanus, aiming higher than the command of the infantry, had won over his army and risen to imperial eminence. 18. Constantius, struck down by the weight of this unexpected mischance as by a thunderbolt of Fate, called a council at about midnight, and all the chief officials hastened to the palace. And when no one's mind or tongue was equal to showing what ought to be done, mention in subdued tones was made of Ursicinus, as a man conspicuous for his sagacity in the art of war, and one who had been without reason provoked by serious injustice. And when he had been summoned by the master of ceremonies [1] (which is the more honourable way) and had entered the council chamber, he was offered the purple to kiss much more graciously than ever before. Now it was the emperor Diocletian who was the first to introduce this foreign and royal form of adoration, whereas we have read that always before our emperors were saluted like the higher officials.[2] 19. So the man who shortly before with malicious slander was called the maelstrom of the East and a seeker after acquisition of imperial power through his sons, then became a most politic leader and mighty fellow-soldier of Constantine's, and the only person to

through the latter, and the actual entrance into the audience chamber was under the direction of the former.

[2] For this meaning of *iudices*, see Index of Officials, s.v.

145

magnus erat commilito, solusque ad extinguendum, probis quidem sed insidiosis rationibus petebatur. Diligens enim opera navabatur, exstingui Silvanum, ut fortissimum perduellem, aut (si secus accidisset) Ursicinum exulceratum iam penitus aboleri, ne superesset scopulus [1] impendio formidandus. 20. Igitur cum de profectione celeranda disponeretur, propulsationem obiectorum criminum eundem ducem parantem praegressus, oratione leni prohibet imperator, non id esse memorans tempus, ut controversa defensio causae susciperetur, cum vicissim restitui in pristinam concordiam partes necessitas subigeret urgentium rerum, antequam cresceret mollienda. 21. Habita igitur deliberatione multiplici, id [2] potissimum tractabatur, quo commento Silvanus gesta etiam tum imperatorem ignorare existimaret. Et [3] probabili argumento ad [4] firmandam fidem reperto monetur honorificis scriptis, ut accepto Ursicino successore cum potestate rediret intacta. 22. Post haec ita digesta protinus iubetur exire, tribunis et protectoribus domesticis decem, ut postularat, ad iuvandas necessitates publicas ei coniunctis, inter quos ego quoque eram cum Veriniano collega, residui omnes propinqui et

---

[1] *scopulus,* Her., cf. Florus, iv. 9, 1 ; *scrupulus,* EBG ; *scropulus,* V.   [2] *id,* added by Gardt. ; V omits.   [3] *et,* added by Val. ; V omits.   [4] *ad,* E²G ; V omits.

extinguish the fire ; but he was really being attacked under motives honourable, to be sure, but yet insidious. For great care was being taken that Silvanus should be destroyed as a very brave rebel ; or, if that should fail, that Ursicinus, already deeply gangrened, should be utterly annihilated, in order that a rock[1] so greatly to be dreaded should not be left. 20. Accordingly, when arrangements were being made for hastening his departure, and the general undertook the refutation of the charges brought against him, the emperor, forestalling him by a mild address, forbade it, declaring that it was not the time for taking up the defence of a disputed case, when the urgency of pressing affairs which should be mitigated before it grew worse, demanded that parties should mutually be restored to their old-time harmony. 21. Accordingly, after a many-sided debate, this point was chiefly discussed, namely, by what device Silvanus might be led to think that the emperor even then had no knowledge of his action. And they invented a plausible means of strengthening his confidence, advising him in a complimentary letter to receive Ursicinus as his successor and return with his dignities unimpaired. 22. After this had been thus settled, Ursicinus was ordered to set forth at once, accompanied (as he had requested) by some tribunes and ten of the body-guard, to assist the exigencies of the state. Among these I myself was one, with my colleague Verinianus ; all the rest were relatives

---

[1] Cf. Florus, iv. 9, 1 ; *cum scopulus et nodus et mora publicae securitatis superesset Antonius*, "a rock in his path" (*L.C.L.*, p. 316).

familiares.[1] 23. Iamque eum egressum solum de se metuens quisque per longa spatia deducebat. Et quamquam ut bestiarii obiceremur intractabilibus feris, perpendentes tamen hoc bonum habere tristia accidentia,[2] quod in locum suum [3] secunda substituunt,[4] mirabamur illam sententiam Tullianam, ex internis veritatis ipsius promulgatam, quae est talis : " Et quamquam optatissimum est perpetuo fortunam quam florentissimam permanere, illa tamen aequalitas vitae non tantum habet sensum, quantum cum ex miseris [5] et perditis rebus ad meliorem statum fortuna revocatur."

24. Festinamus itaque itineribus magnis, ut ambitiosus magister armorum, ante allapsum per Italicos de tyrannide ullum Rumorem, in suspectis finibus appareret, verum cursim nos properantes aeria quadam via [6] antevolans prodiderat Fama, et Agrippinam ingressi, invenimus cuncta nostris conatibus altiora. 25. Namque convena undique multitudine trepide coepta fundante, coactisque copiis multis, pro statu rei praesentis id aptius videbatur, ut ad imperatoris novelli, per ludibriosa auspicia virium accessu firmandi sensum ac voluntatem dux flexibilis [7] verteretur ; quo variis

---

[1] *omnes propinqui et familiares. iamque,* BG ; *omni* (lac. of 21 letters) *Iamque,* V.   [2] *tristia,* EAG ; *accidentia,* Clark ; *haberet tristitia recidentia,* V.   [3] *locum suum,* Her. ; *locos* (from *locis*) *sunt.*   [4] V has lac. of 10 letters at end of page ; no lac., BG.   [5] *miseris,* Kiessling ; *seris,* V.   [6] *aeria quadam uia,* Novák ; *aeria uia quadam,* Clark, cf. xviii. 6, 3 ; *aeraria quadam,* V.   [7] *flexibilis,* Bentley ; *flexilis,* Pet. ; *flebilis,* V.

148

and friends. 23. And when he left, each of us attended him for a long distance in fear only for our own safety. But although we were, like gladiators,[1] cast before ravening wild beasts, yet reflecting that melancholy events after all have this good sequel, that they give way to good fortune, we admired that saying of Tully's, delivered even from the inmost depths of truth itself, which runs as follows: " And although it is most desirable that our fortune always remain wholly favourable, yet that evenness of life does not give so great a sense of satisfaction as when, after wretchedness and disaster, fortune is recalled to a better estate."[2]

24. Accordingly, we hastened by forced marches, since the commander-in-chief of the army, in his zeal, wished to appear in the suspected districts before any report of the usurpation had made its way into Italy. But for all our running haste, Rumour had flown before us by some aerial path and revealed our coming; and on arriving at Cologne we found everything above our reach. 25. For since a great crowd assembled from all sides gave a firm foundation to the enterprise so timidly begun, and large forces had been mustered, it seemed, in view of the state of affairs, more fitting that our general[3] should complaisantly favour the upstart[4] emperor's purpose and desire to be strengthened in the growth of his power by deceptive omens; to the end that by means of manifold devices of flattery his feeling

---

[1] The *bestiarii* were matched against wild beasts.

[2] This passage does not occur in Cicero's extant works. A similar one appears in *Ad Quir. post Reditum*, i. 2.

[3] Ursicinus.

[4] *Novelli* is contemptuous; cf. xxvi. 6, 15.

assentandi figmentis in mollius vergente securitate, nihil metuens hostile deciperetur. 26. Cuius rei finis arduus videbatur ; erat enim cautius observandum, ut appetitus opportunitati obtemperarent, nec praecurrentes eam nec deserentes. Qui si eluxissent intempestive, constabat nos omnes sub elogio uno morte multandos.

27. Susceptus tamen idem dux leniter adactusque, inclinante negotio ipso cervices, adorare sollemniter anhelantem celsius purpuratum, ut spectabilis colebatur et intimus : facilitate aditus honoreque mensae regalis adeo antepositus aliis, ut iam secretius de rerum summa consultaretur. 28. Aegre ferebat Silvanus ad[1] consulatum potestatesque sublimes elatis indignis, se et[2] Ursicinum solos post exsudatos magnos pro re publica labores et crebros, ita fuisse despectos, ut ipse quidem per quaestiones familiarium sub disceptatione ignobili crudeliter agitatus, commisisse in maiestatem arcesseretur, alter vero ab oriente raptus odiis inimicorum addiceretur ; et haec assidue clam querebatur et palam. 29. Terrebant nos tamen, cum dicerentur haec et similia, circumfrementia undique murmura causantis inopiam militis, et rapida celeritate ardentis angustias Alpium perrumpere Cottiarum.

30. In hoc aestu mentis ancipiti, ad effectum tendens consilium occulta scrutabamus indagine,

[1] *ad*, W²BG ; V omits.   [2] *et*, W²BG ; V omits.

[1] In order to march to Italy against Constantius himself.

of security might be made more complete, and he might be caught off his guard against anything hostile. 26. But the issue of this project seemed difficult ; for special care had to be observed that the onsets should take advantage of the right moment, neither anticipating it nor falling short of it. Since if they should break out prematurely, we were all sure to suffer death under a single sentence.

27. However, our general, being kindly received and forcing himself—since our very commission bent our necks—formally to reverence the high-aiming wearer of the purple, was welcomed as a distinguished and intimate friend. In freedom of access and honourable place at the royal table he was so preferred to others that he came to be confidentially consulted about the most important affairs. 28. Silvanus took it ill that while unworthy men were raised to the consulship and to high positions, he and Ursicinus alone, after having toiled through such heavy and repeated tasks for the government, had been so scorned that he himself had been cruelly harassed in an unworthy controversy through the examination of friends of his, and summoned to trial for treason, while Ursicinus, haled back from the East, was delivered over to the hatred of his enemies ; and these continual complaints he made both covertly and openly. 29. We however were alarmed, in spite of these and similar speeches, at the uproarious complaints of the soldiers on every hand, pleading their destitution and eager to burst through the passes of the Cottian Alps [1] with all speed.

30. Amid this perplexing distress of spirit we kept casting about in secret investigation for some plan

sederatque tandem mutatis prae timore saepe senten-
tiis, ut quaesitis magna industria cautis rei ministris,
obstricto religionum consecratione colloquio, Bracchiati sollicitarentur atque Cornuti, fluxioris fidei
et [1] ubertate mercedis ad momentum omne versabiles.
31. Firmato itaque negotio per sequestres quosdam
gregarios, obscuritate ipsa ad id patrandum idoneos,
praemiorum exspectatione accensus solis ortu iam
rutilo, subitus armatorum globus erupit, atque ut
solet in dubiis rebus, audentior caesis custodibus,
regia penetrata, Silvanum [2] extractum aedicula,
quo exanimatus confugerat, ad conventiculum ritus
Christiani tendentem, densis gladiorum ictibus
trucidarunt.

32. Ita dux haut exsilium meritorum hoc genere
oppetit mortis, metu calumniarum, quibus factione
iniquorum irretitus est absens, ut tueri possit
salutem, ad praesidia progressus extrema. 33.
Licet enim ob tempestivam illam cum armaturis
proditionem ante Mursense proelium obligatum
gratia retineret Constantium, ut dubium tamen et
mutabilem verebatur, licet patris quoque Boniti
praetenderet fortia facta, Franci quidem sed pro
Constantini partibus in bello civili acriter contra
Licinianos saepe versati. 34. Evenerat autem

---

[1] *fidei et*, G in lac. of 22 letters ; two letters are erased
at the end.   [2] *Siluanum*, W²G ; *signorum*, Mommsen
(*signiorium*, B) ; *signarum*, V.

---

[1] Against Magnentius ; see note 2, p. 3.

likely to have results ; and in the end, after often changing our minds through fear, we resolved to search with the greatest pains for discreet representatives, to bind our communication with solemn oaths, and try to win over the Bracchiati and Cornuti, troops wavering in their allegiance and ready to be swayed by any influence for an ample bribe. 31. Accordingly, the matter was arranged through some common soldiers as go-betweens, men who through their very inconspicuousness were suited to accomplish it ; and just as sunrise was reddening the sky, a sudden group of armed men, fired by the expectation of rewards, burst forth ; and as usually happens in critical moments, made bolder by slaying the sentinels, they forced their way into the palace, dragged Silvanus from a chapel where he had in breathless fear taken refuge, while on his way to the celebration of a Christian service, and butchered him with repeated sword-thrusts.

32. So fell by this manner of death a general of no slight merits, who through fear due to the slanders in which he was ensnared during his absence by a clique of his enemies, in order to save his life had resorted to the uttermost measures of defence. 33. For although he held Constantius under obligation through gratitude for that timely act of coming over to his side with his soldiers before the battle of Mursa,[1] yet he feared him as variable and uncertain, although he could point also to the valiant deeds of his father Bonitus, a Frank it is true, but one who in the civil war often fought vigorously on the side of Constantine against the soldiers of Licinius. 34. Now it had happened that before

153

ut,[1] antequam huius modi aliquid agitaretur in Galliis, Romae in Circo maximo populus, incertum relatione [2] quadam percitus an praesagio, " Silvanus devictus est " magnis vocibus exclamaret.

35. Igitur Silvano Agrippinae (ut relatum est) interfecto, inaestimabili gaudio re cognita princeps, insolentia coalitus et tumore, hoc quoque felicitatis suae prosperis cursibus assignabat, eo more quo semper oderat fortiter facientes, ut quondam Domitianus, superare tamen quacumque arte contraria cupiebat. 36. Tantumque afuit laudare industrie gesta, ut etiam quaedam scriberet de Gallicanis intercepta thesauris, quos nemo attigerat. Idque scrutari iusserat artius interrogato Remigio, etiam tum rationario apparitionis armorum magistri, cui multo postea Valentiniani temporibus laques vitam in causa Tripolitanae legationis, eripuit. 37. Post quae ita completa, Constantius ut iam caelo contiguus, casibusque imperaturus humanis, magniloquentia sufflabatur adulatorum, quos augebat ipse spernendo proiciendoque id genus parum callentes, ut Croesum legimus ideo regno suo Solonem expulisse praecipitem, quia blandiri nesciebat ; et Dionysium intentasse poetae Philoxeno mortem, cum eum recitantem proprios versus absurdos et

---

[1] *ut antequam*, Traube, Clark (*ut* before *Siluanus*, BG ; before *Romae*, Val.) ; *tantae quam*, V.   [2] *relatione*, Bentley ; *ratione*, V.

---

[1] Cf. Gellius, xv. 18, for a similar prophecy.
[2] Cf. xxviii. 6, **7** and xxx. **2,** 9.
[3] Cf. Herodotus, i. 33.
[4] Cf. Diod. Sic. xv. **6,** and see Index.

anything of the kind was set on foot in Gaul, the
people at Rome in the Great Circus (whether excited by some story or by some presentiment is
uncertain) cried out with a loud voice : " Silvanus
is vanquished." [1]

35. Accordingly, when Silvanus had been slain
at Cologne, as has been related, the emperor learned
of it with inconceivable joy, and swollen with
vanity and pride, ascribed this also to the prosperous course of his own good fortune, in accordance
with the way in which he always hated brave and
energetic men, as Domitian did in times gone by,
yet tried to overcome them by every possible
scheme of opposition. 36. And so far was he from
praising conscientious service, that he actually wrote
that Ursicinus had embezzled funds from the Gallic
treasury, which no one had touched. And he had
ordered the matter to be closely examined, questioning Remigius, who at that time was already auditor
of the general's office of infantry supplies, and whose
fate it was, long afterwards, in the days of Valentinian, to take his life with the halter because of the
affair of the embassy from Tripoli.[2] 37. After this
turn of affairs, Constantius, as one that now touched
the skies with his head and would control all human
chances, was puffed up by the grandiloquence of
his flatterers, whose number he himself increased
by scorning and rejecting those who were not adepts
in that line ; as we read of Croesus,[3] that he drove
Solon headlong out of his kingdom for the reason
that he did not know how to flatter ; and of Dionysius, that he threatened the poet Philoxenus [4] with
death, because when the tyrant was reading aloud

155

inconcinnos, laudantibus cunctis, solus audiret
immobilis. 38. Quae res perniciosa vitiorum est
altrix. Ea demum enim laus grata esse potestati
debet excelsae, cum interdum et vituperationi secus
gestorum pateat locus.

6. *Silvani amici et conscii necati.*

1. Iamque post securitatem quaestiones agitabantur ex more, et vinculis catenisque plures ut noxii
plectebantur. Exsurgebat enim effervens laetitia
Paulus, tartareus ille delator, ad venenatas artes
suas licentius exercendas, et inquirentibus in negotium consistorianis atque militaribus (ut praeceptum
est) Proculus admovetur eculeo, Silvani domesticus,
homo gracilis et morbosus, metuentibus cunctis,
ne vi nimia tormentorum, levi corpore fatigato,
reos atrocium criminum promiscue citari faceret
multos. Verum contra quam speratum est contigit. 2. Memor enim somnii quo vetitus erat per
quietem (ut ipse firmavit) pulsare quendam insontem,
usque ad confinia mortis vexatus, nec nominavit
nec prodidit aliquem, sed asserebat factum Silvani
constanter, id eum cogitasse quod iniit, non cupiditate sed necessitate compulsum, argumento evidenti
demonstrans. 3. Causam enim probabilem ponebat
in medio, multorum testimoniis claram, quod die
quinto antequam infulas susciperet principatus,

156

his own silly and unrythmical verses, and every one
else applauded, the poet alone listened unmoved.
38. But this fault is a pernicious nurse of vices.
For praise ought to be acceptable in high places
only when opportunity is also sometimes given for
reproach of things ill done.

6. *The friends and accomplices of Silvanus are put to
death.*

1. And now after this relief the usual trials were
set on foot, and many men were punished with
bonds and chains, as malefactors. For up rose that
diabolical informer Paulus, bubbling over with joy,
to begin practising his venomous arts more freely ;
and when the councillors and officers (as was ordered)
inquired into the matter, Proculus, Silvanus' adju-
tant, was put upon the rack. Since he was a puny
and sickly man, every one feared that his slight
frame would yield to excessive torture, and that
he would cause many persons of all conditions to
be accused of heinous crimes. But the result was
not at all what was expected. 2. For mindful of
a dream, in which he was forbidden while asleep, as
he himself declared, to strike a certain innocent
person, although tortured to the very brink of death,
he neither named nor impeached anyone, but stead-
fastly defended the action of Silvanus, proving by
credible evidence that he had attempted his enterprise, not driven on from ambition, but compelled by
necessity. 3. For he brought forward a convincing
reason, made clear by the testimony of many persons,
namely, that four days before Silvanus assumed

157

donatum stipendio militem Constanti nomine allocutus est, fortis esset et fidus. Unde apparebat
quod si praesumere fortunae superioris insignia
conaretur, auri tam grave pondus largiretur [1] ut
suum. 4. Post hunc damnatorum sorte Poemenius
raptus ad supplicium interiit, qui (ut supra rettulimus) cum Treveri civitatem Caesari clausissent
Decentio, ad defendendam plebem electus est.
Tum Asclepiodotus et Lutto et Maudio comites
interempti sunt, aliique plures, haec et similia perplexe temporis obstinatione scrutante.

7. *Ab Leontio praefecto urbi populi R. seditiones
repressae. Liberius episcopus sede pulsus.*

1. Dum has exitiorum communium clades sus-
citat turbo feralis, urbem aeternam Leontius regens,
multa spectati iudicis documenta praebebat, in
audiendo celerior,[2] in disceptando iustissimus, natura
benevolus, licet auctoritatis causa servandae acer
quibusdam videbatur, et inclinatior ad damnandum.[3]
2. Prima igitur causa [4] seditionis in eum concitandae
vilissima fuit et levis. Philoromum enim aurigam
rapi praeceptum, secuta plebs omnis, velut defen-
sura proprium pignus, terribili impetu praefectum

---

[1] *largiretur*, Boxhorn, Val. ; *giretur*, V.   [2] *celerior*, or
celerrimus, Clark, c.c. ; *celeri*, V.   [3] *damnandum*,
Bentley, Erfurdt ; *amandum*, V.   [4] *causa*, vulgo ; *ars*,
BG ; *aut*, V.

---

[1] These were improvised for the occasion; see **5, 16**, at
the end.

[2] In one of the lost books.

158

the badges[1] of empire, he paid the soldiers and in Constantius' name exhorted them to be brave and loyal. From which it was clear that if he were planning to appropriate the insignia of a higher rank, he would have bestowed so great a quantity of gold as his own gift. 4. After him Poemenius, doomed like evil doers, was haled to execution and perished ; he was the man (as we have told above)[2] who was chosen to protect his fellow-citizens when Treves closed its gates against Decentius Caesar.[3] Then the counts Asclepiodotus, Lutto and Maudio were put to death, and many others, since the obduracy of the times made an intricate investigation into these and similar charges.

7. *Riots of the Roman people are suppressed by Leontius, prefect of the City. The Bishop Liberius is deposed.*

1. While the dire confusion was causing these calamities of general destruction, Leontius, governor of the Eternal City, gave many proofs of being an excellent judge ; for he was prompt in hearing cases, most just in his decisions, by nature kindly, although for the sake of maintaining his authority he seemed to some to be severe and too apt to condemn. 2. Now the first device for stirring up rebellion against him was very slight and trivial. For when the arrest of the charioteer Philoromus was ordered, all the commons followed, as if to defend their own darling, and with a formidable

[3] Decentius had been given the rank of Caesar by his brother Magnentius.

incessebat ut timidum, sed ille stabilis et erectus, immissis apparitoribus, correptos aliquos vexatosque tormentis, nec strepente ullo nec obsistente, insulari poena multavit. 3. Diebusque paucis secutis cum itidem plebs excita calore quo consuevit, vini causando inopiam, ad Septemzodium convenisset, celebrem locum, ubi operis ambitiosi Nymphaeum Marcus condidit imperator, illuc de industria pergens praefectus, ab omni toga apparitioneque rogabatur enixius, ne in multitudinem se arrogantem immitteret et minacem, ex commotione pristina saevientem ; difficilis ad pavorem, recta tetendit, adeo ut eum obsequentium pars [1] desereret, licet in periculum festinantem abruptum. 4. Insidens itaque vehiculo, cum speciosa fiducia contuebatur acribus oculis tumultuantium undique cuneorum, veluti serpentium vultus, perpessusque multa dici probrosa, agnitum quendam inter alios eminentem vasti corporis rutilique capilli, interrogavit, an ipse esset Petrus Valuomeres (ut audierat) cognomento ; eumque cum esse sonu respondisset obiurgatorio, ut seditiosorum antesignanum olim sibi compertum, reclamantibus multis, post [2] terga manibus vinctis, suspendi praecepit. 5. Quo viso sublimi, tribuliumque adiumentum nequicquam implorante, vulgus

---

[1] *obsequentium pars*, G ; *obsequens praefecturae apparitio*, Seeck ; *obsequen* (lac. of 12 letters), V.   [2] *pos*, V.

---

[1] Probably the well-known building of Severus at the south-eastern corner of the Palatine, named from the seven planets ; see Suet., *L.C.L.* ii. p. 321.

[2] Referring probably to the Septemzodium. See preceding note, and index, *s.v.* Marcus.

onslaught set upon the governor, thinking him to be
timid. But he, firm and resolute, sent his officers
among them—seized some and put them to the torture, and then without anyone protesting or opposing
him he punished them with exile to the islands.
3. And a few days later the people again, excited
with their usual passion, and alleging a scarcity of
wine, assembled at the Septemzodium,[1] a much frequented spot, where the emperor Marcus Aurelius
erected a Nymphaeum [2] of pretentious style. Thither
the governor resolutely proceeded, although earnestly
entreated by all his legal and official suite not to
trust himself to the self-confident and threatening
throng, which was still angry from the former disturbance ; but he, hard to frighten, kept straight
on, so boldly that a part of his following deserted him,
though he was hastening into imminent danger.
4. Then, seated in his carriage, with every appearance of confidence he scanned with keen eyes the
faces of the crowds in their tiers, raging on all sides
of him like serpents, and allowed many insults to be
hurled at him ; but recognising one fellow conspicuous among the rest, of huge stature and red-
headed, he asked him if he were not Peter, surnamed
Valuomeres, as he had heard. And when the man
had replied in insolent tones that he was none
other, the governor, who had known him of old as
the ringleader of the malcontents, in spite of the
outcries of many, gave orders to bind his hands
behind him and hang him up.[3] 5. On seeing him
aloft, vainly begging for the aid of his fellows, the

---

[3] To be flogged.

omne paulo ante confertum, per varia urbis membra
diffusum, ita evanuit ut turbarum acerrimus concitor, tamquam in iudiciali secreto exaratis lateribus,
ad Picenum eiceretur, ubi postea ausus eripere
virginis non obscurae pudorem, Patruini consularis
sententia supplicio est [1] capitali addictus.

6. Hoc administrante Leontio, Liberius Chri-
tianae legis antistes, a Constantio ad comitatum
mitti praeceptus est, tamquam imperatoriis iussis
et plurimorum sui consortium decretis obsistens,
in re quam brevi textu percurram. 7. Athanasium
episcopum eo tempore apud Alexandriam, ultra
professionem altius se efferentem, scitarique conatum externa, ut prodidere rumores assidui, coetus
in unum quaesitus eiusdem legis cultorum [2] (synodus
ut appellant) removit a sacramento quod optinebat.
8. Dicebatur enim fatidicarum sortium fidem,
quaeve augurales portenderent alites, scientissime
callens, aliquotiens praedixisse futura ; super his
intendebantur ei alia quoque, a proposito legis
abhorrentia cui praesidebat. 9. Hunc per sub-
scriptionem abicere sede sacerdotali, paria sentiens
ceteris, iubente principe Liberius monitus, persever-
anter renitebatur, nec visum hominem nec auditum
damnare nefas ultimum saepe exclamans, aperte

---

[1] *est*, W[2], vulgo ; *periit*, Eyssen. ; *oppetit*, Her. ; *ei id*,
V.   [2] *legis cultorum*, Kiessling ; *loci multorum*, V.

---

[1] At Mediolanum, where Constantius then was.

whole mob, until then crowded together, scattered through the various arteries of the city and vanished so completely that this most doughty promoter of riots had his sides well flogged, as if in a secret dungeon, and was banished to Picenum. There later he had the hardihood to offer violence to a maiden of good family, and, under sentence of the governor Patruinus, suffered capital punishment.

6. During the administration of this Leontius, a priest of the Christian religion, Liberius by name, by order of Constantius[1] was brought before the privy council on the charge of opposing the emperor's commands and the decrees of the majority of his colleagues in an affair which I shall run over briefly. 7. Athanasius, at that time bishop of Alexandria, was a man who exalted himself above his calling and tried to pry into matters outside his province, as persistent rumours revealed; therefore an assembly which had been convoked of members of that same sect—a synod, as they call it—deposed him from the rank that he held. 8. For it was reported that, being highly skilled in the interpretation of prophetic lots or of the omens indicated by birds, he had sometimes foretold future events; and besides this he was also charged with other practices repugnant to the purposes of the religion over which he presided. 9. Liberius, when directed by the emperor's order to depose him from his priesthood by endorsing the official decree, though holding the same opinion as the rest strenuously objected, crying out that it was the height of injustice to condemn a man unseen and unheard, thus, of course, openly defying the emperor's will.

scilicet recalcitrans imperatoris arbitrio. 10. Id
enim ille Athanasio semper infestus, licet sciret
impletum, tamen auctoritate quoque potiore aeternae urbis episcopi firmari desiderio nitebatur ardenti ;
quo non impetrato, Liberius aegre populi metu, qui
eius amore flagrabat, cum magna difficultate noctis
medio potuit asportari.

8. *Iulianus, Galli frater, a Constantio Aug. fratre
    patrueli Caesar creatur, ac praeficitur Galliae.*

1. Et haec quidem Romae (ut ostendit textus
superior) agebantur. Constantium vero exagitabant
assidui nuntii,[1] deploratas iam Gallias indicantes,
nullo renitente ad internecionem barbaris vastanti-
bus universa ; aestuansque diu qua vi propulsaret
aerumnas, ipse in Italia residens, ut cupiebat—
periculosum enim existimabat se in partem contru-
dere longe dimotam—repperit tandem consilium
rectum, et Iulianum patruelem fratrem haut ita
dudum ab Achaico tractu accitum, etiam tum
palliatum, in societatem imperii adsciscere cogitabat.
2. Id ubi, urgente malorum impendentium mole,
confessus est proximis, succumbere tot necessitatibus
tamque crebris unum se (quod numquam fecerat)
aperte demonstrans, illi in assentationem nimiam

[1] *nuntii*, added by W²N²BG ; *rumores*, Traube ; V
omits.

---

[1] One of the earliest indications of the growing importance of the Roman bishops.
[2] Cf. Zosimus, iii. 1 ff.
[3] The *pallium* was the characteristic Greek cloak,
worn among others by students.

10. For although Constantius, who was always hostile to Athanasius, knew that the matter had been carried out, yet he strove with eager desire to have it ratified also by the higher power of the bishop of the Eternal City ; [1] and since he could not obtain this, Liberius was spirited away, but only with the greatest difficulty and in the middle of the night, for fear of the populace, who were devotedly attached to him.

8. *Julian, brother of Gallus, is appointed Caesar by his cousin Constantius Augustus, and given command over Gaul.*

1. This, then, was the situation at Rome, as the preceding text has shown. But Constantius was disquieted by frequent messages reporting that Gaul was in desperate case, since the savages were ruinously devastating everything without opposition. And after worrying for a long time how he might forcibly avert these disasters, while himself remaining in Italy as he desired—for he thought it risky to thrust himself into a far-distant region— he at length hit upon the right plan and thought of associating with himself in a share of the empire his cousin Julian,[2] who not so very long before had been summoned from the district of Achaia and still wore his student's cloak.[3]

2. When Constantius, driven by the weight of impending calamities, admitted his purpose to his intimates, openly declaring (what he had never done before) that in his lone state he was giving way before so many and such frequent crises, they,

165

eruditi, infatuabant hominem,[1] nihil esse ita asperum
dictitantes, quod praepotens eius virtus, fortunaque
tam vicina sideribus, non superaret ex more. Adde-
bantque noxarum conscientia stimulante complures,
deinceps caveri debere Caesaris nomen, replicantes
gesta sub Gallo. 3. Quis annitentibus obstinate
opponebat se sola regina, incertum migrationem ad
longinqua pertimescens, an pro nativa prudentia
consulens in commune, omnibusque memorans
anteponi debere propinquum. Post multa itaque [2]
per deliberationes ambiguas actitata, stetit fixa
sententia, abiectisque disputationibus irritis, ad
imperium placuit Iulianum assumere. 4. Et cum
venisset accitus, praedicto die advocato omni quod
aderat commilitio, tribunali ad altiorem suggestum
erecto, quod aquilae circumdederunt et signa,
Augustus insistens [3] eumque manu retinens dextera,
haec sermone placido peroravit:

5. "Adsistimus apud vos—optimi rei publicae
defensores—causae communi uno paene omnium
spiritu vindicandae, quam acturus tamquam apud
aequos iudices succinctius edocebo. 6. Post interitum rebellium tyrannorum, quos ad haec temptanda
quae moverunt, rabies egit et furor, velut impiis
eorum manibus Romano sanguine parentantes,
persultant barbari Gallias, rupta limitum pace;

[1] *infatuabant hominem*, V; *infatuabant imperatorem,
spirantem iam ultra hominem*, Her. [2] *multa itaque*,
Novák; *multaque*, V. [3] *insistens*, Val., Haupt;
inscendens, G; *insiginens*, V.

---

[1] I.e. their offences against Julian, which made them
fear his rise to greater power.

being trained to excessive flattery, tried to cajole him, constantly repeating that there was nothing so difficult that his surpassing ability and a good fortune so nearly celestial could not overcome as usual. And several, since the consciousness of their offences [1] pricked them on, added that the title of Caesar ought henceforth to be avoided, rehearsing what had happened under Gallus. 3. To them in their obstinate resistance the queen alone opposed herself, whether she dreaded journeying to a far country or with her native intelligence took counsel for the common good, and she declared that a kinsman ought to be preferred to every one else. So, after much bandying the matter to and fro in fruitless deliberations, the emperor's resolution stood firm, and setting aside all bootless discussion, he decided to admit Julian to a share in the imperial power. 4. So when he had been summoned and had arrived, on an appointed day all his fellow-soldiers there present were called together, and a platform was erected on a lofty scaffolding, surrounded by the eagles and the standards. On this Augustus stood, and holding Julian by the right hand, in a quiet tone delivered the following address :

5. "We stand before you, valiant defenders of our country, to avenge the common cause with one all but unanimous spirit ; and how I shall accomplish this I shall briefly explain to you, as impartial judges. 6. After the death of those rebellious tyrants whom mad fury drove to attempt the designs which they projected, the savages, as if sacrificing to their wicked Manes with Roman blood, have forced our peaceful frontier and are

167

hac animati fiducia, quod nos per disiunctissimas terras arduae necessitates adstringunt. 7. Huic igitur malo ultra apposita iam proserpenti, si dum patitur tempus, occurrerit nostri vestrique consulti suffragium, et colla superbarum gentium detumescent, et imperii fines erunt intacti. Restat ut venturorum [1] spem quam gero secundo roboretis effectu. 8. Iulianum hunc fratrem meum patruelem (ut nostis,) verecundia qua nobis ita ut necessitudine carus est, recte spectatum, iamque elucentis industriae iuvenem, in Caesaris adhibere potestatem exopto, coeptis (si videntur utilia) etiam vestra consensione firmandis."

9. Dicere super his plura conantem, interpellans contio lenius prohibebat, arbitrium summi numinis id esse non mentis humanae velut praescia venturi proclamans.[2] 10. Stansque imperator immobilis dum silerent, residua fidentius explicavit : " Quia igitur vestrum quoque favorem adesse fremitus indicat laetus, adulescens vigoris tranquilli, cuius temperati mores imitandi sunt potius quam praedicandi, ad honorem prosperante deo delatum [3] exsurgat ; cuius praeclaram indolem bonis artibus institutam, hoc ipso plene videor exposuisse quod elegi. Ergo eum, praesente nutu dei caelestis, amictu principali velabo."

11. Dixit moxque indutum avita purpura Iulianum,

---

[1] *ut uenturorum,* Her., cf. xxi. 10. 2 ; *rotorum,* Hagendahl; *ucturum,* V. [2] *proclamans,* W[2], Clark, c.c. ; *praedans,* V. [3] *prosperante deo delatum,* Novák, cf. xviii. 6, 3, etc., pro *re speratum,* Her. ; *prope speratum,* V.

over-running Gaul, encouraged by the belief that dire straits beset us throughout our far-flung empire. 7. If this evil therefore, which is already creeping on beyond set bounds, is met by the accord of our and your wills while time permits, the necks of these proud tribes will not swell so high, and the frontiers of our empire will remain inviolate. It remains for you to confirm with happy issue the hope of the future which I cherish. 8. This Julian, my cousin as you know, rightly honoured for the modesty through which he is as dear to us as through ties of blood, a young man of ability which is already conspicuous, I desire to admit to the rank of Caesar, and that this project, if it seems advantageous, may be confirmed also by your assent."

9. As he was attempting to say more to this effect, the assembly interrupted and gently prevented him, declaring as if with foreknowledge of the future that this was the will of the supreme divinity rather than of any human mind. 10. And the emperor, standing motionless until they became silent, went on with the rest of his speech with greater assurance : " Since, then," said he, " your joyful acclaim shows that I have your approval also, let this young man of quiet strength, whose temperate behaviour is rather to be imitated than proclaimed, rise to receive this honour conferred upon him by God's favour. His excellent disposition, trained in all good arts, I seem to have fully described by the very fact that I have chosen him. Therefore with the immediate favour of the God of Heaven I will invest him with the imperial robes."

11. This he said and then, after having clothed

169

et Caesarem cum exercitus gaudio declaratum, his alloquitur contractiore vultu submaestum :

12. "Recepisti primaevus originis tuae splendidum florem, amantissime mihi omnium frater; aucta gloria mea, confiteor, qui iustius in deferenda suppari [1] potestate nobilitati mihi propinquae, quam ipsa potestate videor esse sublimis. 13. Adesto igitur laborum periculorumque particeps, et tutelam ministerii suscipe Galliarum, omni beneficentia partes levaturus afflictas : et si hostilibus congredi sit necesse, fixo gradu consiste inter signiferos ipsos, audendi in tempore consideratus hortator, pugnantes accendens praeeundo cautissime, turbatosque subsidiis fulciens, modesteque [2] increpans desides, verissimus testis adfuturus industriis et ignavis. 14. Proinde urgente rei magnitudine, perge vir fortis, ducturus viros itidem fortes. Aderimus nobis vicissim amoris robusta constantia, militabimus simul, una orbem pacatum, deus modo velit quod oramus, pari moderatione pietateque recturi. Mecum ubique videberis praesens, et ego tibi quodcumque acturo non deero. Ad summam i, propera sociis omnium votis, velut assignatam tibi ab ipsa re publica, stationem cura pervigili defensurus."

[1] *suppari*, Cornelissen ; *superari*, V. [2] *modesteque*, Clark ; *modeste* **** (formerly *quid*), V.

Julian in the ancestral purple and proclaimed him Caesar to the joy of the army, he thus addressed him, somewhat melancholy in aspect as he was, and with careworn countenance :

12. " My brother, dearest to me of all men, you have received in your prime the glorious flower of your origin ; with increase of my own glory, I admit, since I seem to myself more truly great in bestowing almost equal power on a noble prince who is my kinsman, than through that power itself. 13. Come, then, to share in pains and perils, and undertake the charge of defending Gaul, ready to relieve the afflicted regions with every bounty. And if it becomes necessary to engage with the enemy, take your place with sure footing amid the standard-bearers themselves ; be a thoughtful advisor of daring in due season, animate the warriors by taking the lead with utmost caution, strengthen them when in disorder with reinforcements, modestly rebuke the slothful, and be present as a most faithful witness at the side of the strong, as well as of the weak. 14. Therefore, urged by the great crisis, go forth, yourself a brave man, ready to lead men equally brave. We shall stand by each other in turn with firm and steadfast affection, we shall campaign at the same time, and together we shall rule over a pacified world, provided only God grants our prayers, with equal moderation and conscientiousness. You will seem to be present with me everywhere, and I shall not fail you in whatever you undertake. In fine, go, hasten, with the united prayers of all, to defend with sleepless care the post assigned you, as it were, by your country herself."

15. Nemo post haec finita reticuit, sed militares omnes horrendo fragore scuta genibus illidentes (quod est prosperitatis indicium plenum ; nam contra cum hastis clipei feriuntur, irae documentum est et doloris)[1] immane quo quantoque gaudio praeter paucos Augusti probavere iudicium, Caesaremque admiratione digna suscipiebant, imperatorii muricis fulgore flagrantem. 16. Cuius oculos cum venustate terribilis, vultumque excitatius gratum, diu multumque contuentes, qui futurus sit colligebant velut scrutatis veteribus libris, quorum lectio per corporum signa pandit animorum interna. Eumque ut potiori reverentia servaretur, nec supra modum laudabant, nec infra quam decebat, atque ideo censorum voces sunt aestimatae, non militum. 17. Susceptus denique ad consessum vehiculi, receptusque in regiam, hunc versum ex Homerico carmine susurrabat :

ἔλλαβε πορφύρεος θάνατος καὶ μοῖρα κραταιή.

Haec diem octavum iduum Novembrium gesta sunt, cum Arbetionem consulem annus haberet et Lollianum. 18. Deinde diebus paucis Helena virgine, Constanti sorore, eidem Caesari iugali foedere

---

[1] Damsté regards *nam contra . . . doloris* as a gloss and incorrect, citing xx. **5**, 8 ; xxi. **5**, 9. Cf. Pighi, *Nov. Stud. Amm.* p. 62.

---

[1] See critical note.
[2] Cf. Gellius, i. 9, 2, (*Pythagoras*) *iam a principio adules-*

15. After this address was ended, no one held his peace, but all the soldiers with fearful din struck their shields against their knees (this is a sign of complete approval; for when, on the contrary, they smite their shields with their spears it is an indication of anger and resentment),[1] and it was wonderful with what great joy all but a few approved Augustus' choice and with due admiration welcomed the Caesar, brilliant with the gleam of the imperial purple. 16. Gazing long and earnestly on his eyes, at once terrible and full of charm, and on his face attractive in its unusual animation, they divined what manner of man he would be, as if they had perused those ancient books, the reading of which discloses from bodily signs the inward qualities of the soul.[2] And that he might be regarded with the greater respect, they neither praised him beyond measure nor less than was fitting, and therefore their words were esteemed as those of censors, not of soldiers. 17. Finally, he was taken up to sit with the emperor in his carriage and conducted to the palace, whispering this verse from the Homeric song [3] :

" By purple death I'm seized and fate supreme."

This happened on the sixth of November of the year when Arbetio and Lollianus were consuls. 18. Then, within a few days, Helena, the maiden sister of Constantius, was joined in the bonds of wedlock to the Caesar ; and when everything had

---

centes ἐφυσιογνωμόνει. Id verbum significat, mores ... de oris et vultus ingenio . . . sciscitari.

[3] Iliad, v. 83; cf. § 20; a play on πορφύρεος as the colour of blood and of royalty.

CONSTANTIUS ET GALLUS

copulata, paratisque universis quae maturitas pro-
ficiscendi poscebat, comitatu parvo suscepto, kalen-
dis Decembribus egressus est deductusque ab
Augusto ad usque locum duabus columnis insignem,
qui Laumellum interiacet et Ticinum, itineribus
rectis Taurinos pervenit, ubi nuntio percellitur
gravi, qui nuper in comitatum Augusti perlatus,
de industria silebatur, ne parata diffluerent. 19. Indicabat autem Coloniam Agrippinam, ampli nominis
urbem in secunda Germania, pertinaci barbarorum
obsidione reseratam magnis viribus et deletam.
20. Quo maerore perculsus, velut primo adventantium malorum auspicio, murmurans querulis vocibus
saepe audiebatur : nihil se plus assecutum, quam ut
occupator interiret. 21. Cumque Viennam venisset, ingredientem optatum quidem et impetrabilem [1]
honorifice susceptura omnis aetas concurrebat et
dignitas, proculque visum plebs universa, cum
vicinitate finitima, imperatorem clementem appellans et faustum, praevia consonis laudibus celebra-
bat, avidius pompam regiam in principe legitimo
cernens : communiumque remedium aerumnarum
in eius locabat adventu, salutarem quendam genium
affulsisse conclamatis negotiis arbitrata. 22. Tunc
anus quaedam orba luminibus, cum percontando
quinam esset ingressus, Iulianum Caesarem comperisset, exclamavit hunc deorum templa repara-
turum.

[1] *impetrabilem*, Val. ; *insperabilem*, Pet. ; *imperabilem*,
V.

been prepared which the imminence of his departure demanded, taking a small suite, he set out on the first of December, escorted by Augustus as far as the spot marked by two columns, lying between Laumello and Pavia, and came by direct marches to Turin. There he was staggered by serious news, which had lately been brought to the emperor's court but had purposely been kept secret, for fear that the preparations might come to nothing. 19. The news stated that Cologne, a city of great renown in Lower Germany, after an obstinate siege by the savages in great force, had been stormed and destroyed. 20. Overwhelmed by sorrow at this, the first omen, as it were, of approaching ills, he was often heard to mutter in complaining tones that he had gained nothing, except to die with heavier work. 21. But when he reached Vienne and entered the city, all ages and ranks flocked together to receive him with honour, as a man both longed for and efficient; and when they saw him afar off, the whole populace with the immediate neighbourhood, saluted him as a commander gracious and fortunate, and marched ahead of him with a chorus of praise, the more eagerly beholding royal pomp in a legitimate prince. And in his coming they placed the redress of their common disasters, thinking that some helpful spirit had shone upon their desperate condition. 22. Then an old woman, who had lost her sight, on inquiring who had entered and learning that it was the Caesar Julian, cried out that he would repair the temples of the Gods.

CONSTANTIUS ET GALLUS

9. *De origine Gallorum; et unde dicti Celtae ac Galatae; deque eorum doctoribus.*

1. Proinde quoniam—ut Mantuanus vates praedixit excelsus—"maius opus moveo"[1] maiorque mihi rerum nascitur ordo, Galliarum tractus et situm ostendere puto nunc tempestivum, ne inter procinctus ardentes, proeliorumque varios casus, ignota quibusdam expediens imitari videar desides nauticos, attrita lintea cum rudentibus, quae licuit parari securius, inter fluctus resarcire coactos et tempestates. 2. Ambigentes super origine prima Gallorum, scriptores veteres notitiam reliquere negotii semiplenam, sed postea Timagenes, et diligentia Graecus et lingua, haec quae diu sunt ignorata collegit ex multiplicibus libris. Cuius fidem secuti, obscuritate dimota, eadem distincte docebimus et aperte. 3. Aborigines primos in his regionibus quidam visos esse firmarunt, Celtas nomine regis amabilis et matris eius vocabulo Galatas dictos—ita enim Gallos sermo Graecus appellat—alii Dorienses antiquiorem secutos Herculem oceani locos inhabitasse confines. 4. Drysidae memorant re vera fuisse

[1] So the text of Ammianus; see note on translation.

---

[1] *Aen.* vii. 44 f, *maior rerum mihi nascitur ordo, Maius opus moveo.*

[2] Timagenes of Alexandria, who, according to Suidas, was brought to Rome as a prisoner of war by Pompey. He wrote a *History of Alexander* and a *History of the Gauls.* Cf. Hor., *Epist.* i. 19, 15; Quint., i. 10, 10; x. i. 75.

[3] "Earlier" seems to be contrasted with "the son of Amphytrion" in **9,** 6, below and "the Theban Hercules" in **10,** 9, whom Ammianus identifies with the son of Amphytrion. The story of a hero similar to Hercules is found in

176

9. *Of the origin of the Gauls ; and why the Celts and Galatians were so called ; and of their learned men.*

1. Now, since—as the lofty bard of Mantua said of old [1]—a greater work I undertake, a greater train of events ariseth before me, I think now a suitable time to describe the regions and situation of the Gauls, for fear that amid fiery encounters and shifting fortunes of battle I may treat of matters unknown to some and seem to follow the example of slovenly sailors, who are forced amid surges and storms to mend their worn sails and rigging, which might have been put in order with less danger. 2. The ancient writers, in doubt as to the earliest origin of the Gauls, have left an incomplete account of the matter, but later Timagenes,[2] a true Greek in accuracy as well as language, collected out of various books these facts that had been long forgotten ; which, following his authority, and avoiding any obscurity, I shall state clearly and plainly. 3. Some asserted that the people first seen in these regions were Aborigines, called Celts from the name of a beloved king, and Galatae (for so the Greek language terms the Gauls) from the name of his mother. Others stated that the Dorians, following the earlier Hercules,[3] settled in the lands bordering on the Ocean. 4. The

Greece, Italy, Egypt, the Orient, and among the Celts and Germans. Cicero, *De Nat. Deor.* iii. 16, 42, names six Herculeses, Serv., *ad Aen.* viii. 564, four : the Tirynthian, Argive, Theban, and Libyan. The Theban Hercules is generally regarded as the son of Amphitryon, but the one here referred to seems to have been the Italic hero, locally called Recaranus and Garanus, who was later identified with the Greek Heracles.

populi partem indigenam, sed alios quoque ab insulis extimis confluxisse et [1] tractibus transrhenanis, crebritate bellorum et alluvione fervidi maris sedibus suis expulsos. 5. Aiunt quidam paucos post excidium Troiae fugitantes Graecos ubique dispersos loca haec occupasse tunc vacua. 6. Regionum autem incolae id magis omnibus asseverant, quod etiam nos legimus in monumentis eorum incisum, Amphitryonis filium Herculem ad Geryonis et Taurisci saevum [2] tyrannorum perniciem festinasse, quorum alter Hispanias, alter Gallias infestabat; superatisque ambobus, coisse cum generosis feminis suscepisseque liberos plures, et eos partes quibus imperitabant suis nominibus appellasse. 7. A Phocaea vero Asiaticus populus, Harpali inclementiam vitans, Cyri regis praefecti, Italiam navigio petit. Cuius pars in Lucania Veliam, alia condidit in Viennensi Massiliam : dein secutis aetatibus oppida, aucta virium copia, instituere non pauca. Sed declinanda varietas saepe satietati coniuncta. 8. Per haec loca hominibus paulatim excultis, viguere studia laudabilium doctrinarum, inchoata per bardos et euhagis et drysidas. Et Bardi quidem fortia virorum illustrium facta, heroicis composita versibus,

---

[1] *et*, G ; *ex*, V.   [2] *saeuum*, V, Norden (cf. xxix. 5, 48) ; *saevium*, Val., Clark ; *saevorum*, BG.

---

[1] Druids.
[2] An error for Harpagus, see Index.
[3] Modern Castellamare della Bruca.
[4] Marseilles.

Drysidae [1] say that a part of the people was in fact indigenous, but that others also poured in from the remote islands and the regions across the Rhine, driven from their homes by continual wars and by the inundation of the stormy sea. 5. Some assert that after the destruction of Troy a few of those who fled from the Greeks and were scattered everywhere occupied those regions, which were then deserted. 6. But the inhabitants of those countries affirm this beyond all else, and I have also read it inscribed upon their monuments, that Hercules, the son of Amphytrion, hastened to destroy the cruel tyrants Geryon and Tauriscus, of whom one oppressed Spain, the other, Gaul; and having overcome them both that he took to wife some high-born women and begat numerous children, who called by their own names the districts which they ruled. 7. But in fact a people of Asia from Phocaea, to avoid the severity of Harpalus, [2] prefect of king Cyrus, set sail for Italy. A part of them founded Velia [3] in Lucania, the rest, Massilia [4] in the region of Vienne. Then in subsequent ages they established no small number of towns, as their strength and resources increased. But I must not discuss varying opinions, which often causes satiety. 8. Throughout these regions men gradually grew civilised and the study of the liberal arts flourished, initiated by the Bards, the Euhages and the Druids. [5] Now, the Bards sang to the sweet strains of the lyre the valorous deeds of famous men composed in heroic

[5] The three are connected also by Strabo (iv. 4. 4), who says that the *bards* were poets; the *euhages* (Οὐάτεις), diviners and natural philosophers; while the Druids studied both natural and moral philosophy. *L.C.L.* ii. p. 245.

cum dulcibus lyrae modulis cantitarunt, Euhages
vero scrutantes sublimia, leges [1] naturae pandere
conabantur internas.[2] Drysidae ingeniis celsiores, ut
auctoritas Pythagorae decrevit, sodaliciis astricti
consortiis, quaestionibus occultarum rerum altar-
umque erecti sunt, et despectantes humana, pro-
nuntiarunt animas immortales.

10. *De Alpibus Gallicanis ; et de variis per eas
itineribus.*

1. Hanc Galliarum plagam ob suggestus montium
arduos, et horrore nivali semper obductos, orbis
residui incolis antehac paene ignotam, nisi qua
litoribus est vicina, munimina claudunt undique
natura velut arte circumdata. 2. Et a latere quidem australi, Tyrrheno alluitur et Gallico mari ;
qua caeleste suspicit plaustrum, a feris gentibus
fluentis distinguitur Rheni ; ubi occidentali subiecta
est sideri, oceano et altitudine Pyrenaea arcetur ;[3]
unde ad solis ortus attollitur, aggeribus cedit
Alpium Cottiarum ; quas rex Cottius perdomitis
Galliis, solus in angustiis latens, inviaque locorum

---

[1] *sublimia, leges naturae*, Novák ; *serviani et sublimia
naturae*, V. [2] *internas*, Novák ; *inter es*, V.
[3] *Pyrenaea arcetur*, Clark ; *Pyrenaei saltus urgetur*,
F. Walter ; *pyrenei surgitur*, V.

---

[1] Properly, Vates (Οὐάτεις)
[2] The *septentriones*, the constellation of *ursa major*,
representing the north.

verse, but the Euhages,[1] investigating the sublime, attempted to explain the secret laws of nature. The Druids, being loftier than the rest in intellect, and bound together in fraternal organisations, as the authority of Pythagoras determined, were elevated by their investigation of obscure and profound subjects, and scorning all things human, pronounced the soul immortal.

10. *Of the Gallic Alps and the various passes through them.*

1. This country of Gaul, because of its lofty chains of mountains always covered with formidable snows, was formerly all but unknown to the inhabitants of the rest of the globe, except where it borders on the coast ; and bulwarks enclose it on every side, surrounding it naturally, as if by the art of man. 2. Now on the southern side it is washed by the Tuscan and the Gallic Sea ; where it looks up to the heavenly Wain,[2] it is separated from the wild nations by the channels[3] of the Rhine. Where it lies under the west-sloping sun[4] it is bounded by the Ocean and the Pyrenaean heights ; and where it rises towards the East it gives place to the bulk of the Cottian Alps. There King Cottius, after the subjugation of Gaul, lay hidden alone in their defiles, trusting to the pathless ruggedness of the

[3] As it enters the sea, the Rhine divides into several branches.

[4] As there is no specific western constellation, *sidus* seems to mean "sun"; cf. Pliny, *N.H.* ii. 12; etc., and *solis ortus*, below, of the east.

asperitate confisus, lenito tandem tumore, in amicitiam principis Octaviani receptus [1] molibus magnis exstruxit, ad vicem memorabilis muneris, compendiarias et viantibus opportunas, medias inter alias Alpes vetustas, super quibus comperta paulo postea referemus. 3. In his Alpibus Cottiis, quarum initium a Segusione est oppido, praecelsum erigitur iugum, nulli fere sine discrimine penetrabile. 4. Est enim e Galliis venientibus prona humilitate devexum, pendentium saxorum altrinsecus visu terribile praesertim verno tempore,[2] cum liquente gelu nivibusque solutis flatu calidiore ventorum, per diruptas utrimque angustias et lacunas, pruinarum congerie latebrosas, descendentes cunctantibus plantis homines et iumenta procidunt et carpenta ; idque remedium ad arcendum exitium repertum est solum, quod pleraque vehicula vastis funibus illigata pone cohibente virorum vel boum nisu valido vix gressu reptante, paulo tutius devolvuntur. Et haec (ut diximus) anni verno contingunt. 5. Hieme vero humus crustata frigoribus et tamquam levigata ideoque labilis incessum praecipitantem impellit ; et patulae valles per spatia plana glacie perfidae vorant non numquam transeuntes. Ob quae locorum callidi eminentes ligneos stilos per cautiora loca defigunt, ut eorum series viatorem ducat innoxium ; qui si

---

[1] *principis* after *receptus*, V ; deleted by Damsté, obelized by Clark c.c. ; transposed by Novák before *Octaviani; principiis*, Her. [2] *tepore*, Damsté ; *tempore*, V.

region ; finally, when his disaffection was allayed, and he was admitted to the emperor Octavian's friendship, in lieu of a remarkable gift he built with great labour short cuts convenient to travellers, since they were midway between other ancient Alpine passes, about which I shall later tell what I have learned. 3. In these Cottian Alps, which begin at the town of Susa, there rises a lofty ridge, which scarcely anyone can cross without danger. 4. For as one comes from Gaul it falls off with sheer incline, terrible to look upon because of overhanging cliffs on either side, especially in the season of spring, when the ice melts and the snows thaw under the warmer breath of the wind ; then over precipitous ravines on either side and chasms rendered treacherous through the accumulation of ice, men and animals descending with hesitating step slide forward, and waggons as well. And the only expedient that has been devised to ward off destruction is this : they bind together a number of vehicles with heavy ropes and hold them back from behind with powerful efforts of men or oxen at barely a snail's pace ; and so they roll down a little more safely. And this, as we have said, happens in the spring of the year. 5. But in winter the ground, caked with ice, and as it were polished and therefore slippery, drives men headlong in their gait and the spreading valleys in level places, made treacherous by ice, sometimes swallow up the traveller. Therefore those that know the country well drive projecting wooden stakes along the safer spots, in order that their line may guide the traveller in safety. But if these are covered with snow and

nivibus operti latuerint, aut montanis [1] defluentibus
rivis eversi, calles [2] agrestibus praeviis difficile per-
vadunt. 6. A summitate autem huius Italici clivi,
planities ad usque stationem nomine Martis per
septem extenditur milia, et hinc alia celsitudo
erectior, aegreque superabilis, ad Matronae porrigitur verticem, cuius vocabulum casus feminae
nobilis dedit. Unde declive quidem iter sed ex-
peditius ad usque castellum Brigantiam patet. 7.
Huius sepulcrum reguli, quem itinera struxisse rettulimus, Segusione est moenibus proximum, manes-
que eius ratione gemina religiose [3] coluntur, quod
iusto moderamine rexerat suos, et asscitus in societatem rei Romanae, quietem genti praestitit sem-
piternam. 8. Et licet haec quam diximus viam
media sit et compendiaria, magisque celebris, tamen
etiam aliae multo antea temporibus sunt con-
structae diversis. 9. Et primam Thebaeus Hercules, ad Geryonem exstinguendum (ut relatum est)
et Tauriscum lenius gradiens, prope maritimas
composuit Alpes, hisque [4] Graiarum [5] indidit nomen ;
Monoeci similiter arcem et portum ad perennem sui
memoriam consecravit. Deinde emensis postea saeculis multis, hac ex causa sunt Alpes excogitatae
Poeninae. 10. Superioris Africani pater Publius

---

[1] *aut montanis*, W[2], Bentley ; *montanisue*, Kellerbauer ;
montanis, V.   [2] *calles*, Pet. ; *glacies*, Bentley ; *gnaris*,
Haupt ; *graves*, V.   [3] *religiose*, vulgo ; *religione*, V.
[4] *hisque*, T, Val. ; *hique*, V.   [5] *Graiarum*, Val. ; *harum*,
V, Gardt.

hidden, or are overturned by the streams running down from the mountains, the paths are difficult to traverse even with natives leading the way. 6. But from the peak of this Italian slope a plateau extends for seven miles, as far as the post named from Mars [1]; from there on another loftier height, equally difficult to surmount, reaches to the peak of the Matrona,[2] so called from an accident to a noble lady. After that a route, steep to be sure, but easier to traverse extends to the fortress of Briançon. 7. The tomb of the prince, who, as we said, built these roads, is at Susa next to the walls, and his shades are devoutly venerated for a double reason : because he had ruled his subjects with a just government, and when admitted to alliance with the Roman state, procured eternal peace for his nation. 8. And although this road which I have described is the middle one, the short cut, and the more frequented, yet there are also others, constructed long before at various times. 9. Now the first of these the Theban Hercules,[3] when travelling leisurely to destroy Geryon and Tauriscus, constructed near the Maritime Alps and gave them the name of the Graian [4] Alps. And in like manner he consecrated the castle and harbour of Monaco to his lasting memory. Then, later, after the passage of many centuries, the name Pennine was devised for these Alps for the following reason. 10. Publius Cornelius Scipio,

---

[1] Modern Oulx, in the *Ant. Itin.* called *mansio Martis ;* in the *Itin. Burdigalense, ad Martis.* Amm. uses *statio* both of a military post, and of a station on the *cursus publicus,* but see Hyde, *R. Alp. Routes,* p. 59.

[2] Mont Genèvre.   [3] See note, p. 176.

[4] " Grecian," but see Hyde, *R. Alpine Routes,* p. 59.

CONSTANTIUS ET GALLUS

Cornelius Scipio, Saguntinis memorabilibus aerumnis et fide, pertinaci destinatione Afrorum obsessis, iturus auxilio, in Hispaniam traduxit onustam manu valida classem, sed civitate potiore Marte deleta, Hannibalem sequi nequiens, triduo ante transito Rhodano, ad partes Italiae contendentem, navigatione veloci intercurso spatio maris haut longo, degressurum montibus apud Genuam observabat, Liguriae oppidum, ut cum eo (si copiam fors dedisset) viarum asperitate fatigato decerneret in planitie. 11. Consulens tamen rei communi, Cn. Scipionem fratrem ire monuit in Hispanias, ut Hasdrubalem exinde similiter erupturum arceret. Quae Hannibal doctus a perfugis, ut erat expeditae mentis et callidae, Taurinis ducentibus accolis, per Tricasinos et oram Vocontiorum extremam, ad saltus Tricorios venit. Indeque exorsus, aliud iter antehac insuperabile fecit ; excisaque rupe in immensum elata, quam cremando vi magna flammarum acetoque infuso dissolvit, per Druentiam flumen, gurgitibus vagis intutum, regiones occupavit Etruscas. Hactenus super Alpibus. Nunc ad restantia veniamus.

---

[1] That is, the Carthaginians, in 218 B.C. See Hyde, pp. 197 ff.

[2] After a siege of eight months.

[3] Cf. Livy, xxi. 37, 1-3 ; Juvenal, x. 153 ; etc. Pliny, *N.H.* xxiii. 57, attributes this power to vinegar, but Polybius does not mention the story, which is doubted for various reasons.

father of the elder Africanus, when the Saguntines, famous both for their catastrophies and their loyalty, were besieged by the Africans [1] with persistent obstinacy, wishing to help them, crossed to Spain with a fleet manned by a strong army. But as the city had been destroyed by a superior force,[2] and he was unable to overtake Hannibal, who had crossed the Rhone three days before and was hastening to the regions of Italy, by swift sailing he crossed the intervening space—which is not great—and watched at Genoa, a town of Liguria, for Hannibal's descent from the mountains, so that if chance should give him the opportunity, he might fight with him in the plain while exhausted by the roughness of the roads. 11. At the same time, having an eye to the common welfare, he advised his brother, Gnaeus Scipio, to proceed to Spain and hold off Hasdrubal, who was planning to burst forth in like manner from that quarter. But Hannibal learned of this from deserters, and being of a nimble and crafty wit, came, under the guidance of natives from among the Taurini, through the Tricasini and the extreme edge of the Vocontii to the passes of the Tricorii. Starting out from there, he made another road, where it hitherto had been impassable; he hewed out a cliff which rose to a vast height by burning it with flames of immense power and crumbling it by pouring on vinegar;[3] then he marched along the river Druentia, dangerous with its shifting eddies, and seized upon the district of Etruria. So much about the Alps; let us now turn to the rest of the country.

CONSTANTIUS ET GALLUS

11. *Brevis divisio ac descriptio Galliarum; et cursus fluminis Rhodani.*

1. Temporibus priscis, cum laterent hae partes ut barbarae, tripertitae fuisse creduntur in Celtas eosdemque Gallos divisae, et Aquitanos et Belgas, lingua institutis legibusque discrepantes. 2. Et Gallos quidem (qui Celtae sunt) ab Aquitanis Garumna disterminat flumen, a Pyrenaeis oriens collibus, postque oppida multa transcursa, in oceano delitescens. 3. Belgis vero eandem gentem Matrona discindit et Sequana, amnes magnitudinis geminae; qui fluentes per Lugdunensem, post circumclausum ambitu insulari Parisiorum castellum, Lutetiam nomine, consociati, meantesque protinus prope castra Constantia funduntur in mare. 4. Horum omnium apud veteres Belgae dicebantur esse fortissimi, ea propter quod ab humaniore cultu longe discreti, nec adventiciis effeminati deliciis, diu cum transrhenanis certavere Germanis. 5. Aquitani enim, ad quorum litora ut proxima placidaque, merces adventiciae convehuntur, moribus ad mollitiem lapsis, facile in dicionem venere Romanam. 6. Regebantur autem Galliae omnes, iam inde uti crebritate bellorum urgenti cessere Iulio dictatori, potestate in partes divisa quattuor, quarum Narbonensis una Viennensem intra se continebat et Lugdunensem; altera Aquitanis praeerat universis;

---

[1] With this part of the account, cf. Caesar, *B.G.*, i. 1.
[2] Paris.
[3] The site of Harfleur.
[4] Referring to Cæsar's campaigns, 58-49 B.C.

11. *A brief description of the various parts of Gaul
and of the course of the Rhone.*

1. In early times, when these regions lay in darkness as savage, they are thought to have been
threefold,[1] divided into Celts (the same as the Gauls),
the Aquitanians, and the Belgians, differing in
language, habits and laws. 2. Now the Gauls (who
are the Celts) are separated from the Aquitanians
by the Garonne river, which rises in the hills of the
Pyrenees, and after running past many towns
disappears in the Ocean. 3. But from the Belgians
this same nation is separated by the Marne and the
Seine, rivers of identical size; they flow through
the district of Lyons, and after encircling in the
manner of an island a stronghold of the Parisii called
Lutetia,[2] they unite in one channel, and flowing
on together pour into the sea not far from Castra
Constantia.[3] 4. Of all these nations the Belgae
had the reputation in the ancient writers of being the
most valiant, for the reason that being far removed
from civilised life and not made effeminate by imported luxuries, they warred for a long time with
the Germans across the Rhine. 5. The Aquitanians,
on the contrary, to whose coasts, as being near at
hand and peaceable, imported wares are conveyed,
had their characters weakened to effeminacy and
easily came under the sway of Rome. 6. All the
Gauls, ever since under the perpetual pressure of
wars[4] they yielded to the dictator Julius, have
been governed by an administration divided into
four parts. Of these Gallia Narbonensis by itself
comprised the districts of Vienne and Lyons; the

superiorem et inferiorem Germaniam Belgasque duae
iurisdictiones eisdem rexere temporibus. 7. At nunc
numerantur provinciae per omnem ambitum Galliarum : secunda Germania, prima ab occidentali
exordiens cardine, Agrippina et Tungris munita,
civitatibus amplis et copiosis. 8. Dein prima
Germania, ubi praeter alia municipia Mogontiacus
est et Vangiones, et Nemetae et Argentoratus,
barbaricis cladibus nota. 9. Post has Belgica prima
Mediomatricos praetendit et Treveros, domicilium
principum clarum. 10. Huic annexa secunda est
Belgica, qua Ambiani sunt, urbs inter alias eminens,
et Catelauni et Remi. 11. Apud Sequanos Bisontios
videmus et Rauracos, aliis potiores oppidis multis.
Lugdunensem primam Lugdunus ornat et Cabyllona
et Senones et Biturigae et moenium Augustuduni
magnitudo vetusta. 12. Secundam enim Lugdunensem Rotomagi et Turini, Mediolanum ostendunt et
Tricasini; Alpes Graiae et Poeninae exceptis
obscurioribus [1] habent et Aventicum, desertam
quidem civitatem sed non ignobilem quondam, ut
aedificia semiruta nunc quoque demonstrant. Haec
provinciae urbesque sunt splendidae Galliarum.
13. In [2] Aquitania quae Pyrenaeos montes et eam
partem spectat oceani quae pertinet ad Hispanos,

---

[1] *obscurioribus*, followed by lac. of 4 letters, V; no lac.,
G.   [2] *in*, added by A ; VBG omit.

---

[1] At the battle of Argentoratus (Strasburg); see **xvi.
12.**

[2] Augusta Trevirorum was the headquarters of the Roman
commanders on the Rhine, and a frequent residence of the

second had control of all Aquitania; Upper and Lower Germany, as well as the Belgians, were governed by two administrations at that same time. 7. But now the provinces over the whole extent of Gaul are reckoned as follows: The first province (beginning on the western front) is Lower, or Second, Germany, fortified by the wealthy and populous cities of Cologne and Tongres. 8. Next comes First, or Upper, Germany where besides other free towns are Mayence and Worms and Spires and Strasburg, famous for the disasters of the savages.[1] 9. After these the First province of Belgium displays Metz and Treves, splendid abode of the emperors.[2] 10. Adjoining this is the Second province of Belgium, in which are Amiens, a city eminent above the rest, and Châlons[3] and Rheims. 11. In the Seine province we see Besançon and Augst, more important than its many other towns. The first Lyonnese province is made famous by Lyons, Châlon-sur-Saône, Sens, Bourges, and Autun with its huge ancient walls. 12. As for the second Lyonnese province, Rouen and Tours make it distinguished, as well as Evreux and Troyes. The Graian and Pennine Alps, not counting towns of lesser note, have Avenche, a city now abandoned, to be sure, but once of no slight importance, as is even yet evident from its half-ruined buildings. These are the goodly provinces and cities of Gaul. 13. In Aquitania, which trends towards the Pyrenees mountains and that part of the Ocean which extends

Roman emperors; Ausonius, in his *Ordo Urbium Nobilium* gives it sixth place.

[3] Châlons-sur-Marne.

prima provincia est Aquitanica, amplitudine civitatum admodum culta omissis aliis multis, Burdigala et Arverni excellunt, et Santones et Pictavi. 14. Novem populos Ausci commendant et Vasatae. In Narbonensi Elusa et Narbona et Tolosa [1] principatum urbium tenent. Viennensis civitatum exultat decore multarum, e [2] quibus potiores sunt Vienna ipsa et Arelate et Valentia ; quibus Massilia iungitur, cuius societate et viribus in discriminibus arduis fultam aliquotiens legimus Romam. 15. His prope Salluvii sunt et Nicaea et Antipolis, insulaeque Stoechades. 16. Et quoniam ad has partes opere contexto pervenimus, silere super Rhodano, maximi nominis flumine, incongruum est et absurdum. A Poeninis Alpibus effusiore copia fontium Rhodanus fluens, et proclivi impetu ad planiora degrediens, proprio agmine ripas occultat, et paludi sese ingurgitat, nomine Lemanno, eamque intermeans, nusquam aquis miscetur externis, sed altrinsecus summitates undae praeterlabens segnioris, quaeritans exitus, viam sibi impetu veloci molitur. 17. Unde sine iactura rerum per Sapaudiam fertur et Sequanos, longeque progressus, Viennensem latere sinistro perstringit, dextro Lugdunensem, et emensus spatia flexuosa, Ararim quem Sauconnam appellant, inter

---

[1] *Tolosa*, N, Val. ; *Tolosa et*, V ; *Tolosa quae*, BG.
[2] *e*, added by Damsté ; V omits.

---

[1] The country between the Garonne and the Pyrenees, Aquitania in the narrower sense. The names of the nine nations are not known.

[2] That is, it receives no tributaries, yet fills its channel full.

towards Spain, the first province is Aquitania, much adorned by the greatness of its cities ; leaving out numerous others, Bordeaux and Clermont are conspicuous, as well as Saintorige and Poitiers. 14. The " Nine Nations "[1] are ennobled by Auch and Bazas. In the Narbonese province Eauze, Narbonne, and Toulouse hold the primacy among the cities. The Viennese province rejoices in the distinction conferred by many cities, of which the most important are Vienne itself, Arles and Valence ; and joined to these is Marseilles, by whose alliance and power we read that Rome was several times supported in severe crises. 15. Near these are Aix-en-Provence, Nice, Antibes, and the Isles d'Hyères. 16. And since we have reached these parts in the course of our work, it would be unfitting and absurd to say nothing of the Rhone, a river of the greatest celebrity. Rising in the Pennine Alps from a plenteous store of springs, the Rhone flows in headlong course towards more level places. It hides its banks with its own stream [2] and bursts into the lagoon called Lake Leman. This it flows through, nowhere mingling with the water outside, but gliding along the surface of the less active water on either hand, it seeks an outlet and forces a way for itself by its swift onset. 17. From there without any loss of volume it flows through [3] Savoy and the Seine Province,[4] and, after going on for a long distance, it grazes the Viennese Province on the left side and the Lyonnese on the right side. Next, after describing many meanders, it receives the Arar,

[3] Really " between."
[4] Maxima Sequanorum.

Germaniam primam fluentem et Sequanos,[1] suum
in nomen ascciscit, qui locus exordium est Galliarum.
Exindeque non millenis passibus sed leugis itinera
metiuntur. 18. Dein Isarae [2] Rhodanus aquis advenis locupletior, vehit grandissimas naves, ventorum difflatu iactari saepius assuetas, finitisque
intervallis quae ei natura praescripsit, spumeus
Gallico mari concorporatur, per patulum sinum
quem vocant Ad gradus, ab Arelate octavo decimo
ferme lapide disparatum. Sit satis de situ locorum.
Nunc figuras et mores hominum designabo.

12. *De moribus Gallorum.*

1. Celsioris staturae et candidi paene Galli sunt
omnes et rutili, luminumque torvitate terribiles,
avidi iurgiorum, et sublatius insolentes. Nec enim
eorum quemquam adhibita uxore rixantem, multo
se [3] fortiore et glauca, peregrinorum ferre poterit
globus, tum maxime cum illa inflata cervice suf-
frendens, ponderansque niveas ulnas et vastas,
admixtis calcibus emittere coeperit pugnos, ut
catapultas tortilibus nervis excussas. 2. Metuendae
voces complurium et minaces, placatorum iuxta et
irascentium, tersi tamen pari diligentia cuncti et
mundi, nec in tractibus illis, maximeque apud
Aquitanos, vir [4] poterit aliquis videri vel femina,

---

[1] *et Sequanos,* Cluverius *;* lac. after *fluentem,* Val. ; no lac.,
V. [2] *Dein Isarae,* Clark ; *hinc Rhodanus,* Val. ; (lac.
3 letters) *han* (lac. 2 letters) *Rhodanus,* V. [3] *multo se,*
Her. ; *multos,* V. [4] *Aquitanos,* Val. ; *A., vir,* Her. ;
aqua (lac. 12 letters) *poterit,* V.

which they call the Sauconna,[1] flowing between
Upper Germany and the Seine Province, and gives it
its own name. This point is the beginning of Gaul,
and from there they measure distances, not in miles
but in leagues. 18. After this the Rhone, enriched
by the tributary waters of the Isère, carries very
large craft, which are frequently wont to be tossed
by gales of wind, and having finished the bounds
which nature has set for it, its foaming waters are
mingled with the Gallic Sea through a broad bay
which they call Ad Gradus [2] at about the eighteenth
milestone distant from Arles. Let this suffice for
the topography of the region ; I shall now describe
the appearance and manners of its people.

12. *The Manners and Customs of the Gauls.*

1. Almost all the Gauls are of tall stature, fair
and ruddy, terrible for the fierceness of their eyes,
fond of quarrelling, and of overbearing insolence.
In fact, a whole band of foreigners will be unable
to cope with one of them in a fight, if he call in his
wife, stronger than he by far and with flashing eyes ;
least of all when she swells her neck and gnashes
her teeth, and poising her huge white arms, proceeds
to rain punches mingled with kicks, like shots discharged by the twisted cords of a catapult. 2. The
voices of most of them are formidable and threatening, alike when they are good-natured or angry.
But all of them with equal care keep clean and
neat, and in those districts, particularly in Aquitania, no man or woman can be seen, be she never

---

[1] Saône.   [2] The Gulf of Lyons ; cf. Grau-du-Roi.

licet perquam pauper, ut alibi frustis squalere pannorum. 3. Ad militandum omnis aetas aptissima, et pari pectoris robore senex ad procinctum ducitur et adultus, gelu duratis artubus et labore assiduo, multa contempturus et formidanda. Nec eorum aliquando quisquam (ut in Italia) munus Martium pertimescens, pollicem sibi praecidit, quos localiter murcos appellant. 4. Vini avidum genus, affectans ad vini similitudinem multiplices potus, et inter eos humiles quidam, obtunsis ebrietate continua sensibus, quam furoris voluntariam speciem esse Catoniana sententia definivit, raptantur discursibus vagis, ut verum illud videatur quod ait defendens Fonteium Tullius : " Gallos post haec dilutius esse poturos quod illi venenum esse arbitrabantur."

5. Hae regiones, praecipueque confines Italicis, paulatim levi sudore sub imperium venere Romanum, primo temptatae per Fulvium, deinde proeliis parvis quassatae per Sextium, ad ultimum per Fabium Maximum domitae. Cui negotii plenus effectus, asperiore Allobrogum gente devicta, hoc indidit cognomentum. 6. Nam omnes Gallias (nisi qua paludibus inviae fuere, ut [1] Sallustio docetur auctore) post decennalis belli mutuas clades subegit Caesar dictator,[2] societatique nostrae foederibus

---

[1] *ut*, E² G ; V omits.   [3] *subegit Caesar, societatique* Lind. (*dictator,* addidi) ;   *sub* (lac. 13 letters) *societatique,* V.

---

[1] Cf. Suet., *Aug.* 24, 1.   [2] Ammianus is the only source for these words.   [3] M. Fulvius Flaccus ; see Index and cf. Livy, *Periochae,* lx. and lxi.

so poor, in soiled and ragged clothing, as elsewhere.
3. All ages are most fit for military service, and the
old man marches out on a campaign with a courage
equal to that of the man in the prime of life ; since
his limbs are toughened by cold and constant toil,
and he will make light of many formidable dangers.
Nor does anyone of them, for dread of the service
of Mars, cut off his thumb, as in Italy [1] : there they
call such men " murci," or cowards.   4. It is a race
greedy for wine, devising numerous drinks similar
to wine, and some among them of the baser sort,
with wits dulled by continual drunkenness (which
Cato's saying pronounced a voluntary kind of
madness) rush about in aimless revels, so that those
words seem true which Cicero spoke when defending
Fonteius [2] : " The Gauls henceforth will drink wine
mixed with water, which they once thought poison."

5. These regions, and especially those bordering
on Italy, came gradually and with slight effort under
the dominion of Rome ; they were first essayed by
Fulvius,[3] then undermined in petty battles by
Sextius,[4] and finally subdued by Fabius Maximus,[5]
on whom the full completion of this business (when
he had vanquished the formidable tribe of the
Allobroges) [5] conferred that surname.[6]   6. Now the
whole of Gaul (except where, as the authority of
Sallust [7] informs us, it was impassable with marshes),
after losses on both sides during ten years of war the
dictator Caesar subdued and joined to us in an

---

[4] C. Sextius Calvinus ; see Index and cf. Livy, *Periocha*,
lxi.   [5] In 121 B.C.
   [6] Allobrogicus.   [7] *Hist.* i. 11, Maurenbrecher.

iunxit aeternis. Evectus sum longius ; sed remeabo tandem ad coepta.

13. *De Musaniano praefecto praetorio per Orientem.*

1. Domitiano crudeli morte consumpto, Musonianus eius sucessor orientem praetoriani regebat potestate praefecti, facundia sermonis utriusque clarus. Unde sublimius quam sperabatur eluxit. 2. Constantinus enim cum limatius superstitionum quaereret sectas, Manichaeorum et similium, nec interpres inveniretur idoneus, hunc sibi commendatum ut sufficientem elegit ; quem, officio functum perite, Musonianum voluit appellari, ante Strategium dictitatum, et ex eo percursis honorum gradibus multis, ascendit ad praefecturam, prudens alia tolerabilisque provinciis, et mitis et blandus, sed ex qualibet occasione, maximeque ex controversis litibus (quod nefandum est) et in totum [1] lucrandi aviditate sordescens, ut inter alia multa, evidenter apparuit in quaestionibus agitatis super morte Theophili Syriae consularis, proditione Caesaris Galli, impetu plebis promiscuae discerpti, ubi damnatis pauperibus, quos cum haec agerentur, peregre fuisse constabat, auctores diri facinoris exutis patrimoniis absoluti sunt divites.

[1] *in totum,* V ; *inlotum,* Her.

---

[1] Cf. xiv. **7,** 16.
[2] Greek and Latin ; cf. Suet., *Claud.* 42, 1.

everlasting covenant of alliance. I have digressed too far, but I shall at last return to my subject.

13. *The doings of the praetorian prefect, Musonianus, in the Orient.*

1. After Domitianus was dispatched by a cruel death,[1] his successor Musonianus governed the East with the rank of pretorian prefect, a man famed for his command of both languages,[2] from which he won higher distinction than was expected. 2. For when Constantine was closely investigating the different religious sects, Manichaeans and the like, and no suitable interpreter could be found, he chose him, as a person recommended to him as competent ; and when he had done that duty skilfully, he wished him to be called Musonianus, whereas he had hitherto had the name of Strategius. From that beginning, having run through many grades of honour, he rose to the prefecture, a man intelligent in other respects and satisfactory to the provinces, mild also and well-spoken, but on any and every occasion, and especially (which is odious) in hard-fought lawsuits and under all circumstances greedily bent upon filthy lucre. This became clearly evident (among many other instances) in the investigations set on foot regarding the death of Theophilus, governor of Syria, who, because of the betrayal of Gallus Caesar, was torn to pieces in an onslaught of the rabble upon him ; on which occasion sundry poor men were condemned, although it was known that they had been away when this happened, while the wealthy perpetrators of the foul crime were set free after being stripped of their property.

3. Hunc Prosper adaequabat, pro magistro equitum agente etiam tum in Galliis, militem regens, abiecte ignavus et (ut ait comicus) arte despecta furtorum rapiens propalam.

4. Quis concordantibus, mutuaque commercia vicissim sibi conciliando locupletatis, Persici duces vicini fluminibus, rege in ultimis terrarum suarum terminis occupato, per praedatorios globos nostra vexabant, nunc Armeniam aliquotiens Mesopotamiam confidentius incursantes, Romanis ductoribus ad colligendas oboedientium exuvias occupatis.

LIBER XVI

1. *Iuliani Caesaris laus.*

1. Haec per orbem Romanum fatorum ordine contexto versante, Caesar apud Viennam in collegium fastorum a consule octiens Augusto adscitus, urgente genuino vigore, pugnarum fragores caedesque barbaricas somniabat, colligere provinciae fragmenta iam parans, si adfuisset fortuna [1] flatu tandem secundo. **2.** Quia igitur res magnae quas per Gallias virtute felicitateque correxit, multis veterum factis fortibus praestant, singula serie

[1] *fortuna,* added by Wagner.

---

[1] Ursicinus (see xiv. **11,** 5).
[2] Plautus, *Epidicus,* 12, *minus iam furtificus sum quam antehac. Quid ita? Rapio propalam.*
[3] That is, Constantius Augustus.

3. He was matched by Prosper, who was at that time still representing the cavalry commander [1] in Gaul and held military authority there, an abject coward and, as the comic poet says,[2] scorning artifice in thieving and plundering openly.

4. While these men were in league and enriching themselves by bringing mutual gain one to the other, the Persian generals stationed by the rivers, while their king was busied in the farthest bounds of his empire, kept raiding our territories with predatory bands, now fearlessly invading Armenia and sometimes Mesopotamia, while the Roman officers were occupied in gathering the spoils of those who paid them obedience.

BOOK XVI

1. *Praise of Julianus Caesar.*

1. While the linked course of the fates was bringing this to pass in the Roman world, Julian Caesar at Vienne was admitted by Augustus,[3] then consul for the eighth time, into the fellowship of the consular fasti. Urged on by his native energy, he dreamed of the din of battle and the slaughter of savages, already preparing to gather up the broken fragments of the province, if only fortune should at last aid him with her favouring breeze. 2. Accordingly, since the great deeds that he had the courage and good fortune to perform in Gaul surpass many valiant achievements of the ancients, I shall describe them one by one in progressive order,

201

progrediente monstrabo, instrumenta omnia mediocris ingenii (si suffecerint) commoturus. 3. Quicquid autem narrabitur, quod non falsitas arguta concinnat, sed fides integra rerum absolvit, documentis evidentibus fulta, ad laudativam paene materiam pertinebit. 4. Videtur enim lex quaedam vitae melioris hunc invenem a nobilibus cunis ad usque spiritum comitata supremum. Namque incrementis velocibus ita domi forisque colluxit, ut prudentia Vespasiani filius Titus alter aestimaretur, bellorum gloriosis cursibus Traiani simillimus, clemens ut Antoninus, rectae perfectaeque rationis indigine congruens Marco, ad cuius aemulationem actus suos effingebat et mores. 5. Et quoniam (ut Tulliana docet auctoritas) "omnium magnarum artium sicut arborum altitudo nos delectat, radices stirpesque non item," sic praeclarae huius indolis rudimenta, tunc multis obnubilantibus tegebantur, quae anteferri gestis eius postea multis et miris, hac ratione deberent, quod adulescens primaevus, ut Erechtheus in secessu Minervae nutritus, ex Academiae quietis umbraculis, non e militari tabernaculo, in pulverem Martium tractus, strata Germania, pacatisque rigentis Rheni meatibus, cruenta spirantium regum hic sanguinem fudit, alibi manus catenis afflixit.

---

[1] This is also stated by Eutropius, x. 16, 5, and by Julian himself in his *Letter to Themistius*, p. 253, 13 ; ii. p. 203, L.C.L.

[2] *Orator*, 43, 147 ; a very free quotation.

endeavouring to put in play all the resources of my modest ability, if only they will suffice. 3. Now whatever I shall tell (and no wordy deceit adorns my tale, but untrammelled faithfulness to fact, based upon clear proofs, composes it) will almost belong to the domain of the panegyric. 4. For some law of a higher life seems to have attended this youth from his noble cradle even to his last breath. For with rapid strides he grew so conspicuous at home and abroad that in his foresight he was esteemed a second Titus, son of Vespasian, in the glorious progress of his wars as very like Trajan, mild as Antoninus Pius, and in searching out the true and perfect reason of things in harmony with Marcus Aurelius, in emulation of whom he moulded his conduct and his character.[1] 5. And since (as the authority of Cicero informs us) [2] "we take delight in the loftiness of all noble arts, as we do of trees, but not so much in their roots and stumps," just so the beginnings of his surpassing ability were then veiled by many overshadowing features. Yet they ought to be preferred to his many admirable later achievements, for the reason that while still in early youth, educated like Erechtheus [3] in Minerva's retreat, and drawn from the peaceful shades of the Academy, not from a soldier's tent, to the dust of battle, he vanquished Germany, subdued the meanders of the freezing Rhine, here shed the blood of kings breathing cruel threats, and there loaded their arms with chains.

[3] One of the earliest kings of Athens, because of his discovery of many useful arts said to have been educated by Minerva; cf. *Iliad*, ii. 546 f.

CONSTANTIUS ET GALLUS

2. *Iulianus Caesar Alamannos adoritur, caedit, capit, et fugat.*

1. Agens itaque negotiosam hiemem apud oppidum ante dictum, inter rumores, qui volitabant assidui, comperit Augustuduni civitatis antiquae muros spatiosi quidem ambitus sed carie vetustatis invalidos, barbarorum impetu repentino insessos, torpente praesentium militum manu, veteranos concursatione pervigili defendisse, ut solet abrupta saepe discrimina salutis ultima desperatio propulsare. **2.** Nihil itaque remittentibus curis, ancillari adulatione posthabita, qua eum proximi ad amoenitatem flectebant et luxum, satis omnibus comparatis, octavum kalendas Iulias Augustudunum pervenit, velut dux diuturnus viribus eminens et consiliis, per diversa palantes barbaros ubi dedisset fors copiam aggressurus. **3.** Habita itaque deliberatione assistentibus locorum peritis, quodnam iter eligeretur ut tutum, multa ultro citroque dicebantur aliis per Arbor [1] . . . quibusdam per Sedelaucum et Coram iri debere firmantibus. **4.** Sed cum subsererent quidam, Silvanum paulo ante magistrum peditum per compendiosas vias, verum suspectas, quia ramorum tenebris [2] multis umbrantur, cum octo auxiliarium milibus aegre transisse, fidentius Caesar audaciam viri fortis imitari magnopere

---

[1] *Arbor* (lac. 13 letters), V.   [2] *ramorum tenebris*, Fletcher, cf. xvi. 12, 59; *nemorum t.*, Her.; *tenebris*, G, Clark; *quiante mumibris*, V.

---

[1] I.e. Vienne.
[2] The name cannot be completed.
[3] In the department Côte d'Or.

2. *Julianus Caesar attacks the Alamanni, slaughters, captures, and vanquishes them.*

1. Accordingly, while he was passing a busy winter in the above-mentioned town,[1] in the thick of rumours which kept persistently flying about, he learned that the walls of the ancient city of Autun, of wide circuit, to be sure, but weakened by the decay of centuries, had been besieged by a sudden onset of the savages ; and then, though the force of soldiers garrisoned there was paralysed, it had been defended by the watchfulness of veterans who hurried together for its aid, as it often happens that the extreme of desperation wards off imminent danger of death. 2. Therefore, without putting aside his cares, and disregarding the servile flattery with which his courtiers tried to turn him to pleasure and luxury, after making adequate preparation he reached Autun on the 24th of June, like some experienced general, distinguished for power and policy, intending to fall upon the savages, who were straggling in various directions, whenever chance should give opportunity. 3. Accordingly, when he held a council, with men present who knew the country, to decide what route should be chosen as a safe one, there was much interchange of opinion, some saying that they ought to go by Arbor [2] . . . others by way of Saulieu [3] and Cora.[4] 4. But when some remarked that Silvanus, commander of the infantry, with 8000 reserve troops had shortly before passed (though with difficulty) by roads shorter but mistrusted because of the heavy shade of the branches, the Caesar with the greater confidence

---

[4] A small place in the neighbourhood of Autun.

nitebatur. 5. Et nequa interveniat mora, adhibitis cataphractariis solis et ballistariis, parum ad tuendum rectorem idoneis, percurso eodem itinere, Autosudorum pervenit. 6. Ubi brevi (sicut solebat) otio cum milite recreatus, ad Tricasinos tendebat, et barbaros in se catervatim ruentes partim, cum timeret ut ampliores, confertis lateribus observabat, alios occupatis habilibus locis, decursu facili proterens, non nullos pavore traditos cepit, residuos in curam celeritatis omne quod poterant conferentes, quia sequi non valebat, gravitate praepeditus armorum, innocuos abire perpessus est. 7. Proinde certiore iam spe ad resistendum ingruentibus confirmatus, per multa discrimina venit Tricasas, adeo insperatus, ut eo portas paene pulsante, diffusae multitudinis barbarae metu, aditus urbis non sine anxia panderetur ambage. 8. Et paulisper moratus, dum fatigato consulit militi, civitatem Remos, nihil prolatandum existimans, petit, ubi in unum congregatum exercitum vehentem unius mensis cibaria[1] iusserat operiri praesentiam suam; cui praesidebat Ursicini successor Marcellus, et ipse Ursicinus, ad usque expeditionis finem agere praeceptus eisdem in locis. 9. Post variatas itaque sententias

---

[1] *mensis cibaria*, added by Val., *unius* by Novák (in lac. 18 letters).

---

[1] The *cataphractarii* were mounted warriors; both horses and men were heavily clad in armour; see xvi. **10, 8.**

[1] The *ballistarii* had charge of the *ballistae*, which took the place of modern artillery; described in xxiii. **4, 1.**

made a strong resolve to emulate the daring of that hardy man. 5. And to avoid any delay, he took only the cuirassiers[1] and the crossbowmen,[2] who were far from suitable to defend a general, and traversing the same road, he came to Auxerre. 6. There with but a short rest (as his custom was) he refreshed himself and his soldiers and kept on towards Troyes; and when troops of savages kept making attacks on him, he sometimes, fearing that they might be in greater force, strengthened his flanks and reconnoitered; sometimes he took advantage of suitable ground, easily ran them down and trampled them under foot, capturing some who in terror gave themselves up, while the remainder exerted all their powers of speed in an effort to escape. These he allowed to get away unscathed, since he was unable to follow them up, encumbered as he was with heavy-armed soldiers. 7. So, as he now had firmer hope of success in resisting their attacks, he proceeded among many dangers to Troyes, reaching there so unlooked for, that when he was almost knocking at the gates, the fear of the widespread bands of savages was such, that entrance to the city was vouchsafed only after anxious debate. 8. And after staying there a short time, out of consideration for his tired soldiers, he felt that he ought not to delay, and made for the city of Rheims. There he had ordered the whole army to assemble with provisions for a month and to await his coming; the place was commanded by Ursicinus' successor Marcellus, and Ursicinus himself was directed to serve in the same region until the end of the campaign. 9. Accordingly, after the expression of

plures, cum placuisset per Decem pagos Alamannam aggredi plebem densatis agminibus, tendebat illuc solito alacrior miles. 10. Et quia dies umectus et decolor, vel contiguum eripiebat aspectum, iuvante locorum gnaritate hostes tramite obliquo discurso, post Caesaris terga legiones duas arma cogentes adorti, paene delessent, ni subito concitus clamor sociorum auxilia coegisset. 11. Hinc et deinde nec itinera nec flumina transire posse sine insidiis putans, erat providus et cunctator, quod[1] praecipuum bonum in magnis ductoribus, opem ferre solet exercitibus et salutem. 12. Audiens itaque Argentoratum, Brotomagum, Tabernas, Salisonem, Nemetas et Vangionas et Mogontiacum civitates barbaros possidentes, territoria earum habitare (nam ipsa oppida ut circumdata retiis busta declinant) primam omnium Brotomagum occupavit, eique iam adventanti Germanorum manus[2] pugnam intentans occurrit. 13. Cumque in bicornem figuram acie divisa, collato pede res agi coepisset, exitioque hostes urgerentur ancipiti, captis non nullis, aliis in ipso proelii fervore truncatis, residui discessere, celeritatis praesidio tecti.

---

[1] *quod*, G ; V omits.   [2] *G. manus p.*, W[2] G ; *G. pugnam* (without lac.), V.

---

[1] Dieuse.

[2] In xxxi. **2**, 4, a similar statement is made of the Huns, that they avoid houses as they would tombs. E. Maass,

many various opinions, it was agreed to attack the
Alamannic horde by way of the Ten Cantons [1] with
closed ranks ; and the soldiers went on in that
direction with unusual alacrity. 10. And because
the day was misty and overcast, so that even objects
close at hand could not be seen, the enemy, aided
by their acquaintance with the country, went around
by way of a crossroad and made an attack on the
two legions bringing up the rear of the Caesar's
army. And they would nearly have annihilated
them, had not the shouts that they suddenly raised
brought up the reinforcements of our allies. 11.
Then and thereafter, thinking that he could cross
neither roads nor rivers without ambuscades, Julian
was wary and hesitant, which is a special merit in
great commanders, and is wont both to help and to
save their armies. 12. Hearing therefore that
Strasburg, Brumath, Saverne, Seltz, Speyer, Worms,
and Mayence were held by the savages, who were
living on their lands (for the towns themselves
they avoid as if they were tombs surrounded by
nets),[2] he first of all seized Brumath, but while he
was still approaching it a band of Germans met him
and offered battle. 13. Julian drew up his forces in
the form of a crescent, and when the fight began
to come to close quarters, the enemy were overwhelmed by a double danger ; some were captured,
others were slain in the very heat of the battle, and
the rest got away, saved by recourse to speed.

Neue Jahrb., xlix. (1922) pp. 205 ff., says that graves of
women who died in childbed, and might return to get their
offspring, were surrounded with nets.

CONSTANTIUS ET GALLUS

3. *Iulianus Caesar Coloniam a Francis captum recipit, et pacem ibi cum Francorum regibus facit.*

1. Nullo itaque post haec repugnante, ad recuperandam ire placuit Agrippinam, ante Caesaris in Gallias adventum excisam, per quos tractus nec civitas ulla visitur nec castellum, nisi quod apud Confluentes, locum ita cognominatum, ubi amnis Mosella confunditur Rheno, Rigomagum oppidum est et una prope ipsam Coloniam turris. 2. Igitur Agrippinam ingressus, non ante motus est exinde, quam Francorum regibus furore mitescente perterritis, pacem firmaret rei publicae interim profuturam, et urbem reciperet munitissimam. 3. Quibus vincendi primitiis laetus, per Treveros hiematurus, apud Senonas oppidum tunc opportunum abscessit. Ubi bellorum inundantium molem umeris suis (quod dicitur) vehens, scindebatur in multiplices curas, ut milites qui a solitis descivere praesidiis reducerentur ad loca suspecta, et conspiratas gentes in noxam Romani nominis disiectaret, ac provideret ne alimenta deessent exercitui per varia discursuro.

---

[1] See xv. **8**, 19.
[2] Near Coblenz, which gets its name from *Confluentes*.

3. *Julian recovers Cologne, which had been captured by the Franks, and there makes peace with the kings of the Franks.*

1. Accordingly, as after this no one offered resistance, Julian decided to go and recover Cologne, which had been destroyed before his arrival in Gaul.[1] In all that region there is no city to be seen and no stronghold, except that at the Confluence, a place so called because there the river Moselle mingles with the Rhine, there is the town of Remagen[2] and a single tower near Cologne itself. 2. So, having entered Cologne, he did not stir from there until he had overawed the Frankish kings and lessened their pugnacity, had made a peace with them which would benefit the state meanwhile, and had recovered that very strongly fortified city. 3. Pleased with these first-fruits of victory, he passed through the land of the Treveri, and went to winter at Sens, a town which was then convenient. There, bearing on his shoulders, as the saying is, the burden of a flood of wars,[3] he was distracted by manifold cares—how the soldiers who had abandoned their usual posts might be taken back to danger-points, how he might scatter the tribes that had conspired to the hurt of the Roman cause, and how to see to it that food should not fail his army, as it was about to range in different directions.

[3] See p. 82, n. 5.

4. *Iulianus Caesar apud Senonas oppidum ab Alemannis obsidetur.*

1. Haec sollicite perpensantem, hostilis aggreditur multitudo, oppidi capiundi spe in maius accensa, ideo confidenter quod ei nec scutarios adesse prodentibus perfugis didicerant nec gentiles, per municipia distributos, ut commodius vescerentur quam antea.[1] 2. Clausa ergo urbe murorumque intuta parte firmata, ipse cum armatis die noctuque inter propugnacula visebatur et pinnas, ira exundante substridens, cum erumpere saepe conatus, paucitate praesentis manus impediretur. Post tricesimum denique diem, abiere barbari tristes, inaniter stulteque cogitasse civitatis obsidium mussitantes. 3. Et [2] (quod indignitati rerum est assignandum) periclitanti Caesari distulit suppetias ferre Marcellus, magister equitum agens in stationibus proximis, cum etiam si civitas absque principe vexaretur, opposita multitudine malis obsidionalibus expediri deberet. 4. Hoc metu solutus, efficacissimus Caesar providebat constanti sollicitudine, ut militum diuturno labori quies succederet aliqua licet brevis, ad recreandas tamen sufficiens vires, quamquam ultima squalentes

---

[1] *quam antea* (without lac.), Heraeus; *cum autem* (lac. 42 letters) *clausa*, V.   [2] *et*, V (Pet. defends); *set*, Clark; *at*, Lind.

---

[1] See note 3, p. 56.
[2] I.e. the ill-treatment of Julian.

4. *Julian is besieged by the Alemanni in the town of Sens.*

1. As he was anxiously weighing these problems, a host of the enemy attacked, fired with increased hope of taking the town, and full of confidence because they had learned from the statements of deserters that neither the targeteers nor the gentiles [1] were at hand ; for they had been distributed in the towns, so as to be more easily provisioned than before. 2. So, having shut the city gates and strengthened a weak section of the walls, Julian could be seen day and night with his soldiers among the bulwarks and battlements, boiling over with rage and fretting because however often he tried to sally forth, he was hampered by the scanty numbers of the troops at hand. Finally, after a month the savages withdrew crestfallen, muttering that they had been silly and foolish to have contemplated the blockade of the city. 3. But—a thing to be regarded as a shameful situation [2]—while Caesar was in jeopardy, Marcellus, master of the horse, although he was stationed in neighbouring posts, postponed sending him reinforcements ; whereas even if the city alone was endangered, to say nothing of the prince's presence there, it ought to have been saved from the hardships of blockade by the intervention of a large force. 4. Once relieved of this fear, Caesar provided with the greatest efficiency and with unfailing solicitude that some rest should follow the long continued toil of the soldiers, a short one perhaps, but enough, at least, to restore their strength ; and yet that region, a wilderness in its

213

inopia terrae, saepe vastitatae exigua quaedam victui congrua suggerebant. 5. Verum hoc quoque diligentia curato pervigili, affusa laetiore spe prosperorum, sublato animo ad exsequanda plurima consurgebat.

5. *Iuliani Caesaris virtutes.*

1. Primum igitur factuque difficile, temperantiam ipse sibi indixit atque retinuit, tamquam adstrictus sumptuariis legibus viveret, quas ex rhetris Lycurgi (id est axibus) Romam translatas, diuque observatas et senescentes, paulatim reparavit Sulla dictator, reputans ex praedictis Democriti, quod ambitiosam mensam fortuna, parcam virtus apponit. 2. Id enim etiam Tusculanus Cato prudenter definiens, cui Censorii cognomentum, castior vitae indidit cultus : " Magna " inquit " cura cibi, magna virtutis incuria." 3. Denique cum legeret libellum assidue, quem Constantius, ut privignum ad studia mittens, manu sua conscripserat, praelicenter disponens quid in convivio Caesaris impendi deberet,

---

[1] The rhetrae (ῥῆτραι) were oracular utterances which Lycurgus professed to have received directly from Apollo at Delphi ; later the word was used generally for the laws of Lycurgus.

[2] The laws of Solon were called ἄξονες because they could be revolved on pivots. Many ancient writers state that the tablets were originally of wood, and they retained this name after they were republished on marble slabs. R. Scholl was probably right in assuming a lacuna after

extreme destitution through having often been
ravaged, provided very little suitable for rations.
5. But when this too had been provided for by his
ever-watchful care, a happier hope of success was
shed upon him, and with spirits revived he rose to
the achievement of numerous enterprises.

5. *The merits of Julianus Caesar.*

1. First, then (and a hard thing to accomplish)
he imposed moderation on himself, and kept to it,
as if he were living bound by the sumptuary laws
which were brought to Rome from the Edicts,[1]
that is, the wooden tablets,[2] of Lycurgus ; and when
they had long been observed, but were going out of
use, the dictator Sulla gradually renewed them,[3]
taking account of one of the sayings of Democritus,
that a pretentious table is set by Fortune, a frugal
one by Virtue. 2. Furthermore, Cato of Tusculum,
whose austere manner of living conferred upon
him the surname Censorius, wisely defined that
point, saying : " Great care about food implies
great neglect of virtue." [4] 3. Lastly, though he constantly read the booklet which Constantius, as it
sending a stepson to the university, had written
with his own hand, making lavish provision for what
should be spent on Caesar's table, he forbade the

Lycurgi, and Ammianus may have included a reference to
Solon's ἄξονες, for ῥῆτραι and ἄξονες were used throughout antiquity of the two lawgivers' works distinctively.
For their history see J. H. Oliver, *Hesperia,* iv. (1935),
pp. 9 ff.
   [3] See Gellius, ii. 24, 11 ; i. 204 f. L.C.L., for details of this
and other sumptuary laws.   [4] P. 110, 22, Jordan.

phasianum et vulvam et sumen exigi vetuit et
inferri, munificis militis vili et fortuito cibo contentus.

4. Hinc contingebat ut noctes ad officia divideret
tripertita, quietis et publicae rei et musarum, quod
factitasse Alexandrum legimus Magnum ; sed multo
hic fortius. Ille namque aenea concha supposita,
brachio extra cubile protento pilam tenebat argenteam, ut cum nervorum vigorem sopor laxasset
infusus, gestaminis lapsi tinnitus abrumperet somnum. 5. Iulianus vero absque instrumento, quotiens voluit evigilavit, et nocte dimidiata semper
exsurgens, non e plumis vel stragulis sericis ambiguo
fulgore nitentibus, sed ex tapete et sisyra [1], quam
vulgaris simplicitas susurnam appellat, occulte
Mercurio supplicabat, quem mundi velociorem
sensum esse motum mentium suscitantem, theo-
logicae prodidere doctrinae ; atque in tanto rerum
defectu, explorate rei publicae munera cuncta [2]
curabat. 6. Post quae ut ardua et seria terminata,
ad procudendum ingenium vertebatur, et incredibile quo quantoque ardore, principalium rerum
notitiam celsam indagans, et quasi pabula quaedam
animo ad sublimiora scandenti conquirens, per
omnia philosophiae membra prudenter disputando
currebat. 7. Sed tamen cum haec effecte pleneque

---

[1] ξυσίρα, bG ; ξισύρα, B ; σισύρα, Lind. ; (lac. **7**
letters at end of page) *syra*, V. [2] *explorate rei publicae
munera*, T, Val. (*cuncta* added by Novák, c.c.) ; *exploranter.
ei. p̄.*, Ⓜ (lac. 5 letters), V (*nter . . . Ⓜ, V²*).

ordering and serving of pheasants and of sow's
matrix and udders, contenting himself with the
coarse and ordinary rations of a common soldier.

4. So it came about that he divided his nights
according to a threefold schedule—rest, affairs of
state, and the Muses, a course which Alexander the
Great, as we read, used to practise ; but Julian
was far more self-reliant. For Alexander used to
set a bronze basin beside his couch and with out-
stretched arm hold a silver ball over it, so that when
the coming of sleep relaxed the tension of his muscles,
the clanging of the ball as it fell might break off his
nap. 5. But Julian could wake up as often as he
wished, without any artificial means. And when
the night was half over, he always got up, not from
a downy couch or silken coverlets glittering with
varied hues, but from a rough blanket and rug,
which the simple common folk call *susurna*.[1] Then
he secretly prayed to Mercury, whom the teaching
of the theologians stated to be the swift intelligence
of the universe, arousing the activity of men's minds ;
and in spite of such great lack of material things
he paid diligent heed to all his public duties. 6.
And after bringing these (as his lofty and serious
tasks) to an end, he turned to the exercise of his
intellect, and it is unbelievable with what great
eagerness he sought out the sublime knowledge of
all chiefest things, and as if in search of some
sort of sustenance for a soul soaring to loftier
levels, ran through all the departments of philosophy in his learned discussions. 7. But yet,

[1] A coarse blanket made from the fur or hide of an
animal.

colligeret, nec humiliora despexit, poeticam medio-
criter et rhetoricam tractans [1] (ut ostendit orationum
epistularumque eius cum gravitate comitas in-
corrupta) et nostrarum externarumque rerum his-
toriam multiformem. Super his aderat Latine
quoque disserendi sufficiens sermo. 8. Si itaque
verum est, quod scriptores varii memorant, Cyrum
regem et Simonidem lyricum, et Hippian Eleum
sophistarum acerrimum, ideo valuisse memoria,
quod epotis quibusdam remediis id impetrarunt,
credendum est hunc etiam tum adultum totum
memoriae dolium (si usquam repperiri potuit) ex-
hausisse. Et haec quidem pudicitiae virtutumque
sunt signa nocturna.

9. Diebus vero quae ornate dixerit et facete,
quaeve in apparatu vel in ipsis egerit congressibus
proeliorum, aut in re civili magnanimitate correxit
et libertate, suo quaeque loco singulatim [2] demon-
strabuntur. 10. Cum exercere proludia disciplinae
castrensis philosophus cogeretur ut princeps, artem-
que modulatius incedendi per pyrricham concinentibus disceret fistulis, vetus illud proverbium " clitellae
bovi sunt impositae; plane non est nostrum onus "
Platonem crebro nominans exclamabat. 11. Cum
inducti essent iussu eius [3] quadam sollemnitate
agentes in rebus [4] in consistorium, ut aurum

---

[1] *tractans*, added by Novák; V omits.　　[2] *singulatim*,
Her.; *singula*, V.　　　[3] *Cum inducti essent iussu eius*,
Novák; *inducet et eius*, V; lac. after *inducet*, Seeck.
[4] *sollemnitate agentes*, Heraeus; *sollemni* (lac. 5 letters)
agens, V.

---

[1] Cic., *ad Att.* v. 15, 3.

though he gained full and exhaustive knowledge in this sphere, he did not neglect more humble subjects, studying poetry to a moderate degree, and rhetoric (as is shown by the undefiled elegance and dignity of his speeches and letters) as well as the varied history of domestic and foreign affairs. Besides all this he had at his command adequate fluency also in Latin conversation. 8. If, then, it is true (as divers writers report) that King Cyrus and the lyric poet Simonides, and Hippias of Elis, keenest of the sophists, had such powerful memories because they had acquired that gift by drinking certain potions, we must believe that Julian, when only just arrived at manhood, had drained the entire cask of memory, if such could be found anywhere. These, then, were the nightly evidences of his self-restraint and his virtues.

9. But how he passed his days in brilliant and witty conversation, in preparation for war or in the actual clash of battle, or in lofty and liberal improvements in civil administration, shall later be shown in detail, each in its proper place. 10. When this philosopher, being a prince, was forced to practise the rudiments of military training and learn the art of marching rhythmically in pyrrhic measure to the harmony of the pipes, he often used to call on Plato's name, quoting that famous old saying :[1]   " A pack-saddle is put on an ox ; that is surely no burden for me." 11. When the agents [2] had been summoned by his order on a festal day to his council chamber, to receive their

[2] The *agentes in rebus* formed the imperial secret service under the *Magister Officiorum ;* see note 2, p. 98.

acciperent inter alios, quidam ex eorum consortio, non (ut moris est) pansa chlamyde, sed utraque manu cavata suscepit. Et imperator " rapere " inquit " non accipere sciunt agentes in rebus." 12. Aditus a parentibus virginis raptae, eum qui violarat convictum relegari decrevit. Hisque indigna pati querentibus, quod non sit morte multatus, res- ponderat hactenus : " Incusent iura clementiam, sed imperatorem mitissimi animi legibus praestare ceteris decet." 13. Egressurum eum ad ex- peditionem plures interpellabant ut laesi, quos audiendos provinciarum rectoribus commendabat ; et reversus, quid egerint singuli quaerens, delic- torum vindictas genuina lenitudine mitigabat. 14. Ad ultimum exceptis victoriis, per quas caden- tes [1] saepe incolumi · contumacia barbaros fudit, quod profuerit anhelantibus extrema penuria Gallis, hinc maxime claret, quod primitus partes eas ingressus, pro capitulis singulis tributi nomine vicenos quinos aureos repperit flagitari, discedens vero septenos tantum munera universa complentes : ob quae tamquam solem sibi serenum post squa- lentes tenebras affulsisse, cum alacritate et tri- pudiis laetabantur. 15. Denique id eum ad usque imperii finem et vitae scimus utiliter observasse, ne per indulgentias (quas appellant) tributariae

---

[1] *audentes*, Birt ; *uagantes*, Novák.

---

[1] The *aureus* was the standard gold coin of Rome, equal to 100 sesterces.

gold with the rest, one of the company took it, not (as the custom is) in a fold of his mantle, but in both his open hands. Whereupon the emperor said, "It is seizing, not accepting, that agents understand." 12. When approached by the parents of a girl who had been assaulted, he ordered that her ravisher, if convicted, should be banished ; and when they complained of the indignity suffered in that he was not punished with death, the emperor merely replied : "The laws may censure my clemency, but it is right for an emperor of very merciful disposition to rise above all other laws." 13. When he was on the point of leaving on a campaign, many persons would appeal to him, as having grievances ; but he used to recommend them to the provincial governors for their hearings. On his return he would inquire what had been decided in each case, and with his native kindliness would mitigate the punishment of the offences. 14. Last of all, not to speak of the victories in which he routed the savages, who often fell with spirits unbroken, what good he did to Gaul, labouring as it was in utmost destitution, appears most clearly from this fact : when he first entered those parts, he found that twenty-five pieces of gold [1] were demanded by way of tribute from every one as a poll- and land-tax ; but when he left, seven only for full satisfaction of all duties. And on account of this (as if clear sunshine had beamed upon them after ugly darkness), they expressed their joy in gaiety and dances. 15. To conclude, we know that to the very end of his reign, and of his life, he observed this rule profitably, not to remit arrears of tribute by so-called "indulgencies." For he had

221

rei concederet reliqua. Norat enim hoc facto se aliquid locupletibus additurum, cum constet ubique, pauperes inter ipsa indictorum[1] exordia solvere universa sine laxamento compelli.

16. Inter has tamen regendi moderandique vias, bonis principibus aemulandas, barbarica rabies exarserat rursus in[2] maius. 17. Utque bestiae custodum neglegentia raptu vivere solitae, ne his quidem remotis, appositisque fortioribus abscesserunt, sed tumescentes inedia, sine respectu salutis, armenta vel greges incursant, ita etiam illi, cunctis quae diripuere consumptis, fame urgente, agebant aliquotiens praedas, interdum antequam contingerent aliquid, oppetebant.

6. *Arbetio vir consularis accusatur, et absolvitur.*

1. Haec per eum annum spe dubia eventu tamen secundo per Gallias agebantur. In comitatu vero Augusti, circumlatrabat Arbetionem invidia, velut summa mox adepturum, decora cultus imperatorii praestruxisse, instabatque ei strepens immania, comes Verissimus nomine, arguens coram, quod a gregario ad magnum militiae culmen evectus, hoc quoque non contentus (ut parvo) locum appeteret principalem. 2. Sed specialiter eum insectabatur

---

[1] *indictorum*, Pithoeus ; *indictionum*, Seeck ; *dictorum*, V.   [2] *rursus in*, added by Heraeus ; *in*, by BG ; *e.m.* without lac., V def. by Löfstedt.

learned that by so doing he would somewhat better the condition of the rich, since it is generally known that poor people at the very beginning of the tax-levying are forced to pay in full without easement.

16. However, in the midst of these courses of wise governing, worthy of the imitation of good emperors, the fury of the savages had blazed forth again more than ever. 17. And as wild beasts accustomed to live by plundering when their guards are slack do not cease even when these guards are removed and stronger ones put in their place, but ravening with hunger rush upon flocks or herds without regard for their own lives : so they too, when they had used up all that they had seized by pillage, urged on by hunger, were continually driving off booty, and sometimes perishing of want before finding anything.

6. *Arbetio, a man of consular rank, is accused and acquitted.*

1. These were the events in Gaul during that year dubious in prospect, but successful in outcome. But in the court of the Augustus envy kept barking on every side at Arbetio, as one that would soon attain the highest rank and had already prepared the insignia of imperial dignity ; and a certain count, Verissimus by name, assailed him with unbridled outcry, openly charging that although he had risen from the common soldiery to the chief military command, he was not satisfied even with this, but thinking it was a slight thing, was aiming at the imperial position. 2. But in particular one

CONSTANTIUS ET GALLUS

Dorus quidam ex medico scutariorum, quem nitentium rerum centurionem sub Magnentio Romae
provectum, retulimus accusasse Adelphium, urbi
praefectum, ut altiora coeptantem. 3. Cumque
res in [1] inquisitionem veniret, necessariisque negotio
tentis, obiectorum probatio speraretur, tamquam
per saturam subito cubiculariis suffragantibus, ut
loquebatur pertinax rumor, et vinculis sunt exutae
personae quae stringebantur ut consciae, et Dorus
evanuit, et Verissimus ilico tacuit, velut aulaeo
deposito scenae.

7. *Iulianus Caesar a praeposito cubiculi sui Eutherio
apud imperatorem defenditur adversus Marcel-
lum ; et laus Eutherii.*

1. Eisdem diebus, allapso rumore Constantius
doctus, obsesso apud Senonas Caesari auxilium
non tulisse Marcellum, eum sacramento solutum
abire iussit in larem. Qui tamquam iniuria gravi
perculsus, quaedam in Iulianum moliebatur, auribus Augusti confisus, in omne patentibus crimen.

---

[1] *in*, added by EGB ; *ad*, by Novák ; V omits ; *in
quaestionem*, Her.

---

[1] In one of the lost books.
[2] Commander of the night-patrol in charge of public
buildings and monuments.
[3] Cf. Sallust, *Jug.*, xxix. 5, where the reference is to
voting on several questions at once ; *lex multis rebus con-
ferta*, Festus, *s.v.*

Dorus, ex-surgeon of the targeteers, kept pursuing him; he it was who (as I stated) [1] when promoted under Magnentius to be centurion in charge of works of art at Rome,[2] accused Adelphius, prefect of the city, of aiming at a higher station. 3. And when the matter came to an investigation, and everything needful for the business was at hand, a proof of the charges was looked for; when suddenly, as if by an irregular vote,[3] at the instance of the chamberlains (as persistent rumour reported) both those persons under restraint as implicated were released from their fetters; Dorus disappeared, and Verissimus at once held his peace, just as when on the stage the curtain is lowered and put away.[4]

7. *Julianus Caesar is defended against Marcellus before the emperor by Eutherius, his chief chamberlain; and praise of Eutherius.*

1. At that same time Constantius, apprised by approaching rumour that when Caesar was blockaded at Sens, Marcellus had not brought aid,[5] discharged the latter from the army and commanded him to depart to his home. Whereupon Marcellus, as if staggered by a grievous insult, began to contrive a plot against Julian, presuming on Augustus, whose ears were open to every slander. 2. And so,

---

[4] We might say "The curtain is dropped," but the lowering of the curtain revealed the stage of the Roman theatre. Here the reference is to putting the curtain away and closing the theatre, as in Juvenal, vi. 67 ff., *quotiens aulaea recondita cessant et vacuo clusoque sonant fora sola theatro.*   [5] Cf. xvi. **4**, 3.

2. Ideoque cum discederet, Eutherius praepositus cubiculi mittitur statim post eum, siquid finxerit convicturus. Verum ille hoc nesciens, mox venit Mediolanum, strepens et tumultuans, (ut erat vanidicus et amenti propior) ; admissus in consistorium, Iulianum ut procacem insimulat, iamque ad evagandum altius validiores sibi pinnas aptare ; ita enim cum motu quodam corporis loquebatur ingenti. 3. Haec eo fingente licentius, Eutherius (ut postulavit) inductus, iussusque loqui quod vellet, verecunde et modice docet, velari veritatem mendaciis. Magistro enim armorum, ut credebatur, cessante consulto, industria vigili Caesarem obsessum apud Senonas diu barbaros reppulisse, apparitoremque fidum auctori suo quoad vixerit fore, obligata cervice sua spondebat.

4. Res monuit super hoc eodem Eutherio pauca subserere, forsitan non credenda, ea re quod si Numa Pompilius vel Socrates bona quaedam dicerent de spadone, dictisque religionum adderent fidem, a veritate descivisse arguebantur. Sed inter vepres rosae nascuntur, et inter feras non nullae mitescunt, itaque carptim eius praecipua, quae sunt comperta, monstrabo. 5. Natus in Armenia sanguine libero, captusque a finitimis hostibus, etiam tum parvulus

when Marcellus was on his way, Eutherius, the head chamberlain, was sent immediately after him, to confute him in case he should trump up anything. But Marcellus, unware of this, presently came to Milan, blustering and making trouble, being a vain talkative fool and all but mad; and when admitted to the council, he charged Julian with being arrogant and already fitting himself with stronger pinions, so as to soar up higher; for thus he spoke with a mighty movement of his body to match his words. 3. While he was freely forging these accusations, Eutherius (as he requested) was brought in, and being commanded to say what he wished, modestly and in few words showed that the truth was veiled with lies. For while the commander of the heavy-armed infantry (as was believed) deliberately held back, Caesar, who had long been blockaded in Sens, had by his watchful energy driven back the bar-barians; and Eutherius staked his own head on the promise that Julian would be a loyal servitor to his superior, so long as he should live.

4. The subject prompts me to add a few facts about this same Eutherius, perhaps hardly to be credited, for the reason that if a Numa Pompilius or a Socrates should give any good report of a eunuch, and should back their statements by a solemn oath, they would be charged with having departed from the truth. But among brambles roses spring up, and among savage beasts some are tamed. Accord-ingly, I shall give a brief summary of the chief facts known about him. 5. He was born in Armenia of free parents, but when still very young he was kid-napped by hostile tribesmen in that neighbourhood,

abstractis geminis Romanis mercatoribus venun-
datus, ad palatium Constantini deducitur; ubi
paulatim adulescens rationem [1] recte vivendi, soller-
tiamque ostendebat, litteris quantum tali fortunae
satis esse poterat eruditus, cogitandi inveniendique
dubia et scrupulosa, acumine nimio praestans,
immensum quantum memoria vigens, benefaciendi
avidus plenusque iusti consilii, quem si Constans
imperator olim ex adulto iamque [2] maturum audiret, honesta suadentem et recta, nulla vel venia
certe digna peccasset. 6. Is praepositus cubiculi
etiam Iulianum aliquotiens corrigebat, Asiaticis
coalitum moribus, ideoque levem. Denique digressus ad otium, asscitusque postea in palatium,
semper sobrius et in primis consistens, ita fidem
continentiamque virtutes coluit amplas, ut nec
prodidisse aliquando arcanum, nisi tuendae causa
alienae salutis, nec exarsisse cupidine plus habendi
arcesseretur, ut ceteri. 7. Unde factum est ut
subinde Romam secedens, ibique fixo domicilio
consenescens, comitem circumferens conscientiam
bonam, colatur a cunctis ordinibus et ametur, cum
soleant id genus homines post partas ex iniquitate divitias latebras captare secretas, ut luci-
fugae vitantes multitudinis laesae conspectus. 8.
Cui spadonum veterum hunc comparare debeam,

[1] *paulatim adulescens rationem*, Val.; *paulatim* (lac.
14 letters) *acules* (lac. 9 letters) *irationem*, V.   [2] *adulto
iamque*, Val.; *adulto* (lac. 14 letters) *tamque*, V.

[1] Text and meaning are uncertain. On the faults of Constans, cf. Aurel. Victor, 41, and Zosimus, ii. 42.
[2] See Introd., xxxv.

who gelded him and sold him to some Roman traders, who brought him to Constantine's palace. There, as he grew up, he gradually gave evidence of virtuous living and intelligence. He received as much training in letters as might suffice for one of that station ; conspicuous for his remarkable keenness in devising and solving difficult and knotty problems, he had extraordinary powers of memory ; he was eager to do kindnesses and full of sound counsel. And if the emperor Constans had listened to him in times past, when Eutherius had grown up and was already mature, and urged honourable and upright conduct upon him, he would have been guilty of no faults, or at least of only pardonable ones.[1] 6. When he had become head chamberlain,[2] he would sometimes criticise even Julian, as trained in the manners of Asia and therefore inconstant. Finally going into retirement, but afterwards summoned to the palace, always temperate and especially consistent, he so cultivated the noble virtues of loyalty and self-restraint that he was never charged, as the rest have been, with having disclosed a secret, unless it were to save another's life, or to have been kindled with a desire to increase his wealth. 7. The result was, that when he presently retired to Rome and grew old there in a permanent home, he carried about with him a good conscience as his companion ; he was honoured and loved by all classes, whereas that type of man, after amassing wealth by iniquitous means, usually seeks out secret lurking-places, like creatures of darkness shunning the sight of the multitude they have wronged. 8. In unrolling many records of the past, to see to which of the

antiquitates replicando complures invenire non
potui. Fuerunt enim apud veteres (licet oppido
pauci) fideles et frugi, sed ob quaedam vitia macu-
losi. Inter praecipua enim, quae eorum quisque
studio possederat vel ingenio, aut rapax aut feritate
contemptior fuit, aut propensior ad laedendum, vel
regentibus [1] nimium blandus, aut potentiae fastu
superbior; ex omni latere autem ita paratum,[2] neque
legisse me neque audisse confiteor, aetatis nostrae
testimonio locupleti confisus. 9. Verum si forte
scrupulosus quidam lector antiquitatum, Menophilum
Mithridatis Pontici regis eunuchum, nobis opponat,
hoc monitu recordetur, nihil super eo relatum praeter
id solum, quod in supremo discrimine gloriose monstravit. 10. Ingenti proelio superatus a Romanis
et Pompeio rex praedictus, fugiensque ad regna
Colchorum, adultam filiam nomine Drypetinam,
vexatam asperitate morborum, in castello Sinhorio
huic Menophilo commissam reliquit. Qui virginem
omni remediorum solacio plene curatam, patri
tutissime servans, cum a Mallio Prisco, imperatoris
legato, munimentum quo claudebatur obsideri
coepisset, defensoresque eius deditionem meditari
sentiret, veritus ne parentis opprobrio puella nobilis
captiva superesset [3] et violata, interfecta illa mox

---

[1] *regentibus*, Erfurdt, Mommsen; *clientibus*, Val.; *lar-
gientibus*, Novák; *ligendi mus*, V.   [2] *paratum*, Damsté,
cf. Cic. in *Cat.* iii. 7, 17; *peritum*, V.   [3] *superesset*,
H²BG; *superasset*, V.

eunuchs of old I ought to compare him, I could find
none. True, there were in times gone by those that
were loyal and virtuous (although very few), but
they were stained with some vice or other. For
along with the excellent qualities which anyone of
them had acquired by studious endeavour or natural
ability he was either extortionate or despicable
for his cruelty, or prone to do mischief, or too
subservient to the rulers, or insolent through pride
of power ; but of one so well equipped in every
direction I confess I have neither read nor heard,
although I have relied on the abundant testimony of
our age. 9. But if haply any curious student of
ancient history should confront me with Menophilus,
the eunuch of Mithridates, king of Pontus, let this
reminder recall to him that nothing was recorded
of Menophilus save this one fact, that in the supreme
crisis he made a glorious showing. 10. The aforesaid king, after having been defeated in a mighty
battle by Pompey and the Romans, fled to the
kingdom of Čolchis ; he left his grown daughter,
Dryp tina by name, who was afflicted with a
grievous disease, in the fortress of Sinhorium under
the charge of this Menophilus. He, resorting to
every healing remedy, entirely cured the girl
and was guarding her in complete security for her
father, when the fortress in which he was beleagured
began to be blockaded by Mallius Priscus, the
Roman commander's lieutenant-general ; and when
Menophilus learned that its defenders were thinking
of surrender, fearing lest, to her father's reproach,
the high-born girl might be taken alive and suffer
outrage, he killed her and then plunged the sword

gladium in viscera sua compegit. Nunc redeam unde diverti.

8. *Delationes et calumniae in castris Constantii Augusti, et aulicorum rapacitas.*

1. Superato ut dixi Marcello, reversoque [1] Serdi-cam, unde oriebatur, in castris Augusti per simula-tionem tuendae maiestatis imperatoriae, multa et nefanda perpetrabantur.[2] 2. Nam si super occentu soricis vel occursu mustelae, vel similis signi gratia consuluisset quisquam [3] peritum, aut anile incanta-mentum ad leniendum adhibuisset dolorem, quod medicinae quoque admittit auctoritas, reus unde non poterat opinari delatus, raptusque in iudicium, poenaliter interibat.

3. Per id tempus fere servum [4] quendam, nomine Danum, terrore tenus uxor rerum levium incusarat: hanc incertum unde notam [5] Rufinus subsedit,[6]—quo indicante quaedam cognita per Gaudentium, agen-tem in rebus, consularem Pannoniae tunc Africanum, cum convivis rettulimus interfectum—apparitionis praefecturae praetorianae tum etiam princeps ob devotionem. 4. Is [7] (ut loquebatur iactantius) ver-sabilem feminam, post nefandum concubitum, in

---

[1] *reuersoque*, Lind; *euersoque*, V. [2] *perpetrabantur* G; *perpetrabant*, V. [3] *quisquam*, Heraeus, cf. xxii. 16, 19; *quemquam*, V. [4] *fere* or *ferme*, Wagner, *seruum*, Heraeus; *fer* (lac. 11 letters) *num*, V. [5] *hanc incertum unde notam*, Heraeus; *incusarat* (lac. of 7 letters) *certum an*cincertum* (c after * added by V²) *undenso tam*, V. [6] *subsedit*, Clark; *subsidebat*, Val.; *subseda*, V. [7] *is*, Val; *bis*, V.

into his own vitals.[1]   Now let me return to the point
from which I digressed.

8. *Slanders and calumnies in the camp of Constantius*
   Augustus, and the greed of the courtiers.

1. After Marcellus had been worsted, as I have
said, and had returned to Serdica,[2] his native place,
in the camp of Augustus, under pretext of upholding his imperial majesty, many abominable acts
were committed. 2. For if anyone consulted a
soothsayer about the squeaking of a shrew-mouse,
the meeting with a weasel on the way, or any like
portent, or used some old wife's charm to relieve pain
(a thing which even medical authority allows), he was
indicted (from what source he could not guess), was
haled into court, and suffered death as the penalty.

3. At about that time a certain slave, Danus by
name, was accused by his wife on trifling charges
merely to intimidate him; this woman was
approached by Rufinus, who had come to know her
in some way or other.   He was the man who had
given certain information that he had learned
through Gaudentius, one of the agents,[3] and had
caused the death of Africanus, then governor-
general of Pannonia, along with his guests, as I
have related;[4] he was even then, because of his
obsequiousness, chief steward of the praetorian prefecture. 4. This Rufinus (as he kept boastfully
saying) led the fickle woman, first into shameful

---

[1] This action is not mentioned elsewhere, not even by
Val. Max., i. 8, 13, where he speaks of Drypetina.
[2] Modern Sophia, Bulgaria.   [3] See note 2, p. 98.   [4] xv. **3**, 7.

233

periculosam fraudem illexit ; suasit consarcinatis
mendaciis laesae maiestatis arcessere maritum insontem, et fingere quod velamen purpureum, a
Diocletiani sepulcro furatus, quibusdam consciis
occultabat. 5. Hisque ad multorum exitium ita
formatis, ipse spe potiorum ad imperatoris pervolat
castra, excitaturus calumnias consuetas. Reque
comperta, iubetur Mavortius, tunc praefectus praetorio, vir sublimis constantiae, crimen acri inquisi-
tione spectare, iuncto ad audiendi societatem
Ursulo (largitionum comite) severitatis itidem non
improbandae. 6. Exaggerato itaque negotio ad
arbitrium temporum, cum nihil post tormenta
multorum inveniretur, iudicesque haererent ambigui,
tandem veritas respiravit oppressa, et in abrupto
necessitatis mulier Rufinum totius machinae con-
fitetur auctorem, nec adulterii foeditate suppressa ;
statimque legibus contemplatis, illi amore recti
concordes et iusti,[1] ambos sententia damnavere
letali. 7. Quo cognito Constantius fremens, et
tamquam vindicem salutis suae lugens exstinctum,
missis equitibus citis, Ursulum redire ad comitatum
minaciter iussit. Qui cum eo venisset adireque
principem vellet, ab aulicis arcebatur, ne defendendae

---

[1] *contemplatis,* Val. ; *illi amore recti,* Novák (*iudices idem,*
scripseram) ; *concordes et iusti,* Eyssen. ; *contem* (lac. 24
letters) *ordes.* V.

---

[1] See Introd., pp. xl f.

relations with him, and then into a dangerous deceit; he induced her by a tissue of lies to charge her guiltless husband with high treason, and to allege that he had stolen a purple robe from Diocletian's tomb and with several accomplices was concealing it. 5. And having thus framed these matters to the destruction of many persons, Rufinus himself, in hope of greater profit, flies to the emperor's camp, to stir up his customary scandals. And when the fact was divulged, Mavortius, then praetorian prefect, a man of high resolution, was bidden to look into the charge with a keen investigation, having associated with him, to hear the case in common, Ursulus, count of the largesses,[1] likewise a man of praiseworthy severity. 6. So when the affair had been exaggerated, after the standard of the times, and after the torture of many persons nothing was discovered, and the judges were hesitating in perplexity, at last truth, crushed to earth, breathed again, and at the point of necessity the woman confessed that Rufinus was the contriver of the whole plot, and did not even keep back the shame of her adultery. And at once the laws were consulted and the judges, unanimous in their love of right and justice, condemned them both to death. 7. Constantius, on learning this, raged and lamented, as if the defender of his own life had perished; he sent fast horsemen and commanded Ursulus in threatening terms to return to the court. And when he had come there and wished to approach the emperor, the courtiers tried to keep him from being able to appear in defence of the truth. But he, scorning those who would hold him back, burst through

posset assistere [1] veritati ; sed ille spretis qui prohibebant, perrupit intrepidus, ingressusque consistorium, ore et pectore libero docuit gesta ; hacque
fiducia linguis adulatorum occlusis, et praefectum et
se discrimine gravi subtraxit.

8. Tunc illud apud Aquitanos evenit, quod latior
fama vulgarat. Veterator quidam ad lautum convivium rogatus et mundum, qualia sunt in his regionibus plurima, cum vidisset linteorum toralium purpureos [2] clavos ita latissimos, ut sibi vicissim arte
ministrantium cohaererent, mensamque operimentis
paribus tectam, anteriorem chlamydis partem utraque manu vehens intrinsecus, structuram omnem
ut amictus adornaverat principalis ; quae res patrimonium dives evertit.

9. Malignitate simili quidam agens in rebus in
Hispania ad cenam itidem invitatus, cum inferentes
vespertina lumina pueros exclamasse audisset ex
usu " vincamus," verbum sollemne [3] interpretatum
atrociter delevit nobilem domum.

10. Haec taliaque ideo magis magisque cresce-
bant, quod Constantius impendio timidus et de vita
sollicitus,[4] semper se ferro peti [5] sperabat, ut Dionysius tyrannus ille Siciliae, qui ob hoc idem vitium

---

[1] *qui cum eo . . . adsistere*, Novák ; *posse adsistere ueri-
tatis et tale*, V. [2] *purpureos*, Günther ; *per duos*, V.
[3] *uerbum*, Her., *sollemne*, Lind. ; *perun* (lac. 8 letters)
lemne (lac. 11 letters), V. [4] *et . . . sollicitus*, Novák
in lac. of 18 letters. [5] *ferro peti*, Novák ; *feriri*,
EBG ; *ferri*, V.

---

[1] The *veterator* showed that the table decorations could
be used for an imperial cloak, and implied that they had
been so used.

fearlessly and, entering the council-chamber, with frank speech and bold heart told what had been done ; and by this confidence having stopped the mouths of the flatterers, he delivered both the prefect and himself from a grave danger.

8. Then a thing happened in Aquitania which fame bruited more widely abroad. A crafty old fellow who was invited to a sumptuous and elegant banquet, such as are very frequent in that country, noticed that the purple borders of the linen couch-covers were so very broad that the skill of the attendants made them seem all one piece, and that the table was covered with similar cloths ; and by turning the front part of his cloak inward with both hands, he so adorned its whole structure, that it resembled an emperor's garment[1] ; and this action ruined a rich estate.

9. With like malice a certain member of the secret service in Spain, who also was invited to a dinner, when he heard the slaves who were bringing in the evening lights cry (as the manner is) : "May we conquer,"[2] gave the expression a serious meaning, and wickedly destroyed a noble house.[3]

10. These and similar actions kept growing more and more common, for the reason that Constantius, who was excessively timid and fearful for his life, always anticipated that a knife was at his throat, like that famous Sicilian despot, Dionysius, who because

---

[2] I.e. the darkness, a formula at lighting up ; cf. Varro, *Ling. Lat.* vi. 4, *Graeci quoque, cum lumen affertur, solent dicere φῶς ἀγαθόν* ; *perun* (see crit. note) may possibly be for *pereundum est nocti.*

[3] *Vincamus* was interpreted as referring to some plot.

et tonstrices docuit filias, necui alieno ora committeret leviganda, aedemque brevem, ubi cubitare sueverat, alta circumdedit fossa eamque ponte solubili superstravit, cuius disiectos asseres et axiculos secum in somnum abiens transferebat, eosdemque compaginabat, lucis initio processurus. 11. Inflabant itidem has malorum civilium bucinas potentes in regia, ea re ut damnatorum petita bona suis accorporarent, essetque materia per vicinitates eorum late grassandi. 12. Namque ut documenta liquida prodiderunt, proximorum fauces aperuit primus omnium Constantinus, sed eos medullis provinciarum saginavit Constantius. 13. Sub hoc enim ordinum singulorum auctores, infinita cupidine divitiarum arserunt, sine iustitiae distinctione vel recti, inter ordinarios iudices Rufinus primus praefectus praetorio, et inter militares equitum magister Arbetio, praepositusque cubiculi Eusebius,[1] . . . anus quaestor, et in urbe Anicii, quorum ad avorum [2] aemulationem posteritas tendens, satiari numquam potuit cum possessione multo maiore.

---

[1] *Eusebius*, Lind. ; *Lucillianus* (?), Val. ; *laps* (lac. 19 letters) *annus*, V.   [2] *quorum ad auorum*, Pet. ; *aniciique* (la c. 27 letters), *uorum*, V.

of that same infirmity actually taught his daughters to be barbers, in order that he might not trust the shaving of his cheeks to an outsider ; and he surrounded the little house in which he used to sleep, with a deep trench and spanned it with a knockdown bridge,[1] the planks and pins of which he took apart and carried with him when he went off to bed ; and reassembled them at daybreak, when he was on his way out. 11. These trumpet-blasts of internal revolt [2] were likewise increased by powerful courtiers, to the end that they might lay claim to the property of condemned persons and incorporate it with their own, and thus have the means of encroaching widely on their neighbours. 12. For as clear proofs bore witness, the first of all to open the jaws of those nearest to him was Constantine, but it was Constantius who fattened them with the marrow of the provinces. 13. For under him the leading men of every rank were inflamed with a boundless eagerness for riches, without consideration for justice or right ; among the civil functionaries first came Rufinus, the praetorian prefect ; among the military, Arbetio, master of the horse, and the head-chamberlain Eusebius, . . . anus,[3] the quaestor, and in Rome itself the members of the Anician family, whose younger generation, striving to outdo their forefathers, could never be satisfied with even much greater possessions.

---

[1] That is, a bridge which could be taken apart.
[2] I.e. signs of coming disturbances in the state.
[3] Only the ending of the name has been preserved.

CONSTANTIUS ET GALLUS

9. *Agitur de pace cum Persis.*

1. At Persae in oriente per furta et latrocinia
potius quam (ut solebant antea) per concursatorias
pugnas, hominum praedas agitabant et pecorum,
quas [1] non numquam lucrabantur ut repentini,
aliquotiens superati multitudine militum amitte-
bant, interdum nihil conspicere [2] prorsus quod
poterat rapi permittebantur. 2. Musonianus tamen
praefectus praetorio, multis (ut ante diximus) bonis
artibus eruditus, sed venalis et flecti a veritate
pecunia facilis, per emissarios quosdam, fallendi
perstringendique gnaros, Persarum scitabatur consilia, assumpto in deliberationes huius modi Cassiano
Mesopotamiae duce, stipendiis et discriminibus
indurato diversis. 3. Qui cum fide concinente
speculatorum aperte cognossent Saporem in extremis
regni limitibus, suorum sanguine fuso multiplici,
aegre propulsare gentes infestas, Tamsaporem ducem
parti nostrae contiguum, occultis per ignotos milites
temptavere colloquiis, ut si copiam fors dedisset,
suaderet regi per litteras pacem tandem aliquando
cum principe Romano firmare, ut hoc facto ab
occidentali latere omni [3] securus, perduelles involea-
ret [4] assiduos. 4. Paruit Tamsapor, hisque fretus
refert ad regem, quod bellis acerrimis Constantius
implicatus, pacem postulat precativam. Dumque ad

---

[1] *quas*, C. F. W. Müller ; *quis*, V.   [2] *conspicere*,
C. F W. Müller (*con* from *cu* in *percumittebantur* of V) ;
prospicere, V.   [3] *ab occidentali latere omni* (*ab uno
latere*, scripseram), Novák ; *a latere damni*, Clark, Mommsen ;
latere adomnis, V.   [4] *inuolaret*, Novák ; *aduolaret*, V.

240

9. *Negotiations for peace with the Persians.*

1. But the Persians in the East, rather by thieving and robbery than (as their former manner was) in set battles, kept driving off booty of men and animals ; sometimes they got away with their loot, being unexpected ; often they lost it, overmarched by the great number of our soldiers ; occasionally they were not allowed to see anything at all which could be carried off. 2. None the less, Musonianus, the praetorian prefect, a man (as I have said before) gifted with many excellent accomplishments, but corrupt and easy to turn from the truth by a bribe, inquired into the designs of the Persians through emissaries of his who were adepts in deceit and incrimination ; and he took into his counsels on this subject Cassianus, duke of Mesopotamia, who had been toughened by various campaigns and dangers. 3. When the two had certain knowledge from the unanimous reports of their scouts that Sapor, on the remotest frontiers of his realm, was with difficulty and with great bloodshed of his troops driving back hostile tribesmen, they made trial of Tamsapor, the commander nearest to our territory, in secret interviews through obscure soldiers, their idea being that, if chance gave an opportunity, he should by letter advise the king finally to make peace with the Roman emperor, in order that by so doing he might be secure on his whole western frontier and could rush upon his persistent enemies. 4. Tamsapor consented and relying on this information, reported to the king that Constantius, being involved in very serious wars, entreated and begged for peace.

CONSTANTIUS ET GALLUS

Chionitas et Eusenos [1] haec scripta mittuntur, in quorum confiniis agebat hiemem Sapor, tempus interstitit longum.

10. *Constantii Aug. militaris ac velut triumphalis in urbem Romam adventus.*

1. Haec dum per eoas partes et Gallias pro captu temporum disponuntur, Constantius quasi cluso [2] Iani templo stratisque hostibus cunctis, Romam visere gestiebat, post Magnenti exitium absque nomine ex sanguine Romano triumphaturus. 2. Nec enim gentem ullam bella cientem per se superavit, aut victam fortitudine suorum comperit ducum, vel addidit quaedam imperio, aut usquam in necessitatibus summis primus vel inter primos est visus, sed ut pompam nimis extentam, rigentiaque auro vexilla, et pulcritudinem stipatorum ostenderet agenti tranquillius populo, haec vel simile quicquam videre nec speranti umquam nec optanti. 3. Ignorans fortasse, quosdam veterum principum in pace quidem lictoribus fuisse contentos, ubi vero proeliorum ardor nihil perpeti poterat segne, alium anhelante rabido flatu ventorum lenunculo se commisisse piscantis, alium ad Deciorum exempla vovisse pro re publica spiritum, alium

---

[1] *Cusenos*, Marquart.
[2] *quasi cluso*, Her. ; *quam recluso*, V.

But while these communications were being sent to the Chionitae and Euseni, in whose territories Sapor was passing the winter, a long time elapsed.

10. *Constantius Augustus in military attire and like a triumphator arrives in Rome.*

1. While these events were so being arranged in the Orient and in Gaul in accordance with the times, Constantius, as if the temple of Janus had been closed and all his enemies overthrown, was eager to visit Rome and after the death of Magnentius to celebrate, without a title, a triumph over Roman blood. 2. For neither in person did he vanquish any nation that made war upon him, nor learn of any conquered by the valour of his generals; nor did he add anything to his empire; nor at critical moments was he ever seen to be foremost, or among the foremost; but he desired to display an inordinately long procession, banners stiff with goldwork, and the splendour of his retinue, to a populace living in perfect peace and neither expecting nor desiring to see this or anything like it. 3. Perhaps he did not know that some of our ancient commanders in time of peace were satisfied with the attendance of their lictors; but when the heat of battle could tolerate no inaction, one, with the mad blast of the winds shrieking, entrusted himself to a fisherman's skiff;[1] another, after the example of the Decii, vowed his life for the commonwealth;[2] a third in his own person together with common soldiers explored the

---

[1] Julius Caesar; see Lucan, v. 533 ff.
[2] Claudius II., in the Gothic war.

hostilia castra per semet ipsum cum militibus in-
fimis explorasse, diversos denique actibus inclaruisse
magnificis, ut glorias suas posteritatis celebri
memoriae [1] commendarent.

4. Ut igitur multa quaeque consumpta sunt in
apparatu regio, pro meritis cuilibet munera reddita,[2]
secunda Orfiti praefectura, transcurso Ocriculo,
elatus honoribus magnis, stipatusque agminibus
formidandis, tamquam acie ducebatur instructa,
omnium oculis in eum [3] contuitu pertinaci intentis.
5. Cumque urbi propinquaret, senatus officia, reve-
rendasque patriciae stirpis effigies, ore sereno contemplans, non ut Cineas ille Pyrri legatus, in unum
coactam multitudinem regum, sed asylum mundi
totius adesse existimabat.   6. Unde cum se ver-
tisset ad plebem, stupebat qua celebritate [4] omne
quod ubique est hominum genus confluxerit Romam.
Et tamquam Euphraten armorum specie territurus
aut Rhenum, altrinsecus praeeuntibus signis, in-
sidebat aureo solus ipse carpento, fulgenti claritudine lapidum variorum, quo micante lux quaedam
misceri videbatur alterna.   7. Eumque post ante-
gressos multiplices alios, purpureis subtegminibus
texti, circumdedere dracones, hastarum aureis
gemmatisque summitatibus illigati, hiatu vasto
perflabiles, et ideo velut ira perciti sibilantes, cau-
darumque volumina relinquentes in ventum.   8. Et

---

[1] *memoriae*, Kiessling ;   *memoria*, V.   [2] *regio . . .
reddita*, BG in lac. of 17 letters.   [3] *eum*, Bentley,
Günther ;   *eo*, V.   [4] *celebritate*, Bentley ; *celeritate*, V.

---

[1] Galerius Maximianus, who in person reconnoitred
the Persian camp.   [2] The imperial standards.

enemy's camp;[1] in short, various among them became famous through splendid deeds, so that they commended their glories to the frequent remembrance of posterity.

4. So soon, then, as much had been disbursed in regal preparation, and every sort of man had been rewarded according to his services, in the second prefecture of Orfitus he passed through Ocriculi, elated with his great honours and escorted by formidable troops; he was conducted, so to speak, in battle array and everyone's eyes were riveted upon him with fixed gaze. 5. And when he was nearing the city, as he beheld with calm countenance the dutiful attendance of the senate and the august likenesses of the patrician stock, he thought, not like Cineas, the famous envoy of Pyrrhus, that a throng of kings was assembled together, but that the sanctuary of the whole world was present before him. 6. And when he turned from them to the populace, he was amazed to see in what crowds men of every type had flocked from all quarters to Rome. And as if he were planning to overawe the Euphrates with a show of arms, or the Rhine, while the standards preceded him on each side, he himself sat alone upon a golden car in the resplendent blaze of shimmering precious stones, whose mingled glitter seemed to form a sort of shifting light. 7. And behind the manifold others that preceded him he was surrounded by dragons,[2] woven out of purple thread and bound to the golden and jewelled tops of spears, with wide mouths open to the breeze and hence hissing as if roused by anger, and leaving their tails winding in the wind. 8. And there marched on either side

CONSTANTIUS ET GALLUS

incedebat hinc inde ordo geminus armatorum,
clipeatus atque cristatus, corusco lumine radians,
nitidis loricis indutus, sparsique cataphracti equites
(quos clibanarios dictitant) personati thoracum
muniti tegminibus, et limbis ferreis cincti, ut Praxi-
telis manu polita crederes simulacra, non viros;
quos laminarum circuli tenues, apti corporis
flexibus ambiebant, per omnia membra diducti,
ut quocumque artus necessitas commovisset, vesti-
tus congrueret, iunctura cohaerenter aptata. 9.
Augustus itaque faustis vocibus appellatus, non
montium [1] litorumque intonante fragore cohorruit,
talem se tamque immobilem, qualis in provinciis
suis visebatur, ostendens. 10. Nam et corpus
perhumile curvabat portas ingrediens celsas, et
velut collo munito, rectam aciem luminum tendens,
nec dextra vultum nec laeva flectebat et [2] (tamquam
figmentum hominis) nec [3] cum rota concuteret
nutans, nec spuens, aut os aut nasum tergens vel
fricans, manumve agitans visus est umquam. 11.
Quae licet affectabat, erant tamen haec et alia
quaedam in citeriore vita, patientiae non mediocris
indicia, ut existimari dabatur, uni illi concessae.
12. Quod autem per omne tempus imperii, nec in
consessum vehiculi quemquam suscepit, nec in
trabea socium privatum asscivit, ut fecere principes
consecrati, et similia multa elatus in arduum super-

---

[1] *appellatus*, EG ; *non*, added by Her. ; *montium*, Val. ;
appella (lac. 10 letters) *otium*, V.   [2] *et*, added by Clark ;
V omits ; asyndeton def. Heilmann.   [3] *nec*, Clark ; *nam*,
V ; *non*, AG.

---

[1] Cuirassiers ; the word is derived from κλίβανον, "oven,"
and means entirely encased in iron ; see Index of Officials,
or Index II.

246

twin lines of infantrymen with shields and crests
gleaming with glittering rays, clad in shining mail;
and scattered among them were the full-armoured
cavalry (whom they call *clibanarii*),[1] all masked,
furnished with protecting breastplates and girt with
iron belts, so that you might have supposed them
statues polished by the hand of Praxiteles, not men.
Thin circles of iron plates, fitted to the curves of
their bodies, completely covered their limbs; so
that whichever way they had to move their members,
their garment fitted, so skilfully were the joinings
made. 9. Accordingly, being saluted as Augustus
with favouring shouts, while hills and shores thun-
dered out the roar, he never stirred, but showed
himself as calm and imperturbable as he was commonly seen in his provinces. 10. For he both
stooped when passing through lofty gates (although
he was very short), and as if his neck were in a vice,
he kept the gaze of his eyes straight ahead, and turned
his face neither to right nor to left, but (as if he were
a lay figure) neither did he nod when the wheel
jolted nor was he ever seen to spit, or to wipe or
rub his face or nose, or move his hands about.
11. And although this was affectation on his part,
yet these and various other features of his more
intimate life were tokens of no slight endurance,
granted to him alone, as was given to be understood.
12. Furthermore, that during the entire period of
his reign he neither took up anyone to sit beside
him in his car, nor admitted any private person to
be his colleague in the insignia of the consulship,
as other anointed princes did, and many like habits
which in his pride of lofty conceit he observed as

cilium, tamquam leges aequissimas observavit, praetereo, memor ea me rettulisse cum incidissent.

13. Proinde Romam ingressus imperii virtutumque omnium larem, cum venisset ad rostra, perspectissimum priscae potentiae forum, obstipuit, perque omne latus quo se oculi contulissent, miraculorum densitate praestrictus, allocutus nobilitatem in curia, populumque e [1] tribunali, in palatium receptus favore multiplici, laetitia fruebatur optata, et saepe, cum equestres ederet ludos, dicacitate plebis oblectabatur, nec superbae nec a libertate coalita desciscentis, reverenter modum ipse quoque debitum servans. 14. Non enim (ut per civitates alias) ad arbitrium suum certamina finiri patiebatur, sed (ut mos est) variis casibus permittebat. Deinde intra septem montium culmina, per acclivitates planitiemque posita urbis membra collustrans et suburbana, quicquid viderat [2] primum, id eminere inter alia cuncta sperabat : Iovis Tarpei delubra, quantum terrenis divina praecellunt ; lavacra in modum provinciarum exstructa ; amphitheatri molem solidatam lapidis Tiburtini compage, ad cuius summitatem aegre visio humana conscendit ; Pantheum velut regionem teretem speciosa celsitudine fornicatam ; elatosque vertices qui [3] scansili [4]

---

[1] e, Val. ; pro, BG ; V omits.   [2] uiderat, Val. ; erat, V.   [3] qui, added by Novák.   [4] uertice scansili, G ; uertices rasili, B ; u. s., Lind ; u. cassili, V.

though they were most just laws, I pass by, remembering that I set them down when they occurred.

13. So then he entered Rome, the home of empire and of every virtue, and when he had come to the Rostra, the most renowned forum of ancient dominion, he stood amazed; and on every side on which his eyes rested he was dazzled by the array of marvellous sights. He addressed the nobles in the senate-house and the populace from the tribunal, and being welcomed to the palace with manifold attentions, he enjoyed a longed-for pleasure; and on several occasions, when holding equestrian games, he took delight in the sallies of the commons, who were neither presumptuous nor regardless of their old-time freedom, while he himself also respectfully observed the due mean. 14. For he did not (as in the case of other cities) permit the contests to be terminated at his own discretion, but left them (as the custom is) to various chances. Then, as he surveyed the sections of the city and its suburbs, lying within the summits of the seven hills, along their slopes, or on level ground, he thought that whatever first met his gaze towered above all the rest: the sanctuaries of Tarpeian Jove so far surpassing as things divine excel those of earth; the baths built up to the measure of provinces; the huge bulk of the amphitheatre, strengthened by its framework of Tiburtine stone,[1] to whose top human eyesight barely ascends; the Pantheon like a rounded city-district,[2] vaulted over in lofty

---

[1] Travertine.
[2] *Regio* here refers to one of the regions, or districts, into which the city was divided.

suggestu consurgunt, priorum principum imita-
menta portantes, et Urbis templum forumque
Pacis, et Pompei theatrum et Odeum et Stadium,
aliaque inter haec decora urbis aeternae. 15. Verum
cum ad Traiani forum venisset, singularem sub
omni caelo structuram, ut [1] opinamur, etiam numinum assensione mirabilem, haerebat attonitus, per
giganteos contextus circumferens mentem, nec
relatu effabiles, nec rursus mortalibus appetendos.
Omni itaque spe huius modi quicquam conandi
depulsa, Traiani equum solum, locatum in atrii
medio, qui ipsum principem vehit, imitari se velle
dicebat et posse. 16. Cui prope adstans regalis
Ormisda, cuius e Perside discessum supra monstravimus, respondit astu gentili : " Ante " inquit
" imperator, stabulum tale condi iubeto, si vales ;
equus [2] quem fabricare disponis, ita late succedat,
ut iste quem videmus." Is ipse interrogatus quid

---

[1] *et ut*, Her.   [2] *ut equus*, Her.

---

[1] The columns of Trajan, Antoninus Pius, and Marcus
Aurelius. The platform at the top was reached by a stair-
way within the column.

[2] The double temple of Venus and Roma, built by
Hadrian and dedicated in A.D. 135.

[3] The Forum Pacis, or Vespasiani, was begun by
Vespasian in A.D. 71, after the taking of Jerusalem, and
dedicated in 75. It lay behind the basilica Aemilia.

[4] Built in 55 B.C. in the Campus Martius.

[5] A building for musical performances, erected by
Domitian, probably near his Stadium.

[6] The Stadium of Domitian in the Campus Martius,
the shape and size of which is almost exactly preserved
by the modern Piazza Navona.

beauty; and the exalted heights which rise with platforms to which one may mount, and bear the likenesses of former emperors; [1] the Temple of the City,[2] the Forum of Peace,[3] the Theatre of Pompey,[4] the Oleum,[5] the Stadium,[6] and amongst these the other adornments of the Eternal City. 15. But when he came to the Forum of Trajan, a construction unique under the heavens, as we believe, and admirable even in the unanimous opinion of the gods, he stood fast in amazement, turning his attention to the gigantic complex about him, beggaring description and never again to be imitated by mortal men. Therefore abandoning all hope of attempting anything like it, he said that he would and could copy Trajan's steed alone, which stands in the centre of the vestibule, carrying the emperor himself. 16. To this prince Ormisda, who was standing near him, and whose departure from Persia I have described above,[7] replied with native wit: " First, Sire," said he, " command a like stable to be built, if you can; let the steed which you propose to create range as widely as this which we see." When Ormisda was asked directly what he thought of Rome, he said that he took comfort [8]

---

[7] In 323 (Zosimus, ii. 27); hence in one of the lost books of Ammianus.

[8] Valesius read *displicuisse*, and was followed by Gibbon. Robert Heron (pseudonym of John Pinkerton) in *Letters of Literature* (London, 1789), xii., p. 68, discusses this remark at some length, disagreeing with Gibbon. He thinks that " the prince's envy at the pleasures of the inhabitants of Rome could only be moderated by the reflection that their pleasures were transitory."

de Roma sentiret, id tantum sibi placuisse aiebat, quod didicisset ibi quoque homines mori. 17. Multis igitur cum stupore visis horrendo, imperator de [1] fama querebatur, ut invalida vel maligna,[2] quod augens omnia semper in maius, erga haec explicanda quae Romae sunt obsolescit, deliberansque diu quid ibi [3] ageret, urbis addere statuit ornamentis, ut in maximo [4] circo erigeret obeliscum, cuius originem formamque loco competenti monstrabo.

18. Inter haec Helenae sorori Constanti, Iuliani coniugi Caesaris, Romam affectionis specie ductae, regina tunc insidiabatur Eusebia, ipsa quoad vixerat sterilis, quaesitumque venenum bibere per fraudem illexit, ut quotienscumque concepisset, immaturum abiceret partum. 19. Nam et pridem in Galliis, cum marem genuisset infantem, hoc perdidit dolo, quod obstetrix corrupta mercede, mox [5] natum, praesecto plus quam convenerat umbilico, necavit ; tanta tamque diligens opera navabatur, ne fortissimi viri soboles appareret.

20. Cupiens itaque augustissima omnium sede morari diutius imperator, ut otio puriore frueretur et voluptate, assiduis nuntiis terrebatur et certis, indicantibus Suebos Raetias incursare, Quadosque

---

[1] *imperator de*, AG ; *imperator in*, Gronov ; *imperatori*, V. See Dessau, Inscr. 736 : C.I.L. vi. 1163.   [2] *maligna*, A ; *magna*, V.   [3] *quid ibi*, suggested by Clark ; *quid*, E²BG ; V omits.   [4] *maximo*, E², Val. ; *proximo*, V.   [5] *mox*, V, 20, 4 ; *modo*, Damsté.

in this fact alone, that he had learned that even there men were mortal.   17. So then, when the emperor had viewed many objects with awe and amazement, he complained of Fame as either incapable or spiteful, because while always exaggerating everything, in describing what there is in Rome, she becomes shabby.   And after long deliberation what he should do there, he determined to add to the adornments of the city by erecting in the Circus Maximus an obelisk, the provenance and figure of which I shall describe in the proper place.[1]

18. Meanwhile Constantius' sister Helena, wife of Julian Caesar, had been brought to Rome under pretence of affection, but the reigning queen, Eusebia, was plotting against her ; she herself had been childless all her life, and by her wiles she coaxed Helena to drink a rare potion, so that as often as she was with child she should have a miscarriage.   19. For once before, in Gaul, when she had borne a baby boy, she lost it through this machination : a midwife had been bribed with a sum of money, and as soon as the child was born cut the umbilical cord more than was right, and so killed it ; such great pains and so much thought were taken that this most valiant man might have no heir.

20. Now the emperor desired to remain longer in this most majestic abode of all the world, to enjoy freer repose and pleasure ; but he was alarmed by constant trustworthy reports, stating that the Suebi were raiding Raetia and the Quadi Valeria,[2]

---

[1] xvii. **4,** 6 ff.

[2] A division of Pannonia, named from Valeria, daughter of Diocletian and wife of Galerius ; see xix. **11,** 4.

Valeriam, et Sarmatas, latrocinandi peritissimum
genus, superiorem Moesiam et secundam populari
Pannoniam ; quibus percitus tricensimo postquam
ingressus est die, quartum kal. Iunias ab urbe
profectus, per Tridentum iter in Illyricum festinavit.
21. Unde misso in locum Marcelli Severo, bellorum
usu et maturitate firmato, Ursicinum ad se venire
praecepit. Et ille litteris gratanter acceptis, Sirmium venit, comitantibus sociis,[1] libratisque diu
super pace consiliis, quam fundari posse cum Persis
Musonianus rettulerat, in orientem cum magisterii
remittitur potestate, provectis e consortio nostro
ad regendos milites natu maioribus, adulescentes
eum sequi iubemur, quicquid pro re publica man-
daverit impleturi.

11. *Iulianus Caesar Alamannos in insulis Rheni, quo*
      se et sua receperant, aggreditur, et Tres Tabernas
      adversus eos reparat.

1. At Caesar exacta apud Senonas hieme turbu-
lenta, Augusto novies seque iterum consule, Ger-
manicis undique circumfrementibus minis, secundis
ominibus motus, Remos properavit alacrior, magisque laetus quod exercitum regebat Severus, nec

----

[1] *sociis*, BG ; *solis* (lac.), Clark ; *solis*, V.

----

[1] Trent.
[2] See index.
[3] Cf. **7, 1,** above.

while the Sarmatians, a tribe most accomplished in brigandage, were laying waste Upper Moesia and Lower Pannonia. Excited by this news, on the thirtieth day after entering Rome he left the city on May 29th, and marched rapidly into Illyricum by way of Tridentum.[1] 21. From there he sent Severus, a general toughened by long military experience, to succeed Marcellus, and ordered Ursicinus to come to him. The latter received the letter with joy and came to Sirmium[2] with his companions; and after long deliberations about the peace which Musonianus had reported might be established with the Persians, Ursicinus was sent back to the Orient with the powers of commander-in-chief; the elder members of our company were promoted to the command of his soldiers, while we younger men were directed to escort him and be ready to perform whatever he should direct on behalf of the commonwealth.

11. *Julianus Caesar attacks the Alamanni on the islands of the Rhine, to which they had fled with their belongings, and refits Tres Tabernae against them.*

1. But Julianus Caesar, after having passed a troubled winter at Sens,[3] in the year when the emperor was consul for the ninth time and he for the second, with the threats from the Germans thundering on every side, stirred by favourable omens hastened to Rheims. He felt the greater eagerness and pleasure because Severus was commanding the army, a man neither insubordinate nor overbearing

discors nec arrogans, sed longa militiae frugalitate
compertus, et eum recta praeeuntem secutus,[1] ut
ductorem morigerus [2] miles.   2. Parte alia Barbatio,
post Silvani interitum promotus ad peditum magis-
terium, ex Italia iussu principis cum XXV milibus
armatorum Rauracos venit.   3. Cogitatum est enim,
sollicteque praestructum, ut saevientes ultra solitum Alamanni vagantesque fusius, multitudine
geminata nostrorum, forcipis specie, trusi in angustias
caederentur.   4. Dum haec tamen rite disposita
celerantur, Laeti barbari ad tempestiva furta soller-
tes, inter utriusque exercitus castra occulte transgressi, invasere Lugdunum incautam, eamque populatam vi subita [3] concremassent, ni clausis aditibus
repercussi, quicquid extra oppidum potuit inveniri
vastassent.   5. Qua clade cognita, agili studio
Caesar missis cuneis tribus equitum expeditorum
et fortium, tria observavit itinera, sciens per ea
erupturos procul dubio grassatores; nec conatus ei
insidianti [4] irritus fuit.   6. Cunctis enim qui per eos
tramites exiere truncatis, receptaque praeda omni
intacta, hi soli innoxii absoluti sunt, qui per vallum
Barbationis transiere securi, ideo labi permissi,
quod Bainobaudes tribunus, et Valentinianus postea

---

[1] secutus, Clark, c.c.; secuturus, V.   [2] morigerus,
Petavius; morigerum, EBG; murigerum, V.   [3] subita,
Hermann; summa, Gronov; uisu (lac. 8 letters) aconcre-
massent, V.   [4] ei insidianti, Novák; neco (V[2] in lac.
9 letters) inanti, V.

---

[1] The forceps or forfex was a military formation with
diverging wings for meeting and baffling a cuneus; cf.
Vegetius, iii. 19, nam ex lectissimis militibus in V litteram

but well known for his long excellent record in the army, who had followed Julian as he advanced straight ahead, as an obedient soldier follows his general. 2. From another direction Barbatio, who had been promoted after Silvanus' death to the command of the infantry, came from Italy at the emperor's order with twenty-five thousand soldiers to Augst. 3. For it was planned and carefully arranged beforehand that the Alamanni, who were raging beyond their customary manner and ranging more afield, should be driven into straits as if with a pair of pliers[1] by twin forces of our soldiers, and cut to pieces. 4. But while these well-laid plans were being hurried on, the Laeti, a savage tribe skilled in seasonable raids, passed secretly between the encampments of both armies and made an unlooked for attack on Lyons; and with their sudden onset they would have sacked and burned the town, had they not been driven back from the closed gates but made havoc of whatever they could find outside the town. 5. This disaster was no sooner known than Caesar, with quick grasp of the situation, sent three squadrons of brave light cavalry and watched three roads, knowing that the raiders would doubtless burst forth by them; and his ambuscade was not in vain. 6. For all who passed out by those roads were butchered and all their booty recovered intact, and only those escaped unharmed who made their way undisturbed past the rampart of Barbatio; being allowed so to slip by because Bainobaudes, the tribune,

---

ordo componitur, et illum cuneum excipit atque utraque parte concludit. The open part of the V of course faced the enemy. Here *forceps* is perhaps used in its literal sense.

imperator, cum equestribus turmis quas regebant,
ad exsequendum id ordinati, a Cella tribuno scutariorum, qui Barbationi sociatus venerat ad procinctum,
iter observare sunt vetiti, unde redituros didicere
Germanos. 7. Quo non contentus, magister peditum ignavus et gloriarum Iuliani pervicax obtrec-
tator, sciens se id contra utilitatem Romanae rei [1]
iussisse—hoc enim cum argueretur, Cella confessus
est—relatione fefellit Constantium, finxitque hos
eosdem tribunos, ad sollicitandos milites quos
duxerat per speciem venisse negotii publici ; qua
causa abrogata potestate ad lares rediere privati.

8. Eisdem diebus, exercituum adventu perterriti
barbari, qui domicilia fixere cis Rhenum, partim
difficiles vias et suapte natura clivosas, concaedibus
clausere sollerter, arboribus immensi roboris caesis ;
alii occupatis insulis sparsis crebro per flumen
Rhenum, ferum [2] ululantes et lugubre, conviciis
Romanos incessebant et Caesarem ; qui graviore
motu animi percitus, ad corripiendos aliquos septem
a Barbatione petierat naves, ex his quas velut transiturus amnem ad compaginandos paraverat pontes ;

---

[1] *Romanae rei*, Mommsen ; *Romanam*, W[2] G ; *Romaniae*,
V. [2] *ferum*, added by Schneider ; in place of *Rhenum*,
Heraeus, c.c. ; V omits.

and Valentinian, afterwards emperor, who with the
cavalry troops they commanded had been ordered
to attend to that matter, were forbidden by Cella, tribune of the targeteers, who had come to the campaign
as Barbatio's colleague, to watch the road over which
they were informed that the Germans would return.
7. And not content with that, the infantry commander, who was a coward and a persistent de-
tractor of Julian's reputation, knowing that what
he had ordered was against the interests of the
Roman cause (for when Cella was charged with
this, he confessed it), deceived Constantius in
his report and pretended that these same tribunes
had come, under the pretext of public business,
to tamper with the soldiers whom he had been
commanding; and for that reason they were cashiered and returned to their homes in a private
capacity.

8. At that same time the savages who had established their homes on our side of the Rhine, were
alarmed by the approach of our armies, and some
of them skilfully blocked the roads (which are difficult and naturally of heavy grades) by barricades
of felled trees of huge size; others, taking possession of the islands which are scattered in numbers
along the course of the Rhine, with wild and
mournful cries heaped insults upon the Romans
and Caesar. Whereupon he was inflamed with a
mighty outburst of anger, and in order to catch
some of them, asked Barbatio for seven of the ships
which he had got ready for building bridges with
the intention of crossing the river; but Barbatio
burned them all, in order that he might be unable

qui, nequid per eum impetraretur, omnes incendit.
9. Doctus denique exploratorum delatione recens
captorum, aestate iam torrida fluvium vado posse
transiri, hortatus auxiliares velites cum Bainobaude
Cornutorum misit tribuno,[1] facinus memorabile
si iuvisset fors patraturos, qui nunc incedendo per
brevia, aliquotiens scutis in modum alveorum sup-
positis, nando ad insulam venere propinquam,
egressique promiscue virile et muliebre secus sine
aetatis ullo discrimine trucidabant ut pecudes,
nanctique vacuas lintres, per eas licet vacillantes
evecti, huius modi loca plurima perruperunt, et ubi
caedendi satias cepit, opimitate praedarum onusti,
cuius partem vi fluminis amiserunt, rediere omnes
incolumes. 10. Hocque comperto, residui Germani,
ut infido praesidio insularum relicto, ad ulteriora
necessitudines et fruges opesque barbaricas contulerunt. 11. Conversus hinc Iulianus ad reparan-
das Tres Tabernas (munimentum ita cognominatum,)
haut ita dudum obstinatione subversum hostili, quo
aedificato constabat ad intima Galliarum (ut consueverant) adire Germanos arceri, et opus spe
celerius consummavit, et victum defensoribus ibi
locandis, ex barbaricis messibus non sine discriminis
metu collectum militis manu, condidit ad usus anni
totius. 12. Nec sane hoc solo contentus, sibi

---

[1] *misit tribuno*, tr. by Heilmann; *tribuno dimisit*, Clark,
c.c.; *misit*, V.

---

[1] Cf. xiv. **2**, 10, *cavatis arborum truncis*; xxxi. **4**, 5,
navibus ratibusque et cavatis arborum alveis.
[2] The Three Taverns; modern Saverne, Germ. Rhein-
zabern.

260

to give any help. 9. Finally Julian, learning from
the report of some scouts just captured, that now
in the heat of summer the river could be forded,
with words of encouragement sent the light-armed
auxiliaries with Bainobaudes, tribune of the Cornuti,
to perform a memorable feat, if fortune would
favour them; and they, now wading through the
shallows, now swimming on their shields, which
they put under them like canoes,[1] came to a neighbouring island and landing there they butchered
everyone they found, men and women alike, without distinction of age, like so many sheep. Then,
finding some empty boats, they rowed on in these,
unsteady as they were, and raided a large number
of such places; and when they were sated with
slaughter, loaded down with a wealth of booty
(a part of which they lost through the force of
the current) they all came back safe and sound.
10. And the rest of the Germans, on learning of
this, abandoned the islands as an unsafe refuge
and carried off into the interior their families, their
grain, and their rude treasures. 11. From here
Julian turned aside to repair the fortress called Tres
Tabernae,[2] destroyed not long before by the enemy's
obstinate assault, the rebuilding of which ensured
that the Germans could not approach the interior
of Gaul, as they had been wont to do. And he both
finished this work sooner than was expected and,
for the garrison that was to be stationed there, he
stored up food for the needs of a whole year, gathered
together by the hands of the soldiers, not without
fear of danger, from the savages' crops. 12. And
not content with that alone, he gathered for

quoque viginti dierum alimenta parata collegit.
Libentius enim bellatores quaesito dexteris propriis
utebantur, admodum indignati, quoniam ex com-
meatu, qui eis recens advectus est, ideo nihil sumere
potuerunt, quod partem eius Barbatio, cum transiret
iuxta, superbe praesumpsit ; residuumque quod [1]
superfuit congestum in acervum exussit, quae
utrum ut vanus gerebat et demens, an mandatu
principis confidenter nefanda multa [2] temptabat,[3]
usque in id temporis latuit. 13. Illud tamen rumore
tenus ubique iactabatur, quod Iulianus non levaturus
incommoda Galliarum electus est, sed ut possit per
bella deleri saevissima, rudis etiam tum ut existi-
mabatur, et ne sonitum quidem duraturus armorum.
14. Dum castrorum opera [4] mature consurgunt,[5]
militisque pars stationes praetendit agrarias, alia
frumenta insidiarum metu colligit caute, multitudo
barbarica rumorem nimia velocitate praeversa,
Barbationem cum exercitu quem regebat (ut praedictum est) Gallico vallo discretum impetu repentino
aggressa, sequensque fugientes ad usque Rauracos
et ultra quoad potuit, rapta sarcinarum et iumentorum cum calonibus parte maxima redit ad suos.[6]
15. Et ille tamquam expeditione eventu prospero
terminata, milite disperso per stationes hibernas, ad
comitatum imperatoris revertit, crimen compositurus
in Caesarem (ut solebat).[7]

[1] *que quod*, Günther (*quod*, EBG) ; *quae*, V.   [2] *multa*,
E[2] G ; *ut multi*, Her. ; *multi*, V.   [3] *temptabat*, Her. ;
tentabant, Val. ; *temptabatus que tamen* . . . , added by V[2] in
margin.   [4] *castrorum opus militum opera*, Mommsen.
[5] *consurgunt*, G ; *consurgit*, V.   [6] lac. 13 letters at end
of page, V.   [7] lac. 6 letters at end of line, V ; *graviter
semper incessens*, BG.

himself also rations to serve for twenty days. For the
warriors the more willingly made use of what they
had won by their own right hands, being greatly
incensed because from the supplies which had just
been brought them they could get nothing, since
Barbatio had arrogantly appropriated a part of
them, when they were passing near him ; and piled
in a heap what remained over and burned it.
Whether he did this like an empty-headed fool, or
at the emperor's bidding brazenly perpetrated his
many abominable acts, has remained obscure up
to this time. 13. However, it was current rumour
everywhere, that Julian was not chosen to relieve
the distress of Gaul, but that he might meet his
death in the cruellest of wars, being even then (as
it was thought) inexperienced and one who could
not stand even the clash of arms. 14. While the
fortifications of the camp were rapidly rising and
part of the soldiers were garrisoning the country
posts, part gathering in grain warily for fear of
ambush, a horde of savages, outstripping by their
extraordinary speed any rumour of their coming,
with a sudden attack set upon Barbatio and the
army he commanded, which was (as has been said)
separated from the Gallic camp ; and they followed
them in their flight as far as Augst, and as much
farther as they could ; then, after seizing the greater
part of his baggage and pack-animals, together with
the camp-followers, they returned home again.
15. And Barbatio, as if he had ended the campaign
successfully, distributed his soldiers in winter quarters and returned to the emperor's court, to frame
some charge against Caesar, as was his custom.

CONSTANTIUS ET GALLUS

12. *Iulianus C. vii Alamannorum reges Galliam
incubantes aggreditur, et barbaros apud Argentoratum acie fundit.*

1. Quo dispalato foedo terrore, Alamannorum reges
Chonodomarius et Vestralpus, Urius quin etiam et
Ursicinus, cum Serapione et Suomario et Hortario,
in unum robore virium suarum omni collecto,
bellicumque canere bucinis iussis, venere [1] prope
urbem Argentoratum, extrema metuentem Caesarem arbitrati retrocessisse, cum ille tum [2] etiam
perficiendi munimenti studio stringeretur. **2.** Erexit
autem confidentiam caput altius attollentum scu-
tarius perfuga, qui commissi criminis metuens
poenam, transgressus ad eos post ducis fugati discessum, armatorum tredecim milia tantum reman-
sisse cum Iuliano docebat—is enim numerus eum
sequebatur—barbara feritate certaminum rabiem
undique concitante. **3.** Cuius asseveratione eadem
subinde replicantis, ad maiora stimulati fiducia,
missis legatis, satis pro imperio Caesari mandaverunt,
ut terris abscederet virtute sibi quaesitis et ferro ;
qui ignarus pavendi, nec ira nec dolore perculsus,
sed fastus barbaricos ridens, tentis legatis ad usque
perfectum opus castrorum, in eodem gradu constantiae stetit immobilis.

---

[1] *canere bucinis iussis,* Novák ; *canentibus bucinis uenere,*
Her. ; *belli. cumque foedere,* V.   [2] *tum,* Val. ; *dum,* V.

12. *Julianus Caesar attacks the seven kings of the Alamanni, who were oppressing the Gauls, and routs the savages in a battle at Argentoratum (Strasburg).*

1. When this disgraceful panic had been spread abroad, the kings of the Alamanni, Chonodomarius and Vestralpus, as well as Urius and Ursicinus, together with Serapio and Suomarius and Hortarius, collected all the flower of their forces in one spot and having ordered the horns to sound the war-note, approached the city of Strasburg, thinking that Caesar had retired through fear of the worst, whereas he was even then busily employed in his project of completing the fort. 2. Moreover, as they tossed their heads proudly, their confidence was increased by a deserter from the targeteers; who, in fear of punishment for a crime he had committed, went over to them after the departure of his defeated leader, and informed them that only thirteen thousand soldiers had stayed with Julian; and in fact that was the number of his followers, while savage ferocity was arousing the frenzy of battle on every side. 3. Through this deserter's frequent repetition of that statement their confidence was raised still higher; they sent delegates to Caesar and imperiously enough commanded him to depart from the lands which they had won by valour and the sword. But he, a stranger to fear, neither lost his temper nor felt aggrieved, but laughing at the presumption of the savages, he detained the envoys until the work of fortification was ended and remained steadfast in the same attitude of resolution.

265

CONSTANTIUS ET GALLUS

4. Agitabat autem miscebatque omnia, sine modo ubique sese diffunditans, et princeps audendi periculosa, rex Chonodomarius, ardua subrigens supercilia, ut saepe secundis rebus elatus. **5.** Nam et Decentium Caesarem superavit, aequo Marte congressus, et civitates erutas multas vastavit et opulentas, licentiusque diu nullo refragante Gallias persultavit. Ad cuius roborandam fiduciam, recens quoque fuga ducis accessit, numero praestantis et viribus. **6.** Alamanni enim scutorum insignia contuentes, norant eos milites permisisse paucis suorum latronibus terram, quorum metu aliquotiens, antequam[1] gradum conferrent, amissis pluribus abiere dispersi. Quae anxie ferebat sollicitus Caesar, quod trudente ipsa necessitate, digresso periculi socio,[2] cum paucis (licet fortibus) populosis gentibus occurrere cogebatur.

7. Iamque solis radiis rutilantibus, tubarumque concinente clangore, pedestres copiae lentis incessibus educuntur, earumque lateri equestres iunctae[3] sunt turmae, inter quas cataphractarii erant et sagittarii, formidabile genus armorum. **8.** Et quoniam a loco, unde Romana promota sunt signa, ad usque vallum barbaricum quarta leuga signabatur et decima, id est unum et viginti milia passuum, utilitati securitatique recte consulens Caesar, revocatis procursatoribus[4] iam antegressis, indictaque

---

[1] *antequam*, C. F. W. Müller, Haupt.; *inaliquam*, V.
[2] *periculi socio*, Günther, Mommsen (*s.p.*, Madvig); *periculis*, V.   [3] *iunctae*, E, C. F. W. Müller; *cunctae*, V.
[4] *procursatoribus*, Her.; *praecursoribus*, BG; *praecursatoribus*, V.

---

[1] Namely, Barbatio.   [2] See note 1, p. 206.

4. Now King Chonodomarius was raising general disturbance and confusion, making his presence felt everywhere without limit, a leader in dangerous enterprises, lifting up his brows in pride, being as he was conceited over frequent successes. 5. For he both met Decentius Caesar on equal terms and defeated him, and had destroyed and sacked many wealthy cities, and for a long time freely overran Gaul without opposition. To strengthen his confidence, there was added besides the recent rout of a general superior in numbers and strength.[1] 6. For the Alamanni, on seeing the devices of their shields, realised that these soldiers, who had given ground before a few of their brigands, were the men in fear of whom they had at times in the past scattered and fled with heavy losses, before coming to close quarters. All this caused Julian worry and anxiety, because at the instance of urgent necessity, with the partner of his danger gone, he was forced with only a few (though brave) troops to meet swarming tribes.

7. Already the beams of the sun were reddening the sky, and the blare of the trumpets was sounding in unison, when the infantry forces were led out at a moderate pace, and to their flank were joined the squadrons of cavalry, among whom were the cuirassiers [2] and the archers, a formidable branch of the service. 8. And since from the place where the Roman standards had begun advancing, the distance to the enemy's camp was figured to be fourteen leagues—that is, twenty-one miles—Caesar had proper regard for both advantage and security, and having recalled his outposts, who had already

267

solitis vocibus quiete, cuneatim circumsistentes alloquitur, genuina placiditate sermonis :

9. " Urget ratio salutis tuendae communis, ut parcissime dicam, non iacentis animi Caesarem hortari vos et orare,—commilitones mei—ut adulta robustaque virtute confisi, cautiorem viam potius eligamus, ad toleranda vel ad depellenda quae sperantur, non praeproperam et ancipitem. 10. Ut enim in periculis iuventutem impigram esse convenit et audacem, ita (cum res postulat) regibilem et consultam. Quid igitur censeo, si arbitrium affuerit vestrum, iustaque sustinet indignatio, paucis absolvam. 11. Iam dies in meridiem vergit, lassitudine nos itineris fatigatos, scrupulosi tramites excipient et obscuri, nox senescente luna nullis sideribus adiuvanda, terrae protinus aestu flagrantes, nullis aquarum subsidiis fultae ; quae si dederit quisquam commode posse transiri, ruentibus hostium examinibus post otium cibique refectionem et potus, quid nos agamus ?[1] Quo vigore inedia siti laboreque membris marcentibus occurramus ? 12. Ergo quoniam negotiis difficillimis quoque[2] saepe dispositio tempestiva prospexit, et statum nutantium rerum, recto consilio in bonam partem accepto, aliquotiens divina remedia repararunt, hic quaeso

---

[1] *agamus,* Clark, c.c. ; *agimus,* V. [2] *quoque* before *saepe,* Her. ; *q.* before *Ergo,* V.

gone ahead, and having proclaimed silence by the usual announcements, with his native calmness of speech he addressed the soldiers, who stood about him in companies, as follows :

9. " Regard for maintaining our common safety (to speak most sparingly) urges me, a Caesar far from pusillanimous, to urge and entreat you, fellow soldiers, to have confidence in our mature and sturdy courage, and to choose for all of us rather the path of caution, not the over-hasty and doubtful one, if we are to withstand or to repulse what we have to expect. 10. For in the midst of peril, while it is proper that young men should be energetic and daring, they should also (when occasion requires) be docile and circumspect. Let me therefore in few words detail what my opinion is and see if you will give me leave, and your just anger upholds it. 11. The day is already nearing noon ; we are exhausted by the fatigue of the march ; steep and blind paths will receive us ; the moon is waning and the night will be relieved by no stars ; the country is fairly ablaze with heat and relieved by no supply of water. If anyone should grant us the ability to pass through all this comfortably, what are we to do when the enemy's swarms rush upon us, refreshed as they will be with rest and food and drink ? What strength can we have, when our limbs are enfeebled with hunger, thirst and toil, to offer resistance ? 12. Therefore, since even the most difficult situations have often been met by timely arrangement, and when suitable advice has been taken in good part, heaven-sent remedies have frequently restored the condition of affairs which threatened ruin,

vallo fossaque circumdati, divisis vigiliis, quiescamus,
somnoque et victu congruis potiti pro tempore,
pace dei sit dictum, triumphaturas aquilas et
vexilla victricia primo lucis moveamus exordio."

13. Nec finiri perpessi quae dicebantur, stridore
dentium infrendentes, ardoremque pugnandi hastis
illidendo scuta monstrantes, in hostem se duci iam
conspicuum exorabant, caelestis dei favore, fiduciaque sui, et fortunati rectoris expertis virtutibus
freti, atque (ut exitus docuit) salutaris quidam
genius praesens ad dimicandum eos (dum adesse
potuit), incitabat. 14. Accessit huic alacritati plenus
celsarum potestatum assensus, maximeque Florenti
praefecti praetorio, periculose quidem sed ratione
secunda pugnandum esse censentis, dum starent [1]
barbari conglobati, qui si diffluxissent, motum militis in seditiones nativo calore propensioris ferri non
posse aiebat, extortam sibi victoriam (ut putavit)
non sine ultimorum conatu graviter toleraturi.[2]
15. Addiderat autem fiduciam nostris consideratio
gemina, recordantibus quod anno nuper emenso,
Romanis per transrhenana spatia fusius volitantibus,
nec visus est quisquam laris sui defensor, nec obvius

---

[1] *starent*, Haupt; *instarent*, V.   [2] *toleraturi*, G (with
following lac. c.c. Her.) ; *tolleratur*, V.

here, I ask of you, protected by a rampart and a
trench and with our sentinels picketed, let us rest
and for the present enjoy sleep and food suitable to
the occasion; and then (with God's leave be it
spoken) let us advance our triumphant eagles and
victorious standards at the first break of day."

13. The soldiers did not allow him to finish what
he was saying, but gnashed and ground their teeth
and showed their eagerness for battle by striking
their spears and shields together, and besought
him that they might be led against an enemy
who was already in sight, trusting in the favour of
God in Heaven, in their own self-confidence, and in
the tried valour of their lucky general; and (as the
event showed) a sort of helpful guardian spirit was
urging them to the fray, so long as he could be at
hand. 14. To add to this eagerness there was the
full approval of the high command and especially of
Florentius, the praetorian prefect, who judged that
though it was risky, they must none the less fight
with hope of success while the savages were standing massed together; but if they scattered, the
resentment of our soldiers, who, he said, are inclined
by their native hotness of temper towards insubordi-
nation, would be impossible to withstand; for that
victory (as they thought) should be wrested from
their hands they would hardly endure without
recourse to the last extremity. 15. Furthermore,
our men's confidence had been increased by a twofold consideration, since they recalled that during
the year just elapsed, when the Romans were
ranging freely all through the country beyond the
Rhine, not a man was seen to defend his own home

stetit, sed concaede arborum densa undique semitis clausis, sidere urente brumali, aegre vixere barbari longius amendati, quodque imperatore terras eorum ingresso, nec resistere ausi, nec apparere, pacem impetraverunt, suppliciter obsecrantes. 16. Sed nullus mutatam rationem temporis advertebat, quod tunc tripertito exitio premebantur, imperatore urgente per Raetias, Caesare proximo nusquam elabi permittente, finitimis, quos hostes fecere discordiae, modo non occipitia conculcantibus hinc indeque cinctorum. Postea vero pace data discesserat imperator, et sedata iurgiorum materia, vicinae gentes iam concordabant, et turpissimus ducis Romani digressus ferociam natura conceptam auxit in maius. 17. Alio itidem modo res est aggravata Romana, ex negotio tali. Regii duo fratres vinculo pacis adstricti, quam anno praeterito impetraverant a Constantio, nec tumultuare nec commoveri sunt ausi. Sed paulo postea uno ex his Gundomado, qui potior erat, fideique firmioris, per insidias interempto, omnis eius populus cum nostris hostibus conspiravit et confestim Vadomarii plebs (ipso invito,[1] ut asserebat) agminibus bella cientium barbarorum sese coniunxit.

---

[1] *ipso inuito,* Clark, c.c.; *ipso repugnante,* Haupt; lac. 12 letters at end of line, V.

or to make a stand against them ; but after blocking
the paths everywhere with a thick barricade of
felled trees, the savages, frost-bitten by winter climate,
had much ado to live, moving far out of the way ;
and once the emperor had entered into their country
they did not dare either to resist or show themselves, and obtained peace by suppliant entreaties.
16. But no one noticed that now the state of the
case was changed, since then they were threatened
with ruin from three sides ; the emperor was menacing them by way of Raetia, Caesar was near at hand
and would not allow them to slip out anywhere, and
their neighbours (whom civil strife had made their
enemies) were all but treading on their necks while
they were hemmed in on all sides. But later, peace
was granted and the emperor had departed ; the
source of their quarrels having disappeared, the
border tribes were now in agreement ; and the shameful departure of the Roman commander had greatly
increased the savageness implanted in them by
nature. 17. In another way also the Roman situation was made worse in consequence of the following
occurrence : there were two brothers of royal blood,
who, bound by the obligation of the peace which
they had obtained from Constantius the year before,
dared neither to raise a disturbance nor to make
any move ; but a little later, when one of them,
Gundomadus, who was the stronger of the two and
truer to his promise, had been treacherously murdered, all his tribe made common cause with our
enemies, and at once the subjects of Vadomarius
(against his will, as he insisted) united with the armies
of the savages who were clamouring for war.

CONSTANTIUS ET GALLUS

18. Cunctis igitur summis infimisque approbanti-
bus tunc opportune congrediendum, nec de rigore
animorum quicquam remittentibus, exclamavit
subito signifer " Perge, felicissime omnium Caesar,
quo te fortuna prosperior ducit ; tandem per te virtutem et consilia militare sentimus. Praevius [1]
ut faustus antesignanus et fortis, experieris quid
miles sub conspectu bellicosi ductoris testisque
individui gerendorum, modo adsit superum numen,
viribus efficiet excitatis." 19. His auditis cum
nullae laxarentur indutiae, promotus exercitus
prope collem advenit molliter editum, opertum
segetibus iam maturis, a superciliis Rheni haut
longo intervallo distantem ; ex cuius summitate
speculatores hostium tres equites exciti, subito
nuntiaturi Romanum exercitum adventare, festi-
narunt ad suos, unus vero pedes qui sequi non
potuit, captus agilitate nostrorum, indicavit per
triduum et trinoctium flumen transisse Germanos.
20. Quos cum iam prope densantes semet in cuneos
nostrorum conspexere ductores, steterunt vestigiis
fixis, antepilanis hastatisque et ordinum primis,
velut insolubili muro fundatis, et pari cautela hostes

---

[1] *praevius*, V (defended by Her.) ; *i praevius*, G ; *praei
nos*, Clark.

---

[1] The meaning is uncertain. The *antepilani* were the
soldiers of the first two lines, the *hastati*, or spearmen, were
also part of the first line, so that there seems to be a
repetition. Büchele thought that the *hastati* were the
standard-bearers (*signiferi* and *draconarii*), citing *Petulan-*

274

18. So, since the whole army, from the highest to the lowest, agreed that then was the suitable time to fight, and did not in the least abate their inflexibility of spirit, one of the standard bearers suddenly cried : " Forward, most fortunate of all Caesars, whither your lucky star guides you ; in you at last we feel that both valour and good counsel are in the field. Leading the way for us like a lucky and valiant commander, you will find what the soldier will accomplish when his strength is called out to the full, under the eyes of a warlike general, the immediate witness of his achievements, if only the favour of the supreme deity be present." 19. On hearing this no delay was permitted, but the army moved forward and approached a hill of gentle slope, covered with grain already ripe, and not far distant from the banks of the Rhine. From its top three of the enemy's cavalry scouts galloped off and hastened to their troops, to bring speedy word of the Roman army's approach. But one infantryman, who could not keep up with them, was caught through the quickness of our men, and reported that the Germans had been crossing the river for three days and three nights. 20. When our leading officers espied them, now near at hand, taking their places in close wedge-formation, they halted and stood fast, making a solid line, like an impregnable wall, of the vanguard, the standard bearers, and the staff-officers ; [1] and with like wariness the enemy held their ground in wedge-

tium hastatus, xx. 4, 18, where *hastatus* clearly has that sense, and that the *ordinum primi* were officers ranking between the centurions and the tribunes, citing Frontinus, *Strat.*, xx. 4, which seems probable.

stetere cuneati. 21. Cumque ita ut ante dictus
docuerat perfuga, equitatum omnem a dextro latere
sibi vidissent oppositum, quicquid apud eos per
equestres copias praepollebat, in laevo cornu locavere confertum. Eisdemque sparsim pedites mis-
cuere discursatores et leves, profecto ratione tuta
poscente. 22. Norant enim licet prudentem ex
equo bellatorem cum clibanario nostro congressum,
frena retinentem et scutum, hasta una manu vibrata,
tegminibus ferreis abscondito bellatori nocere non
posse, peditem vero inter ipsos discriminum vertices,
cum nihil caveri solet praeter id quod occurrit,
humiliter et [1] occulte reptantem, latere forato
iumenti, incautum rectorem praecipitem agere,
levi negotio trucidandum. 23. Hoc itaque disposito, dextrum sui latus struxere clandestinis
insidiis et obscuris. Ductabant autem populos
omnes pugnaces et saevos Chonodomarius et Serapio,
potestate excelsiores ante alios reges. 24. Et
Chonodomarius quidem nefarius turbinis [2] totius
incentor, cuius vertici flammeus torulus aptabatur,
anteibat cornu sinistrum, audax et fidens ingenti
robore lacertorum, ubi ardor proelii sperabatur,
immanis, equo spumante sublimior, erectus in
iaculum formidandae vastitatis, armorumque nitore
conspicuus ante alios,[3] et strenuus [4] miles et utilis
praeter ceteros ductor. 25. Latus vero dextrum
Serapio agebat etiam tum adultae lanuginis iuvenis,

---

[1] *et*, added by Clark; V omits.   [2] *turbinis*, Her.;
belli, AG; *boni*, V.   [3] *ante alios*, Mommsen (with
conspicuus, Her.).   [4] *et strenuus*, transposed by Clark, *et*
deleted by Her.; *antea strenuus et miles*, V.

formation. 21. And when (just as the above-mentioned deserter had told us) they saw all our cavalry opposite them on the right flank, they put all their strongest cavalry forces on their left flank in close order. And among them here and there they intermingled skirmishers and light-armed infantry, as safe policy certainly demanded. 22. For they realised that one of their warriors on horseback, no matter how skilful, in meeting one of our cavalry in coat-of-mail, must hold bridle and shield in one hand and brandish his spear with the other, and would thus be able to do no harm to a soldier hidden in iron armour; whereas the infantry soldier in the very hottest of the fight, when nothing is apt to be guarded against except what is straight before one, can creep about low and unseen, and by piercing a horse's side throw its unsuspecting rider headlong, whereupon he can be slain with little trouble. 23. Having made this arrangement, they provided their right flank with secret and puzzling ambuscades. Now all these warlike and savage tribes were led by Chonodomarius and Serapio, kings higher than all the rest in authority. 24. And Chonodomarius, who was in fact the infamous instigator of the whole disturbance, rode before the left wing with a flame-coloured plume on his helmet, a bold man, who relied upon his mighty muscular strength, a huge figure wherever the heat of battle was looked for; erect on his foaming steed, he towered with a lance of formidable size; made conspicuous above others by the gleam of his armour, he was both a doughty soldier and a skilful general beyond all the rest. 25. But the right wing was led by Serapio, who was

efficacia praecurrens aetatem ; Mederichi fratris Chonodomarii filius, hominis quoad vixerat perfidissimi ; ideo sic appellatus, quod pater eius diu obsidatus pignore tentus in Galliis, doctusque Graeca quaedam arcana, hunc filium suum, Agenarichum genitali vocabulo dictitatum, ad Serapionis transtulit nomen.   26. Hos sequebantur potestate proximi reges, numero quinque, regalesque decem, et optimatum series magna, armatorumque milia triginta et quinque, ex variis nationibus partim mercede, partim pacto vicissitudinis reddendae quaesita.

27. Iamque torvum concrepantibus tubis, Severus dux Romanorum, aciem dirigens laevam, cum prope fossas armatorum refertas venisset, unde dispositum erat ut abditi repente exorti cuncta turbarent, stetit impavidus, suspectiorque de obscuris, nec referre gradum nec ulterius ire temptavit.   28. Quo viso, animosus contra labores maximos Caesar, ducentis equitibus saeptus, ut ardor negotii flagitabat, agmina peditum impetu [1] veloci discurrerent, verbis hortabatur et gestu.[2]   29. Et quoniam alloqui pariter omnes nec longitudo spatiorum extenta, nec in unum coactae multitudinis permitteret crebritas, (et alioqui vitabat gravioris invidiae pondus, ne videretur id affectasse quod soli sibi deberi Augustus existimabat) incautior sui hostium

---

[1] *ut impetu*, suggested by Clark.   [2] *et gestu*, added by Novák, cf. xix. 11, 9.

---

[1] The name is connected with Serapis, as that of a god similar to Dis ; cf. Caesar, *BG.* vi. 18 ; *Galli se omnes ab Dite patre prognatos praedicant.*

still a young man with downy cheeks, but his ability outran his years; he was the son of Mederichus, Chonodomarius' brother, a man of the utmost treachery all his life; and he was so named because his father, who had for a long time been kept as a hostage in Gaul and had been taught certain Greek mysteries, changed his son's original native name of Agenarichus to that of Serapio.[1] 26. These were followed by the kings next in power, five in number, by ten princes, with a long train of nobles, and 35,000 troops levied from various nations, partly for pay and partly under agreement to return the service.

27. And now as the trumpets blared ominously, Severus, the Roman general in command of the left wing, on coming near the trenches filled with soldiers, from which it had been arranged that the men in concealment should rise up suddenly and throw everything into confusion, halted fearlessly, and being somewhat suspicious of ambuscades, made no attempt either to draw back or to go further. 28. On seeing this, Caesar, who was courageous in the face of the greatest dangers, surrounded himself with an escort of two hundred horsemen, as the violence of this affair demanded, and with word and action urged the lines of infantry to deploy with swift speed. 29. And since to address them all at once was impossible, both on account of the wide extent of the field and the great numbers of the multitude that had been brought together (and besides he avoided the heavy burden of jealousy, for fear of seeming to have affected that which the emperor supposed to be due to himself alone) without

279

tela praetervolans, his et similibus notos pariter et ignotos ad faciendum fortiter accendebat. 30. "Advenit—o socii—iustum pugnandi iam tempus, olim exoptatum mihi vobiscum, quod antehac arcessentes, arma inquietis [1] motibus poscebatis." 31. Item cum ad alios postsignanos, in acie locatos extrema, venisset, "En" inquit "commilitones, diu speratus praesto est dies, compellens nos omnes, elutis pristinis maculis, Romanae maiestati reddere proprium decus. Hi sunt barbari quos rabies et immodicus furor ad perniciem rerum suarum coegit occurrere, nostris viribus opprimendos." 32. Alios itidem bellandi usu diutino callentes, aptius ordinans, his exhortationibus adiuvabat : "Exsurgamus—viri fortes—propulsemus [2] fortitudine congrua illisa nostris partibus probra, quae contemplans Caesaris nomen cunctando suscepi." 33. Quoscumque autem pugnae signum inconsulte poscentes, rupturosque imperium irrequietis motibus praevideret, "Quaeso" inquit "ne hostes vertendos in fugam sequentes avidius, futurae victoriae gloriam violetis, neu quis ante necessitatem ultimam cedat. Nam fugituros procul dubio deseram, hostium terga caesuris adero

---

[1] *inquietis*, V, Damsté, cf. xvii. 1, 13 ; *irrequietis*, Kellerbauer (cf. § 33), Clark.　　[2] *propulsemus*, Her. ; *propellamus*, BG ; *propellemus*, V, def. by Pighi.

thought of his own safety he flew past the enemy's weapons and by these and similar speeches animated the soldiers, strangers as well as acquaintances, to deeds of valour. 30. "There has come now, comrades, the real time for fighting, which you and I have long since desired, and which you were just now demanding, when you were tumultuously calling for your weapons." 31. Also, when he had come to others, who were stationed behind the standards and in the extreme rear, he said : "Behold, fellow-soldiers, the long-hoped-for day is now here, forcing us all to wash away the old-time stains and restore its due honour to the majesty of Rome. These are the savages whom madness and excessive folly have driven on to the ruin of their fortunes, doomed as they are to be overwhelmed by our might." 32. In the same way, as he arranged in better order others who were experienced by long practice in warfare, he cheered them with such words of encouragement as these : "Let us bestir ourselves, brave soldiers, and by seasonable valour do away with the reproaches inflicted upon our cause, in consideration of which I have hesitatingly accepted the title of Caesar." 33. But whenever he saw any soldiers who were calling for the battle-signal out of season, and foresaw that they would by their riotous actions break discipline, he said : "I beg of you, do not mar the glory of our coming victory by following too eagerly the enemy whom you are about to put to flight ; and let none yield ground before the extremity of need. For I shall surely abandon those who are likely to flee, but I shall be inseparably present with those who shall wound their foemen's

indiscretus, si hoc pensatione moderata fiat et cauta."

34. Haec aliaque in eundem modum saepius replicando, maiorem exercitus partem primae barbarorum opposuit fronti, et subito Alamannorum peditum fremitus, indignationi mixtus auditus est, unanimi conspiratione vociferantium, relictis equis secum oportere versari regales, ne siquid contigisset adversum, deserta miserabili plebe, facilem discedendi copiam reperirent. 35. Hocque comperto, Chonodomarius iumento statim [1] desiluit, et secuti eum residui idem fecere,[2] nihil morati ; nec enim eorum quisquam ambigebat partem suam fore victricem.

36. Dato igitur aeneatorum accentu sollemniter signo ad pugnandum utrimque, magnis concursum est viribus. Paulisper [3] praepilabantur missilia, et properantes concito [4] quam considerato cursu Germani, telaque dextris explicantes, involavere nostrorum equitum turmas, frendentes immania, eorumque ultra solitum saevientium, comae fluentes horrebant, et elucebat quidam ex oculis furor, quos contra pertinax miles, scutorum obicibus vertices tegens, eiectansque gladios, vel tela concrispans, mortem minitantia perterrebat. 37. Cumque in ipso proeliorum articulo eques se fortiter conturmaret, et muniret latera sua firmius pedes, frontem artissimis conserens parmis, erigebantur crassi

---

[1] *id statim*, V ; *id* deleted by Novák ; *ipse s.*, Eyssen.
[2] *fecere*, Kiessling ; *facere*, V.   [3] *paulisper*, Mommsen ; *populis*, V.   [4] *concito*, Schneider, Clark ; *cito*, E G ; *cuto*, V.

backs, provided that it be done with regard for judgment and caution.

34. While he kept often repeating these and other words to the same effect, he placed the greater part of his army opposite the forefront of the savages, and suddenly there was heard the outcry of the German infantry, mingled with indignation, as they shouted with one accord that their princes ought to leave their horses and keep company with them, for fear that they, if anything adverse should occur, abandoning the wretched herd, would easily make shift to escape. 35. On learning of this, Chonodomarius at once sprang down from his horse, and the rest, following his example, did the same without delay ; for not one of them doubted that their side would be victorious.

36. So, when the call to battle had been regularly given on both sides by the notes of the trumpeters, they began the fight with might and main ; for a time missiles were hurled, and then the Germans, running forward with more haste than discretion, and wielding their weapons in their right hands, flew upon our cavalry squadrons ; and as they gnashed their teeth hideously and raged beyond their usual manner, their flowing hair made a terrible sight, and a kind of madness shone from their eyes. Against them our soldiers resolutely protected their heads with the barriers of their shields, and with sword thrusts or by hurling darts threatened them with death and greatly terrified them. 37. And when in the very crisis of the battle the cavalry formed massed squadrons valiantly and the infantry stoutly protected their flanks by making a front of

pulveris nubes, variique fuere discursus, nunc
resistentibus, nunc cedentibus nostris, et obnixi
genibus quidam barbari peritissimi bellatores, hostem propellere laborabant, sed destinatione nimia
dexterae dexteris miscebantur et umbo trudebat
umbonem, caelumque exsultantium cadentiumque
resonabat a vocibus magnis, et cum cornu sinistrum
artius [1] gradiens, urgentium tot agmina Germanorum
vi nimia pepulisset, iretque in barbaros fremens,
equites nostri cornu tenentes dextrum, praeter
spem incondite discesserunt, dumque primi fugien-
tium postremos impediunt, gremio legionum pro-
tecti, fixerunt integrato proelio gradum. 38. Hoc
autem exinde acciderat, quod dum ordinum res-
tituitur series, cataphracti equites viso rectore suo
leviter vulnerato, et consorte quodam per cervicem
equi labente,[2] pondere armorum oppressi, dilapsi
qua quisque poterat, peditesque calcando cuncta
turbassent, ni conferti illi sibique vicissim innexi [3]
stetissent immobiles. Igitur cum equites nihil
praeter fugae circumspectantes praesidia, vidisset
longius Caesar, concito equo, eos velut repagulum
quoddam cohibuit. 39. Quo agnito per purpureum [4]
signum draconis, summitati hastae longioris aptatum,

[1] *artius*, Pet. ; *altius*, V.   [2] *labente*, Cornelissen,
labentis, V.   [3] *innexi*, Her. ; *innixi*, V.   [4] *per
purpureum*, W²G ; *perpureum*, V.

284

their bucklers joined fast together, clouds of thick
dust arose. Then there were various manœuvres,
as our men now stood fast and now gave ground,
and some of the most skilful warriors among the
savages by the pressure of their knees tried to force
their enemy back; but with extreme determination
they came to hand-to-hand fighting, shield-boss
pushed against shield, and the sky re-echoed with the
loud cries of the victors or of the falling. And although our left wing, marching in close formation had
driven back by main force the onrushing hordes of
Germans and was advancing with shouts into the
midst of the savages, our cavalry, which held the right
wing, unexpectedly broke ranks and fled; but while
the foremost of these fugitives hindered the hind-
most, finding themselves sheltered in the bosom of
the legions, they halted, and renewed the battle. 38.
Now that had happened for the reason that while the
order of their lines was being re-established, the
cavalry in coat-of-mail, seeing their leader slightly
wounded and one of their companions slipping over
the neck of his horse, which had collapsed under the
weight of his armour, scattered in whatever direction
they could; the cavalry would have caused complete confusion by trampling the infantry under foot,
had not the latter, who were packed close together
and intertwined one with the other, held their ground
without stirring. So, when Caesar had seen from
a distance that the cavalry were looking for nothing
except safety in flight, he spurred on his horse and
held them back like a kind of barrier. 39. On
recognising him by the purple ensign of a dragon,
fitted to the top of a very long lance and spreading

velut senectutis pandentis exuvias, stetit unius turmae tribunus, et pallore timoreque perculsus, ad aciem
integrandam recurrit. 40. Utque in rebus amat fieri
dubiis, eosdem lenius increpans Caesar, " Quo "
inquit " cedimus, viri fortissimi ? an ignoratis, fugam
quae salutem numquam repperit, irriti conatus
stultitiam indicare ? Redeamus ad nostros, saltim
gloriae futuri participes, si eos pro re publica dimicantes reliquimus inconsulte." 41. Haec reverenter
dicendo, reduxit omnes ad munia subeunda bellandi,
imitatus salva differentia veterem Sullam, qui cum
contra Archelaum (Mithridatis ducem) educta acie
proelio fatigabatur ardenti, relictus a militibus
cunctis, cucurrit in ordinem primum, raptoque et
coniecto vexillo in partem hostilem, " Ite " dixerat
" socii periculorum electi, et scitantibus ubi relictus
sim imperator, respondete nihil fallentes : ' solus
in Boeotia pro omnibus nobis cum dispendio sanguinis sui decernens.' "

42. Proinde Alamanni, pulsis disiectisque equitibus nostris, primam aciem peditum incesserunt,
eam abiecta resistendi animositate pulsuri. 43.
Sed postquam comminus ventum est, pugnabatur
paribus diu momentis. Cornuti enim et Bracchiati,
usu proeliorum diuturno firmati, eos iam gestu
terrentes, barritum ciere vel maximum : qui clamor

out like the slough of a serpent, the tribune of one of the squadrons stopped, and pale and struck with fear rode back to renew the battle. 40. Whereupon Caesar, as is the custom to do in times of panic, rebuked them mildly and said : " Whither are we fleeing, my most valiant men ? Do you know not that flight never leads to safety, but shows the folly of a useless effort ? Let us return to our companions, to be at least sharers in their coming glory, if it is without consideration that we are abandoning them as they fight for their country." 41. By his tactful way of saying this he recalled them all to perform their duty as soldiers, following (though with some difference) the example of Sulla of old. For when he had led out his forces against Mithradates' general Archelaus and was being exhausted by the heat of battle and deserted by all his men, he rushed to the front rank, caught up a standard, flung it towards the enemy, and cried : " Go your way, you who were chosen to be companions of my dangers, and to those who ask you where I, your general, was left, answer truthfully : ' Fighting alone in Boeotia, and shedding his blood for all of us.' "

42. Then the Alamanni, having beaten and scattered our cavalry, charged upon the front line of the infantry, supposing that their courage to resist was now lost and that they would therefore drive them back. 43. But as soon as they came to close quarters, the contest continued a long time on equal terms. For the Cornuti and the Bracchiati, toughened by long experience in fighting, at once intimidated them by their gestures, and raised their mighty battle-cry. This shout in the very heat of

ipso fervore certaminum, a tenui susurro exoriens,
paulatimque adulescens ritu extollitur fluctuum,
cautibus illisorum ; iaculorum deinde stridentium
crebritate, hinc indeque convolante, pulvis aequali
motu adsurgens, et prospectum eripiens arma armis
corporaque corporibus obtrudebat. 44. Sed violentia iraque incompositi, barbari in modum exarsere
flammarum, nexamque scutorum compagem, quae
nostros in modum testudinis tuebatur, scindebant
ictibus gladiorum assiduis. 45. Quo cognito opitu-
latum conturmalibus suis celeri cursu Batavi venere
cum Regibus, formidabilis manus, extremae necessitatis articulo circumventos, (si iuvisset fors) ereptura,
torvumque canentibus classicis, adultis viribus
certabatur. 46. Verum Alamanni bella alacriter
ineuntes, altius anhelabant, velut quodam furoris
afflatu,[1] opposita omnia deleturi.   Spicula tamen
verrutaque missilia non cessabant, ferrataeque
arundines fundebantur, quamquam etiam comminus mucro feriebat contra mucronem, et loricae
gladiis findebantur, et vulnerati nondum effuso
cruore ad audendum exsertius consurgebant. 47.
Pares enim quodam modo coiere cum paribus,
Alamanni robusti et celsiores, milites usu nimio
dociles ; illi feri et turbidi, hi quieti et cauti ; animis
isti fidentes, grandissimis illi corporibus freti. 48.
Resurgebat tamen aliquotiens armorum pondere

1 *afflatu*, Bentley, Hertz ; *adfectu*, V.

---

[1] In this formation the soldiers held their shields close
together over their heads ; here, before their bodies.
[2] The *Reges* (cf. *regii* in *Notitia Imp. Occident.*, p. 1466)

combat rises from a low murmur and gradually grows louder, like waves dashing against the cliffs. Then a cloud of hissing javelins flew hither and thither, the dust arose with steady motion on both sides and hid the view, so that weapon struck blindly on weapon and body against body. 44. But the savages, thrown into disorder by their violence and anger, flamed up like fire, and hacked with repeated strokes of their swords at the close-jointed array of shields, which protected our men like a tortoise-formation.[1] 45. On learning this, the Batavians, with the " Kings "[2] (a formidable band) came at the double quick to aid their comrades and (if fate would assist) to rescue them, girt about as they were, from the instant of dire need ; and as their trumpets pealed savagely, they fought with all their powers. 46. But the Alamanni, who enter eagerly into wars, made all the greater effort, as if to destroy utterly everything in their way by a kind of fit of rage. Yet darts and javelins did not cease to fly, with showers of iron-tipped arrows, although at close quarters also blade clashed on blade and breastplates were cleft with the sword ; the wounded too, before all their blood was shed, rose up to some more conspicuous deed of daring. 47. For in a way the combatants were evenly matched ; the Alamanni were stronger and taller, our soldiers disciplined by long practice ; they were savage and uncontrollable, our men quiet and wary, these relying on their courage, while the Germans presumed upon their huge size. 48. Yet frequently the Roman,

seem to have been a select body of household troops. The Batavians had no kings at this time.

pulsus loco Romanus, lassatisque impressus genibus
laevum reflectens poplitem barbarus subsidebat,
hostem ultro lacessens, quod indicium est obstina-
tionis extremae.   49. Exsiluit itaque subito ardens
optimatium globus, inter quos decernebant et reges,
et sequente vulgo ante alios agmina nostrorum
irrupit, et iter sibi aperiendo,[1] ad usque Primanorum
legionem pervenit locatam in medio—quae confir-
matio castra praetoria dictitatur,—ubi densior et
ordinibus frequens, miles instar turrium fixa firmitate consistens, proelium maiore spiritu repetivit,
et vulneribus declinandis intentus, seque in modum
mirmillonis operiens, hostium latera, quae nudabat
ira flagrantior, districtis gladiis perforabat.   50.
At illi prodigere vitam pro victoria contendentes,
temptabant agminis nostri laxare compagem.   Sed
continuata serie peremptorum, quos Romanus iam
fidentior stravit, succedebant barbari superstites
interfectis, auditoque occumbentium gemitu crebro,
pavore perfusi torpebant.   51. Fessi denique tot
aerumnis, et ad solam deinceps strenui fugam,
per diversos tramites tota celeritate digredi [2] festinabant, ut e mediis saevientis pelagi fluctibus, quocumque avexerit ventus, eici nautici properant et

---

[1] *aperiendo*, EBG ;   *pandendo*, Her. ;   *rapiendo*, suggested by Clark, cf. xviii. 9, 3 ;   *pariendo*, V.   [2] *digredi*,
Her. cf. *deici*, § 51 ;   *egredi*, W[2] ;   *gredi*, V.

---

[1] The *Primani* formed a part of the household troops,
under command of the *magister militum*.   Here, probably, a
select legion forming a reserve corps.

[2] *Turres* was also a military formation (Gell., x, 9, 1), but
here the word is clearly used in its literal sense ; see note
on *forceps*, xvi. 11, 3.

driven from his post by the weight of armed men,
rose up again; and the savage, with his legs giving
way from fatigue, would drop on his bended left
knee and even thus attack his foe, a proof of extreme
resolution. 49. And so there suddenly leaped forth
a fiery band of nobles, among whom even the kings
fought, and with the common soldiers following they
burst in upon our lines before the rest; and opening
up a path for themselves they got as far as the legion
of the Primani,[1] which was stationed in the centre—
a strong feature called praetorian camp; there our
soldiers, closely packed and in fully-manned lines.
stood their ground fast and firm, like towers,[2] and
renewed the battle with greater vigour; and being
intent upon avoiding wounds, they protected themselves like murmillos,[3] and with drawn swords
pierced the enemy's sides, left bare by their frenzied
rage. 50. But the enemy strove to lavish their lives
for victory and kept trying to break the fabric of our
line. But as they fell in uninterrupted succession,
and the Romans now laid them low with greater
confidence, fresh savages took the places of the
slain; but when they heard the frequent groans of
the dying, they were overcome with panic and lost
their courage. 51. Worn out at last by so many
calamities, and now being eager for flight alone,
over various paths they made haste with all speed
to get away, just as sailors and passengers hurry to

[3] The *murmillones*, a kind of gladiator, so called from
a fish which they wore on their helmets, were armed in
Gallic fashion. They were matched against the *retiarii*,
who tried to throw a net over them; Festus, p. 358,
Lind (p. 285, M.).

vectores ; quod voti magis quam spei fuisse fatebitur quilibet tunc praesens. 52. Aderatque propitiati numinis arbitrium clemens, et secans terga cedentium miles cum interdum flexis ensibus feriendi non suppeterent instrumenta, erepta [1] ipsis barbaris tela eorum vitalibus immergebat, nec quisquam vulnerantium sanguine iram explevit nec satiavit caede multiplici dexteram, vel miseratus supplicantem abscessit. 53. Iacebant itaque plurimi transfixi letaliter, remedia mortis compendio postulantes, alii semineces, labente iam spiritu, lucis usuram oculis morientibus inquirebant, quorundam capita discissa trabalibus telis, et pendentia iugulis cohaerebant, pars per [2] limosum [3] et lubricum solum, in sociorum cruore relapsi,[4] intactis ferro corporibus, acervis superruentium obruti necabantur. 54. Quae ubi satis evenere prosperrime, validius instante victore, acumina densis ictibus hebescebant, splendentesque galeae sub pedibus volvebantur et scuta, ultimo denique trudente discrimine, barbari, cum elati cadaverum aggeres exitus impedirent, ad subsidia fluminis petivere, quae sola restabant, eorum terga iam perstringentis. 55. Et quia cursu sub

---

[1] *erepta,* added by Haupt (*rapta,* Novák) ; V omits.
[2] *per,* added by W²G ; V omits. [3] *limosum,* Clark ; *scruposum,* Her. ; *lutosum,* BG ; *cliuosum,* W² ; *lubrosum,* omitting *per,* V. [4] *relapsi,* Clark, *prolapsi,* Her.c.c.; *lapse,* V.

be cast up on land out of the midst of the billows of a raging sea, no matter where the wind has carried them ; and anyone there present will admit that it was a means of escape more prayed for than expected. 52. Moreover, the gracious will of an appeased deity was on our side, and our soldiers slashed the backs of the fugitives ; when sometimes their swords were bent, and no weapons were at hand for dealing blows, they seized their javelins from the savages themselves and sank them into their vitals ; and not one of those who dealt these wounds could with their blood glut his rage or satiate his right hand by continual slaughter, or take pity on a suppliant and leave him. 53. And so a great number of them lay there pierced with mortal wounds, begging for death as a speedy relief ; others half-dead, with their spirit already slipping away, sought with dying eyes for longer enjoyment of the light ; some had their heads severed by pikes heavy as beams, so that they hung down, connected only by their throats ; some had fallen in their comrades' blood on the miry, slippery ground, and although their persons were untouched by the steel, they were perishing, buried beneath the heaps of those who kept falling above them. 54. When all this had turned out so very successfully, our victorious troops pressed on with greater vigour, blunting the edges of their swords with stroke after stroke, while gleaming helms and shields rolled about under foot. At last the savages, driven on by the utmost extremity, since the heaps of corpses were so high as to block their passage, made for the only recourse left, that of the river, which now almost grazed their backs. 55. And since

armis concito, fugientes miles indefessus urgebat, quidam nandi peritia eximi se posse discriminibus arbitrati, animas fluctibus commiserunt. Qua causa celeri corde futura praevidens Caesar, cum tribunis et ducibus clamore obiugatorio prohibebat, ne hostem avidius sequens, nostrorum quisquam se gurgitibus committeret verticosis. 56. Unde id observatum est, ut marginibus insistentes, confoderent telorum varietate Germanos, quorum siquem morti velocitas subtraxisset, iacti corporis pondere ad ima fluminis subsidebat. 57. Et velut in quodam theatrali spectaculo, aulaeis miranda monstrantibus multa, licebat iam sine metu videre nandi strenuis quosdam nescios adhaerentes, fluitantes alios cum expeditioribus linquerentur ut stipites, et velut luctante amnis violentia vorari quosdam fluctibus involutos, non nullos clipeis vectos, praeruptas undarum occursantium molis, obliquatis meatibus declinantes, ad ripas ulteriores post multa discrimina pervenire. Spumans denique cruore barbarico, decolor alveus insueta stupebat augmenta.

58. Dum haec ita aguntur,[1] rex Chonodomarius reperta copia discedendi, lapsus per funerum strues, cum satellitibus paucis, celeritate rapida properabat

---

[1] *ita aguntur*, Novák, cf. xvii. 11, 5, etc. (*aguntur* added by AG ; V omits).

our indefatigable soldiers, running fast even under
their armour, pressed upon them as they fled, some
of them, thinking that by their skill in swimming
they could save themselves from the dangers,
committed their lives to the waves. Whereupon
Caesar, with swift intelligence foreseeing what might
happen, joined with the tribunes and higher officers
in restraining shouts, forbidding any of our men
in their over-eager pursuit of the enemy to entrust
themselves to the eddying flood. 56. As a result
it was seen that they stood on the banks and trans-
fixed the Germans with various kinds of darts; and
if any of them by his speed escaped this death, he
would sink to the bottom of the river through the
weight of his struggling body. 57. And just as
in some theatrical scene, when the curtain displays
many wonderful sights, so now one could without
apprehension see how some who did not know how
to swim clung fast to good swimmers; how others
floated like logs when they were left behind by
those who swam faster; and some were swept into
the currents and swallowed up, so to speak, by the
struggling violence of the stream; some were carried
along on their shields, and by frequently changing
their direction avoided the steep masses of the
onrushing waves, and so after many a risk reached
the further shores. And at last the reddened river's
bed, foaming with the savages' blood, was itself
amazed at these strange additions to its waters.

58. While this was thus going on, King Chonodomarius found means to get away by slipping
through the heaps of corpses with a few of his attendants, and hastened at top speed towards the

ad castra, quae prope Tribuncos et Concordiam munimenta Romana, fixit intrepidus, ut escensis navigiis, dudum paratis ad casus ancipites, in secretis[1] secessibus se[2] amendaret.[3] 59. Et quia non nisi Rheno transito ad territoria sua poterat pervenire, vultum ne agnosceretur operiens, sensim retulit pedem. Cumque propinquaret iam ripis, lacunam palustribus aquis interfusam circumgrediens ut transiret, calcata mollitie glutinosa, equo est evolutus, et confestim licet obeso corpore gravior, ad subsidium vicini collis evasit, quem agnitum (nec enim potuit celare qui fuerit, fortunae prioris magnitudine proditus), statim anhelo cursu cohors cum tribuno secuta, armis circumdatum aggerem nemorosum, cautius obsidebat, perrumpere verita, ne fraude latenti inter ramorum tenebras exciperetur occultas. 60. Quibus visis, compulsus ad ultimos metus, ultro se dedidit[4] solus egressus, comitesque eius ducenti numero et tres amici iunctissimi, flagitium arbitrati post regem vivere, vel pro rege non mori, si ita tulerit casus, tradidere se vinciendos. 61. Utque nativo more sunt barbari humiles in adversis, disparesque in secundis, servus alienae voluntatis trahebatur pallore confusus, claudente noxarum conscientia linguam, immensum quantum

---

[1] *in secretis,* V ; *in* deleted by Her.   [2] *se,* added by Val. before *secessibus ;* transposed by Novák ; V omits.   [3] *amendaret,* Val. ; *se mandaret,* Mommsen ; *emendaret,* V.   [4] *dedidit,* Bentley ; *dedit,* V.

---

[1] Near Strasburg.   [2] Drusenheim.

camp which he had boldly pitched near the Roman fortifications of Tribunci[1] and Concordia,[2] his purpose being to embark in some boats which he had sometime before got ready for any emergency, and hide himself away in some secret retreat. 59. And since he could not reach his own territories except by crossing the Rhine, he covered his face for fear of being recognised and slowly retired. But when he was already nearing the river-bank and was skirting a lagoon which had been flooded with marsh water, in order to get by, his horse stumbled on the muddy and sticky ground and he was thrown off; but although he was fat and heavy, he quickly escaped to the refuge of a neighbouring hill. But he was recognised (for he could not conceal his identity, being betrayed by the greatness of his former estate); and immediately a cohort with its tribune followed him with breathless haste and surrounded the wooded height with their troops and cautiously invested it, afraid to break in for fear that some hidden ambush might meet them among the dark shadows of the branches. 60. On seeing them he was driven to the utmost fear and surrendered of his own accord, coming out alone; and his attendants, two hundred in number, with three of his closest friends, thinking it a disgrace to survive their king, or not to die for their king if an emergency required it, gave themselves up to be made prisoners. 61. And as the savages are by nature humble in adversity and overbearing in success, subservient as he now was to another's will he was dragged along pale and abashed, tongue-tied by the consciousness of his crimes—how vastly different from

297

ab eo differens, qui post feros lugubresque terrores,
cineribus Galliarum insultans, multa minabatur et
saeva.

62. Quibus ita favore superni numinis terminatis,
post exactum iam diem, occinente liticine revocatus
invitissimus miles, prope supercilia Rheni tendebat,
scutorumque ordine multiplicato vallatus, victu
fruebatur et somno.   63. Ceciderunt autem in hac
pugna Romani quidem CCXL et III, rectores vero
IIII : Bainobaudes Cornutorum tribunus, adaeque
Laipso et Innocentius cataphractarios ducens, et
vacans quidam tribunus, cuius non suppetit nomen ;
ex Alamannis vero sex [1] milia corporum numerata
sunt, in campo constrata, et alii [2] inaestimabiles
mortuorum acervi per undas fluminis ferebantur.
64. Tunc Iulianus, ut erat fortuna sui spectatior,
meritisque magis quam imperio potens, Augustus
acclamatione concordi totius exercitus appellatus,
ut agentes petulantius milites increpabat, id se
nec sperare nec adipisci velle iurando confirmans.
65. Et ut augeret eventus secundi laetitiam, concilio convocato propositisque praemiis, propitio ore [3]
Chonodomarium sibi iussit offerri.   Qui primo cur-
vatus, deinde humi suppliciter fusus, gentilique
prece veniam poscens, bono animo esse est iussus.
66. Et diebus postea paucis ductus ad comitatum

[1] *sex aliis*, V ; *sex*, G, Her. (cf. note 2) ; *sex aut septem*
(ĀVII), Clark.   [2] *alii*, added by Her. (cf. note 1).
[3] *conuocato . . . ore*, Gardt. ;   *concilio omni spectante*
(*contione*, Kiessling), ʽHaupt ;   *concilio* (lac. 9 letters)
mus peciare, V.

the man who, after savage and woeful outrages, trampled upon the ashes of Gaul and threatened many dire deeds.

62. So the battle was thus finished by the favour of the supreme deity; the day had already ended and the trumpet sounded; the soldiers, very reluctant to be recalled, encamped near the banks of the Rhine, protected themselves by numerous rows of shields, and enjoyed food and sleep. 63. Now there fell in this battle on the Roman side two hundred and forty-three soldiers and four high officers: Bainobaudes, tribune of the Cornuti, and also Laipso; and Innocentius, commander of the mailed cavalry, and one unattached tribune, whose name is not available to me. But of the Alamanni there were counted six thousand corpses lying on the field, and heaps of dead, impossible to reckon, were carried off by the waves of the river. 64. Thereupon, since Julian was a man of greater mark than his position, and more powerful in his deserts than in his command, he was hailed as Augustus by the unanimous acclamation of the entire army; but he rebuked the soldiers for their thoughtless action, and declared with an oath that he neither expected nor desired to attain that honour. 65. And to enhance their rejoicing over their success, he called an assembly and offered rewards, and then courteously gave orders that Chonodomarius should be brought before him; the king at first bowed down and then humbly prostrated himself on the ground; and when he begged for forgiveness in his native tongue, he was told to be of good courage. 66. And a few days later he was

imperatoris, missusque exinde Romam, in castris
peregrinis, quae in monte sunt Caelio, morbo veterni
consumptus est.

67. His tot ac talibus prospero peractis eventu, in
palatio Constanti quidam Iulianum culpantes, ut
princeps ipse delectaretur, irrisive Victorinum ideo
nominabant, quod verecunde referens quotiens
imperaret, superatos indicabat saepe Germanos.
68. Interque exaggerationem inanium laudum, osten-
tationemque aperte lucentium, inflabant ex usu
imperatorem, suopte ingenio nimium, quicquid per
omnem terrae ambitum agebatur, felicibus eius
auspiciis assignantes. 69. Quocirca magniloquentia
elatus adulatorum, tunc et deinde edictis propositis,
arroganter satis multa mentiebatur, se solum (cum
gestis non adfuisset) et dimicasse et vicisse et supplices reges gentium erexisse aliquotiens scribens, et
si verbi gratia eo agente tunc in Italia, dux quidam
egisset fortiter contra Persas, nulla eius mentione
per textum longissimum facta, laureatas litteras ad
provinciarum damna mittebat, se inter primores
versatum cum odiosa sui iactatione significans.
70. Exstant denique eius dicta, in tabulariis principis[1]
publicis condita,[2] in quibus ambitiose[3] delata
narrandi extollendique semet in caelum. Ab Argen-
torato cum pugnaretur, mansione quadragesima

---

[1] *principis*, put after *eius* by Val. ; *tabulariis principiis*
(*principis*, W²BG), V.   [2] *condita*, W²ED ; *condi*
(lac. 27 letters) *delata*, V.   [3] *in quibus ambitiose*,
added by Val.

---

[1] They were a detriment because of the expense they
caused for celebrations, and "graft" by the *agentes in
rebus.*

conducted to the emperor's court and thence sent
to Rome; there in the Castra Peregrina, which is
on the Caelian Hill, he died from senile decay.

67. On the successful outcome of these exploits,
so numerous and so important, some of the courtiers
in Constantius' palace found fault with Julian, in
order to please the emperor himself, or facetiously
called him Victorinus, on the ground that, although
he was modest in making reports whenever he led
the army in battle, he often mentioned defeats of
the Germans. 68. And between piling on empty
praise, and pointing to what was clearly evident,
they as usual puffed up the emperor, who was
naturally conceited, by ascribing whatever was
done anywhere in the world to his favourable
auspices. 69. As a consequence, he was elated by the
grandiloquence of his sycophants, and then and later
in his published edicts he arrogantly lied about a
great many matters, frequently writing that he
alone (although he had not been present at the
action) had both fought and conquered, and had
raised up the suppliant kings of foreign nations. If,
for example, when he himself was then in Italy, one
of his generals had fought bravely against the Persians, he would make no mention of him in the course
of a very long account, but would send out letters
wreathed in laurel to the detriment [1] of the provinces,
indicating with odious self-praise that he had fought
in the front ranks. 70. In short, there are extant
statements filed among the public records of this emperor, in which ostentatious reports are given, of his
boasting and exalting himself to the sky.[2] When this

---

[2] The text is uncertain, but the general sense is clear.

disparatus, describens proelium aciem ordinasse,
et stetisse inter signiferos, et barbaros fugasse praecipites, sibique oblatum falso indicat Chonodomarium
(pro rerum indignitas) super Iuliani gloriosis actibus
conticescens, quos sepelierat penitus, ni fama res
maximas, **vel** obumbrantibus plurimis, silere ne-
sciret.

LIBER XVII

1. *Iulianus C. transito Rheno Alamannorum vicos
diripit ac incendit ; ibi munimentum Traiani
reparat, et decimestres indutias barbaris concedit.*

1. Hac rerum varietate, quam iam digessimus,
ita [1] conclusa, Martius iuvenis, Rheno post Argen-
toratensem pugnam otiose fluente, securus, sollici-
tusque idem ne dirae [2] volucres consumerent corpora peremptorum, sine discretione cunctos humari
mandavit, absolutisque legatis, quos ante certamen
superba quaedam portasse praediximus, ad Tres
Tabernas revertit. 2. Unde cum captivis omnibus
praedam Mediomatricos servandam ad reditum
usque suum duci praecipit, et petiturus ipse Mogontiacum, ut ponte compacto transgressus, in suis

---

[1] *varietate . . . ita,* Clark ; *quis varietatem iam digessimus ita,* V.　　[2] *idem ne dirae,* Her. ; *ne dire,* EBG ;
inedire, V.

battle was fought near Strasburg, although he was distant forty days' march, in his description of the fight he falsely asserts that he arranged the order of battle, and stood among the standard-bearers, and drove the barbarians headlong, and that Chonodomarius was brought to him, saying nothing (Oh, shameful indignity!) of the glorious deeds of Julian, which he would have buried in oblivion, had not fame been unable to suppress his splendid exploits, however much many people would have obscured them.

BOOK XVII

1. *Julianus Caesar, having crossed the Rhine, sacks and burns the villages of the Alamanni; he repairs a fortress of Trajan and grants the barbarians a truce of ten months.*

1. After this conclusion of the variety of events which I have now summarised the young warrior, with mind at ease, since the Rhine flowed on peacefully after the battle of Strasburg, took care to keep birds of prey from devouring the bodies of the slain; and he gave orders that they should all be buried without distinction. Then, having dismissed the envoys, who (as we have related) had brought some insolent messages before the battle, he returned to Savernes. 2. From there he ordered the booty, with all the captives, to be taken to Metz and kept there until his return; he was himself planning to go to Mayence with the purpose of building a bridge, crossing the Rhine, and searching out the

regionibus [1] requireret barbaros, cum nullum reliquisset in nostris, refragante vetabatur exercitu; verum facundia iucunditateque sermonum allectum, in voluntatem traduxerat suam. Amor enim post documenta flagrantior, sequi libenter hortatus est omnis operae conturmalem, auctoritate magnificum ducem, plus laboris indicere sibi quam militi, sicut perspicue contigit, assuetum. Moxque ad locum praedictum est ventum, flumine pontibus constratis transmisso, occupavere terras hostiles. 3. At barbari perstricti negotii magnitudine, qui se in tranquillo positos otio, tunc parum inquietari posse sperabant, aliorum exitio quid fortunis suis immineret anxie cogitantes, simulata pacis petitione, ut primae vertiginis impetum declinarent, misere legatos cum verbis compositis, quae denuntiarent concordem foederum firmitatem ; incertumque quo consilio statim instituto,[2] mutata voluntate, per alios cursu celeri venire compulsos, acerrimum nostris minati sunt bellum, ni eorum regionibus excessissent. 4. Quibus clara fide compertis, Caesar noctis prima quiete, navigiis modicis et velocibus octingentos imposuit milites, ut spatio stadiorum xx [3] sursum versum decurso egressi, quicquid invenire potuerint,

---

[1] *regionibus,* added by Damsté, cf. § 3.   [2] *statim instituto* or *statim impetu restituto,* Mommsen ; *stat institutos,* V.   [3] *ut spatio stadiorum xx,* Novák ; *militis eorum xx,* V.

savages on their own ground, since he had left none
of them in our territory; but he was opposed by
the protests of the army. However, by his eloquence
and the charm of his language he won them over
and converted them to his will. For their affection,
warmer after their experiences with him, prompted
them to follow willingly one who was a fellow-soldier
in every task, a leader brilliant in his prestige, and
accustomed to prescribe more drudgery for himself
than for a common soldier, as was clearly evident.
And as soon as they came to the place above mentioned, crossing the river on the bridges which they
made, they possessed themselves of the enemy's
country. 3. But the savages, thunderstruck at the
vastness of the feat, since they little expected that
they could be molested, settled as they were amid undisturbed peace, gave anxious thought to what might
threaten their own fortunes, in view of the destruction of the others; and so under pretence of a prayer
for peace, with the purpose of avoiding the brunt of
the first onslaught, they sent envoys with set
speeches, to declare the harmonious validity of the
treaties with them; but for some unknown design
that they suddenly formed they changed their
minds, and by other messengers whom they forced
to come post haste, they threatened our men with
most bitter warfare, unless they should withdraw
from their territory.

4. On learning this from a sure source, Caesar
at the first quiet of nightfall embarked eight hundred
soldiers on small, swift boats, so that they might
go up the Rhine for a distance of twenty stadia,
disembark, and with fire and sword lay waste

ferro violarent et flammis. 5. Quo ita disposito, solis primo exortu, visis per montium vertices barbaris, ad celsiora ducebatur alacrior miles, nulloque invento (hoc si quidem opinati discessere confestim) eminus ingentia fumi volumina visebantur, indicantia nostros perruptas populari terras hostiles. 6. Quae res Germanorum perculit animos, atque desertis insidiis, quas per arta loca et latebrosa struxerant nostris, trans Menum nomine fluvium ad opitulandum suis necessitudinibus avolarunt. 7. Ut enim in [1] rebus amat fieri dubiis et turbatis, hinc equitum nostrorum accursu, inde navigiis vectorum militum impetu repentino perterrefacti, evadendi subsidium velox locorum invenere prudentes, quorum digressu miles libere gradiens, opulentas pecore villas et frugibus rapiebat, nulli parcendo, extractisque captivis, domicilia cuncta, curatius ritu Romano constructa, flammis subditis exurebat. 8. Emensaque aestimatione decimi lapidis, cum prope silvam venisset squalore tenebrarum horrendam, stetit dux [2] diu cunctando, indicio perfugae doctus per subterranea quaedam occulta, fossasque multifidas, latere hostium [3] plurimos, ubi habile visum fuerit erupturos. 9. Ausi tamen omnes accedere fidentissime, ilicibus incisis et fraxinis, roboreque

---

[1] *in*, added by Kellerbauer, cf. xvi. 12, 40.   [2] *dux*, added by Clark; V omits.   [3] *hostium*, added by Novák; lac. after *latere*, Clark, c.c.

---

[1] Main.

whatever they could find. 5. This arrangement thus made, at the very break of day the savages were seen drawn up along the hill-tops, and the soldiers in high spirits were led up to the higher ground; but they found no one there (since the enemy, suspecting this, had hastily decamped), and then great columns of smoke were seen at a distance, revealing that our men had burst in and were devastating the enemy's territory. 6. This action broke the Germans' spirit, and abandoning the ambuscades which they had laid for our men in narrow and dangerous places, they fled across the river, Menus [1] by name, to bear aid to their kinsfolk. 7. For, as is apt to happen in times of doubt and confusion, they were panic-stricken by the raid of our cavalry on the one side, and on the other by the sudden onset of our infantry, who had rowed up the river in their boats; and with their knowledge of the ground they had quick recourse to flight. Upon their departure our soldiers marched on undisturbed and plundered farms rich in cattle and crops, sparing none; and having dragged out the captives, they set fire to and burned down all the houses, which were built quite carefully in Roman fashion. 8. After having advanced approximately ten miles, they came to a forest formidable with its forbidding shade and their general stood in hesitation for some time, being informed by the report of a deserter that large forces were lurking in some hidden underground passages and wide-branching trenches, ready to burst forth when they saw an opportunity. 9. Yet they all ventured to draw near with the greatest confidence, but found the

abietum magno, semitas invenere constratas. Ideoque gradientes cautius retro, non nisi per anfractus
longos et asperos ultra progredi posse, vix indignationem capientibus animis, advertebant. 10. Et
quoniam aeris urente saevitia cum discriminibus
ultimis laboratur in cassum (aequinoctio quippe
autumnali exacto, per eos tractus superfusae nives
opplevere montes simul et campos) opus arreptum
est memorabile. 11. Et dum nullus obsisteret,
munimentum quod in Alamannorum solo conditum
Traianus suo nomine voluit appellari, dudum violen-
tius oppugnatum, tumultuario studio reparatum
est ; locatisque ibi pro tempore defensoribus, ex
barbarorum visceribus alimenta congesta sunt.
12. Quae illi maturata ad suam perniciem contemplantes, metuque rei peractae volucriter congregati,
precibus et humilitate suprema, petiere missis oratori-
bus pacem ; quam Caesar omni consiliorum via
firmatam,[1] causatus veri similia plurima, per decem
mensium tribuit intervallum ; id nimirum sollerti
colligens mente, quod castra supra quam optari
potuit occupata sine obstaculo, tormentis muralibus
et apparatu deberent valido communiri. 13. Hac
fiducia tres immanissimi reges venerunt tandem
aliquando iam trepidi, ex his qui misere victis apud
Argentoratum auxilia, iurantes conceptis ritu patrio

---

[1] firmatam, Wagner ; firmata, V.

paths heaped with felled oak and ash-trees and a great quantity of fir. And so they warily retreated, their minds hardly containing their indignation, as they realised that they could not advance farther except by long and difficult detours. 10. And since the rigorous climate was trying to them and they struggled in vain with extreme difficulties (for the autumnal equinox had passed, and in those regions the fallen snows covered mountains and plains alike) they took in hand a memorable piece of work. 11. And while there was no one to withstand them, with eager haste they repaired a fortress which Trajan had built in the territory of the Alamanni and wished to be called by his name, and which had of late been very forcibly assaulted. There a temporary garrison was established and provisions were brought thither from the heart of the savages' country. 12. When the enemy saw these preparations rapidly made for their destruction, they quickly assembled, dreading the completion of the work, and with prayers and extreme abasement sent envoys and sued for peace. And Caesar granted this for the space of ten months, since it was recommended by every kind of consideration, and he could allege very many plausible reasons for it; for doubtless he appreciated with his keen mind that the stronghold which, beyond any possible hope, he had seized without opposition, ought to be fortified with artillery on the walls and powerful appliances of war. 13. Confiding in this peace, three very savage kings finally appeared, though still somewhat apprehensive since they were of the number of those who had sent aid to the vanquished

verbis nihil inquietum [1] acturos, sed foedera **ad prae-**
stitutum usque diem, quia id nostris placuerat,
cum munimento servaturos intacto, frugesque por-
taturos humeris suis,[2] si defuisse sibi docuerint defensores. Quod utrumque, metu perfidiam frenante,
fecerunt.

14. Hoc memorabili bello, comparando quidem
Punicis et Teutonicis, sed dispendiis **rei Romanae**
peracto levissimis, ut faustus Caesar exultabat **et**
felix ; credique obtrectatoribus potuit, ideo fortiter
eum ubique fecisse fingentibus, quod oppetere dimi-
cando gloriose magis optabat, quam damnatorum
sorte (sicut sperabat,) ut frater Gallus occidi, **ni**
pari proposito post excessum quoque Constanti
actibus mirandis inclaruisset.

2. *Iulianus Caesar DC Francos, Germaniam II*
   vastantes obsidet, et ad deditionem fame com-
   pellit.

1. Quibus ut in tali re compositis firmiter, ad
sedes revertens hibernas, sudorum reliquias repperit tales. Remos Severus magister equitum
per Agrippinam petens et Iuliacum, Francorum

---

[1] *uerbis nihil inquietum*, G (*uerbis*, EH) ; *uero* (lac. 10
letters) *linquietum*, V. [2] *suis*, added by Clark, Her.
c.c., or tr. *p.h.*, Clark, Novák.

at Strasburg ; and they took oath in words formally drawn up after the native manner that they would not disturb the peace, but would keep the agreement up to the appointed day, since that was our pleasure, and leave the fortress untouched ; and they would even bring grain in on their shoulders, in case the defenders would let them know that they needed any ; both of which things they did, since fear curbed their treacherous disposition.

14. In this memorable war, which in fact deserves to be compared with those against the Carthaginians and the Teutons, but was achieved with very slight losses to the Roman commonwealth, Caesar took pride as a fortunate and successful general. And one might well believe his detractors, who pretended that he had acted so courageously on all occasions because he chose rather to perish fighting gloriously than to be put to death like a condemned criminal (as he expected), after the manner of his brother Gallus—had he not with equal resolution, even after Constantius' death, increased his renown by marvellous exploits.

2. *Julianus Caesar besieges six hundred Franks, who were devastating Second Germany, and starves them into surrender.*

1. Matters thus being firmly settled, so far as circumstances would permit, he returned to winter quarters and found the following sequel to his exertions. Severus, master of the horse, while on his way to Rheims by way of Cologne and Juliers, fell in with some very strong companies of Franks, to

validissimos cuneos, in sexcentis velitibus (ut
postea claruit,) vacua praesidiis loca vastantes,
offendit; hac opportunitate in scelus audaciam eri-
gente, quod Caesare in Alamannorum secessibus
occupato, nulloque vetante, expleri se posse praedarum opimitate sunt arbitrati. Sed metu iam
reversi exercitus, munimentis duobus, quae olim
exinanita sunt, occupatis, se quoad fieri poterat,
tuebantur. 2. Hac Iulianus rei novitate perculsus,
et coniciens quorsum erumperet, si eisdem transisset
intactis, retento milite circumvallare disposuit
castella munita, quae Mosa [1] fluvius praeterlambit,
et ad usque quartum et quinquagesimum diem,
Decembri scilicet et Ianuario mense, obsidionales
tractae sunt morae, destinatis barbarorum animis
incredibili pertinacia reluctantibus.[2] 3. Tunc pertimescens sollertissimus Caesar, ne observata nocte
inluni, barbari gelu vinctum amnem pervaderent,
cotidie a sole in vesperam flexo, ad usque lucis
principium, lusoriis navibus discurrere flumen ultro
citroque milites ordinavit, ut crustis pruinarum
diffractis, nullus ad erumpendi copiam facile perveniret.[3] Hocque commento, inedia et vigiliis et
desperatione postrema lassati, sponte se propria

---

[1] *castella munita, quae,* scripsi ; *castellum oppidum, quod
Mosa,* BG ; *disposuit* (lac. 16 letters) *osa,* V.   [2] *reluctantibus,* EW[2], Mommsen ; *reluctantis,* V.   [3] lac. 12
letters, end of page, V ; no lac., EBG.

the number (as appeared later) of six hundred light-armed skirmishers, who were plundering the districts unprotected by garrisons; the favourable opportunity that had roused their boldness to the point of action was this, that they thought that while Caesar was busily employed among the retreats of the Alamanni, and there was no one to prevent them, they could load themselves with a wealth of booty. But in fear of the army, which had now returned, they possessed themselves of two strongholds, which had long since been left empty, and there defended themselves as well as they could. 2. Julian, disturbed by the novelty of the act, and guessing what might come of it if he passed by leaving them unmolested, halted his army and made his plans to surround the strongholds, which the river Meuse flows past; and for fifty-four days (namely in the months of December and January) the delays of the siege were dragged out, while the savages with stout hearts and incredible resolution withstood him. 3. Then Caesar, being very shrewd and fearing that the savages might take advantage of some moonless night and cross the frozen river, gave orders that every day, from near sunset to the break of dawn, soldiers should row up and down stream in scouting vessels,[1] so as to break up the cakes of ice and let no one get an opportunity of easy escape. And because of this device, since they were worn out by hunger, sleeplessness, and extreme desperation, they surrendered of their

---

[1] The Romans kept such armed vessels on the rivers which formed the boundaries of the empire; cf. *lusoriae* (*naves*), Vopiscus, *Bonosus*, 15, 1.

dederunt, statimque ad comitatum Augusti sunt
missi. 4. Ad quos eximendos periculo, multitudo
Francorum egressa, cum captos comperisset et
asportatos, nihil amplius ausa, repedavit ad sua,
hisque perfectis, acturus hiemem revertit Parisios
Caesar.

3. *Iulianus C. Gallos tributis oppressos levare
conatur.*

1. Quia igitur plurimae gentes vi maiore col-
laturae capita sperabantur, dubia bellorum coniec-
tans, sobrius rector magnis curarum molibus stringebatur. Dumque per indutias, licet negotiosas et
breves, aerumnosis possessorum damnis mederi
posse credebat, tributi ratiocinia dispensavit. 2.
Cumque Florentius praefectus praetorio, cuncta
permensus (ut contendebat,) quicquid in capitatione
deesset, ex conquisitis se supplere firmaret, talium
gnarus, animam prius amittere quam hoc sinere
fieri memorabat. 3. Norat enim huius modi provisionum, immo eversionum, ut verius dixerim,
insanabilia vulnera, saepe ad ultimam egestatem
provincias contrusisse,[1] quae res (ut docebitur
postea,) penitus evertit Illyricum. 4. Ob quae praefecto praetorio ferri non posse clamante, se repente

---

[1] *contrusisse*, Bentley ; *conduxisse*, Mommsen ; *contrax-
isse*, V.

---

[1] The words *provisionum* and *eversionum* seem to be
chosen for the sake of a word-play. He means that the
arrangement proposed would amount to confiscation and
the ruin of the province.

314

own accord and were sent at once to Augustus'
court. 4. A large troop of Franks had set out to rescue
them from their danger ; but on learning that they
had been captured and carried off, without ven-
turing on anything further they retired to their
strongholds. And Caesar after these successes returned to Paris to pass the winter.

3. *Julianus Caesar tries to relieve the Gauls of oppressive tributes.*

1. Now since it was expected that a great number
of tribes with greater forces would make head together, our cautious commander, weighing the doubtful issue of wars, was perplexed with great burdens
of anxiety. So, thinking that during the truce,
short though it was and full of business, some
remedy might be found for the calamitous losses
incurred by the land-holders, he set in order the
system of taxation. 2. And whereas Florentius, the
praetorian prefect, after having reviewed the whole
matter (as he asserted) stated that whatever was lacking in the poll-tax and land-tax accounts he supplied
out of special levies, Julian, knowing about such
measures, declared that he would rather lose his life
than allow it to be done. 3. For he knew that the
incurable wounds of such arrangements, or rather de-
rangements [1] (to speak more truly) had often driven
provinces to extreme poverty—a thing which (as
will be shown later) was the complete ruin of Illyricum.[2] 4. For this reason, though the praetorian
prefect exclaimed that it was unbearable that he

[2] See xix. **11**, 2 ff.

factum infidum, cui Augustus summam commiserit rerum, Iulianus eum sedatius leniens, scrupulose computando et vere, docuit non sufficere solum, verum etiam exuberare capitationis calculum ad commeatuum necessarios apparatus. 5. Nihilo minus tamen, diu postea indictionale augmentum oblatum sibi nec recitare nec subnotare perpessus, humi proiecit. Litterisque Augusti monitus ex relatione praefecti, non agere ita perplexe, ut videretur parum Florentio credi, rescripsit, gratandum esse si provincialis, hinc inde vastatus, saltem sollemnia praebeat nedum incrementa quae nulla supplicia egenis possent hominibus extorquere. Factumque est tunc et deinde, unius animi firmitate, ut praeter solita nemo Gallis quicquam exprimere conaretur. 6. Denique,[1] inusitato exemplo, id petendo Caesar impetraverat a praefecto, ut secundae Belgicae multiformibus malis oppressae, dispositio sibi committeretur, ea videlicet lege, ut nec praefectianus nec praesidialis apparitor ad solvendum quemquam urgeret. Quo levati solatio cuncti, quos in curam susceperat suam,[2] nec interpellati, ante praestitutum tempus debita contulerunt.

---

[1] conaretur. Denique, Val.; conaretur (lac. 21 letters) inique, V. [2] curam susceperat suam W²; cura (lac. 11 letters) separat suam, V.

should suddenly become distrusted, when Augustus had conferred upon him the supreme charge of the state; Julian calmed him by his quiet manner, and by an exact and accurate computation proved that the amount of the poll-tax and land-tax was not only sufficient, but actually in excess of the inevitable requirements for government provisions. 5. But when long afterwards an increase of taxation was nevertheless proposed to him, he could not bring himself to read it or sign it, but threw it on the ground. And when he was advised by a letter of Augustus, after the prefect's report, not to act so meticulously as to seem to discredit Florentius, he wrote back that it would be a cause for rejoicing if the provincials, harried as they were on every side, might at least have to furnish only the prescribed taxes, not the additional amounts, which no tortures could wring from the poverty-stricken. And so it came to pass then and thereafter, that through the resolution of one courageous spirit no one tried to extort from the Gauls anything beyond the normal tax. 6. Finally, contrary to precedent, Caesar by entreaty had obtained this favour from the prefect, that he should be entrusted with the administration of the province of Second Belgium, which was overwhelmed by many kinds of calamities, and indeed with the proviso that no agent either of the prefect or of the governor should force anyone to pay the tax. So every one whom he had taken under his charge was relieved by this comforting news, and without being dunned they brought in their dues before the appointed date.

CONSTANTIUS ET GALLUS

4. *Iussu Constantii Aug. obeliscus Romae in Circo Maximo subrectus constituitur ; et de obeliscis ac de notis hieorglyphicis.*

1. Inter haec recreandarum exordia Galliarum, administrante secundum adhuc Orfito praefecturam, obeliscus Romae in circo erectus est maximo. Super quo nunc (quia tempestivum est) pauca discurram. 2. Urbem priscis saeculis conditam, ambitiosa moenium strue et portarum centum quondam aditibus celebrem, hecatompylos Thebas, institutores ex facto cognominarunt, cuius vocabulo provincia nunc usque Thebais appellatur. 3. Hanc inter exordia pandentis se late Carthaginis, improviso excursu duces oppressere Poenorum, posteaque reparatam, Persarum rex ille Cambyses, quoad vixerat alieni cupidus et immanis, Aegypto perrupta aggressus est, ut opes exinde raperet invidendas, ne deorum quidem donariis parcens. 4. Qui dum inter praedatores turbulente concursat, laxitate praepeditus indumentorum, concidit pronus, ac suomet pugione, quem aptatum femori dextro gestabat, subita vi ruinae nudato, vulneratus paene letaliter interisset. 5. Longe autem postea Cornelius Gallus Octaviano res tenente Romanas, Aegypti procurator, exhausit civitatem plurimis interceptis, reversusque cum furtorum arcesseretur, et populatae provinciae, metu nobilitatis acriter indignatae, cui

---

[1] *Iliad*, ix. 383 ff. ; Mela, i. 9.
[2] I.e. Thebes.
[3] Gallus was *praefectus Aegypti* (not *procurator*) from 30 to 26 B.C.

4. *By order of Constantius Augustus an obelisk is set up at Rome in the Circus Maximus ; also an account of obelisks and hieroglyphics.*

1. During these first steps towards the rehabilitation of Gaul, and while Orfitus was still conducting his second praefecture, an obelisk was set up at Rome in the Circus Maximus ; and of it, since this is a suitable place, I shall give a brief account. 2. The city of Thebes, founded in primitive times and once famous for the stately structure of its walls and for the hundred approaches formed by its gates, was called by its builders from that feature Hecatompylos,[1] or Hundred-gated Thebes ; and from this name [2] the province is to this day called the Thebaïd. 3. When Carthage was in its early career of wide expansion, Punic generals destroyed Thebes by an unexpected attack ; and when it was afterwards rebuilt, Cambyses, that renowned king of Persia, all his life covetous of others' possessions, and cruel, overran Egypt and attacked Thebes, in the hope of carrying off therefrom its enviable wealth, since he did not spare even gifts made to the gods. 4. But while he was excitedly running about among the plundering troops, tripped by the looseness of his garments he fell headlong ; and his own dagger, which he wore fastened to his right thigh, was unsheathed by the sudden force of the fall and wounded him almost mortally. 5. Again, long afterwards, when Octavian was ruling Rome, Cornelius Gallus, procurator [3] of Egypt, drained the city by extensive embezzlements ; and when on his return he was accused of peculation and the robbery of the province, in his fear of the bitterly exasperated nobility,

319

negotium spectandum dederat imperator, stricto
incubuit ferro. Is est (si recte existimo) Gallus
poeta, quem flens quodam modo in postrema Bucoli-
corum parte Vergilius carmine leni decantat.

6. In hac urbe inter delubra [1] ingentia, diversasque
moles, figmenta Aegyptiorum numinum exprimentes,
obeliscos vidimus plures, aliosque iacentes et com-
minutos, quos antiqui reges bello domitis gentibus,
aut prosperitatibus summarum rerum elati, montium
venis vel apud extremos orbis incolas perscrutatis
excisos, et [2] erectos dis superis in religione dicarunt.
7. Est autem obeliscus asperrimus lapis, in figuram
metae cuiusdam sensim ad proceritatem consurgens
excelsam, utque radium imitetur, gracilescens paulatim, specie quadrata in verticem productus angustum, manu levigatus artifici. 8. Formarum autem
innumeras notas, hieroglyphicas appellatas, quas
ei undique videmus incisas, initialis sapientiae vetus
insignivit auctoritas. 9. Volucrum enim ferarumque
etiam alieni mundi genera multa sculpentes, ut [3] ad
aevi quoque sequentis aetates, impetratorum vulgatius perveniret memoria, promissa vel soluta
regum vota monstrabant. 10. Non enim ut nunc
litterarum numerus praestitutus et facilis exprimit,

---

[1] *delubra*, Cornelissen ; *labra*, V.   [2] *et*, added by
Clark ;   V omits ;   *erectosque*, BG.   [3] *ut* before *ad*,
Clark ;   after *aetates*, Val. ;   *uti*, Gronov ;   V omits.

---

[1] *Eclogue*, x.
[2] A *meta* was one of the three conical columns on the
end of the *spina* of a circus.

to whom the emperor had committed the investigation of the case, he drew his sword and fell upon it. He was (if I am right in so thinking) the poet Gallus, whom Vergil laments in a way in the latter part of the *Bucolics* [1] and celebrates in gentle verse.

6. In this city, amid mighty shrines and colossal works of various kinds, which depict the likenesses of the Egyptian deities, we have seen many obelisks, and others prostrate and broken, which kings of long ago, when they had subdued foreign nations in war or were proud of the prosperous condition of their realms, hewed out of the veins of the mountains which they sought for even among the remotest dwellers on the globe, set up, and in their religious devotion dedicated to the gods of heaven. 7. Now an obelisk is a very hard stone, rising gradually somewhat in the form of a turning-post [2] to a lofty height; little by little it grows slenderer, to imitate a sunbeam; it is four-sided, tapers to a narrow point, and is polished by the workman's hand. 8. Now the infinite carvings of characters called hieroglyphics, which we see cut into it on every side, have been made known by an ancient authority of primeval wisdom. [3] 9. For by engraving many kinds of birds and beasts, even of another world, in order that the memory of their achievements might the more widely reach generations of a subsequent age, they registered the vows of kings, either promised or performed. 10. For not as nowadays, when a fixed and easy series of letters

[3] Cf. Diod. Siculus, iii. 3, 5, who says that hieroglyphics were understood by the priests alone, and that the knowledge was handed down from father to son.

quicquid humana mens concipere potest, ita prisci quoque scriptitarunt Aegyptii, sed singulae litterae singulis nominibus serviebant et verbis ; non numquam significabant integros sensus. 11. Cuius rei scientiam [1] his interim duobus exemplis monstrari sufficiet : [2] per vulturem naturae vocabulum pandunt, quia mares nullos posse inter has alites inveniri, rationes memorant physicae, perque speciem apis mella conficientis, indicant regem, moderatori cum iucunditate aculeos quoque innasci debere his rerum insignibus [3] ostendentes. Et similia plurima.

12. Et quia sufflantes adulatores ex more Constantium id sine modo strepebant, quod cum Octavianus Augustus obeliscos duos ab Heliupolitana civitate transtulisset Aegyptia, quorum unus in Circo Maximo alter in Campo locatus est Martio, hunc recens advectum, difficultate magnitudinis territus, nec contrectare ausus est nec movere, discant qui ignorant, veterem principem translatis aliquibus hunc intactum ideo praeterisse, quod Deo Soli speciali munere dedicatus, fixusque intra ambitiosi templi delubra, quae contingi non poterant, tamquam apex omnium eminebat. 13. Verum Constantinus id parvi ducens, avulsam hanc molem sedibus suis, nihilque committere in religionem

---

[1] *scientiam,* Eyssen. ; *scientia in,* V.   [2] *duobus exemplis monstrari sufficiet,* Novák (*d.e. expediam,* Schneider) ; lac. indicated by Clark ; *exemplum* without lac., V. [3] *rerum insignibus,* Novák ; *signibus (signis,* V³), V.

---

[1] The females were said to be impregnated by the south or the east winds ; Aelian, *Hist. Anim.* ii. 46 ; cf. Plutarch, *Quaest. Rom.* 93.

expresses whatever the mind of man may conceive, did the ancient Egyptians also write ; but individual characters stood for individual nouns and verbs ; and sometimes they meant whole phrases. 11. The principle of this thing for the time it will suffice to illustrate with these two examples : by a vulture they represent the word "nature," because, as natural history records, no males can be found among these birds ;[1] and under the figure of a bee making honey they designate "a king," showing by this imagery that in a ruler sweetness should be combined with a sting as well ;[2] and there are many similar instances.

12. And because sycophants, after their fashion, kept puffing up Constantius and endlessly dinning it into his ears that, whereas Octavianus Augustus had brought over two obelisks from the city of Heliopolis in Egypt, one of which was set up in the Circus Maximus, the other in the Campus Martius, as for this one recently brought in, he neither ventured to meddle with it nor move it, overawed by the difficulties caused by its size—let me inform those who do not know it that that early emperor, after bringing over several obelisks, passed by this one and left it untouched because it was consecrated as a special gift to the Sun God, and because being placed in the sacred part of his sumptuous temple, which might not be profaned, there it towered aloft like the peak of the world. 13. But Constantine,[3] making little account of that, tore the huge mass from its foundations ; and since he rightly thought that he was committing no

---

[2] Seneca, *De Clem.* i. 19, 2 ff., compares a king to a bee.
[3] That is, Constantine the Great.

recte existimans, si ablatum uno templo miraculum
Romae sacraret, id est in templo mundi totius, iacere
diu perpessus est, dum translationi pararentur utilia.
Quo convecto per alveum Nili, proiectoque Alex-
andriae, navis amplitudinis antehac inusitatae
aedificata est, sub trecentis remigibus agitanda.
14. Quibus ita provisis, digressoque vita principe
memorato, urgens effectus intepuit, tandemque
sero impositus navi, per maria fluentaque Tibridis,
velut paventis, ne quod paene ignotus miserat
Nilus, ipse parum sub emeatus [1] sui discrimine moenibus alumnis inferret, defertur in vicum Alexandri,
tertio lapide ab urbe seiunctum. Unde chamulcis
impositus, tractusque lenius per Ostiensem portam
piscinamque publicam, Circo illatus est Maximo.
15. Sola post haec restabat erectio, quae vix aut
ne vix quidem sperabatur posse compleri. At ea
ita est facta : aggestis erectisque digestisque ad
perpendiculum [2] altis trabibus (ut machinarum
cerneres nemus) innectuntur vasti funes et longi,
ad speciem multiplicium liciorum, caelum densitate
nimia subtexentes. Quibus colligatus mons ipse
effigiatus scriptilibus elementis, paulatimque in

[1] *emeatus*, G, Clark ; *emeatu*, V. [2] *at ea . . .
erectisque*, Novák ; *digestis ad perpendiculum*, Haupt ;
idestisque periculum, V.

---

[1] The origin of the name is unknown ; it was obviously
on the Tiber, below Rome.
[2] *Chamulcus*, which occurs only here, is the Greek
χαμουλκός glossed by Latin *traha* (cf. Virg. *Georg.* i. 164).
Here, a kind of sledge or platform without wheels, on which
ships were launched or drawn up on the shore.

sacrilege if he took this marvel from one temple and consecrated it at Rome, that is to say, in the temple of the whole world, he let it lie for a long time, while the things necessary for its transfer were being provided. And when it had been conveyed down the channel of the Nile and landed at Alexandria, a ship of a size hitherto unknown was constructed, to be rowed by three hundred oarsmen. 14. After these provisions, the aforesaid emperor departed this life and the urgency of the enterprise waned, but at last the obelisk was loaded on the ship, after long delay, and brought over the sea and up the channel of the Tiber, which seemed to fear that it could hardly forward over the difficulties of its outward course to the walls of its foster-child the gift which the almost unknown Nile had sent. But it was brought to the vicus Alexandri [1] distant three miles from the city. There it was put on cradles [2] and carefully drawn through the Ostian Gate and by the Piscina Publica [3] and brought into the Circus Maximus. 15. After this there remained only the raising, which it was thought could be accomplished only with great difficulty, perhaps not at all. But it was done in the following manner : to tall beams which were brought and raised on end (so that you would see a very grove of derricks) were fastened long and heavy ropes in the likeness of a manifold web hiding the sky with their excessive numbers. To these was attached that veritable mountain engraved over with written characters, and it was gradually drawn up on high through the empty

---

[3] One of the regions of the city, a part of the Aventine Hill.

arduum per inane [1] protentus, diu [2] pensilis, hominum milibus multis tamquam molendinarias rotantibus metas, cavea locatur in media, eique sphaera superponitur ahenea, aureis lamminis nitens, qua confestim vi ignis divini contacta, ideoque sublata, facis imitamentum infigitur [3] aereum, itidem auro imbracteatum, velut abundanti flamma candentis. 16. Secutaeque aetates alios transtulerunt, quorum unus in Vaticano, alter in hortis Sallusti, duo in Augusti monumento erecti sunt. 17. Qui autem notarum textus obelisco incisus est veteri, quem videmus in Circo, Hermapionis librum secuti interpretatum litteris subiecimus Graecis.[4]

ΑΡΧΗΝ ΑΠΟ ΤΟΥ ΝΟΤΙΟΥ ΔΙΕΡΜΗΝΕΥ-
ΜΕΝΑ ΕΧΕΙ ΣΤΙΧΟΣ ΠΡΩΤΟΣ ΤΑΔΕ
ΛΕΓΕΙ

18. ῞Ηλιος βασιλεῖ ῾Ραμέστῃ · δεδώρημαί σοι
ἀνὰ πᾶσαν οἰκουμένην μετὰ χαρᾶς βασιλεύειν, ὃν

---

[1] *in arduum per inane,* Eyssen.; *id per arduum inane,*
V.   [2] *diuqꝛe,* BG ; *diutius,* Her.   [3] *infigitur,*
Val.; *infigura,* V.   [4] The entire inscr. is preserved
only in G. V has two unintelligible lines with lac. of
1½ pages. Several MSS. omit the Greek, a greater number
have the same amount of Greek as V. It seems best to
refer to Clark's crit. app. for the numerous variants and
conjectures.

---

[1] Here *meta* must refer to the upper (outer) part of the
mill, which was turned around the inner stone.
[2] *Cavea,* regularly used for the spectators' seats, here

air, and after hanging for a long time, while **many**
thousand men turned wheels [1] resembling millstones,
it was finally placed in the middle of the circus [2]
and capped by a bronze globe gleaming with gold-
leaf ; this was immediately struck by a bolt of the
divine fire and therefore removed and replaced
by a bronze figure of a torch, likewise overlaid
with gold-foil and glowing like a mass of flame.
16. And subsequent generations have brought over
other obelisks, of which one was set up on the
Vatican,[3] another in the gardens of Sallust,[4] and two
at the mausoleum of Augustus.[5] 17. Now the text
of the characters cut upon the ancient obelisk which
we see in the Circus [6] I add below in its Greek translation, following the work of Hermapion.[7] The
translation of the first line, beginning on the South
side, reads as follows : 18. " The Sun speaks to King
Ramestes. I have granted to thee that thou
shouldst with joy rule over the whole earth, thou

means the circus as a whole ; cf. Plautus, *Truc.* 931, *quod
verbum in cavea dixit histrio ;* Cic., *De Leg.* ii. 15, 38.
  [3] On the *spina* of the *Circus Gai et Neronis ;* it is now
in front of St. Peter's ; it is 25.36 m. high and without hieroglyphics.
  [4] These now belonged to the imperial house ; the
obelisk is at present in the *Piazza della Trinità dei Monte ;*
it is 13 m. high and has a copy, made in Rome, of the hieroglyphics on the obelisk set up by Augustus in the Circus
Maximus.
  [5] These are before the church of Santa Maria Maggiore
and on the Quirinal ; the former is 14.40 m. high, the latter
somewhat less ; neither has hieroglyphics.
  [6] This obelisk, the greatest of them all (32.50 m.), was set
up at the Lateran by Fontana in 1588.
  [7] He seems to have lived in the time of Augustus.

Ἥλιος φιλεῖ. — [καὶ] Ἀπόλλων κρατερὸς φιλαλήθης υἱὸς Ἥρωνος, θεογέννητος κτιστὴς τῆς οἰκουμένης, ὃν Ἥλιος προέκρινεν, ἄλκιμος Ἄρεως
βασιλεὺς Ῥαμέστης. ᾧ πᾶσα ὑποτέτακται ἡ γῆ
μετὰ ἀλκῆς καὶ θάρσους. βασιλεὺς Ῥαμέστης
Ἡλίου παῖς αἰωνόβιος.

ΣΤΙΧΟΣ ΔΕΥΤΕΡΟΣ

19. Ἀπόλλων κρατερός, ὁ ἑστὼς ἐπ᾿ ἀληθείας,
δεσπότης διαδήματος, τὴν Αἴγυπτον δοξάσας κεκτη-
μένος, ὁ ἀγλαοποιήσας Ἡλίου πόλιν, καὶ κτίσας
τὴν λοιπὴν οἰκουμένην, καὶ πολυτιμήσας τοὺς ἐν
Ἡλίου πόλει θεοὺς ἀνιδρυμένους, ὃν Ἥλιος φιλεῖ.

ΤΡΙΤΟΣ ΣΤΙΧΟΣ

20. Ἀπόλλων κρατερὸς Ἡλίου παῖς παμφεγγής,
ὃν Ἥλιος προέκρινεν καὶ Ἄρης ἄλκιμος ἐδωρή-
σατο. οὗ τὰ ἀγαθὰ ἐν παντὶ διαμένει καιρῷ. ὃν
Ἄμμων ἀγαπᾷ, πληρώσας τὸν νέων τοῦ φοίνικος
ἀγαθῶν. ᾧ οἱ θεοὶ ζωῆς χρόνον ἐδωρήσαντο.

Ἀπόλλων κρατερὸς υἱὸς Ἥρωνος βασιλεὺς
οἰκουμένης Ῥαμέστης, ὃς ἐφύλαξεν Αἴγυπτον τοὺς
ἀλλοεθνεῖς νικήσας, ὃν Ἥλιος φιλεῖ, ᾧ πολὺν
χρόνον ζωῆς ἐδωρήσαντο θεοί. δεσπότης οἰκουμένης Ῥαμέστης αἰωνόβιος.

328

whom the Sun loveth—and powerful Apollo, lover
of truth, son of Heron, god-born, creator of the
world, whom the Sun hath chosen, the doughty
son of Mars, King Ramestes. Unto him the whole
earth is made subject through his valour and boldness. King Ramestes, eternal child of the Sun."

SECOND LINE.

19. " Mighty Apollo, seated upon truth, Lord of
the Diadem, who hath gloriously honoured Egypt
as his peculiar possession, who hath beautified Heliopolis, created the rest of the world, and adorned
with manifold honours the Gods erected in Heliopolis—he whom the Sun loveth."

THIRD LINE.

20. " Mighty Apollo, child of the Sun, all-radiant,
whom the Sun hath chosen and valiant Mars en-
dowed ; whose blessings shall endure forever ; whom
Ammon [1] loveth, as having filled his temple with the
good fruits of the date palm ; unto whom the Gods
have given length of life.

" Apollo, mighty son of Heron, Ramestes,[2] king
of the world, who hath preserved Egypt by con-
quering other nations ; whom the Sun loveth ; to
whom the Gods have granted length of life ; Lord
of the world, Ramestes ever-living."

---

[1] Ammon (or Hammon), was an important Egyptian
and Libyan god, identified by the Romans with Jupiter,
cf. Virg., *Aen.* iv. 198 ff.
[2] See Index.

CONSTANTIUS ET GALLUS

ΛΙΒΟΣ ΣΤΙΧΟΣ ΔΕΥΤΕΡΟΣ

21. Ἥλιος θεὸς μέγας δεσπότης οὐρανοῦ. δεδώρημαί σοι βίον ἀπρόσκοπον. Ἀπόλλων κρατερὸς κύριος διαδήματος ἀνείκαστος, ὃς τῶν θεῶν
ἀνδριάντας ἀνέθηκεν ἐν τῇδε τῇ βασιλείᾳ, δεσπότης
Αἰγύπτου, καὶ ἐκόσμησεν Ἡλίου πόλιν ὁμοίως καὶ
αὐτὸν Ἥλιον δεσπότην οὐρανοῦ. συνετελεύτησεν
ἔργον ἀγαθὸν Ἡλίου παῖς βασιλεὺς αἰωνόβιος.

ΤΡΙΤΟΣ ΣΤΙΧΟΣ

22. Ἥλιος θεὸς δεσπότης οὐρανοῦ Ῥαμέστῃ
βασιλεῖ. δεδώρημαι τὸ κράτος καὶ τὴν κατὰ
πάντων ἐξουσίαν. ὃν Ἀπόλλων φιλαλήθης δεσπότης χρόνων καὶ Ἥφαιστος ὁ τῶν θεῶν πατὴρ
προέκρινεν διὰ τὸν Ἄρεα. βασιλεὺς παγχαρὴς
Ἡλίου παῖς, καὶ ὑπὸ Ἡλίου φιλούμενος.

ΑΦΗΛΙΩΤΗΣ. ΠΡΩΤΟΣ ΣΤΙΧΟΣ

23. Ὁ ἀφ' Ἡλίου πόλεως μέγας θεὸς ἐνουράνιος
Ἀπόλλων κρατερός, Ἥρωνος υἱός, ὃν Ἥλιος
ἠγάπησεν, ὃν οἱ θεοὶ ἐτίμησαν, ὁ πάσης γῆς
βασιλεύων, ὃν Ἥλιος προέκρινεν, ὁ ἄλκιμος διὰ
τὸν Ἄρεα βασιλεύς, ὃν Ἄμμων φιλεῖ. καὶ ὁ
παμφεγγὴς συγκρίνας αἰώνιον βασιλέα et reliqua.

330

WEST SIDE, SECOND LINE.[1]

21. " The Sun, great God, Lord of Heaven ; I have granted to thee life hitherto unforeseen. Apollo the mighty, Lord incomparable of the Diadem, who hath set up statues of the Gods in this kingdom, ruler of Egypt, and he adorned Heliopolis just as he did the Sun himself, Ruler of Heaven ; he finished a good work, child of the Sun, the king ever-living."

THIRD LINE.

22. " The God Sun, Lord of Heaven, to Ramestes the king. I have granted to thee the rule and the authority over all men ; whom Apollo, lover of truth, Lord of seasons, and Vulcan, father of the Gods, hath chosen for Mars. King all-gladdening, child of the Sun and beloved of the Sun."

EAST SIDE, FIRST LINE.

23. " The great God of Heliopolis, heavenly, mighty Apollo, son of Heron, whom the Sun hath loved, whom the Gods hath honoured, the ruler over all the earth, whom the Sun hath chosen, a king valiant for Mars, whom Ammon loveth, and he that is all-radiant, having set apart the king eternal " ; and so on.

---

[1] There seems to be no reason to suspect lacunae. Ammianus gave only parts of the inscriptions as specimens, in order not to weary his readers by repetitions of the same general purport.

CONSTANTIUS ET GALLUS

5. *Constantius Aug. et Sapor Persarum rex frustra de pace per litteras et legatos agunt.*

1. Datiano et Cereali consulibus, cum universa per Gallias studio cautiore disponerentur, formidoque praeteritorum barbaricos hebetaret excursus, rex Persarum in confiniis agens adhuc gentium extimarum, iamque cum Chionitis et Gelanis, omnium acerrimis bellatoribus, pignore icto societatis, rediturus ad sua, Tamsaporis scripta suscepit, pacem Romanum principem nuntiantis poscere precativam. 2. Ideoque non nisi infirmato imperii robore temptari talia suspicatus, latius semet extentans, pacis amplectitur nomen, et condiciones proposuit graves, missoque cum muneribus Narseo quodam legato, litteras ad Constantium dedit nusquam a genuino fastu declinans, quarum hunc fuisse accepimus sensum:

3. " Rex regum Sapor, particeps siderum, frater Solis et Lunae, Constantio Caesari fratri meo salutem plurimam dico.

" Gaudeo tandemque mihi placet, ad optimam viam te revertisse, et incorruptum aequitatis agnovisse suffragium, rebus ipsis expertum pertinax alieni cupiditas quas aliquotiens ediderit strages. 4. Quia igitur veritatis ratio soluta esse debet et

332

5. *Constantius Augustus and Sapor, king of the Persians, negotiate for peace through letters and envoys ; but to no purpose.*

1. In the consulship of Datianus and Cerealis, while all provisions in Gaul were being made with very careful endeavour, and dismay due to past losses halted the raids of the savages, the king of Persia was still encamped in the confines of the frontier tribes ; and having now made a treaty of alliance with the Chionitae and Gelani, the fiercest warriors of all, he was on the point of returning to his own territories, when he received Tamsapor's letter, stating that the Roman emperor begged and entreated for peace. 2. Therefore, imagining that such a step would not be attempted unless the fabric of the empire were weakened, he swelled with still greater pride, embraced the name of peace, and proposed hard conditions ; and dispatching one Narseus with gifts as his envoy, he sent a letter to Constantius, in no wise deviating from his native haughtiness, the tenor of which, as we have learned, was as follows :—

3. " I Sapor, King of Kings, partner with the Stars, brother of the Sun and Moon, to my brother Constantius Caesar offer most ample greeting.

" I rejoice and at last take pleasure that you have returned to the best course and acknowledged the inviolable sanction of justice, having learned from actual experience what havoc has been caused at various times by obstinate covetousness of what belongs to others. 4. Since therefore the consideration of truth ought to be free and untrammelled,

libera, et celsiores fortunas idem loqui decet atque
sentire, propositum meum in pauca conferam
reminiscens, haec quae dicturus sum me saepius
replicasse. 5. Ad usque Strymona flumen et Mace-
donicos fines tenuisse maiores imperium [1] meos,
antiquitates quoque vestrae testantur ; haec me
convenit flagitare (ne sit arrogans quod affirmo)
splendore virtutumque insignium serie, vetustis
regibus antistantem. Sed ubique mihi cordi est
recta ratio,[2] cui coalitus ab adulescentia prima, nihil
umquam paenitendum admisi. 6. Ideoque Armeniam recuperare cum Mesopotamia debeo, avo
meo composita fraude praereptam. Illud apud nos
numquam in acceptum feretur,[3] quod asseritis vos
exsultantes, nullo discrimine virtutis ac doli, prosperos omnes laudari debere bellorum eventus. 7
Postremo si morem gerere suadenti volueris recte,
contemne partem exiguam, semper luctificam et
cruentam, ut cetera regas securus, prudenter reputans medellarum quoque artifices urere non numquam et secare et partes corporum amputare, ut
reliquis uti liceat integris, hocque bestias factitare :
quae cum advertant cur maximo opere capiantur,
illud propria sponte amittunt, ut vivere deinde
possint impavidae. 8. Id sane pronuntio, quod
si haec mea legatio redierit irrita, post tempus

---

[1] *imperium*, added by Clark c.c. ; V omits. [2] *recta
ratio*, Erfurdt ; *moderatio* or *ratio*, Val. ; *recordatio*, V.
[3] *feretur*, Haupt ; *fretus*, V.

and it befits those in high station to speak as they
feel, I shall state my proposal in brief terms, recalling that what I am about to say I have often
repeated. 5. That my forefathers' empire reached
as far as the river Strymon and the boundaries of
Macedonia even your own ancient records bear
witness ; these lands it is fitting that I should demand, since (and may what I say not seem arrogant)
I surpass the kings of old in magnificence and array
of conspicuous virtues. But at all times right reason
is dear to me, and trained in it from my earliest
youth, I have never allowed myself to do anything
for which I had cause to repent. 6. And therefore
it is my duty to recover Armenia with Mesopotamia,
which double-dealing wrested from my grandfather.
That principle shall never be brought to acceptance
among us which you exultantly maintain, that
without any distinction between virtue and deceit
all successful events of war should be approved.
7. Finally, if you wish to follow my sound advice,
disregard this small tract, always a source of woe
and bloodshed, so that you may rule the rest in
security, wisely recalling that even expert physicians
sometimes cauterize, lance, and even cut away some
parts of the body, in order to save the rest sound for
use ; and that even wild beasts do this : for when they
observe for what possession they are being relent-
lessly hunted, they give that up of their own accord,
so as afterwards to live free from fear.[1] 8. This
assuredly I declare, that if this embassy of mine
returns unsuccessful, after the time of the winter

---

[1] Cf. Cic., *pro Scauro*, 2, 7 ; Juv. xii. 34 f., of the beaver.

hiemalis quietis exemptum, viribus totis accinctus, fortuna condicionumque aequitate spem successus secundi fundante, venire, quoad ratio siverit, festinabo."

9. His litteris diu libratis, recto pectore (quod dicitur) considerateque responsum est, hoc modo :

10. " Victor terra marique Constantius, semper Augustus, fratri meo Sapori regi salutem plurimam dico.

Sospitati quidem tuae gratulor ut futurus (si velis,) amicus, cupiditatem vero semper indeflexam fusiusque vagantem, vehementer insimulo. 11. Mesopotamiam poscis ut tuam, perindeque Armeniam, et suades integro corpori adimere membra quaedam, ut salus eius deinceps locetur in solido, quod infindendum [1] est potius quam ulla consensione firmandum. Accipe igitur veritatem, non obtectam praestigiis, sed perspicuam, nullisque minis inanibus perterrendam. 12. Praefectus praetorio meus, opinatus aggredi negotium publicae utilitati conducens, cum duce tuo per quosdam ignobiles, me inconsulto, sermones conseruit super pace. Non refutamus hanc nec repellimus : adsit modo cum decore et honestate, nihil pudori nostro praereptura vel maiestati. 13. Est enim absonum et insipiens nunc cum [2] gestarum rerum ordines (placatae sint aurae invidiae !) nobis multipliciter

---

[1] *infindendum*, Damsté, cf. Val. Flacc. i. 687 ; *infringendum*, Haupt ; *in fundendum*, V. [2] *nunc cum*, Clark ; *cum*, E² BG ; *nam*, Bentley ; *num*, V.

rest is past I shall gird myself with all my strength and with fortune and the justice of my terms upholding my hope of a successful issue, I shall hasten to come on, so far as reason permits."

9. After this letter had long been pondered, answer was made with upright heart, as they say, and circumspectly, as follows :—

10. " I, Constantius, victor by land and sea, perpetual Augustus, to my brother King Sapor, offer most ample greeting.

" I rejoice in your health, and if you will, I shall be your friend hereafter; but this covetousness of yours, always unbending and more widely encroaching, I vehemently reprobate. 11. You demand Mesopotamia as your own and likewise Armenia, and you recommend lopping off some members of a sound body, so that its health may afterwards be put upon a firm footing—advice which is rather to be refuted than to be confirmed by any agreement. Therefore listen to the truth, not obscured by any juggling, but transparent and not to be intimidated by any empty threats. 12. My praetorian prefect, thinking to undertake an enterprise conducing to the public weal, entered into conversations with a general of yours, through the agency of some individuals of little worth and without consulting me, on the subject of peace. This we neither reject nor refuse, if only it take place with dignity and honour, without at all prejudicing our self-respect or our majesty. 13. For at this time, when the sequence of events (may envy's breezes be placated !) has beamed in manifold form upon us, when with the overthrow of the

illuxerunt, cum deletis tyrannis, totus orbis Romanus nobis obtemperat, ea prodere, quae contrusi[1] in orientales angustias, diu servavimus inlibata. 14. Cessent autem quaeso formidines, quae nobis intentantur ex more, cum ambigi nequeat, non inertia nos sed modestia, pugnas interdum excepisse potius quam intulisse, et nostra quotiens lacessimur, fortissimo bonae conscientiae[2] spiritu defensare, id experiendo legendoque scientes, in proeliis quibusdam raro rem titubasse Romanam, in summa vero bellorum numquam ad deteriora prolapsam."

15. Hanc legationem nullo impetrato remissam,—nec enim effrenatae regis cupiditati responderi amplius quicquam potuit—post paucissimos dies secutus est Prosper comes et Spectatus tribunus, et notarius itemque Eustathius, Musoniano suggerente philosophus, ut opifex suadendi ; imperatoris scripta perferentes et munera, enisuri apparatum interim Saporis arte quadam suspendere, ne[3] supra humanum modum provinciae munirentur arctoae.

---

[1] *contrusi*, Bentley, Haupt; *contra si*, V.   [2] *bonae conscientiae*, Novák, cf. xvi. 7, 7, etc. ; *benevolentiae*, V. [3] *ne*, added by Clark ; *ut*, BG ; *dum*, Bentley ; V omits.

---

[1] That is, when Constantius shared the rule with his brothers and governed only the eastern provinces.

usurpers the whole Roman world is subject to us, it is absurd and silly to surrender what we long preserved unmolested when we were still confined within the bounds of the Orient.[1] 14. Furthermore, pray make an end of those intimidations which (as usual) are directed against us, since there can be no doubt that it was not through slackness, but through self-restraint that we have sometimes accepted battle rather than offered it, and that when we are set upon, we defend our territories with the most valiant spirit of a good conscience ; for we know both by experience and by reading that while in some battles, though rarely, the Roman cause has stumbled, yet in the main issue of our wars it has never succumbed to defeat."

15. This embassy having been sent back without obtaining anything—for no fuller answer could be made to the king's unbridled greed—after a very few days it was followed by Count Prosper,[2] Spectatus, tribune and secretary,[3] and likewise, at the suggestion of Musonianus,[4] the philosopher Eustathius,[5] as a master of persuasion ; they carried with them letters of the emperor and gifts, and meanwhile planned by some craft or other to stay Sapor's preparations, so that his northern provinces might not be fortified beyond the possibility of attack.

[2] See xiv. 11, 5 ; xv. 13, 3.
[3] There were three classes of secretaries. The highest held the rank of tribune ; see Introd., pp. xliii f.
[4] See xv. 13, 1 ; xvi. 9, 2.
[5] From Cappadocia, a pupil of Iamblichus.

CONSTANTIUS ET GALLUS

6. *Iuthungi, gens Alamannica, in Raetiis quas populabantur, a Romanis caesi fugatique.*

1. Inter quae ita ambigua, Iuthungi Alamannorum pars Italicis conterminans tractibus, obliti pacis et foederum, quae adepti sunt obsecrando, Raetias turbulente vastabant, adeo ut etiam oppidorum temptarent obsidia praeter solitum. 2. Ad quos repellendos cum valida manu missus Barbatio, in locum Silvani peditum promotus magister, ignavus sed verbis effusior, alacritate militum vehementer erecta, prostravit acerrime multos, ita ut exigua portio, quae periculi metu se dedit in fugam, aegre dilapsa, lares [1] suos non sine lacrimis reviseret et lamentis. 3. Huic pugnae Nevitta, postea consul, equestris praepositus turmae, et adfuisse et fortiter fecisse firmatur.

7. *Nicomedia terrae motu prostrata ; et quot modis terra quatiatur.*

1. Eisdem diebus terrae motus horrendi, per Macedoniam Asiamque et Pontum, assiduis pulsibus oppida multa concusserunt et montes. Inter monu-menta tamen multiformium aerumnarum, eminuere Nicomediae clades, Bithyniae urbium matris, cuius ruinarum eventum vere breviterque absolvam.

[1] *lares,* N² E², Gardt. ; *res,* V.

6. *The Juthungi, a tribe of the Alamanni, who were devastating Raetia, were defeated and put to flight by the Romans.*

1. In the midst of these uncertainties the Juthungi, a branch of the Alamanni bordering on Italian territory, forgetful of the peace and the treaty which they had obtained by their prayers, were laying waste Raetia with such violence as even to attempt the besieging of towns, contrary to their habit. 2. To drive them back Barbatio was sent with a strong force ; he had been promoted in place of Silvanus to be infantry commander. He was a coward but a fluent speaker, and having thoroughly roused the enthusiasm of the soldiers he utterly defeated a large number of the foe, so that only a small remnant, who for fear of danger had taken to flight, barely escaped and returned to their homes, not without tears and lamentations. 3. In this battle, we are assured, Nevitta, commander of a troop of cavalry and afterwards consul,[1] was present and conducted himself manfully.

7. *Nicomedia is destroyed by an earthquake ; the different ways in which the earth is shaken.*

1. At that same time fearful earthquakes throughout Asia, Macedonia, and Pontus with their repeated shocks shattered numerous cities and mountains. Now among the instances of manifold disaster was pre-eminent the collapse of Nicomedia, the metropolis of Bithynia ; and of the misfortune of its destruction I shall give a true and concise account.

[1] With Mamertinus in 362.

CONSTANTIUS ET GALLUS

2. Primo lucis exortu, diem nonum kal. Septembrium, concreti nubium globi nigrantium, laetam paulo ante caeli speciem confuderunt, et amendato solis splendore, nec contigua vel apposita cernebantur; ita oculorum obtutu praestricto, humo involutus crassae caliginis squalor insedit. 3. Dein velut numine summo fatales contorquente manubias, ventosque ab ipsis excitante cardinibus, magnitudo furentium incubuit procellarum, cuius impetu pulsorum auditus est montium gemitus, et elisi litoris fragor, haecque secuti typhones atque presteres, cum horrifico tremore terrarum, civitatem et suburbana funditus everterunt. 4. Et quoniam acclivitate collium aedes pleraeque vehebantur, aliae super alias concidebant, reclangentibus cunctis sonitu ruinarum immenso. Inter quae clamoribus variis celsa culmina resultabant, quaeritantium coniugium liberosque, et siquid necessitudines artae constringunt. 5. Post horam denique secundam (multo [1] ante tertiam) aer iam sudus et liquidus latentes retexit funereas strages. Non nulli enim superruentium ruderum vi nimia constipati, sub ipsis interiere ponderibus; quidam collo tenus aggeribus

[1] *non multo*, Eyssen.; *paulo*, Bentley; *multo*, V.

---

[1] Augural language; see Seneca, *N.Q.* ii. 41; for the usual meaning of *manubiae*, see Gellius, xiii. 25; he does not seem to know this use of the word.

[2] *Cardines* are the four cardinal points, north, south,

2. On the twenty-fourth of August, at the first break of day, thick masses of darkling clouds overcast the face of the sky, which had just before been brilliant ; the sun's splendour was dimmed, and not even objects near at hand or close by could be discerned, so restricted was the range of vision, as a foul, dense mist rolled up and settled over the ground. 3. Then, as if the supreme deity were hurling his fateful bolts [1] and raising the winds from their very quarters,[2] a mighty tempest of raging gales burst forth ; and at its onslaught were heard the groans of the smitten mountains and the crash of the wave-lashed shore ; these were followed by whirlwinds and waterspouts, which, together with a terrific earthquake, completely overturned the city and its suburbs. 4. And since most of the houses were carried down the slopes of the hills, they fell one upon another, while everything re-sounded with the vast roar of their destruction. Meanwhile the highest points re-echoed all manner of outcries, of those seeking their wives, their children, and whatever near kinsfolk belonged to them. 5. Finally, after the second hour, but well before the third, the air, which was now bright and clear, revealed the fatal ravages that lay concealed. For some who had been crushed by the huge bulk of the debris falling upon them perished under its very weight ; some were buried up to their necks

east, and west. Gellius, ii. 22, in his description of the winds, does not use *cardines* (probably because he speaks also of winds coming from between the *cardines*), but *loca, regiones* (§ 2), *limites regionesque* (§ 3), *regiones caeli* (§ 13), *caeli partibus* (§ 17).

obruti, cum superesse possent siqui iuvissent,
auxiliorum inopia necabantur; alii lignorum ex-
stantium acuminibus fixi pendebant. 6. Uno ictu
caesi complures, paulo ante homines tunc promiscae
strages cadaverum cernebantur. Quosdam domo-
rum inclinata fastigia intrinsecus servabant[1] intactos,
angore et inedia consumendos. Inter quos Aristaenetus affectatam recens dioecensin curans vicaria
potestate, quam Constantius ad honorem uxoris
Eusebiae, Pietatis cognominarat, animam hoc casu
cruciatam diutius exhalavit. 7. Alii subita magnitudine ruinae oppressi, eisdem adhuc molibus
conteguntur. Collisis quidam capitibus, vel umeris
praesectis aut cruribus, inter vitae mortisque confinia, aliorum adiumenta paria perferentium im-
plorantes, cum obtestatione magna deserebantur. 8.
Et superesse potuit aedium sacrarum et privatarum,
hominumque pars maior, ni palantes abrupti
flammarum ardores per quinque dies et noctes, quicquid consumi poterat exussissent.

9. Adesse tempus existimo, pauca dicere quae de
terrae pulsibus coniectura veteres collegerunt. Ad
ipsius enim veritatis arcana, non modo haec nostra
vulgaris inscitia, sed ne sempiterna quidem lucubra-
tionibus longis nondum exhausta, physicorum iurgia
penetrarunt. 10. Unde et in ritualibus et pontificio[2] sacerdotio obtemperantibus libris super auctore

[1] *seruabant*, N. Bentley, Novák; *serabant*, E, Haupt;
sepiebant, R. Unger; *serebant*, V.   [2] *pontificio . . .
dicitur*, Novák (lac. suspected by Clark); *pontificiis*
(without lac.) *obtemperantur optemperantibus observantibus
sacerdotiis*, V.

---

[1] Some refer this to the disabled, others to those who
were fleeing. I think it refers to both; cf. in a parallel

in the heaps of rubbish, and might have survived
had anyone helped them, but died for want of
assistance ; others hung impaled upon the sharp
points of projecting timbers. 6. The greater number were killed at one blow, and where there were
just now human beings, were then seen confused
piles of corpses. Some were imprisoned unhurt
within slanting houseroofs, to be consumed by the
agony of starvation. Among these was Aristaenetus,
vice-governor of the recently created diocese which
Constantius, in honour of his wife, Eusebia, had
named Pietas ; by this kind of mishap he slowly
panted out his life amid torments. 7. Others,
who were overwhelmed by the sudden magnitude
of the disaster, are still hidden under the same
ruins ; some who with fractured skulls or amputated
arms or legs hovered between life and death, im-
ploring the aid of others in the same case, were
abandoned, despite their pleas and protestations.[1]
8. And, the greater part of the temples and private
houses might have been saved, and of the population
as well, had not a sudden onrush of flames, sweeping
over them for five days and nights, burned up
whatever could be consumed.

9. I think the time has come to say a few words
about the theories which the men of old have brought
together about earthquakes ; for the hidden depths
of the truth itself have neither been sounded by
this general ignorance of ours, nor even by the
everlasting controversies of the natural philosophers,
which are not yet ended after long study. 10. Hence
in the books of ritual [2] and in those which are in

[1] case Curtius iv. 16, 12 *qui sequi non poterant inter mutuos
gemitus deserebantur.*

[2] See Cic., *de Div.* i. 33, 72 ; Festus, p. 285 M.

motus terrae nihil dicitur caute, ne alio deo pro alio
nominato, cum qui eorum terram concutiat, sit
in abstruso, piacula committantur. 11. Accidunt
autem, (ut opiniones aestimant inter quas Aristoteles
aestuat et laborat), aut in cavernis minutis terrarum,
quas Graece σύριγγας appellamus, impulsu crebriore
aquis undabundis ; aut certe (ut Anaxagoras
affirmat,) ventorum vi subeuntium ima terrarum ;
qui cum soliditatibus concrustatis inciderint, erup-
tiones nullas reperientes, eas partes soli convibrant,
quas subrepserint tumidi.[1] Unde plerumque ob-
servatur, terra tremente, ventorum apud nos spira-
mina nulla sentiri, quod in ultimis eius secessibus
occupantur. 12. Anaximander ait, arescentem nimia
aestuum siccitate, aut post madores imbrium
terram rimas pandere grandiores, quas penetrat
supernus aer violentus et nimius, ac per eas vehe-
menti spiritu quassatam, cieri propriis sedibus.
Qua de causa terrores huius modi, vaporatis temporibus, aut nimia aquarum caelestium superfusione,
contingunt. Ideoque Neptunum, umentis sub-
stantiae potestatem, Ennosigaeon et Sisichthona
poetae veteres et theologi nuncuparunt.

[1] *tumidi*, suggested by Gardt. ; *umidi*, V ; Cornelissen
deleted as dittography.

---

[1] The *pontificales libri* of Seneca, *Epist.* 108, 31.
[2] The Roman ritual required that in addressing a god,
the identity of the god must be made sure and he must
be called by his proper name ; cf. for example, Horace,
Sat. ii. 6, 20, *Matutine pater, seu " Iane " libentius audis,*
and the altar at the foot of the Palatine, *sei deo sei deivae
sacrum.*
[3] *Meteorologica*, ii. 8.   [4] Subterranean passages.

conformity with the pontifical priesthood,[1] nothing is
said about the god that causes earthquakes, and this
with due caution, for fear that by naming one deity
instead of another,[2] since it is not clear which of them
thus shakes the earth, impieties may be perpetrated.
11. Now earthquakes take place (as the theories
state, and among them Aristotle [3] is perplexed and
troubled) either in the tiny recesses of the earth,
which in Greek we call σύριγγαι,[4] under the
excessive pressure of surging waters ; or at any rate
(as Anaxagoras asserts) through the force of the
winds, which penetrate the innermost parts of the
earth ; for when these strike the solidly cemented
walls and find no outlet, they violently shake those
stretches of land under which they crept when swollen.
Hence it is generally observed that during an earthquake not a breath of wind is felt where we are,[5]
because the winds are busied in the remotest recesses of the earth. 12. Anaximander says that
when the earth dries up after excessive summer
drought, or after soaking rainstorms, great clefts
open, through which the upper air enters with excessive violence ; and the earth, shaken by the
mighty draft of air through these, is stirred from
its very foundations. Accordingly such terrible
disasters happen either in seasons of stifling heat or
after excessive precipitation of water from heaven.
And that is why the ancient poets and theologians
call Neptune (the power of the watery element)
Ennosigaeos [6] and Sisichthon.[7]

---

[5] But compare the *procellae* of § 3, above.
[6] "Earthshaker," Juv. x. 182
[7] "Earthquaker," Gell. ii. 28, 1.

13. Fiunt autem terrarum motus modis quattuor:
aut enim brasmatiae sunt, qui humum more aestus
imitus [1] suscitantes, sursum propellunt immanissimas
moles, ut in Asia Delos emersit, et Hiera et Anaphe
et Rhodus, Ophiusa et Pelagia, prioribus saeculis
dictitata, aureo quondam imbri perfusa, et Eleusin
in Boeotia, et apud Tyrrenos Vulcanus, insulaeque
plures; aut climatiae qui limes ruentes atque [2] obliqui,
urbes aedificia montesque complanant; aut chasmatiae qui grandiore motu patefactis subito vora-
trinis, terrarum partes absorbent, ut in Atlantico
mari, Europaeo orbe spatiosior insula, et in Crisaeo
sinu Helice et Bura, et in Ciminia Italiae parte,
oppidum Saccumum, ad Erebi profundos hiatus
abactae, aeternis tenebris occultantur. **14.** Inter
haec tria genera terrae motuum, mycematiae
sonitu audiuntur minaci, cum dissolutis elementa
compagibus, ultro assiliunt, vel relabuntur con-
sidentibus terris. Tunc enim necesse est velut
taurinis reboare mugitibus, fragores fremitusque
terrenos. Sed hinc ad exorsa.

---

[1] *aestus imitus,* Her., Clark; *imitus,* Haupt; *itus,* V[1]; *itus
molestus,* V[2].   [2] *atque,* suggested by Clark, c.c.; *et,* V.

---

[1] A Greek word from βράζειν. "boil up."
[2] Cf. Claudian, *De Cons. Stil.* iii. 226, *Auratos Rhodiis
imbres nascente Minerva indulsisse Iovem perhibent: Iliad*
ii. 670; Pindar, *Olymp.* 7, 59 ff. (L.C.L. pp. 72 f.)
[3] An ancient town of Boeotia near Lake Copais.   It was
not swallowed up by an earthquake, but destroyed by an

13. Now earthquakes take place in four ways; for they are either *brasmatiae*,[1] or upheavings, which lift up the ground from far within, like a tide and force upward huge masses, as in Asia Delos came to the surface, and Hiera, Anaphe, and Rhodes, called in former ages Ophiusa and Pelagia, and once drenched with a shower of gold;[2] also Eleusis[3] in Boeotia, Vulcanus in the Tyrrhenian Sea, and many more islands. Or they are *climatiae*[4] which rush along to one side and obliquely, levelling cities, buildings, and mountains. Or they are *chasmatiae*, or gaping, which with their intensive movement suddenly open abysses and swallow up parts of the earth; as in the Atlantic Ocean an island more extensive than all Europe,[5] and in the Crisaean Gulf,[6] Helice and Bura; and in the Ciminian district of Italy the town of Saccumum;[7] these were all sunk into the deep abysses of Erebus, and lie hidden in eternal darkness. 14. Among these three sorts of earthquakes the *mycematiae*[8] are heard with a threatening roar, when the elements break up into their component parts and clash of their own accord, or slide back when the ground settles. For then of necessity the crashing and rumbling of the earth must resound like the bellowing of a bull. But to return to the episode which we began.

inundation (Strabo, ix. 2, 18; Paus. ix. 24, 2); and it was not an island.

[4] Moving sidewise.

[5] Atlantis; see Plato, *Timaeus*, pp. 24e-25a.

[6] Salona Bay, a part of the Corinthian Gulf; see Diod. xiv. 48, 49.

[7] Its exact location is unknown: it was near Lago di Vico.   [8] Bellowing.

8. *Iulianus C. Salios, gentem Francicam, in deditionem accipit ; Chamavorum alios caedit, alios capit, reliquis pacem tribuit.*

1. At Caesar hiemem apud Parisios agens, Alamannos praevenire studio maturabat ingenti, nondum in unum coactos, sed ad [1] insaniam post Argentoratum audaces omnes et saevos, opperiensque Iulium mensem, unde sumunt Gallicani procinctus exordia, diutius angebatur. Nec enim egredi poterat, antequam ex Aquitania aestatis remissione, solutis frigoribus et pruinis, veheretur annona. 2. Sed ut est difficultatum paene omnium diligens ratio victrix, multa mente versans et varia, id tandem repperit solum, ut anni maturitate non exspectata, barbaris occurreret insperatus, firmatoque consilio, XX dierum frumentum, ex eo quod erat in sedibus consumendum, ad usus diuturnitatem excoctum, bucellatum (ut vulgo appellant,) umeris imposuit libentium militum, hocque subsidio fretus, secundis (ut ante,) auspiciis profectus est, intra mensem quintum vel sextum, duas expeditiones consummari posse urgentes et necessarias arbitratus. 3. Quibus paratis, petit primos omnium Francos, eos videlicet quos consuetudo Salios appellavit,

---

[1] *ad*, A, Novák ; *in*, Lind. ; V omits.

8. *Julianus Caesar receives the surrender of the Salii,*
a Frankish people ; he kills a part of the Chamavi,
captures others, and grants peace to the rest.

1. Now Caesar, while wintering in Paris, hastened
with the greatest diligence to forestall the Alamanni,
who were not yet assembled in one body, but were
all venturesome and cruel to the point of madness
after the battle of Strasburg ; and while waiting for
the month of July, when the campaigns in Gaul
begin, he was for a long time in much anxiety. For
he could not leave until the grain supply was brought
up from Aquitania during the mild summer season,
after the breaking up of the cold weather and
frost. 2. But as careful planning is victorious
over nearly all difficulties, he turned over in his
mind many various possibilities ; and this at last
he found to be the only one, namely, without
waiting for the height of the season, to fall upon the
savages before he was looked for. And having
settled on this plan, he had the grain allowance for
twenty days taken from what was to be consumed
in the winter quarters, and baked up to serve for
some time ; he put this hard-tack (as they commonly
call it) on the backs of his willing soldiers, and
relying on this supply he set out under favourable
auspices (as he did before), thinking that within
the fifth or sixth month two urgent and inevitable campaigns might be brought to completion.
3. After these preparations he first of all aimed at the
Franks, those namely whom custom calls the Salii,[1]
who once had the great assurance to venture to

---

[1] They dwelt between the Maas and the Schelde.

ausos olim in Romano solo apud Toxiandriam locum habitacula sibi figere praelicenter. Cui cum Tungros venisset, occurrit legatio praedictorum, opinantium reperiri imperatorem etiam tum in hibernis, pacem sub hac lege praetendens, ut quiescentes eos tamquam in suis, nec lacesseret quisquam nec vexaret. Hos legatos negotio plene digesto, oppositaque condicionum perplexitate, ut in eisdem tractibus moraturus, dum redeunt, muneratos absolvit. 4. Dictoque citius secutus profectos, Severo duce misso per ripam, subito cunctos aggressus, tamquam fulminis turbo perculsit, iamque precantes potius quam resistentes, in opportunam clementiae partem effectu victoriae flexo, dedentes se cum opibus liberisque suscepit. 5. Chamavos itidem ausos similia adortus, eadem celeritate partim cecidit, partim acriter repugnantes, vivosque captos, compegit in vincula, alios praecipiti fuga repedantes [1] ad sua, ne militem spatio longo defatigaret, abire interim permisit innocuos ; quorum legatis paulo postea missis precatum consultumque rebus suis, humi prostratis sub obtutibus eius, pacem hoc tribuit pacto, ut ad sua redirent incolumes.

---

[1] *repedantes*, Bentley ; *trepidantes*, V.

---

[1] The capital of the Toxiandri, who dwelt in modern Zeeland and the northern part of Flanders. It was then connected territory, but intersected by many marshes; modern Tessender Lo.

[2] In the Belgian part of the province of Limberg ; see Tac., *Germ.* 2.

[3] A German people, living at the mouth of the Rhine ;

fix their abodes on Roman soil at Toxiandria.[1] But when he had reached Tongres,[2] a deputation of the aforesaid people met him, expecting to find the commander even then in winter quarters ; and they offered peace on these terms, that while they remained quiet, as in their own territories, no one should attack or molest them. After having fully discussed the matter and proposed in reply some puzzling conditions, as if intending to remain in the same district until they returned, he gave these envoys gifts and dismissed them. 4. But quicker than a flash he followed them up after their departure, and sending his general Severus along the river bank, fell upon the whole troop suddenly and smote them like a thunderstorm ; at once they took to entreaties rather than to resistance, and he turned the outcome of his victory into the timely direction of mercy by receiving them in surrender with their property and their children. 5. The Chamavi[3] also had ventured to make a similar attempt ; with the same rapidity he attacked these, killed a part of them, and a part, who resisted stoutly and were taken alive, he put in irons ; others, who made tracks for home in headlong flight, he allowed for the time to get away unharmed, in order not to tire his soldiers by a long chase. A little later they sent delegates to make supplication and to provide for their safety, and as they lay prostrate on the ground before his eyes he granted them peace on condition that they should return unmolested to their homes.

they later crossed the river, to drive the Salii from their homes.

CONSTANTIUS ET GALLUS

9. *Iulianus C. tria munimenta ad Mosam eversa
a barbaris instaurat, et a milite famem patiente
probris ac minis incessitur.*

1. Cunctis igitur ex voto currentibus, studio
pervigili properans, modis omnibus utilitatem fun-
dare provinciarum, munimenta tria recta serie
superciliis imposita fluminis Mosae, subversa dudum
obstinatione barbarica, reparare pro tempore cogitabat, et ilico sunt instaurata, procinctu paulisper
omisso. 2. Atque [1] ut consilium prudens celeritas
faceret tutum, ex annona decem dierum et septem,
quam in [2] expeditionem pergens vehebat cervicibus
miles, portionem subtractam in eisdem condidit
castris, sperans ex Chamavorum segetibus id sup-
pleri posse quod ablatum est. 3. Longe autem
aliter accidit. Frugibus enim nondum etiam maturis,
miles, expensis quae portabat, nusquam reperiens
victus, extrema minitans Iulianum compellationibus
incessebat et probris, Asianum appellans Graeculum
et fallacem, et specie sapientiae stolidum. Utque
inveniri solent quidam inter armatos verborum
volubilitate conspicui, haec et similia multa strepebant : 4. " Quo trahimur spe meliorum abolita,

---

[1] *atque*, BG ; *utque*, V ; *utque id*, Novák, Pet.   [2] *in*,
E[2] G ; *ad*, A ; V omits.

---

[1] Cf. Quint. xii. 10, 17, *Asiana gens tumidior alioqui
atque iactantior, vaniore etiam dicendi gloria inflata est.*
[2] Cf. Juvenal, iii. 78 ff.

9. *Julianus Caesar rebuilds three fortresses on the Meuse that had been destroyed by the savages, and is assailed with insults and threats by the soldiers, who are suffering from hunger.*

1. So, as everything was proceeding in accordance with his prayers, he made haste with watchful solicitude to put the well-being of the provinces in every way on a firm footing; and he planned to repair (as time would permit) three forts situated in a straight line along the banks overhanging the river Meuse, which had long since been overthrown by the obstinate assaults of the savages; and they were immediately restored, the campaign being interrupted for a short time. 2. And to the end that speed might make his wise policy safe, he took a part of the seventeen days' provisions, which the soldiers, when they marched forward on their expedition carried about their necks, and stored it in those same forts, hoping that what had been deducted might be replaced from the harvests of the Chamavi. 3. But it turned out far otherwise; for the crops were not yet even ripe, and the soldiers, after using up what they carried, could find no food anywhere; and resorting to outrageous threats, they assailed Julian with foul names and opprobrious language, calling him an Asiatic,[1] a Greekling [2] and a deceiver, and a fool with a show of wisdom. And as some are usually to be found among the soldiers who are noteworthy for their volubility, they kept bawling out such words as these and many others to the same purport: 4. "Where are we being dragged, robbed of the

olim quidem dura et perpessu asperrima per nives
tolerantes et acumina crudelium pruinarum ? Sed
nunc (pro nefas !) cum ultimis hostium fatis in-
stamus, fame, ignavissimo mortis genere tabes-
centes. 5. Et nequi nos turbarum existimet concitores, pro vita loqui sola testamur, non aurum
neque argentum petentes, quae olim nec contrectare
potuimus nec videre, ita nobis negata, velut contra
rem publicam, tot suscepisse labores et pericula
confutatis." 6. Et erat ratio iusta querellarum.
Inter tot enim rerum probabilium cursus, arti-
culosque necessitatum ancipites, sudoribus Gallicanis miles exhaustus, nec donativum meruit nec
stipendium, iam inde ut Iulianus illo est missus,
ea re quod nec ipsi quod daret suppetere poterat
usquam, nec Constantius erogari more solito permittebat. 7. Hocque exinde claruit fraude potius
quam tenacitate committi, quod cum idem Caesar
petenti ex usu gregario cuidam, ut barbas detonderet,
dedisset aliquid vile, contumeliosis calumniis appetitus est a Gaudentio tunc notario, ad explorandos
eius actus diu morato per Gallias, quem postea ipse
interfici iusserat, ut[1] loco monstrabitur competenti.

---

[1] *ut*, added by EG ; V omits.

---

[1] He appears as *agens in rebus*, xv. 3, 8, and as set as a
spy over Julian in xxi. 7, 2. He was finally executed by
Julian's order.
[2] xxii. 11, 1.

hope of a better lot ? We have long endured hardships of the bitterest kind to bear, in the midst of
snows and the pinch of cruel frosts ; but now (Oh
shameful indignity !), when we are pressing on to the
final destruction of the enemy it is by hunger, the
most despicable form of death, that we are wasting
away. 5. And let no man imagine us incitors to
mutiny ; we protest that we are speaking for our lives
alone, asking for neither gold nor silver, which we
have not been able to handle or even look upon for
a long time, and which are denied us just as if it were
against our country that we had been convicted of
having undertaken so much toil and danger." 6. And
they had good reason for their complaints. For
through all their career of laudable achievements, and
the critical moments of hazard, the soldiers, though
worn out by their labours in Gaul, had received
neither donative nor pay from the very day that
Julian was sent there, for the reason that he himself
had no funds available anywhere from which to give,
nor did Constantius allow any to be expended in
the usual manner. 7. And it was evident that this
was done through malice rather than through
niggardliness, from the fact that when this same
Julian was asked by a common soldier, as they
often do, for money for a shave, and had given him
some small coin, he was assailed for it with slan-
derous speeches by Gaudentius,[1] who was then a
secretary. He had remained in Gaul for a long
time to watch Julian's actions, and Caesar afterwards ordered that he be put to death, as will be
shown in the proper place.[2]

10. *Suomarius et Hortarius, Alamannorum reges, captivis redditis, ab Iuliano Caes. pacem impetrant.*

1. Lenito tandem tumultu, non sine blanditiarum genere vario, contextoque navali ponte transito Rheno,[1] terris Alamannorum calcatis, Severus magister equitum, bellicosus ante haec et industrius, repente commarcuit. 2. Et qui saepe universos ad fortiter faciendum hortabatur et singulos, tunc dissuasor pugnandi, contemptus videbatur et timidus, mortem fortasse metuens adventantem, ut in Tageticis libris legitur vel [2] Vegoicis [3] fulmine mox tangendos adeo hebetari, ut nec tonitruum [4] nec maiores aliquos possint audire fragores. Et iter ignaviter egerat praeter solitum, ut ductores, viarum praeeuntes alacri gradu, ultima minitando terreret, ni omnes conspirantes in unum, se loca penitus ignorare firmarent. Qui interdicti, metuentes auctoritatem, nusquam deinde sunt progressi.

3. Inter has tamen moras, Alamannorum rex Suomarius ultro cum suis improvisus occurrit, ferox ante saeviensque in damna Romana, sed tum

---

[1] *transito Rheno,* tr. by Clark, Novák, c.c. ; *R. flumine transito,* Her. ; *R. transito,* V. [2] *uel,* added by Preller, Haupt; *et,* Gardi; V omits. [3] *Vegoicis,* Kiessling; *uegonicus,* V. [4] *tonitruum,* E ; *tonitrum,* BG ; *nectores nitrum,* V.

---

[1] According to Censorinus, *De Die Nat.* 4, 13, and others, these books came from a certain Tages, who came up from the ground when a peasant was ploughing near Tarquinii in Etruria, and taught the people who flocked to him the secrets of prophecy. He is described as a boy with the wisdom of an old man ; see Cic., *De Div.* ii. 23, 50 and Pease's note. The Tarquitian books of xxv. 2, 7 are perhaps the same.

10. *Suomarius and Hortarius, kings of the Alamanni, on giving back their prisoners are granted peace by Julianus Caesar.*

1. At length, after the mutiny had been quelled, not without various sorts of fair words, they built a pontoon bridge and crossed the Rhine ; but when they set foot in the lands of the Alamanni, Severus, master of the horse, who had previously been a warlike and energetic officer, suddenly lost heart. 2. And he that had often encouraged one and all to brave deeds, now advised against fighting and seemed despicable and timid—perhaps through fear of his coming death, as we read in the books of Tages [1] or of Vegoe [2] that those who are shortly to be struck by lightning are so dulled in their senses that they can hear neither thunder nor any louder crashes whatsoever. And contrary to his usual custom, he had marched so lazily that he intimidated the guides, who were leading the way rapidly, and threatened them with death unless they would all agree, and unanimously make a statement, that they were wholly ignorant of the region. So they, being thus forbidden, and in fear of his authority, on no occasion went ahead after that. 3. Now in the midst of these delays Suomarius, king of the Alamanni, of his own initiative met the Romans unexpectedly with his troops, and although he had previously been haughty and cruelly bent upon harming the Romans, at that time on the

---

[2] Cf. Servius, on *Aen.* vi. 72, *libri Begoes nymphae, quae artem scripserat fulguritorum apud Tuscos.* The correct spelling is *Vegoe.*

lucrum existimans insperatum, si propria retinere permitteretur. Et quia vultus incessusque supplicem indicabat, susceptus bonoque animo esse iussus et placido, nihil arbitrio suo relinquens, pacem genibus curvatis oravit. 4. Et eam cum concessione praeteritorum sub hac meruit lege, ut captivos redderet nostros, et quotiens sit necesse, militibus alimenta praeberet, susceptorum vilium more securitates accipiens pro illatis : quas si non ostendisset in tempore, sciret se rursus eadem flagitandum.[1]

5. Quod ita recte dispositum est, impraepedite completo, Hortari nomine petendus erat regis alterius pagus, et quia nihil videbatur deesse praeter ductores, Nesticae tribuno scutariorum, et Chariettoni viro fortitudinis mirae, imperaverat Caesar, ut magna quaesitum industria, comprehensumque offerrent sibi captivum, et correptus velociter, adulescens ducitur Alamannus, pacto obtinendae salutis pollicitus itinera se monstraturum. 6. Hoc progresso secutus exercitus, celsarum arborum obsistente concaede, ire protinus vetabatur. Verum per circuitus longos et flexuosos ubi [2] ventum est tandem ad loca, ira quisque percitus armorum urebat agros et [3] pecora diripiebat et homines,

---

[1] *eadem flagitandum*, Pet., Niemeyer ; *ea defatigandum*, V.   [2] *flexuosos ubi*, Her. ; *flexu dissos*, V.   [3] *et*, before *pecora*, Her., Clark ; before *ira*, V.

---

[1] That is, he was to receive receipts from those in charge of the supplies, and show them to Julian.

contrary he thought it an unlooked-for gain if he were allowed to keep what belonged to him. And inasmuch as his looks and his gait showed him to be a suppliant, he was received and told to be of good cheer and set his mind at rest ; whereupon he completely abandoned his own independence and begged for peace on bended knee. 4. And he obtained it, with pardon for all that was past, on these terms : that he should deliver up his Roman captives and supply the soldiers with food as often as it should be needed, receiving security [1] for what he brought in just like any ordinary contractor. And if he did not present it on time, he was to know that the same amount would again be demanded of him.

5. When this, which was properly arranged, had been carried out without a hitch, since the territory of a second king, Hortarius by name, was to be attacked and nothing seemed to be lacking but guides, Caesar had given orders to Nestica, a tribune of the targeteers, and Charietto, a man of extraordinary bravery, to take great pains to seek out and catch one and bring him in captive. Quickly a young Alamann was seized and led in, and on condition of having his life spared he promised to show the way. 6. He led and the army followed, but it was prevented from going forward by a barricade of tall felled trees. But when they finally, by long and circuitous detours, reached the spot, every man in the army,[2] wild with anger, joined in setting the fields on fire and raiding flocks and men ; and if

---

[2] For this use of *armorum*, cf. xxxi. **10**, 5, *cum quadraginta armorum milibus ;* etc.

resistentesque sine ulla parsimonia contruncabant.
7. His malis perculsus, rex cum multiplices legiones,[1]
vicorumque reliquias cerneret exustorum, ultimas
fortunarum iacturas adesse iam contemplatus,
oravit ipse quoque veniam, facturum se imperanda
iurandi exsecratione promisit.[2] Captivos [3] resti-
tuere universos—id enim cura agebatur impensiore—
iussus fidem non praestitit.[4] Detentisque plurimis
reddidit paucos. 8. Quo cognito ad indignationem
iustam Iulianus erectus, cum munerandus venisset
ex more, quattuor comites eius, quorum ope et
fide maxime nitebatur, non ante absolvit, dum
omnes rediere captivi. 9. Ad colloquium tandem
accitus a Caesare, trementibus oculis adorato,
victorisque superatus aspectu, condicione difficili
premebatur, hac scilicet ut quoniam consentaneum
erat, post tot secundos eventus, civitates quoque
reparari, vi barbarorum excisas, carpenta et materias
ex opibus suis suorumque praeberet; et haec
pollicitus imprecatusque (si perfidum quicquam
egisset,) luenda sibi cruore supplicia, ad propria
remeare permissus est. Annonam enim transferre,
ita ut Suomarius, ea re compelli non potuit, quod
ad internicionem regione eius vastata, nihil inveniri
poterat quod daretur.

10. Ita reges illi tumentes quondam immaniter,
rapinisque ditescere assueti nostrorum, Romanae

---

[1] *legiones*, Hadr. Val.; *regiones*, V; *regionum direptiones*,
Her. [2] *promisit*, tr. after *exsecratione*, Novák; after
universos. V. [3] *captivos*, scripsi; *captivosque* added by
Haupt; lac. after *exsecratione*, Her., Clark. [4] *iussus
. . . praestitit*, added by Novák; lac. indicated by Clark,
Her.

they resisted, they butchered them, without compunction. 7. The king was overwhelmed by these calamities, and when he saw the numerous legions and the ruins of his villages which they had burned down, now fully convinced that the final wreck of his fortunes was at hand, he too begged for pardon and under the solemn sanction of an oath promised that he would do what might be ordered. Being bidden to restore all prisoners—for that was insisted on with special earnestness—he did not keep faith but held back a large number and gave up only a few. 8. On learning this, Julian was roused to righteous indignation, and when the king came to receive presents, as was usual, he would not release his four attendants, on whose aid and loyalty he chiefly relied, until all the captives returned. 9. Finally the king was summoned by Caesar to an interview and reverenced him with trembling eyes ; and overcome at the sight of the conqueror, he was forced to accept these hard terms, namely, that inasmuch as it was fitting that after so many successes the cities also should be rebuilt which the violence of the savages had destroyed, the king should furnish carts and timber from his own supplies and those of his subjects. And when he had promised this and taken oath that if he did any disloyal act, he should expiate it with his heart's blood, he was allowed to return to his own domains. For as to supplying grain, as Suomarius did, he could not be coerced, for the reason that his country had been ravaged to the point of ruin, and nothing to give to us could be found.

10. So those kings, who in times past were inordinately puffed up with pride, and accustomed to

potentiae iugo subdidere colla iam domita, et velut
inter tributarios nati et educati, obsecundabant
imperiis ingravate. Quibus hoc modo peractis,
disperso per stationes milite consuetas, ad hiberna
regressus est Caesar.

11. *Iulianus Caes., post res in Gallia bene gestas, in
aula Constantii Aug. ab invidis deridetur,
segnisque et timidus appellatur.*

1. Haec cum in comitatu Constantii subinde
noscerentur—erat enim necesse, tamquam appari-
torem, Caesarem super omnibus gestis ad Augusti
referre scientiam—omnes qui plus poterant in
palatio, adulandi professores iam docti, recte consulta prospereque completa vertebant in deridiculum,
talia sine modo strepentes insulse : " In odium
venit cum victoriis suis capella, non homo," ut
hirsutum Iulianum carpentes, appellantesque " lo-
quacem talpam " et " purpuratam simiam " et
" litterionem Graecum," et his congruentia plurima.
Atque ut tintinnabula [1] principi resonantes, audire
haec taliaque gestienti, virtutes eius obruere verbis
impudentibus conabantur ut segnem incessentes
et timidum et umbratilem, gestaque secus verbis
comptioribus exornantem ; quod non tunc primitus
accidit. 2. Namque ut solet amplissima quaeque [2]
gloria obiecta esse semper invidiae, legimus in veteres

---

[1] *tintinnabula*, R. Unger; *tintinnacula*, V, Clark.
[2] *amplissima quaeque*, Bentley, Eyssen. ; *amplissimaque*,
V.

enrich themselves with the spoils of our subjects, put their necks, now bowed down, under the yoke of Roman dominion, and ungrudgingly obeyed our commander, as if born and brought up among our tributaries. And after this conclusion of events the soldiers were distributed among their usual posts and Caesar returned to winter quarters.

11. *Julianus Caesar, after these successful campaigns in Gaul, is derided by envious courtiers at the palace of Constantius, and called slothful and timid.*

1. Presently, when all this became known at Constantius' court—for it was necessary that Caesar, like any subordinate, should render an account to Augustus of all his acts—all those who had the chief influence in the palace and were now past masters in flattery turned Julian's well-devised and successful achievements into mere mockery by endless silly jests of this sort : " This fellow, a nanny-goat and no man, is getting insufferable with his victories," jibing at him for being hairy, and calling him a " chattering mole " and " an ape in purple," and " a Greekish pedant," and other names like these ; and by ringing bells, so to speak, in the ears of an emperor eager to hear these and similar things, they tried to bury his merits with shameless speeches, railing at him as a lazy, timid, unpractical person, and one who embellished his ill success with fine words ; all of which did not take place then for the first time. 2. For as the greatest glory is always habitually subject to envy,

quoque magnificos duces vitia criminaque, etiam si
inveniri non poterant, finxisse malignitatem, spec-
tatissimis actibus eorum offensam.   3. Ut Cim-
onem Miltiadis filium, insimulatum incesti,[1] qui
saepe ante et[2] prope Eurymedonta Pamphylium
flumen Persarum populum delevit innumerum,
coegitque gentem insolentia semper elatam obsecrare
suppliciter pacem; Aemilianum itidem Scipionem
ut somniculosum aemulorum incusari malivolentia,
cuius impetrabili vigilantia, obstinatae in perniciem
Romae, duae potentissimae sunt urbes excisae.
4. Nec non etiam in Pompeium obtrectatores iniqui,
multa scrutantes, cum nihil unde vituperari deberet,
inveniretur, duo haec observarunt ludibriosa et
irrita : quod genuino quodam more caput digito
uno scalpebat, quodque aliquandiu tegendi ulceris
causa deformis fasciola candida crus colligatum
gestabat :[3] quorum alterum factitare ut dissolutum,
alterum ut novarum rerum cupidum asserebant;
nihil interesse oblatrantes argumento subfrigido,
quam partem corporis redimiret regiae maiestatis
insigni ; eum virum, quo nec fortior nec autem
cautior[4] quisquam patriae fuit, ut documenta prae-
clara testantur.

5. Dum haec ita aguntur, Romae Artemius curans
vicariam praefecturam, pro Basso quoque agebat,

---

[1] *incesti*, added by Lind.; lac. before *saepe*, Gardt.;
intemperantiae, Val.   [2] *ante qui prope*, BG ; *saepe ante et* V
(no lac.).   [3] *colligatum gestabat* (*habebat*, Novák), Her., cf.
Val. Max. vi. 2, 7 ; *collibatam*, V.   [4] *nec autem cautior*,
Walter ; *nec cautior*, WBG ; *nec amantior*, Haupt ; *ne
cautautior*, V.

we read that even against the renowned leaders
of ancient days faults and charges were trumped
up, even if none could be discovered, by spiteful
persons incensed by their brilliant exploits. 3. As,
for example, Cimon, the son of Miltiades, was accused
of incest, although often before and particularly
near the river Eurymedon in Pamphylia he annihilated a countless host of the Persians, and compelled a nation always swollen with pride to sue
humbly for peace. Likewise Scipio Aemilianus was
accused of inactivity by the malice of his rivals,
although by his effective vigilance two most powerful cities, bent on the destruction of Rome, were
razed to the ground. 4. And also even in the case
of Pompey, some malevolent critics, who after much
search found nothing for which he could be blamed,
noted these two laughable and silly facts : that in
a certain characteristic way he used to scratch his
head with one finger, and that for some time, to
cover up an ugly ulcer, he wore a white bandage
tied around his leg ; the one of these things he did,
they affirmed, because he was dissipated, the other
because he planned a revolution, snarling at him
with the somewhat pointless reason, that it mattered
not what part of his body he bound with the emblem
of kingly majesty[1]—and this to a man than whom,
as the clearest of proofs show, none was more valiant
or circumspect with regard to his country.

5. While these things were thus happening, at
Rome Artemius, who held the office of vice-prefect,

---

[1] The white fillet, to which the bandage was likened,
was emblematic of royalty ; see Suet., *Jul.* 79, 1.

qui recens promotus urbi praefectus, fatali decesserat
sorte, cuius administratio seditiones perpessa est
turbulentas, nec memorabile quicquam habuit quod
narrari sit dignum.

12. *Constantius Aug. Sarmatas dominos olim, tum
exules, et Quados, Pannoniarum et Moesiae
vastatores, ad obsides dandos et captivos
reddendos compellit ; atque exulibus Sarmatis,
in libertatem avitasque sedes restitutis, regem
imposuit.*

1. Augusto inter haec quiescenti per hiemem
apud Sirmium, indicabant nuntii graves et crebri,
permixtos Sarmatas et Quados, vicinitate et similitudine morum armaturaeque concordes, Pannonias
Moesiarumque alteram cuneis incursare dispersis.
2. Quibus ad latrocinia magis quam aperto habilibus
Marti, hastae sunt longiores et loricae ex cornibus
rasis et laevigatis, plumarum specie linteis indumentis innexae ; equorumque plurimi ex usu cas-
trati, ne aut feminarum visu exagitati, raptentur,
aut in subsidiis ferocientes, prodant hinnitu densiore
vectores. **3.** Et per spatia discurrunt amplissima,
sequentes alios vel ipsi terga vertentes, insidendo

---

[1] Junius Bassus died in 359 ; according to Prudentius,
contra Symm. i. 559, he was the first of his family to become
a Christian.

[2] That is, First and Second (Lower) Pannonia ; the
province was divided by Galerius.

[3] Pausanias, i. 21, 6, says that the Sarmatians made
such armour from horses' hoofs, having no iron, and that

also succeeded Bassus,[1] who a short time after he had been promoted to be prefect of the city had died a natural death. His administration suffered from mutinous disturbances, but had no remarkable incident which is worth relating.

12. *Constantius Augustus compels the Sarmatians, formerly rulers, but now exiles, and the Quadi, who were laying waste Pannonia and Moesia, to give hostages and return their prisoners ; and over the exiled Sarmatians, whom he restored to freedom and their ancestral abode, he appointed a king.*

1. As Augustus meanwhile was taking his winter rest at Sirmium, frequent serious reports showed that the Sarmatians and the Quadi, who were in agreement because they were neighbours and had like customs and armour, had united and were raiding the Pannonias [2] and Second Moesia in detached bands. **2.** These people, better fitted for brigandage than for open warfare, have very long spears and cuirasses made from smooth and polished pieces of horn, fastened like scales to linen shirts ; [3] most of their horses are made serviceable by gelding, in order that they may not at sight of mares become excited and run away, or when in ambush become unruly and betray their riders by loud neighing. **3.** And they run over very great distances, pursuing others or themselves turning their backs,

in the temple of Aesculapius at Athens, he saw a specimen, in which pieces of horn looked like clefts on a pine-cone.

velocibus equis et morigeris, trahentesque singulos,
interdum et binos, uti permutatio vires foveat
iumentorum, vigorque otio integretur alterno.

4. Aequinoctio itaque temporis verni confecto,
imperator coacta militum valida manu, ductu
laetioris fortunae profectus, cum ad locum aptissimum pervenisset, flumen Histrum exundantem [1]
pruinarum iam resoluta congerie, super navium
foros ponte contexto transgressus, populandis barbarorum incubuit terris. Qui itinere festinato
praeventi, catervasque bellatoris exercitus iugulis
suis imminere cernentes, quem nondum per anni
tempus colligi posse rebantur, nec spirare ausi
nec stare, sed vitantes exitium insperatum, semet
omnes effuderunt in fugam. 5. Stratisque plurimis,
quorum gressus vinxerat timor, si [2] quos exemit
celeritas morti, inter latebrosas convalles montium
occultati, videbant patriam ferro pereuntem, quam
vindicassent profecto, si vigore quo discesserant
restitissent. 6. Gerebantur haec in ea parte Sar-
matiae, quae secundam prospectat Pannoniam,
parique fortitudine circa [3] Valeriam opes barbaras
urendo rapiendoque occurrentia militaris turbo
vastabat. 7. Cuius cladis immensitate permoti,
posthabito latendi consilio, Sarmatae petendae
specie pacis, agmine tripertito agentes, securius

[1] *exundans* (with comma), Novák, c.c. ; *exundantem*, V.
[2] *si*, Mommsen ; *hi*, E² A ; *ii*, BG ; *his*, V.   [3] *circa*,
W² HTE, Val. ; *contra*, DG ; *c̄c̄*, V.

---

[1] See note 2, p. 253.

being mounted on swift and obedient horses and leading one, or sometimes even two, to the end that an exchange may keep up the strength of their mounts and that their freshness may be renewed by alternate periods of rest.

4. And so, when the spring equinox was past, the emperor mustered a strong force of soldiers and set out under the guidance of a more propitious fortune; and although the river Ister was in flood since the masses of snow and ice were now melted, having come to the most suitable place, he crossed it on a bridge built over the decks of ships and invaded the savages' lands with intent to lay them waste. They were outwitted by his rapid march, and on seeing already at their throats the troops of a fighting army, which they supposed could not yet be assembled owing to the time of year, they ventured neither to take breath nor make a stand, but to avoid unlooked-for destruction all took to precipitate flight. 5. The greater number, since fear clogged their steps, were cut down; if speed saved any from death, they hid in the obscure mountain gorges and saw their country perishing by the sword; and they might undoubtedly have protected her, had they resisted with the same vigour that had marked their flight. 6. This took place in that part of Sarmatia which faces Second Pannonia, and with equal courage our soldiers, like a tempest, laid waste the enemies possessions round about Valeria,[1] burning and plundering everything before them. 7. Greatly disturbed by the vastness of this disaster, the Sarmatians abandoned their plan of hiding, and forming in three divisions, under pretence of suing for peace

CONSTANTIUS ET GALLUS

nostros aggredi cogitarunt ut [1] nec expedire tela
nec vim vulnerum declinare, nec quod est in rebus
artissimis ultimum, verti possent in fugam. 8.
Aderant autem ilico Sarmatis periculorum Quadi
participes, qui noxarum saepe socii fuerant indis-
creti, sed ne eos quidem prompta iuvit audacia, in
discrimina ruentes aperta. 9. Caesis enim compluribus, pars quae potuit superesse, per notos
calles [2] evasit ; quo eventu vires et animos incitante,
iunctis densius cuneis, ad Quadorum regna properabat
exercitus, qui ex praeterito casu impendentia formidantes, rogaturi suppliciter pacem, fidentes ad
principis venere conspectum, erga haec et [3] similia
lenioris, dictoque die statuendis condicionibus pari [4]
modo Zizais quoque etiam tum regalis, ardui [5]
corporis iuvenis, ordines Sarmatarum more certa-
minis instruxit ad preces ; visoque imperatore,
abiectis armis pectore toto procubuit, exanimis
stratus. Et amisso vocis officio prae timore, tum
cum orare deberet, maiorem misericordiam movit,
conatus aliquotiens, parumque impediente singultu,
permissus explicare quae poscebat. 10. Recreatus
denique tandem, iussusque exsurgere, genibus
nixus, usu linguae recuperato, concessionem delictorum sibi tribui supplicavit et veniam, eoque ad

[1] *ut*, added by A in lac. indicated by Langen, Mommsen ;
V omits without lac.   [2] *calles*, Kiessling, Gardt. ; *colles*,
V.   [3] *et* added in EG ; V omits.   [4] *pari*, Her.
in lac. ind. by Eyssen.   (Lind. deleted *modo*.)   [5] *ardui*,
Novák ; *haud parui*, G ; *apud ui*, V.

372

they planned to attack our soldiers with little danger, so that they could neither get their weapons ready nor parry the force of wounds, nor turn to flight, which is the last recourse in times of stress. 8. Furthermore the Quadi, who had often been their inseparable companions in raids, came at once to share the perils of the Sarmatians; but their ready boldness did not help them either, rushing as they were upon evident hazards. 9. For after very many of them had been cut down, the part that could save themselves escaped by paths familiar to them, and our army, their strength and courage aroused by this success, formed in closer order and hastened to the domain of the Quadi. They, dreading from their past disaster what impended, planned to sue suppliantly for peace and confidently presented themselves before the emperor, who was somewhat too lenient towards those and similar offences; and on the day named for settling the terms in like fashion, Zizais, a tall young man who was even then a royal prince, drew up the ranks of the Sarmatians in battle array to make their petition. And on seeing the emperor he threw aside his weapons and fell flat on his breast, as if lying lifeless. And since the use of his voice failed him from fear at the very time when he should have made his plea, he excited all the greater compassion; but after several attempts, interrupted by sobbing, he was able to set forth only a little of what he tried to ask. 10. At last, however, he was reassured and bidden to rise, and getting up on his knees and recovering the use of his voice, he begged that indulgence for his offences, and pardon, be granted him. Upon this the throng

precandum admissa multitudo, cuius ora formido
muta claudebat, periculo adhuc praestantioris
ambiguo, ubi ille solo iussus attolli orandi signum
exspectantibus diu monstravit, omnes clipeis telisque
proiectis, manus precibus dederunt plura excogi-
tantes, ut vincerent humilitate supplicandi regalem.
11. Duxerat potior cum ceteris Sarmatis etiam
Rumonem et Zinafrum et Fragiledum subregulos,
plurimosque optimates, cum impetrandi spe similia
petituros. Qui, licet elati gaudio salutis indultae,
condicionum sarcina compensare inimice facta
pollicebantur, seque cum facultatibus et liberis et
coniugibus terrarumque suarum ambitu Romanae
potentiae libenter offerrent. Praevaluit tamen aequi-
tati iuncta benignitas, iussique obtinere sedes impavidi, nostros reddidere captivos. Duxeruntque
obsides postulatos, et obedire praeceptis deinde
promptissime spoponderunt. 12. Hortante hoc exemplo clementiae, advolarunt regalis [1] cum suis
omnibus Araharius, et Usafer inter optimates
excellens, agminum gentilium duces, quorum alter
Transiugitanorum Quadorumque parti, alter quibusdam Sarmatis praeerat, locorum confiniis et
feritate iunctissimis ; quorum plebem veritus [2]
imperator, ne ferire foedera simulans, in arma

---

[1] *regalis,* Clark ; *regales,* V.   [2] *ueritus,* Val. ; *arcuit,*
G ; *acrius,* V.

was admitted to make its entreaties, but mute **terror** closed their lips, so long as the fate of their superior was uncertain. But when he was told to get up from the ground and gave the long awaited signal for their petition, all threw down their shields and spears, stretched out their hands with prayers, and succeeded in many ways in outdoing their prince in lowly supplication. 11. Their superior had also brought with the rest of the Sarmatians Rumo, Zinafer and Fragiledus, who were petty kings, and a number of nobles, to make like requests, which they hoped would be granted. They, though overjoyed that their lives were spared, offered to make up for their hostile acts by burdensome conditions, and would have willingly submitted themselves with their possessions, their children, their wives, and the whole of their territories to the power of the Romans. However, kindness combined with equity prevailed, and when they were told to retain their homes without fear, they returned all their Roman prisoners. They also brought in the hostages that were demanded and promised from that time on to obey orders with the utmost promptness. 12. Encouraged by this instance of mercy, there hastened to the spot with all their subjects the prince Araharius, and Usafer, a prominent noble, who were leaders of the armies of their countrymen ; one of them ruled a part of the Transiugitani and the Quadi, the other some of the Sarmatians, peoples closely united by the same frontiers and like savagery. Since the emperor feared their people, lest under pretence of striking a treaty they might suddenly rise to arms, he separated the united divisions and bade those

repente consurgeret, discreto consortio, pro Sarmatis obsecrantes iussit paulisper abscedere, dum Araharii et Quadorum negotium spectaretur. 13. Qui cum reorum [1] ritu oblati, stantes curvatis corporibus, facinora gravia purgare non possent, ultimae sortis infortunia metuentes, dederunt obsides imperatos, numquam antea pignora foederis exhibere compulsi. 14. His ex aequo bonoque compositis Usafer in preces admissus est, Arahario pertinaciter obstrepente, firmanteque pacem quam ipse meruit, ei quoque debere proficere, ut participi licet inferiori, et obtemperare suis imperiis consueto. 15. Verum quaestione discussa, aliena potestate eripi Sarmatae iussi (ut semper Romanorum clientes,) offerre obsides quietis vincula conservandae, gratanter amplexi sunt. 16. Ingerebat autem se post haec maximus numerus catervarum confluentium nationum et regum, suspendi a iugulis suis gladios obsecrantium, postquam Araharium impune compererat abscessisse; et pari modo ipsi quoque adepti pacem quam poscebant, accitos ex intimis regni procerum filios obsidatus sorte opinione celerius obtulerunt, itidemque captivos (ut placuerat) nostros, quos haut minore gemitu perdidere quam suos.

---

[1] *reorum*, Lind. ; *eorum*, V.

---

[1] Lindenbrog and Wagner translate : "that swords should be placed at their throats as a symbol of an oath and what would happen to them if they broke it"; cf. xxi. 5, 10, *gladiis cervicibus suis admotis sub exsecrationibus diris iuravereo ;* here "begging that the swords be withdrawn" would give a doubtful meaning to *suspendi.*

who were interceding for the Sarmatians to withdraw for a time, while the case of Araharius and the Quadi was being considered. 13. When these presented themselves in the manner of criminals, standing with bended bodies, and were unable to clear themselves of serious misdeeds, in fear of calamities of the worst kind they gave the hostages which were demanded, although never before had they been forced to present pledges for a treaty. 14. When they had been justly and fairly disposed of, Usafer was admitted to make supplication, although Araharius stoutly objected and insisted that the terms which he himself had obtained ought to be valid also for the other as his partner, although Usafer was of inferior rank and accustomed to obey his commands. 15. But after a discussion of the question, orders were given that the Sarmatians (as permanent dependents of the Romans) should be freed from the domination of others and should present hostages as bonds for keeping the peace ; an offer which they gladly accepted. 16. Moreover, after this there offered themselves a very great number of kings and nations, coming together in companies, and begged that swords be poised at their very throats,[1] as soon as they learned that Araharius had got off scot-free. And they too in the same way gained the peace which they sought, and sooner than was expected they summoned from the innermost parts of the kingdom and brought in as hostages the sons of eminent men, and also our prisoners (as had been stipulated), from whom they parted with as deep sighs as they did from their own countrymen.

CONSTANTIUS ET GALLUS

17. Quibus ordinatis translata est in Sarmatas cura, miseratione dignos potius quam simultate. Quibus incredibile quantum prosperitatis [1] haec attulit causa : ut verum illud aestimaretur, quod opinantur quidam, fatum vinci principis potestate vel fieri. 18. Potentes olim ac nobiles [2] erant huius indigenae regni, sed coniuratio clandestina servos armavit in facinus. Atque ut barbaris esse omne ius in viribus adsuevit, vicerunt dominos ferocia pares, et [3] numero praeminentes. 19. Qui confundente metu consilia, ad Victohalos discretos longius confugerunt, obsequi defensoribus, (ut in malis) optabile, quam servire [4] mancipiis arbitrati ; quae deplorantes, post impetratam veniam recepti in fidem, poscebant praesidia libertati, eosque iniquitate rei permotus, inspectante omni exercitu, convocatos allocutus verbis mollioribus imperator, nulli nisi sibi ducibusque Romanis parere praecepit. 20. Atque ut restitutio libertatis haberet dignitatis augmentum, Zizaim regem eisdem praefecit, conspicuae fortunae tum insignibus aptum profecto, (ut res docuit) et fidelem, nec discedere quisquam post haec gloriose gesta permissus est, antequam (ut placuerat) remearent nostri captivi. 21. His in barbarico gestis, Bregetionem castra commota

---

[1] *prosperitatis*, G ; *in prosperitatis*, V. [2] *ac nobiles*, Lind. ; *potente soli magnobiles*, V. [3] *et*, V. ; *sed*, vulgo. [4] *seruire*, W[2] A, Novák ; *seruire suis*, G ; *seruire seruitutem* (cf. Gell. i. 12, 5), Her. ; *seruitute*, V.

---

[1] Since Julius Capitolinus, *Ant. Phil.* xiv. 1, mentions them in connection with the Marcomanni, they probably lived in the region of Bohemia.

17. These affairs once set in order, his attention was turned to the Sarmatians, who were deserving rather of pity than of anger; and to them this situation brought an incredible degree of prosperity; so that the opinion of some might well be deemed true, that fortune is either mastered or made by the power of a prince 18. The natives of this realm were once powerful and noble, but a secret conspiracy armed their slaves for rebellion; and since with savages all right is commonly might, they vanquished their masters, being their equals in courage and far superior in number. 19. The defeated, since fear prevented deliberation, fled to the Victohali,[1] who dwelt afar off, thinking that to submit to protectors (considering their evil plight) was preferable to serving slaves. Bewailing this situation, after they had gained pardon and been assured of protection they asked that their freedom be guaranteed; whereupon the emperor, deeply moved by the injustice of their condition, in the presence of the whole army called them together, and addressing them in gracious terms, bade them yield obedience to none save himself and the Roman generals. 20. And to give their restoration to freedom an increase of dignity, he set over them as their king Zizais,[2] a man even then surely suited for the honours of a conspicuous fortune and (as the result showed) loyal; but no one was allowed, after these glorious achievements, to leave the place, until (as had been agreed) the Roman prisoners should come back. 21. After these achievements in the savages' country, the camp

[2] See p. 373, above.

sunt, ut etiam ibi belli Quadorum reliquias, circa
illos agitantium tractus, lacrimae vel sanguis ex-
tingueret. Quorum regalis Vitrodorus, Viduari filius
regis, et Agilimundus subregulus, aliique optimates
et iudices, variis populis praesidentes, viso exercitu
in gremio regni solique genitalis, sub gressibus
militum iacuere,[1] et adepti veniam iussa fecerunt,
sobolemque suam obsidatus pignore (ut obsecuturi
condicionibus impositis) tradiderunt, eductisque
mucronibus, quos [2] pro numinibus colunt, iuravere
se permansuros in fide.

13. *Constantius Aug. Limigantes Sarmatas servos,*
post magnam ipsorum caedem factam, cogit
sedibus suis emigrare, ac milites suos alloquitur.

1. His (ut narratum est) secundo finitis eventu,
ad Limigantes, Sarmatas servos, ocius signa transferri utilitas publica flagitabat, quos erat admodum
nefas, impune multa et nefaria perpetrasse. Nam
velut obliti priorum, tunc erumpentibus Liberis,
ipsi quoque tempus aptissimum nancti, limitem
perrupere Romanum, ad hanc solam fraudem domi-
nis suis hostibusque concordes. 2. Deliberatum est

---

[1] *militum iacuere,* Clark, Novák, c.c.; *i.m.,* V.
[2] *quos,* added by EW[2]BG ; V omits.

---

[1] Apparently Flecken Szöny in Hungary, not far from
Komorn.
[2] For this meaning of *iudices* see Index of Officials, s.v.
[3] For their revolt, see **12**, 18, above. Limigantes seems
to be the name that they assumed (Gibbon, ch. xviii.)

was moved to Bregetio,[1] to the end that there also
tears or blood might quench what was left of the
war of the Quadi, who were astir in those regions.
Then their prince Vitrodorus, son of King Viduarius,
and Agilimundus, his vassal, along with other
nobles and officials [2] governing various nations,
seeing the army in the heart of their kingdom and
native soil, prostrated themselves before the marching soldiers, and having gained pardon, did what
was ordered, giving their children as hostages by
way of pledge that they would fulfil the conditions
imposed upon them. Then, drawing their swords,
which they venerate as gods, they swore that they
would remain loyal.

13. *Constantius Augustus compels the Limigantes,
former slaves of the Sarmatians, after inflicting
great bloodshed upon them, to leave their abodes ;
then he addresses his soldiers.*

1. When these events had been brought to a
successful issue, as has been told, the public welfare
required that the standards quickly be transported to
the Limigantes, former slaves of the Sarmatians,[3] for
it was most shameful that they had with impunity
committed many infamous outrages. For as if for-
getting the past, when the free Sarmatians rebelled,
those others also found the opportunity most favourable and broke over the Roman frontier, for this outrage alone making common cause with their masters
and enemies. 2. Nevertheless, it was determined

after driving out their former masters ; according to others,
the Limigantes were a tribe of the Sarmatians.

tamen, id quoque lenius vindicari, quam criminum
magnitudo poscebat, hactenus ultione porrecta, ut
ad longinqua translati, amitterent copiam nostra
vexandi, quos pericula formidare monebat scelerum
conscientia diutius commissorum. 3. Ideoque in se
pugnae molem suspicati vertendam, dolos parabant
et ferrum et preces. Verum aspectu primo exercitus
tamquam fulminis ictu perculsi, ultimaque cogitantes, vitam precati, tributum annuum delectumque
validae iuventutis et servitium spoponderunt,
abnuere parati si iuberentur aliorsum migrare, ut
gestibus indicabant et vultibus, locorum confisi
praesidio, ubi lares post exactos dominos fixere
securi. 4. Has enim terras Parthiscus irruens
obliquatis meatibus, Histro miscetur. Sed dum
solus licentius fluit, spatia longa et lata sensim praelabens,[1] et ea coartans prope exitum in angustias,
accolas ab impetu Romanorum alveo Danubii
defendit, a barbaricis vero excursibus suo tutos
praestat obstaculo, ubi pleraque umidioris soli
natura, et incrementis fluminum redundantia,
stagnosa sunt et referta salicibus, ideoque invia,
nisi perquam gnaris ; et super his insularem an-

---

[1] *praelabens*, Novák, *praeterluens*, Clark, c.c. ; *praeterlabens*, V.

---

[1] The modern Theiss.   [2] The Danube.

after deliberation that this act also should be punished
less severely than the heinousness of their crimes demanded, and vengeance was confined to transferring
them to remote places, where they would lose the opportunity of molesting our territories; yet the consciousness of their long series of misdeeds warned
them to fear danger. 3. Accordingly, suspecting that
the weight of war would be directed against them,
they got ready wiles and arms and entreaties. But
at the first sight of our army, as if smitten by a
stroke of lightning and anticipating the utmost,
after having pleaded for life they promised a yearly
tribute, a levy of their able youth, and slavery; but
they were ready, as they showed by gestures and
expression, to refuse if they should be ordered to
move elsewhere, trusting to the protection of the
situation in which they had established themselves
in security, after driving out their masters. 4. For
the Parthiscus [1] rushing into those lands with winding course, mingles with the Hister. [2] But while it
flows alone and unconfined, it slowly traverses
a long expanse of broad plain; near its mouth,
however, it compresses this into a narrow tract,
thus protecting those who dwell there from a Roman
attack by the channel of the Danube, and making
them safe from the inroads of other savages by the
opposition of its own stream; for the greater part
of the country is of a marshy nature, and since it
is flooded when the rivers rise, is full of pools and
overgrown with willows, and therefore impassable
except for those well acquainted with the region.
Besides this the larger river, enclosing the winding
circuit of an island, which almost reaches the mouth

fractum, aditu Parthisci paene contiguum, amnis potior ambiens, terrae consortio separavit. 5. Hortante igitur principe, cum genuino fastu ad citeriorem venere fluminis ripam, ut exitus docuit, non iussa facturi, sed ne viderentur militis praesentiam formidasse, stabantque contumaciter, ideoque propinquasse monstrantes, ut iubenda repudiarent. 6. Quae imperator accidere posse contemplans, in agmina plurima clam distributo exercitu, celeritate volucri morantes [1] intra suorum acies clausit. Stansque in aggere celsiore cum paucis, et stipatorum praesidio tectus, eos ne ferocirent lenius admonebat. 7. Sed fluctuantes ambiguitate mentium in diversa rapiebantur, et furori mixta versutia, temptabant cum precibus proelium, vicinumque sibi in nostros parantes excursum, proiecere [2] consulto longius scuta, ut ad ea recuperanda sensim progressi, sine ullo fraudis indicio spatia furarentur.

8. Iamque vergente in vesperum die, cum moras rumpere lux moneret excedens, erectis vexillis in eos igneo miles impetu ferebatur. Qui conferti acieque densiore contracta, adversus ipsum principem stantem (ut dictum est) altius, omnem impetum contulerunt, eum oculis incessentes et vocibus truculentis. 9. Cuius furoris amentiam

---

[1] *morantes*, Novák; *pigrantes*, Pet.; *mirantes*, Her.; *migrantes*, V. [2] *proiecere*, EA; *proiicere*, BG; *proicere*, V.

of the Parthiscus, separates it from connection with the land. 5. So, at the emperor's request, they came with their native arrogance to their bank of the river, not, as the event proved, intending to do what they were bidden, but in order not to appear to have feared the presence of the soldiers; and there they stood defiantly, thus giving the impression that they had come there to reject any orders that might be given. 6. But the emperor, suspecting that this might happen, had secretly divided his army into several bands, and with swift speed enclosed them, while they were delaying, within the lines of his own soldiers; then standing with a few followers on a loftier mound, protected by the defence of his guards, in mild terms he admonished them not to be unruly. 7. But they, wavering in uncertainty of mind, were distracted different ways, and with mingled craft and fury they thought both of entreaties and of battle; and preparing to sally out on our men where we lay near to them, they purposely threw forward their shields a long way, so that by advancing step by step to recover them they might without any show of treachery gain ground by stealth.

8. When the day was now declining to evening and the waning light warned them to do away with delay, the soldiers lifted up their standards and rushed upon them in a fiery attack. Thereupon the foe massed themselves together, and, huddled in close order, directed all their attack against the emperor himself, who, as was said, stood on higher ground, charging upon him with fierce looks and savage cries. 9. The furious madness of this onset

385

CONSTANTIUS ET GALLUS

exercitus ira ferre non potuit, eosque imperatori
(ut dictum est) acriter imminentes, desinente in
angustum fronte (quem habitum caput porci simplicitas militaris appellat,) impetu disiecit ardenti,
et dextra pedites catervas peditum obtruncabant,
equites laeva equitum se turmis agilibus infuderunt.
10. Cohors praetoria ex adverso Augustum cautius
stipans, resistentium pectora moxque terga fugien-
tium incidebat, et cadentes insuperabili contumacia
barbari non tam mortem [1] dolere, quam nostrorum
laetitiam, horrendo stridore monstrabant, et iacentes
absque mortuis plurimi, succisis poplitibus ideoque
adempto fugiendi subsidio, alii dexteris amputatis,
non nulli ferro quidem intacti, sed superruentium
collisi ponderibus, cruciatus alto silentio perferebant. 11. Nec eorum quisquam inter diversa supplicia veniam petit aut ferrum proiecit, aut exoravit
celerem mortem, sed arma iugiter retinentes, licet
afflicti, minus criminis aestimabant, alienis viribus
potius quam conscientiae suae iudicio vinci ; mussan-
tesque audiebantur interdum, fortunae non meriti
fuisse quod evenit. Ita in semihorae curriculo
discrimine proeliorum emenso, tot procubuere
subito barbari, ut pugnam fuisse sola victoria
declararet.

[1] *suam mortem,* C. F. W. Müller ; *mortem,* V.

---

[1] Vegetius, iii. 19, says that the soldiers gave the name
caput porcinum to the *cuneus,* a V-shaped formation, with
the apex towards the enemy. It was the opposite of the
forceps, or *forfex* (xvi. **11, 3**).

so angered our army that it could not brook it, and as the savages hotly menaced the emperor (as was said), they took the form of a wedge (an order which the soldier's naïve parlance calls " the pig's head,") [1] and scattered them with a hot charge ; then on the right our infantry slaughtered the bands of their infantry, while on the left our cavalry poured into the nimble squadrons of their cavalry. 10. The praetorian cohort, which stood before Augustus and was carefully guarding him, fell upon the breasts of the resisting foe, and then upon their backs as they took flight. And the savages with invincible stubbornness showed as they fell, by their awful shrieking, that they did not so much resent death as the triumph of our soldiers ; and besides the dead many lay about hamstrung and thus deprived of the means of flight, others had their right hands cut off, some were untouched by any steel but crushed by the weight of those who rushed over them ; but all bore their anguish in deep silence. 11. And amid their varied torments not a single man asked for pardon or threw down his weapon, or even prayed for a speedy death, but they tightly grasped their weapons, although defeated, and thought it less shameful to be overcome by an enemy's strength than by the judgement of their own conscience,[2] while sometimes they were heard to mutter that what befell them was due to fortune, not to their deserts. Thus in the course of half an hour the decision of this battle was reached, and so many savages met a sudden death that the victory alone showed that there had been a fight.

[2] That is, to be overcome by a superior force rather than yield voluntarily.

12. Vix dum populis hostilibus stratis, gregatim peremptorum necessitudines ducebantur, humilibus extractae tuguriis, aetatis sexusque promiscui, et fastu vitae prioris abolito, ad infimitatem obsequiorum venere servilium, et exiguo temporis intervallo decurso, caesorum aggeres et captivorum agmina cernebantur. 13. Incitante itaque fervore certaminum, fructuque vincendi, consurrectum est in perniciem eorum qui deseruerant[1] proelia, vel in tuguriis latitantes occultabantur. Hos, cum ad loca venisset avidus barbarici sanguinis miles, disiectis culmis levibus obtruncabant, nec quemquam casa, vel trabibus compacta firmissimis, periculo mortis extraxit. 14. Denique cum inflammarentur omnia nullusque latere iam posset, cunctis vitae praesidiis circumcisis, aut obstinate igni peribat absumptus, aut incendium vitans, egressusque uno supplicio declinato, ferro sternebatur hostili. 15. Fugientes tamen aliqui tela, incendiorumque magnitudinem, amnis vicini se commisere gurgitibus, peritia nandi ripas ulteriores occupare posse sperantes, quorum plerique summersi necati sunt, alii iaculis periere confixi, adeo ut abunde cruore diffuso, meatus fluminis spumaret immensi; ita per elementum utrumque, Sarmatas vincentium ira virtusque delevit.

16. Placuerat igitur post hunc rerum ordinem

---

[1] *deseruerant,* suggested by Clark, c.c. ; *deseruere,* V.

---

[1] With which the houses were thatched.
[2] Cf. xvi. **12,** 57.

12. Hardly yet had the hordes of the enemy been laid low, when the kinsfolk of the slain, dragged from their humble cots, were led forth in droves without regard to age or sex, and abandoning the haughtiness of their former life, were reduced to the abjectness of servile submission ; and only a brief space of time had elapsed, when heaps of slain and throngs of captives were to be seen. 13. Then, excited by the heat of battle and the fruits of victory, our soldiers roused themselves to destroy those who had deserted the battle or were lurking in concealment in their huts. And these, when the soldiers had come to the spot thirsting for the blood of the savages, they butchered after tearing to pieces the light straw ; [1] and no house, even though built with the stoutest of timbers, saved a single one from the danger of death. 14. Finally, when everything was in flames and none could longer hide, since every means of saving their lives was cut off, they either fell victims to fire in their obstinacy, or, fleeing the flames and coming out to avoid one torture, fell by the enemy's steel. 15. Yet some escaped the weapons and the fires, great as they were, and plunged into the depths of the neighbouring river, hoping through skill in swimming to be able to reach the opposite banks ; of these the most lost their lives by drowning, others were pierced by darts and perished, in such numbers that the whole course of the immense river foamed with the blood that flowed everywhere in abundance.[2] Thus with the aid of two elements the wrath and valour of the victors annihilated the Sarmatians.

16. Then it was decided, after this course of events,

cunctis adimi spem omnem vitaeque solacium. Et
post lares incensos, raptasque familias, navigia
iussa sunt colligi, ad indagandos eos quos a nostrorum acie ulterior discreverat ripa. 17. Statimque
ne alacritas intepesceret pugnatorum, impositi
lintribus, per abdita ducti, velites expediti occuparunt
latibula Sarmatarum, quos repentinus fefellit aspectus, gentiles lembos et nota remigia conspicantes.
18. Ubi vero procul micantibus telis, quod vere-
bantur, propinquare senserunt, ad suffugia locorum
palustrium se [1] contulerunt, eosque secutus infestius
miles, caesis plurimis ibi victoriam repperit, ubi
nec caute posse consistere, nec audere aliquid credebatur. 19. Post absumptos paene diffusosque Amicenses, petiti sunt sine mora Picenses, ita ex regionibus appellati conterminis ; quos tutiores fecere
sociorum aerumnae, rumorum assiduitate com-
pertae. Ad quos opprimendos, (erat enim arduum
sequi per diversa conspersos, imprudentia viarum
arcente,) Taifalorum auxilium et Liberorum adaeque Sarmatarum assumptum est. 20. Cumque
auxiliorum agmina locorum ratio separaret, tractus
contiguos Moesiae sibi miles elegit, Taifali proxima

---

[1] *se*, added by NG (deleted by Löfstedt) ; V omits.

---

[1] A Sarmatian people ; *T.L.L.*
[2] Put by Ptolemy in Upper Moesia.
[3] A tribe of the West Goths ; cf. xxxi. **3, 7.**

that every hope and comfort of life should be taken from all, and after their homes had been burned and their families carried off, orders were given that boats should be brought together, for the purpose of hunting down those whom the opposite bank had kept aloof from our army. 17. And at once, for fear that the ardour of the warriors might cool, light-armed troops were put into skiffs, and taking the course which offered the greatest secrecy, came upon the lurking-places of the Sarmatians; and the enemy were deceived as they suddenly came in sight, seeing their native boats and the manner of rowing of their own country. 18. But when from the glittering of the weapons afar off they perceived that what they feared was approaching, they took refuge in marshy places; but the soldiers, following them still more mercilessly, slew great numbers of them, and gained a victory in a place where it seemed impossible to keep a firm footing or venture upon any action. 19. After the Amicenses [1] had been scattered and all but wholly destroyed, the army immediately attacked the Picenses,[2] so named from the adjoining regions, who had been put on their guard by the disasters to their allies, which were known from persistent rumours. To subdue these (for it was hard to pursue them, since they were scattered in divers places, and unfamiliarity with the roads was a hindrance) they resorted to the help of the Taifali [3] and likewise of the free Sarmatians. 20. And as consideration of the terrain made it desirable to separate the troops of the allies, our soldiers chose the tracts near Moesia, the Taifali undertook those next to their own homes, and the

suis sedibus obtinebant, Liberi terras occupaverant
e regione sibi oppositas.

21. Quae [1] perpessi [2] Limigantes territique subactorum exemplis et subitum [3] prostratorum, diu
haesitabant ambiguis mentibus, utrum oppeterent
an rogarent, cum utriusque rei suppeterent documenta non levia. Vicit tamen ad ultimum coetu
seniorum urgente, dedendi sese [4] consilium. Variae-
que palmae victoriarum accessit eorum quoque
supplicatio, qui armis libertatem invaserant, et
reliqui eorum [5] cum precibus, ut superatos et imbelles dominos aspernati, fortioribus visis inclinavere
cervices.

22. Accepta itaque publica fide, deserto montium
propugnaculo, ad castra Romana convolavit eorum
pars maior, diffusa per spatia ampla camporum,
cum parentibus et natis atque coniugibus, opumque
vilitate, quam eis celeritatis ratio furari permisit.
23. Et qui animas amittere potius, quam cogi solum
vertere putabantur, dum licentem amentiam libertatem existimarent, parere imperiis, et sedes alias
suscipere sunt assensi, tranquillas et fidas, ut nec
bellis vexari, nec mutari seditionibus possint. Eisdemque ex sententia (ut credebatur,) acceptis,

---

[1] *quae,* restored and lac. indicated by Clark.   [2] *perpessi,* added by Pet.;   *contemplantes,* by Günther.
[3] *subitum,* Pet.; *subacie,* D²W²; *subacrum,* V.   [4] *sese,*
Her. c.c.; *se,* V.   [5] *reliqui eorum,* G; *re iniquiore,*
Her.; *reliqui ore,* V.

free Sarmatians occupied the lands directly opposite to them.

21. The Limigantes [1] having now suffered this fate, and terrified by the example of those who had been conquered and suddenly slain, hesitated long with wavering minds whether to die or plead, since for either course they had lessons of no slight weight ; finally, however, the urgency of an assembly of the older men prevailed, and the resolve to surrender. Thus to the laurels of various victories there was added also the entreaties of those who had usurped freedom by arms ; and such of them as survived bowed their necks with prayers before their former masters, whom they had despised as vanquished and weak, but now saw to be the stronger.

22. And so, having received a safe-conduct, the greater number of them forsook the defence of the mountains and hastened to the Roman camp, pouring forth over the broad and spacious plains with their parents, their children and wives, and as many of their poor possessions as haste allowed them to snatch up in time. 23. And those who (as it was supposed) would rather lose their lives than be compelled to change their country, since they believed mad licence to be freedom, now consented to obey orders and take other quiet and safe abodes, where they could neither be harried by wars nor affected by rebellions. And these men, being taken under protection according to their own wish (as was believed) remained quiet for a short time ; later, through their inborn savagery they were aroused

[1] See note on 13, 1, above.

quievere paulisper, post feritate nativa in exitiale
scelus erecti, ut congruo docebitur textu.

24. Hoc rerum prospero currente successu, tutela
Illyrico competens gemina est ratione firmata,
cuius negotii duplicem magnitudinem imperator
aggressus utramque perfecit. Infidis attritis stratisque,[1] exsules populos (licet mobilitate suppares [2])
acturos tamen paulo verecundius, tandem reductos
in avitis sedibus collocavit. Eisdemque ad gratiae
cumulum, non ignobilem quempiam regem, sed
quem ipsi antea sibi praefecere regalem, imposuit,
bonis animi corporisque praestantem. 25. Tali
textu recte factorum, Constantius iam metuente
sublimior, militarique consensu, secundo Sarmaticus
appellatus, ex vocabulo subactorum, iamque dis-
cessurus, convocatis cohortibus, et centuriis, et
manipulis omnibus, tribunali [3] insistens, signisque
ambitus et aquilis, et agmine multiplicium potestatum, his exercitum allocutus est, ore omnium
favorabilis, (ut solebat).

26. " Hortatur recordatio rerum gloriose gestarum, omni iucunditate viris fortibus gratior, ea [4]
ad modum verecundiae replicare, quae divinitus
delata sorte vincendi, et ante proelia et in ipso cor-
reximus fervore pugnarum, Romanae rei fidissimi
defensores. Quid enim tam pulchrum tamque

---

[1] *attritis stratisque*, scripsi (cf. 28 below,), in lac. indicated by Haupt ; *infidis exules populus* without lac., V.
[2] *suppares*, Haupt ; *supra*res*, V.   [3] *tribunali*, Kellerbauer ;
tribunal, V.   [4] *gratior*, EAG ; *gratior ea*, Novák ; *gratiore
ad*, V.

---

[1] See xix. **11.**
[2] That is, Zizais, see **12**, 9, above.

to an outrage which brought them destruction, as will be shown in the proper place.[1]

24. Through this successful sequel of events adequate protection was provided for Illyricum in a twofold manner ; and the emperor having in hand the greatness of this task fulfilled it in both ways. The unfaithful were laid low and trodden under foot, but exiled peoples (although equally unstable) who yet seemed likely to act with somewhat more respect, were at length recalled and settled in their ancestral homes. And as a crowning favour, he set over them, not some low-born king, but one whom they themselves had previously chosen as their ruler, a man eminent for his mental and physical gifts.[2]

25. After such a series of successes Constantius, now raised above any fear, by the unanimous voice of the soldiers was hailed a second time as Sarmaticus, after the name of the conquered people ; and now, on the point of departure, he called together all the cohorts, centuries, and maniples, and standing on a tribunal, surrounded by standards, eagles and a throng of many officers of high rank, he addressed the army with these words, being greeted (as usual) with the acclaim of all :

26. " The recollection of our glorious deeds, more grateful to brave men than any pleasure, moves me to rehearse to you, with due modesty, what abuses we most faithful defenders of the Roman state have corrected by the fortune of victory vouch-safed us by Providence both before our battles and in the very heat of combat. For what is so noble, or so justly worthy to be commended to the memory of posterity, as that the soldier should rejoice in his

posteritatis memoriae iusta ratione mandandum,
quam ut miles strenue factis, ductor prudenter con-
sultis exultet ? 27. Persultabat Illyricum furor
hostilis, absentiam inanitate tumenti
despiciens, dum Italos tueremur et Gallos, variisque
discursibus vastabat extima limitum, nunc cavatis
roboribus, aliquotiens peragrans pedibus flumina,
non congressibus nec armis fretus aut viribus, sed
latrociniis assuetus occultis, astu et ludificandi
varietate, iam inde ab instituta gente nostris quoque
maioribus formidatus ; quae longius disparati, qua [1]
ferri poterant tulimus, saeviores [2] iacturas efficacia
ducum vitari [3] posse sperantes. 28. Ubi vero per
licentiam scandens in maius, ad funestas provinciarum clades erepsit et crebras, communitis aditibus
Raeticis, tutelaque pervigili Galliarum securitate
fundata, terrore nullo relicto post terga, venimus
in Pannonias, si placuerit [4] numini sempiterno,
labentia firmaturi ; cunctisque paratis (ut nostis,)
vere adulto egressi, arripuimus negotiorum maximas
moles : primum ne struendo textis compagibus
ponti, telorum officeret multitudo, quo opera levi
perfecto, visis terris hostilibus et calcatis, obstinatis
ad mortem animis conatos resistere Sarmatas,
absque nostrorum dispendio stravimus, parique
petulantia ruentes in agmina nobilium legionum,
Quados Sarmatis adiumenta ferentes attrivimus.

---

[1] *qua*, Lind. ; *quae*, V. [2] *saeviores*, Fletcher, cf.
Tac., *Ann.* ii. 26, 3 ; *leviores*, V. [3] *uitari*, Cornelissen ;
uetari, V. [4] *si placuerit*, Bentley ; *si placebit*, suggested by Clark ; *placuit*, V.

---

[1] See xiv. **2**, 10, end.

valiant deeds, and the leader in the sagacity of his plans. 27. Our enemies in their madness were overrunning all Illyricum, with arrogant folly despising us in our absence, while we were defending Italy and Gaul, and in successive raids were laying waste our farthest frontiers, crossing the rivers now in dug-out canoes [1] and sometimes on foot; they did not trust to engagements nor to arms and strength, but, as is their custom, to lurking brigandage, with the craft and various methods of deceit dreaded also by our forefathers from our very first knowledge of the race. These outrages we, being far away, endured as well as they could be borne, hoping that any more serious losses could be obviated by the efficiency of our generals. 28. But when, encouraged by impunity, they mounted higher and burst forth in destructive and repeated attacks upon our provinces, after securing the approaches to Raetia and by vigilant guard ensuring the safety of Gaul, leaving no cause of fear behind us, we came into Pannonia, intending, if it should please eternal God, to strengthen whatever was tottering. And sallying forth when all was ready (as you know) and spring was well advanced, we took in hand a mighty burden of tasks: first, to build a close-jointed bridge, without being overwhelmed by a shower of missiles, a work which was easily completed; and when we had seen and set foot upon the enemy's territories, without any loss of our men we laid low the Sarmatians who, with spirits regardless of death attempted to resist us. And when with like impudence the Quadi bore aid to the Sarmatians and rushed upon the ranks of our noble legions, we

CONSTANTIUS ET GALLUS

Qui post aerumnosa dispendia, inter discursus et repugnandi minaces anhelitus, quid nostra valeat virtus experti, manus ad dimicandum aptatas, armorum abiecto munimine, pone terga vinxerunt, restareque solam salutem contemplantes in precibus, affusi sunt vestigiis Augusti clementis, cuius proelia saepe compererant exitus habuisse felices. 29. His sequestratis Limigantes quoque fortitudine superavimus pari, interfectisque pluribus, alios periculi declinatio adegit suffugia petere latebrarum palustrium. 30. Hisque secundo finitis eventu, lenitatis tempus aderat tempestivae. Limigantes ad loca migrare compulimus longe discreta, ne in perniciem nostrorum se commovere possent ulterius et pepercimus plurimis, et Zizaim praefecimus Liberis, dicatum nobis futurum et fidum, plus aestimantes creare quam auferre barbaris regem, hoc decore augente sollemnitatem, quod eisdem quoque rector tributus antehac electus est et acceptus. 31. Quadruplex igitur praemium, quod unus procinctus absolvit, nos quaesivimus et res publica, primo ultione parta de grassatoribus noxiis, deinde quod vobis abunde sufficient ex hostibus capta.[1] His enim virtutem oportet esse contentam, quae sudore quaesivit et dexteris. 32. Nobis amplae facultates opumque sunt magni thesauri, si [2] integra

---

[1] *capta*, Novák ; *captivis*, V.   [2] *si*, added by Bentley, Haupt ; V omits.

trod them under foot. The latter, after grievous losses, having learned amid their raids and menacing efforts at resistance what our valour could effect, cast aside the protection of arms and offered hands that had been equipped for battle to be bound behind their backs; and seeing that their only safety lay in entreaties, they prostrated themselves at the feet of a merciful Augustus, whose battles they had often learned to have come to a happy issue. 29. These barely disposed of, we vanquished the Limigantes as well with equal valour, and after many of them had been slain, avoidance of danger forced the rest to seek the protection of their lairs in the marshes. 30. When these enterprises were brought to a successful issue, the time for seasonable mildness was at hand. The Limigantes we forced to move to remote places, so that they could make no further attempts to destroy our subjects, and very many of them we spared. And over the free Sarmatians we set Zizais, knowing that he would be devoted and loyal to us, and thinking it better to appoint a king for the savages than to take one from them; and it added to the happiness of the occasion, that a ruler was assigned them whom they had previously chosen and accepted. 31. Hence a fourfold prize, the fruit of a single campaign, was won by us and by our country: first, by taking vengeance on wicked robbers; then, in that you will have abundant booty taken from the enemy; for valour ought to be content with what it has won by toil and a strong arm. 32. We ourselves have ample wealth and great store of riches, if our labours and courage have preserved safe and sound

omnium patrimonia nostri labores et fortitudo
servarint. Hoc enim boni principis menti, hoc
successibus congruit prosperis. 33. Postremo ego
quoque hostilis vocabuli spolium prae me fero,
secundo Sarmatici cognomentum, quod vos unum
idemque sentientes, mihi (ne sit arrogans dicere,)
merito tribuistis."

Post hunc dicendi finem contio omnis alacrior
solito, aucta spe potiorum et lucris, vocibus festis in
laudes imperatoris adsurgens, deumque ex usu
testata non posse Constantium vinci, tentoria
repetit laeta. Et reductus imperator ad regiam,
otioque bidui recreatus, Sirmium cum pompa triumphali regressus est, et militares numeri destinatas
remearunt ad [1] sedes.

14. *Romani legati de pace, re infecta revertuntur ex
Perside, Sapore Armeniam et Mesopotamiam
repetente.*

14. 1. Hisce eisdem diebus, Prosper et Spectatus
atque Eustathius, legati ad Persas (ut supra docuimus) missi, Ctesiphonta reversum regem adiere,
litteras perferentes [2] imperatoris et munera, poscebantque rebus integris pacem, et mandatorum

---

[1] *ad*, added by Clark, c.c. ; before *destinatas*, C. F. W.
Müller ; V omits. [2] *perferentes*, Kellerbauer ; *praeferentes*, V.

the patrimonies of all; for this it is that beseems the mind of a good prince, this accords with prosperous successes. 33. Lastly, I also display the spoil of an enemy's name, surnamed as I am Sarmaticus for the second time, a title not undeserved (without arrogance be it said), which you have with one accord bestowed upon me."

After this speech was thus ended, the entire assembly with more enthusiasm than common, since the hope of betterment and gains had been increased, broke out into festal cries in praise of the emperor, and in customary fashion calling God to witness that Constantius was invincible, went back to their tents rejoicing. And when the emperor had been escorted to his palace and refreshed by two days' rest, he returned in triumphal pomp to Sirmium, and the companies of soldiers went back to the quarters assigned them.

14. *The Roman envoys about peace return from Persia without result, since Sapor was bent on recovering Armenia and Mesopotamia.*

1. On these very same days Prosper, Spectatus, and Eustathius, who had been sent as envoys to the Persians (as we have shown above),[1] approached the king on his return to Ctesiphon,[2] bearing letters and gifts from the emperor, and demanded peace with no change in the present status. Mindful of the emperor's instructions, they sacrificed no whit

[1] xvii. 5, 15.
[2] A city of Assyria, on the Tigris, the capital of the Parthian (Persian) king.

principis [1] memores, nusquam ab utilitate Romanae
rei maiestateque discedebant, amicitiae foedus
sub hac lege firmari debere adseverantes, ne super
turbando Armeniae vel Mesopotamiae statu quicquam moveretur. 2. Diu igitur ibi morati, cum
obstinatissimum regem, nisi harum regionum dom-
inio sibi adiudicato, obdurescentem ad suscipiendam
cernerent pacem, negotio redierunt infecto. 3.
Post quod id ipsum condicionum robore pari im-
petraturi, Lucillianus missus est comes, et Procopius
tunc notarius, qui postea nodo quodam violentae
necessitatis adstrictus, ad res consurrexerat [2] novas.

LIBER XVIII

1. *Iulianus Caesar Gallorum commodis consulit, et ubique ab omnibus ius servandum curat.*

1. Haec per orbis varias partes uno eodemque
anno sunt gesta. At in Galliis cum in meliore statu
res essent, et Eusebium atque Hypatium fratres
sublimarent vocabula consulum, Iulianus contextis
successibus clarus, apud Parisios hibernans,[3] sequestratis interim sollicitudinibus bellicis, haut minore
cura provinciarum fortunis multa conducentia dis-
ponebat, diligenter observans nequem tributorum
sarcina praegravaret, neve potentia praesumeret

---

[1] *principis*, added by Clark, c.c.   [2] *consurrexerat*,
Novák; *consurrexit*, HAG; *consurrexerit*, V.   [3] *apud
Parisios hibernans*, Clark; *apud hibernans* (*ns* from *s*,
V[2]*), V.

---

of the advantage and majesty of Rome, insisting
that a treaty of friendship ought to be established
with the condition that no move should be made to
disturb the position of Armenia or Mesopotamia.
2. Having therefore tarried there for a long time,
since they saw that the king was most obstinately
hardened against accepting peace, unless the
dominion over those regions should be made over
to him, they returned without fulfilling their mission.
3. Afterwards Count Lucillianus was despatched, together with Procopius, at that time state secretary,
to accomplish the self-same thing with like insistence
on the conditions ; the latter afterwards, bound as
it were by a knot of stern necessity, rose in revolution.[1]

BOOK XVIII

1. *Julianus Caesar looks out for the welfare of Gaul, and sees to it that justice be observed everywhere by every one.*

1. Such are the events of one and the same year
in various parts of the world. But in Gaul, now
that affairs were in a better condition and the
brothers Eusebius and Hypatius had been honoured
with the high title of consul, Julian, famed for his
series of successes and in winter quarters at Paris,
laid aside for a time the cares of war and with no
less regard made many arrangements leading to
the well-being of the provinces, diligently providing
that no one should be overloaded with a burden of
tribute ; that the powerful should not grasp the

403

aliena, aut hi versarentur in medio, quorum patrimonia publicae clades augebant, vel iudicum quisquam ab aequitate deviaret impune.   2. Idque ea re
levi labore correxit, quod ipse iurgia dirimens, ubi
causarum cogebat magnitudo vel personarum, erat
indeclinabilis iustorum iniustorumque distinctor.
3. Et licet multa sint eius laudanda in huius modi
controversiis, unum tamen sufficiet poni, ad cuius
similitudinem acta vel dicta sunt.   4. Numerium
Narbonensis paulo ante rectorem, accusatum ut
furem, inusitato censorio vigore, pro tribunali
palam admissis volentibus audiebat, qui cum infitiatione defenderet obiecta, nec posset in quoquam
confutari, Delphidius orator acerrimus, vehementer
eum impugnans, documentorum inopia percitus,
exclamavit : " Ecquis, florentissime Caesar, nocens
esse poterit usquam, si negare sufficiet ? " Contra
quem Iulianus prudenter motus ex tempore,
" Ecquis " ait " innocens esse poterit, si accusasse
sufficiet ? " Et haec quidem et huius modi multa
civilia.

2. *Iulianus C. castellorum ad Rhenum quae receperat
    moenia reparat ; Rhenum transit, et hostili
    Alamanniae parte vastata, V Alamannorum
    reges ad pacem petendam et captivos reddendos
    compellit.*

1. Egressurus autem ad procinctum urgentem,
cum Alamannorum pagos aliquos esse reputaret

---

[1] For this meaning of *iudex* see Index of Officials, s.v.

property of others, or those hold positions of authority whose private estates were being increased by public disasters; and that no official[1] should with impunity swerve from equity. 2. And this last abuse he reformed with slight difficulty, for the reason that he settled controversies himself whenever the importance of the cases or of the persons required, and distinguished inflexibly between right and wrong. 3. And although there are many praiseworthy instances of his conduct in such cases, yet it will suffice to cite one, as a sample of his acts and words. 4. Numerius, shortly before governor of Gallia Narbonensis, was accused of embezzlement, and Julian examined him with unusual judicial strictness before his tribunal publicly, admitting all who wished to attend. And when the accused defended himself by denying the charge, and could not be confuted on any point, Delphidius, a very vigorous speaker, assailing him violently and, exasperated by the lack of proofs, cried: "Can anyone, most mighty Caesar, ever be found guilty, if it be enough to deny the charge?" And Julian was inspired at once to reply to him wisely: "Can anyone be proved innocent, if it be enough to have accused him?" And this was one of many like instances of humanity.

2. *Julianus Caesar repairs the walls of the fortresses on the Rhine which he had recovered. He crosses the Rhine, and after laying waste the hostile part of Alamannia compels five of their kings to sue for peace and return their prisoners.*

1. But being on the point of entering upon an urgent campaign, since he considered that some

hostiles, et ausuros immania, ni ipsi quoque ad
ceterorum sternerentur exempla, haerebat anxius
qua vi qua celeritate, cum primum ratio copiam
tribuisset, rumore praecurso, terras eorum invaderet
repentinus. 2. Seditque tandem multa et varia
cogitanti, id temptare quod utile probavit eventus.
Hariobaudem vacantem tribunum, fidei fortitudinis-
que notae, nullo conscio legationis specie ad Hor-
tarium miserat regem iam pacatum, ut exinde
facile ad collimitia progressus eorum, in quos erant
arma protinus commovenda, scitari possit quid molirentur, sermonis barbarici perquam gnarus. 3. Quo
fidenter ad haec patranda digresso, ipse anni
tempore opportuno, ad expeditionem undique milite
convocato, profectus, id inter potissima mature
duxit implendum, ut ante proeliorum fervorem,
civitates multo ante excisas ac vacuas [1] introiret,
receptasque communiret, horrea quin etiam ex-
strueret pro incensis, ubi condi possit annona, a
Britanniis sueta transferri. 4. Et utrumque perfectum est spe omnium citius. Nam et horrea veloci
opere surrexerunt, alimentorumque in eisdem satias
condita, et civitates occupatae sunt septem : Castra
Herculis Quadriburgium Tricensima et Novesium,

---

[1] *excisas ac vacuas*, Her. ; *excisa quas*, V.

---

[1] Apparently a fortress on the Rhine.
[2] Schenkenschanz.
[3] Kellen, also called *Colonia Traiani*, xvii. 1, 11.
[4] Nuys.   [5] Bonn.

districts of the Alamanni were hostile and would venture on outrages unless they also were overthrown after the example of the rest, he was anxious and doubtful with what force and with what speed (as soon as prudence gave an opportunity) he might anticipate the news of his coming and invade their territories unexpected. 2. And after thinking over many varied plans he at last decided to try the one which the outcome proved to be expedient. Without anyone's knowledge he had sent Hariobaudes, an unattached tribune of tried fidelity and courage, ostensibly as an envoy to Hortarius, a king already subdued, with the idea that he could easily go on from there to the frontiers of those against whom war was presently to be made, and find out what they were plotting ; for he was thoroughly acquainted with the language of the savages. 3. When the tribune had fearlessly set out to execute these orders, Julian, since the season of the year was favourable, called together his soldiers from all quarters for a campaign, and set forth ; and he thought that above all things he ought betimes to attend to this, namely, before the heat of battle to enter the cities long since destroyed and abandoned, regain and fortify them, and even build granaries in place of those that had been burned, in which he could store the grain which was regularly brought over from Britain ; and both things were accomplished sooner than anyone expected. 4. For not only did the granaries quickly rise, but a sufficiency of food was stored in them ; and the cities were seized, to the number of seven : Castra Herculis,[1] Quadriburgium,[2] Tricensima [3] and Novesium,[4] Bonna,[5]

CONSTANTIUS ET GALLUS

Bonna Antennacum et Vingo, ubi laeto quodam eventu, etiam Florentius praefectus apparuit subito, partem militum ducens, et commeatuum perferens copiam, sufficientem usibus longis.

5. Post haec impetrata, restabat adigente necessitatum articulo, receptarum urbium moenia reparari, nullo etiam tum interturbante; idque [1] claris indiciis apparet, ea tempestate utilitati publicae metu barbaros oboedisse, rectoris amore Romanos. 6. Reges ex pacto superioris anni aedificiis habilia multa suis misere carpentis, et auxiliarii milites semper munia spernentes huius modi, ad obsequendi sedulitatem Iuliani blanditiis deflexi, quinquagenarias longioresque materias vexere cervicibus ingravate, et fabricandi ministeriis opem maximam contulerunt.

7. Quae dum diligenti maturantur effectu, Hariobaudes exploratis omnibus rediit, docuitque comperta. Post cuius adventum incitatis viribus omnes venere Mogontiacum, ubi Florentio et Lupicino (Severi successore) destinate certantibus, per pontem illic constitutum transiri debere, renitebatur firmissime Caesar, asserens pacatorum terras non debere calcari, ne (ut saepe contigit) per incivilitatem [2] militis [3] occurrentia vastitantis, abrupte foedera frangerentur.

8. Alamanni tamen omnes quos petebat exercitus, confine periculum cogitantes, Suomarium regem

[1] *idque,* G ; *et que,* V ; *consociato labore cunctorum mox est perfectum ; unde,* Novák between *idque* and *claris.* [2] *indiuitatem,* V (emended by a later hand). [3] *militis,* G ; *militio,* V.

---

[1] Andernach. [2] Bingen. [3] See § 9, below.

Antennacum [1] and Vingo,[2] where by a happy stroke
of fortune the prefect Florentius also appeared unexpectedly, leading a part of the forces and bringing
a store of provisions sufficient to last a long time.

5. After this had been accomplished, one pressing
necessity remained, namely, to repair the walls of
the recovered cities, since even then no one hindered ;
and it is evident from clear indications that the
savages through fear, and the Romans through love
for their commander, at that time served the
public welfare. 6. The kings, according to the compact of the preceding year, sent in their wagons an
abundance of building material, and the auxiliary
soldiers, who always disdain such tasks, induced
to diligent compliance by Julian's fair words, willingly
carried on their shoulders timbers fifty feet or more
in length, and in the work of building rendered the
greatest service.

7. While these works were being pushed on with
diligence and success, Hariobaudes returned after examining into everything, and reported what he had
learned. After his arrival all came at top speed to
Mayence ; and there, when Florentius and Lupicinus
(successor to Severus) strongly insisted that they ought
to build a bridge at that place and cross the river,[3]
Caesar stoutly opposed, declaring that they ought not
to set foot in the lands of those who had submitted,
for fear that (as often happens) through the rudeness
of the soldiers, destroying everything in their way,
the treaties might be abruptly broken.

8. However, the Alamanni as a whole, against
whom our army was marching, thinking danger
to be close at hand, with threats warned king

amicum nobis ex pactione praeterita monuerunt
minaciter, ut a transitu Romanos arceret. Eius
enim pagi Rheni ripis ulterioribus adhaerebant.
Quo testante resistere solum non posse, in unum
coacta barbara multitudo venit prope Mogontiacum,
prohibitura viribus magnis exercitum, ne transmit-
teret flumen. 9. Gemina itaque ratione visum est
habile quod suaserat Caesar, ne pacatorum terrae
corrumperentur, neve renitente pugnacissima plebe,
pons cum multorum discrimine iungeretur iri [1] in
locum ad compaginandum pontem aptissimum.
10. Quod hostes sollertissime contemplati, per
contrarias ripas leniter incedentes, ubi nostros figere
tentoria, procul cernebant, ipsi quoque noctes agebant exsomnes, custodientes pervigili studio, ne
transitus temptaretur. 11. Verum cum nostri locum
adventarent provisum, vallo fossaque quievere
circumdati, et asscito Lupicino in consilium, Caesar
certis imperavit tribunis, ut trecentenos pararent
cum sudibus milites expeditos, quid agi quove iri
deberet penitus ignorantes. 12. Et collecti nocte
provecta, impositique omnes quos lusoriae naves
quadraginta quae tunc aderant solae, ceperunt,
decurrere iubentur per flumen, adeo taciti, ut etiam
remi suspenderentur, ne barbaros sonitus excitaret
undarum, atque mentis agilitate et corporum, dum

---

[1] lac. ind. Her., Clark; *iri,* added by Val., *ni* by T[2];
no lac. in V.

---

[1] Text and exact meaning are uncertain; see crit. note.
[2] See note, p. 313.

Soumarius, a friend of ours through a previous treaty, to debar the Romans from passing over; for his territories adjoined the opposite bank of the Rhine. And when he declared that he could not resist single-handed, the savages united their forces and came to the neighbourhood of Mayence, intending with might and main to prevent our army from crossing the river. 9. Therefore for a twofold reason what Caesar had advised seemed fitting, namely, that they should not ravage the lands of peaceful natives, nor against the opposition of a most warlike people construct the bridge with loss of life to many of our men, but should go [1] to the place best suited for building a bridge. 10. This step the enemy observed with the greatest care, slowly marching along the opposite bank; and when from afar they saw our men pitching their tents, they themselves also passed sleepless nights, keeping guard with watchful diligence to prevent an attempt at crossing. 11. Our soldiers, however, on coming to the appointed place rested, protected by a rampart and a trench, and Caesar, after taking counsel with Lupicinus, ordered trusty tribunes to provide with stakes three hundred light-armed troops, who as yet were wholly unaware what was to be done or where they were to go. 12. And having been brought together when night was well advanced, all were embarked whom forty scouting boats [2] (as many as were available at the time) would hold, and ordered to go down stream so quietly that they were even to keep their oars lifted for fear that the sound of the waters might arouse the savages; and while the enemy were watching our campfires, the soldiers

411

hostes nostrorum ignes observant, adversas perrumpere milites [1] ripas.

13. Dum haec celerantur, Hortarius rex nobis antea foederatus, non novaturus quaedam, sed amicus finitimis quoque suis, reges omnes et regales et regulos ad convivium corrogatos retinuit, epulis ad usque vigiliam tertiam gentili more extentis ; quos discedentes inde casu nostri ex improviso adorti, nec interficere nec corripere ullo genere potuerunt, tenebrarum equorumque adiumento, quo dubius impetus trusit, abreptos ; lixas vero vel servos, qui eos pedibus sequebantur, (nisi quos exemit discrimine temporis obscuritas) occiderunt.

14. Cognito denique transitu Romanorum,[2] qui tunc perque expeditiones praeteritas, ibi levamen sumere laborum opinabantur, ubi hostem contingeret inveniri, perculsi reges eorumque populi, qui pontem ne strueretur, studio servabant intento, metu exhorrescentes diffuse vertuntur in pedes ; et indomito furore sedato, necessitudines opesque suas transferre longius festinabant. Statimque difficultate omni depulsa, ponte constrato, sollicitarum gentium opinione praeventa, visus in barbarico miles per Hortarii regna transibat intacta. 15. Ubi vero terras infestorum etiam tum tetigit

---

[1] *milites*, V, deleted by Eyssen., Novák   *limitis*, G.
[2] *transitu Romanorum*, Clark, c.c.   *R.t.*, V.

were ordered with nimbleness of mind and body to force the opposite bank.

13. While this was being done with all haste, Hortarius, a king previously allied with us, not intending any disloyalty but being a friend also to his neighbours, invited all the kings, princes, and kinglets to a banquet and detained them until the third watch, prolonging the feasting after the native fashion. And as they were leaving the feast, it chanced that our men unexpectedly attacked them, but were in no way able to kill or take any of them, aided as they were by the darkness and their horses, which carried them off wherever panic haste drove them ; they did, however, slay the lackeys or slaves, who followed their masters on foot, except such as the darkness of the hour saved from danger.

14. When word at last came of the crossing of the Romans, who then, as in former campaigns, expected to find rest from their labours wherever they should succeed in finding the enemy, the panic-striken kings and their peoples, who were watching with eager intentness and dreading the building of the bridge, shuddering with fear, took to their heels in all directions ; and their unbridled anger now laid aside, they hastened to transport their kindred and their possessions to a greater distance. And at once every difficulty was removed, the bridge was built, and before the anxious nations expected it our soldiers appeared in the land of the savages, and were passing through the realms of Hortarius without doing any damage. 15. But when they reached the territories of kings that were still hostile, they burned and pillaged everything,

413

regum, urens omnia rapiensque,[1] per medium rebellium solum grassabatur intrepidus.

Postque saepimenta fragilium penatium in-
flammata, et obtruncatam hominum multitudinem,
visosque cadentes multos aliosque supplicantes, cum
ventum fuisset ad regionem (cui Capillacii vel Palas
nomen est) ubi terminales lapides Alamannorum [2]
et Burgundiorum confinia distinguebant, castra sant
posita, ea propter ut Macrianus et Hariobaudus,
germani fratres et reges, susciperentur impavidi,
qui propinquare sibi perniciem sentientes, venerant
pacem anxiis animis precaturi. 16. Post quos
statim rex quoque Vadomarius venit, cuius erat
domicilium contra Rauracos, scriptisque Constantii [3]
principis, quibus commendatus est artius, allegatis,
leniter susceptus est (ut [4] decebat), olim ab Augusto
in clientelam rei Romanae susceptus. 17. Et
Macrianus quidem cum fratre inter aquilas admissus
et signa, stupebat armorum viriumque [5] varium
decus, visa tunc primitus, proque suis orabat.
Vadomarius vero nostris coalitus (utpote vicinus
limiti) mirabatur quidem apparatum ambitiosi procinctus, sed vidisse se talia saepe ab adulescentia
meminerat prima. 18. Libratis denique diu consiliis, concordi assensione cunctorum, Macriano
quidem et Hariobaudo pax est attributa, Vadomario

---

[1] *rapiensque*, G ; *rapinisque*, V.   [2] *Romanorum*, V,
def. Norden.   [3] *Constantii*, Clark, c.c. ; *Constanti*, V.
[4] *ut*, added by Henr. Val. ; *ut conducebat*, Hadr. Val. ;
V omits.   [5] *viriumque*, del. Gardt. as dittography.

ranging without fear through the midst of the rebel country.

After firing the fragile huts that sheltered them, killing a great number of men, and seeing many falling and others begging for mercy, our soldiers reached the region called Capillacii or Palas [1] where boundary stones marked the frontiers of the Alamanni and the Burgundians. There they encamped with the design of capturing Macrianus and Hariobaudus, kings and own brothers, before they took alarm ; for they, perceiving the ruin that threatened them, had come with anxious minds to sue for peace. 16. The kings were at once followed also by Vadomarius, whose abode was over against the Rauraci, and since he presented a letter of the emperor Constantius, in which he was strongly commended, he was received kindly (as was fitting), since he had long before been taken by Augustus under the protection of the Roman empire. 17. And Macrianus indeed, when admitted with his brother among the eagles and ensigns, was amazed at the variety and splendour of the arms and the forces, things which he saw then for the first time, and pleaded for his subjects. But Vadomarius, who was familiar with our affairs (since he lived near the frontier) did indeed admire the equipment of the splendid array, but remembered that he had often seen the like from early youth. 18. Finally, after long deliberation, by the unanimous consent of all, peace was indeed granted to Macrianus and Hariobaudus ; but to Vadomarius, who had come to secure his own

---

[1] A district of the Alamanni on the frontier of the Burgundians.

vero, qui suam locaturus securitatem in tuto, et
legationis nomine precator venerat, pro Urio et
Ursicino et Vestralpo regibus pacem itidem obsecrans, interim responderi non poterat, ne (ut sunt
fluxioris fidei barbari) post abitum recreati nostrorum, parum acquiescerent per alios impetratis.
19. Sed cum ipsi quoque missis legatis, post messes
incensas et habitacula, captosque plures et inter-
fectos, ita supplicarent tamquam ipsi [1] haec deliquis-
sent in nostros, pacem condicionum similitudine
meruerunt. Inter quas id festinatum [2] est maxime,
ut captivos restituerent omnes, quos rapuerant
excursibus crebris.

3. *Barbationi magistro peditum et uxori eius cur capita abscissa sint iussu Constantii Aug.*

1. Haec dum in Galliis caelestis corrigit cura, in
comitatu Augusti turbo novarum exoritur rerum, a
primordiis levibus ad luctus et lamenta progressus.
In domo Barbationis, pedestris militiae tunc rectoris,
examen apes fecere [3] perspicuum. Superque hoc
ei prodigiorum gnaros sollicite consulenti, discrimen
magnum portendi responsum est, coniectura videlicet tali, quod hae volucres post compositas sedes,

---

[1] *ipsi*, V ; *non ipsi*, Mommsen.   [2] *festinatum*, V ;
destinatum, Cornelissen.   [3] *fecere*, G ; *texere*, A,
Mommsen; *struxere*, Pet ; *pestexere*, V (*ex* above the
line, *ere* added by V[2]).

---

[1] This was not always true. Cf. Pliny, *N.H.* xi. 55 ff.:
Tunc (apes) ostenta faciunt privata ac publica, uva de-
pendente in domibus templisque, saepe expiata magnis

safety, but at the same time as an envoy and inter-cessor, begging for peace in behalf of the kings Urius, Ursicinus and Vestralpus, no immediate reply could be given, for fear that (since savages are of unstable loyalty) they might take courage after the departure of our army and not abide by a peace secured through others. 19. But when they them-selves also, after the burning of their harvests and homes and the capture or death of many men, sent envoys and made supplication as if they too had committed these sins against our people, they won peace on the same terms; and among these conditions it was especially stressed that they should give up all the prisoners whom they had taken in their frequent raids.

3. *Why Barbatio, commander of the infantry, and his wife were beheaded by order of Constantius.*

1. While in Gaul the providence of Heaven was reforming these abuses, in the court of Augustus a tempest of sedition arose, which from small beginnings proceeded to grief and lamentation. In the house of Barbatio, then commander of the in-fantry forces, bees made a conspicuous swarm; and when he anxiously consulted men skilled in prodigies about this, they replied that it portended great danger,[1] obviously inferring this from the belief, that

eventibus. Sedere in ore infantis tum etiam Platonis, suavitatem illam praedulcis eloqui portendentes. Sedere in castris Drusi imperatoris cum prosperrime pugnatum apud Arbalonem est, haud quaquam perpetua haruspicum coniectura, qui dirum id ostentum existimant semper.

opesque congestas, fumo pelluntur, et turbulento
sonitu cymbalorum. 2. Huic uxor erat Assyria
nomine, nec taciturna nec prudens, quae eo ad
expeditionem profecto, et multiplici metu suspenso,
ob ea quae meminerat sibi praedicta, perculsa
vanitate muliebri, ancilla asscita notarum perita,
quam e patrimonio Silvani possederat, ad maritum
scripsit intempestive, velut flens obtestans ne post
obitum Constanti propinquantem, in imperium ipse
ut sperabat admissus, despecta se anteponeret
Eusebiae matrimonium tunc reginae, decore corporis inter multas feminas excellentis. 3. Quibus
litteris occulte quantum fieri potuit missis, ancilla,
quae domina dictante perscripserat, reversis omnibus e procinctu, exemplum ferens ad Arbetionem
noctis prima quiete confugit, avideque suscepta,
chartulam prodidit. 4. Hocque indicio ille confisus,
ut erat ad criminandum aptissimus, principi detulit,
atque ex usu, nec mora ulla negotio tributa nec
quiete, Barbatio epistulam suscepisse confessus,
et mulier scripsisse documento convicta non levi,
cervicibus interiere praecisis. 5. Hisque punitis,
quaestiones longe serpebant, vexatique multi no-
centes sunt et innocentissimi.[1] Inter quos etiam

---

[1] *innocentissimi*, Damsté, c.c. ; *innocentes*, V ; Fletcher
would delete *sunt*, or write *n. simul et innocentes.*

418

when these insects have made their homes and
gathered their treasures, they are only driven out
by smoke and the wild clashing of cymbals.   2. Barbatio had a wife, Assyria by name, who was talkative and indiscreet. She, when her husband had
gone forth on a campaign and was worried by many
fears because of what he remembered had been foretold him, overcome by a woman's folly, confided
in a maidservant skilled in cryptic writing, whom
she had acquired from the estate of Silvanus.
Through her Assyria wrote at this untimely moment
to her husband, entreating him in tearful accents
that when, after Constantius' approaching death,
he himself had become emperor, as he hoped, he
should not cast her off and prefer marriage with
Eusebia, who was then queen and was conspicuous
among many women for the beauty of her person.
3. After this letter had been sent with all possible
secrecy, the maidservant, who had written it at
her mistress' dictation, as soon as all had returned
from the campaign took a copy of it and ran off to
Arbetio in the first quiet of the night ; and being
eagerly received, she handed over the note. 4.
Arbetio, who was of all men most clever in framing
an accusation, trusting to this evidence reported
the matter to the emperor. The affair was investigated, as usual, without delay or rest, and when
Barbatio admitted that he had received the letter,
and strong evidence proved that the woman had
written it, both were beheaded.   5. When they had
been executed, far-reaching inquisitions followed,
and many suffered, the most innocent as well as
the guilty. Among these also Valentinus, formerly

CONSTANTIUS ET GALLUS

Valentinus ex primicerio protectorum tribunus, ut
conscius inter complures alios tortus aliquotiens
supervixit, penitus quid erat gestum ignorans. Ideoque ad iniuriae periculique compensationem, ducis
in Illyrico meruit potestatem.

6. Erat autem idem Barbatio subagrestis, arro-
gantisque propositi, ea re multis exosus, quod et
dum domesticos protectores sub Gallo regeret Caesare,
proditor erat et perfidus, et post eius excessum, nobi-
lioris militiae fastu elatus, in Iulianum itidem Caesarem paria confingebat, crebroque detestantibus
bonis, sub Augusti patulis auribus multa garriebat
et saeva. 7. Ignorans profecto veteris [1] Aristotelis
sapiens dictum, qui Callisthenem sectatorem et
propinquum suum ad regem Alexandrum mittens,
ei saepe mandabat, ut quam rarissime et iucunde
apud hominem loqueretur, vitae potestatem et necis
in acie linguae portantem. 8. Ne sit hoc mirum,
homines profutura discernere non numquam et
nocentia, quorum mentes cognatas caelestibus arbi-
tramur, animalia ratione carentia salutem suam
interdum alto tueri silentio solent, ut exemplum
est hoc perquam notum. 9. Linquentes orientem
anseres ob calorem, plagamque petentes occiduam,
cum montem penetrare coeperint Taurum, aquilis
abundantem, timentes fortissimas volucres, rostra
lapillis occludunt, ne eis eliciat vel necessitas extrema clangorem, eisdemque collibus agiliore volatu

---

[1] *ueteris*, Cornelissen, Schneider ; *uetus*, **V.**

captain of the guard and then a tribune, was suspected with many others of being implicated and, although wholly ignorant of what had been done, was tortured several times, but survived. And so, as compensation for his wrongs and his peril, he gained the position of a general in Illyricum.

6. Now the aforesaid Barbatio was a somewhat boorish fellow, of arrogant intentions, who was hated by many for the reason that, while he commanded the household troops under Gallus Caesar, he was a perfidious traitor ; and after Gallus' death, puffed up with pride in his higher military rank, he made like plots against Julian, when he became Caesar ; and to the disgust of all good men he chattered into the open ears of the Augustus many cruel accusations. 7. He surely was unaware of the wise saying of Aristotle of old, who, on sending his disciple and relative Callisthenes to King Alexander, charged him repeatedly to speak as seldom and as pleasantly as possible in the presence of a man who had at the tip of his tongue the power of life and death. 8. And it should not cause surprise that men, whose minds we regard as akin to the gods, sometimes distinguish what is advantageous from what is harmful ; for even unreasoning animals are at times wont to protect their lives by deep silence, as appears from this well-known fact. 9. The geese, when leaving the east because of heat and flying westward, no sooner begin to traverse Mount Taurus, which abounds in eagles, than in fear of those mighty birds they close their beaks with little stones, so that even extreme necessity may not call forth a clamour from them ; and after they have passed over those same hills in

transcursis, proiciunt calculos, atque ita securius pergunt.

4. *Rex Persarum Sapor Romanos totis viribus aggredi parat.*

1. Dum apud Sirmium haec diligentia quaeruntur impensa, Orientis fortuna periculorum terribiles tubas reflabat. Rex enim Persidis, ferarum gentium quas placarat adiumentis accinctus, augendique regni cupiditate supra homines flagrans, arma viresque parabat et commeatus, consilia tartareis manibus miscens, et superstitiones [1] omnes consulens de futuris ; hisque satis collectis, pervadere cuncta prima verni temperie cogitabat.

2. Et cum haec primo rumores, dein nuntii certi perferrent, omnesque suspensos adventantium calamitatum complicaret magna formido, comitatensis fabrica eandem incudem (ut dicitur) diu noctuque tundendo, ad spadonum arbitrium, imperatori suspicaci ac timido intendebat Ursicinum, velut vultus Gorgonei torvitatem, haec saepe taliaque replicans, quod interempto Silvano, quasi paenuria meliorum, ad tuendas partes eoas denuo missus, altius anhelabat. 3. Hac autem assentandi nimia foeditate, mercari complures nitebantur Eusebi favorem, cubiculi tunc praepositi, apud quem (si vere dici debeat) multa Constantius posuit,[2]

---

[1] *superstitiones*, Her. ; *praesciones*, Gronov ; *praestionis*, V.   [2] *posuit*, Damsté ; *potuit*, V.

speedier flight, they cast out the pebbles and so go on with greater peace of mind.

4. *Sapor, king of the Persians, prepares to attack the Romans with all his forces.*

1. While at Sirmium these matters were being investigated with all diligence, the fortune of the Orient kept sounding the dread trumpets of danger; for the king of Persia, armed with the help of the savage tribes which he had subdued, and burning with superhuman desire of extending his domain, was preparing arms, forces, and supplies, embroiling his plans with infernal powers and consulting all superstitions about the future; and having assembled enough of these, he planned with the first mildness of spring to overrun everything. 2. And when news of this came, at first by rumours and then by trustworthy messengers, and great dread of impending disasters held all in suspense, the forge of the courtiers, hammering day and night at the instigation of the eunuchs on the same anvil (as the saying is), held up Ursicinus to the suspicious and timid emperor as a grim-visaged gorgon, often reiterating these and similar charges : that he, having on the death of Silvanus been sent as if in default of better men, to defend the east, was panting for higher honours. 3. Furthermore, by this foul and excessive flattery very many strove to purchase the favour of Eusebius, then head-chamberlain, upon whom (if the truth must be told) Constantius greatly depended, and who was vigorously attacking the safety of the aforesaid commander of the cavalry

ante dicti magistri equitum salutem acriter impugnantis ratione bifaria, quod omnium solus nec opes [1] eius augebat,[2] ut ceteri, et domo sua non cederet Antiochiae, quam molestissime flagitabat. 4. Qui ut coluber copia virus exuberans, natorum multitudinem etiam tum aegre serpentium, excitans ad nocendum, emittebat cubicularios iam adultos, ut inter ministeria vitae secretioris, gracilitate vocis semper puerilis et blandae, apud principis aures nimium patulas, existimationem viri fortis invidia gravi pulsarent. Et brevi iussa fecerunt. 5. Horum et similium taedio iuvat veterem laudare Domitianum, qui licet patris fratrisque dissimilis, memoriam nominis sui inexpiabili detestatione perfudit, tamen receptissima inclaruit lege, qua minaciter interdixerat ne intra terminos iuris dictionis Romanae castraret quisquam puerum ; quod ni contigisset, quis eorum ferret examina, quorum raritas [3] difficile toleratur ? 6. Actum est tamen cautius, ne (ut fingebat) rursus accitus idem Ursicinus, metu cuncta turbaret, sed cum fors copiam detulisset, raperetur ad mortem.

7. Haec operientibus illis, et ancipiti cogitatione districtis, nobis apud Samosatam, Commageni

---

[1] *opes*, Her. ; *opis*, G ; *opus*, V.   [2] *augebat*, Her. ; *agebat*, V.   [3] *raritas*, Boxh. ; *paritas*, V.

[1] Suetonius, *Dom.* vii.

for a double reason : because he alone of all was not, like the rest, adding to Eusebius' wealth, and would not give up to him his house at Antioch, which the head-chamberlain most importunately demanded. 4. Eusebius then, like a viper swelling with abundant poison and arousing its multitudinous brood to mischief when they were still barely able to crawl, sent out his chamberlains, already well grown, with directions that, amid the duties of their more private attendance, with the soft utterances of voices always childish and persuasive they should with bitter hatred batter the reputation of that brave man in the too receptive ears of the prince. And they promptly did what they were ordered. 5. Through disgust with these and their kind, I take pleasure in praising Domitian of old, for although, unlike his father and his brother, he drenched the memory of his name with indelible detestation, yet he won distinction by a most highly approved law, by which he had under heavy penalties forbidden anyone within the bounds of the Roman jurisdiction to geld a boy ;[1] for if this had not happened, who could endure the swarms of those whose small number is with difficulty tolerated ? 6. However, Eusebius proceeded warily, lest (as he pretended) that same Ursicinus, if again summoned to court, should through fear cause general disturbance, but actually that he might, whenever chance should give the opportunity, be haled off to execution.

7. While they held these plots in abeyance and were distracted by anxious thoughts, and I was staying for a time at Samosata, the famous seat of the

425

quondam regni clarissimam sedem, parumper moran-
tibus, repente novi motus rumoribus densis audiuntur et certis.[1] Quos docebit orationis progrediens
textus.

5. *Antoninus protector cum suis omnibus ad Saporem
transfugit ; eumque in bellum Romanum sponte
iam motum impellit.*

1. Antoninus quidam ex mercatore opulento
rationarius apparitor Mesopotamiae ducis, tunc
protector exercitatus et prudens, perque omnes
illas notissimus terras, aviditate quorundam nexus
ingentibus damnis, cum iurgando contra potentis,
se magis magisque iniustitia frangi contemplaretur,
ad deferendam potioribus gratiam, qui spectabant
negotium, inclinatis, ne contra acumina calcitraret,
flexus [2] in blanditias molliores, confessusque debitum per colludia in nomen fisci translatum,
iamque ausurus immania, rimabatur tectius rei
publicae membra totius, et utriusque linguae litteras
sciens, circa ratiocinia versabatur, qui vel quarum
virium milites ubi agant, vel procinctus tempore
quo sint venturi [3] describens, itidem armorum et
commeatuum copiae, aliaque usui bello futura,
an abunde suppetant indefessa scitatione [4] per-
contans. 2. Et cum [5] totius Orientis didicisset

---

[1] *certis*, Val. ; *contextis*, Petschenig ; *concertis*, V.
[2] *flexus*, Pet. ; *flectens*, Mommsen ; *flectis*, V.   [3] *quo
sint uenturi*, C. F. W. Müller ; *q.s. ituri*, Bentley ; *quos in-
tuentiri*, V.   [4] *scitatione*, BG, Novák ; *sciscitatione*, EA ;
indefessas cititatione, V.   [5] *cum*, Val. ; *dum*, V.

---

[1] See note 2, p. 198.

former kingdom of Commagene, on a sudden repeated and trustworthy rumours were heard of new commotions ; and of these the following chapter of my history shall tell.

5. *Antoninus, of the household troops, goes over with all his household to Sapor, and urges him to the war against the Romans which he had already set on foot of his own accord.*

1. There was a certain Antoninus, at first a rich merchant, then an accountant in the service of the governor of Mesopotamia, and finally one of his body-guard, a man of experience and sagacity, who was widely known throughout all that region. This man, being involved in great losses through the greed of certain powerful men, found on contending against them that he was more and more oppressed by unjust means, since those who examined the case were inclined to curry favour with men of higher position. Accordingly, in order not to kick against the pricks, he turned to mildness and flattery and acknowledged the debt, which by collusion had been transferred to the account of the privy purse. And then, planning to venture upon a vast enterprise, he covertly pried into all parts of the entire empire, and being versed in the language of both tongues,[1] busied himself with calculations, making record of what troops were serving anywhere or of what strength, or at what time expeditions would be made, inquiring also by tireless questioning whether supplies of arms, provisions, and other things that would be useful in war were at hand in abundance. 2. And

interna, virorum stipendiique parte maxima per
Illyricum distributa, ubi distinebatur ex negotiis
seriis imperator, allapsuro iam praestituto die
solvendae pecuniae, quam per syngrapham debere
se confiteri, vi metuque compulsus est, cum omnibus
se prospiceret undique periculis opprimendum,
largitionum comite ad alterius gratiam infestius
perurgente, fugam ad Persas cum coniuge liberis
et omni vinculo caritatum, ingenti molimine conabatur. 3. Atque ut lateret stationarios milites,
fundum in Iaspide (qui locus Tigridis fluentis ad-
luitur,) pretio non magno mercatur. Hocque commento cum nullus causam veniendi ad extremas
Romani limitis partes, iam possessorem cum plurimis
auderet exigere, per familiares fidos peritosque
nandi, occultis saepe colloquiis cum Tamsapore
habitis, qui tractus omnes adversos ducis potestate
tunc tuebatur, et antea cognitus, misso a Persicis
castris auxilio virorum pernicium, lembis impositus,
cum omni penatium [1] dulcedine, nocte concubia
transfretatur [2] ex [3] contraria specie Zopyri illius
similis Babylonii proditoris.

4. Rebus per Mesopotamiam in hunc statum de-
ductis, Palatina cohors palinodiam in exitium concinens nostrum, invenit tandem amplam nocendi
fortissimo viro, auctore et incitatore coetu spadonum,

---

[1] *penatium*, Bentley ; *penatum*, AG ; *paena dum*, V.
[2] *transfretatur*, Clark ; *transfretat rex*, V.   [3] *ex*, Mommsen ; *rex*, V.

---

[1] The chief treasurer ; see Introd., pp. xl. f.
[2] Zopyrus pretended to desert to Babylon, in order to
betray the city to his king, Darius. Antoninus actually
deserted, to betray his native country.

when he had learned the internal affairs of the entire Orient, since the greater part of the troops and the money for their pay were distributed through Illyricum, where the emperor was distracted with serious affairs, and as the stipulated time would soon be at hand for paying the money which he was compelled by force and threats to admit by written bond that he owed, foreseeing that he must be crushed by all manner of dangers on every side, since the count of the largesses [1] through favour to his creditor was pressing him more urgently, he made a great effort to flee to the Persians with his wife, his children, and all his dear ones. 3. And to the end that he might elude the sentinels, he bought at no great price a farm in Iaspis, a place washed by the waters of the Tigris. And since because of this device no one ventured to ask one who was now a landholder with many attendants his reason for coming to the utmost frontier of the Roman empire, through friends who were loyal and skilled in swimming he held many secret conferences with Tamsapor, then acting as governor of all the lands across the river, whom he already knew ; and when active men had been sent to his aid from the Persian camp, he embarked in fishing boats and ferried over all his beloved household in the dead of night, like Zopyrus, that famous betrayer of Babylon, but with the opposite intention.[2]

4. After affairs in Mesopotamia had been brought to this pass, the Palace gang, chanting the old refrain with a view to our destruction, at last found an opportunity for injuring the most valiant of men, aided and abetted by the corps of eunuchs, who

qui feri et acidi semper, carentesque necessitudinibus
ceteris, divitias solas ut filiolas iucundissimas
amplectuntur. 5. Stetitque sententia, ut Sabinianus cultus [1] quidem senex et bene nummatus, sed
imbellis et ignavus et ab impetranda magisterii
dignitate per obscuritatem adhuc longe discretus,
praeficiendus eois partibus mitteretur, Ursicinus
vero curaturus pedestrem militiam, et successurus
Barbationi, ad comitatum reverteretur, quo praesens
rerum novarum avidus concitor, (ut iactabant,)
a gravibus inimicis et metuendis incesseretur.

6. Dum haec in castris Constantii quasi per lustra
aguntur et scaenam, et diribitores venundatae subito
potestatis pretium per potiores diffunditant domos,
Antoninus ad regis hiberna perductus, aventer
suscipitur, et apicis nobilitatus auctoritate, quo
honore participantur mensae regales, et meritorum
apud Persas ad suadendum, ferendasque sententias
in contionibus ora panduntur, non contis nec
remulco (ut aiunt,) id est non flexiloquis ambagibus
vel obscuris, sed velificatione plena in rem publicam
ferebatur, eundemque incitans regem, ut quondam
Maharbal lentitudinis Hannibalem [2] increpans, posse
eum vincere, sed victoria uti nescire, assidue praedicabat. 7. Educatus enim in medio, ut rerum

---

[1] *cultus*, Her. ; *uegetus*, Cornelissen and Novák ; *victus*
V.   [2] *Hannibalem increpans*, transposui, c.c. ; *i. H.*, V.

---

[1] For *bene nummatus*, cf. Hor., *Epist.* i. 6, 38.
[2] The *diribitores* were originally those who sorted and
counted the ballots at elections ; in 7 B.C. Agrippa built
the *diribitorium* in the Campus Martius for their use ;
see Suet., *Claud.* 18. *Diribitores* seems to have acquired

are always cruel and sour, and since they lack other offspring, embrace riches alone as their most dearly beloved daughters. 5. So it was decided that Sabinianus, a cultivated man, it is true, and well-to-do,[1] but unfit for war, inefficient, and because of his obscurity still far removed from obtaining magisterial rank, should be sent to govern the eastern regions; but that Ursicinus should return to court to command the infantry and succeed Barbatio : to the end that by his presence there that eager inciter to revolution (as they persisted in calling him) might be open to the attacks of his bitter and formidable enemies.

6. While this was being done in the camp of Constantius, after the manner of brothels and the stage, and the distributors [2] were scattering the price of suddenly purchased power through the homes of the powerful, Antoninus was conducted to the king's winter quarters and received with open arms, being graced with the distinction of the turban, an honour shared by those who sit at the royal table and allowing men of merit among the Persians to speak words of advice and to vote in the assemblies. Thus, not with poles or tow-rope (as the saying is), that is, not by ambiguous or obscure subterfuges, but under full sail he attacked his country, urging on the aforesaid king, as long ago Maharbal chided the slowness of Hannibal, and kept insisting that he could win victories, but not take advantage of them.[3] 7. For having been brought up in their

the meaning of " distributors of bribes " ; see Suet., *Aug.* 40, 2, where however the word itself does not occur.

[3] Livy, xxii. 51 ; Florus, i. 22, 19.

omnium gnarus, auditorum nanctus vegetos [1] sensus,
et aurium delenimenta captantes, nec laudantium,
sed secundum Homericos Phaeacas cum silentio
admirantium, iam inde quadragesimi anni memoriam
replicabat, post bellorum assiduos casus, et maxime
apud Hileiam et Singaram, ubi acerrima illa nocturna
concertatione pugnatum est, nostrorum copiis
ingenti strage confossis, quasi dirimente quodam
medio fetiali, Persas nondum Edessam nec pontes
Euphratis tetigisse victores quos armipotentia
fretos, successibusque magnificis, ita dilatasse decuerat regna,[2] ut [3] toti Asia imperarent,[4] eo maxime
tempore quo diuturnis bellorum civilium motibus,
sanguis utrimque Romani roboris fundebatur.

8. His ac talibus subinde inter epulas sobrius
perfuga, ubi de apparatu bellorum et seriis rebus
apud eos Graiorum more veterum consultatur, regem
incendebat ardentem, ut exacta hieme statim arma
fretus fortunae suae magnitudine concitaret, ipse
quoque in multis ac necessariis operam suam
fidenter promittens.

---

[1] *uegetos* (*eius* a corr. of *iliis*) cf, xxii. 1 ɔ̃. 1 ˙ Her.; *vigiles*,
G; *vigiliis eius*, V.   [2] lac. after *decuerat* indic.
Eyssen.; *regna* added by Schneider; *decue ratarenteo*, V.
[3] *ut*, added by Eyssen.   [4] *toti Asiae imper(arent)*, added
by Novák.

midst, as a man well informed on all matters, finding eager hearers, desirous of having their ears tickled, who did not praise him but like Homer's Phaeacians [1] admired him in silence, he would rehearse the history of the past forty years. He showed that after constant successes in war, especially at Hileia and Singara,[2] where that furious contest at night took place and our troops were cut to pieces with great carnage, as if some fetial priest were intervening [3] to stop the fight, the Persians did not yet reach Edessa nor the bridges of the Euphrates, in spite of being victorious ; whereas trusting to their prowess and their splendid successes, they ought so to have extended their kingdom as to rule over all Asia, especially at a time when through the continual commotions of civil wars Rome's stoutest soldiers were shedding their blood on two sides.

8. With these and similar speeches from time to time at banquets, where after the old Greek custom they used to consult about preparations for war and other serious affairs, the deserter kept sober and fired the already eager king, so soon as winter was over, at once to take the field, trusting to his good fortune, and Antoninus himself confidently promised to aid him in many important ways.

---

[1] Cf. *Odyssey*, xiii. 1, and Index.

[2] In 348, see Gibbon, ch. xviii.

[3] The fetiales had to do with treaties and declaring war. Their persons were sacrosanct and they sometimes intervened to present terms of peace when the opposing armies were drawn up ready for battle.

CONSTANTIUS ET GALLUS

6. *Ursicinus magister militum ex Oriente evocatus,
cum iam venisset in Thraciam, remittitur in
Mesopotamiam ; quo reversus, per Marcellinum
Saporis adventum explorat.*

1. Sub eisdem fere diebus, Sabinianus adepta
repentina potestate sufflatus, et Ciliciae fines ingressus, decessori suo principis litteras dedit, hor-
tantis ut ad comitatum dignitate afficiendus superiore citius properaret, eo necessitatum articulo,
quo etiam si apud Thulen moraretur Ursicinus, acciri
eum magnitudo rerum ratione probabili flagitabat,
utpote disciplinae veteris et longo usu bellandi
artis Persicae scientissimum. 2. Quo rumore provinciis percitis, ordines civitatum et populi, decretis
et acclamationibus densis, iniecta manu detinebant
paene publicum defensorem, memores quod relictus
ad sui tutelam, cum inerti et umbratili milite,
nihil amiserat per decennium ; simul metuentes
saluti, quod tempore dubio, remoto illo advenisse
hominem compererant inertissimum. 3. Credimus
(neque enim dubium est) per aerios tramites Famam
praepetem volitare, cuius indicio haec gesta pandente,
consiliorum apud Persas summa proponebatur [1] ; et
multis ultro citroque deliberatis, placuit Antonino

---

[1] *proponebatur*, Lind. ; *praeponebatur*, V.

---

[1] Looked on by the Romans as a land north of Britain,
perhaps Norway confused with Iceland, but of which
they had no definite conception. It is a proverbial
expression for " the ends of the earth."

6. *Ursicinus, commander of the army in the Orient, being summoned from there and having already reached Thrace, is sent back to Mesopotamia; on his return he tries to learn through Marcellinus of the coming of Sapor.*

1. At about that same time Sabinianus, puffed up by his suddenly acquired power, entered the confines of Cilicia and handed his predecessor the emperor's letter, which directed him to make all haste to the court, to be invested with a higher rank; and that too at a crisis when, even if Ursicinus were living in Thule,[1] the weight of affairs with good reason demanded that he be sent for,[2] well acquainted as he was with the old-time discipline and with the Persian methods of warfare from long experience. 2. The rumour of this action greatly disquieted the provinces, and the senates and peoples of the various cities, while decrees and acclamations came thick and fast, laid hands on him and all but held fast their public defender, recalling that though he had been left to protect them with weak and ease-loving soldiers, he had for ten years suffered no loss; and at the same time they feared for their safety on learning that at a critical time he had been deposed and a most inefficient man had come to take his place. 3. We believe (and in fact there is no doubt of it) that Rumour flies swiftly through the paths of air, since it was through her circulation of the news of these events that the Persians held council as to their course of action. And after long

---

[2] That is, to go to the seat of war against Sapor, instead of to the emperor's court.

suadente, ut Ursicino procul amoto, despectoque
duce novello,[1] posthabitis civitatum perniciosis
obsidiis, perrumperetur Euphrates, ireturque prorsus, ut occupari possint provinciae, fama celeritate
praeventa, omnibus ante bellis (nisi temporibus
Gallieni,) intactae, paceque longissima locupletes,
cuius rei prosperante deo ductorem commodissimum
fore spondebat. 4. Laudato firmatoque concordi
omnium voluntate consilio, conversisque universis
ad ea quae erant citius congerenda, commeatus
milites arma ceteraque instrumenta, quae poscebat
procinctus adventans, perpetua hieme parabantur.

5. Nos interea paulisper cis Taurum morati,
ex imperio ad partes Italiae festinantes, prope
flumen venimus Hebrum, ex Odrysarum montibus
decurrentem, ibique principis scripta suscepimus,
iubentia omni causatione posthabita, reverti Mesopotamiam, sine apparitione ulla expeditionem cura-
turi periculosam, ad alium omni potestate translata.
6. Quod ideo per molestos formatores imperii struebatur, ut si Persae frustra habiti redissent ad sua,

---

[1] *duce novello*, transposui c.c. ; *n.d.*, V.

---

[1] Rufius Festus, ch. xxiii., says that in the time of
Gallienus the Persians invaded Mesopotamia and thought
themselves masters of Syria, when Odenatus (*decurio* in
Palmyra and husband of Zenobia) gathered a band of
Syrian farmers, defeated the Persians several times, and
pressed on as far as Ctesiphon.

debate to and fro it was decided, on the advice of
Antoninus, that since Ursicinus was far away and
the new commander was lightly regarded, they should
give up the dangerous sieges of cities, pass the barrier
of the Euphrates, and push on with the design of
outstripping by speed the news of their coming and
seizing upon the provinces, which in all previous wars
(except in the time of Gallienus) [1] had been untouched
and had grown rich through long-continued peace ;
and Antoninus promised that with God's favour
he would be a most helpful leader in this enterprise. 4. When this plan had been commended and
approved by unanimous consent, all turned their
attention to such things as must be amassed with
speed ; and so the preparation of supplies, soldiers,
weapons, and other equipment which the coming
campaign required, went on all winter long.

5. We [2] meanwhile lingered for a time on this
side the Taurus, and then in accordance with our
orders were hastening to the regions of Italy and
had come to the vicinity of the river Hebrus,[3] which
flows down from the mountains of the Odrysae ;
there we received the emperor's dispatch, which
without offering any excuse ordered us to return
to Mesopotamia without any attendants and take
charge of a perilous campaign, after all power
had been transferred to another. 6. This was devised by the mischievous moulders of the empire
with the idea that, if the Persians were baffled and
returned to their own country, the glorious deed

[2] Ammianus accompanied Ursicinus to the emperor's
court.

[3] A river of Thrace, the modern Maritza.

ducis novi virtuti facinus adsignaretur egregium ;
si fortuna sequior ingruisset, Ursicinus reus proditae [1]
rei publicae deferretur.   7. Agitatis itaque [2] rationibus, diu cunctati reversique, fastidii plenum Sabinianum invenimus, hominem mediocris staturae,
et parvi angustique animi, vix sine turpi metu
sufficientem ad levem convivii, nedum proelii
strepitum, perferendum.

8. Tamen quoniam speculatores apparatus omnes
apud hostes fervere, constanti asseveratione perfugis concinentibus, affirmabant, oscitante homun-
culo, Nisibin propere venimus, utilia paraturi, ne
dissimulantes obsidium, Persae civitati super-
venirent incautae.   9. Dumque intra muros matur-
anda perurgerentur, fumus micantesque ignes assidue a [3] Tigride per Castra Maurorum et Sisara et
collimitia reliqua, ad usque civitatem continui
perlucebant, solito crebriores, erupisse hostium
vastatorias manus superato flumine permonstrantes.
10. Qua causa ne occuparentur itinera, celeri cursu
praegressi, cum ad secundum lapidem venissemus,
liberalis formae puerum torquatum, (ut coniectaba-
mus) octennem, in aggeris medio vidimus heiu-
lantem, ingenui cuiusdam filium (ut aiebat) ; quem

---

[1] *proditae*, Cornelissen ; *ut proditor*, Bentley ; *proditor*, V.
[2] *itaque*, Bentley, Haupt ; *ita siue*, V.   [3] *a*, added by
Lind. ; *adsiduae trigidae*, V.

---

[1] Sabinianus : see xviii. **5**, 5 ; **7**, 7 ; and for his small
size, **6**, 7, above. His inaction is vividly expressed by
oscitante.
[2] A city of Mesopotamia, in Mygdonia, surrendered to
the Persians in the time of Jovian ; modern Nisibin.
[3] See also xxv. **7**, 9. It lay north of Nisibis and was

would be attributed to the ability of the new leader ; but if Fortune proved unfavourable, Ursicinus would be accused as a traitor to his country. 7. Accordingly, after careful consideration, and long hesitation, we returned, to find Sabinianus a man full of haughtiness, but of insignificant stature and small and narrow mind, barely able to endure the slight noise of a banquet without shameful apprehension, to say nothing of the din of battle.

8. Nevertheless, since scouts, and deserters agreeing with them, most persistently declared that the enemy were pushing all their preparations with hot haste, while the manikin [1] yawned, we hastily marched to Nisibis,[2] to prepare what was useful, lest the Persians, masking their design of a siege, might surprise the city when off its guard. 9. And while within the walls the things that required haste were being pushed vigorously, smoke and gleaming fires constantly shone from the Tigris on past Castra Maurorum [3] and Sisara and all the neighbouring country as far as the city, in greater number than usual and in a continuous line, clearly showing that the enemy's bands of plunderers had burst forth and crossed the river. 10. Therefore, for fear that the roads might be blocked, we hastened on at full speed, and when we were within two miles, we saw a fine-looking boy, wearing a neck-chain, a child eight years old (as we guessed) and the son of a man of position (as he said), crying in the

called by the Arabic geographers by a name meaning *pagus mororum*, or " the place of mulberries," of which *Maurorum* seems to be a corruption. Sisara is a neighbouring fortress.

mater dum imminentium hostium terrore percita
fugeret, impeditior trepidando reliquerat solum.
Hunc dum imperatu ducis miseratione [1] commoti,
impositum equo, prae me ferens ad civitatem reduco;
circumvallato murorum ambitu praedatores latius
vagabantur. 11. Et quia me obsidionales aerumnae
terrebant, intra semiclausam posticam exposito
puero, nostrorum agmen agilitate volucri repetebam
exanimis, nec multum afuit [2] quin caperer. 12. Nam
cum Abdigildum [3] quendam tribunum, fugientem
cum calone ala sequeretur hostilis, lapsoque per
fugam domino servum deprehensum, cum ego
rapido ictu transirem, interrogassent, quisnam provectus [4] sit iudex, audissentque Ursicinum paulo
ante urbem ingressum, montem Izalam petere ;
occiso indice in unum quaesiti complures nos irrequietis cursibus sectabantur. 13. Quos cum
iumenti agilitate praegressus, apud Amudin munimentum infirmum, dispersis per pabulum equis,
recubantes nostros securius invenissem, porrecto
extentius brachio, et summitatibus sagi contortis
elatius, adesse hostes signo solito demonstrabam,
eisdemque iunctus impetu communi ferebar, equo
iam fatiscente. 14. Terrebat autem nos plenilunium
noctis, et planities supina camporum, nulla (si
occupasset artior casus,) latibula praebere sufficiens,

---

[1] *miseratione*, Her. ; *miserati*, V.   [2] *afuit*, Bentley,
C. F. W. Müller, Haupt ; *fuit*, V (def. Löfstedt, Pighi).
[3] *Abdigildum*, Her. ; *Abdigidum*, G ; *abdigitdum*, V.
[4] *provectus*, Val. ; *profectus*, V.

440

middle of the highway ; his mother, while she was fleeing, wild with fear of the pursuing enemy, being hampered and agitated had left him alone. While I, at the command of my general, who was filled with pity, set the boy before me on my horse and took him back to the city, the pillagers, after building a rampart around the entire wall, were ranging more widely. 11. And because the calamities of a siege alarmed me, I set the boy down within a half-open postern gate and with winged speed hastened breathless to our troop ; and I was all but taken prisoner. 12. For a tribune called Abdigildus was fleeing with his camp-servant, pursued by a troop of the enemy's cavalry. And while the master made his escape, they caught the slave and asked him (just as I passed by at full gallop) who had been appointed governor. And when they heard that Ursicinus had entered the city a short time before and was now on his way to Mount Izala, they killed their informant and a great number, got together into one body, followed me with tireless speed. 13. When through the fleetness of my mount I had outstripped them and come to Amudis, a weak fortress, I found our men lying about at their ease, while their horses had been turned out to graze. Extending my arm far forward and gathering up my cloak and waving it on high, I showed by the usual sign that the enemy were near, and joining with them I was hurried along at their pace, although my horse was now growing tired. 14. We were alarmed, moreover, by the fact that it was full moon at night and by the level stretch of plain, which (in case any pressing emergency surprised us) could offer no hiding-places,

CONSTANTIUS ET GALLUS

ubi nec arbores nec frutecta nec quicquam praeter herbas humiles visebatur. 15. Excogitatum est ergo ut ardente superposita lampade, et circumligata ne rueret, iumentum solum quod eam vehebat solutum, sine rectore laevorsus ire permitteretur, cum nos ad montanos excessus dextra positos tenderemus, ut praelucere sebalem facem duci lenius gradienti, Persae credentes, eum tenerent potissimum cursum ; quod ni fuisset praevisum, circumventi et capti, sub dicionem venissemus hostilem.

16. Hoc extracti periculo, cum ad nemorosum quendam locum vineis arbustisque pomiferis consitum, Meiacarire nomine venissemus, cui fontes dedere vocabulum gelidi, dilapsis [1] accolis omnibus, solum in remoto secessu latentem invenimus militem, qui oblatus duci et locutus varia prae timore, ideoque suspectus, adigente metu qui intentabatur,[2] pandit rerum integram fidem, docetque quod apud Parisios natus in Galliis, et equestri militans turma, vindictam quondam commissi facinoris timens, ad Persas abierat profugus, exindeque morum probitate spectata, sortita coniuge liberisque susceptis, speculatorem se missum ad nostra, saepe

---

[1] *dilapsis*, Cornelissen ; *lapsis*, **V.**   [2] *intentatur*, suggested by Clark, c.c.

---

[1] *Sebalis fax*, which seems to occur only here, is the same as *sebacea*, a torch or candle made of tallow (*sebum*) instead of wax.

since neither trees nor shrubs were to be seen, but nothing except short grass. 15. Therefore we devised the plan of placing a lighted lantern on a single pack-animal, binding it fast, so that it should not fall off, and then turning loose the animal that carried the light and letting him go towards the left without a driver, while we made our way to the mountain heights lying on the right, in order that the Persians, supposing that a tallow torch [1] was carried before the general as he went slowly on his way, should take that course rather than any other ; and had it not been for this stratagem, we should have been surrounded and captured and come into the power of the enemy.

16. Saved from this danger, we came to a wooded tract planted with vineyards and fruitbearing orchards, called Meiacarire,[2] so named from its cold springs. There all the inhabitants had decamped, but we found one soldier hiding in a remote spot. He, on being brought before the general, because of fear gave contradictory answers and so fell under suspicion. But influenced by threats made against him, he told the whole truth, saying that he was born at Paris in Gaul and served in a cavalry troop ; but in fear of punishment for a fault that he had once committed he had deserted to the Persians. Then, being found to be of upright character, and to have married and reared children, he was sent as a spy to our territories and often brought back trustworthy news. But now

---

[2] According to Valesius, from Syrian *maia* or *maio*, "water," and *carire*, "cold"; the former word appears also in *Emmaus*.

veros nuntios reportasse. At nunc se a Tamsapore et Nohodare optimatibus missum, qui catervas ductaverant praedatorum, ad eos redire quae didicerat perlaturum. Post haec, adiectis quae agi in parte diversa norat, occiditur.

17. Proinde curarum crescente sollicitudine, inde passibus citis Amidam pro temporis copia venimus, civitatem postea secutis cladibus inclutam. Quo reversis exploratoribus nostris, in vaginae internis notarum figuris membranam repperimus scriptam, a Procopio ad nos perferri mandatam, quem legatum ad Persas antea missum cum comite Lucilliano praedixi, haec consulto obscurius indicantem, ne captis baiulis, sensuque intellecto scriptorum, excitaretur materia funestissima.

18. " Amendatis procul Graiorum legatis, forsitan et necandis, rex ille [1] longaevus non contentus Hellesponto, iunctis Grenici [2] et Rhyndaci pontibus, Asiam cum numerosis populis pervasurus adveniet, suopte ingenio irritabilis et asperrimus, auctore et incensore Hadriani quondam Romani Principis successore ; actum et conclamatum est, ni caverit Graecia."

19. Qui textus significabat Persarum regem transitis fluminibus Anzaba et Tigride, Antonino hortante,

---

[1] *ill(e)*, added by Clark ; *vel*, E. Meurig Davies ; *flongeuus* V.   [2] *Grenici*, Her. ; *graenicia*, V.

---

[1] Modern Diarbekir, see Gibbon, ii. p. 269, Bury.
[2] Ch. ix. below, and xix, **1-8**.
[3] Two rivers of Mysia, in north-western Asia Minor, the former celebrated for the victory of Alexander the Great

he had been sent out by the grandees Tamsapor and Nohodares, who had led the bands of pillagers, and was returning to them, to report what he had learned. After this, having added what he knew about what the enemy were doing, he was put to death.

17. Then with our anxious cares increasing we went from there as quickly as circumstances allowed to Amida,[1] a city afterwards notorious for the calamities which it suffered.[2] And when our scouts had returned there, we found in the scabbard of a sword a parchment written in cipher, which had been brought to us by order of Procopius, who, as I said before, had previously been sent as an envoy to the Persians with Count Lucillianus. In this, with intentional obscurity, for fear that, if the bearers were taken and the meaning of the message known, most disastrous consequences would follow, he gave the following message :—

18. " Now that the envoys of the Greeks have been sent far away and perhaps are to be killed, that aged king, not content with Hellespontus, will bridge the Granicus and the Rhyndacus [3] and come to invade Asia with many nations. He is naturally passionate and very cruel, and he has as an instigator and abetter the successor of the former Roman emperor Hadrian ;[4] unless Greece takes heed, it is all over with her and her dirge chanted."

19. This writing meant that the king of the Persians had crossed the rivers Anzaba and Tigris, and, urged on by Antoninus, aspired to the rule of the

over the Persians, the latter for the defeat of Mithradates by Lucullus.

[4] Referring of course to the deserter Antoninus.

dominium Orientis affectare totius. His ob perplexitatem nimiam aegerrime lectis, consilium suscipitur prudens.

20. Erat eo tempore satrapa Corduenae, quae obtemperabat potestati Persarum, Iovinianus nomine appellatus in solo Romano,[1] adulescens nobiscum occulte sentiens ea gratia, quod obsidatus sorte in Syriis detentus, et dulcedine liberalium studiorum illectus, remeare ad nostra ardenti desiderio gestiebat. 21. Ad hunc missus ego cum centurione quodam fidissimo, exploratius noscendi gratia quae gerebantur, per avios montes angustiasque praecipites veni. Visusque et agnitus, comiterque susceptus, causam praesentiae meae uni illi confessus, adiuncto taciturno aliquo locorum perito, mittor ad praecelsas rupes exinde longe distantes, unde nisi oculorum deficeret acies, ad quinquagesimum usque lapidem, quodvis etiam minutissimum apparebat. 22. Ibi morati integrum biduum, cum sol tertius affulsisset, cernebamus terrarum omnes ambitus subiectos, quos ὁρίζοντας appellamus, agminibus oppletos innumeris, et antegressum regem vestis claritudine rutilantem. Quem iuxta laevus incedebat Grumbates, Chionitarum rex nervositate[2]

---

[1] *Romano, adulescens,* Mommsen ; lac. after *R.* Cornelissen, or *educatus* for *adulescens.* [2] *neruositate,* Pet. ; *uenustate,* Her. ; *nobilitate,* Mommsen ; *nobis aetate,* V.

---

[1] A mountainous region in Armenia, taken by Caesar Maximianus from the Persians in the time of Galerius,

entire Orient. When it had been read, with the greatest difficulty because of its excessive ambiguity, a sagacious plan was formed.

20. There was at that time in Corduene,[1] which was subject to the Persian power, a satrap called Jovinianus on Roman soil, a youth who had secret sympathy with us for the reason that, having been detained in Syria as a hostage and allured by the charm of liberal studies, he felt a burning desire to return to our country. 21. To him I was sent with a centurion of tried loyalty, for the purpose of getting better informed of what was going on ; and I reached him over pathless mountains and through steep defiles. After he had seen and recognized me, and received me cordially, I confided to him alone the reason for my presence. Thereupon with one silent attendant who knew the country he sent me to some lofty cliffs a long distance from there, from which, unless one's eyesight was impaired, even the smallest object was visible at a distance of fifty miles. 22. There we stayed for two full days, and at dawn of the third day we saw below us the whole circuit of the lands (which we[2] call ὁρίζοντες[3]) filled with innumerable troops with the king leading the way, glittering in splendid attire. Close by him on the left went Grumbates, king of the Chionitae,[4] a man of moderate strength, it is true, and with shrivelled limbs, but of a certain

but not yet wholly freed from their rule. Later it was separated from the Persian dominion by Jovian : cf. xxv. 2.

[2] That is, the Greeks.　　　[3] The horizon.

[4] Sapor had recently made peace with them ; see xvi. 9, 4.

quidem media rugosisque membris, sed mente
quadam grandifica, multisque victoriarum insignibus
nobilis ; dextra rex Albanorum, pari loco atque
honore sublimis ; post duces varii, auctoritate et po-
testatibus eminentes, quos ordinum omnium multitudo sequebatur, ex vicinarum gentium roboribus
lecta, ad tolerandam rerum asperitatem diuturnis
casibus erudita. 23. Quo usque nobis Doriscum
Thraciae oppidum, et agminatim intra consaepta
exercitus, recensitos Graecia fabulosa narrabis ?
cum nos cauti vel (ut verius dixerim) timidi, nihil
exaggeremus, praeter ea quae fidei testimonia neque
incerta monstrarunt.

7. *Sapor cum Chionitarum et Albanorum regibus
Mesopotamiam intrat. Romani suos ipsi agros
incendunt, agrestes in oppida compellunt, ac
citeriorem ripam Euphratis castellis praesidiisque
communiunt.*

1. Postquam reges Nineve Adiabenae ingenti
civitate transmissa, in medio pontis Anzabae
hostiis caesis, extisque prosperantibus, transiere
laetissimi, coniectantes nos residuam plebem omnem
aegre penetrare post triduum posse, citius exinde ad
satrapen reversi quievimus, hospitalibus officiis
recreati. 2. Unde per loca itidem deserta et sola,
magno necessitatis ducente solacio, celerius quam

---

[1] Dwelling in what is now Georgia.
[2] Cf. Herodotus, vii. 59. Xerxes, in order to reckon
the size of his army, assembled ten thousand men and

greatness of mind and distinguished by the glory of many victories. On the right was the king of the Albani,[1] of equal rank, high in honour. After them came various leaders, prominent in reputation and rank, followed by a multitude of every degree, chosen from the flower of the neighbouring nations and taught to endure hardship by long continued training. 23. How long, storied Greece, will you continue to tell us of Doriscus, the city of Thrace, and of the armies drawn up in troops within enclosures and numbered?[2] For I am too cautious, or (to speak more truly) too timid, to exaggerate anything beyond what is proven by trustworthy and sure evidence.

7. *Sapor with the kings of the Chionitae and the Albani invades Mesopotamia. The Romans set fire to their own fields, drive the peasants into the towns, and fortify our bank of the Euphrates with strongholds and garrisons.*

1. After the kings had passed by Nineveh, a great city of Adiabene, and after sacrificing victims in the middle of the bridge over the Anzaba and finding the omens favourable, had crossed full of joy, I judged that all the rest of the throng could hardly enter in three days; so I quickly returned to the satrap and rested, entertained with hospitable attentions. 2. Then I returned, again passing through deserted and solitary places, more quickly

drew a circle around them; then he filled the space again and again with men, until the whole army was thus counted.

potuit sperari reversi, confirmavimus animos haesitantium, unum e navalibus pontem transisse reges absque ulla circumitione perdoctos. 3. Extemplo igitur equites citi mittuntur ad Cassianum, Mesopotamiae ducem, rectoremque provinciae tunc[1] Euphronium, compulsuri agrestes cum familiis et pecoribus universis ad tutiora transire,[2] et agiliter deseri Carras, oppidum invalidis circumdatum muris; super his campos omnes incendi, ne pabulorum suppeteret copia. 4. Et imperatis sine mora completis, iniecto igni furentis elementi vis maxima, frumenta omnia cum iam stipula flaventi turgerent, herbasque pubentes ita contorruit, ut ad usque Euphraten, ab ipsis marginibus Tigridis, nihil viride cerneretur. Tunc exustae sunt ferae complures, maximeque leones, per ea loca saevientes immaniter, consumi vel caecari sueti paulatim hoc modo. 5. Inter harundineta Mesopotamiae fluminum et frutecta, leones vagantur innumeri, clementia hiemis ibi mollissimae semper innocui. At ubi solis radiis exarserit tempus, in regionibus aestu ambustis, vapore sideris et magnitudine culicum agitantur, quorum examinibus per eas terras referta sunt omnia. Et quoniam oculos, quasi umida

---

[1] *tunc* after *Cassianum*, Günther, Mommsen; after *prouinciae*, V. [2] *transire compelli et*, VEBG, Bentley (*confestim*, Pet.).

than could be expected, led as I was by the great consolation of necessity, and cheered the spirits of those
who were troubled because they were informed that
the kings, without any detour, had crossed on a single
bridge of boats. 3. Therefore at once swift horsemen were sent to Cassianus, commander in Mesopotamia, and to Euphronius, then governor of the
province, to compel the peasants with their house-
holds and all their flocks to move to safer quarters,
directing also that the city of Carrhae should
quickly be abandoned, since the town was surrounded
only by weak fortifications ; and in addition that
all the plains be set on fire, to prevent the enemy
from getting fodder. 4. These orders were executed without delay, and when the fires had been
kindled, the mighty violence of that raging element
consumed all the grain, which was filled out on
the now yellowing stalk, and every kind of growing
plant, so utterly that from the very banks of the
Tigris all the way to the Euphrates not a green
thing was to be seen. At that time many wild
beasts were burned up, especially lions, which
are excessively savage in those regions and usually
perish or are gradually blinded in the following
manner. 5. Amid the reed-beds and thickets of
the Mesopotamian rivers lions range in countless
numbers ; and during the moderate winter, which
is there very mild, they are always harmless. But
when the sun's rays have brought the season of
burning heat, in regions parched by drought they
are tormented both by the sultry breath of the sun
and by crowds of gnats, swarms of which fill all parts
of that land. And since these same insects make

451

et lucentia membra, eaedem appetunt volucres,
palpebrarum libramentis mordicus insidentes, idem
leones, cruciati diutius, aut fluminibus mersi sor-
bentur, ad quae remedii causa confugiunt, aut amissis
oculis, quos unguibus crebro lacerantes effodiunt,
immanius efferascunt ; quod ni fieret, universus
oriens huius modi bestiis abundaret.

6. Dum campi cremantur (ut dictum est) tribuni
cum protectoribus missi, citerioris ripae Euphratis
castellis et praeacutis sudibus omnique praesidiorum
genere communibant, tormenta, qua parum [1] erat
voraginosum, locis opportunis aptantes.

7. Dum haec celerantur, Sabinianus inter rapienda
momenta periculorum communium lectissimus mode-
rator belli internecivi, per Edessena sepulchra,
quasi fundata cum mortuis pace, nihil formidans,
more vitae remissioris fluxius agens, militari pyrrice [2] sonantibus modulis pro histrionicis gestibus,
in silentio summo delectabatur, ominoso sane et
incepto et loco,[3] cum haec et huius modi factu
dictuque tristia, futuros praenuntiantia [4] motus,
vitare optimum quemque debere saeculi progressione
discamus. 8. Interea reges, Nisibi pro statione [5]

---

[1] *qua parum erat*, Günther ;   *qua flumen parum erat*,
Mommsen ; *quarum erat*, V.   [2] *pyrrice*, Clark ; *pyrrica*,
Val. ;   *pyrrico*, V.   [3] *et loco*, Wagner ;   *et inloco*, V.
[4] *praenuntiantia*, Günther, Mommsen ; *pronuntiant*, V ;
futuros . . . motus, del. Val.   [5] *pro statione*, G ;
prostratione, V.

---

[1] So that the Persians would be likely to try to cross.
[2] Of course, ironical.

for the eyes, as the moist and shining parts of the body, and settling along the eyelids bite them, those same lions, after suffering long torture, either plunge into the rivers, to which they flee for protection, and are drowned, or after losing their eyes, which they dig out by constantly scratching them with their claws, become frightfully savage. And were it not for this, the entire Orient would be overrun by such beasts.

6. While the plains were burning (as was said), tribunes were sent with the guard and fortified the nearer bank of the Euphrates with towers, sharp stakes, and every kind of defence, planting hurling-engines in suitable places, where the river was not full of eddies.[1]

7. While these preparations were being hastened, Sabinianus, that splendid choice [2] of a leader in a deadly war, when every moment should have been seized to avert the common dangers, amid the tombs of Edessa, as if he had nothing to fear when he had made his peace with the dead, and acting with the wantonness of a life free from care, in complete inaction was being entertained by his soldiers with a pyrrhic dance,[3] in which music accompanied the gestures of the performers— conduct ominous both in itself and in its occasion, since we learn that these and similar things that are ill-omened in word and deed ought to be avoided by every good man as time goes on as foreboding coming troubles. 8. Meanwhile the kings passed

---

[3] These were originally war dances in armour, but their scope was extended to pantomime of all kinds ; see Suet., *Nero*, 12, 1 and 2.

CONSTANTIUS ET GALLUS

vili transmissa, incendiis arida nutrimentorum
varietate crescentibus, fugitantes inopiam pabuli,
sub montium pedibus per valles gramineas incedebant. 9. Cumque Bebasen villam venissent, unde
ad Constantinam usque oppidum, quod centesimo
lapide disparatur, arescunt omnia siti perpetua,
nisi quod in puteis aqua reperitur exilis, quid agerent
diu cunctati, iamque suorum duritiae fiducia tran-
situri, exploratore fido docente, cognoscunt Euph-
ratem, nivibus tabefactis inflatum, late fusis gurgitibus evagari, ideoque vado nequaquam posse
transiri. 10. Convertuntur ergo ad ea quae amplec-
tenda fortuita daret occasio, spe concepta praeter
opinionem exclusi, ac proposito pro abrupto rerum
praesentium statu urgenti consilio, Antoninus dicere
quid sentiat iussus, orditur, flecti iter suadens in
dexterum latus, ut per longiorem circumitum, omnium rerum usu regionum feracium, et consideratione ea qua rectus pergeret hostis, adhuc intac-
tarum, castra duo praesidiaria Barzalo et Claudias [1]
peterentur, sese ductante, ubi tenuis fluvius prope
originem et angustus, nullisque adhuc aquis advenis
adolescens, facile penetrari poterit ut vadosus.
11. His auditis laudatoque suasore, et iusso ducere

---

[1] *Barzalo et Claudias,* Kellerbauer ; *Barzala et Laudias,*
G ; *barzaloc te laudias,* V.

---

[1] Formerly Antoninupolis, renamed after its restoration
by Constantine, see **9, 1,** below.
[2] That is, the Romans had not devastated that part of

454

by Nisibis as an unimportant halting place, and since fires were spreading because of the variety of dry fuel, to avoid a scarcity of fodder were marching through the grassy valleys at the foot of the mountains. 9. And now they had come to a hamlet called Bebase, from which as far as the town of Constantina,[1] which is a hundred miles distant, everything is parched by constant drought except for a little water to be found in wells. There they hesitated for a long time what to do, and finally were planning to cross, being confident of the hardiness of their men, when they learned from a faithful scout that the Euphrates was swollen by the melted snows and overflowing in wide pools, and hence could not be forded anywhere. 10. Therefore, being unexpectedly disappointed in the hope that they had conceived, they turned to embrace whatever the chance of fortune should offer ; and on holding a council, with reference to the sudden urgent difficulties of their present situation, Antoninus, on being bidden to say what he thought, began by advising that they should turn their march to the right, in order to make a long detour through regions abounding in all sorts of supplies, and still untouched by the Romans in the belief that the enemy would march straight ahead,[2] and that they should go under his guidance to the two garrison camps of Barzalo and Claudias : for there the river was shallow and narrow near its source, and as yet increased by no tributaries, and hence was fordable and easy to cross. 11. When this proposition had been heard and its author

the country because they thought that the enemy would march straight to the river without making a detour.

qua norat, agmina cuncta, ab instituto itinere
conversa, praevium sequebantur.

8. *Septingenti equites Illyriciani necopinantes a*
    Persis coniiciuntur in fugam. Evadunt hinc
    Ursicinus, inde Marcellinus.

  1. Quo certis speculationibus cognito, nos dis-
posuimus properare Samosatam, ut superato exinde
flumine, pontiumque apud Zeugma et Capersana
iuncturis abscisis, hostiles impetus (si iuvisset fors
ulla,) repelleremus. 2. Sed contigit atrox et silentio
omni dedecus obruendum. Namque duarum turmarum equites circiter septingenti, ad subsidium
Mesopotamiae recens ex Illyrico missi, enerves
et timidi, praesidium per eos tractus [1] agentes,
nocturnasque paventes insidias, ab aggeribus publicis vesperi, quando custodiri magis omnes tramites
conveniret, longius discedebant. 3. Hocque ob-
servato, eos vino oppressos et somno, viginti milia
fere Persarum, Tamsapore et Nohodare ductantibus,
nullo prospiciente transgressa, post tumulos celsos
vicinos Amidae, occultabantur armata.

  4. Moxque (ut dictum est) cum abituri Samosatam
luce etiam tum dubia pergeremus, ab alta quadam
specula radiantium armorum splendore perstricti,
hostisque adesse excitatius clamitantes, signo dato

---

[1] *tractus*, Lind. ; *traductus*, V.

commended and bidden to lead them by the way that he knew, the whole army changed its intended line of march and followed its guide.

8. *Seven hundred Illyrian horsemen are surprised and put to flight by the Persians. Ursicinus and Marcellinus escape in different directions.*

1. When this was known through trustworthy scouts, we planned to hasten to Samosata, in order to cross the river from there and break down the bridges at Zeugma and Capersana, and so (if fortune should aid us at all) repel the enemy's attacks. 2. But there befell a terrible disgrace, which deserves to be buried in utter silence. For about seven hundred horsemen, belonging to two squadrons who had recently been sent to the aid of Mesopotamia from Illyricum, a spiritless and cowardly lot, were keeping guard in those parts. And dreading a night attack, they withdrew to a distance from the public roads at evening, when all the paths ought to be better guarded. 3. This was observed by the Persians, and about twenty thousand of them, under the command of Tamsapor and Nohodares, passed by the horsemen unobserved, while these were overcome with wine and sleep, and hid themselves with arms behind some high mounds near Amida.

4. And presently, when we were on the point of going to Samosata (as has been said) and were on our way while it was still twilight, from a high point our eyes caught the gleam of shining arms, and an excited cry was raised that the enemy were upon

457

quod ad proelium solet hortari, restitimus conglobati, nec fugam capessere, cum essent iam in
contuitu qui sectarentur, nec congredi cum hoste
equitatu et numero praevalente, metu indubitatae
mortis cautum existimantes.   5. Denique ex ultima
necessitate manibus iam conserendis, cum quid agi
oporteat cunctaremur, occiduntur quidam nostrorum,
temere procursantes, et urgente utraque parte,
Antoninus ambitiosius [1] praegrediens agmen,[2] ab
Ursicino agnitus, et obiurgatorio sonu vocis increpi-
tus, proditorque et nefarius appellatus, sublata
tiara, quam capiti summi [3] ferebat honoris insigne,
desiluit equo, curvatisque membris, humum vultu
paene contingens, salutavit patronum appellans
et dominum, manus post terga conectens, quod
apud Assyrios supplicis indicat formam. 6. Et
" Ignosce mihi " inquit " amplissime comes, necessitate non voluntate ad haec quae novi [4] scelesta,
prolapso ; egere me praecipitem iniqui [5] flagitatores,
ut nosti, quorum avaritiae ne tua quidem excelsa
illa fortuna, propugnans miseriis meis, potuit re-
fragari." Simul haec dicens, e medio prospectu
abscessit, non aversus, sed dum evanesceret, verecunde retrogradiens et pectus ostentans.

7. Quae dum in curriculo semihorae aguntur,
postsignani nostri, qui tenebant editiora collis
exclamant, aliam cataphractorum multitudinem

---

[1] *ambitiosius*, Mommsen ; *ambitiosum*, V.   [2] *agmen*,
Her. ;   *agmini*, Mommsen ;   *agmina bursicino*,   V.
[3] *summi*, Damsté ;   *summo*, V.   [4] *novi*, HBG ; *moui*,
Kellerbauer, Eyssen. ;   *nonis*, V.   [5] *iniqui*, Haupt ;
inquit, EBG ;   *inquid*, V.

us ; then the usual signal for summoning to battle was given and we halted in close order, thinking it prudent neither to take flight when our pursuers were already in sight, nor yet (through fear of certain death) to engage with a foe far superior in cavalry and in numbers. 5. Finally, after it became absolutely necessary to resort to arms, while we were hesitating as to what ought to be done, some of our men ran forward rashly and were killed. And as both sides pressed forward, Antoninus, who was ostentatiously leading the troops, was recognised by Ursicinus and rated with chiding language ; and after being called traitor and criminal, Antoninus took off the tiara which he wore on his head as a token of high honour, sprang from his horse, and bending his body so that he almost touched the ground with his face, he saluted Ursicinus, calling him patron and lord, clasping his hands together behind his back, which among the Assyrians is a gesture of supplication. 6. Then, " Pardon me," said he, " most illustrious Count, since it is from necessity and not voluntarily that I have descended to this conduct, which I know to be infamous. It was unjust duns, as you know, that drove me mad, whose avarice not even your lofty station, which tried to protect my wretchedness, could check." As he said these words he withdrew from sight, not turning about, but respectfully walking backwards until he disappeared, and presenting his breast.

7. While all this took place in the course of half an hour, our soldiers in the rear, who occupied the higher part of the hill, cry out that another force,

equitum pone visam, celeritate quam maxima propinquare. 8. Atque ut in rebus solent afflictis, ambigentes cuinam deberet aut posset occurri, trudente pondere plebis immensae, passim qua cuique proximum videbatur, diffundimur universi, dumque se quisque expedire discrimine magno conatur, sparsim disiecti hosti concursatori miscemur. 9. Itaque spreta iam vivendi cupiditate, fortiter decernentes, ad ripas pellimur Tigridis, alte excisas. Unde quidam praecipites pulsi, implicantibus armis, haeserunt, ubi vadosus est amnis, alii lacunarum hausti vertigine, vorabantur, non nulli cum hoste congressi, vario eventu certabant, quidam cuneorum densitate perterriti, petebant proximos Tauri montis excessus. 10. Inter quos dux ipse agnitus pugnatorumque mole circumdatus, cum Aiadalthe tribuno, caloneque uno, equi celeritate ereptus, abscessit.

11. Mihi dum avius ab itinere comitum quid agerem circumspicio, Verennianus domesticus protector occurrit, femur sagitta confixus, quam dum avellere obtestante collega conarer, cinctus undique antecedentibus Persis, civitatem petebam, anhelo cursu rependo, ex eo latere quo incessebamur in

of heavy-armed cavalry, was to be seen behind the others, and that they were approaching with all possible speed. 8. And, as is usual in times of trouble, we were in doubt whom we should, or could, resist, and pushed onward by the weight of the vast throng, we all scattered here and there, wherever each saw the nearest way of escape ; and while every one was trying to save himself from the great danger, we were mingled in scattered groups with the enemy's skirmishers. 9. And so, now scorning any desire for life and fighting manfully, we were driven to the banks of the Tigris, which were high and steep. From these some hurled themselves headlong, but entangled by their weapons stuck fast in the shoals of the river ; others were dragged down in the eddying pools and swallowed up ; some engaged the enemy and fought with varying success ; others, terrified by the dense array of hostile ranks, sought to reach the nearest elevations of Mount Taurus. 10. Among these the commander himself was recognised and surrounded by a horde of warriors, but he was saved by the speed of his horse and got away, in company with Aiadalthes, a tribune, and a single groom.

11. I myself, having taken a direction apart from that of my comrades, was looking around to see what to do, when Verennianus, one of the guard, came up with an arrow in his thigh ; and while at the earnest request of my colleague I was trying to pull it out, finding myself surrounded on all sides by the foremost Persians, I moved ahead at breathless speed and aimed for the city, which from the point where we were attacked lay high up and could

arduo sitam, unoque ascensu perangusto meabilem,
quem scissis collibus molinae,[1] ad calles aptandas [2]
aedificatae, densius constringebant. 12. Hic mixti
cum Persis, eodem ictu procurrentibus ad superiora
nobiscum, ad usque ortum alterius solis immobiles
stetimus, ita conferti, ut caesorum cadavera multitudine fulta, reperire ruendi spatium nusquam
possent, utque miles ante me quidam, discriminato
capite, quod in aequas partes ictus gladii fiderat
validissimus, in stipitis modum undique coartatus
haereret. 13. Et licet multiplicia tela, per tormentorum omnia genera, volarent e propugnaculis, hoc
tamen periculo murorum nos propinquitas eximebat,
tandemque per posticam civitatem[3] ingressus, re-
fertam inveni, confluente ex finitimis virili et muliebri secus. Nam et casu illis ipsis diebus, in subur-
banis peregrina commercia, circumacto anno solita
celebrari,[4] multitudo convenarum augebat agrestium.
14. Interea sonitu vario cuncta miscentur, partim
amissos gementibus, aliis cum exitio sauciis, multis
caritates diversas, quas prae angustiis videre non
poterant, invocantibus.

9. *Descriptio Amidae, et quot tum ibi legiones ac
turmae in praesidio fuerint.*

1. Hanc civitatem olim perquam brevem, Caesar
etiam tum Constantius, ut accolae suffugium possint

---

[1] *molinae,* V ; *molimina,* Mommsen. [2] *aptandas,*
Clark ; *artandas,* V. [3] *civitatem,* added by Corn.
[4] *celebrari* (*i* corr. from *um*), V ; *celebrare,* G. Langen,
Mommsen.

---

[1] That is, apparently, for preparing the material of
which the paths were made.

be approached only by a single very narrow ascent;
and this was made still narrower by mills which
had been built on the cliffs for the purpose of making
the paths.[1] 12. Here, mingled with the Persians,
who were rushing to the higher ground with the same
effort as ourselves, we remained motionless until
sunrise of the next day, so crowded together that
the bodies of the slain, held upright by the throng,
could nowhere find room to fall, and that in front
of me a soldier with his head cut in two, and split
into equal halves by a powerful sword stroke, was
so pressed on all sides that he stood erect like a
stump. 13. And although showers of weapons from
all kinds of artillery flew from the battlements,
nevertheless the nearness of the walls saved us from
that danger, and when I at last entered the city by
a postern gate I found it crowded, since a throng of
both sexes had flocked to it from the neighbouring
countryside. For, as it chanced, it was at that very
time that the annual fair was held in the suburbs,
and there was a throng of country folk in addition
to the foreign traders. 14. Meanwhile there was a
confusion of varied cries, some bewailing their
lost kindred, others wounded to the death, many
calling upon loved ones from whom they were
separated and could not see because of the press.

9. *A description of Amida, and the number of the
legions and troops of cavalry that were on guard
there.*

1. This city was once very small, but Constantius,
when he was still a Caesar, in order that the neighbours

habere tutissimum, eo tempore quo Antoninupolim
oppidum aliud struxit, turribus circumdedit amplis
et moenibus, locatoque ibi conditorio muralium
tormentorum, fecit hostibus formidatam, suoque
nomine voluit appellari. 2. Et a latere quidem
australi, geniculato Tigridis meatu subluitur, propius
emergentis ; qua Euri opponitur flatibus, Mesopotamiae plana despectat ; unde aquiloni obnoxia
est, Nymphaeo amni vicina, verticibus Taurinis
umbratur, gentes Transtigritanas dirimentibus et
Armeniam ; spiranti zephyro contraversa Guma-
thenam contingit, regionem ubere et [1] cultu iuxta
fecundam, in qua vicus est Abarne nomine, sospita-
lium aquarum lavacris calentibus notus. In ipso
autem Amidae meditullio sub arce fons dives
exundat, potabilis quidem, sed vaporatis aestibus
non numquam faetens. 3. Cuius oppidi praesidio
erat semper Quinta Parthica legio destinata, cum
indigenarum turma non contemnenda. Sed tunc
ingruentem Persarum multitudinem sex legiones,
raptim percursis itineribus antegressae, muris ad-
stitere firmissimis, Magnentiaci et Decentiaci, quos
post consummatos civiles procinctus, ut fallaces et
turbidos, ad Orientem venire compulit imperator,
ubi nihil praeter bella timetur externa, et Tricensi-
mani Decimanique, Fortenses et Superventores

---

[1] *ubere et*, Cornelissen ; *uberem*, V.

[1] The soldiers enrolled by Magnentius and called by
his name and that of his brother.

[2] Also called Ulpia.

[3] Called in early inscriptions Fretenses.

[4] According to the *Notit. Imp.* these were light-armed
horsemen ; the former were used in surprise attacks, the
latter as scouts.

might have a secure place of refuge, at the same time that he built another city called Antoninupolis, surrounded Amida with strong walls and towers; and by establishing there an armoury of mural artillery, he made it a terror to the enemy and wished it to be called after his own name. 2. Now, on the south side it is washed by the winding course of the Tigris, which rises near-by; where it faces the blasts of Eurus it looks down on Mesopotamia's plains; where it is exposed to the north wind it is close to the river Nymphaeus and lies under the shadow of the peaks of Taurus, which separate the peoples beyond the Tigris from Armenia; opposite the breath of Zephyrus it borders on Gumathena, a region rich alike in fertility and in tillage, in which is the village called Abarne, famed for its warm baths of healing waters. Moreover, in the very heart of Amida, at the foot of the citadel, a bountiful spring gushes forth, drinkable indeed, but sometimes malodorous from hot vapours. 3. Of this town the regular garrison was formed by the Fifth Legion, Parthica, along with a force of no mean size of natives. But at that time six additional legions, having outstripped the advancing horde of Persians by rapid marches, were drawn up upon its very strong walls. These were the soldiers of Magnentius and Decentius,[1] whom, after finishing the campaigns of the civil wars, the emperor had forced, as being untrustworthy and turbulent, to come to the Orient, where none but foreign wars are to be feared; also the soldiers of the Thirtieth,[2] and the Tenth, also called Fortenses,[3] and the Superventores and Praeventores[4] with Aelianus, who was then a count; these

CONSTANTIUS ET GALLUS

atque Praeventores, cum Aeliano iam comite,
quos tirones tum etiam novellos, hortante memorato
adhuc protectore, erupisse a Singara, Persasque
fusos [1] in somnum retulimus trucidasse complures.
4. Aderat comitum quoque sagittariorum pars
maior, equestris [2] videlicet turmae ita cognominatae,
ubi merent omnes ingenui barbari, armorum viriumque firmitudine inter alios eminentes.

10. *Sapor duo castella Romana in fidem recipit.*

1. Haec dum primi impetus turbo [3] conatibus
agitat insperatis, rex cum populo suo gentibusque
quas ductabat, a Bebase loco itinere flexo dextrorsus
ut monuerat Antoninus, per Horren et Meiacarire
et Charcha, ut transiturus Amidam, cum prope
castella Romana venisset, quorum unum Reman,
alterum Busan appellatur, perfugarum indicio
didicit, multorum opes illuc translatas servari, ut
in munimentis praecelsis et fidis, additumque
est, ibi cum suppellectili pretiosa, inveniri feminam
pulchram cum filia parvula, Craugasii Nisibeni
cuiusdam uxorem, in municipali ordine genere
fama potentiaque circumspecti.[4] 2. Aviditate itaque rapiendi aliena festinans, petit impetu fidenti
castella, unde subita animi consternatione defensores

[1] *Persasque fusos*, tr. in G ; *f. Persasque*, V. [2] *equestris*,
Mommsen ; *equestres*, V. [3] *turbo*, added in G ; *uertigo*,
Her. ; V omits. [4] lac. of 23 letters at end of page, V.

---

[1] In one of the lost books.

466

troops, when still raw recruits, at the urging of the same Aelianus, then one of the guard, had made a sally from Singara (as I have said[1]) and slain great numbers of the Persians while they were buried in sleep. 4. There were also in the town the greater part of the *comites sagittarii*[2] (household archers), that is to say, a squadron of horsemen so-named, in which all the freeborn foreigners serve who are conspicuous above the rest for their prowess in arms and their bodily strength.

10. *Sapor receives two Roman fortresses in surrender.*

1. While the storm of the first attack was thus busied with unlooked-for undertakings, the king with his own people and the nations that he was leading turned his march to the right from the place called Bebase, as Antoninus had recommended, through Horre and Meiacarire and Charcha, as if he would pass by Amida ; but when he had come near two fortresses of the Romans, of which one is called Reman and the other Busan, he learned from the information of deserters that the wealth of many people had been brought there and was kept in what were regarded as lofty and safe fortifications ; and it was added that there was to be found there with a costly outfit a beautiful woman with her little daughter, the wife of a certain Craugasius of Nisibis, a man distinguished among the officials of his town for family, reputation, and influence. 2. Accordingly the king, with a haste due to his greed for seizing others' property, attacked the fortresses

---

[2] Apparently a division of the household cavalry ; see **xv. 4, 10,** note 2, and Index II. (Index of Officials).

armorum varietate praestricti, se[1] cunctosque
prodidere, qui ad praesidia confugerunt, et digredi
iussi confestim claves obtulere portarum, pate-
factisque aditibus, quicquid ibi congestum erat
eruitur, et productae sunt attonitae metu mulieres,
et infantes matribus implicati, graves aerumnas
inter initia tenerioris aetatis experti.[2] 3. Cumque
rex percontando cuiusnam coniux esset, Craugasii
comperisset, vim in se metuentem, prope venire
permisit intrepidam, et confisam[3] opertamque
ad usque[4] labra ipsa atro velamine, certiore
iam spe mariti recipiendi, et pudoris inviolati
mansuri, benignius confirmavit. Audiens enim
coniugem miro eius amore flagrare, hoc praemio
Nisibenam proditionem mercari se posse arbitra-
batur. 4. Inventas tamen alias quoque[5] virgines,
Christiano ritu cultui divino sacratas, custodiri
intactas, et religioni servire solito more, nullo
vetante, praecepit, lenitudinem profecto in tempore
simulans, ut omnes quos antehac diritate crudeli-
tateque terrebat, sponte sua metu remoto venirent,
exemplis recentibus docti, humanitate eum et
moribus iam placidis magnitudinem temperasse
fortunae.

---

[1] *praestricti se*, Val. ; *praestrictis*, V.   [2] lac. after
experti, Clark.   [3] *confisam*, Novák ; *invisam*, Damsté ;
uisam, V.   [4] *ad usque*, Gronovius pater, Bentley ;
absque, V.   [5] *alias quoque*, Lind. ; *aliasque*, V.

with fiery confidence, whereupon the defenders, overcome with sudden panic and dazzled by the variety of arms, surrendered themselves and all those who had taken refuge with the garrison ; and when ordered to depart, they at once handed over the keys of the gates. When entrance was given, whatever was stored there was brought out, and the women, paralysed with fear, were dragged forth with the children clinging to their mothers and experiencing grievous woes at the beginning of their tender years. 3. And when the king by inquiring whose wife the lady was had found that her husband was Craugasius, he allowed her, fearing as she did that violence would be offered her, to approach nearer without apprehension ; and when she had been reassured and covered as far as her very lips with a black veil, he courteously encouraged her with sure hope of regaining her husband and of keeping her honour unsullied. For hearing that her husband ardently loved her, he thought that at this price he might purchase the betrayal of Nisibis. 4. Yet finding that there were others also who were maidens and consecrated to divine service according to the Christian custom, he ordered that they be kept uninjured and allowed to practise their religion in their wonted manner without any opposition ; to be sure he made a pretence of mildness for the time, to the end that all whom he had heretofore terrified by his harshness and cruelty might lay aside their fear and come to him of their own volition, when they learned from recent instances that he now tempered the greatness of his fortune with kindliness and gracious deportment.

CONSTANTIUS ET GALLUS

LIBER XIX

1. Sapor, dum Amidenses ad deditionem hortatur, a praesidiariis sagittis et tragulis petitur. Idem dum temptat Grumbates rex, filius eius interficitur.

1. Hoc miserae nostrorum captivitatis eventu rex laetus, successusque operiens similes, egressus exinde paulatimque incedens, Amidam die tertio venit. 2. Cumque primum aurora fulgeret, universa quae videri poterant armis stellantibus coruscabant, ac ferreus equitatus campos opplevit et colles. 3. Insidens autem equo, ante alios celsior, ipse praeibat agminibus cunctis, aureum capitis arietini figmentum, interstinctum lapillis, pro diademate gestans, multiplici vertice dignitatum, et gentium diversarum comitatu sublimis. Satisque eum constabat, colloquio tenus defensores moenium temptaturum, aliorsum Antonini [1] consilio festinantem. 4. Verum caeleste numen ut Romanae rei totius aerumnas intra unius regionis concluderet ambitum, adegerat in immensum se extollentem, credentemque quod viso statim obsessi omnes metu exanimati, supplices venirent in preces. 5. Portis obequitabat,[2] comitante cohorte regali, qui dum se prope confidentius inserit, ut etiam vultus eius possit aperte cognosci, sagittis missilibusque ceteris, ob

---

[1] *Antonini dignitate* (*d.* del. m. 1 ?), **V.**   [2] *obequitabat,* **V ;**   *obequita* (lac. 1 line) *bat,* **Clark.**

470

BOOK XIX

1. *Sapor, while urging the people of Amida to surrender, is attacked by the garrison with arrows and spears. While King Grumbates attempts the same thing, his son is slain.*

1. The king, rejoicing in the wretched imprisonment of our men that had come to pass, and anticipating like successes, set forth from there, and slowly advancing, came to Amida on the third day. 2. And when the first gleam of dawn appeared, everything so far as the eye could reach shone with glittering arms, and mail-clad cavalry filled hill and dale. 3. The king himself, mounted upon a charger and overtopping the others, rode before the whole army, wearing in place of a diadem a golden image of a ram's head set with precious stones, distinguished too by a great retinue of men of the highest rank and of various nations. But it was clear that he would merely try the effect of a conference on the defenders of the walls, since by the advice of Antoninus he was in haste to go elsewhere. 4. However, the power of heaven, in order to compress the miseries of the whole Roman empire within the confines of a single region, had driven the king to an enormous degree of self-confidence, and to the belief that all the besieged would be paralysed with fear at the mere sight of him, and would resort to suppliant prayers. 5. So he rode up to the gates attended by his royal escort, and while with too great assurance he came so near that even his features could clearly be recognised, because of his

471

decora petitus insignia, corruisset, ni pulvere iaculantium adimente conspectum parte indumenti tragulae ictu discissa, editurus postea strages innumeras evasisset. 6. Hinc quasi in sacrilegos violati saeviens templi, temeratumque tot regum et gentium dominum praedicans, eruendae urbis apparatu nisibus magnis instabat, et orantibus potissimis ducibus ne profusus in iram a gloriosis descisceret coeptis, leni summatum petitione placatus, postridie quoque super deditione moneri decreverat defensores.

7. Ideoque cum prima lux advenisset, rex Chionitarum Grumbates, fidenter domino suam [1] operam navaturus, tendebat ad moenia, cum manu promptissima stipatorum, quem ubi venientem iam telo forte contiguum contemplator peritissimus advertisset, contorta ballista, filium eius primae pubis adulescentem, lateri paterno haerentem, thorace cum pectore perforato perfodit,[2] proceritate et decore corporis aequalibus antestantem. 8. Cuius occasu in fugam dilapsi populares eius omnes, moxque ne raperetur, ratione iusta regressi, numerosas gentes ad arma clamoribus dissonis concitarunt, quarum concursu ritu grandinis hinc inde convolantibus telis, atrox committitur pugna. 9. Et post interneciva certamina, ad usque finem diei protenta,

---

[1] *domino*, Thörnell; *Sapori s.*, Clark; *suam*, Eyssen.; *ano per amna baturus* (*b* to *u*, V[2]), V. [2] *perfodit*, G; *praecipitem fudit*, Novák; *praefudit*, V.

---

[1] Which would be delayed by the siege of Amida.

conspicuous adornment he became the target of arrows and other missiles, and would have fallen, had not the dust hidden him from the sight of his assailants, so that after a part of his garment was torn by the stroke of a lance he escaped, to cause the death of thousands at a later time. 6. In consequence of this attack he raged as if against sacrilegious violators of a temple, and declaring that the lord of so many kings and nations had been outraged, he pushed on with great effort every preparation for destroying the city ; but when his most distinguished generals begged that he would not under stress of anger abandon his glorious enterprises,[1] he was appeased by their soothing plea and decided that on the following day the defenders should again be warned to surrender.

7. And so, at the first dawn of day, Grumbates, king of the Chionitae, wishing to render courageous service to his lord, boldly advanced to the walls with a band of active attendants ; but a skilful observer caught sight of him as soon as he chanced to come within range of his weapon, and discharging a ballista, pierced both cuirass and breast of Grumbates' son, a youth just come to manhood, who was riding at his father's side and was conspicuous among his companions for his height and his handsome person. 8. Upon his fall all his countrymen scattered in flight, but presently returned in well-founded fear that his body might be carried off, and with harsh outcries roused numerous tribes to arms ; and on their onset weapons flew from both sides like hail and a fierce fight ensued. 9. After a murderous contest, protracted to the very end of

cum iam noctis esset initium, per acervos caesorum
et scaturigines sanguinis aegre defensum caligine
tenebrarum extrahitur corpus, ut apud Troiam quondam super comite Thessali ducis exanimi socii [1]
Marte acerrimo conflixerunt. 10. Quo funere regia
maesta, et optimatibus universis cum parente
subita clade perculsis, indicto iustitio, iuvenis nobilitate commendabilis et dilectus ritu nationis pro-
priae lugebatur. Itaque ut armari solebat elatus,
in amplo quodam suggestu locatur et celso, circaque
eum lectuli decem sternuntur, figmenta vehentes
hominum mortuorum, ita curate pollincta, ut imagines essent corporibus similes iam sepultis, ac per
dierum spatium septem, viri quidem omnes per con-
tubernia et manipulos epulis indulgebant, saltando,
et cantando tristia quaedam genera naeniarum,
regium iuvenem lamentantes. 11. Feminae vero
miserabili planctu, in primaevo flore succisam spem
gentis solitis fletibus conclamabant, ut lacrimare
cultrices Veneris saepe spectantur, in sollemnibus
Adonidis sacris, quod simulacrum aliquod esse
frugum adultarum religiones mysticae docent.

2. *Amida circumsidetur, et intra biduum bis oppug-
natur a Persis.*

1. Post incensum corpus ossaque in argenteam
urnam collecta,[2] quae ad gentem humo mandanda

---

[1] *exanimi socii Marte*, Pet. ; *exanimes aciem arte*, V.
[2] *conlecta*, C. F. W. Müller ; *coniecta*, Val. ; *contecta*, V.

---

[1] Patroclus, comrade of Achilles.

the day, at nightfall the body, which had with difficulty been protected amid heaps of slain and streams
of blood, was dragged off under cover of darkness,
as once upon a time before Troy his companions
contended in a fierce struggle over the lifeless comrade [1] of the Thessalian leader. 10. By this death
the palace was saddened, and all the nobles, as
well as the father, were stunned by the sudden
calamity ; accordingly a truce was declared and the
young man, honoured for his high birth and beloved,
was mourned after the fashion of his own nation.
Accordingly he was carried out, armed in his usual
manner, and placed upon a large and lofty platform,
and about him were spread ten couches bearing
figures of dead men, so carefully made ready that
the images were like bodies already in the tomb. For
the space of seven days all men by communities and
companies [2] feasted (lamenting the young prince)
with dances and the singing of certain sorrowful
dirges. 11. The women for their part, woefully
beating their breasts and weeping after their wonted
manner, loudly bewailed the hope of their nation
cut off in the bloom of youth, just as the priestesses
of Venus are often seen to weep at the annual festival of Adonis, which, as the mystic lore of religion
tells us, is a kind of symbol of the ripened grain.

2. *Amida is besieged and assaulted twice within two*
days by the Persians.

1. After the body had been burned and the ashes
collected and placed in a silver urn, since the father

---

[2] That is, those that were associated by their living
quarters or their places in the ranks.

475

portari statuerat pater, agitata summa consiliorum, placuerat busto urbis subversae expiare [1] perempti iuvenis manes ; nec enim Grumbates, inulta unici pignoris umbra, ire ultra patiebatur. 2. Biduoque ad otium dato, ac missis abunde qui pacis modo patentes agros pingues cultosque vastarent, quinquiens ordine multiplicato scutorum, cingitur civitas ac tertiae principio lucis, corusci globi turmarum impleverunt cuncta quae prospectus humanus potuit undique contueri, et sorte loca divisa, clementi gradu incedentes ordines occuparunt. 3. Persae omnes murorum ambitus obsidebant. Pars, quae orientem spectabat, Chionitis evenit, qua funestus nobis ceciderat adulescens, cuius manibus excidio urbis parentari debebat, Gelani [2] meridiano lateri sunt destinati, tractum servabant septentrionis Albani, occidentali portae oppositi sunt Segestani, acerrimi omnium bellatores, cum quibus elata in arduum specie elephantorum agmina rugosis horrenda corporibus, leniter incedebant, armatis onusta, ultra omnem diritatem taetri spectaculi formidanda, ut rettulimus saepe.

4. Cernentes populos tam indimensos, ad orbis Romani incendium diu quaesitos, in nostrum conversos exitium, salutis rata desperatione, gloriosos vitae exitus deinde curabamus, iamque omnibus nobis optatos. 5. A sole itaque orto usque diei ultimum, acies immobiles stabant, ut fixae nullo

[1] *expiari* suggested by Clark. [2] *manibus . . . Gelani,* added by Novák ; cf. xv. 8, 6 ; xix. 7, 1.

---

[1] That is, the burned city should take the place of the *bustum* where his body was burned ; see *A.J.P.* liv. pp. 362 f.

had decided that they should be taken to his native
land to be consigned to the earth, they debated
what it was best to do; and it was resolved to pro-
pitiate the spirit of the slain youth by burning [1] and
destroying the city; for Grumbates would not allow
them to go farther while the shade of his only son
was unavenged.   2. Accordingly, after two days
had been given to rest, a large force was sent to
devastate the rich, cultivated fields, which were
unprotected as in time of peace; then the city was
begirt by a fivefold line of shields, and on the morning
of the third day gleaming bands of horsemen filled
all places which the eye could reach, and the ranks,
advancing at a quiet pace, took the places assigned
them by lot.   3. The Persians beset the whole
circuit of the walls.   The part which faced the east
fell to the lot of the Chionitae, the place where the
youth so fatal to us was slain, whose shade was
destined to be appeased by the destruction of the
city.   The Gelani were assigned to the southern
side, the Albani guarded the quarter to the north,
and to the western gate were opposed the Segestani,
the bravest warriors of all.   With them, making a
lofty show, slowly marched the lines of elephants,
frightful with their wrinkled bodies and loaded with
armed men, a hideous spectacle, dreadful beyond
every form of horror, as I have often declared.

4. Beholding such innumerable peoples, long
got together to set fire to the Roman world and
bent upon our destruction, we despaired of any hope
of safety and henceforth strove to end our lives gloriously, which was now our sole desire.   5. And so from
sunrise until the day's end the battle lines stood fast.

variato vestigio, nec sonitu vel equorum audito
hinnitu, eademque figura digressi qua venerant, cibo
recreati et somno, cum superesset exiguum noctis,
aeneatorum clangore ductante, urbem ut mox
casuram terribili corona cinxerunt. 6. Vixque ubi
Grumbates hastam infectam sanguine ritu patrio
nostrique more coniecerat fetialis, armis exercitus
concrepans, involat [1] muros, confestimque lacrima-
bilis belli turbo crudescit, rapido turmarum processu,
in procinctum alacritate omni tendentium, et contra
acri intentaque occursatione nostrorum.

7. Proinde diffractis capitibus, multos hostium
scorpionum iactu moles saxeae colliserunt, alii
traiecti sagittis, pars confixi tragulis humum corporibus obstruebant, vulnerati alii socios fuga
praecipiti repetebant. 8. Nec minores in civitate
luctus aut mortes, sagittarum creberrima nube
auras spissa multitudine obumbrante, tormentorumque machinis, quae direpta Singara possederant
Persae, vulnera inferentibus plura. 9. Namque
viribus collectis propugnatores, omissa vicissim
certamina repetentes, in maximo defendendi ardore
saucii perniciose cadebant, aut laniati volvendo
stantes proxime subvertebant, aut certe spicula
membris infixa, viventes adhuc vellendi peritos

---

[1] *inuolat,* Eyssen. ; *inuolanti,* V (second *n* del. V[2]).

as though rooted in the same spot; no sound was heard, no neighing of horses; and they withdrew in the same order in which they had come, and then refreshed with food and sleep, when only a small part of the night remained, led by the trumpeters' blast they surrounded the city with the same awful ring, as if it were soon to fall. 6. And hardly had Grumbates hurled a bloodstained spear, following the usage of his country and the custom of our fetial priest, than the army with clashing weapons flew to the walls, and at once the lamentable tempest of war grew fiercer, the cavalry advancing at full speed as they hurried to the fight with general eagerness, while our men resisted with courage and determination.

7. Then heads were shattered, as masses of stone, hurled from the scorpions, crushed many of the enemy; others were pierced by arrows, some were struck down by spears and the ground strewn with their bodies, while others that were only wounded retreated in headlong flight to their companions. 8. No less was the grief and no fewer the deaths in the city, since a thick cloud of arrows in compact mass darkened the air, while the artillery which the Persians had acquired from the plunder of Singara inflicted still more wounds. 9. For the defenders, recovering their strength and returning in relays to the contest they had abandoned, when wounded in their great ardour for defence fell with destructive results; or if only mangled, they overturned in their writhing those who stood next to them, or at any rate, so long as they remained alive kept calling for those who had the skill to pull

quaeritabant. 10. Ita strages stragibus implicatas, et ad extremum usque diei productas, ne vespertinae quidem hebetaverunt tenebrae, ea re quod obstinatione utrimque magna decernebatur. 11. Agitatis itaque sub onere armorum vigiliis, resultabant altrinsecus exortis clamoribus colles, nostris virtutes Constanti Caesaris extollentibus, ut domini rerum et mundi, Persis Saporem saansaan appellantibus et pirosen, quod rex regibus imperans, et bellorum victor interpretatur.

12. Ac priusquam lux quinta occiperet, signo per lituos dato, ad fervorem similium proeliorum excitae undique inaestimabiles copiae in modum alituum ferebantur, unde longe ac late prospici poterat, campis et convallibus nihil praeter arma micantia ferarum gentium demonstrantibus. 13. Moxque clamore sublato, cunctis temere prorumpentibus, telorum vis ingens volabat e muris, utque opinari dabatur, nulla frustra mittebantur inter hominum cadentia densitatem. Tot enim nos circumstantibus malis, non obtinendae causa salutis, (ut dixi) sed fortiter moriendi studio flagrabamus, et a diei principio ad usque lucem obscuram, neutrubi proelio inclinato, ferocius quam consultius pugnabatur. Exsurgebant enim terrentium paventiumque[1] clamores, ut prae alacritate consistere sine vulnere vix quisquam possit. 14. Tandemque nox finem caedibus fecit, et satias aerumnarum

---

[1] *paventiumque,* Her., cf. Livy, xxii. 5, 4; *territorum terrentiumque* E. Meurig Davies; *ruentium ferientiumque* Val.; *terrentiumque,* V.

out the arrows implanted in their bodies. 10. Thus slaughter was piled upon slaughter and prolonged to the very end of the day, nor was it lessened even by the darkness of evening, with such great determination did both sides fight. 11. And so the night watches were passed under the burden of arms, while the hills re-echoed from the shouts rising from both sides, as our men praised the power of Constantius Caesar as lord of the world and the universe, and the Persians called Sapor " saansaan " and " pirosen," which being interpreted is " king of kings " and " victor in wars."

12. And before the dawn of the fifth day the signal was given on the trumpets and the countless forces were aroused anew from all sides to battles of equal heat, rushing to the strife like birds of prey ; and the plains and dales as far and as wide as the eye could reach revealed nothing save the flashing arms of savage nations. 13. Presently a shout was raised and all rushed blindly forward, a vast shower of weapons flew from the walls, and as might be supposed, not one that fell among that dense throng of men was discharged in vain. For since so many ills hedged us about, we burned, not with the desire of saving our lives, but, as I have said, of dying bravely ; and from the beginning of the day until the light was dim we fought with more fury than discretion, without a turn of the battle to either side. For the shouts of those who would terrify and of those who feared constantly rang out, and such was the heat of battle that scarcely anyone could stand his ground without a wound. 14. At length night put an end to the bloodshed and satiety

481

indutias partibus dederat longiores. Ubi enim
quiescendi nobis tempus est datum, exiguas quae
supererant vires, continuus cum insomnia labor
absumpsit, sanguine et pallente exspirantium facie
perterrente, quibus ne suprema quidem humandi
solacia tribui sinebant angustiae spatiorum, intra
civitatis ambitum non nimium amplae, legionibus
septem et promiscua advenarum civiumque sexus
utriusque plebe, et militibus aliis paucis, ad usque
numerum milium centum [1] viginti cunctis [2] inclusis.
15. Medebatur ergo suis quisque vulneribus pro
possibilitate vel curantium copia, cum quidam
graviter saucii, cruore exhausto, spiritus reluctantes
efflarent, alii confossi mucronibus frustraque curati,[3]
animis in ventum solutis, proiciebantur exstincti,
aliquorum foratis undique membris mederi periti
vetabant, ne offensionibus cassis animae vexarentur
afflictae, non nulli vellendis sagittis in ancipiti
curatione graviora morte supplicia perferebant.

3. *Ursicinus noctu obsidentibus supervenire frustra
conatur, Sabiniano magistro militum repugnante.*

1. Dum apud Amidam hac partium destinatione
pugnatur, Ursicinus maerens, quod ex alterius pendebat arbitrio, auctoritatis tunc in regendo milite
potioris, Sabinianum etiam tum sepulcris haerentem,
crebro monebat, ut compositis velitaribus cunctis,

---

[1] *centum*, added by Clark.   [2] *cunctis*, Eyssen.;
quinque, Mommsen; *concitis*, V.   [3] *frustraque curati*,
Novák; *post irritam curam*, Fletcher; *prostratique humi*,
Clark, cf. xvii. 8, 5, xxii. 1, 2; *prostrati curam*, V.

---

[1] See xviii. **7,** 7.

of woes had brought both sides a longer rest from
fighting; for even when time for rest was given
us, constant toil and sleeplessness sapped the little
strength that remained, and we were terrified by the
blood and the pale faces of the dying, to whom not
even the last consolation of burial could be given
because of the confined space; for within the limits
of a city that was none too large there were shut
seven legions, a promiscuous throng of strangers
and citizens of both sexes, and a few other soldiers,
to the number of 120,000 in all. 15. Therefore each
cured his wounds according to his ability or the
supply of helpers; some, who were severely hurt,
gave up the ghost slowly from loss of blood; others,
pierced through by arrows, after vain attempts to
relieve them, breathed out their lives, and were cast
out when death came; others, whose limbs were
gashed everywhere, the physicians forbade to be
treated, lest their sufferings should be increased
by useless infliction of pain; still others plucked out
the arrows and through this doubtful remedy endured torments worse than death.

3. *Ursicinus vainly attempts to surprise the besiegers
by night, being opposed by Sabinianus, commander of the infantry.*

1. While the fight was going on at Amida with such
determination on both sides, Ursicinus, grieving
because he was dependent upon the will of another,
who was then of greater authority in the command
of the soldiers, frequently admonished Sabinianus,
who was still clinging to his graves,[1] that, getting

per imos pedes montium occultis itineribus properarent, quo levium armorum auxilio, siqua fors iuvisset, stationibus interceptis, nocturnas hostium aggrederentur excubias, quae ingenti circumitu vallaverant muros, aut lacessitionibus crebris occuparent obsidioni fortiter adhaerentes. 2. Quibus Sabinianus renitebatur ut noxiis, palam quidem litteras imperiales praetendens, intacto ubique milite, quicquid geri potuisset impleri debere aperte iubentes, clam vero corde altissimo retinens, saepe in comitatu sibi mandatum, ut amplam omnem adipiscendae laudis decessori suo ardenti studio gloriae circumcideret, etiam ex re publica processuram. 3. Adeo vel cum exitio provinciarum festinabatur, ne bellicosus homo memorabilis alicuius facinoris auctor nuntiaretur aut socius. Ideoque his attonitus malis, exploratores ad nos saepe mittendo, licet ob custodias artas nullus facile oppidum poterat introire, et utilia agitando complura, nihil proficiens visebatur, ut leo magnitudine corporis et torvitate terribilis, inclusos intra retia catulos periculo ereptum ire non audens, unguibus ademptis et dentibus.

484

together all his skirmishers, he should hasten by
secret paths along the foot of the mountains, so
that with the help of these light-armed troops [1] (if
fortune was at all favourable) he might surprise the
pickets and attack the night-watches of the enemy,
who had surrounded the walls in wide extent, or by
repeated assaults distract the attention of those who
were stoutly persisting in the siege.   2. These pro-
posals Sabinianus opposed as dangerous, publicly
offering as a pretext letters of the emperor, which ex-
pressly directed that whatever could be done should
be effected without injury to the soldiers anywhere,
but secretly in his inmost heart keeping in mind
that he had often been instructed at court to cut
off from his predecessor, because of his burning desire for glory, every means of gaining honour, even
though it promised to turn out to the advantage
of the state.   3. Such great haste was made, even
though attended with the destruction of the provinces, that this valiant warrior should not receive
mention as author of, or participant in, any noteworthy action.   Therefore, alarmed by this unhappy
situation, Ursicinus often sent us scouts, although
because of the strict guard no one could easily enter
the town, and attempted many helpful things ;
but he obviously could accomplish nothing, being
like a lion of huge size and terrible fierceness which
did not dare to go to save from danger his whelps
that were caught in a net, because he had been
robbed of his claws and teeth.

---

[1] For this meaning of *armorum* see xvii. **10**, 6, note ; also
xvi. 12, 7.

CONSTANTIUS ET GALLUS

4. *Pestilentia Amidae orta, intra decimum diem exiguo imbre sedatur. Et de causis ac generibus pestilentiae.*

1. Sed in civitate, ubi sparsorum per vias cadaverum multitudo humandi officia superaret, pestilentia tot malis accessit, verminantium corporum lue tabifica, vaporatis aestibus varioque plebis languore nutrita, quae genera morborum unde oriri solent breviter explicabo.

2. Nimietatem frigoris aut caloris, vel umoris vel siccitatis, pestilentias gignere philosophi et illustres medici tradiderunt. Unde accolentes loca palustria vel umecta tusses et oculares[1] casus et similia perferunt, contra confines caloribus tepore[2] febrium arescunt.[3] Sed quanto ignis materies ceteris est efficacior,[4] tanto ad perimendum celerior siccitas. 3. Hinc cum decennali bello Graecia desudaret, ne peregrinus poenas dissociati regalis matrimonii lucraretur, huius modi grassante pernicie, telis Apollinis periere complures (qui sol aestimatur). 4. Atque ut Thucydides exponit, clades illa, quae in Peloponnesiaci belli principiis Athenienses acerbo genere morbi vexavit, ab usque ferventi Aethiopiae

---

[1] *humecta tusses et oculares,* Lind. ; *umectatus sese ioculares,* V. [2] *tepore,* G ; *tempore,* V. [3] *arescunt,* G ; *arescentes,* V ; lac. after *arescentes,* Novák ; *arescunt frequentes,* Her. [4] *materia est acrior ceteris et efficacior* suggested by Novák.

---

[1] Paris, the cause of the Trojan War.

4. *A plague which broke out in Amida is ended within ten days by a light rain. Remarks on the causes and varieties of plagues.*

1. But within the city, where the quantity of corpses scattered through the streets was too great to admit of burial, a plague was added to so many ills, fostered by the contagious infection of maggot-infested bodies, the steaming heat, and the weakness of the populace from various causes. The origin of diseases of this kind I shall briefly set forth.

2. Philosophers and eminent physicians have told us that an excess of cold or heat, or of moisture or dryness, produces plagues. Hence those who dwell in marshy or damp places suffer from coughs, from affections of the eyes, and from similar complaints ; on the other hand, the inhabitants of hot climates dry up with the heat of fever. But by as much as the substance of fire is fiercer and more effective than the other elements, by so much is drought the swifter to kill. 3. Therefore when Greece was toiling in a ten years' war in order that a foreigner [1] might not evade the penalty for separating a royal pair, a scourge of this kind raged and many men perished by the darts of Apollo,[2] who is regarded as the sun. 4. And, as Thucydides shows,[3] that calamity which, at the beginning of the Peloponnesian war, harassed the Athenians with a grievous kind of sickness, gradually crept

[2] See *Iliad*, i. 9 ff. and 43 ff. Apollo was angry because the request of his priest was denied. Ammianus rationalizes the myth, attributing the pestilence to the heat of the sun, and likening its rays to the arrows of the god.

[3] Cf. Thuc. ii. 4, 7.

plaga paulatim proserpens, Atticam occupavit.
5. Aliis placet auras (ut solent) aquasque vitiatas
faetore cadaverum, vel similibus, salubritatis vio-
lare maximam partem, vel certe aeris permutationem
subitam aegritudines parere leviores. 6. Affirmant
etiam aliqui, terrarum halitu densiore crassatum
aera, emittendis corporis spiraminibus resistentem,
necare non nullos, qua causa animalia praeter
homines cetera iugiter prona, Homero auctore, et
experimentis deinceps multis, cum talis incesserit
labes, ante novimus interire. 7. Et prima species
luis pandemus appellatur, quae efficit in aridioribus
locis agentes, caloribus crebris interpellari, secunda
epidemus, quae tempore ingruens, acies hebetat
luminum, et concitat periculosos umores, tertia
loemodes, quae itidem temporaria est, sed volucri
velocitate letabilis.

8. Hac exitiali peste quassatis,[1] paucis intem-
perantia aestuum[2] consumptis, quos multitudo
augebat, tandem nocte quae diem consecuta est
decimum, exiguis imbribus disiecto concreto spiritu
et crassato, sospitas retenta est corporum firma.

---

[1] *quassatis*, Dederichs, Pet. ; *quassati*, V.   [2] *intem-
perantia aestuum*, Her. ; *intemperanti* (second *n* added
by V[2]) *aestu*, V.

all the way from the torrid region of Africa and laid hold upon Attica.   5. Others believe that when the air, as often happens, and the waters are polluted by the stench of corpses or the like, the greater part of their healthfulness is spoiled, or at any rate that a sudden change of air causes minor ailments. 6. Some also assert that when the air is made heavy by grosser exhalations from the earth, it checks the secretions that should be expelled from the body, and is fatal to some ; and it is for that reason, as we know on the authority of Homer [1] as well as from many later experiences, that when such a pestilence has appeared, the other animals besides man, which constantly look downward, are the first to perish.   7. Now the first kind of plague is called endemic, and causes those who live in places that are too dry to be cut off by frequent fevers.   The second is epidemic, which breaks out at certain seasons of the year, dimming the sight of the eyes and causing a dangerous flow of moisture. The third is *loemodes*,[2] which is also periodic, but deadly from its winged speed.

8. After we had been exhausted by this destructive plague and a few had succumbed to the excessive heat and still more from the crowded conditions, at last on the night following the tenth day the thick and gross exhalations were dispelled by light showers, and sound health of body was regained.

[1] *Iliad*, i. 50, οὐρῆας μὲν πρῶτον ἐπῴχετο καὶ κύνας ἀργούς.
[2] Pestilential.

CONSTANTIUS ET GALLUS

5. *Amida hinc circum muros, inde per subterraneos*
fornices duce transfuga oppugnatur.

1. Verum inter haec inquies Persa vineis civitatem
pluteisque [1] circumdabat, et erigi aggeres coepti,
turresque fabricabantur, frontibus ferratis excelsae,
quarum fastigiis ballistae locatae sunt singulae, ut
a propugnaculis propellerent defensores, levia tamen
per funditores et sagittarios proelia ne puncto
quidem brevi cessabant. 2. Erant nobiscum duae
legiones Magnentiacae recens e Galliis ductae (ut
praediximus) virorum fortium et pernicium, ad
planarios conflictus aptorum, ad eas vero belli artes
quibus stringebamur, non modo inhabiles, sed
contra nimii turbatores, qui cum neque in [2] machinis
neque in operum constructione iuvarent, aliquotiens [3]
stolidius [4] erumpentes, dimicantesque fidentissime
minuto numero revertebant, tantum proficientes,
quantum in publico (ut aiunt) incendio, aqua unius
hominis manu adgesta. 3. Postremo obseratis
portis praecaute vetantibusque [5] tribunis, egredi
nequeuntes, frendebant ut bestiae. Verum secutis
diebus efficacia eorum eminuit (ut docebimus).

4. In summoto loco partis meridianae murorum,
quae despectat fluvium Tigrim, turris fuit in sub-
limitatem exsurgens, sub qua hiabant rupes abscisae,
ut despici sine vertigine horrenda non posset, unde
cavatis fornicibus subterraneis, per radices montis

---

[1] *pluteisque*, Bentley, Kiessling ; *et pluteis*, Pet., Mommsen ; *pluteis*, V.   [2] *neque in*, E, Lind. ; *nequem*, V.
[3] *aliquotiens*, Clark ; *aliquem*, V.   [4] *stolidius*, G ; *studio-*
sius, Fletcher ; *studius*, V.   [5] *praecaute uetantibusque*
(*u.*, Bentley, Cornelissen), Novák ; *praecantibusque*, V.

[1] Cf. xviii. 9, 3.

5. *Amida is attacked on one side about the walls, and on the other, under the lead of a deserter, by underground passages.*

1. But meanwhile the restless Persian was surrounding the city with sheds and mantlets, and mounds began to be raised and towers were constructed; these last were lofty, with ironclad fronts, and on the top of each a ballista was placed, for the purpose of driving the defenders from the ramparts; yet not even for a moment did the skirmishing by the slingers and archers slacken. 2. There were with us two Magnentian legions, recently brought from Gaul (as I have said) [1] and composed of brave, active men, experienced in battle in the open field, but to the sort of warfare to which we were constrained they were not merely unsuited, but actually a great hindrance; for whereas they were of no help with the artillery or in the construction of fortifications, they would sometimes make reckless sallies and after fighting with the greatest confidence return with diminished numbers, accomplishing just as much as would the pouring of a single handful of water (as the saying is) upon a general conflagration. 3. Finally, when the gates were very carefully barred, and their officers forbade them to go forth, they gnashed their teeth like wild beasts. But in the days that followed (as I shall show) their efficiency was conspicuous. 4. In a remote part of the walls on the southern side, which looks down on the river Tigris, there was a tower rising to a lofty height, beneath which yawned rocks so precipitous that one could not look down without

scalae ad usque civitatis ducebant planitiem, quo
ex amnis alveo haurirentur aquae furtim, ut in
omnibus per eas regiones munimentis quae contingunt flumina vidimus, fabre politae. 5. Per
has tenebras ob derupta neglectas, oppidano transfuga quodam ductante, qui ad diversam partem
desciverat, septuaginta sagittarii Persae ex agmine
regio arte fiduciaque praestantes, silentio summoti
loci defensi, subito singuli noctis medio ad contig-
nationem turris tertiam ascenderunt, ibique occultati, mane sago punici coloris elato, quod erat
subeundae indicium pugnae, cum ex omni parte
circumveniri urbem suis copiis inundantibus advertissent, exinanitis proiectisque ante pedes phare-
tris, clamoris ululabilis incendio tela summa peritia
dispergebant.   Moxque acies omnes densae petebant
multo infestius quam antea civitatem.   6. Inter [1]
incertos nos et ancipites, quibus occurri deberet,
instantibus supra, an multitudini transcensu scala-
rum iam propugnacula ipsa prensanti, dividitur
opera, et translatae leviores quinque ballistae,
contra turrim locantur, quae ocius lignea tela fun-
dentes, non numquam et [2] binos forabant, e quibus
pars graviter vulnerati ruebant, alii machinarum

----

[1] *inter*, added by G ; V omits.   [2] *et*, added by Her., cf.
xvii. 12, 3.

shuddering dizziness.   From these rocks subterranean arches had been hollowed out, and skilfully made steps led through the roots of the mountain as far as the plateau on which the city stood, in order that water might be brought secretly from the channel of the river, a device which I have seen in all the fortifications in those regions which border on streams.   5. Through these dark passages, left unguarded because of their steepness, led by a deserter in the city who had gone over to the opposite side, seventy Persian bowmen from the king's bodyguard who excelled in skill and bravery, protected by the silence of the remote spot, suddenly one by one in the middle of the night mounted to the third story of the tower and there concealed themselves ; in the morning they displayed a cloak of red hue, which was the signal for beginning battle, and when they saw the city surrounded on all sides with the floods of their forces, emptying their quivers, and throwing them at their feet, with a conflagration of shouts and yells they sent their shafts in all directions with the utmost skill.   And presently all the Persian forces in dense array attacked the city with far greater fury than before.   6. We were perplexed and uncertain where first to offer resistance, whether to those who stood above us or to the throng mounting on scaling-ladders and already laying hold of the very battlements ; so the work was divided among us and five of the lighter ballistae were moved and placed over against the tower, rapidly pouring forth wooden shafts, which sometimes pierced even two men at a time.   Some of the enemy fell, severely wounded ; others, through

metu stridentium praecipites acti, laniatis corporibus
interibant. 7. Quibus hac celeritate confectis, re-
latisque ad loca sueta tormentis, paulo securius
moenia omnium concursu defendebantur. 8. Et
quoniam augebat iras [1] militum scelestum facinus
perfugae, quasi decurrentes in planum, ita iaculantes
diversa missilia lacertis fortibus incumbebant, ut
vergente in [2] meridiem die, gentes [3] acri repulsa
disiectae,[4] lacrimantes complurium mortes, tentoria
repeterent vulnerum [5] metu.

6. *Gallicanarum legionum eruptio Persis exitiabilis.*

1. Adspiravit auram quandam salutis fortuna,
innoxio die cum hostili clade emenso, cuius reliquo
tempore ad quietem reficiendis corporibus dato,
posterae lucis initio ex arce innumeram cernimus
plebem, quae Ziata capto castello, ad hosticum
ducebatur, quem in locum ut capacissimum et
munitum—spatio quippe decem stadiorum ambitur
—promiscua confugerat multitudo. 2. Nam etiam
alia munimenta eisdem diebus rapta sunt et incensa,
unde hominum milia extracta complura, servituri
sequebantur, inter quos multi senecta infirmi,
et mulieres iam grandaevae, cum ex variis de-
ficerent causis, itineris longinquitate offensae, abiecta

---

[1] *iras*, Günther; *cumras*, V.   [2] *uergente in*, Gardt.;
uergentem, V[2] (*uertem*, V[1]).   [3] *die gentes*, Gardt.;
degentes, V.   [4] *disiectae*, Gardt.; *disiecta*, V.
[5] *uulnerum*, tr. before *metu*, Clark; before *acri*, V.

fear of the clanging engines, leaped off headlong and were dashed to pieces. 7. This being so quickly accomplished and the engines restored to their usual places, with a little greater confidence all ran together to defend the walls. 8. And since the wicked deed of the deserter increased the soldiers' wrath, as if they were entering a level ground in a sham fight they used such strength of arm as they hurled their various weapons, that as the day inclined towards noon the enemy were scattered in bitter defeat, and lamenting the death of many of their number, retreated to their tents through fear of wounds.

6. *A sally of the Gallic legions, destructive to the Persians.*

1. Fortune thus breathed upon us some hope of safety, since a day had passed without harm to us and with disaster to the enemy; so the remainder of that day was devoted to rest, for refreshing our bodies. But at the arrival of the following dawn we saw from the citadel a countless throng which after the capture of the fortress of Ziata was being taken to the enemy's camp; for in that stronghold, which was both capacious and well fortified (it has a circuit of ten stadia) a multitude of people of all sorts had taken refuge. 2. For other fortifications also were seized and burned during those same days, and from them many thousands of men had been dragged, and were following into slavery, among them many feeble old men, and women already advanced in years, who, when they gave out for various reasons, discouraged by the long march and

vivendi cupiditate, suris vel suffraginibus relinque-
bantur exsectis.

3. Has miserabiles turmas Galli milites contuentes, rationabili quidem sed intempestivo motu,
conferendae cum hostibus manus copiam sibi dari
poscebant, mortem tribunis vetantibus, primisque
ordinibus minitantes, si deinceps prohiberent. 4.
Utque dentatae [1] in caveis bestiae, taetro paedore
acerbius efferatae, evadendi spe repagulis versa-
bilibus illiduntur, ita gladiis portas caedebant, quas
supra diximus obseratas, admodum anxii, ne urbe
excisa ipsi quoque sine ullo specioso facinore delean-
tur, aut exuta periculis, nihil egisse operae pretium
pro magnanimitate Gallica memorentur, licet antea
saepe egressi, structoresque aggerum confossis [2]
quibusdam impedire conati, paria pertulerunt.

5. Inopes nos consilii, et quid opponi deberet
saevientibus ambigentes, id potissimum aegre eisdem
assentientibus, tandem elegimus, ut quoniam ultra
ferri non poterant, paulisper morati, custodias
aggredi permitterentur hostiles, quae non procul
erant a coniectu locatae telorum, ut eis perruptis,
pergerent prorsus. Apparebat enim eos (si im-
petrassent) strages maximas edituros. 6. Quae
dum parantur, per varia certaminum genera de-
fensabantur acriter muri, laboribus et vigiliis, et

---

[1] *dentatae*, G; *tentate*, V (*tentatae*, def. Val.); *ut retentatae*,
Bentley.   [2] *confossis*, Lind.; *confusis*, VG.

---

[1] The wild beasts for the arena were kept in cages of
iron lattice work, at the top of which was a bar that turned
when struck by their claws and threw them back to the
floor of the cage.

abandoning the desire to live, were left behind with their calves or hams cut out.

3. The Gallic soldiers, seeing these throngs of wretches, with a reasonable, but untimely, impulse demanded that the opportunity be given them of encountering the enemy, threatening death to the tribunes who forbade them, and to the higher officers, if they in their turn prevented them. 4. And just as ravening beasts in cages, roused to greater fierceness by the odour of carrion, in hope of getting out dash against the revolving bars,[1] so did they hew with swords at the gates, which (as I said above) were locked, being exceedingly anxious lest, if the city should be destroyed, they also might perish without any glorious action, or if it were saved from peril, they should be said to have done nothing worth while, as Gallic greatness of heart demanded; and yet before this they had made frequent sallies and attempted to interfere with the builders of mounds, had killed some, and had suffered the like themselves.

5. We, at our wit's end and in doubt what opposition ought to be made to the raging Gauls, at last chose this course as the best, to which they reluctantly consented: that since they could no longer be restrained, they should wait for a while and then be allowed to attack the enemy's outposts, which were stationed not much farther than a bowshot away, with the understanding that if they broke through them, they might keep right on. For it was apparent that, if their request were granted, they would deal immense slaughter. 6. While preparations for this were going on, the walls were being vigorously defended by various kinds of effort: by toil and

tormentis, ad emittenda undique saxa telaque
dispositis. Duo tamen aggeres celsi Persarum
peditum manu, e regione et ex pugnaculo [1] civitatis,
struebantur [2] operibus lentis, contra quos nostrorum
quoque impensiore cura moles excitabantur altissi-
mae, fastigio adversae celsitudinis aequatae, pro-
pugnatorum vel nimia pondera duraturae.

7. Inter haec Galli morarum impatientes, securi-
bus gladiisque succincti, patefacta sunt egressi
postica, observata nocte squalida et inluni,[3]
orantes caeleste praesidium, ut propitium adesset
et libens. Atque ipsum spiritum reprimentes, cum
prope venissent, conferti valido cursu, quibusdam
stationariis interfectis, exteriores castrorum vigiles
(ut in nullo tali metu) sopitos obtruncant, et [4]
supervenire ipsi regiae (si prosperior iuvisset eventus)
occulte meditabantur. 8. Verum audito licet levi
reptantium [5] sonitu, gemituque caesorum, discusso
somno excitatis multis et ad arma pro se quoque
clamitante, steterunt milites vestigiis fixis, progredi ultra non ausi; nec enim cautum deinde
videbatur,[6] expergefactis quos petebant insidiae,
in apertum properare discrimen, cum iam undique
frendentium catervae Persarum in proelia venirent
accensae. 9. Contra Galli corporum robore, auda-
ciaque quoad poterant inconcussi, gladiis secantes

---

[1] *e regione et ex pugnaculo*, Her.; *erecti et expugnatio*, V.
[2] *struebantur*, Clark; *struebatur*, V.   [3] *inluni*, edd. before
Lind.; *interlunio*, Corn.; *interluni*, V.   [4] *obtruncant
et*, Her.; *obstrunccatis*, V.[2]   [5] *leui reptantium*, Haupt;
reue temp dentium, V.   [6] *videbatur*, added by Clark.

498

watchfulness and by placing engines so as to scatter stones and darts in all directions. However, two lofty mounds were constructed by a troop of Persian infantry, and the storming of the city was being prepared with slowly built siege-works ; and in opposition to these troops our soldiers also with extreme care were rearing earthworks of great height, equal in elevation to those of the enemy and capable of supporting the greatest possible weight of fighting men.

7. Meanwhile the Gauls, impatient of delay, armed with axes and swords rushed out through an opened postern gate, taking advantage of a gloomy, moonless night and praying for the protection of heaven, that it might propitiously and willingly aid them. And holding their very breath when they had come near the enemy, they rushed violently upon them in close order, and having slain some of the outposts, they butchered the outer guards of the camp in their sleep (since they feared nothing of the kind), and secretly thought of a surprise attack even on the king's quarters, if a favourable fortune smiled on them. 8. But the sound of their cautious advance, slight though it was, and the groans of the dying were heard, and many of the enemy were roused from sleep and sprang up, while each for himself raised the call to arms. Our soldiers stood rooted to the spot, not daring to advance farther ; for it no longer seemed prudent, when those against whom the surprise was directed were aroused, to rush into open danger, since now throngs of raging Persians were coming to battle from every side, fired with fury. 9. But the Gauls faced them, relying on

499

adversos, parte suorum strata vel sagittarum undique volantium crebritate confixa, cum unum in locum totam periculi molem conversam, et concurrentium hostium agmina advertissent, nullo terga vertente, evadere festinabant, et velut repedantes sub modulis, sensim extra vallum protrusi, cum manipulos confertius invadentes sustinere non possent, tubarum perciti clangore castrensium, discedebant. 10. Et resultantibus e civitate lituis multis, portae panduntur, recepturae nostros si pervenire illuc usque valuissent, tormentorumque machinae stridebant sine iaculatione ulla telorum, ut stationibus praesidentes, post interemptos socios, quae pone [1] agerentur ignari, urbis oppositi moenibus nudarent intuta [2] et porta [3] viri fortes susciperentur innoxii. 11. Hacque arte Galli portam prope confinia lucis introiere minuto, numero quidam perniciose, pars leviter vulnerati, quadringentis ea nocte desideratis, qui non Rhesum nec cubitantes pro muris Iliacis Thracas, sed Persarum regem armatorum centum milibus circumsaeptum, ni obstitisset violentior casus, in ipsis tentoriis obtruncarant. 12. Horum campiductoribus,[4] ut fortium factorum antesignanis, post civitatis excidium, armatas statuas apud Edessam in regione

---

[1] *quae*, added by Her., Novák.   [2] *intuta et*, added by Novák.   [3] *porta*, Clark; *in aperta*, Novák; *mizperta*, V. [4] *campiductoribus*, V; *campidoctoribus*, Cornelissen (see Val. *ad loc.*).

---

[1] Text and exact meaning are uncertain.
[2] *Iliad*, x. 435 ff.; Virgil, *Aen.*, i. 469 ff.

their strength of body and keeping their courage
unshaken as long as they could, cut down their
opponents with the sword, while a part of their own
number were slain or wounded by the cloud of arrows
flying from every side. But when they saw that
the whole weight of peril and all the troops of the
enemy were turned against one spot, although
not one of them turned his back, they made haste
to get away ; and as if retreating to music, they were
gradually forced out beyond the rampart, and being
now unable to withstand the bands of foemen
rushing upon them in close order, and excited by
the blare of trumpets from the camp, they withdrew.
10. And while many clarions sounded from the city,
the gates were thrown open to admit our men, if
they could succeed in getting so far, and the hurling-
engines roared constantly, but without discharging
any missiles, in order that since those in command
of the outposts, after the death of their comrades
were unaware of what was going on behind them,
the men stationed before the walls of the city
might abandon their unsafe position, and the brave
men might be admitted through the gate without
harm.[1] 11. By this device the Gauls entered the
gate about daybreak in diminished numbers, a part
severely others slightly wounded (the losses of that
night were four hundred) ; and if a mightier fate
had not prevented, they would have slain, not
Rhesus nor the Thracians encamped before the
walls of Troy,[2] but the king of the Persians in
his own tent, protected by a hundred thousand
armed men. 12. In honour of their officers, as
leaders in these brave deeds, after the destruction

celebri locari iusserat imperator, quae ad praesens
servantur intactae.

13. Retectis sequenti luce funeribus, cum inter
caesorum cadavera optimates invenirentur, et
satrapae, clamoresque dissoni fortunam aliam alibi
cum lacrimis indicabant, luctus ubique et indignatio
regum audiebatur, arbitrantium per stationes muris
obiectas irrupisse Romanos indutiisque ob haec
tridui datis assensu communi, nos quoque spatium
ad respirandum accepimus.

7. *Turres et alia opera urbis muris admoventur;*
incenduntur a Romanis.

1. Perculsae deinde novitate rei efferataeque
gentes, omissa omni cunctatione, operibus (quoniam
vis minime procedebat) decernere iam censebant,
et concito extremo belli ardore, omnes oppetere
gloriose iam properabant, aut ruina urbis animis
litasse caesorum.

2. Iamque apparatu cunctorum alacritate perfecto, exsiliente lucifero, operum variae species
cum turribus ferratis admovebantur, quorum in
verticibus celsis aptatae ballistae propugnatores
agitantes humilius disiectabant. 3. Et albescente
iam die, ferrea munimenta membrorum caelum
omne subtexunt, densetaeque [1] acies non in-
ordinatim ut antea, sed tubarum sonitu leni

---

[1] *densetaeque*, Cornelissen ; *densataeque*, G, Bentley ;
densetaequeacie, C. F. W. Müller ; *tensitate quae*, V.

of the city the emperor ordered statues in full armour
to be made and set up in a frequented spot at Edessa,
and they are preserved intact to the present time.

13. When on the following day the slaughter
was revealed, and among the corpses of the slain
there were found grandees and satraps, and dissonant
cries and tears bore witness to the disasters in this
or that place, everywhere mourning was heard and
the indignation of the kings at the thought that the
Romans had forced their way in through the guards
posted before the walls. And as because of this
event a truce of three days was granted by common
consent, we also gained time to take breath.

7. *Towers and other siege-works are brought up to the
walls of the city; they are set on fire by the
Romans.*

1. Then the enemy, horrified and maddened by
the unexpected mishap, set aside all delay, and
since force was having little effect, now planned to
decide the contest by siege-works; and all of them,
fired with the greatest eagerness for battle, now hastened to meet a glorious death or with the downfall
of the city to make offering to the spirits of the slain.

2. And now through the zeal of all the preparations were completed, and as the morning star shone
forth various kinds of siege-works were brought up,
along with ironclad towers, on the high tops of
which ballistae were placed, and drove off the defenders who were busy lower down. 3. And day was
now dawning, when mail-clad soldiers underspread
the entire heaven, and the dense forces moved
forward, not as before in disorder, but led by the

CONSTANTIUS ET GALLUS

ductante, nullis procursantibus incedebant, machinarum operti tegminibus, cratesque vimineas prae-
tendentes. 4. Cumque propinquantes ad coniec-
tum venere telorum, oppositis scutis, Persae pedites
sagittas tormentis excussas e muris aegrius evitantes
laxaverant[1] aciem, nullo paene iaculi genere in
vanum cadente ; etiam cataphracti hebetati et
cedentes animos auxere nostrorum. 5. Tamen quia
hostiles ballistae ferratis impositae turribus, in humiliora ex supernis valentes, ut loco dispari ita eventu
dissimili, nostra[2] multo cruore foedabant, ingruente
iam vespera, cum requiescerent partes, noctis spatium
maius consumptum est, ut excogitari possit quid
exitio ita atroci obiectaretur.

6. Et tandem multa versantibus nobis, sedit consilium quod tutius celeritas fecit, quattuor eisdem
ballistis scorpiones opponi, qui dum translati e
regione, caute (quod artis est difficillimae) collo-
cantur, lux nobis advenit maestissima, Persarum
manipulos formidatos ostentans, adiectis elephantorum agminibus, quorum stridore immanitateque
corporum nihil humanae mentes terribilius cernunt.
7. Cumque omni ex latere armorum et operum
beluarumque molibus urgeremur, per scorpionum
ferreas fundas e propugnaculis subinde rotundi

[1] *laxaverant,* suggested by Clark, c.c. ; *laxarunt,* V.
[2] *nostros,* Mommsen.

[1] The scorpion was an engine for hurling stones, also
called *onager,* " wild ass." It is described in xxiii. 4, 4 ff.

504

slow notes of the trumpets and with no one running forward, protected too by pent-houses and holding before them wicker hurdles. 4. But when their approach brought them within bowshot, though holding their shields before them the Persian infantry found it hard to avoid the arrows shot from the walls by the artillery, and took open order, and almost no kind of dart failed to find its mark; even the mail-clad horsemen were checked and gave ground, and thus increased the courage of our men. 5. However, because the enemy's ballistae, mounted as they were upon iron-clad towers, were effective from their higher place against those lower down, on account of their different position they had a different result and caused terrible carnage on our side; and when evening was already coming on and both sides rested, the greater part of the night was spent in trying to devise a remedy for this awful slaughter.

6. And at last, after turning over many plans, we resolved upon a plan which speedy action made the safer, namely, to oppose four scorpions [1] to those same ballistae; but while they were being moved exactly opposite and cautiously put in place (an act calling for the greatest skill) the most sorrowful of days dawned upon us, showing as it did formidable bands of Persians along with troops of elephants, than whose noise and huge bodies the human mind can conceive nothing more terrible. 7. And while we were hard pressed on every side by weight of armed men, siege-works, and monsters, round stones hurled at intervals from the battlements by the iron arms of our scorpions shattered

505

lapides iacti,[1] dissolutis turrium coagmentis, **ballistas earumque tortores ita fudere praecipites, ut** quidam citra vulnerum noxas, alii [2] obtriti magnitudine ponderum interirent, elephantis vi magna propulsis, quos flammis coniectis undique circumnexos, iam corporibus tactis, gradientesque retrosus regere [3] magistri non poterant, postque [4] exustis operibus, nulla quies certaminibus data. 8. Rex enim ipse Persarum, qui numquam adesse certaminibus cogitur, his turbinum infortuniis percitus, novo et nusquam antea cognito more, proeliatoris militis ritu prosiluit in confertos, et quia conspectior tegentium multitudine procul speculantibus visebatur, petitus crebritate telorum, multis stipatoribus stratis, abscessit, alternans regibilis acies, et ad extremum diei, nec mortium truci visu [5] nec vulnerum territus, tandem tempus exiguum tribui quieti permisit.

8. *Amida per celsos aggeres muris proximos temptatur a Persis ac invaditur. Marcellinus post captam urbem nocte evadit, ac fuga Antiochiam petit.*

1. Verum nocte proelia dirimente, somno per breve otium capto, nitescente iam luce, ad potiunda

---

[1] *iacti* Pet.; *acti*, V.   [2] *alii*, V; *at*, Mommsen; *sola*, Her.   [3] *regere*, W[2], Val.; *retinere*, NBG; *retere*, V.   [4] *post quae*, Pet.   [5] *uisu*, C[2] A; *viso*, BG; *visione*, Günther, Pet.; *visio*, V.

---

[1] That is, by the fall from the high towers.

the joints of the towers, and threw down the ballistae and those who worked them in such headlong fashion, that some perished [1] without injury from wounds, others were crushed to death by the great weight of debris. The elephants, too, were driven back with great violence, for they were surrounded by firebrands thrown at them from every side, and as soon as these touched their bodies, they turned tail and their drivers were unable to control them. But though after that the siege-works were burned up, there was no cessation from strife. 8. For even the king of the Persians himself, who is never compelled to take part in battles, aroused by these storms of ill-fortune, rushed into the thick of the fight like a common soldier (a new thing, never before heard of) and because he was more conspicuous even to those who looked on from a distance because of the throng of his body-guard, he was the mark of many a missile; and when many of his attendants had been slain he withdrew, inter-changing the tasks of his tractable forces, and at the end of the day, though terrified by the grim spectacle neither of the dead nor of the wounded he at last allowed a brief time to be given to rest.

8. *Amida is attacked by the Persians over lofty mounds close to the walls, and is stormed. Marcellinus after the capture of the city escapes by night and flees to Antioch.*

1. But night put an end to the conflict; and having taken a nap during the brief period of rest,

sperata ira et dolore exundans, nec fas ullum prae
oculis habiturus, gentes in nos excitabat. Cumque
crematis operibus (ut docuimus), pugna per aggeres
celsos muris proximos temptaretur, ex aggestis
erectis intrinsecus, quantum facere nitique poterant,
nostri aequis viribus per ardua resistebant.

2. Et diu cruentum proelium stetit, nec metu
mortis quisquam ex aliqua parte a studio propug-
nandi removebatur, eoque producta contentione,
cum sors partium eventu regeretur indeclinabili,
diu laborata moles illa nostrorum, velut terrae
quodam tremore quassata [1] procubuit, et tamquam
itinerario aggere, vel superposito ponte, complana-
tum spatium, quod inter murum [2] congestamque
forinsecus struem hiabat, patefecit hostibus transi-
tum, nullis obicibus impeditum, et pars pleraque
militum deiectorum oppressa vel debilitata cessavit.[3]
3. Concursum est tamen undique ad propulsationem
periculi tam abrupti, et festinandi studio aliis im-
pedientibus alios, audacia hostium ipso successu
crescebat. 4. Accitis igitur regis imperio proelia-
toribus [4] universis, strictoque comminus ferro, cum
sanguis utrubique immensis caedibus funderetur,
oppilatae [5] sunt corporibus fossae latiorque via ideo
pandebatur, et concursu copiarum ardenti iam

---

[1] *quassata*, EW²G ; *quasina*, V.   [2] *murum*, G ;
muros, Kiessling ; *murorum*, V ; *murorum ambitum*, Her.
[3] *cessauit*, Clark ; *cessabat*, EBG ; *cessabit*, V.   [4] *proelia-
toribus*, vulgo ; *praedatoribus*, V.   [5] *oppilatae*,
Gronov. pater ; *oppletae*, W² ; *appellatae*, V.

the king, as soon as dawn appeared, boiling with
wrath and resentment and closing his eyes to all
right, aroused the barbarians against us, to win what
he hoped for ; and when the siege-works had been
burned (as I have shown) they attempted battle
over high mounds close to the walls, whereupon our
men erected heaps of earth on the inside as well as
they could with all their efforts, and under difficulties
resisted with equal vigour.

2. For a long time the sanguinary battle remained
undecided, and not a man anywhere through fear
of death gave up his ardour for defence ; and the
contest had reached a point when the fate of both
parties was governed by some unavoidable hap,
when that mound of ours, the result of long toil,
fell forward as if shattered by an earthquake.
Thus the gulf which yawned between the wall and
the heap built up outside was made a level plain,
as if by a causeway or a bridge built across it, and
opened to the enemy a passage blocked by no obstacles, while the greater part of the soldiers that
were thrown down ceased fighting, being either
crushed or worn out. 3. Nevertheless others rushed
to the spot from all sides, to avert so sudden a danger ;
but in their desire for haste they impeded one another,
while the boldness of the enemy was increased by
their very success. 4. Accordingly, by the king's
command all the warriors were summoned and there
was a hand-to-hand contest with drawn swords ;
blood streamed on all sides from the vast carnage ;
the trenches were blocked with bodies and so a
broader path was furnished. And now the city
was filled with the eager rush of the enemy's forces,

civitate oppleta, cum omnis defendendi vel fugiendi
spes esset abscisa, pecorum ritu armati et imbelles
sine sexus discrimine truncabantur.

5. Itaque vespera tenebrante, cum adhuc licet
iniqua reluctante fortuna, multitudo nostrorum
manu conserta distringeretur, in abstrusa quadam
parte oppidi cum duobus aliis latens, obscurae
praesidio noctis postica per quam nihil servabatur
evado, et squalentum peritia locorum, comitumque
adiutus celeritate, ad decimum lapidem tandem
perveni. 6. In qua statione lenius recreati, cum
ire protinus pergeremus, et incedendi nimietate
iam superarer, ut insuetus ingenuus, offendi dirum
aspectum, sed fatigato mihi lassitudine gravi levamen impendio tempestivum. 7. Fugaci equo nudo
et infreni calonum quidam sedens (ne labi possit)
ex more habenam qua ductabatur sinistra manu
artius illigavit, moxque decussus, vinculi nodum
abrumpere nequiens, per avia saltusque membratim
discerptus, iumentum exhaustum cursu pondere
cadaveris detinebat, cuius dorsuali [1] comprensi
servitio usus in tempore, cum eisdem sociis ad fontes
sulphureos aquarum, suapte natura calentium,
aegre perveni. 8. Et quia per aestum arida siti
reptantes, aquam diu quaeritando, profundum
bene [2] vidimus puteum, et neque descendendi prae

---

[1] *dorsuali,* Langen ; *dorsuatis,* V.   [2] *bene,* Lind. ;
paenae, V ; *pene,* WBG.

and since all hope of defence or of flight was cut off, armed and unarmed alike without distinction of sex were slaughtered like so many cattle.

5. Therefore when the darkness of evening was coming on and a large number of our soldiers, although adverse fortune still struggled against them, were joined in battle and thus kept busy, I hid with two others in a secluded part of the city, and under cover of a dark night made my escape through a postern gate at which no guard was kept ; and, aided by my familiarity with desert places and by the speed of my companions, I at length reached the tenth milestone. 6. At the post-house there we got a little rest, and when we were making ready to go farther and I was already unequal to the excessive walking, to which as a gentleman I was unused, I met a terrible sight, which however furnished me a most timely relief, worn out as I was by extreme weariness. 7. A groom, mounted on a runaway horse without saddle or bit, in order not to fall off had tied the rein by which, in the usual manner, the horse was guided, tightly to his left hand ; and afterwards, being thrown off and unable to loose the knot, he was torn limb from limb as he was dragged through desert places and woods, while the animal, exhausted by running, was held back by the weight of the dead body ; so I caught it and making timely use of the service of its back, with those same companions I with difficulty reached some springs of sulphurous water, naturally hot. 8. And since the heat had caused us parching thirst, for a long time we went slowly about looking for water. And we fortunately found a deep well,

altitudine, nec restium aderat copia, necessitate
docente postrema, indumenta lintea, quibus tegebamur,[1] in oblongos discidimus pannulos, unde
explicato fune ingenti, centonem quem sub galea
unus ferebat e nostris, ultimae aptavimus summitati,
qui per [2] funem coniectus, aquasque hauriens ad
peniculi modum, facile sitim qua urgebamur[3] ex-
stinxit. 9. Unde citi ferebamur ad flumen Euphra-
tem, ulteriorem ripam petituri per navem, quam
transfretandi causa iumenta et homines, in eo tractu
diuturna consuetudo locarat. 10. Ecce autem
Romanum agmen cum equestribus signis disiectum,
eminus cernimus, quod persequebatur multitudo
Persarum, incertum unde impetu tam repentino
terga viantum aggressa. 11. Quo exemplo terri-
genas illos, non sinibus terrae emersos, sed exuber-
anti pernicitate credimus natos, qui quoniam inopini per varia visebantur, σπαρτοί vocitati, humo
exsiluisse, vetustate rem [4] fabulosius extollente, sunt
aestimati. 12. Hoc malo [5] conciti, cum omne iam
esset in celeritate salutis praesidium, per dumeta
et silvas montes petimus celsiores, exindeque
Melitinam minoris Armeniae oppidum venimus,

---

[1] *tegebamur*, BGA ; *tegebatur*, V ; *lectulus tegebatur*, Clark.
[2] *qui per*, added in G (lac. indicated by Clark).   [3] *urgebamur*, Her. ; *hauriebamur*, EBG ; *hariebamur*, V.   [4] *rem*,
Novák, Her. ; *materiem*, Kiessling ; *ut cetera*, G ; *rem viatere*
(see note 5), V.   [5] *malo* (for *viatere*, Her.), put after
hoc by G.

---

[1] Damsté, reading *tegebatur*, thinks that the groom's
clothing is meant. But he seems to have been left some
distance behind, and it is doubtful whether his garments
were in a condition to use. Clark adds *lectulus*, but where
they would find a couch is not clear.

but it was neither possible to go down into it because of its depth, nor were there ropes at hand; so taught by extreme need, we cut the linen garments in which we were clad[1] into long strips and from them made a great rope. To the extreme end of this we tied the cap which one of us wore under his helmet, and when this was let down by the rope and sucked up the water after the manner of a sponge, it readily quenched the thirst by which we were tormented. 9. From there we quickly made our way to the Euphrates river, planning to cross to the farther bank by a boat which long continued custom had kept in that vicinity for the transport of men and animals. 10. But lo! we saw afar off a scattered band of Romans with cavalry standards, pursued by a great force of Persians; and we could not understand how they appeared so suddenly behind us as we went along. 11. Judging from this instance, we believe that the famous "sons of earth" did not come forth from the bosom of the land, but were born with extraordinary swiftness —those so-called sparti,[2] who, because they were seen unexpectedly in sundry places, were thought to have sprung from the earth, since antiquity gave the matter a fabulous origin. 12. Alarmed by this danger, since now all hope of life depended upon speed, through thickets and woods we made for the higher mountains, and came from there to the town of Melitina in lesser Armenia, where we

---

[2] Σπαρτοί (from σπείρω, "sow") was a name applied to the Thebans, because of the fable of the dragon's teeth sown by Cadmus. The Athenians, who claimed to be earthborn, were called αὐτόχθονες.

mox[1] repertum ducem comitatique[2] iam profecturum, Antiochiam revisimus insperati.[3]

9. *Amidae ex ducibus Rom. alii supplicio affecti, alii vincti. Craugasius Nisibenus desiderio uxoris captivae transfugit ad Persas.*

At Persae quia tendere iam introrsus autumno praecipiti haedorumque iniquo[4] sidere exorto prohibebantur, captivos agentes et praedas, remeare cogitabant ad sua. 2. Inter haec tamen funera direptionesque civitatis excisae, Aeliano comite et tribunis, quorum efficacia diu defensa sunt moenia, stragesque multiplicatae Persarum, patibulis sceleste suffixis, Iacobus et Caesius, numerarii apparitionis magistri equitum aliique protectores, post terga vinctis manibus ducebantur, Transtigritanis qui sollicita quaerebantur industria, nullo infimi summique discrimine, ad unum omnibus contruncatis.

3. Uxor vero Craugasii, quae retinens pudorem inviolatum, ut matrona nobilis colebatur, maerebat velut orbem alium sine marito visura, quamquam sperabat documentis praesentibus altiora. 4. In rem itaque consulens suam, et accidentia longe

---

[1] *mox*, Pet.; *ubi*, W[2], vulgo; *uos*, V.   [2] *comitatique*, Her.; *comitatumque*, Gardt.; *comitateque*, V.   [3] *insperati. At*, Her.; *interea Sapor et*, G; *iam impetrata re*, Clark; *iamimperator et*, V (*im*, added by V[2]).   [4] *haedorumque iniquo*, Pet.; *haedorum quem pro*, V.

---

[1] Three stars in the constellation Auriga; they rise at the beginning of October and bring stormy weather; cf. Horace, *Odes*, iii. **1, 28.**   [2] I.e. Persian deserters.

presently found and accompanied an officer, who was just on the point of leaving ; and so we returned unexpectedly to Antioch.

9. *At Amida some of the Roman leaders are executed, others imprisoned. Craugasius of Nisibis, through longing for his captive wife, deserts to the Persians.*

1. But the Persians, since the rapidly approaching end of autumn and the rising of the unfavourable constellation of the Kids [1] prevented them from marching farther inland, were thinking of returning to their own country with their prisoners and their booty. 2. But in the midst of the slaughter and pillage of the destroyed city Count Aelianus and the tribunes, by whose efficient service the walls had been so long defended and the losses of the Persians increased, were shamefully gibbeted ; Jacobus and Caesius, paymasters of the commander of the cavalry, and other officers of the bodyguard, were led off with their hands bound behind their backs ; and those who had come from across the Tigris [2] were hunted down with extreme care and butchered to a man, highest and lowest without distinction.

3. But the wife of Craugasius, who retained her chastity inviolate and was honoured as a woman of rank, grieved that she was likely to see another part of the world without her husband, although from present indications she had reason to hope for a loftier fortune. 4. Therefore, looking out for her own interests and foreseeing long beforehand what would happen, she was tormented by two-

ante prospiciens, anxietate bifaria stringebatur, viduitatem detestans et nuptias. Ideo familiarem suum perquam fidum, regionumque Mesopotamiae gnarum, per Izalam montem, inter castella praesidiaria duo Maride et Lorne introiturum, Nisibin occulte dimisit, mandatis arcanisque vitae secretioris, maritum exorans, ut auditis quae contigerint, veniret secum beate victurus. 5. Quibus conventis,[1] expeditus viator per saltuosos tramites et frutecta, Nisibin passibus citis ingressus, causatusque se domina nusquam visa, et forsitan interempta, data evadendi copia castris hostilibus abscessisse, et ideo ut vilis neglectus, docet Craugasium gesta ; moxque accepta fide quod si tuto licuerit, sequetur coniugem libens, evasit, exoptatum mulieri nuntium ferens, quae hoc cognito per Tamsaporem ducem supplicaverat regi, ut si daretur facultas, antequam Romanis excederet finibus, in potestatem suam iuberet propitius maritum adscisci.

6. Praeter spem itaque omnium digresso advena repentino, qui postliminio reversus, statim sine ullius evanuit conscientia, perculsus suspicione dux Cassianus, praesidentesque ibi proceres alii, minitantes ultima Craugasium incessebant, non sine eius

---

[1] *conventis*, Damsté, cf. Livy xxx. 43, 7 ; *contentus*, V ; *contextis*, Cornelissen, Petschenig.

---

[1] *Postliminium* is literally " a return behind the threshold"; *i.e.* a complete return home with restoration of one's former rank, privileges, and condition. The slave seems to have been captured by the Persians with his mistress, and pretended to have escaped from the enemy. On his return to Nisibis, he again became the slave of Craugasius.

fold anxiety, dreading both separation from her husband and marriage with another. Accordingly, she secretly sent a slave of hers, who was of tried fidelity and acquainted with the regions of Mesopotamia, to go over Mount Izala between the strongholds of Maride and Lorne to Nisibis, and take a message to her husband and certain tokens of their more private life, begging him that on hearing what had happened he should come to live happily with her. 5. When this had been arranged, the messenger, being lightly equipped, made his way with quick pace through forest paths and thickets and entered Nisibis. There giving out that he had seen his mistress nowhere, that she was perhaps slain, and that he himself, taking advantage of an opportunity to escape, had fled from the enemy's camp, he was accordingly disregarded as of no consequence. Thereupon he told Craugasius what had happened and then, after receiving assurance that if it could safely be done he would gladly follow his wife, the messenger departed, bearing to the woman the desired news. She on hearing it begged the king through his general Tamsapor that, if the opportunity offered before he left the Roman territory, he would graciously give orders that her husband be received under his protection.

6. The sudden departure, contrary to every one's expectation, of the stranger, who had returned by the right of postliminium [1] and immediately vanished without anyone's knowledge, aroused the suspicions of the general Cassianus and the other important officials in Nisibis, who assailed Craugasius with dire threats, loudly insisting that the man had

voluntate vel venisse vel abisse hominem clamitantes. 7. Qui proditoris[1] metuens crimen, im-
pendioque sollicitus, ne transitione perfugae uxor
eius superesse doceretur et tractari piissime, per
simulationem matrimonium alterius splendidae virginis affectavit. Et velut paraturus necessaria
convivio nuptiali, egressus ad villam octavo lapide
ab urbe distantem, concito equo ad Persarum
vastatorium globum, quem didicerat adventare,
confugit, susceptusque aventer, qui esset ex his
cognitus quae loquebatur, Tamsapori post diem
traditur quintum, perque eum regi oblatus, opibus
et necessitudine omni recuperata cum coniuge,
quam paucos post menses amiserat, erat[2] secundi
loci post Antoninum, ut ait poeta praeclarus " longo
proximus intervallo." 8. Ille enim ingenio et usu
rerum diuturno firmatus, consiliis validis sufficiebat
in cuncta quae conabatur, hic natura simplicior,
nominis tamen itidem pervulgati. Et haec quidem
haut diu postea contigerunt.

9. Rex vero licet securitatem praeferens[3] vultu,
exultansque specie tenus urbis excidio videbatur,
profundo tamen animi graviter aestuabat, reputans
in obsidionalibus malis saepe luctuosas se pertulisse
iacturas multoque ampliores se ipsum populos perdi-
disse, quam e nostris ceperat vivos, vel certe per
diversas fuderat pugnas, ut apud Nisibin aliquotiens
evenit, et Singaram, parique modo cum septuaginta

---

[1] *proditoris*, W[2]. Lind. ; *proditores*, V.   [2] *amiserat*,
erat, Her. ; *amisit*, *erat*, Val. ; *amiserat*, V.   [3] *prae-*
ferens, Val., Bentley ; *referens*, V[2] (*refens*, V).

---

[1] Cf. Virgil, *Aen.* v. 320.

neither come nor gone without his wish. 7. He, then, fearing a charge of treason and greatly troubled lest through the coming of the deserter it should become known that his wife was alive and treated with great respect, as a blind sought marriage with another, a maiden of high rank, and, under pretence of preparing what was needed for the wedding-banquet, went to a country house of his eight miles distant from the city; then, at full gallop he fled to a band of Persian pillagers that he had learned to be approaching. He was received with open arms, being recognized from the story that he told, and five days later was brought to Tamsapor, and by him taken to the king. And after recovering his property and all his kindred, as well as his wife, whom he had lost after a few months, he held the second place after Antoninus, but was, as the eminent poet says, " next by a long interval." [1] 8. For Antoninus, aided by his talent and his long experience of the world, had available plans at hand for all his enterprises, while Craugasius was by nature most simple, yet of an equally celebrated reputation. And these things happened not long afterward.[2]

9. But the king, although making a show of ease of mind in his expression, and to all appearance seeming to exult in the destruction of the city, yet in the depths of his heart was greatly troubled, recalling that in unfortunate sieges he had often suffered sad losses, and had sacrificed far more men himself than he had taken alive of ours, or at any rate had killed in the various battles, as happened several times at Nisibis and at Singara; and in the

[1] That is, not long after the fall of Amida.

519

tresque dies Amidam multitudine circumsedisset armorum, triginta milia perdidit bellatorum, quae paulo postea per Discenen tribunum et notarium numerata sunt, hac discretione facilius, quod nostrorum cadavera mox caesorum fatiscunt ac [1] diffluunt,[2] adeo ut nullius mortui facies post quatriduum agnoscatur, interfectorum vero Persarum inarescunt in modum stipitum corpora, ut nec liquentibus membris, nec sanie perfusa, madescant, quod vita parcior facit, et ubi nascuntur exustae caloribus terrae.

10. *Plebs Romana inopiam frumenti metuens, seditiones movet.*

1. Dum haec per varios turbines in Orientis extimo festinantur, difficultatem adventantis inopiae frumentorum urbs verebatur aeterna, vique minacissimae plebis, famem ultimum malorum omnium exspectantis, subinde Tertullus vexabatur, ea tempestate praefectus, irrationabiliter plane ; nec enim per eum steterat quo minus tempore congruo alimenta navibus veherentur, quas maris casus asperiores solitis ventorumque procellae reflantium, delatas in proximos sinus, introire portum Augusti discriminum magnitudine perterrebant. 2. Quocirca idem saepe praefectus seditionibus agitatus,

---

[1] *ac*, Kellerbauer ; *et*, EBG ; V, see note 2.   [2] *diffluunt*, C. F. W. Müller ; *fatiscunctaede fluunt* (*nc* from *m*, V[2]), V.

---

[1] Prefect of the City.

same way, when he had invested Amida for seventy-
three days with a great force of armed men, he lost
30,000 warriors, as was reckoned a little later by
Discenes, a tribune and secretary, the more readily
for this difference : that the corpses of our men
soon after they are slain fall apart and waste away,
to such a degree that the face of no dead man is
recognisable after four days, but the bodies of the
slain Persians dry up like tree-trunks, without
their limbs wasting or becoming moist with corruption—a fact due to their more frugal life and the
dry heat of their native country.

10. *The Roman commons rebel, fearing a scarcity of
grain.*

1. While these storms were swiftly passing one
after the other in the extreme East, the eternal city
was fearing the disaster of a coming shortage of
grain, and from time to time Tertullus, who was
prefect[1] at the time, was assailed by the violent
threats of the commons, as they anticipated famine,
the worst of all ills ; and this was utterly unreason-
able, since it was no fault of his that food was not
brought at the proper time in the ships, which
unusually rough weather at sea and adverse gales of
wind drove to the nearest harbours, and by the
greatness of the danger kept them from entering
the Port of Augustus.[2] 2. Therefore that same
prefect, since he had often been disquieted by up-
risings, and the common people, in fear of imminent

[2] The hexagonal basin at Ostia built by Trajan ; also
called *Portus urbis,* or simply *Portus.*

521

ac plebe iam saeviente immanius, quoniam[1] verebatur impendens exitium, ab omni spe tuendae
salutis exclusus, ut aestimabat, tumultuanti acriter
populo, sed accidentia considerare sueto prudenter,
obiecit parvulos filios, et lacrimans 3. " En "
inquit " cives vestri (procul omen dii caelestes
avertant!) eadem perlaturi vobiscum, ni fortuna
affulserit laetior. Si itaque his abolitis nil triste
accidere posse existimatis, praesto in potestate
sunt vestra." Qua miseratione vulgus ad clementiam[2] suapte natura proclive, lenitum conticuit,
aequanimiter venturam operiens sortem. 4. Moxque divini arbitrio numinis, quod auxit ab incunabulis Romam, perpetuamque fore spopondit,[3] dum
Tertullus apud Ostia in aede sacrificat Castorum,
tranquillitas mare mollivit, mutatoque in austrum
placidum vento, velificatione plena portum naves
ingressae, frumentis horrea referserunt.

11. *Limigantes Sarmatae, dum simulata petitione*
pacis deceptum imperatorem invadunt, maxima
suorum strage reprimuntur.

1. Inter haec ita ambigua, Constantium Sirmi
etiam tum hiberna quiete curantem, permovebant
nuntii metuendi et graves, indicantes id quod tunc
magnopere formidabat, Limigantes Sarmatas, quos
expulisse paternis avitisque sedibus dominos suos
ante monstravimus, paulatim posthabitis locis

---

[1] *quoniam,* Clark ; *quam,* V. [2] *clementiam,* EG ;
clementia, V ; *clementiora,* Her. [3] *spopondit,* E,
Bentley, Haupt ; *spondit,* V.

[1] xvii. **12,** 18.

destruction, were now raging still more cruelly, being shut off from all hope of saving his life, as he thought, held out his little sons to the wildly riotous populace, who had however been wont to take a sensible view of such accidents, and said with tears :
3. "Behold your fellow citizens, who with you (but may the gods of heaven avert the omen!) will endure the same fate, unless a happier fortune shine upon us. If therefore you think that by the destruction of these no heavy calamity can befall you, here they are in your power." Through pity at this sight the mob, of their own nature inclined to mercy, was appeased and held its peace, awaiting with patience the fortune that should come. 4. And presently by the will of the divine power that gave increase to Rome from its cradle and promised that it should last forever, while Tertullus was sacrificing in the temple of Castor and Pollux at Ostia, a calm smoothed the sea, the wind changed to a gentle southern breeze, and the ships entered the harbour under full sail and again crammed the storehouses with grain.

11. *The Limigantes of Sarmatia deceive the emperor by a pretended request for peace and attack him; but they are repulsed with great slaughter.*

1. In the midst of such troubles Constantius, who was still enjoying his winter rest at Sirmium, was disturbed by fearful and serious news, informing him of what he then greatly dreaded, namely, that the Sarmatian Limigantes, who (as we have already pointed out)[1] had driven their masters from their ancestral abodes, having gradually abandoned the

523

quae eis anno praeterito utiliter sunt destinata,
ne (ut sunt versabiles) aliquid molirentur inicum,[1]
regiones confines limitibus occupasse, vagarique
licentius genuino more (ni pellerentur,) omnia
turbaturos.

2. Quae superbius incitanda prope diem imperator dilato negotio credens, coacta undique multitudine militis ad bella promptissimi, nec dum
adulto vere ad procinctum egressus est gemina consideratione alacrior, quod expletus praedarum
opimitate exercitus, aestate nuper emensa, similium
spe fidenter in effectus animabitur prosperos, quodque Anatolio regente tunc per Illyricum praefecturam, necessaria cuncta, vel ante tempus coacta,
sine ullius dispendiis affluebant. 3. Nec enim
dispositionibus umquam alterius praefecturae (ut
inter omnes constat) ad praesens Arctoae provinciae
bonis omnibus floruerunt, correctione titubantium
benevola et sollerti, vehiculariae rei iacturis ingentibus, quae clausere domos innumeras, et censuali
professione speciosa fiducia relevatae; indemnesque
deinde et innoxii earum incolae partium, querellarum
sopitis materiis viverent, ni postea exquisitorum
detestanda nomina titulorum, per offerentes sus-
cipientesque criminose in maius exaggerata, his pro-
pugnare sibi nitentibus potestates, illis attenuatis

---

[1] *inicum* Haupt; *incon,* V[1]; *incum,* V[2].

---

[1] He was a Syrian from Berytus, who came to Rome
and filled all the grades of rank up to the prefecture. He
was noted for his energy, his eloquence, and his high
character.

places which for the public good had been assigned
them the year before for fear that they (as they are
inconstant) might attempt some wrongful act, had
seized upon the regions bordering upon their frontiers, were ranging freely in their native fashion, and
unless they were driven back would cause general
confusion.

2. The emperor, believing that these outrages
would soon be pushed to greater heights if the matter
were postponed, assembled from every quarter a
great number of soldiers most eager for war and took
the field before spring had yet fully come ; he was
the more eager for action from two considerations :
first, because an army glutted with the rich booty
of the past summer, by the hope of similar booty
would be confidently encouraged to achieve successful enterprises, and because under Anatolius,[1] who
at that time was prefect of Illyricum, all necessary
supplies had been brought together even ahead of
time and were still coming in without trouble to
anyone. 3. For never under the management of
any other prefect up to the present time, as was
generally agreed, had the northern provinces so
abounded in all blessings, since by his kindly and
skilful correction of abuses they were relieved of
the great cost of the courier-service, which had
closed homes without number, and there was considerable hope of freedom from the income tax. The
dwellers in those parts might have lived thereafter
happy and untroubled without grounds for complaint, had not later the most hated forms of taxation that could be imagined, criminally amplified
by both tax-payers and tax-collectors, since the

omnium opibus, se fore sperantibus tutos, ad usque proscriptiones miserorumque suspendia pervenerunt.

4. Rem igitur emendaturus urgentem, profectus cum instrumentis ambitiosis, imperator (ut dictum est) Valeriam venit, partem quondam Pannoniae, sed ad honorem Valeriae Diocletiani filiae et institutam et ita cognominatam, sub pellibusque exercitu diffuso per Histri fluminis margines, barbaros observabat ante adventum suum amicitiae velamento, Pannonias furtim vastandas, invadere hiemis durissimo cogitantes, cum nec dum solutae vernis caloribus nives amnem undique pervium faciunt, nostrique pruinis subdivales moras difficile tolerabunt.

5. Confestim itaque missis ad Limigantes duobus tribunis cum interpretibus singulis, explorabat modestius percunctando, quam ob rem relictis laribus post pacem et foedera petentibus attributa,[1] ita palarentur per [2] varia, limitesque contra interdicta pulsarent. 6. Qui vana quaedam causantes et irrita, pavore adigente mentiri, principem exorabant in veniam, obsecrantes ut simultate abolita, transmisso flumine ad eum venire permitterentur, docturi quae sustinerent incommoda, paratique intra spatia orbis Romani (si id placuerit) terras

---

[1] *adtributa*, Eyssen.; *adtributis*, V.   [2] *per*, added by C. F. W. Müller, Cornelissen ; V omits.

---

[1] The Danube ; usually its lower course, but used also of the whole river.

latter hoped to gain the protection of the governors in their efforts and the former hoped for safety if all were impoverished, resulted finally in proscriptions and the suicide of the wretched victims.

4. Well, then, the emperor (as I have said), in order to improve the pressing situation, set out with splendid equipment and came to Valeria, once a part of Pannonia, but made into a province and named in honour of Valeria, the daughter of Diocletian. There, with his army encamped along the banks of the river Hister,[1] he watched the savages, who before his coming, under pretext of friendship but really intending secretly to devastate the country, were planning to enter Pannonia in the dead of winter, when the snows are not yet melted by the warmth of spring and so the river can be crossed everywhere, and when our soldiers would with difficulty, because of the frosts, endure life in the open.

5. Then having quickly sent two tribunes to the Limigantes, each with an interpreter, by courteous questioning he tried to find out why they had left their homes after the treaty of peace which had been granted to them at their own request, and were thus roaming at large and disturbing the frontiers, notwithstanding orders to the contrary. 6. They gave some frivolous and unsatisfactory excuses, since fear forced them to lie, and begged for pardon, entreating the emperor to forget his anger and allow them to cross the river and come to him, in order to inform him of the difficulties that they were suffering. They were ready to take up far distant lands, but within the compass of the Roman world,

527

suscipere longe discretas, ut diuturno otio involuti,
et Quietem colentes (tamquam salutarem deam)
tributariorum onera subirent et nomen.

7. His post reditum tribunorum compertis, imperator exsultans, ut negotio quod rebatur inexplicabile
sine ullo pulvere consummando, cunctos admisit,
aviditate plus habendi incensus, quam adulatorum
cohors augebat, id sine modo strepentium, quod
externis sopitis, et ubique pace composita, prole-
tarios lucrabitur plures, et tirocinia cogere poterit
validissima : aurum quippe gratanter provinciales
pro [1] corporibus dabunt, quae spes rem Romanam
aliquotiens aggravavit.[2] 8. Proinde vallo prope
Acimincum locato, celsoque aggere in speciem
tribunalis erecto, naves vehentes quosdam legionarios
expeditos alveum fluminis proximum ripis observare
sunt iussae, cum Innocentio quodam agrimensore,
huius auctore consilii, ut si barbaros tumultuare
sensissent, aliorsum intentos post terga pervaderent
improvisi. 9. Quae Limigantes licet properari sentirent, nihil tamen praeter preces [3] fingentes, stabant

[1] *pro*, added by Reinesius, Mommsen ; V omits.
[2] *adgrauauit*, G ; *adgrauit*, V ; *exaggerauit*, Pet.
[3] *praeter preces*, Val. ; *praeces*, V.

---

[1] I.e. they would rather contribute money than personal
service or recruits.

528

if he would allow them, in order that wrapped in lasting repose and worshipping Quiet (as a saving goddess), they might submit to the burdens and the name of tributaries.

7. When this was known after the return of the tribunes, the emperor, exulting in the accomplishment without any toil of a task which he thought insuperable, admitted them all, being inflamed with the desire for greater gain, which his crew of flatterers increased by constantly dinning it into his ears that now that foreign troubles were quieted, and peace made everywhere, he would gain more child-producing subjects and be able to muster a strong force of recruits; for the provincials are glad to contribute gold to save their bodies,[1] a hope which has more than once proved disastrous to the Roman state.[2] 8. Accordingly, having placed a rampart near Acimincum[3] and erected a high mound in the manner of a tribunal, ships carrying some light-armed legionaries were ordered to patrol the channel of the river near the banks, with one Innocentius, a field-measurer, who had recommended the plan, in order that, if they should see the savages beginning disorder, they might attack them in the rear, when their attention was turned elsewhere. 9. But although the Limigantes knew that these plans were being hastened, yet they stood with bared heads, as if composing nothing save entreaties,

[2] It was in fact this hope that led the Romans to allow the Goths to cross the Danube, and thus brought on the defeat at Adrianople in 378; see xxxi., **4**, 4, *pro militari supplemento quod provinciatim annuum pendebatur, thesauris accederet auri cumulus magnus.*

[3] A city of Pannonia.

incurvi, longe alia quam quae gestu praeferebant
et verbis altis mentibus perpensantes.

10. Visoque imperatore ex alto suggestu, iam
sermonem parante lenissimum, meditanteque alloqui velut morigeros iam futuros, quidam ex illis,
furore percitus truci, calceo suo in tribunal contorto,
" Marha marha " (quod est apud eos signum belli-
cum) exclamavit, eumque secuta incondita multitudo, vexillo elato repente barbarico, ululans ferum,
in ipsum principem ferebatur. 11. Qui cum ex alto
despiciens, plena omnia discurrentis turbae cum
missilibus vidisset, retectisque gladiis et verrutis iam
propinquante [1] pernicie, externis mixtus et suis,
ignotusque dux esset an miles, quia neque cunctandi
aderat tempus, neque cessandi, equo veloci impositus,
cursu effuso evasit. 12. Stipatores tamen pauci
dum ignis more inundantes conabantur arcere, aut
vulnerati interierunt, aut ponderibus superruentium
solis afflicti, sellaque regalis cum aureo pulvinari,
nullo vetante, direpta est.

13. Mox autem audito, quod ad ultimum paene
tractus exitium, in abrupto staret adhuc imperator,
antiquissimum omnium exercitus ratus eum iuvare
(nondum enim exemptum periculis aestimavit
salutis) fastu fidentior, licet ob procursionem subitam semitectus, sonorum et Martium frendens,

---

[1] *propinquante pernicie*, Clark, cf. xxii. 3, 5 ; *propinquam
perniciem*, W[2] G ; *propinquam pernicie*, V.

530

but meditating deep in their hearts quite other things than their attitude and their words suggested. 10. And when the emperor was seen on the high tribunal and was already preparing to deliver a most mild address, intending to speak to them as future obedient subjects, one of their number, struck with savage madness, hurling his shoe at the tribunal, shouted " Marha, marha " (which is their warcry), and the rude crowd following him suddenly raised a barbarian banner and with savage howls rushed upon the emperor himself. 11. He, looking down from his high place and seeing everything filled with a mob running about with missiles, and death already imminent from their drawn swords and javelins, in the midst as he was of the enemy and of his own men, and with nothing to indicate whether he was a general or a common soldier, since there was no time for hesitation or delay mounted a swift horse and galloped off at full speed. 12. However, a few of his attendants, while they were trying to keep off the savages, who poured upon them like a stream of fire, were either wounded to the death or trampled down by the mere weight of those who rushed over them ; and the royal seat with its golden cushion was seized without resistance.

13. But when presently it was heard that the emperor had all but been drawn into extreme peril and was not yet on safe ground, the soldiers considered it their first duty to aid him (for they thought him not yet free from danger of death) ; so, with greater confidence because of their contempt of the enemy, although the attack was so

barbarorum mori obstinatorum catervis semet
immersit. 14. Et quia virtute dedecus purgatura,
ardens copia nostrorum erupit, iras in hostem
perfidum parans, obvia quaeque obtruncabat, sine
parsimonia vivos conculcans et semineces et per-
emptos ; et antequam exsatiaret caedibus barbaricis
manus, acervi constipati sunt mortuorum. 15.
Urgebantur enim rebelles, aliis trucidatis, aliis terrore disiectis, quorum pars spem vitae cassis precibus
usurpando multiplicatis ictibus caedebantur, postque
deletos omnes in receptum canentibus lituis, nostri
quoque licet rari videbantur exanimes, quos impetus
conculcaverat vehemens, aut furori resistentes
hostili, lateraque nudantes intecta, ordo fatalis
absumpsit. 16. Mors tamen eminuit inter alios
Cellae Scutariorum tribuni, qui inter confligendi
exordia, primus omnium in medios semet [1] Sarmatarum globos immisit.

17. Post quae tam saeva, digestis pro securitate
limitum [2] quae rationes monebant urgentes, Constantius Sirmium redit, ferens de hoste fallaci
vindictam, et maturatis quae necessitates temporis
poscebant instantes, egressus exinde Constantinopolim petit, ut Orienti iam proximus, cladibus apud

---

[1] *se,* added by G (*semet,* Novák) before *immisit ;* **V** omits.
[2] *limitum,* **Val.** ; *militum,* **V.**

sudden that they were only partly armed, with a loud battlecry they plunged into the bands of the savages, who were regardless of their lives. 14. And so eagerly did our forces rush forth in their desire to wipe out the disgrace by valour, at the same time venting their wrath on the treacherous foe, that they butchered everything in their way, trampling under foot without mercy the living, as well as those dying or dead; and before their hands were sated with slaughter of the savages, the dead lay piled in heaps. 15. For the rebels were completely overthrown, some being slain, others fleeing in terror in all directions; and a part of them, who hoped to save their lives by vain entreaties, were cut down by repeated strokes. And after all had been killed and the trumpets were sounding the recall, some of our men also, though few, were found among the dead, either trampled under foot in the fierce attack or, when they resisted the fury of the enemy and exposed their unprotected sides, destroyed by the fatal course of destiny. 16. But conspicuous above the rest was the death of Cella, tribune of the Targeteers, who at the beginning of the fight was first to rush into the thick of the Sarmatian forces.

17. After this cruel carnage Constantius, having made such arrangements for the safety of the frontiers as considerations of urgency recommended, returned to Sirmium after taking vengeance on a treacherous foe. Then, having quickly attended to what the pressing necessities of the time required, he set out from there and went to Constantinople, in order that being now nearer the Orient he might remedy the disaster which he had suffered at Amida,

Amidam mederetur acceptis, et redintegrato supple-
mentis exercitu, impetus regis Persarum pari virium
robore cohiberet, quem constabat (ni caelestis ratio
impensiorque repelleret cura multorum) Mesopotamia relicta post terga, per extenta spatia signa
moturum.

12. *Laesae maiestatis multi arcessiti atque damnati.*

1. Inter has tamen sollicitudines, velut ex re-
cepto quodam antiquitus more, ad vicem bellorum
civilium, inflabant litui quaedam colorata laesae
crimina maiestatis, quorum exsecutor et administer,
saepe dictus Tartareus [1] ille notarius missus est
Paulus, qui peritus artium cruentarum, ut lanista
ex commerciis libitinae vel ludi, ipse quoque ex
eculeo vel carnifice quaestum fructumque captabat.
2. Ut enim erat obstinatum fixumque eius propositum ad laedendum, ita nec furtis abstinuit, inno-
centibus exitialis causas affingens,[2] dum in calami-
tosis stipendiis versaretur.
3. Materiam autem in infinitum quaestionibus
extendendis dedit occasio vilis et parva. Oppidum
est Abydum in Thebaidis partis situm extremo.[3]
Hic Besae dei localiter appellati, oraculum quondam

---

[1] *dictus Tartareus,* Her. (*dictus,* W[2]) ; *dictandus,* Val. ;
dictaneus, V ; *dictus Catena,* Langen (cf. xiv. 5, 8 ; xv.
3, 4). [2] *adfingens dum,* G ; *adfringen* *** *dum* (from
dum dum), V ; *adfingendo,* Cornelissen. [3] *partis situm
extremo,* Pet. ; *partis dum extremo,* V ; *parte situm extrema,*
AG.

---

[1] "The Diabolical," from Tartarus. He is called
Catena in xiv. **5,** 8 and xv. **3,** 4.

and by supplying the army there with reinforcements might with an equally strong force check the inroads of the Persian king; for it was clear that the latter (unless the will of heaven and the supreme efforts of many men repelled him) would leave Mesopotamia behind and seek a wider field for his arms.

12. *Many are tried and condemned for high treason.*

1. Yet in the midst of these anxieties, as if it were prescribed by some ancient custom, in place of civil wars the trumpets sounded for alleged cases of high treason; and to investigate and punish these there was sent that notorious state-secretary Paulus, often called Tartareus.[1] He was skilled in the work of bloodshed, and just as a trainer of gladiators seeks profit and emolument from the traffic in funerals [2] and festivals, so did he from the rack or the executioner. 2. Therefore, as his determination to do harm was fixed and obstinate, he did not refrain from secret fraud, devising fatal charges against innocent persons, provided only he might continue his pernicious traffic.

3. Moreover, a slight and trivial occasion gave opportunity to extend his inquisitions indefinitely. There is a town called Abydum, situated in the remotest part of the Thebaïs [3]; here the oracle of a god called in that place. Besa in days of old revealed the future and was wont to be honoured in

---

[2] Gladiatorial shows were given at the funerals of distinguished Romans, as well as at festivals.

[3] A nome, or province, of Egypt.

futura pandebat, priscis circumiacentium regionum
caerimoniis solitum coli. 4. Et quoniam quidam
praesentes, pars per alios desideriorum indice missa
scriptura, supplicationibus expresse conceptis, consulta numinum scitabantur, chartulae sive [1] mem-
branae, continentes quae petebantur, post data
quoque responsa, interdum remanebant in fano.
5. Ex his aliqua ad imperatorem maligne sunt missa,
qui (ut erat angusti pectoris [2]) obsurdescens in aliis
etiam nimium seriis, in hoc titulo ima (quod aiunt)
auricula mollior, et suspicax et minutus, acri felle
concaluit ; statimque ad Orientem ocius ire monuit
Paulum, potestate delata, ut instar ducis rerum
experientia clari, ad arbitrium suum audiri efficeret
causas. 6. Datumque est negotium Modesto (etiam
tum per Orientem comiti) apto ad haec et similia.
Hermogenes enim Ponticus ea tempestate praefectus praetorio, ut lenioris ingenii, spernebatur.

7. Perrexit (ut praeceptum est) Paulus funesti
furoris et anhelitus plenus, dataque calumniae
indulgentia plurimis,[3] ducebantur ab orbe prope
terrarum, iuxta nobiles et obscuri, quorum aliquos
vinculorum afflixerant nexus, alios claustra poenalia
consumpserunt. 8. Et electa est spectatrix sup-
pliciorum feralium civitas in Palaestina Scythopolis,
gemina ratione visa magis omnibus opportuna, quod

---

[1] *sive,* Clark ; *seu,* EBG ; *saevi,* V.   [2] *angusti pectoris,*
G ; *augusti rectoris,* V.   [3] *plurimis,* Clark with V, corr.
l from *r* ; *plurimi,* E²BG.

---

[1] So also at the temple of Jupiter at Baalbek.

the ancient ceremonials of the adjacent regions.
4. And since some in person, a part through others,
by sending a written list of their desires,[1] inquired
the will of the deities after definitely stating their
requests, the papers or parchments containing their
petitions sometimes remained in the shrine even
after the replies had been given. 5. Some of these
were with malicious intent sent to the emperor
who (being narrow-minded), although deaf to other
very serious matters, on this point was softer than
an earlobe,[2] as the proverb has it ; and being
suspicious and petty, he grew furiously angry. At
once he admonished Paulus to proceed quickly to
the Orient, conferring on him, as a leader renowned
for his experience, the power of conducting trials
according to his good pleasure. 6. A commission was
also given to Modestus (at that very time count in the
Orient) a man fitted for these and similar affairs.
For Hermogenes of Pontus, at that time praetorian
prefect, was rejected as being of too mild a temper.

7. Off went Paulus (as he was ordered) in panting
haste and teeming with deadly fury, and since free
rein was given to general calumny, men were brought
in from almost the whole world, noble and obscure
alike ; and some of them were bowed down with
the weight of chains, others wasted away from the
agony of imprisonment. 8. As the theatre of torture
and death Scythopolis was chosen, a city of Palestine
which for two reasons seemed more suitable than
any other : because it is more secluded, and because
it is midway between Antioch and Alexandria,

[2] Cf. Cic., Q.F. ii. 154, *me . . . fore auricula infima
scito molliorem ;* Catull. 25, 2 (*mollior*) *imula auricilla.*

secretior est [1] et inter Antiochiam Alexandriamque
media, unde multi plerumque ad crimina trahebantur.
9. Ductus est itaque inter primos Simplicius,
Philippi filius, ex praefecto et consule, reus hac
gratia postulatus, quod super adipiscendo in-
terrogasse dicebatur imperio, perque elogium principis torqueri praeceptus, qui in his casibus nec
peccatum aliquando pietati dederat nec erratum,
fato quodam arcente, corpore immaculato lata [2] fuga
damnatus est. 10. Dein Parnasius (ex praefecto
Aegypti) homo simplicium morum, eo [3] adductus [4]
periculi, ut pronuntiaretur capitis reus, itidem pulsus
est in exsilium, saepe auditus multo antehac rettulisse,
quod cum Patras Achaicum oppidum, ubi genitus
habuit larem, impetrandae causa cuiusdam relin-
queret potestatis, per quietem deducentia se habitus
tragici figmenta viderat multa. 11. Andronicus
postea, studiis liberalibus et claritudine carminum
notus, in iudicium introductus cum secura mente
nullis suspicionibus urgeretur, purgando semet [5]
fidentius, absolutus est. 12. Demetrius itidem
Cythras cognomento philosophus, grandaevus quidem sed [6] corpore durus et animo, sacrificasse aliquotiens confutatus, infitiari non potuit, asserens

---

[1] *est* (before or after *secretior*), Novák, Pet.; V omits.
[2] *lata*, V; G omits; Cornelissen del. as dittography. [3] *eo*,
added in NG; V omits. [4] *adductus*, Clark, cf. xiv.
11, 8; *deductus*, V (for which Her. cites Val. Max., viii.
1, abs. 6). [5] *semet*, Bentley, Günther; *semper et*, V.
[6] *sed*, N[2] G; *set*, Hermann; *et*, V.

---

[1] On *elogium*, see p. 31, note 3.

from which cities the greater number were brought to meet charges.

9. Among the first, then, to be summoned was Simplicius, son of Philippus, a former prefect and consul, who was indicted for the reason that he had (as was said) inquired about gaining imperial power; and by a note [1] of the emperor, who in such cases never condoned a fault or an error because of loyal service, he was ordered to be tortured; but, protected by some fate, he was banished to a stated place,[2] but with a whole skin. 10. Then Parnasius (ex-prefect of Egypt), a man of simple character, was brought into such peril that he was tried for his life, but he likewise was sent into exile; he had often been heard to say long before this, that when, for the purpose of gaining a certain office, he left Patrae, a town of Achaia where he was born and had his home, he had dreamt that many shadowy figures in tragic garb escorted him. 11. Later Andronicus, known for his liberal studies and the fame of his poems, was haled into court; but since he had a clear conscience, was under no suspicion, and most confidently asserted his innocence, he was acquitted. 12. Also Demetrius, surnamed Cythras, a philosopher of advanced years, it is true, but hardy of body and mind, being charged with offering sacrifice [3] several times, could not deny it;

[2] According to Marcianus, *Digest*, xlviii. 22, 5, there were three kinds of exile; exclusion from certain places specifically named (*liberum exsilium*); confinement to a designated place (*lata fuga*); banishment to an island (*insulae vinculum*).

[3] To Besa.

539

propitiandi causa numinis haec a prima adulescentia factitasse, non temptandi sublimiora scrutatis ; nec enim quemquam id noverat affectare. Diu itaque adhaerens eculeo, cum fiducia gravi fundatus, nequaquam varians eadem oraret intrepidus, Alexandriam (unde oriebatur) innoxius abire permissus est.

13. Et hos quidem aliosque paucos aequa sors, veritatis adiutrix, periculis eximit abruptis. Criminibus vero serpentibus latius, per implicatos nexus sine fine distentos, quidam corporibus laniatis exstinguebantur, alii poenis ulterioribus damnati sunt bonis ereptis, Paulo succentore fabularum crudelium, quasi e[1] promptuaria cella, fallaciarum et nocendi species suggerente complures, cuius ex nutu (prope dixerim) pendebat incedentium[2] omnium salus. 14. Nam siqui remedia quartanae vel doloris alterius collo gestaret, sive per monumentum transisse vesperi, malivolorum argueretur indiciis, ut veneficus, sepulchrorumque horrores, et errantium ibidem[3] animarum ludibria colligens vana, pronuntiatus reus capitis interibat. 15. Et prorsus ita res agebatur, quasi Clarum, Dodonaeas arbores, et effata Delphorum olim sollemnia, in imperatoris

---

[1] *quasi e*, W, Lind. ; *quas ce*, V.   [2] *incedentium*, V ; *incidentium*, Clark, cf. xxvi. 10, 10.   [3] *ibidem*, Lind. ; *intidem*, V.

---

[1] A city of Ionia near Colophon, the seat of a famous oracle of Apollo.

he declared, however, that he had done so from early youth for the purpose of propitiating the deity, not of trying to reach a higher station by his investigations ; for he did not know of anyone who had such aspirations. Therefore, after being long kept upon the rack, supported by his firm confidence he fearlessly made the same plea without variation ; whereupon he was allowed to go without further harm to his native city of Alexandria.

13. These and a few others a just fate in alliance with truth saved from imminent danger. But as these charges made their way further by entangling snares extended endlessly, some died from the mangling of their bodies, others were condemned to further punishment and had their goods seized, while Paulus was the prompter of these scenes of cruelty, supplying as if from a storehouse many kinds of deception and cruelty ; and on his nod (I might almost say) depended the life of all who walk the earth. 14. For if anyone wore on his neck an amulet against the quartan ague or any other complaint, or was accused by the testimony of the evil-disposed of passing by a grave in the evening, on the ground that he was a dealer in poisons, or a gatherer of the horrors of tombs and the vain illusions of the ghosts that walk there, he was condemned to capital punishment and so perished. 15. In fact, the matter was handled exactly as if many men had importuned Claros,[1] the oaks of Dodona,[2] and the once famous oracles of Delphi with regard

[2] A city of Epirus, in the country of the Molossians, where there was in an oak grove a celebrated temple and oracle of Zeus.

exitium sollicitaverint multi. 16. Unde blanditiarum taetra commenta, palatina cohors exquisite
confingens, immunem eum fore malorum communium asserebat, fatum eius vigens semper et
praesens in abolendis adversa conantibus eluxisse,
vocibus magnis exclamans.

17. Et inquisitum in haec negotia fortius, nemo
qui quidem recte sapiat reprehendet. Nec enim
abnuimus salutem legitimi principis, propugnatoris
bonorum et defensoris, unde salus quaeritur aliis,
consociato studio muniri debere cunctorum ; cuius
retinendae [1] causa validius, ubi maiestas pulsata
defenditur, a quaestionibus vel cruentis, nullam
Corneliae leges exemere fortunam. 18. Sed exsultare
maestis casibus effrenate non decet, ne videantur
licentia regi subiecti, non potestate. Imitandus
sit Tullius, cum parcere vel laedere potuisset, ut
ipse affirmat, ignoscendi quaerens causas, non
puniendi occasiones, quod iudicis lenti et considerati
est proprium.

19. Tunc apud Daphnen, amoenum illud et ambitiosum Antiochiae suburbanum, visu relatuque
horrendum natum est monstrum, infans ore gemino
cum dentibus binis et barba, quattuorque oculis,

[1] *retinendae*, EN, Gardt. ; *redimendae*, WBG ; *redinendae*
V.

---

[1] On the Cornelian Laws (*Lex Cornelia maiestatis*),
see Cicero *in Pisonem*, 21. They were emended and en-
larged by Julius Caesar as the *Lex Iulia maiestatis*.

to the death of the emperor. 16. Therefore the palace band of courtiers, ingeniously fabricating shameful devices of flattery, declared that he would be immune to ordinary ills, loudly exclaiming that his destiny had appeared at all times powerful and effective in destroying those who made attempts against him.

17. And that into such doings strict investigation was made no man of good sense will find fault. For we do not deny that the safety of a lawful prince, the protector and defender of good men, on whom depends the safety of others, ought to be safeguarded by the united diligence of all men; and in order to uphold him the more strongly when his violated majesty is defended, the Cornelian laws [1] exempted no one of whatever estate from examination by torture, even with the shedding of blood.[2] 18. But it is not seemly for a prince to rejoice beyond measure in such sorrowful events, lest his subjects should seem to be ruled by despotism rather than by lawful power. And the example of Tully ought to be followed, who, when it was in his power to spare or to harm, as he himself tells us,[3] sought excuses for pardoning rather than opportunities for punishing; and that is the province of a mild and considerate official.

19. At that same time in Daphne, that charming and magnificent suburb of Antioch, a portent was born, horrible to see and to report: an infant,

[2] See *Cod. Theod.* ix., Tit. 35, *in maiestatis crimine omnibus aequa est condicio.*

[3] A fragment of Cicero preserved only by Ammianus; perhaps from the *Oratio Metellina* (Cic., *ad Att.* 1, 13, 5).

et brevissimis duabus auriculis, qui partus ita dis-
tortus praemonebat rem publicam in statum verti
deformem. 20. Nascuntur huius modi saepe por-
tenta, indicantia rerum variarum eventus, quae
quoniam non expiantur, ut apud veteres publice,
inaudita praetereunt et incognita.

13. *Lauricius comes Isaurorum lactrocinia compescit.*

1. His temporibus Isauri diu quieti post gesta
quae superior continet textus, temptatumqe Seleuciae civitatis obsidium, paulatim reviviscentes,
ut solent verno tempore foveis exsilire serpentes,
saltibus degressi scrupulosis et inviis, confertique
in cuneos densos per furta et latrocinia finitimos
afflictabant, praetenturas militum (ut montani)
fallentes, perque rupis et dumeta ex usu facile discurrentes. 2. Ad quos vi vel ratione sedandos
Lauricius, adiecta comitis dignitate, missus est
rector, homo civilis prudentiae, qui minis potius
quam acerbitate pleraque correxit, adeo ut eo diu
provinciam obtinente, nihil accideret, quod animad-
versione dignum aestimaretur.

namely, with two heads, two sets of teeth, a beard, four eyes and two very small ears ; and this mis-shapen birth foretold that the state was turning into a deformed condition. 20. Portents of this kind often see the light, as indications of the outcome of various affairs ; but as they are not expiated by public rites, as they were in the time of our forefathers, they pass by unheard of and unknown.

13. *Count Lauricius checks the raids of the Isaurians.*

1. In these days the Isaurians, who had long been quiet after the acts of which an account is given above [1] and the attempted siege of the city of Seleucia, gradually coming to life again just as snakes are wont to dart forth from their holes in the spring time, sallying forth from their rocky and inaccessible mountain fastnesses, and massed together in dense bands, were harrying their neighbours with thefts and brigandage, eluding the frontier-defences of our soldiers by their skill as mountaineers and from experience easily running over rocks and through thickets. 2. In order to quiet them by force or by reason, Lauricius was sent as governor with the added rank of count ; being a man skilled in statesmanship, he corrected many evils by threats rather than by actual severity, so that for a long time, while he governed the province, nothing occurred which was thought deserving of punishment.

---

[1] See xiv. 2, 1 ff.

I.—INDEX OF NAMES [1]

Abarne, a village of Mesopotamia, located by Ammianus in Gumathena (*q.v.*), xviii. **9**, 2.

Abdigildus, xviii. **6**, 12.

Abora, a river of Mesopotamia, a tributary of the Euphrates, the Hermas or Alhauali, xiv. **3**, 4.

Aborigines, a name applied to the earliest inhabitants of various countries ; to the Celtae in Gaul, xv. **9**, 3.

Abydum (Abydus), a city of Egypt, under the native kings ranking next to Thebes, xix. **12**, 3, note. It was the seat of the palace of Memnon, and of a temple of Osiris, Pliny, *N.H.* v. 60.

Achaicus, -a, -um, adj. from Achaia, a district on the northern coast of the Peloponnesus : *oppidum*, xix. **12**, 10. Used also of the whole of Greece : *tractus*, xv. **8**, 1.

Achilleus, the famous Greek hero, xix. **1**, 9.

Acilius Glabrio, M', consul in 191 B.C. and commander against Antiochus. He was the first Roman to be honoured with a golden statue. His son of the same name dedicated a temple of Pietas at Rome, and placed the statue of his father in it, xiv. **6**, 8.

Acimincum (Acumincum), a city of Lower Pannonia, xix. **11**, 8.

Adelphius (Clodius), prefect of Rome under Magnentius in 350, xvi. **6**, 2.

Ad Gradus, a part of the Gulf of Lyons at the mouth of the Rhone. *Gradus* means " a landing-place " (Val. Max. iii. 6, 1) and is found in connection with the mouths of other rivers, xv. **11**, 18, note.

Adiabene, a district of Assyria, Modern Hadjab, xviii. **7**, 1.

Adonis, a beautiful youth, son of Cinyras, king of Cyprus, beloved by Aphrodite. He was killed by a boar, but was allowed to spend half of each year with Aphrodite. His death and return to life were celebrated at Alexandria and elsewhere by festivals (*Adonia*), typical of the death of nature in winter and its revival in the spring, xix. **1**, 11.

Adramyttenus (Adramyttenus), adj. from Adramytteum (Adramyttium), a town on the river Caicus in Mysia, on the road between the Hellespont and Pergamum, xiv. **11**, 31 ; see Andriscus.

Adrastia, used as another name for Nemesis, the goddess of retributive justice, xiv. **11**, 25.

Adrasteus pallor, xiv. **11**, 22, note.

Aedesius (Sextilius Agesilaus), xv. **5**, 4, 14. Cf. *C.I.L.* vi. 510.

Aegyptia civitas, xvii. **4**, 6.

---

[1] Historical, geographical, and mythological, as they appear in Vol. I. only. Additional information found in later books is given in the Indices to Vols. II. and III. Where nothing can be added to the information given in the text and the notes, usually only the reference is given.

INDEX OF NAMES

548

INDEX OF NAMES

549

INDEX OF NAMES

INDEX OF NAMES

INDEX OF NAMES

INDEX OF NAMES

553

INDEX OF NAMES

INDEX OF NAMES

INDEX OF NAMES

INDEX OF NAMES

557

INDEX OF NAMES

558

INDEX OF NAMES

559

INDEX OF NAMES

560

INDEX OF NAMES

561

INDEX OF NAMES

INDEX OF NAMES

INDEX OF NAMES

564

INDEX OF NAMES

565

INDEX OF NAMES

INDEX OF NAMES

567

INDEX OF NAMES

INDEX OF NAMES

INDEX OF NAMES

INDEX OF NAMES

INDEX OF NAMES

INDEX OF NAMES

INDEX OF NAMES

INDEX OF NAMES

II.—INDEX OF OFFICIALS [1]

Not confined to Vol. I. and including bodies of troops and other military terms.

INDEX OF OFFICIALS

Bracchiati—continued.
   Lydus, *De Mag.* i. 46, βραχιᾶτοι
   ἤτοι ἀρμιλλιγεροι, ψελιοφόροι,
   "wearers of bracelets," xv. **5**,
   30; xvi. **12**, 43.

Caesares, see note 3, p. 3, and
   Introd., p. xxiv. The following
   references throw light on the
   subordination of the Caesars
   to the Augustus, xiv. **11**, 10;
   xvii. **9**, 6; xx. **8**, 6.

campidoctores, xv. **3**, 10; see
   note. They trained the soldiers
   also in military exercises, martial dancing, and rhythmical
   marching (see *pyrricha*).

campiductores, subordinate military officers, xix. **6**, 12; regarded by some as equivalent
   to *campigeni* (= *antesignani*) in
   Vegetius, ii. 7.

candidati militares, two bodies of
   the court troops, divided into
   seniores and *iuniores*. They were
   selected because of their height
   and handsome appearance, had
   the rank of subaltern officers,
   and were in line for appointment
   as tribunes; they sometimes
   formed an imperial bodyguard,
   xv. **5**, 16; xxv. **3**, 6; xxxi. **13**, 14.

capita scholarum, the *capita con-
   tuberniorum* of Vegetius, ii. 8
   and 13. They had charge of
   the troops occupying the same
   quarters or tents, xxv. **10**, 8.

castra praetoria, the praetorian
   camp, used by Ammianus (xvi.
   12, 49) for the centre of the
   battle-line, "forte quia imperator, quoties in exercitu est,
   eo in loco tutiore consistere
   solet . . . praetorium erat in
   medio castrorum" (*Valesius*).

castrensis sacri palatii (*comes*),
   marshal of the court, in charge
   of pages, chamberlains, cooks,
   etc., Introd. p. xxxvi; cf. *ex
   cura palatii*, xxii. **3**, 7.

cataphractarii, xvi. **2**, 5; see note.
   They are also called *clibanarii* in
   xvi. **10**, 8, see note. See also
   Claudian, *In Ruf.* ii. 357 ff. and
   De VI Cons. Honor. 569 ff.

Celtae et Petulantes, bodies of
   Roman auxiliary troops (see
   Petulantes), xx. **4**, 2, 20; xxi.
   3, 2; xxii. 12, 6; xxxi. **10**, 4.

centurio rerum nitentium, xvi. **6**,
   2, note; later we find a *tribunus*
   (*Not. Imp. Occid.*, p. 1818), and
   still later a *comes rerum nitentium* (Cassiod., *Varia*, vii.,
   Epist. xiii.). The *centurio* was
   perhaps a subordinate of the
   curator statuarum.

clarissimi, see Introd., p. xxviii.,
   xxvi. **6**, 18; xxviii. **1**, 27.

clibanarii, see *cataphractarii*.

comes, see Introd., pp. xxviii. f.
   We also find *comites* in charge of
   provinces: *Aegypti*, xxiii. **3**, 5;
   Africae, xxi. **7**, 4; see also *comes
   Orientis*, xiv. 1, 3.

comes domesticorum, see Introd.,
   p. xlii.; xiv. **10**, 8 note; **11**,
   14, 19.

comes rei castrensis, vicarius of the
   magister militum, xiv. **11**, 5;
   xxx. **7**, 3.

comes rerum privatarum, see
   Introd., pp. xli. f.; cf. *comes
   rei privatae*, xv. **5**, 4; **3**, 7.

comes sacrarum largitionum see
   Introd., pp. xl. f.; xiv. **7**, 9;
   xvi. **8**, 5; xviii. **5**, 2. Cf. *qui
   largitiones curat*, xxi. **8**, 1;
   qui aerarium tuebatur, xx. **11**, 5.

comitatenses milites, household
   troops which were taken on
   campaigns; distinguished from
   palatini and from *limitanei* and
   ripenses, xxix. **5**, 4.

comitatensis fabrica, see *fabrica*.

comites thesaurorum, who collected
   the revenues in the provinces
   and rendered an account to the
   comes largitionum : per Thracias,
   xxix. **1**, 26; *qui Gallicanos
   tuebatur thesauros*, xxii. **3**, 7; cf.
   xv. **5**, 36.

comites sagittarii, mounted archers
   who accompanied the emperor
   on a campaign, xviii. **9**, 4, a
   division of the *comitum turmae
   equestres*.

comitum turma equestris, a troop
   of select barbarian horsemen,
   xv. **4**, 10, note; xviii. **9**, 4.

INDEX OF OFFICIALS

compulsores, collectors of money due to the fiscus, xxii. 6, 1.

consiliarius, a general term for members of the *consistorium*, xxv. 3, 14 ; xxviii. 1, 21 ; 6, 12.

consistoriani, members of the *consistorium*, xxxi. 12, 10. As distinguished from *militares* it designated the civil members, xv. 5, 12 ; 6, 1.

consistorium, see Introd., pp. xxix. f. ; xiv. 7, 11 note ; xv. 5, 18 ; xxv. 10, 10.

consulares, see xv. 5, 14, note ; *consularis Piceni*, xv: 7, 5 ; *Syriae*, xiv. 7, 5.

consules, see Introd., pp. xxx. ff. ; *amplissimus magistratus*, xxvi. 9, 1.

Cornuti, a body of Roman soldiers, divided into *seniores* and *iuniores ;* cf. *Bracchiati*, with whom they are associated in xv. 5, 30 ; xvi. 12, 43. According to the *Notit. Dig. Orient.* 6. 48 there was also a mounted troop. They perhaps derived their name from Cornutum in Pannonia.

correctores, xv. 5, 14, note.

cubicularii, chamberlains, **xx. 8,** 4.

cubiculi praepositus, see xiv. 10, 5, note ; xv. 3, 2 ; xvi. 7, 2.

curans summitatem necessitatum castrensium, chief commissary officer, xxvi. 1, 4.

curator, a marshal of the court, xiv. 7, 19, *agens palatii Caesaris curam ; curator urbis*, usually a Roman senator sent to the provinces as a city official ; he ranked above the local *decuriones*, but below the *duumviri*, xiv. 7, 17.

curiales, used by Ammianus in the sense of courtiers in xxi. 12, 20 ; in that of *decuriones* in xxii. 9, 12 ; xxvii. 7, 7.

(*cursus publicus*), the state courier-service, consisting of relays of horses and vehicles at stations along the highways, for the use of those who were sent to the provinces on official business, or

(*cursus publicus*)—continued.
summoned to the court ; see *vehiculis publicis*, xxi. 13, 7 ; the *clavularis cursus* (xx. 4, 11, note) apparently refers to the use of *clavulae*, vehicles of some special sort, but the derivation and meaning of *clavularis* are uncertain ; see, however, xx. 4, 11, note.

Decimani, the soldiers of the Tenth legion ; see *Fortenses*.

decuriones, senators in municipal towns and colonies, xxviii, 6, 10.

decurio palatii, one of the three officers in charge of the thirty *silentiarii*, whose duty it was to preserve the necessary quiet in the presence of the emperor, xx. 4, 20, note.

diogmitae, light-armed soldiers, used especially in the pursuit of the enemy, xxvii. 9, 6.

Divitenses et Tungricani, **xxvi. 6,** 12 ; **7,** 14 ; xxvii. 1, 2. Auxiliary troops at the disposition of the commander of the infantry, *Not. Imperii*, p. 1483.

domestici, household troops, commanded by a *comes domesticorum* (xxvi. 5, 3) ; see *scholae.*

domesticus, apparently = *apparitor ;* see *apparitores*, xv. 6, 1.

draconarius, a standard bearer, xvi. 10, 7, where the *dracones* are described, cf. Claudian, *In Ruf.*, ii. 177 ; xvi. 12, 39 ; xx. 4, 18.

dracones, standards of the cohorts in the form of dragons, adopted during the reign of Trajan, xiv. 5, 16 ; see *draconarius*.

duces, used generally of leaders of armies (xv. 5, 25) ; in a narrower sense, generals or governors of varying rank and importance, distinguished as *militares* and *provinciarum*. They ranked below the *comites* (xxiii. 3, 5) ; in the west there were two *comites* and thirteen *duces ;* in the east six *comites* and twelve *duces ;* used of a Persian, xviii. 5, 3. *Dux Aegypti*, xxiii. 3, 5 ; xxiv. 1, 9.

578

INDEX OF OFFICIALS

579

INDEX OF OFFICIALS

INDEX OF OFFICIALS

581

---

[1] The name of a praetorian prefect.

INDEX OF OFFICIALS

Victores, the name of a legion, xxiv. 4, 23; xxix. 3, 7; associated with the Jovii, xxv. 6, 3; xxvi. 7, 13; xxvii. 8, 7.

xystarcha, the head of a wrestling school, xxi. 1, 4.

Zabdiceni sagittarii, xx. 7, 1, in the *Not. Imperii* included under the command of the *dux* of Mesopotamia, of which country the Zabdiceni were natives.

Zinnanorum legio, xxv. 1, 19. In the *Not. Imp. Orentalis*, Tzanni are mentioned among the troops of the *magister militum per Thracias*; the Tzanni, called *Sani* in early times, were neighbours of the Armenians and the Lazi, dwelling on the river Phasis in Colchis (Procopius, ii. 29, 14; i., p. 136 ff. *L.C.L.*).

Note.—The latest complete Index of Names is that of Gardthausen, 1875; of Officials that of Wagner-Erfurdt, 1808. The Index to Clark's edition is not available. The *Thes. Ling Lat.* is helpful so far as it has been published, as well as works mentioned in the Bibliographical Note (p. xlix), but not a few uncertainties remain.

PRINTED IN GREAT BRITAIN BY
THE ABERDEEN UNIVERSITY PRESS.

THE LOEB CLASSICAL LIBRARY

VOLUMES ALREADY PUBLISHED

LATIN AUTHORS

AMMIANUS MARCELLINUS. Translated by J. C. Rolfe. 3 Vols.

APULEIUS: THE GOLDEN ASS (METAMORPHOSES). W. Adlington (1566). Revised by S. Gaselee.

ST. AUGUSTINE: CITY OF GOD. 7 Vols., Vol. I. G. H. McCracken. Vol. VI. W. C. Greene.

ST. AUGUSTINE, CONFESSIONS OF. W. Watts (1631). 2 Vols.

ST. AUGUSTINE, SELECT LETTERS. J. H. Baxter.

AUSONIUS. H. G. Evelyn White. 2 Vols.

BEDE. J. E. King. 2 Vols.

BOETHIUS: TRACTS AND DE CONSOLATIONE PHILOSOPHIAE. Rev. H. F. Stewart and E. K. Rand.

CAESAR: ALEXANDRINE, AFRICAN AND SPANISH WARS. A. G. Way.

CAESAR: CIVIL WARS. A. G. Peskett.

CAESAR: GALLIC WAR. H. J. Edwards.

CATO AND VARRO: DE RE RUSTICA. H. B. Ash and W. D. Hooper.

CATULLUS. F. W. Cornish ; TIBULLUS. J. B. Postgate ; PERVIGILIUM VENERIS. J. W. Mackail.

CELSUS: DE MEDICINA. W. G. Spencer. 3 Vols.

[CICERO]: RHETORICA AD HERENNIUM. H. Caplan.

CICERO: BRUTUS AND ORATOR. G. L. Hendrickson and H. M. Hubbell.

CICERO : DE FATO; PARADOXA STOICORUM; DE PARTITIONE ORATORIA. H. Rackham. (With De Oratore, Vol. II.)

CICERO: DE FINIBUS. H. Rackham.

CICERO: DE INVENTIONE, etc. H. M. Hubbell.

THE LOEB CLASSICAL LIBRARY

CICERO: DE NATURA DEORUM AND ACADEMICA. H. Rackham.

CICERO: DE OFFICIIS. Walter Miller.

CICERO: DE ORATORE. E. W. Sutton and H. Rackham. 2 Vols.

CICERO: DE REPUBLICA AND DE LEGIBUS. Clinton W. Keyes.

CICERO: DE SENECTUTE, DE AMICITIA, DE DIVINATIONE. W. A. Falconer.

CICERO: IN CATILINAM, PRO MURENA, PRO SULLA, PRO FLACCO. Louis E. Lord.

CICERO: LETTERS TO ATTICUS. E. O. Winstedt. 3 Vols.

CICERO: LETTERS TO HIS FRIENDS. W. Glynn Williams. 3 Vols.

CICERO: PHILIPPICS. W. C. A. Ker.

CICERO: PRO ARCHIA, POST REDITUM, DE DOMO, DE HARUSPICUM RESPONSIS, PRO PLANCIO. N. H. Watts.

CICERO: PRO CAECINA, PRO LEGE MANILIA, PRO CLUENTIO, PRO RABIRIO. H. Grose Hodge.

CICERO: PRO MILONE, IN PISONEM, PRO SCAURO, PRO FONTEIO, PRO RABIRIO POSTUMO, PRO MARCELLO, PRO LIGARIO, PRO REGE DEIOTARO. N. H. Watts.

CICERO: PRO QUINCTIO, PRO ROSCIO AMERINO, PRO ROSCIO COMOEDO, CONTRA RULLUM. J. H. Freese.

CICERO: PRO SESTIO, IN VATINIUM. R. Gardner.

CICERO: TUSCULAN DISPUTATIONS. J. E. King.

CICERO: VERRINE ORATIONS. L. H. G. Greenwood. 2 Vols.

CLAUDIAN. M. Platnauer. 2 Vols.

COLUMELLA: DE RE RUSTICA, DE ARBORIBUS. H. B. Ash, E. S. Forster and E. Heffner. 3 Vols.

CURTIUS, Q: HISTORY OF ALEXANDER. J. C. Rolfe. 2 Vols.

FLORUS. E. S. Forster; and CORNELIUS NEPOS. J. C. Rolfe.

FRONTINUS: STRATAGEMS AND AQUEDUCTS. C. E. Bennett and M. B. McElwain.

FRONTO: CORRESPONDENCE. C. R. Haines. 2 Vols.

GELLIUS. J. C. Rolfe. 3 Vols.

HORACE: ODES AND EPODES. C. E. Bennett.

HORACE: SATIRES, EPISTLES, ARS POETICA. H. R. Fairclough.

JEROME: SELECT LETTERS. F. A. Wright.

JUVENAL and PERSIUS. G. G. Ramsay.

2

THE LOEB CLASSICAL LIBRARY

LIVY. B. O. Foster, F. G. Moore, Evan T. Sage and A. C. Schlesinger and R. M. Geer (General Index). 14 Vols.

LUCAN. J. D. Duff.

LUCRETIUS. W. H. D. Rouse.

MARTIAL. W. C. A. Ker. 2 Vols.

MINOR LATIN POETS: from PUBLILIUS SYRUS to RUTILIUS NAMATIANUS, including GRATTIUS, CALPURNIUS SICULUS, NEMESIANUS, AVIANUS, with "Aetna," "Phoenix" and other poems. J. Wight Duff and Arnold M. Duff.

OVID: THE ART OF LOVE AND OTHER POEMS. J. H. Mozley.

OVID: FASTI. Sir James G. Frazer.

OVID: HEROIDES and AMORES. Grant Showerman.

OVID: METAMORPHOSES. F. J. Miller. 2 Vols.

OVID: TRISTIA and EX PONTO. A. L. Wheeler.

PETRONIUS. M. Heseltine; SENECA APOCOLOCYNTOSIS. W. H. D. Rouse.

PLAUTUS. Paul Nixon. 5 Vols.

PLINY: LETTERS. Melmoth's translation revised by W. M. L. Hutchinson. 2 Vols.

PLINY: NATURAL HISTORY. 10 Vols. Vols. I-V and IX. H. H. Rackham. Vols. VI-VIII. W. H. S. Jones. Vol. X. D. E. Eichholz.

PROPERTIUS. H. E. Butler.

PRUDENTIUS. H. J. Thomson. 2 Vols.

QUINTILIAN. H. E. Butler. 4 Vols.

REMAINS OF OLD LATIN. E. H. Warmington. 4 Vols. Vol. I. (Ennius and Caecilius.) Vol. II. (Livius, Naevius, Pacuvius, Accius.) Vol. III. (Lucilius, Laws of XII Tables.) Vol. IV. (Archaic Inscriptions.)

SALLUST. J. C. Rolfe.

SCRIPTORES HISTORIAE AUGUSTAE. D. Magie. 3 Vols.

SENECA: APOCOLOCYNTOSIS. Cf. PETRONIUS.

SENECA: EPISTULAE MORALES. R. M. Gummere. 3 Vols.

SENECA: MORAL ESSAYS. J. W. Basore. 3 Vols.

SENECA: TRAGEDIES. F. J. Miller. 2 Vols.

SIDONIUS: POEMS AND LETTERS. W. B. Anderson. 2 Vols.

SILIUS ITALICUS. J. D. Duff. 2 Vols.

STATIUS. J. H. Mozley. 2 Vols.

SUETONIUS. J. C. Rolfe. 2 Vols.

TACITUS: DIALOGUS. Sir Wm. Peterson; and AGRICOLA AND GERMANIA. Maurice Hutton.

THE LOEB CLASSICAL LIBRARY

TACITUS: HISTORIES AND ANNALS. C. H. Moore and J. Jackson. 4 Vols.

TERENCE. John Sargeaunt. 2 Vols.

TERTULLIAN: APOLOGIA AND DE SPECTACULIS. T. R. Glover; MINUCIUS FELIX. G. H. Rendall.

VALERIUS FLACCUS. J. H. Mozley.

VARRO: DE LINGUA LATINA. R. G. Kent. 2 Vols.

VELLEIUS PATERCULUS and RES GESTAE DIVI AUGUSTI. F. W. Shipley.

VIRGIL. H. R. Fairclough. 2 Vols.

VITRUVIUS: DE ARCHITECTURA. F. Granger. 2 Vols.

GREEK AUTHORS

ACHILLES TATIUS. S. Gaselee.

AELIAN: ON THE NATURE OF ANIMALS. 3 Vols. Vols. I. II. and III, A. F. Scholfield.

AENEAS TACTICUS, ASCLEPIODOTUS AND ONASANDER. The Illinois Greek Club.

AESCHINES. C. D. Adams.

AESCHYLUS. H. Weir Smyth. 2 Vols.

ALCIPHRON, AELIAN AND PHILOSTRATUS: LETTERS. A. R. Benner and F. H. Fobes.

APOLLODORUS. Sir James G. Frazer. 2 Vols.

APOLLONIUS RHODIUS. R. C. Seaton.

THE APOSTOLIC FATHERS. Kirsopp Lake. 2 Vols.

APPIAN'S ROMAN HISTORY. Horace White. 4 Vols.

ARATUS. Cf. CALLIMACHUS.

ARISTOPHANES. Benjamin Bickley Rogers. 3 Vols. Verse trans.

ARISTOTLE: ART OF RHETORIC. J. H. Freese.

ARISTOTLE: ATHENIAN CONSTITUTION, EUDEMIAN ETHICS, VIRTUES AND VICES. H. Rackham.

ARISTOTLE: GENERATION OF ANIMALS. A. L. Peck.

ARISTOTLE: METAPHYSICS. H. Tredennick. 2 Vols.

ARISTOTLE: METEOROLOGICA. H. D. P. Lee.

ARISTOTLE: MINOR WORKS. W. S. Hett. "On Colours", "On Things Heard", "Physiognomics", "On Plants", "On Marvellous Things Heard", "Mechanical Problems", "On Indivisible Lines", "Situations and Names of Winds", "On Melissus, Xenophanes, and Gorgias".

ARISTOTLE: NICOMACHEAN ETHICS. H. Rackham.

4

THE LOEB CLASSICAL LIBRARY

ARISTOTLE: OECONOMICA and MAGNA MORALIA. G. C. Armstrong. (With Metaphysics, Vol. II.)

ARISTOTLE: ON THE HEAVENS. W. K. C. Guthrie.

ARISTOTLE: ON THE SOUL, PARVA NATURALIA, ON BREATH. W. S. Hett.

ARISTOTLE: CATEGORIES, ON INTERPRETATION, PRIOR ANALYTICS. H. P. Cooke and H. Tredennick.

ARISTOTLE: POSTERIOR ANALYTICS, TOPICS. H. Tredennick and E. S. Forster.

ARISTOTLE: ON SOPHISTICAL REFUTATIONS, ON COMING TO BE AND PASSING AWAY, ON THE COSMOS. E. S. Forster and D. J. Furley.

ARISTOTLE: PARTS OF ANIMALS. A. L. Peck; MOTION AND PROGRESSION OF ANIMALS. E. S. Forster.

ARISTOTLE: PHYSICS. Rev. P. Wicksteed and F. M. Cornford. 2 Vols.

ARISTOTLE: POETICS and LONGINUS. W. Hamilton Fyfe; DEMETRIUS ON STYLE. W. Rhys Roberts.

ARISTOTLE: POLITICS. H. Rackham.

ARISTOTLE: PROBLEMS. W. S. Hett. 2 Vols.

ARISTOTLE: RHETORICA AD ALEXANDRUM. H. Rackham. (With Problems, Vol. II.)

ARRIAN: HISTORY OF ALEXANDER AND INDICA. Rev. E. Iliffe Robson. 2 Vols.

ATHENAEUS: DEIPNOSOPHISTAE. C. B. Gulick. 7 Vols.

ST. BASIL: LETTERS. R. J. Deferrari. 4 Vols.

CALLIMACHUS: FRAGMENTS. C. A. Trypanis.

CALLIMACHUS and LYCOPHRON. A. W. Mair; ARATUS. G. R. Mair.

CLEMENT OF ALEXANDRIA. Rev. G. W. Butterworth.

COLLUTHUS. Cf. OPPIAN.

DAPHNIS AND CHLOE. Cf. LONGUS.

DEMOSTHENES I: OLYNTHIACS, PHILIPPICS AND MINOR ORATIONS I.-XVII. and XX. J. H. Vince.

DEMOSTHENES II: DE CORONA and DE FALSA LEGATIONE. C. A. Vince and J. H. Vince.

DEMOSTHENES III: MEIDIAS, ANDROTION, ARISTOCRATES, TIMOCRATES, ARISTOGEITON. J. H. Vince.

DEMOSTHENES IV-I: PRIVATE ORATIONS AND IN NEAERAM. A. T. Murray.

DEMOSTHENES VI: FUNERAL SPEECH, EROTIC ESSAY, EXORDIA AND LETTERS. N. W. and N. J. DeWitt.

5

THE LOEB CLASSICAL LIBRARY

DIO CASSIUS: ROMAN HISTORY. E. Cary. 9 Vols.

DIO CHRYSOSTOM. J. W. Cohoon and H. Lamar Crosby. 5 Vols.

DIODORUS SICULUS. 12 Vols. Vols. I.-VI. C. H. Oldfather. Vol. VII. C. L. Sherman. Vol. VIII. C. B. Welles. Vols. IX. and X. R. M. Greer. Vol. XI. F. Walton.

DIOGENES LAERTIUS. R. D. Hicks. 2 Vols

DIONYSIUS OF HALICARNASSUS: ROMAN ANTIQUITIES. Spelman's translation revised by E. Cary. 7 Vols.

EPICTETUS. W. A. Oldfather. 2 Vols.

EURIPIDES. A. S. Way. 4 Vols. Verse trans.

EUSEBIUS: ECCLESIASTICAL HISTORY. Kirsopp Lake and J. E. L. Oulton. 2 Vols.

GALEN: ON THE NATURAL FACULTIES. A. J. Brock.

THE GREEK ANTHOLOGY. W. R. Paton. 5 Vols.

THE GREEK BUCOLIC POETS (THEOCRITUS, BION, MOSCHUS). J. M. Edmonds.

GREEK ELEGY AND IAMBUS WITH THE ANACREONTEA. J. M. Edmonds. 2 Vols.

GREEK MATHEMATICAL WORKS. Ivor Thomas. 2 Vols.

HERODES. Cf. THEOPHRASTUS: CHARACTERS.

HERODOTUS. A. D. Godley. 4 Vols.

HESIOD AND THE HOMERIC HYMNS. H. G. Evelyn White.

HIPPOCRATES and the FRAGMENTS OF HERACLEITUS. W. H. S. Jones and E. T. Withington. 4 Vols.

HOMER: ILIAD. A. T. Murray. 2 Vols

HOMER: ODYSSEY. A. T. Murray. 2 Vols.

ISAEUS. E. S. Forster.

ISOCRATES. George Norlin and LaRue Van Hook. 3 Vols.

ST. JOHN DAMASCENE: BARLAAM AND IOASAPH. Rev. G. R. Woodward and Harold Mattingly.

JOSEPHUS: 9 Vols. Vols. I-IV. H. Thackeray. Vol. V. H. Thackeray and R. Marcus. Vols. VI-VII. R. Marcus. Vol. VIII. R. Marcus and Allen Wikgren.

JULIAN. Wilmer Cave Wright. 3 Vols.

LONGUS: DAPHNIS AND CHLOE. Thornley's translation revised by J. M. Edmonds; and PARTHENIUS. S. Gaselee.

LUCIAN. Vols. I.-V. A. M. Harmon; Vol. VI. K. Kilburn. Vol. VII, M. D. Macleod. 8 Vols.

LYCOPHRON. Cf. CALLIMACHUS.

LYRA GRAECA. J. M. Edmonds. 3 Vols.

LYSIAS. W. R. M. Lamb.

THE LOEB CLASSICAL LIBRARY

MANETHO. W. G. Waddell: PTOLEMY: TETRABIBLOS. F. E. Robbins.

MARCUS AURELIUS. C. R. Haines.

MENANDER. F. G. Allinson.

MINOR ATTIC ORATORS. K. J. Maidment and J. O. Burtt. 2 Vols.

NONNOS: DIONYSIACA. W. H. D. Rouse. 3 Vols.

OPPIAN, COLLUTHUS, TRYPHIODORUS. A. W. Mair.

PAPYRI. 5 Vols. NON-LITERARY SELECTIONS. A. S. Hunt and C. C. Edgar. 2 Vols. LITERARY SELECTIONS Vol. I. (Poetry). D. L. Page.

PARTHENIUS. *Cf.* LONGUS.

PAUSANIUS: DESCRIPTION OF GREECE. W. H. S. Jones. 5 Vols. and Companion Vol. arranged by R. E. Wycherley.

PHILO. 10 Vols. Vols. I.-V. F. H. Colson and Rev. G. H. Whitaker; Vols. VI.-IX. F. H. Colson. Vol. X. F. H. Colson and the Rev. J. W. Earp.

PHILO. 2 supplementary Vols. (*Translation only.*) Vols. I. and II. R. Marcus.

PHILOSTRATUS: THE LIFE OF APOLLONIUS OF TYANA. F. C. Coneybeare. 2 Vols.

PHILOSTRATUS: IMAGINES; CALLISTRATUS: DESCRIPTIONS. A. Fairbanks.

PHILOSTRATUS and EUNAPIUS: LIVES OF THE SOPHISTS. Wilmer Cave Wright.

PINDAR. Sir J. E. Sandys.

PLATO: CHARMIDES, ALCIBIADES, HIPPARCHUS, THE LOVERS, THEAGES, MINOS and EPINOMIS. W. R. M. Lamb.

PLATO: CRATYLUS, PARMENIDES, GREATER HIPPIAS, LESSER HIPPIAS. H. N. Fowler.

PLATO: EUTHYPHRO, APOLOGY, CRITO, PHAEDO, PHAEDRUS. H. N. Fowler.

PLATO: LACHES, PROTAGORAS, MENO, EUTHYDEMUS. W. R. M. Lamb.

PLATO: LAWS. Rev. R. G. Bury. 2 Vols.

PLATO: LYSIS, SYMPOSIUM, GORGIAS. W. R. M. Lamb.

PLATO: REPUBLIC. Paul Shorey. 2 Vols.

PLATO: STATESMAN, PHILEBUS. H. N. Fowler; ION. W. R. M. Lamb.

PLATO: THEAETETUS AND SOPHIST. H. N. Fowler.

PLATO: TIMAEUS, CRITIAS, CLITOPHO, MENEXENUS, EPISTULAE. Rev. R. G. Bury.

THE LOEB CLASSICAL LIBRARY

PLUTARCH: MORALIA. 14 Vols. Vols. I.-V. F. C. Babbitt;
   Vol. VI. W. C. Helmbold; Vol. VII. P. H. De Lacy and
   B. Einarson; Vol. IX. E. L. Minar, Jr., F. H. Sandbach,
   W. C. Helmbold; Vol. X. H. N. Fowler; Vol. XII. H.
   Cherniss and W. C. Helmbold.
PLUTARCH: THE PARALLEL LIVES. B. Perrin. 11 Vols.
POLYBIUS. W. R. Paton. 6 Vols.
PROCOPIUS: HISTORY OF THE WARS. H. B. Dewing. 7 Vols.
PTOLEMY: TETRABIBLOS. Cf. MANETHO.
QUINTUS SMYRNAEUS. A. S. Way. Verse trans.
SEXTUS EMPIRICUS. Rev. R. G. Bury. 4 Vols.
SOPHOCLES. F. Storr. 2 Vols. Verse trans.
STRABO: Geography. Horace L. Jones. 8 Vols.
THEOPHRASTUS: CHARACTERS. J. M. Edmonds. HERODES,
   etc. A. D. Knox.
THEOPHRASTUS: ENQUIRY INTO PLANTS. Sir Arthur Hort.
   2 Vols.
THUCYDIDES. C. F. Smith. 4 Vols.
TRYPHIODORUS. Cf. OPPIAN.
XENOPHON: CYROPAEDIA. Walter Miller. 2 Vols.
XENOPHON: HELLENICA, ANABASIS, APOLOGY, and SYM-
   POSIUM. C. L. Brownson and O. J. Todd. 3 Vols.
XENOPHON: MEMORABILIA and OECONOMICUS. E. C.
   Marchant.
XENOPHON: SCRIPTA MINORA. E. C. Marchant.

VOLUMES IN PREPARATION

ARISTOTLE: HISTORIA ANIMALIUM. A. L. Peck. (Greek)
PLOTINUS. A. H. Armstrong. (Greek)
BABRIUS (Greek) and PHAEDRUS (Latin) B. E. Perry.

DESCRIPTIVE PROSPECTUS ON APPLICATION

LONDON   WILLIAM HEINEMANN LTD.
CAMBRIDGE, MASS.   HARVARD UNIVERSITY PRESS